Applying Software Metrics

Paul Oman
Shari Lawrence Pfleeger

IEEE Computer Society Press
Los Alamitos, California

Washington • Brussels • Tokyo

Library of Congress Cataloging-in-Publication Data

Applying software metrics / [compiled by] Paul Oman, Shari Lawrence Pfleeger.
   p.   cm.
   Includes bibliographical references.
   ISBN 0-8186-7645-0
   1. Computer software—Quality control.   I. Oman, Paul W.   II. Pfleeger, Shari Lawrence.
QA76.76.Q35A67   1997
005.1 ' 4—dc20   96-29059
                                                                     CIP

IEEE Computer Society Press
10662 Los Vaqueros Circle
P.O. Box 3014
Los Alamitos, CA 90720-1314

IEEE Computer Society Press Order Number BP07645
Library of Congress Number 96-29059
ISBN 0-8186-7645-0

Additional copies can be ordered from

IEEE Computer Society Press	IEEE Service Center	IEEE Computer Society	IEEE Computer Society
Customer Service Center	445 Hoes Lane	13, avenue de l'Aquilon	Ooshima Building
10662 Los Vaqueros Circle	P.O. Box 1331	B-1200 Brussels	2-19-1 Minami-Aoyama
P.O. Box 3014	Piscataway, NJ 08855-1331	BELGIUM	Minato-ku, Tokyo 107
Los Alamitos, CA 90720-1314	Tel: (908) 981-1393	Tel: +32-2-770-2198	JAPAN
Tel: (714) 821-8380	Fax: (908) 981-9667	Fax: +32-2-770-8505	Tel: +81-3-3408-3118
Fax: (714) 821-4641	mis.custserv@computer.org	euro.ofc@computer.org	Fax: +81-3-3408-3553
Email: cs.books@computer.org			tokyo.ofc@computer.org
http://www.computer.org/cspress			

Assistant Publisher: Matt Loeb
Technical Editor: Carl K. Chang
Acquisitions Editor: Bill Sanders
Acquisitions Assistant: Cheryl Smith
Advertising/Promotions: Tom Fink
Production Editor: Lisa O'Conner
Cover Design: Joe Daigle

The Institute of Electrical and Electronics Engineers, Inc.

Contents

Acknowledgments

The idea for this book came from True Seaborn, publisher for the IEEE Computer Society Press, who recognized back in 1993 that there really wasn't a good tutorial explaining how and why to use metrics at the practitioner's level. While we were working on special issues of *Computer* and *IEEE Software* that would be devoted to metrics, True suggested putting together a tutorial expressly aimed at the working software engineer. The theme issues later appeared as "Metrics in Software," (*Computer*, September 1994) and "Measurement-Based Process Improvement," (*IEEE Software*, July 1994). This book is an outgrowth of that work. We gratefully acknowledge True's encouragement and appreciate the early collaboration of Taghi Khoshgoftaar and Hans Dieter Rombach, our coeditors for the special issues.

While compiling this book we received much advice, assistance, and encouragement from our laboratory colleagues. The support and camaraderie at the Centre for Software Reliability, City University, London, and the Software Engineering Test Lab at the University of Idaho are well remembered and much appreciated. Special thanks are due to Ben Colborn, University of Idaho, for assistance in compiling and editing early versions of the manuscript.

We also recognize and wish to acknowledge the expertise and contributions of the IEEE Computer Society volunteers and staff. Without the tireless enthusiasm of volunteers like Ted Lewis and Carl Chang, there would be little connectivity between the computing professionals and the computing press. The expertise and dedication of people like Angela Burgess and the production and editorial staff at the IEEE Computer Society Press have improved our writing style and readability.

—*Paul W. Oman and Shari Lawrence Pfleeger, September 1996*

Foreword

The need for measurement

From the smoothness of an electric razor's shave to the flight path of an approaching aircraft, the quality of the controlling software affects the quality of our daily lives. With software's ubiquity comes our responsibility for making software safe and reasonably priced as well as functional and useful. Measurement is an essential part of that responsibility, both in understanding what affects quality, timeliness, utility and functionality and in improving software-related products and processes. As practitioners, we are counseled to measure as part of software development or maintenance. As researchers, we are told to use measurement to support experimentation or analysis. Textbooks tell us how to define metrics, but there is little guidance about exactly how to start and what has proven most effective in actual use.

This book helps bridge that gap by bringing together important and practical papers on applying software metrics. Each chapter addresses a significant question whose answer is essential to building an effective measurement program. To answer each question, we have chosen papers and book chapters that provide information based on actual experience with successful measurement programs. Included with each chapter is a case study to focus on technology transfer: how to make measurement become a natural part of everyday software development. Included in every chapter is a set of recommended references, pointing to additional books or papers that embellish the ideas introduced by the selected papers.

To understand how to apply software metrics, we must first understand what measurement means and why we need it. Measurement lets us quantify concepts or attributes in order to manipulate them and learn more about them. A measure is a mapping from the empirical world (that is, the real world in which we live and function) to a more formal, mathematical world. We identify an entity to study, and then an attribute of that entity. Next, we map the attribute to its mathematical representation, where manipulation of the mathematical symbols may reveal more about the entity or attribute than our direct observation (in the real world) would allow. For example, we may choose to examine a code module (the entity) and capture its size (the attribute) using a measure such as lines of code. The measure is the mapping that tells us how to count the lines of code from any module: counting comments or not, counting reused code or not, and so on. Thus, for each module, we can generate a mathematical representation: the number of lines of code. We evaluate the number of lines of code for each of a set of modules so that we can compare and contrast the modules. The measure helps us see if one module is larger or smaller than another, or if one module is growing as changes and fixes are implemented. Finally, we interpret the mathematical changes in terms of their meaning in the empirical world, and we act accordingly. For instance, if the measure tells us that a frequently changed module is getting very large, we may choose to split the module into smaller ones, either to isolate the part that is changed frequently, or simply to make the code easier to understand.

This technique is not exclusive to software engineering. For example, we use measurement to help us understand the properties of materials; we describe an entity mathematically in terms of its height, weight, thickness, melting point, and other numerical characteristics. These numbers help us distinguish one element from another in a way that cannot be done easily in the empirical world. Similarly, we can define measures, such as size, number of defects, and cyclomatic number, that help us understand how one module differs from another of the same functionality. Kitchenham, Pfleeger, and Fenton have formalized these notions in a framework for software measurement.[1] The framework shows how measurement requires an entity and an attribute, relating them to values, units, and scale types, sometimes with a model or equation to relate multiple measures. Figure 1 illustrates the framework for indirect measures, while Figure 2 shows the variation needed to measure multidimensional attributes.

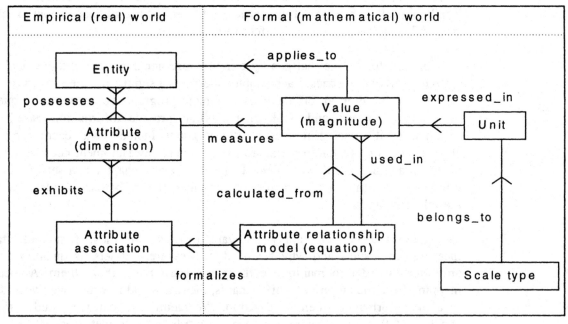

Figure 1. A structural model for indirect measures of simple attributes (from Kitchenham, Pfleeger, and Fenton).

[1] B. Kitchenham, S. Lawrence Pfleeger, and N. Fenton, "Towards a Framework for Software Measurement Validation," *IEEE Trans. Software Eng.*, Vol. 21, No. 12, Dec. 1995, pp. 929-944.

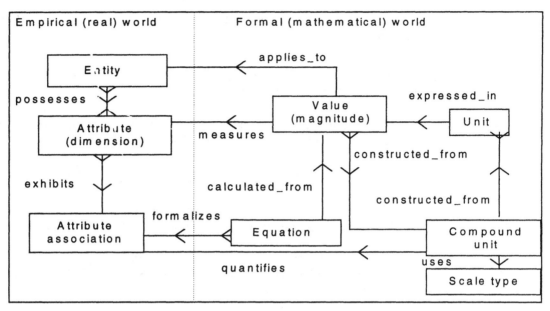

Figure 2. A structural model for measuring multidimensional attributes (from Kitchenham, Pfleeger, and Fenton).

The mapping need not be numerical; characters and categories can be useful, too. For example, we can define a measure of failure severity for each failure that occurs during system use. We might say that a failure is "critical" if it halts the system's functioning, "moderate" if it halts only nonessential functions, or "minor" if the problems are only cosmetic in nature. Here, the measure maps the failure in the real world to a triple: <critical, moderate, minor>. Even though we have no numerical representation, we still have a formal representation that helps us understand the system. For instance, we can examine counts of failures in each of the three categories to help us determine overall system quality.

Measurements can be applied to projects, processes, and resources, as well as to products. For example, we can use measures to tell us about project success (did it finish on time and within budget?), process effectiveness (did the addition of inspections improve product quality?), and resource sufficiency (did the more-experienced programmers write more reliable code than less-experienced ones?). And we can perform our measurement in many different ways. For example, we can measure size by counting lines of code, computing function points, or summing the number of objects and methods. Different approaches address different types of questions to be answered, so the actual metric must be chosen with a particular goal or question in mind.

However, this book focuses not on the metrics themselves but rather on the application of those metrics.[2] We look at what questions can be or have been addressed by measurement, and how the results are used to make key decisions about projects, products, processes, and resources. As we will see, many of these questions are identified up front, before a project begins, so that measurement can be performed as a

---

[2] There are several good books that describe metrics choices, including Fenton and Pfleeger's *Software Metrics: A Rigorous Approach*, second edition, International Thomson Press, London, 1996.

natural part of software development. That is, measurement *planning* should be part of more comprehensive project-planning activities.

Every measurement program should be based on a comprehensive measurement **plan**. The plan should address the following:

- *Why* measurement is needed: What are the product, process, resource, and project goals that must be addressed by the metrics?

- *What* is to be measured: Which project, process, product, and resource attributes are to be characterized quantitatively?

- *Who* will be involved: Who will define the metrics, collect the data, analyze the data and present the results, and who needs to see the results?

- *Where* measurement is needed: Which processes and subprocesses (such as quality assurance or configuration management) are to be instrumented with metrics?

- *When* will the measurements be taken: When during the development or maintenance process will the metrics be collected, and how often?

- *How* the metrics will be gathered and analyzed: What manual or automated techniques will be used for metrics capture, storage, and analysis?

The answers to these questions are essential for successful measurement. Knowing *why* we are measuring gives us the purpose and reason for capturing and evaluating the data. Knowing *what*, *where*, and *when* to measure tells us how measurement will be merged with the day-to-day activities of development. And knowing *how* to measure and *who* will be involved explains who is responsible for data gathering, storage, and presentation.

The chapters of this book address each of the questions in a measurement plan. Chapter 1, explaining why we measure, lays the groundwork for establishing the rationale of a metrics program. Chapter 2 addresses what to measure, examining process, product, and resource measurement. In Chapter 3, we look at how measuring is done, incorporating who is involved, when the measurements are taken, and where in the process the data are captured. Once the data are available, Chapter 4 tells us how the metrics are used; it explores methods of presentation as well as analysis. Finally, Chapter 5 reminds us that the measurement process can be assessed and improved; it examines existing metrics programs and looks at criteria for success.

Each chapter contains

- a list of the included papers,

- an editors' introduction summarizing the papers,

- the featured papers, and

- a list of references for further information.

A glossary is provided at the end of this book.

The selected papers represent current thinking about software measurement. We have tried to include viewpoints that are representative, reflecting a broad spectrum of approaches rather than our own particular preferences. We leave to you the task of evaluating the ideas and techniques, given your own context and organizational needs. And we encourage you to be both skeptical and adventurous, fashioning a measurement program by learning from others and trying new methods.

Chapter 1

Why Measure?

The papers

Measuring for understanding
Norman Fenton, Shari Lawrence Pfleeger, and Robert L. Glass, "Science and Substance: A Challenge to Software Engineers," *IEEE Software*, Vol. 11, No. 4, July 1994, pp. 86–95. Describes how measurement is key to understanding and evaluating the factors that affect our products, processes, and resources.

Measuring for experimentation
Victor R. Basili, Richard W. Selby, and David H. Hutchens, "Experimentation in Software Engineering," *IEEE Trans. Software Eng.*, Vol. SE-12, No. 7, July 1986, pp. 733–743. Presents a framework for analyzing experimentation in software engineering to help structure the experimental process and provide a means of classifying previous work.

Measuring for project control
Barry W. Boehm, "Software Risk Management: Principles and Practices," *IEEE Software*, Vol. 8, No. 1, Jan. 1991, pp. 32–41. Uses four subsets of risk management techniques to identify risk items and rate a project's current status, ranking risk items by their risk exposure values.

Measuring for process improvement
Michael K. Daskalantonakis, "Achieving Higher SEI Levels," *IEEE Software*, Vol. 11, No. 4, July 1994, pp. 17–24. Describes how to conduct and monitor incremental assessments when improved SEI capability maturity level is the long-term goal.

Measuring for product improvement
Robert B. Grady, "Successfully Applying Software Metrics," *Computer*, Vol. 27, No. 9, Sept. 1994, pp. 18–25. Uses examples from real projects to show that a project's success depends on using clearly defined measures to aid design and management decisions.

Measuring for prediction

Edward F. Weller, "Using Metrics to Manage Software Projects," *Computer*, Vol. 27, No. 9, Sept. 1994, pp. 27–33. Shows how defect data collected over time can be used to plan projects and schedule delivery, with an overall improvement in software process maturity.

Case study

George Stark, Robert C. Durst, and C.W. Vowell, "Using Metrics in Management Decision Making," *Computer*, Vol. 27, No. 9, Sept. 1994, pp. 42–48. Explains how metrics defined using the Goal-Question-Metric paradigm and standardized tool kits help managers at NASA's Mission Operations Directorate to understand better their processes and products.

Editors' introduction

As with any other profession, the quality of our practitioners and processes is judged by the quality of our products. And software's ubiquity means that our reputations are continually on the line. In *The Decline and Fall of the American Programmer* (Prentice Hall, 1991), Ed Yourdon tells us that

> "Today, the world-class software company knows that it cannot be satisfied with what it's doing. [...] Software is now a global industry, and a lot of hungry people around the world are aching to eat your lunch."

To get ahead and stay ahead, a company must deliver products that are better than its competition's. It must strive to improve the status quo. To produce an excellent product, the successful software company must make improvements to every step of the software life cycle. But to do that, each step must be understood. Measurement is critical to understanding; as Lord Kelvin reminded us, "One does not understand what one cannot measure."

We begin our book by examining the reasons for measuring software. There are three major reasons to measure:

- understanding
- predicting
- controlling

As we saw in the foreword, measurement allows us to manipulate symbols in a formal, mathematical way so that we learn more about what is happening in the real, empirical world. Metrics help us to identify unusual cases (good and bad) and to describe a typical or usual situation (that is, to establish a baseline). We can also determine cost, effort, and duration requirements for various types of products or process activities.

By knowing what is typical, we can begin to predict what is likely to happen later in an on-going project, or on future projects. For example, given a metrics database of information about past projects, we can estimate resource requirements on similar projects that may be proposed. Likewise, we can use information about defects already discovered to help us predict the likely number of defects still remaining in our code, and thus the amount of testing required before the product can be delivered. Figure 3 illustrates opportunities for prediction throughout the development process.

Finally, the predictions enable us to control projects. We can estimate the cost, effort, and schedule required to complete a project, and track the actual values against our estimates. By examining information about changes to requirements, design, code, and test cases, we can determine whether the effort and schedule allotments should be revised. We can use defect and test coverage information to set entry and exit criteria for testing and quality assurance activities. And we can use information about unusual cases to determine our testing strategy.

Our measurements offer us control in another sense. Many organizations are concentrating on improving their software products and processes. Metrics information can assist by revealing which activities are resulting in demonstrable improvement. That is, we can use metrics information to help us understand which activities are most effective at accomplishing our goals. For example, Bob Grady compared the efficiency of different kinds of testing techniques, as shown in Table 1. (See [Grady 1992] in this chapter's "To probe further.") His experiment and similar research results confirm that inspections are one of the cheapest and most effective testing techniques for finding faults.

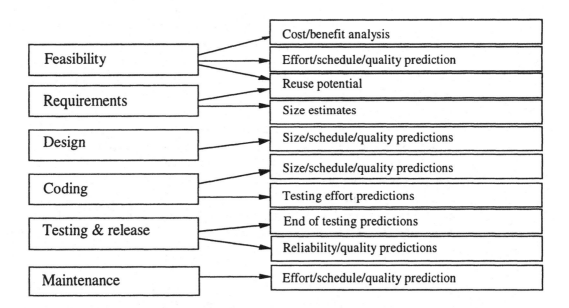

Figure 3. Example predictions needed for software development decision-making (Fenton and Pfleeger 1996).

Table 1. Comparison of testing efficiency. [Grady 1992]

Testing Type	Efficiency (Defects found per hour)
Regular Use	.210
Black Box	.282
White Box	.322
Reading/Inspections	1.057

The papers in this first chapter focus on the importance of measurement and the rationale for instituting a comprehensive measurement program. In "Science and Substance: A Challenge to Software Engineers," Norman Fenton, Shari Lawrence Pfleeger, and Bob Glass explain that measurement is critical in evaluating the effectiveness of any proposed technology. They explain that careful experimentation is needed to determine the effects of new techniques or tools on the resulting software quality. By presenting guidelines for evaluating experiments and case studies, they help us not only to improve our own evaluative work but also to assess the reported work of others.

In our second paper, "Experimentation in Software Engineering," Victor Basili, Rick Selby, and David Hutchens propose a framework for experimentation in the software environment. The framework is then used to evaluate several reported experimental studies. Thus, the first two papers show us that measurement is simply good engineering practice, and that we cannot be good scientists without it.

Next, we turn to project management to see how measurement can help us to predict and control a project's outcome. Associated with every project are a number of risks, many of which relate to allocation of limited resources. In "Software Risk Management: Principles and Practices," Barry Boehm sets forth a model for managing these risks. Using his model, a development organization can try to reduce the probability of exposure to severe risk. Boehm illustrates his approach with examples, showing that projects using the "concept of risk exposure ... tended to avoid pitfalls and produce good products."

Project management also involves controlling the software process. Successful software managers use experiences on previous projects to help improve the next ones. In "Achieving Higher SEI Levels," Michael Daskalantonakis describes how Motorola conducts and monitors incremental assessments to help projects reach their long-term process improvement goals. Whether you use the Software Engineering Institute's capability maturity levels or some other measure of process quality (such as SPICE, Bootstrap, or ISO-9001), the techniques described here are useful in providing interim feedback toward long-term improvement.

Hewlett-Packard is well-known for its successful corporate measurement program based on H-P's goal of improving product quality. Bob Grady shares his experiences at H-P by instructing us in "Successfully Applying Software Metrics." Grady suggests particular courses of action for metrics managers, using real-life examples to support his arguments. Ed Weller tells us about "Using Metrics to Manage Software Projects" at

Honeywell. Weller's article complements Grady's, showing that metrics collected from past projects can aid in planning future ones.

The first chapter closes with a case study of the successful introduction of metrics at NASA's Johnson Space Center. Realizing that NASA software failures could be catastrophic, the Mission Operations Directorate initiated a measurement program in May 1990 to "better understand and manage these risks." The article discusses the reasons for program implementation, how metrics have aided in management decisions, which tools have been useful, and how the metrics have been used effectively.

To probe further

B. Boehm, *Software Engineering Economics*, Prentice Hall, Englewood Cliffs, N.J., 1981. One of the first books to apply measurement to software engineering, it describes in detail a model for estimating effort and schedule from measurable project, process, and resource characteristics.

B. Curtis, "Measurement and experimentation in software engineering," *Proceedings of the IEEE*, Vol. 68, No. 9, 1980, pp. 1,144–1,157. This seminal paper includes the first description of the scales of measurement made in a software engineering context.

N. Fenton and S. Lawrence Pfleeger, *Software Metrics: A Rigorous Approach*, second edition, International Thomson Press, London, 1996. A thorough overview of software metrics, including measurement theory and descriptions of many product, process, and resource metrics. Includes new information about implementing a metrics program and validating software measures.

R. Grady and D. Caswell, *Software Metrics: Establishing a Company-Wide Program*, Prentice Hall, Englewood Cliffs, N.J., 1987. A clear and thorough description of the goals and activities of the Hewlett-Packard corporate measurement program.

R. Grady, *Practical Software Metrics for Project Management and Process Improvement*, Prentice Hall, Englewood Cliffs, N.J., 1992. A well-written guide to implementing a corporate metrics program, based on Grady's experience at Hewlett-Packard.

T. Khoshgoftaar and P. Oman (eds.), "Metrics in Software," *Computer*, Vol. 27, No. 9, Sept. 1994. A theme issue devoted to industrial applications of software metrics.

S. Lawrence Pfleeger, "Experimental Design and Analysis in Software Engineering," *Annals of Software Engineering*, Vol. 1, No. 1, 1995, pp. 219–253. The first of the published papers from the UK's DESMET project, it describes the basic issues in designing and carrying out software engineering experiments.

S. Lawrence Pfleeger and H. Dieter Rombach (eds.), "Measurement-Based Process Improvement," *IEEE Software*, Vol. 11, No. 4, July 1994. A theme issue devoted to software process improvement driven by measurement and metrics.

5

SCIENCE AND SUBSTANCE: A CHALLENGE TO SOFTWARE ENGINEERS

For 25 years, software researchers have proposed improving software development and maintenance with new practices whose effectiveness is rarely, if ever, backed up by hard evidence. We suggest several ways to address the problem, and we challenge the community to invest in being more scientific.

NORMAN FENTON and
SHARI LAWRENCE PFLEEGER
City University, London
ROBERT L. GLASS
Computing Trends

Software researchers and engineers are always seeking ways to improve their ability to build software. This search has resulted in such methods as

- structured design and programming,
- abstract data types,
- object-oriented design and programming,
- CASE tools,
- statistical process control,
- maturity models,
- fourth-generation languages, and
- formal methods,

among others. But in spite of such "advances," software engineering in practice continues to be a labor-intensive, intellectually complex, and costly activity in which good management and communication seem to count for much more than technology.

At the same time, the January 1993 issue of the *IEEE CS Technical Committee on Software Engineering Newsletter* reported that since 1976 the Software Engineering Standards Committee of the IEEE Computer Society has developed 19 standards in the areas of terminology, requirements documentation, design documentation, user documentation, testing, verification and validation, reviews, and audits. And if you include all the major national standards bodies, there are in fact more than 250 software-engineering standards.

The existence of these standards raises some important questions. How do we know which practices to standardize? And are the standards not working or being ignored, since many development projects generate less-than-desirable products? The answer is that much of what we believe about which approaches are best is based on anecdotes, gut feelings, expert opinions, and flawed research, not on careful, rigorous software-engineering experimentation.

In this article, we examine some of the past and current problems with software-engineering research and technology transfer and suggest several ways to redirect our efforts toward improving our ability to build and maintain software.

RESEARCH CLAIMS

Developers who want to improve their productivity or the quality of their product are faced with an enormous choice of methods, tools, and standards. Adopting one or more often involves considerable time, expense, and trouble. Rational managers and their subordinates are prepared to invest in a new technology if they have evidence that using it will ultimately produce benefits. Although a single evaluation can never cover all possible situations, it is reasonable to seek some evidence of a new technology's likely *efficacy* when used under certain conditions.

But evidence is rare. Vendors' quantitative descriptions are often no more than sweeping claims like
- productivity gains of 250 percent,
- maintenance effort reduced by 80 percent, and
- integration time cut by five sixths.
Similar claims are often made by eminent experts. How can practitioners distinguish valid claims from invalid? And how can they determine that a particular method or technology is suited to their situation?

One way is to examine claims carefully from the viewpoint of scientific experimentation. As described by Vic Basili, Rick Selby, and David Hutchens in their classic paper on software-engineering experimentation, there *is* a scientifically sound way to design and carry out software-engineering investigations.[1] Their paper gives many examples of good research practice, plus guidelines for future experiments, but very few experiments reported since its publication have followed those recommendations.

Admittedly, experimentation in software engineering is notoriously difficult: Not only is it potentially expensive, but it can be daunting to try to control variables and environments. We applaud those who have performed an empirical study to confirm or refute their understanding of likely effects, even as we criticize certain experiments. Our intent is to suggest improvements to software-engineering research practices, in the hope that the results of future research will reflect a more solid scientific foundation. To do that, we compare good experiments with flawed ones, to illustrate the scrutiny required to determine if a recommended practice lives up to its claims.

RESEARCH REALITIES

Five questions should be (but rarely are) asked about any claim arising from software-engineering research:
- Is it based on empirical evaluation and data?
- Was the experiment designed correctly?
- Is it based on a toy or a real situation?
- Were the measurements used appropriate to the goals of the experiment?
- Was the experiment run for a long enough time?

Empiricism versus intuition. In many ways, software-engineering research got off to a bad start. Early researchers

HOW CAN YOU TELL IF CLAIMS ARE VALID? ASK FIVE QUESTIONS THAT ADDRESS EXPERIMENTAL TECHNIQUE.

often assumed that if sufficient brilliance and analysis were put into conceiving a technique, benefits would surely follow. As a result, many research findings published can be characterized as "analytical advocacy research." That is, the authors describe a new concept in considerable detail, derive its potential benefits analytically, and recommend the concept be transferred to practice. Time passes, and other researchers derive similar conclusions from similar analyses. Eventually the consensus among researchers is that the concept has clear benefits. Yet practitioners often seem unenthused. Researchers, satisfied that their communal analysis is correct, become frustrated. Heated discussion and finger-pointing ensues.

Something important is missing from this picture: rigorous, quantitative experimentation. In the traditional scientific method used by researchers in other disciplines, the formulation of an idea and its related hypothesis is followed by evaluative research to investigate if the hypothesis is true or false. Only when research results confirm the hypothesis do researchers advocate broad-based technology transfer. Moreover, the research tries to quantify the magnitude, as well as the existence, of a benefit.

Evaluative research must involve realistic projects with realistic subjects, and it must be done with sufficient rigor to ensure that any benefits identified are clearly derived from the concept in question. This type of research is time-consuming and expensive and, admittedly, difficult to employ in all software-engineering research. It is not surprising that little of it is being done.

On the other hand, claims made by analytical advocacy are insupportable. Today, practitioners must place their

MEASUREMENT SCALES AND MEANINGFUL ANALYSIS

Measurement is the process of assigning a number or descriptor (a measure) to an entity to characterize a specific attribute of the entity. By manipulating these numbers, instead of the entities themselves, you make judgments about the entities. However, you must use the measures in mathematically correct ways if your judgments are to make sense. The type of measurement determines what analysis is acceptable.

Measurement types. You must assign measures that preserve your empirical observations about the attribute you are interested in. For example, if the attribute of the entity person that you want to measure is height, then you must assign a number to each person in a way that preserves empirical observations about height. If person A is taller than person B (an empirical observation), the measurement $M(A)$ must be greater than $M(B)$.

Sometimes there are many ways to assign numbers that preserve all empirical observations. For example, $M(A)$ is greater than $M(B)$ regardless of whether M is inches, feet, centimeters, or furlongs. Furthermore, the relationship among entities is preserved when you convert the attribute data from one measure to another, such as from inches to centimeters. Such a conversion is called an *admissible transformation.*

So any two valid measures, M and M', of the same attribute are related in a very specific way. For example, if M and M' are measures of height, there is always some constant c, greater than 0, such that $M = cM'$. If M is inches and M' is centimeters, then c is 2.54.

The kind of admissible transformations determines the measurement scale type. Height, for example, is a ratio scale type because multiplication is an admissible transformation. In general, the more restrictive the admissible transformations, the more sophisticated the scale type and the analyses that can be done. Table A defines the most common scale types, in increasing order of sophistication.

Usually, an attribute's scale type is not known a priori. Instead, you start with a crude understanding of an attribute, devise a simple way to measure it, accumulate data, and see if the results reflect the empirical behavior of the attribute. Then you clarify and reevaluate the attribute: Are you measuring what you really want to measure? This analysis helps you refine definitions and introduce new empirical relations, improving the accuracy of the measurement and, usually, increasing the sophistication of the measurement scale.

A goal of software measurement is to define measures that are on the most sophisticated scale possible, given the constraints of the real world. However, we still have only very crude empirical relations — and hence crude measurement scales — for attributes like soft-

ware quality and productivity. Consider the software-failure attribute "criticality." Today we usually measure this by identifying different kinds of failures and relating them with a single binary relation, "is more critical than." This kind of empirical relational system defines a (relatively unsophisticated) ordinal scale type.

Meaningful measures. This formal definition of scale type based on admissible transformations lets you determine rigorously what kind of statements about your measurement are meaningful. Formally, a statement involving measurement is meaningful if its truth or falsity remains unchanged under any admissible transformation of the measures involved.

If you say "Fred is twice as tall as Jane," your statement implies that the measures are at least on the ratio scale, because multiplication is an admissible transformation. No matter which measure of height you use, the

---

faith in the reputation of the advocates who, although sometimes correct in the past, may not always be correct in the future. Consider the initial engineering attempts to allow humans to fly. Experts carefully studied the flight of birds, then developed flexible wings that would mimic it as closely as possible. This sounded fine in theory but was disastrous in practice. It was not until a completely new paradigm, using rigid wings and Bernoulli's laws, was conceived and tested that flight became possible. Empirical testing and analysis were critical to the discovery of the new paradigm.

Unfortunately, software methods and techniques often find their way into standards even when there is no reported empirical, quantitative evidence of their benefit. This is true of even the most sophisticated methods, developed with mathematical care and precision. For example, although there is some limited empirical evidence that fault-tolerant design for high-integrity systems (such as those that are safety-critical) is effective, there appears to be little or no published empirical work that supports the claims made on behalf of formal methods.

The case of formal methods is an especially interesting and instructive example of a revolutionary technique that has gained widespread appeal without rigorous experimentation. Formal methods are based on the use of mathematically precise specification and design notations. In its purest form, formal development is based on refinement and proof of correctness at each stage in the life cycle. In general,

adopting formal methods requires a revolutionary change in development practices. There is no simple migration path, because the effective use of formal methods requires a radical change right at the beginning of the traditional life-cycle, when customer requirements are captured and recorded. Thus, the stakes are particularly high.

Yet, when Susan Gerhart, Dan Craigen, and Ted Ralston performed an extensive survey of formal methods use in industrial environments,[2] they concluded

There is no simple answer to the question: do formal methods pay off? Our cases provide a wealth of data but only scratch the surface of information available to address these questions. All cases involve so many interwoven factors that it is impossi-

truth or falsity of the statement remains consistent.

But if you say, "The temperature in Tokyo today is twice that in London," your statement also implies the ratio scale, but in this case the ratio scale is not meaningful because air temperature is measured in Celsius and Fahrenheit. So, while it might be 40°C in Tokyo and 20°C in London (making your statement true), it would also be 104°F in Tokyo and 68°F in London (truth is not preserved). Thus, scalar multiplication is an inadmissible transformation, and this is an inappropriate use of measurement.

But suppose you said, "The difference in temperature between Tokyo and London today is twice what it was yesterday." This statement implies that the distance between two measures is meaningful, a condition that is part of the interval scale. The statement is meaningful, because Fahrenheit and Celsius are related by the affine transformation F = 9/5C + 32,

which ensures that ratios of differences (as opposed to just ratios) are preserved. If it was 35°C yesterday in Tokyo and 25°C in London (a difference of 10) and today it is 40°C in Tokyo and 20°C in London (a difference of 20), the difference will be preserved when you transform the temperatures to the Fahrenheit scale: 95°F in Tokyo and 77°F London (a difference of 18) and 104°F in Tokyo and 68°F in London (a difference of 36).

Unfortunately, there are

no such transformations for the software-failure attribute. The statement, "Failure x is twice as critical as failure y" is not meaningful because we have only an ordinal scale for failure criticality.

It is important to remember that meaningfulness is not the same as truth. Although the statement "Mickey Mouse is 102 years old" is clearly false, it is nevertheless a meaningful statement involving the age measure.

The notion of meaningfulness lets us determine

what kind of operations we can perform on different measures. For example, it is meaningful to use the mean to compute the average of a data set measured on a ratio scale but not on an ordinal scale. Medians are meaningful for an ordinal scale but not for a nominal scale. These basic observations have been ignored in many software-measurement studies, in which a common mistake is to use the mean (rather than median) as the measure of average for data that is only ordinal.

TABLE A
COMMON SCALE TYPES

Scale type	Admissible transformations	Examples
Nominal	$M'=F(M)$ where F is any one-to-one mapping	Classification, for example software fault types (data, control, other)
Ordinal	$M'=F(M)$ where F is any monotonic increasing mapping that is, $M(x) \geq M(y)$ implies $M'(x) > M'(y)$	Ordering, for example, software failure by severity (negligible, marginal, critical, catastrophic)
Intervals	$M'=aM+b$ $(a>0)$	Calendar time, temperature (restricted to Fahrenheit and Celsius)
Ratio	$M'=aM$ $(a>0)$	Time interval, length
Absolute	$M'=M$	Counting

ble to allocate payoff from formal methods versus other factors, such as quality of people or effects of other methodologies. Even where data was collected, it was difficult to interpret the results across the background of the organization and the various factors surrounding the application.

One of the situations investigated by the Gerhart team was a joint project between IBM Hursley and the Programming Research Group at Oxford University.[3] For 12 years, this project used the Z specification language to respecify parts of Customer Information Control System-ESA Version 3 Release 1 as it was updated. The project made a serious attempt to quantify the benefits of using Z. As a result, the CICS project is widely believed to provide the best quantita-

tive evidence to support the efficacy of formal methods, an observation confirmed by the Gerhart study.

The project would appear to be a huge success — so successful that IBM and PRG shared the prestigious Queen's Award for Technology. The project participants estimated that using Z reduced their costs by almost $5.5 million, a savings of nine percent overall. In addition, they claimed a 60 percent decrease in product failure rate. These results led the PGR's Geraint Jones to assert in his 1992 e-mail broadcast announcing the Queen's Award, "The moral of this tale is that formal methods cannot only improve quality, but also the timeliness and cost of producing state-of-the-art products." However, the quantified evidence to support these widely publi-

cized claims is missing from the published results.

Another study casts doubt on the claim that formal methods are a universal solution to poor software quality. In a recent article, Peter Naur[4] reports that the use of formal notations does not lead inevitably to higher quality specifications, even when used by the most mathematically sophisticated minds. In his experiment, the use of a formal notation often led to more, not fewer, defects.

These studies suggest that the benefits of formal methods are not self-evident and argue for experiments. Yet there seems to be a widespread consensus that formal methods should be used on projects in which the software is safety-critical. For example, John McDermid[5] asserts that "these mathematical approaches provide us with the best available approach to the development of high-integrity safety-critical systems." In addition, the interim UK defense standard for such systems, DefStd 00-55, makes the use of formal methods mandatory.[6]

The assumption seems to be that no expense should be spared to improve confidence in the reliability of critical systems. Unfortunately, no real project has unlimited funds. Even safety-critical projects must use the most cost-effective way to ensure reliability. Rather than abandon formal methods, we suggest their use be embedded in the context of an experiment so that their effect on software quality and reliability can be studied and assessed. At present, there is no hard evidence to show that

♦ formal methods have been used cost-effectively on a realistic, safety-critical development;

♦ using formal methods delivers reliability more cost-effectively than, say, traditional structured methods with enhanced testing; and

♦ developers and users can be trained in sufficient numbers to use formal methods properly.

There is also the problem of choosing among competing formal methods, which we assume are not equally effective in a given situation. By thinking about a more scientific context before using formal methods, a project can try them and contribute to the larger body of software-engineering understanding.

There *are* some techniques that have become standards or standard practice after careful, empirical analysis. A good example is the use of inspections to uncover defects in code. Table 1 compares the efficiency of different kinds of testing techniques, as reported by Bob Grady.[7] This and similar research experiments confirm one

of the few consensus views to emerge in empirical studies: Inspections are the cheapest and most effective testing techniques for finding faults.

Even here, it is important to keep the objective of the experiment in mind. The table shows overall testing efficiency, but does not report efficiency with respect to particular kinds of faults. Nevertheless, analyzing empirical data in the context of a rigorous investigation provides a sounder basis for changing practice than anecdote or intuition.

CURRICULA FOR THE MOST PART DO NOT COVER HOW TO ESTABLISH AND EVALUATE THE DESIGN OF EXPERIMENTS.

Experimental design. The experimental design must be correct for the hypothesis being tested. Some of the best publicized studies have subsequently been challenged on the basis of inappropriate experimental design. For example, an experiment by Ben Shneiderman and his colleagues showed that flowcharts did not help programmers comprehend documentation any better than pseudocode.[8] As a result, flowcharts were shunned in the software-engineering community and textbooks almost invariably use pseudocode instead of flowcharts to describe specific algorithms.

However, some years later David Scanlan demonstrated that structured flowcharts are preferable to pseudocode for program documentation.[9] Scanlan compared flowcharts and pseudocode with respect to the relative time needed to understand the algorithm and the relative time needed to make (accurate) changes to the algorithm. In both dimensions, flowcharts were clearly superior to pseudocode. Although some of Scanlan's criticisms of Shneiderman's study are controversial, he appears to have exposed a number of experimental flaws that explain the radically different conclusions about the two types of documentation. In particular, Scanlan demonstrated

that Shneiderman overlooked several key variables in his experimental design.

Similar flaws in experimental design have misled the community about the benefits of structured programming. Harlan Mills' claims are typical:[10]

When a program was claimed to be 90 percent done with solid top-down structured programming, it would take only 10 percent more effort to complete it (instead of possibly another 90 percent!).

But Iris Vessey and Ron Weber examined in detail the published empirical evidence to support the use of structured programming. They concluded that the evidence was "equivocal" and argued that the problems surrounding experimentation on structured programming are "a manifestation of poor theory, poor hypothesis, and poor methodology."[11]

The classic experiment by Gerald Weinberg on meeting goals shows that if you don't choose the attributes for determining success carefully, it is easy to maximize any single one as a success criterion.[12] Weinberg and Schulman gave each of six teams a different programming goal, and each team optimized its performance (and "succeeded") with respect to its goal — but performed poorly in terms of the other five goals. You can expect similar results if you run experiments out of context, because you will be narrowly defining "success" according to only one attribute.

These examples show that it is critical to examine experimental design carefully. Many software engineers are not familiar with how to establish or evaluate a proper design. This is due in no small part to the almost total absence of topics like experimental design, statistical analysis, and measurement principles in most computer-science and software-engineering curricula. The guidelines presented by Basili and his colleagues are a good first step, but the paper does not present important material in enough detail.

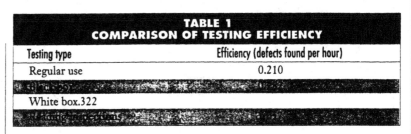

TABLE 1 COMPARISON OF TESTING EFFICIENCY	
Testing type	Efficiency (defects found per hour)
Regular use	0.210
White box.322	

To address this problem, the British Department of Trade and Industry is now funding two projects in the UK: SMARTIE is producing guidelines about how to evaluate the effectiveness of standards and methods, and DESMET is preparing handbooks for software researchers and engineers on experimental design and statistical analysis.[13]

Toy versus real. Because of the cost of designing and running large-scale studies, exploratory research in software engineering is all too often conducted on artificial problems in artificial situations. Practitioners refer to these as toy projects in toy situations. The number of research studies using experienced practitioners (instead of students or novice programmers) on realistic projects is minuscule.

This is particularly noticeable in studies of programmers, a field in which evaluative and experimental research is the norm. At its major conference, Empirical Studies of Programmers, the community's leaders continue to recommend that researchers study real projects and real programmers, yet many of the findings reported at the conference continue to involve small, student projects. Because of cost and time constraints, even this community refrains from doing large-scale, realistic studies.

To be sure, evaluative research in the small is better than no evaluative research at all. And a small project may be appropriate for an initial foray into testing an idea or even a research design. For example, Vessey conducted an interesting experiment using students and small projects that indicates object orientation is not the natural approach to systems analysis and design that its advocates claim it to be.[14] The results are not conclusive, especially for experienced practitioners on real software projects, but it does indicate directions for further investigation. Similarly, Naur's experiment[4] was small but exposed a weakness in a popularly held belief about formal notations.

In another small but valuable study, Elliot Soloway, Jeffrey Bonar, and Kate Ehrlich examined which looping constructs novice programmers found most natural.[15] Popular assumptions about structured programming are reflected in the fact that many languages supply a while-do loop (exit at the top) and a repeat-until loop (exit at the bottom). But the Soloway study revealed that the most natural looping structure was neither of these, but a loop that allows an exit in the middle, a technique disallowed in structured programming. This result implies that language designers, who followed common wisdom in not supplying such a loop, may inavertently make programming tasks more difficult than they need to be.

How do the results from toy studies scale up to larger, more realistic situations? Although some studies have addressed this question (as we describe later in discussing Cleanroom), little research has been done to answer that question. The best that can be said is that, just as software-development-in-the-small differs from software-development-in-the-large, research-in-the-small may differ from research-in-the-large. There is something about

EXPERIMENTS MAY BE DESIGNED PROPERLY BUT MEASURE OR ANALYZE THE WRONG DATA.

the nature of software tasks and the required communication among team members that prevents our understanding of small-scale work from yielding an understanding of large-scale work.

Obviously, there is no easy solution to this problem. It is not possible for a lone researcher, operating on a relatively small budget, to conduct the kind of research needed. Credible studies require the cooperation and financial backing of major research institutions and software-development organizations. To date, such support has been rare.

Appropriate measures. Sometimes an experiment is designed properly but it measures and analyzes insufficient data or the wrong data.

Measuring the right attribute? The most common example is success criteria. For example, a study to demonstrate the effectiveness of using abstract data types used program size, measured in lines of code, as a measure of product quality.[16] Often purely subjective measures are used in the absence of objective measures. This is sometimes unavoidable; for example, in measuring user satisfaction. However, the conclusions you can draw from subjective data are very limited. For example, Virginia Gibson and James Senn[17] show that maintainers' subjective perceptions of which systems are most easily maintained differ wildly from objective data that measured maintainability.

Another measure that is commonly misleading is reliability. One of the most effective ways to demonstrate a method's efficacy is to show that it leads to more reliable software. How-

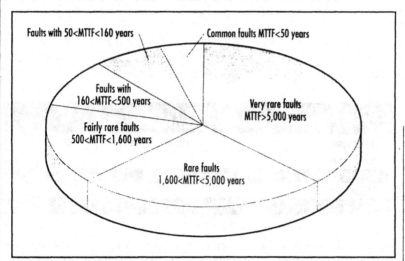

Figure 1. *The relationship between faults and failures, which shows that focusing on faults instead of failures can be fatal. Studies that compare testing methods by using faults may be inappropriate and misleading.*

ever, measuring reliability involves tracking operational failures over time, and it is not always practical to wait until software is completed to evaluate its reliability. The most common "substitute" measure is the number of faults or defects discovered during development and testing, a number that can be very misleading.

At IBM, Ed Adams examined data from nine large software products, each with many thousands of years of logged use worldwide.[18] Figure 1 shows the relationship he discovered between detected faults and their manifestation as failures. For example, 33 percent of all faults led to a mean-time-to-failure greater than 5,000 years. In practical terms, such faults will almost never manifest as failures. Conversely, about two percent of faults led to an MTTF of less than 50 years. These faults are important to find, because a significant number of users will eventually be affected by the failures they cause.

It follows that finding and removing large numbers of faults may not necessarily improve reliability. The crucial task is to find the important two percent of faults. Thus, a focus on faults instead of failures can be fatal, unless a technique can identify the faults that have a short MTTF or greatly affect system behavior. Many studies have compared the effectiveness of different testing methods, but if the comparison is done in terms of general faults discovered, they may be inappropriate and misleading.

What scale? In addition to measuring the correct attribute, researchers must take care to evaluate and manipulate the measurements in a way that is appropriate to the design and the kind of data collected, as the box on pp. 88-89 briefly explains.

Data falls into one of five scales: nominal, ordinal, interval, ratio, and absolute. Each scale reflects the data's properties and can be manipulated only in certain ways. For example, nominal data includes labels or classifications, such as when you classify requirements as data requirements, interface requirements, and so on. Nominal data can be analyzed statistically in terms of frequency and mode, but not in terms of mean or median. In other words, only nonparametric statistical tests are valid on nominal data. The software-engineering literature is rife with experiments in which means and standard deviations are applied to nominal data, but their results are meaningless in the sense of formal measurement theory.

Likewise, there is an embarrassingly large set of literature in which inappropriate statistical techniques are applied. For example, a researcher might compare correlation coefficients across disparate sets of data instead of using the more appropriate analysis of variance. One of the most talked-about measures in software engineering is the Software Engineering Institute's process-maturity level. This five-point ordinal scale is only a valid measure of an organiza-

tion's process maturity if it can be demonstrated that, in general, organizations at level $n + 1$ normally produce better software than organizations at level n. This relationship has not yet been demonstrated, although the SEI has told us that relevant studies are underway.

Long-term view. Sometimes research is designed and measured properly but just isn't carried on long enough. Short-term results masquerade as long-term effects. For example, speakers at the annual NASA Goddard Software Engineering Conference often report on an experiment at the Software Engineering Laboratory to investigate the benefits of using Ada instead of Fortran. The researchers examined a set of new Ada projects and found that the productivity and quality of the resulting Ada programs fell short of equivalent programs written in Fortran. However, the SEL did not stop there and report that Ada was a failure. It continued to develop programs in Ada, until each team had experience with at least three major Ada developments. These later results indicated that there were indeed significant benefits of Ada over Fortran.

The SEL concluded that the learning curve for Ada is long, and that the first set of projects represented programmers' efforts to code Fortran-like programs in Ada. By the third development, the programmers were taking advantage of Ada characteristics not available in Fortran, and these characteristics had measurable benefits. Thus, the long-term view led to conclusions very different from the short-term view.

The CASE Research Corp. found something similar when it considered the empirical evidence supporting the use of CASE tools.[19] They found that, contrary to the revolutionary improvements vendors invariably claimed, productivity normally decreased in the first year of CASE use, followed by modest improvement. Again, the short- and long-term assessments yielded opposite conclusions. However, the study found that the eventual improvement was rarely more than 10 percent and might be explained by factors other than the use of CASE (or may even fall within the margin of error). Moreover, compared with acquisition and upgrade costs, such modest improvements may indicate that CASE is not even cost-effective.

Researchers must take a long-term view of practices that promise to have a profound effect on development and maintenance, especially since the resistance of personnel to new techniques and the problems inherent in making radical changes quickly can mislead those who take only a short-term view.

RECENT EXAMPLES

Although most software-engineering research does not meet the requirements we outline here, some interesting examples do.

Cleanroom. Perhaps the single most complete research study involves Cleanroom.[20] Studies at the SEL, done in conjunction with the University of Maryland at College Park and Computer Sciences Corp., examined the Cleanroom error-detection and testing methodology using
 ♦ student subjects on small projects,
 ♦ NASA staff members on small real projects, and
 ♦ experienced industry practitioners on a sizable real project.
The findings used data collected both prestudy and within each context. For example, baseline data from projects not using the Cleanroom approach showed an error rate of six per thousand lines of code and productivity of 24 lines of code per day. The study of NASA staff using Cleanroom showed 4.5 errors per thousand LOC and productivity of 40 LOC per day, and the industry practitioners' Cleanroom project showed 3.2 errors per thousand LOC and productivity of 26 LOC per day. (Note how reliability improved significantly as Cleanroom was scaled up to a large program, but productivity did not.)

This study meets nearly all the criteria for good software-engineering research:
 ♦ It involved empirical evaluation and data.
 ♦ Its design was reasonable, given that the projects were "real."
 ♦ It involved both toy and real situations.
 ♦ The measurements were appropriate to the goals.
 ♦ The experiment was conducted over a period of time sufficient to encompass the effects of change in practice.

Object-oriented design. The SEL is also involved in a more mixed example of software-engineering research. In this case, it is gathering data over several years on eight major software projects using the object-oriented approach to building software. The series of studies is not finished, and the scaled-up study is not due for completion until 1996, but researchers are already reporting that the approaches studied represent "the most important methodology studies by the SEL to date."[21]

So far, researchers have reported that the amount of reuse rises dramatically when OO techniques are used, from 20 to 30 percent to 80 percent, and OO programs are about three-quarters the length (in lines of code) of comparable traditional solutions. On the other hand, OO projects have reported performance problems (although it is unclear how much of these problems are the result of OO), and OO appears to require significant domain analysis and project tailoring.

Unfortunately, the projects under study are also using Ada, and the studies have not separated the effects of OO from those of Ada. And because many of the benefits appear to be the result of increased reuse, it is not clear what gains are due to Ada, OO, or reuse.

So these studies meet many of, but not all, the goals for good research because
 ♦ They involve empirical evaluation and data.
 ♦ Use questionable experimental design.
 ♦ Involve real situations.
 ♦ Use measurements appropriate to the experimental goals.
 ♦ Are being run over an appropriate period of time.

4GLs. More typical of research approaches in the last decade are the studies of the benefits of fourth-generation languages. Several interesting studies published in the late 1980s compare Cobol and various 4GLs for implementing relatively simple business systems applications.[22-24] The findings of these studies are fascinating but hardly definitive. Some report productivity improving with the use of 4GLs by a factor of 4 to 5, while others describe only 29 to 39 percent differences. In some cases, object-code performance degraded by a factor of 15 to 174 for 4GLs, while other 4GLs produced code that was six times as fast!

It is apparent from the studies that measured effects are highly dependent on the 4GL studied, the project's application, and the people doing the job (for example, end users versus software specialists).

Examining the 4GL studies with the same criteria for good research in mind, we can make the following statements:
 ♦ The studies were based on empirical evidence and data.
 ♦ The experimental designs were reasonable.
 ♦ The projects were not toys, but neither were they sizable.
 ♦ The measurements were appropriate to the study goals.
 ♦ The experiments were not done over an extended period of time.

> **THERE ARE FAR TOO FEW EXAMPLES OF MODERATELY EFFECTIVE RESEARCH.**

(Interestingly, two of the studies involved the same author, implying that the author may have made a second attempt at research in the topic area.)

Thus, recent examples of evaluative research paint a mixed picture. There are examples of effective research, but they are far too few in number. There are examples of moderately good research, and we can learn interesting things from them; however, follow-up, long-term, significant project studies are needed. And there are many examples of research that does no evaluation whatsoever. Given this spectrum, one thing is clear: there is considerable room for improvement.

We continue to look for new technologies to improve our ability to build and maintain software. But there is very little empirical evidence to confirm that technological fixes, such as introducing specific methods, tools and techniques, can radically improve the way we develop software systems. Even when improvements can be made by using specific methods, there is an urgent need to quantify the benefits and costs involved, and to compare these with competing technologies. At present, little quantitative data is available to help software managers make informed decisions about which method to use when change is needed.

The difficulty in performing the well-designed, quantitative assessments necessary to evaluate technologies in an objective manner is small compared with the massive resistance to change. Until there is widespread demand and expectation for objective measurement-based evaluation, software managers and standards bodies will continue to place their trust in unsubstantiated advertising claims, misleading or incomplete research reports, and anecdotal evidence.

Thus, we challenge the software-engineering community to take three major steps toward producing more rigorous and meaningful analyses of current and proposed practices:

♦ *For the software manager*: Insist on quantitative data and well-designed experimental research to substantiate any claims made for new or changed practices. And be willing to participate in such experiments to further your knowledge in particular and the software-engineering community's in general.

♦ *For the software developer or maintainer*: Be flexible and willing to participate in experiments involving existing or new techniques or methods. Try to be objective in providing data to researchers, and help them identify behaviors, attitudes, or practices that

ACKNOWLEDGMENTS

Norman Fenton is supported in part by the SMARTIE and PDCS2 projects. We thank Chris Kemerer, Bev Littlewood, Peter Mellor, and Stella Page for their contributions to this article. The final version was considerably improved as a result of the comments of several anonymous referees.

REFERENCES

1. V.R. Basili, R.W. Selby, and D.H. Hutchens, "Experimentation in Software Engineering," *IEEE Trans. Software Eng.*, June 1986, pp. 758-773.
2. S. Gerhart, D. Craigen, and A. Ralston, "Observation on Industrial Practice Using Formal Methods," *Proc. Int'l Conf. Software Eng.*, IEEE CS Press, Los Alamitos, Calif., 1993, pp. 24-33.
3. I. Houston and S. King, "CICS Project Report: Experiences and Results from the use of Z," *Lecture Notes in Computer Science*, Vol. 551, 1991.
4. P. Naur, "Understanding Turing's Universal Machine Personal Style in Program Description," *Computer J.*, No. 4, 1993, pp. 351-371.
5. J.A. McDermid, "Safety-Critical Software: A Vignette," *IEE Software Eng. J.*, No. 1, 1993, pp. 2-3.
6. *Interim Defence Standard 00-55: The Procurement of Safety-Critical Software in Defence Equipment*, Ministry of Defence Directorate of Standardization, Glasgow, Scotland, 1991.
7. R.B. Grady, *Practical Software Metrics for Project Management and Process Improvement*, Prentice-Hall, Englewood Cliffs, N.J., 1992.
8. B. Shneiderman et al., "Experimental Investigations of the Utility of Detailed Flowcharts in Programming," *Comm. ACM*, June 1977, pp. 373-381.
9. D.A. Scanlan, "Structured Flowcharts Outperform Pseudocode: An Experimental Comparison," *IEEE Software*, Sept. 1989, pp. 28-36.
10. H. Mills, "Structured Programming: Retrospect and Prospect," *IEEE Software*, Nov. 1986, pp. 58-66.
11. I. Vessey and R. Weber, "Research on Structured Programming: An Empiricist's Evaluation," *IEEE Trans. Software Eng.*, July 1984, pp. 397-407.
12. G. Weinberg and E. Schulman, "Goals and Performance in Computer Programming," *Human Factors*, No. 1, 1974, pp. 70-77.
13. W.-E. Mohamed, C.J. Sadler, and D. Law, "Experimentation in Software Engineering: A New Framework," *Proc. Software Quality Management '93*, Elsevier Science, Essex, U.K. and Computational Mechanics Publications, Southampton, U.K., 1993.
14. I. Vessey and S. Conger, "Requirements Specification: Learning Object, Process, and Data Methodologies," *Comm. ACM*, May 1994.
15. E. Soloway, J. Bonar, and K. Ehrlich, "Cognitive Strategies and Looping Constructs: An Empirical Survey," *Comm. ACM*, Nov. 1983, pp. 853-860.
16. J. Mitchell, J.E. Urban, and R. McDonald, "The Effect of Abstract Data Types on Program Development," *Computer*, Aug. 1987, pp. 85-88.
17. V.R. Gibson and J.A. Senn, "System Structure and Software Maintenance Performance," *Comm. ACM*, Mar. 1989, pp. 347-358.
18. E. Adams, "Optimizing Preventive Service of Software Products," *IBM J. Research and Development*, No. 1, 1984, pp. 2-14.
19. CASE Research Group, *The Second Annual Report on CASE*, Bellevue, Wash., 1990.
20. A. Kouchakdjian and V.R. Basili, "Evaluation of the Cleanroom Methodology in the SEL," *Proc. Software Eng. Workshop*, NASA Goddard, Greenbelt, MD., 1989.
21. M. Stark, "Impacts of Object-Oriented Technologies: Seven Years of Software Engineering," *J. Systems and Software*, Nov. 1993.
22. S.K. Misra and P.J. Jalics, "Third-Generation versus Fourth-Generation Software Development," *IEEE Software*, July 1988, pp. 8-14.
23. V. Matos and P.J. Jalics, "An Experimental Analysis of the Performance of Fourth-Generation Tools on PCs," *Comm. ACM*, Nov. 1989.
24. J. Verner and G. Tate, "Estimating Size and Effort in Fourth-Generation Development," *IEEE Software*, July 1988, pp. 15-22.

might affect the aspects of the project being studied.

♦ *For the software researcher*: Employ evaluative research as a necessary component in exploring new ideas. Learn about rigorous experimentation, and design your projects accordingly. Try to quantify as much as possible, and identify the degree to which you have control over each of the variables you are studying.

By taking these steps, the entire community should benefit. Finding willing industrial partners for research should be made easier, as the potential benefit to all participants is clear. The European Community has recognized the urgent need for quantitative evaluation performed by industry-research partnerships. A new program called the European Systems and Software Initiative has been defined and funded (initial funding is $50 million) to support projects that aim to evaluate specific software methods or tools. Eventually, with programs such as these, the practice of software engineering will benefit from better approaches resulting from scientific investigation and demonstrated improvement. ♦

Experimentation in Software Engineering

VICTOR R. BASILI, SENIOR MEMBER, IEEE, RICHARD W. SELBY, MEMBER, IEEE, AND
DAVID H. HUTCHENS, MEMBER, IEEE

Abstract—Experimentation in software engineering supports the advancement of the field through an iterative learning process. In this paper we present a framework for analyzing most of the experimental work performed in software engineering over the past several years. We describe a variety of experiments in the framework and discuss their contribution to the software engineering discipline. Some useful recommendations for the application of the experimental process in software engineering are included.

Index Terms—Controlled experiment, data collection and analysis, empirical study, experimental design, software metrics, software technology measurement and evaluation.

I. INTRODUCTION

AS any area matures, there is the need to understand its components and their relationships. An experimental process provides a basis for the needed advancement in knowledge and understanding. Since software engineering is in its adolescence, it is certainly a candidate for the experimental method of analysis. Experimentation is performed in order to help us better evaluate, predict, understand, control, and improve the software development process and product.

Experimentation in software engineering, as with any other experimental procedure, involves an iteration of a hypothesize and test process. Models of the software process or product are built, hypotheses about these models are tested, and the information learned is used to refine the old hypotheses or develop new ones. In an area like software engineering, this approach takes on special importance because we greatly need to improve our knowledge of how software is developed, the effect of various technologies, and what areas most need improvement. There is a great deal to be learned and intuition is not always the best teacher.

In this paper we lay out a framework for analyzing most of the experimental work that has been performed in soft-

Manuscript received July 15, 1985; revised January 15, 1986. This work was supported in part by the Air Force Office of Scientific Research under Contract AFOSR-F49620-80-C-001 and by the National Aeronautics and Space Administration under Grant NSG-5123 to the University of Maryland. Computer support was provided in part by the Computer Science Center at the University of Maryland.

V. R. Basili is with the Department of Computer Science, University of Maryland, College Park, MD 20742.

R. W. Selby was with the Department of Computer Science, University of Maryland, College Park, MD 20742. He is now with the Department of Information and Computer Science, University of California, Irvine, CA 92717.

D. H. Hutchens is with the Department of Computer Science, Clemson University, Clemson, SC 29634.

IEEE Log Number 8608188.

ware engineering over the past several years. We then discuss a variety of these experiments, their results, and the impact they have had on our knowledge of the software engineering discipline.

II. OBJECTIVES

There are three overall goals for this work. The first objective is to describe a framework for experimentation in software engineering. The framework for experimentation is intended to help structure the experimental process and to provide a classification scheme for understanding and evaluating experimental studies. The second objective is to classify and discuss a variety of experiments from the literature according to the framework. The description of several software engineering studies is intended to provide an overview of the knowledge resulting from experimental work, a summary of current research directions, and a basis for learning from past experience with experimentation. The third objective is to identify problem areas and lessons learned in experimentation in software engineering. The presentation of problem areas and lessons learned is intended to focus attention on general trends in the field and to provide the experimenter with useful recommendations for performing future studies. The following three sections address these goals.

III. EXPERIMENTATION FRAMEWORK

The framework of experimentation, summarized in Fig. 1, consists of four categories corresponding to phases of the experimentation process: 1) definition, 2) planning, 3) operation, and 4) interpretation. The following sections discuss each of these four phases.

A. Experiment Definition

The first phase of the experimental process is the study definition phase. The study definition phase contains six parts: 1) motivation, 2) object, 3) purpose, 4) perspective, 5) domain, and 6) scope. Most study definitions contain each of the six parts; an example definition appears in Fig. 2.

There can be several motivations, objects, purposes, or perspectives in an experimental study. For example, the motivation of a study may be to understand, assess, or improve the effect of a certain technology. The "object of study" is the primary entity examined in a study. A study may examine the final software product, a development process (e.g., inspection process, change process), a model (e.g., software reliability model), etc. The

I. Definition					
Motivation	Object	Purpose	Perspective	Domain	Scope
Understand	Product	Characterise	Developer	Programmer	Single project
Assess	Process	Evaluate	Modifier	Program/project	Multi-project
Manage	Model	Predict	Maintainer		Replicated project
Engineer	Metric	Motivate	Project manager		Blocked subject-project
Learn	Theory		Corporate manager		
Improve			Customer		
Validate			User		
Assure			Researcher		

II. Planning		
Design	Criteria	Measurement
Experimental designs	Direct reflections of cost/quality	Metric definition
Incomplete block	Cost	Goal-question-metric
Completely randomised	Errors	Factor-criteria-metric
Randomized block	Changes	Metric validation
Fractional factorial	Reliability	Data collection
Multivariate analysis	Correctness	Automatability
Correlation	Indirect reflections of cost/quality	Form design and test
Factor analysis	Data coupling	Objective vs. subjective
Regression	Information visibility	Level of measurement
Statistical models	Programmer comprehension	Nominal/classificatory
Non-parametric	Execution coverage	Ordinal/ranking
Sampling	Size	Interval
	Complexity	Ratio

III. Operation		
Preparation	Execution	Analysis
Pilot study	Data collection	Quantitative vs. qualitative
	Data validation	Preliminary data analysis
		Plots and histograms
		Model assumptions
		Primary data analysis
		Model application

IV. Interpretation		
Interpretation context	Extrapolation	Impact
Statistical framework	Sample representativeness	Visibility
Study purpose		Replication
Field of research		Application

Fig. 1. Summary of the framework of experimentation.

Definition element	example
Motivation	To improve the unit testing process,
Purpose	characterise and evaluate
Object	the processes of functional and structural testing
Perspective	from the perspective of the developer
Domain: programmer	as they are applied by experienced programmers
Domain: program	to unit-size software
Scope	in a blocked subject-project study.

Fig. 2. Study definition example.

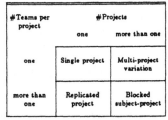

Fig. 3. Experimental scopes.

purpose of a study may be to characterize the change in a system over time, to evaluate the effectiveness of testing processes, to predict system development cost by using a cost model, to motivate[1] the validity of a theory by analyzing empirical evidence, etc. In experimental studies that examine "software quality," the interpretation usually includes correctness if it is from the perspective of a developer or reliability if it is from the perspective of a customer. Studies that examine metrics for a given project type from the perspective of the project manager may interest certain project managers, while corporate managers may only be interested if the metrics apply across several project types.

Two important domains that are considered in experimental studies of software are 1) the individual programmers or programming teams (the "teams") and 2) the programs or projects (the "projects"). "Teams" are (possibly single-person) groups that work separately, and "projects" are separate programs or problems on which teams work. Teams may be characterized by experience, size, organization, etc., and projects may be characterized by size, complexity, application, etc. A general classification of the scopes of experimental studies can be obtained by examining the sizes of these two domains considered (see Fig. 3). Blocked subject-project studies examine one or more objects across a set of teams and a set of projects. Replicated project studies examine ob-

---

[1] For clarification, the usage of the word "motivate" as a study purpose is distinct from the study "motivation."

ject(s) across a set of teams and a single project, while multiproject variation studies examine object(s) across a single team and a set of projects. Single project studies examine object(s) on a single team and a single project. As the representativeness of the samples examined and the scope of examination increase, the wider-reaching a study's conclusions become.

B. Experiment Planning

The second phase of the experimental process is the study planning phase. The following sections discuss aspects of the experiment planning phase: 1) design, 2) criteria, and 3) measurement.

The design of an experiment couples the study scope with analytical methods and indicates the domain samples to be examined. Fractional factorial or randomized block designs usually apply in blocked subject–project studies, while completely randomized or incomplete block designs usually apply in multiproject and replicated project studies [33], [41]. Multivariate analysis methods, including correlation, factor analysis, and regression [75], [80], [89], generally may be used across all experimental scopes. Statistical models may be formulated and customized as appropriate [89]. Nonparametric methods should be planned when only limited data may be available or distributional assumptions may not be met [100]. Sampling techniques [40] may be used to select representative programmers and programs/projects to examine.

Different motivations, objects, purposes, perspectives, domains, and scopes require the examination of different criteria. Criteria that tend to be direct reflections of cost/ quality include cost [114], [108], [86], [5], [28], errors/ changes [49], [24], [112], [2], [81], [13], reliability [42], [64], [56], [69], [70], [76], [77], [95], and correctness [51], [61], [68]. Criteria that tend to be indirect reflections of cost/quality include data coupling [62], [48], [104], [78], information visibility [85], [83], [55], programmer understanding [99], [103], [109], [113], execution coverage [105], [15], [18], and size/complexity [11], [59], [71].

The concrete manifestations of the cost/quality aspects examined in the experiment are captured through measurement. Paradigms assist in the metric definition process: the goal-question-metric paradigm [17], [25], [19], [93] and the factor-criteria-metric paradigm [39], [72]. Once appropriate metrics have been defined, they may be validated to show that they capture what is intended [7], [21], [45], [50], [108], [116]. The data collection process includes developing automated collection schemes [16] and designing and testing data collection forms [25], [27]. The required data may include both objective and subjective data and different levels of measurement: nominal (or classificatory), ordinal (or ranking), interval, or ratio [100].

C. Experiment Operation

The third phase of the experimental process is the study operation phase. The operation of the experiment consists of 1) preparation, 2) execution, and 3) analysis. Before conducting the actual experiment, preparation may include a pilot study to confirm the experimental scenario, help organize experimental factors (e.g., subject expertise), or inoculate the subjects [45], [44], [63], [18], [113], [73]. Experimenters collect and validate the defined data during the execution of the study [21], [112]. The analysis of the data may include a combination of quantitative and qualitative methods [30]. The preliminary screening of the data, probably using plots and histograms, usually precedes the formal data analysis. The process of analyzing the data requires the investigation of any underlying assumptions (e.g., distributional) before the application of the statistical models and tests.

D. Experiment Interpretation

The fourth phase of the experimental process is the study interpretation phase. The interpretation of the experiment consists of 1) interpretation context, 2) extrapolation, and 3) impact. The results of the data analysis from a study are interpreted in a broadening series of contexts. These contexts of interpretation are the statistical framework in which the result is derived, the purpose of the particular study, and the knowledge in the field of research [16]. The representativeness of the sampling analyzed in a study qualifies the extrapolation of the results to other environments [17]. Several follow-up activities contribute to the impact of a study: presenting/publishing the results for feedback, replicating the experiment [33], [41], and actually applying the results by modifying methods for software development, maintenance, management, and research.

IV. Classification of Analyses

Several investigators have published studies in the four general scopes of examination: blocked subject–project, replicated project, multiproject variation, or single project. The following sections cite studies from each of these categories. Note that surveys on experimentation methodology in empirical studies include [35], [96], [74], [98]. Each of the sections first discusses one experiment in moderate depth, using italicized keywords from the framework for experimentation, and then chronologically presents an overview of several others in the category. In any survey of this type it is almost certain that some deserving work has been accidentally omitted. For this, we apologize in advance.

A. Blocked Subject–Project Studies

With a *motivation* to improve and better understand unit testing, Basili and Selby [18] conducted a study whose *purpose* was to characterize and evaluate the processes (i.e., *objects*) of code reading, functional testing, and structural testing from the *perspective* of the developer. The testing processes were examined in a blocked subject–project *scope*, where 74 student through professional programmers (from the programmer *domain*) tested four unit-size programs (from the program *domain*) in a replicated fractional factorial *design*. Objective *measurement* of the testing processes was in several *criteria* areas: fault detection effectiveness, fault detection cost, and classes of faults detected. Experiment *preparation* included a pilot study [63], *execution* incorporated both manual and automated monitoring of testing activity, and *analysis* used analysis of variance methods [33], [90]. The major results (in the *interpretation context* of the study purpose) included: 1) with the professionals, code reading detected more software faults and had a higher fault detection rate than did the other methods; 2) with the professionals, functional testing detected more faults than did structural testing, but they were not different in fault detection rate; 3) with the students, the three techniques were not different in performance, except that structural testing detected fewer faults than did the others in one study phase; and 4) overall, code reading detected more interface faults and functional testing detected more control faults than did the other methods. A major result (in the *interpretation context* of the field of research) was that the study suggested that nonexecution based fault detection, as in code reading, is at least as effective as on-line methods. The particular programmers and programs sampled qualify the *extrapolation* of the results. The *impact* of the study was an advancement in the understanding of effective software testing methods.

In order to understand program debugging, Gould and Drongowski [58] evaluated several related factors, including effect of debugging aids, effect of fault type, and effect of particular program debugged from the perspective of the developer and maintainer. Thirty experienced programmers independently debugged one of four one-page programs that contained a single fault from one of three classes. The major results of these studies were: 1) debugging is much faster if the programmer has had previous experience with the program, 2) assignment bugs were harder to find than other kinds, and 3) debugging aids did not seem to help programmers debug faster. Consistent results were obtained when the study was conducted on ten additional experienced programmers [57]. These results and the identification of possible "principles" of debugging contributed to the understanding of debugging methodology.

In order to improve experimentation methodology and its application, Weissman [113] evaluated programmers' ability to understand and modify a program from the perspective of the developer and modifier. Various measures of programmer understanding were calculated, in a series of factorial design experiments, on groups of 16–48 university students performing tasks on two small programs. The study emphasized the need for well-structured and well-documented programs and provided valuable testimony on and worked toward a suitable experimentation methodology.

In order to assess the impact of language features on the programming process, Gannon and Horning [54] characterized the relationship of language features to software reliability from the perspective of the developer. Based on an analysis of the deficiencies in a programming language, nine different features were modified to produce a new version. Fifty-one advanced students were divided into two groups and asked to complete implementations of two small but sophisticated programs (75–200 line) in the original language and its modified version. The redesigned features in the two languages were contrasted in program fault frequency, type, and persistence. The experiment identified several language-design decisions that significantly affected reliability, which contributed to the understanding of language design for reliable software.

In order to understand the unit testing process better, Hetzel [60] evaluated a reading technique and functional and "selective" testing (a composite approach) from the perspective of the developer. Thirty-nine university students applied the techniques to three unit-size programs in a Latin square design. Functional and "selective" testing were equally effective and both superior to the reading technique, which contributed to our understanding of testing methodology.

In order to improve and better understand the maintenance process, Curtis *et al.* [44] conducted two experiments to evaluate factors that influence two aspects of software maintenance, program understanding, and modification, from the perspective of the developer and maintainer. Thirty-six junior through advanced professional programmers in each experiment examined three classes of small (36–57 source line) programs in a factorial design. The factors examined include control flow complexity, variable name mnemonicity, type of modification, degree of commenting, and the relationship of programmer performance to various complexity metrics. In [45] they continued the investigation of how software characteristics relate to psychological complexity and presented a third experiment to evaluate the ability of 54 professional programmers to detect program bugs in three programs in a factorial design. The series of experiments suggested that software science [59] and cyclomatic complexity [71] measures were related to the difficulty experienced by programmers in locating errors in code.

In order to improve and better understand program debugging, Weiser [110] evaluated the theory that "programmers use 'slicing' (stripping away a program's statements that do not influence a given variable at a given statement) when debugging" from the perspective of the developer, maintainer, and researcher. Twenty-one university graduate students and programming staff debugged a fault in three unit-size (75–150 source line) programs in a nonparametric design. The study results supported the slicing theory, that is, programmers during debugging routinely partitioned programs into a coherent, discontiguous piece (or slice). The results advanced the understanding of software debugging methodology.

In order to improve design techniques, Ramsey, Atwood, and Van Doren [87] evaluated flowcharts and program design languages (PDL) from the perspective of the developer. Twenty-two graduate students designed two small (approximately 1000 source line) projects, one using flowcharts and the other using PDL. Overall, the results suggested that design performance and designer-programmer communication were better for projects using PDL.

In order to validate a theory of programming knowledge, Soloway and Ehrlich [102] conducted two studies, using 139 novices and 41 professional programmers, to evaluate programmer behavior from the perspective of the researcher. The theory was that programming knowledge contained programming plans (generic program fragments representing common sequences of actions) and rules of programming discourse (conventions used in composing plans into programs). The results supported the existence and use of such plans and rules by both novice and advanced programmers.

Other blocked subject–project studies include [82], [115], and [111].

B. Replicated Project Studies

With a *motivation* to assess and better understand team software development methodologies, Basili and Reiter [16] conducted a study whose *purpose* was to characterize and evaluate the development processes (i.e., *objects*) of a 1) disciplined-methodology team approach, 2) ad hoc team approach, and 3) ad hoc individual approach from the *perspective* of the developer and project manager. The development processes were examined in a replicated project *scope*, in which advanced university students comprising seven three-person teams, six three-person teams, and six individuals (from the programmer *domain*) used the approaches, respectively. They separately developed a small (600–2200 line) compiler (from the program *domain*) in a nonparametric *design*. Objective *measurement* of the development approaches was in several *criteria* areas: number of changes, number of program runs, program data usage, program data coupling/binding, static program size/complexity metrics, language usage, and modularity. Experiment *preparation* included presentation of relevant material [68], [8], [34], *execution* included automated monitoring of on-line development activity and *analysis* used nonparametric comparison methods. The major results (in the *interpretation context* of the study purpose) included: 1) the methodological discipline was a key influence on the general efficiency of the software development process; 2) the disciplined team methodology significantly reduced the costs of software development as reflected in program runs and changes; and 3) the examination of the effect of the development approaches was accomplished by the use of quantitative, objective, unobtrusive, and automatable process and product metrics. A major result (in the *interpretation context* of the field of research) was that the study supported the belief that incorporating discipline in software development reflects positively on both the development process and final product. The particular programmers and program sampled qualify the *extrapolation* of the results. The *impact* of the study was an advancement in the understanding of software development methodologies and their evaluation.

In order to improve the design and implementation processes, Parnas [84] evaluated system modularity from the perspective of the developer. Twenty university undergraduates each developed one of four different types of implementations for one of five different small modules. Then each of the modules were combined with others to form several versions of the whole system. The results were that minor effort was required in assembling the systems and that major system changes were confined to small, well-defined subsystems. The results supported the ideas on formal specifications and modularity discussed in [83] and [85], and advanced the understanding of design methodology.

In order to assess the impact of static typing of programming languages in the development process, Gannon [53] evaluated the use of a statically typed language (having integers and strings) and a "typeless" language (e.g., arbitrary subscripting of memory) from the perspective of the developer. Thirty-eight students programmed a small (48–297 source line) problem in both languages, with half doing it in each order. The two languages were compared in the resulting program faults, the number of runs containing faults, and the relation of subject experience to fault proneness. The major result was that the use of a statically typed language can increase programming reliability, which improved our understanding of the design and use of programming languages.

In order to improve program composition, comprehension, debugging, and modification, Shneiderman [99] evaluated the use of detailed flowcharts in these tasks from the perspective of the developer, maintainer, modifier, and researcher. Groups of 53–70 novice through intermediate subjects, in a series of five experiments, performed various tasks using small programs. No significant differences were found between groups that used and those that did not use flowcharts, questioning the merit of using detailed flowcharts.

In order to improve and better understand the unit testing process, Myers [79] evaluated the techniques of three-person walk-throughs, functional testing, and a control group from the perspective of the developer. Fifty-nine junior through advanced professional programmers applied the techniques to test a small (100 source line) but nontrivial program. The techniques were not different in the number of faults they detected, all pairings of techniques were superior to single techniques, and code reviews were less cost-effective than the others. These results improved our understanding of the selection of appropriate software testing techniques.

In order to validate a particular metric family, Basili and Hutchens [11] evaluated the ability of a proposed metric family to explain differences in system development methodologies and system changes from the perspective of the developer, project manager, and researcher. The metrics were applied to 19 versions of a small (600–2200) compiler, which were developed by teams of advanced university students using three different development approaches (see the first study [16] described in this section). The major results included: 1) the metrics were able to differentiate among projects developed with different development methodologies; and 2) the differences among individuals had a large effect on the relationships between the metrics and aspects of system development. These results provided insights into the formulation and appropriate use of software metrics.

In order to improve the understanding of why software errors occur, Soloway *et al.* [65], [101] characterized programmer misconceptions, cognitive strategies, and their manifestations as bugs in programs from the perspective of the developer and researcher. Two hundred and four novice programmers separately attempted implementations of an elementary program. The results supported the programmers' intended use of "programming plans" [103] and revealed that most people preferred a read–process strategy over a process–read strategy. The results advanced the understanding of how individuals write programs, why they sometimes make errors, and what programming language constructs should be available.

In order to understand the effect of coding conventions on program comprehensibility, Miara *et al.* [73] conducted a study to evaluate the relationship between indentation levels and program comprehension from the perspective of the developer. Eighty-six novice through professional subjects answered questions about one of seven program variations with different level and type of indentation. The major result was that an indentation level of two or four spaces was preferred over zero or six spaces.

In order to improve software development approaches, Boehm, Gray, and Seewaldt [29] characterized and evaluated the prototyping and specifying development approaches from the perspective of the developer, project manager, and user. Seven two- and three-person teams, consisting of university graduate students, developed versions of the same application software system (2000–4000 line); four teams used a requirement/design specifying approach and three teams used a prototyping approach. The systems developed by prototyping were smaller, required less development effort, and were easier to use. The systems developed by specifying had more coherent designs, more complete functionality, and software that was easier to integrate. These results contributed to the understanding of the merits and appropriateness of software development approaches.

In order to validate the theoretical model for *N*-version programming [3], [66], Knight and Leveson [67] conducted a study to evaluate the effectiveness of *N*-version programming for reliability from the perspective of the customer and user. *N*-version programming uses a high-level driver to connect several separately designed versions of the same system, the systems "vote" on the correct solution, and the solution provided by the majority of the systems is output. Twenty-seven graduate students were asked to independently design an 800 source line

system. The factors examined included individual system reliability, total *N*-version system reliability, and classes of faults that occurred in systems simultaneously. The major result was that the assumption of independence of the faults in the programs was not justified, and therefore, the reliability of the combined "voting" system was not as high as given by the model.

In order to improve and better understand software development approaches, Selby, Basili, and Baker [94] characterized and evaluated the Cleanroom development approach [46], [47], in which software is developed without execution (i.e., completely off-line), from the perspective of the developer, project manager, and customer. Fifteen three-person teams of advanced university students separately developed a small system (800–2300 source line); ten teams used Cleanroom and five teams used a traditional development approach in a nonparametric design. The major results included: 1) most developers using the Cleanroom approach were able to build systems without program execution; and 2) the Cleanroom teams' products met system requirements more completely and succeeded on more operational test cases than did those developed with a traditional approach. The results suggested the feasibility of complete off-line development, as in Cleanroom, and advanced the understanding of software development methodology.

Other replicated project studies include [37], [4], and [63].

C. Multiproject Variation Studies

With a *motivation* to improve the understanding of resource usage during software development, Bailey and Basili [5] conducted a study whose *purpose* was to predict development cost by using a particular model (i.e., *object*) and to evaluate it from the *perspective* of the project manager, corporate manager, and researcher. The particular model generation method was examined in a multiproject *scope*, with baseline data from 18 large (2500–100 000 source line) software projects in the NASA S.E.L. [27], [26], [38], [91] production environment (from the program *domain*), in which teams contained from two to ten programmers (from the programmer *domain*). The study *design* incorporated multivariate methods to parameterize the model. Objective and subjective *measurement* of the projects was based on 21 *criteria*[2] in three areas: methodology, complexity, and personnel experience. Study *preparation* included preliminary work [52], *execution* included an established set of data collection forms [27], and *analysis* used forward multivariate regression methods. The major results (in the *interpretation context* of the study purpose) included 1) the estimation of software development resource usage improved by considering a set of both baseline and customization factors; 2) the application in the NASA environment of

---

[2] Twenty-one factors were selected after examining a total of 82 factors that possibly contributed to project resource expenditure, including 36 from [108] and 16 from [28].

the proposed model generation method, which considers both types of factors, produced a resource usage estimate for a future project within one standard deviation of the actual; and 3) the confirmation of the NASA S.E.L. formula that the cost per line of reusing code is 20 percent of that of developing new code. A major result (in the *interpretation context* of the field of research) was that the study highlighted the difference of each software development environment, which improved the selection and use of resource estimation models. The particular programming environment and projects sampled qualify the *extrapolation* of the results. The *impact* of the study was an advancement in the understanding of estimating software development resource expenditure.

In order to assess, manage, and improve multiproject environments, several researchers [28], [20], [108], [10], [36], [21], [62], [112], [97], [107] have characterized, evaluated, and/or predicted the effect of several factors from the perspective of the developer, modifier, project manager, and corporate manager. All the studies examined moderate to large projects from production environments. The relationships investigated were among various factors, including structured programming, personnel background, development process and product constraints, project complexity, human and computer resource consumption, error-prone software identification, error/change distributions, data coupling/binding, project duration, staff size, degree of management control, and productivity. These studies have provided increased project visibility, greater understanding of classes of factors sensitive to project performance, awareness of the need for project measurement, and efforts for standardization of definitions. Analysis has begun on incorporating project variation information into a management tool [9], [14].

In order to improve and better understand the software maintenance process, Vessey and Weber [106] conducted an experiment to evaluate the relationship between the rate of maintenance repair and various product and process metrics from the perspective of the developer, user, and the project manager. A total of 447 small (up to 600 statements) commercial and clerical Cobol programs from one Australian organization and two U.S. organizations were analyzed. The product and process metrics included program complexity, programming style, programmer quality, and number of system releases. The major results were: 1) in the Australian organization, program complexity and programming style significantly affected the maintenance repair rate; and 2) in the U.S. organizations, the number of times a system was released significantly affected the maintenance repair rate.

In order to improve the software maintenance process, Adams [1] evaluated operational faults from the perspective of the user, customer, project manager, and corporate manager. The fault history for nine large production products (e.g., operating system releases or their major components) were empirically modeled. He developed an approach for estimating whether and under what circumstances preventively fixing faults in operational software

in the field was appropriate. Preventively fixing faults consisted of installing fixes to faults that had yet to be discovered by particular users, but had been discovered by the vendor or other users. The major result was that for the typical user, corrective service was a reasonable way of dealing with most faults after the code had been in use for a fairly long period of time, while preventively fixing high-rate faults was advantageous during the time immediately following initial release.

In order to assess the effectiveness of the testing process, Bowen [31] evaluated estimations of the number of residual faults in a system from the perspective of the customer, developer, and project manager. The study was based on fault data collected from three large (2000–6000 module) systems developed in the Hughes–Fullerton environment. The study partitioned the faults based on severity and analyzed the differences in estimates of remaining faults according to stage of testing. Insights were gained into relationships between fault detection rates and residual faults.

D. Single Project Studies

With a *motivation* to improve software development methodology, Basili and Turner [22] conducted a study whose *purpose* was to characterize the process (i.e., *object*) of iterative enhancement in conjunction with a top-down, stepwise refinement development approach from the *perspective* of the developer. The development process was examined in a single project *scope*, where the authors, two experienced individuals (from the programmer *domain*), built a 17 000 line compiler (from the program *domain*). The study *design* incorporated descriptive methods to capture system evolution. Objective *measurement* of the system was in several *criteria* areas: size, modularity, local/global data usage, and data binding/coupling [62], [104]. Study *preparation* included language design [23], *execution* incorporated static analysis of system snapshots, and *analysis* used descriptive statistics. The results (in the *interpretation context* of the statistical framework) included: 1) the percentage of global variables decreased over time while the percentage of actual versus possible data couplings across modules increased, suggesting the usage of global data became more appropriate over time; and 2) the number of procedures and functions rose over time while the number of statements per procedure or function decreased, suggesting increased modularity. The major result of the study (in the *interpretation context* of the study purpose) was that the iterative enhancement technique encouraged the development of a software product that had several generally desirable aspects of system structure. A major result (in the *interpretation context* of the field of research) was that the study demonstrated the feasibility of iterative enhancement. The particular programming team and project examined qualify the *extrapolation* of the results. The *impact* of the study was an advancement in the understanding of software development approaches.

In order to improve, better understand, and manage the

software development process, Baker [6] evaluated the effect of applying chief programming teams and structured programming in system development from the perspective of the user, developer, project manager, and corporate manager. The large (83 000 line) system, known as "The New York Times Project," was developed by a team of professionals organized as a chief programmer team, using structured code, top-down design, walk-throughs, and program libraries. Several benefits were identified, including reduced development time and cost, reduced time in system integration, and reduced fault detection in acceptance testing and field use. The results of the study demonstrated the feasibility of the chief programmer team concept and the accompanying methodologies in a production environment.

In order to improve their development environments, several researchers [49], [24], [2], [81], [13] have each conducted single project studies to characterize the errors and changes made during a development project. They examined the development of a moderate to large software project, done by a multiperson team, in a production environment. They analyzed the frequency and distribution of errors during development and their relationship with several factors, including module size, software complexity, developer experience, method of detection and isolation, effort for isolation and correction, phase of entrance into the system and observance, reuse of existing design and code, and role of the requirements document. Such analyses have produced fault categorization schemes and have been useful in understanding and improving a development environment.

In order to better understand and improve the use of the Ada® language, Basili et al. [55], [12] examined a ground-support system written in Ada to characterize the use of Ada packages from the perspective of the developer. Four professional programmers developed a project of 10 000 source lines of code. Factors such as how package use affected the ease of system modification and how to measure module change resistance were identified, as well as how these observations related to aspects of development and training. The major results were 1) several measures of Ada programs were developed, and 2) there was an indication that a lot of training will be necessary if we are to expect the facilities of Ada to be properly used.

In order to assess and improve software testing methodology, Basili and Ramsey [15], [88] characterized and evaluated the relationship between system acceptance tests and operational usage from the perspective of the developer, project manager, customer, and researcher. The execution coverage of functionally generated acceptance test cases and a sample of operational usage cases was monitored for a medium-size (10 000 line) software system developed in a production environment. The results calculated that 64 percent of the program statements were executed during system operation and that the acceptance test cases corresponded reasonably well to the operational

®Ada is a registered trademark of the U.S. Department of Defense (Ada Joint Program Office).

usage. The results gave insights into the relationships among structural coverage, fault detection, system testing, and system usage.

V. Problem Areas in Experimentation

The following sections identify several problem areas of experimentation in software engineering. These areas may serve as guidelines in the performance of future studies. After mentioning some overall observations, considerations in each of the areas of experiment definition, planning, operation, and interpretation are discussed.

A. Experimentation Overall

There appears to be no "universal model" or "silver bullet" in software engineering. There are an enormous number of factors that differ across environments, in terms of desired cost/quality goals, methodology, experience, problem domain, constraints, etc. [108], [20], [5], [10], [28]. This results in every software development/maintenance environment being different. Another area of wide variation is the many-to-one (e.g., 10:1) differential in human performance [11], [43], [18]. The particular individuals examined in an empirical study can make an enormous difference. Among other considerations, these variations suggest that metrics need to be validated for a particular environment and a particular person to show that they capture what is intended [11], [21]. Thus, experimental studies should consider the potentially vast differences among environments and among people.

B. Experiment Definition

In the definition of the purpose for the experiment, the formulation of intuitive problems into precisely stated goals is a nontrivial task [17], [25]. Defining the purpose of a study often requires the articulation of what is meant by "software quality." The many interpretations and perceptions of quality [32], [39], [72] highlight the need for considering whose perspective of quality is being examined. Thus, a precise specification of the problem to be investigated is a major step toward its solution.

C. Experiment Planning

Experimental planning should have a horizon beyond a first experiment. Controlled studies may be used to focus on the effect of certain factors, while their results may be confirmed in replications [92], [99], [102], [113], [58], [57], [45], [44], [18] and/or larger case studies [5], [16]. When designing studies, consider that a combination of factors may be effective as a "critical mass," even though the particular factors may be ineffective when treated in isolation [16], [107]. Note that formal designs and the resulting statistical robustness are desirable, but we should not be driven exclusively by the achievement of statistical significance. Common sense must be maintained, which allows us, for example, to experiment just to help develop and refine hypotheses [13], [112]. Thus, the experimental planning process should include a series of experiments for exploration, verification, and application.

D. Experiment Operation

The collection of the required data constitutes the primary result of the study operation phase. The data must be carefully defined, validated, and communicated to ensure their consistent interpretation by all persons associated with the experiment: subjects under observation, experimenters, and literature audience [21]. There have been papers in the literature that do not define their data well enough to enable a comparison of results across many projects and environments. We have often contacted experimenters and discovered that different entities were being measured in different studies. Thus, the experimenter should be cautious about the definition, validation, and communication of data, since they play a fundamental role in the experimental process.

E. Experiment Interpretation

The appropriate presentation of results from experiments contributes to their correct interpretation. Experimental results need to be qualified by the particular samples (e.g., programmers, programs) analyzed [17]. The extrapolation of results from a particular sample must consider the representativeness of the sample to other environments [40], [114], [108], [86], [5], [28]. The visibility of the experimental results in professional forums and the open literature provides valuable feedback and constructive criticism. Thus, the presentation of experimental results should include appropriate qualification and adequate exposure to support their proper interpretation.

VI. Conclusion

Experimentation in software engineering supports the advancement of the field through an iterative learning process. The experimental process has begun to be applied in a multiplicity of environments to study a variety of software technology areas. From the studies presented, it is clear that experimentation has proven effective in providing insights and furthering our domain of knowledge about the software process and product. In fact, there is a learning process in the experimentation approach itself, as has been shown in this paper.

We have described a framework for experimentation to provide a structure for presenting previous studies. We also recommend the framework as a mechanism to facilitate the definition, planning, operation, and interpretation of past and future studies. The problem areas discussed are meant to provide some useful recommendations for the application of the experimental process in software engineering. The experimental framework cannot be used in a vacuum; the framework and the lessons learned complement one another and should be used in a synergistic fashion.

References

[1] E. N. Adams, "Optimizing preventive service of software products," *IBM J. Res. Develop.*, vol. 28, no. 1, pp. 2–14, Jan. 1984.

[2] J.-L. Albin and R. Ferreol, "Collecte et analyse de mesures de logiciel (Collection and analysis of software data)," *Technique et Science Informatiques*, vol. 1, no. 4, pp. 297–313, 1982 (Rairo ISSN 0752-4072).

[3] A. Avizienis, P. Gunningberg, J. P. J. Kelly, L. Strigini, P. J. Traverse, K. S. Tso, and U. Voges, "The UCLA Dedix system: A distributed testbed for multiple-version software," in *Dig. 15th Int. Symp. Fault-Tolerant Comput.*, Ann Arbor, MI, June 19–21, 1985.

[4] J. W. Bailey, "Teaching Ada: A comparison of two approaches," in *Proc. Washington Ada Symp.*, Washington, DC, 1984.

[5] J. W. Bailey and V. R. Basili, "A meta-model for software development resource expenditures," in *Proc. 5th Int. Conf. Software Eng.*, San Diego, CA, 1981, pp. 107–116.

[6] F. T. Baker, "System quality through structured programming," in *AFIPS Proc. 1972 Fall Joint Comput. Conf.*, vol. 41, 1972, pp. 339–343.

[7] V. R. Basili, *Tutorial on Models and Metrics for Software Management and Engineering*. New York: IEEE Computer Society, 1980.

[8] V. R. Basili and F. T. Baker, "Tutorial of structured programming," in *Proc. 11th IEEE COMPCON*, IEEE Cat. No. 75CH1049-6, 1975.

[9] V. R. Basili and C. Doerflinger, "Monitoring software development through dynamic variables," in *Proc. COMPSAC*, Chicago, IL, 1983.

[10] V. R. Basili and K. Freburger, "Programming measurement and estimation in the software engineering laboratory," *J. Syst. Software*, vol. 2, pp. 47–57, 1981.

[11] V. R. Basili and D. H. Hutchens, "An empirical study of a syntactic metric family," *IEEE Trans. Software Eng.*, vol. SE-9, pp. 664–672, Nov. 1983.

[12] V. R. Basili, E. E. Katz, N. M. Panilio-Yap, C. L. Ramsey, and S. Chang, "A quantitative characterization and evaluation of a software development in Ada," *Computer*, Sept. 1985.

[13] V. R. Basili and B. T. Perricone, "Software errors and complexity: An empirical investigation," *Commun. ACM*, vol. 27, no. 1, pp. 42–52, Jan. 1984.

[14] V. R. Basili and C. L. Ramsey, "Arrowsmith-P—A prototype expert system for software engineering management," in *Proc. Symp. Expert Systems in Government*, Mclean, VA, Oct. 1985.

[15] V. R. Basili and J. R. Ramsey, "Analyzing the test process using structural coverage," in *Proc. 8th Int. Conf. Software Eng.*, London, Aug. 28–30, 1985, pp. 306–312.

[16] V. R. Basili and R. W. Reiter, "A controlled experiment quantitatively comparing software development approaches," *IEEE Trans. Software Eng.*, vol. SE-7, May 1981.

[17] V. R. Basili and R. W. Selby, "Data collection and analysis in software research and management," *Proc. Amer. Statistical Association and Biometric Society Joint Statistical Meetings*, Philadelphia, PA, August 13–16, 1984.

[18] ——, "Comparing the effectiveness of software testing strategies," Dep. Comput. Sci., Univ. Maryland, College Park, Tech. Rep. TR-1501, May 1985.

[19] ——, "Four applications of a software data collection and analysis methodology," in *Proc. NATO Advanced Study Institute: The Challenge of Advanced Computing Technology to System Design Methods*, Durham, U. K., July 29–Aug. 10, 1985.

[20] ——, "Calculation and use of an environment's characteristic software metric set," in *Proc. 8th Int. Conf. Software Eng.*, London, Aug. 28–30, 1985, pp. 386–393.

[21] V. R. Basili, R. W. Selby, and T. Y. Phillips, "Metric analysis and data validation across FORTRAN projects," *IEEE Trans. Software Eng.*, vol. SE-9, pp. 652–663, Nov. 1983.

[22] V. R. Basili and A. J. Turner, "Iterative enhancement: A practical technique for software development," *IEEE Trans. Software Eng.*, vol. SE-1, Dec. 1975.

[23] ——, *SIMPL-T: A Structured Programming Language*. Geneva, IL: Paladin House, 1976.

[24] V. R. Basili and D. M. Weiss, "Evaluation of a software requirements document by analysis of change data," in *Proc. 5th Int. Conf. Software Eng.*, San Diego, CA, Mar. 9–12, 1981, pp. 314–323.

[25] ——, "A methodology for collecting valid software engineering data*," *IEEE Trans. Software Eng.*, vol. SE-10, pp. 728–738, Nov. 1984.

[26] V. R. Basili and M. V. Zelkowitz, "Analyzing medium-scale software developments," in *Proc. 3rd Int. Conf. Software Eng.*, Atlanta, GA, May 1978, pp. 116–123.

[27] V. R. Basili, M. V. Zelkowitz, F. E. McGarry, R. W. Reiter, Jr., W. F. Truszkowski, and D. L. Weiss, "The software engineering laboratory," Software Eng. Lab., NASA/Goddard Space Flight Center, Greenbelt, MD, Rep. SEL-77-001, May 1977.

[28] B. W. Boehm, *Software Engineering Economics*. Englewood Cliffs, NJ: Prentice-Hall, 1981.

[29] B. W. Boehm, T. E. Gray, and T. Seewaldt, "Prototyping versus specifying: A multiproject experiment," *IEEE Trans. Software Eng.*, vol. SE-10, pp. 290-303, May 1984.

[30] R. C. Bogdan and S. K. Biklen, *Qualitative Research for Education: An Introduction to Theory and Methods.* Boston, MA: Allyn and Bacon, 1982.

[31] J. Bowen, "Estimation of residual faults and testing effectiveness," in *Proc. 7th Minnowbrook Workshop Software Performance Evaluation*, Blue Mountain Lake, NY, July 24-27, 1984.

[32] T. P. Bowen, G. B. Wigle, and J. T. Tsai, "Specification of software quality attributes," Rome Air Development Center, Griffiss Air Force Base, NY, Tech. Rep. RADC-TR-85-37 (3 vols.), Feb. 1985.

[33] G. E. P. Box, W. G. Hunter, and J. S. Hunter, *Statistics for Experimenters.* New York: Wiley, 1978.

[34] F. P. Brooks, Jr., *The Mythical Man-Month.* Reading, MA: Addison-Wesley, 1975.

[35] R. E. Brooks, "Studying programmer behavior: The problem of proper methodology, *Commun. ACM*, vol. 23, no. 4, pp. 207-213, 1980.

[36] W. D. Brooks, "Software technology payoff: Some statistical evidence," *J. Syst. Software*, vol. 2, pp. 3-9, 1981.

[37] F. O. Buck, "Indicators of quality inspections," IBM Systems Products Division, Kingston, NY, Tech. Rep. 21.802, Sept. 1981.

[38] D. N. Card, F. E. McGarry, J. Page, S. Eslinger, and V. R. Basili, "The software engineering laboratory," Software Eng. Lab., NASA/Goddard Space Flight Center, Greenbelt, MD, Rep. SEL-81-104, Feb. 1982.

[39] J. P. Cavano and J. A. McCall, "A Framework for the measurement of software quality," in *Proc. Software Quality and Assurance Workshop*, San Diego, CA, Nov. 1978, pp. 133-139.

[40] W. G. Cochran, *Sampling Techniques.* New York: Wiley, 1953.

[41] W. G. Cochran and G. M. Cox, *Experimental Designs.* New York: Wiley, 1950.

[42] P. A. Currit, M. Dyer, and H. D. Mills, "Certifying the reliability of software," *IEEE Trans. Software Eng.*, vol. SE-12, pp. 3-11, Jan. 1986.

[43] B. Curtis, "Cognitive science of programming," *6th Minnowbrook Workshop Software Performance Evaluation*, Blue Mountain Lake, NY, July 19-22, 1983.

[44] B. Curtis, S. B. Sheppard, P. Milliman, M. A. Borst, and T. Love, "Measuring the psychological complexity of software maintenance tasks with the Halstead and McCabe metrics," *IEEE Trans. Software Eng.*, pp. 96-104, Mar. 1979.

[45] B. Curtis, S. B. Sheppard, and P. M. Milliman, "Third time charm: Stronger replication of the ability of software complexity metrics to predict programmer performance," in *Proc. 4th Int. Conf. Software Eng.*, Sept. 1979, pp. 356-360.

[46] M. Dyer, "Cleanroom software development method," IBM Federal Systems Division, Bethesda, MD, Oct. 14, 1982.

[47] M. Dyer and H. D. Mills, "Developing electronic systems with certifiable reliability," in *Proc. NATO Conf.*, Summer 1982.

[48] T. Emerson, "A discriminant metric for module cohesion," in *Proc. 7th Int. Conf. Software Eng.*, Orlando, FL, 1984, pp. 294-303.

[49] A. Endres, "An analysis of errors and their causes in systems programs," *IEEE Trans. Software Eng.*, pp. 140-149, vol. SE-1, June 1975.

[50] A. R. Feuer and E. B. Fowlkes, "Some results from an empirical study of computer software," in *Proc. 4th Int. Conf. Software Eng.*, 1979, pp. 351-355.

[51] R. W. Floyd, "Assigning meaning to programs," *Amer. Math. Soc.*, vol. 19, J. T. Schwartz, Ed., Providence, RI, 1967.

[52] K. Freburger and V. R. Basili, "The software engineering laboratory: Relationship equations," Dep. Comput. Sci., Univ. Maryland, College Park, Tech. Rep. TR-764, May 1979.

[53] J. D. Gannon, "An experimental evaluation of data type conventions," *Commun. ACM*, vol. 20, no. 8, pp. 584-595, 1977.

[54] J. D. Gannon and J. J. Horning, "The impact of language design on the production of reliable software," *IEEE Trans. Software Eng.*, vol. SE-1, pp. 179-191, 1975.

[55] J. D. Gannon, E. E. Katz, and V. R. Basili, "Characterizing Ada programs: Packages," in *The Measurement of Computer Software Performance*, Los Alamos Nat. Lab., Aug. 1983.

[56] A. L. Goel, "Software reliability and estimation techniques," Rome Air Development Center, Griffiss Air Force Base, NY, Rep. RADC-TR-82-263, Oct. 1982.

[57] J. D. Gould, "Some psychological evidence on how people debug computer programs," *Int. J. Man-Machine Studies*, vol. 7, pp. 151-182, 1975.

[58] J. D. Gould and P. Drongowski, "An exploratory study of computer program debugging," *Human Factors*, vol. 16, no. 3, pp. 258-277, 1974.

[59] M. H. Halstead, *Elements of Software Science.* New York: North-Holland, 1977.

[60] W. C. Hetzel, "An experimental analysis of program verification methods," Ph.D. dissertation, Univ. North Carolina, Chapel Hill, 1976.

[61] C. A. R. Hoare, "An axiomatic basis for computer programming," *Commun. ACM*, vol. 12, no. 10, pp. 576-583, Oct. 1969.

[62] D. H. Hutchens and V. R. Basili, "System structure analysis: Clustering with data bindings," *IEEE Trans. Software Eng.*, vol. SE-11, Aug. 1985.

[63] S.-S. V. Hwang, "An empirical study in functional testing, structural testing, and code reading/inspection*," Dep. Comput. Sci., Univ. Maryland, College Park, Scholarly Paper 362, Dec. 1981.

[64] Z. Jelinski and P. B. Moranda, "Applications of a probability-based model to a code reading experiment," in *Proc. IEEE Symp. Comput. Software Rel.*, New York, 1973, pp. 78-81.

[65] W. L. Johnson, S. Draper, and E. Soloway, "An effective bug classification scheme must take the programmer into account," in *Proc. Workshop High-Level Debugging*, Palo Alto, CA, 1983.

[66] J. P. J. Kelly, "Specification of fault-tolerant multi-version software: Experimental studies of a design diversity approach," Ph.D. dissertation, Univ. California, Los Angeles, 1982.

[67] J. C. Knight and N. G. Leveson, "An experimental evaluation of the assumption of independence in multiversion programming," *IEEE Trans. Software Eng.*, vol. SE-12, pp. 96-109, Jan. 1986.

[68] R. C. Linger, H. D. Mills, and B. I. Witt, *Structured Programming: Theory and Practice.* Reading, MA: Addison-Wesley, 1979.

[69] B. Littlewood, "Stochastic reliability growth: A model for fault renovation computer programs and hardware designs," *IEEE Trans. Rel.*, vol. R-30, Oct. 1981.

[70] B. Littlewood and J. L. Verrall, "A Bayesian reliability growth model for computer software," *Appl. Statist.*, vol. 22, no. 3, 1973.

[71] T. J. McCabe, "A complexity measure," *IEEE Trans. Software Eng.*, vol. SE-2, pp. 308-320, Dec. 1976.

[72] J. A. McCall, P. Richards, and G. Walters, "Factors in software quality," Rome Air Development Center, Griffiss Air Force Base, NY, Tech. Rep. RADC-TR-77-369, Nov. 1977.

[73] R. J. Miara, J. A. Musselman, J. A. Navarro, and B. Shneiderman, "Program indentation and comprehensibility," *Commun. ACM*, vol. 26, no. 11, pp. 861-867, Nov. 1983.

[74] T. Moher and G. M. Schneider, "Methodology and experimental research in software engineering," *Int. J. Man-Machine Studies*, vol. 16, no. 1, pp. 65-87, 1982.

[75] S. A. Mulaik, *The Foundations of Factor Analysis.* New York: McGraw-Hill, 1972.

[76] J. D. Musa, "A theory of software reliability and its application," *IEEE Trans. Software Eng.*, vol. SE-1, pp. 312-327, 1975.

[77] —, "Software reliability measurement," *J. Syst. Software*, vol. 1, no. 3, pp. 223-241, 1980.

[78] G. L. Myers, *Composite/Structured Design.* New York: Van Nostrand Reinhold, 1978.

[79] —, "A controlled experiment in program testing and code walkthroughs/inspections," *Commun. ACM*, pp. 760-768, Sept. 1978.

[80] J. Neter and W. Wasserman, *Applied Linear Statistical Models.* Homewood, IL: Richard D. Irwin, 1974.

[81] T. J. Ostrand and E. J. Weyuker, "Collecting and categorizing software error data in an industrial environment*," *J. Syst. Software*, vol. 4, pp. 289-300, 1983.

[82] D. J. Panzl, "Experience with automatic program testing," in *Proc. NBS Trends and Applications*, Nat. Bureau Standards, Gaithersburg, MD, May 28, 1981, pp. 25-28.

[83] D. L. Parnas, "On the criteria to be used in decomposing systems into modules," *Commun. ACM*, vol. 15, no. 12, pp. 1053-1058, 1972.

[84] —, "Some conclusions from an experiment in software engineering techniques," in *AFIPS Proc. 1972 Fall Joint Comput. Conf.*, vol. 41, 1972, pp. 325-329.

[85] —, "A technique for module specification with examples," *Commun. ACM*, vol. 15, May 1972.

[86] L. Putnam, "A general empirical solution to the macro software sizing and estimating problem," *IEEE Trans. Software Eng.*, vol. SE-4, July 1978.

[87] H. R. Ramsey, M. E. Atwood, and J. R. Van Doren, "Flowcharts versus program design languages: An experimental comparison," *Commun. ACM*, vol. 26, no.6, pp. 445–449, June 1983.

[88] J. Ramsey, "Structural coverage of functional testing," in *Proc. 7th Minnowbrook Workshop Software Perform. Eval.*, Blue Mountain Lake, NY, July 24–27, 1984.

[89] *Statistical Analysis System (SAS) User's Guide*, SAS Inst. Inc., Box 8000, Cary, NC 27511, 1982.

[90] H. Scheffe, *The Analysis of Variance*. New York: Wiley, 1959.

[91] "Annotated bibliography of software engineering laboratory (SEL) literature," Software Eng. Lab., NASA/Goddard Space Flight Center, Greenbelt, MD, Rep. SEL-82-006, Nov. 1982.

[92] R. W. Selby, "An empirical study comparing software testing techniques," in *Proc. 6th Minnowbrook Workshop Software Perform. Eval.*, Blue Mountain Lake, NY, July 19–22, 1983.

[93] ——, "Evaluations of software technologies: Testing, CLEANROOM, and metrics," Ph.D. dissertation, Dep. Comput. Sci., Univ. Maryland, College Park, Tech. Rep. TR-1500, 1985.

[94] R. W. Selby, V. R. Basili, and F. T. Baker, "CLEANROOM software development: An empirical evaluation," Dep. Comput. Sci., Univ. Maryland, College Park, Tech. Rep. TR-1415, Feb. 1985.

[95] J. G. Shanthikumar, "A statisical time dependent error occurrence rate software reliability model with imperfect debugging," in *Proc. 1981 Nat. Comput. Conf.*, June 1981.

[96] B. A. Sheil, "The psychological study of programming," *Comput. Surveys*, vol. 13, pp. 101–120, Mar. 1981.

[97] V. Y. Shen, T. J. Yu, S. M. Thebaut, and L. R. Paulsen, "Identifying error-prone software—An empirical study," *IEEE Trans. Software Eng.*, vol. SE-11, pp. 317–324, Apr. 1985.

[98] B. Shneiderman, *Software Psychology: Human Factors in Computer and Information Systems*. Winthrop, 1980.

[99] B. Shneiderman, R. E. Mayer, D. McKay, and P. Heller, "Experimental investigations of the utility of detailed flowcharts in programming," *Commun. ACM*, vol. 20, no. 6, pp. 373–381, 1977.

[100] S. Siegel, *Nonparametric Statistics for the Behavioral Sciences*. New York: McGraw-Hill, 1955.

[101] E. Soloway, J. Bonar, and K. Ehrlich, "Cognitive strategies and looping constructs: An empirical study," *Commun. ACM*, vol. 26, no.11, pp. 853–860, Nov. 1983.

[102] E. Soloway and K. Ehrlich, "Empirical studies of programming knowledge," *IEEE Trans. Software Eng.*, vol. SE-10, pp. 595–609, Sept. 1984.

[103] E. Soloway, K. Ehrlich, J. Bonar, and J. Greenspan, "What do novices know about programming?" in *Directions in Human–Computer Interactions*, A. Badre and B. Shneiderman, Eds. Norwood, NJ: Ablex, 1982.

[104] W. P. Stevens, G. L. Myers, and L. L. Constantine, "Structural design," *IBM Syst. J.*, vol. 13, no. 2, pp. 115–139, 1974.

[105] L. G. Stucki, "New directions in automated tools for improving software quality," in *Current Trends in Programming Methodology*, R. T. Yeh, Ed. Englewood Cliffs, NJ: Prentice-Hall, 1977.

[106] I. Vessey and R. Weber, "Some factors affecting program repair maintenance: An empirical study," *Commun. ACM*, vol. 26, no. 2, pp. 128–134, Feb. 1983.

[107] J. Vosburgh, B. Curtis, R. Wolverton, B. Albert, H. Malec, S. Hoben, and Y. Liu, "Productivity factors and programming environments," in *Proc. 7th Int. Conf. Software Eng.*, Orlando, FL, 1984, pp. 143–152.

[108] C. E. Walston and C. P. Felix, "A method of programming measurement and estimation," *IBM Syst. J.*, vol. 16, no. 1, pp. 54–73, 1977.

[109] G. Weinberg, *The Psychology of Computer Programming*. New York: Van Nostrand Rheinhold, 1971.

[110] M. Weiser, "Programmers use slices when debugging," *Commun. ACM*, vol. 25, pp. 446–452, July 1982.

[111] M. Weiser and J. Shertz, "Programming problem representation in novice and expert programmers," *Int. J. Man–Machine Studies*, vol. 19, pp. 391–398, 1983.

[112] D. M. Weiss and V. R. Basili, "Evaluating software development by analysis of changes: Some data from the software engineering laboratory," *IEEE Trans. Software Eng.*, vol. SE-11, pp. 157–168, Feb. 1985.

[113] L. Weissman, "Psychological complexity of computer programs: An experimental methodology," *SIGPLAN Notices*, vol. 9, no. 6, pp. 25–36, June 1974.

[114] R. Wolverton, "The cost of developing large scale software," *IEEE Trans. Comput.*, vol. C-23, June 1974.

[115] S. N. Woodfield, H. E. Dunsmore, and V. Y. Shen, "The effect of modularization and comments on program comprehension," Dep. Comput. Sci., Arizona State Univ., Tempe, AZ, Working Paper, 1981.

[116] J. C. Zolnowski and D. B. Simmons, "Taking the measure of program complexity," in *Proc. Nat. Comput. Conf.*, 1981, pp. 329–336.

Software Risk Management: Principles and Practices

BARRY W. BOEHM,
Defense Advanced Research Projects Agency

◆ *Identifying and dealing with risks early in development lessens long-term costs and helps prevent software disasters.*

It is easy to begin managing risks in your environment.

Like many fields in their early stages, the software field has had its share of project disasters: the software equivalents of the Beauvais Cathedral, the *HMS Titanic*, and the "Galloping Gertie" Tacoma Narrows Bridge. The frequency of these software-project disasters is a serious concern: A recent survey of 600 firms indicated that 35 percent of them had at least one runaway software project.[1]

Most postmortems of these software-project disasters have indicated that their problems would have been avoided or strongly reduced if there had been an explicit early concern with identifying and resolving their high-risk elements. Frequently, these projects were swept along by a tide of optimistic enthusiasm during their early phases that caused them to miss some clear signals of high-risk issues that proved to be their downfall later.

Enthusiasm for new software capabilities is a good thing. But it must be tempered with a concern for early identification and resolution of a project's high-risk elements so people can get these resolved early and then focus their enthusiasm and energy on the positive aspects of their product.

Current approaches to the software process make it too easy for projects to make high-risk commitments that they will later regret:

◆ The sequential, document-driven waterfall process model tempts people to overpromise software capabilities in contractually binding requirements specifications before they understand their risk implications.

◆ The code-driven, evolutionary development process model tempts people to say, "Here are some neat ideas I'd like to put into this system. I'll code them up, and

Reprinted from *IEEE Software,* Vol. 8, No. 1, Jan. 1991, pp. 32–41.

if they don't fit other people's ideas, we'll just evolve things until they work." This sort of approach usually works fine in some well-supported minidomains like spreadsheet applications but, in more complex application domains, it most often creates or neglects unsalvageable high-risk elements and leads the project down the path to disaster.

At TRW and elsewhere, I have had the good fortune to observe many project managers at work firsthand and to try to understand and apply the factors that distinguished the more successful project managers from the less successful ones. Some successfully used a waterfall approach, others successfully used an evolutionary development approach, and still others successfully orchestrated complex mixtures of these and other approaches involving prototyping, simulation, commercial software, executable specifications, tiger teams, design competitions, subcontracting, and various kinds of cost-benefit analyses.

One pattern that emerged very strongly was that the successful project managers were good *risk managers*. Although they generally didn't use such terms as "risk identification," "risk assessment," "risk-management planning," or "risk monitoring," they were using a general concept of risk exposure (potential loss times the probability of loss) to guide their priorities and actions. And their projects tended to avoid pitfalls and produce good products.

The emerging discipline of software risk management is an attempt to formalize these risk-oriented correlates of success into a readily applicable set of principles and practices. Its objectives are to identify, address, and eliminate risk items before they become either threats to successful software operation or major sources of software rework.

BASIC CONCEPTS

Webster's dictionary defines "risk" as "the possibility of loss or injury." This definition can be translated into the fundamental concept of risk management: risk exposure, sometimes also called "risk im-

pact" or "risk factor." Risk exposure is defined by the relationship

$$RE = P(UO) * L(UO)$$

where RE is the risk exposure, P(UO) is the probability of an unsatisfactory outcome and L(UO) is the loss to the parties affected if the outcome is unsatisfactory. To relate this definition to software projects, we need a definition of "unsatisfactory outcome."

Given that projects involve several classes of participants (customer, developer, user, and maintainer), each with different but highly important satisfaction criteria, it is clear that "unsatisfactory outcome" is multidimensional:

♦ For customers and developers, budget overruns and schedule slips are unsatisfactory.

♦ For users, products with the wrong functionality, user-interface shortfalls, performance shortfalls, or reliability shortfalls are unsatisfactory.

♦ For maintainers, poor-quality software is unsatisfactory.

These components of an unsatisfactory outcome provide a top-level checklist for identifying and assessing risk items.

A fundamental risk-analysis paradigm is the decision tree. Figure 1 illustrates a potentially risky situation involving the software controlling a satellite experiment. The software has been under development by the experiment team, which understands the experiment well but is inexperienced in and somewhat casual about software development. As a result, the satellite-platform manager has obtained an estimate that there is a probability P(UO) of 0.4 that the experimenters' software will have a critical error: one that will wipe out the entire experiment and cause an associated loss L(UO) of the total $20 million investment in the experiment.

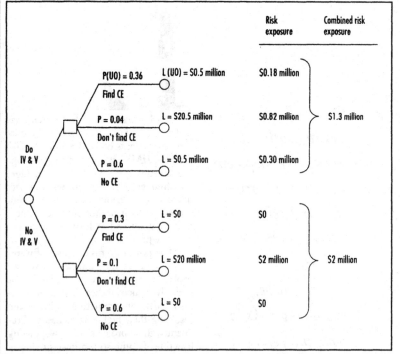

FIGURE 1. DECISION TREE FOR WHETHER TO PERFORM INDEPENDENT VALIDATION AND VERIFICATION TO ELIMINATE CRITICAL ERRORS IN A SATELLITE-EXPERIMENT PROGRAM. L(UO) IS THE LOSS ASSOCIATED WITH AN UNSATISFACTORY OUTCOME, P(UO) IS THE PROBABILITY OF THE UNSATISFACTORY OUTCOME, AND CE IS A CRITICAL ERROR.

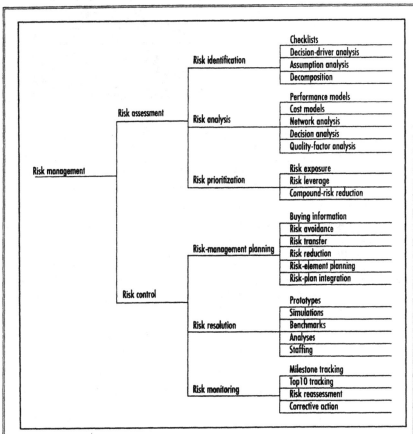

FIGURE 2. SOFTWARE RISK MANAGEMENT STEPS.

The satellite-platform manager identifies two major options for reducing the risk of losing the experiment:

♦ Convincing and helping the experiment team to apply better development methods. This incurs no additional cost and, from previous experience, the manager estimates that this will reduce the error probability P(UO) to 0.1.

♦ Hiring a contractor to independently verify and validate the software. This costs an additional $500,000; based on the results of similar IV&V efforts, the manager estimates that this will reduce the error probability P(UO) to 0.04.

The decision tree in Figure 1 then shows, for each of the two major decision options, the possible outcomes in terms of the critical error existing or being found and eliminated, their probabilities, the losses associated with each outcome, the risk exposure associated with each outcome, and the total risk exposure (or expected loss) associated with each decision option. In this case, the total risk exposure associated with the experiment-team option is only $2 million. For the IV&V option, the total risk exposure is only $1.3 million, so it represents the more attractive option.

Besides providing individual solutions for risk-management situations, the decision tree also provides a framework for analyzing the sensitivity of preferred solutions to the risk-exposure parameters. Thus, for example, the experiment-team option would be preferred if the loss due to a critical error were less than $13 million, if the experiment team could reduce its critical-error probability to less than 0.065, if the IV&V team cost more than $1.2 million, if the IV&V team could not reduce the probability of critical error to less than 0.075, or if there were various partial combinations of these possibilities.

This sort of sensitivity analysis helps deal with many situations in which probabilities and losses cannot be estimated well enough to perform a precise analysis. The risk-exposure framework also supports some even more approximate but still very useful approaches, like range estimation and scale-of-10 estimation.

RISK MANAGMENT

As Figure 2 shows, the practice of risk management involves two primary steps each with three subsidiary steps.

The first primary step, risk assessment, involves risk identification, risk analysis, and risk prioritization:

♦ Risk identification produces lists of the project-specific risk items likely to compromise a project's success. Typical risk-identification techniques include checklists, examination of decision drivers, comparison with experience (assumption analysis), and decomposition.

♦ Risk analysis assesses the loss probability and loss magnitude for each identified risk item, and it assesses compound risks in risk-item interactions. Typical techniques include performance models, cost models, network analysis, statistical decision analysis, and quality-factor (like reliability, availability, and security) analysis.

♦ Risk prioritization produces a ranked ordering of the risk items identified and analyzed. Typical techniques include risk-exposure analysis, risk-reduction leverage analysis (particularly involving cost-benefit analysis), and Delphi or group-consensus techniques.

The second primary step, risk control, involves risk-management planning, risk resolution, and risk monitoring:

♦ Risk-management planning helps prepare you to address each risk item (for example, via information buying, risk avoidance, risk transfer, or risk reduction), including the coordination of the individual risk-item plans with each other and with the overall project plan. Typical techniques include checklists of risk-resolution techniques, cost-benefit analysis, and standard risk-management plan outlines, forms, and elements.

♦ Risk resolution produces a situation in which the risk items are eliminated or otherwise resolved (for example, risk avoidance via relaxation of requirements). Typical techniques include prototypes, simulations, benchmarks, mission analyses, key-personnel agreements, design-to-cost approaches, and incremental development.

♦ Risk monitoring involves tracking the project's progress toward resolving its risk items and taking corrective action where appropriate. Typical techniques include milestone tracking and a top-10 risk-item list that is highlighted at each

weekly, monthly, or milestone project review and followed up appropriately with reassessment of the risk item or corrective action.

In addition, risk management provides an improved way to address and organize the life cycle. Risk-driven approaches, like the spiral model of the software process,[2] avoid many of the difficulties encountered with previous process models like the waterfall model and the evolutionary development model. Such risk-driven approaches also show how and where to incorporate new software technologies like rapid prototyping, fourth-generation languages, and commercial software products into the life cycle.

SIX STEPS

Figure 2 summarized the major steps and techniques involved in software risk management. This overview article covers

four significant subsets of risk-management techniques: risk-identification checklists, risk prioritization, risk-management planning, and risk monitoring. Other techniques have been covered elsewhere.[3,4]

Risk-identification checklists. Table 1 shows a top-level risk-identification checklist with the top 10 primary sources of risk on software projects, based on a survey of several experienced project managers. Managers and system engineers can use the checklist on projects to help identify and resolve the most serious risk items on the project. It also provides a corresponding set of risk-management techniques that have been most successful to date in avoiding or resolving the source of risk.

If you focus on item 2 of the top-10 list in Table 1 (unrealistic schedules and budgets), you can then move on to an example of a next-level checklist: the risk-probabil-

ity table in Table 2 for assessing the probability that a project will overrun its budget. Table 2 is one of several such checklists in an excellent US Air Force handbook[5] on software risk abatement.

Using the checklist, you can rate a project's status for the individual attributes associated with its requirements, personnel, reusable software, tools, and support environment (in Table 2, the environment's availability or the risk that the environment will not be available when needed). These ratings will support a probability-range estimation of whether the project has a relatively low (0.0 to 0.3), medium (0.4 to 0.6), or high (0.7 to 1.0) probability of overrunning its budget.

Most of the critical risk items in the checklist have to do with shortfalls in domain understanding and in properly scoping the job to be done — areas that are generally underemphasized in computer-science literature and education. Recent

TABLE 1. TOP 10 SOFTWARE RISK ITEMS.	
Risk item	Risk-management technique
Personnel shortfalls	Staffing with top talent, job matching, team building, key personnel agreements, cross training.
Unrealistic schedules and budgets	Detailed multisource cost and schedule estimation, design to cost, incremental development, software reuse, requirements scrubbing.
Developing the wrong functions and properties	Organization analysis, mission analysis, operations-concept formulation, user surveys and user participation, prototyping, early users' manuals, off-nominal performance analysis, quality-factor analysis.
Developing the wrong user interface	Prototyping, scenarios, task analysis, user participation.
Gold-plating	Requirements scrubbing, prototyping, cost-benefit analysis, designing to cost.
Continuing stream of requirements changes	High change threshold, information hiding, incremental development (deferring changes to later increments).
Shortfalls in externally furnished components	Benchmarking, inspections, reference checking, compatibility analysis.
Shortfalls in externally performed tasks	Reference checking, preaward audits, award-fee contracts, competitive design or prototyping, team-building.
Real-time performance shortfalls	Simulation, benchmarking, modeling, prototyping, instrumentation, tuning.
Straining computer-science capabilities	Technical analysis, cost-benefit analysis, prototyping, reference checking.

TABLE 2.
QUANTIFICATION OF PROBABILITY AND IMPACT FOR COST FAILURE.

Cost drivers	Probability		
	Improbable (0.0-0.3)	Probable (0.4-0.6)	Frequent (0.7-1.0)
Requirements			
Size	Small, noncomplex, or easily decomposed	Medium to moderate complexity, decomposable	Large, highly complex, or not decomposable
Resource constraints	Little or no hardware-imposed constraints	Some hardware-imposed constraints	Significant hardware-imposed constraints
Application	Nonreal-time, little system interdependency	Embedded, some system interdependencies	Real-time, embedded, strong interdependency
Technology	Mature, existent, in-house experience	Existent, some in-house experience	New or new application, little experience
Requirements stability	Little or no change to established baseline	Some change in baseline expected	Rapidly changing, or no baseline
Personnel			
Availability	In place, little turnover expected	Available, some turnover expected	Not available, high turnover expected
Mix	Good mix of software disciplines	Some disciplines inappropriately represented	Some disciplines not represented
Experience	High experience ratio	Average experience ratio	Low experience ratio
Management environment	Strong personnel management approach	Good personnel management approach	Weak personnel management approach
Reusable software			
Availability	Compatible with need dates	Delivery dates in question	Incompatible with need dates
Modifications	Little or no change	Some change	Extensive changes
Language	Compatible with system and maintenance requirements	Partial compatibility with requirements	Incompatible with system or maintenance requirements
Rights	Compatible with maintenance and competition requirements	Partial compatibility with maintenance, some competition	Incompatible with maintenance concept, noncompetitive
Certification	Verified performance, application compatible	Some application-compatible test data available	Unverified, little test data available
Tools and environment			
Facilities	Little or no modification	Some modifications, existent	Major modifications, nonexistent
Availability	In place, meets need dates	Some compatibility with need dates	Nonexistent, does not meet need dates
Rights	Compatible with maintenance and development plans	Partial compatibility with maintenance and development plans	Incompatible with maintenance and development plans
Configuration management	Fully controlled	Some controls	No controls
Impact			
	Sufficient financial resources	Some shortage of financial resources, possible overrun	Significant financial shortages, budget overrun likely

initiatives, like the Software Engineering Institute's masters curriculum in software engineering, are providing better coverage in these areas. The SEI is also initiating a major new program in software risk management.

Risk analysis and prioritization. After using all the various risk-identification checklists, plus the other risk-identification techniques in decision-driver analysis, assumption analysis, and decomposition, one very real risk is that the project will identify so many risk items that the project could spend years just investigating them. This is where risk prioritization and its associated risk-analysis activities become essential.

The most effective technique for risk prioritization involves the risk-exposure quantity described earlier. It lets you rank the risk items identified and determine which are most important to address.

One difficulty with the risk-exposure

TABLE 3.
RISK EXPOSURE FACTORS FOR SATELLITE EXPERIMENT SOFTWARE.

Unsatisfactory outcome	Probability of unsatisfactory outcome	Loss caused by unsatisfactory outcome	Risk exposure
A. Software error kills experiment	3-5	10	30-50
B. Software error loses key data	3-5	8	24-40
C. Fault-tolerant features cause unacceptable performance	4-8	7	28-56
D. Monitoring software reports unsafe condition as safe	5	9	45
E. Monitoring software reports safe condition as unsafe	5	3	15
F. Hardware delay causes schedule overrun	6	4	24
G. Data-reduction software errors cause extra work	8	1	8
H. Poor user interface causes inefficient operation	6	5	30
I. Processor memory insufficient	1	7	7
J. Database-management software loses derived data	2	2	4

quantity, as with most other decision-analysis quantities, is the problem of making accurate input estimates of the probability and loss associated with an unsatisfactory outcome. Checklists like that in Table 2 provide some help in assessing the probability of occurrence of a given risk item, but it is clear from Table 2 that its probability ranges do not support precise probability estimation.

Full risk-analysis efforts involving prototyping, benchmarking, and simulation generally provide better probability and loss estimates, but they may be more expensive and time-consuming than the situation warrants. Other techniques, like betting analogies and group-consensus techniques, can improve risk-probability estimation, but for risk prioritization you can often take a simpler course: assessing the risk probabilities and losses on a relative scale of 0 to 10.

Table 3 and Figure 3 illustrate this risk-prioritization process by using some potential risk items from the satellite-experiment project as examples. Table 3 summarizes several unsatisfactory outcomes with their corresponding ratings for P(UO), L(UO), and their resulting risk-exposure estimates. Figure 3 plots each unsatisfactory outcome with respect to a set of constant risk-exposure contours.

Three key points emerge from Table 3 and Figure 3:

♦ Projects often focus on factors having either a high P(UO) or a high L(UO), but these may not be the key factors with a high risk-exposure combination. One of the highest P(UO)s comes from item G

(data-reduction errors), but the fact that these errors are recoverable and not mission-critical leads to a low loss factor and a resulting low RE of 7. Similarly, item I (insufficient memory) has a high potential loss, but its low probability leads to a low RE of 7. On the other hand, a relatively

low-profile item like item H (user-interface shortfalls) becomes a relatively high-priority risk item because its combination of moderately high probability and loss factors yield a RE of 30.

♦ The RE quantities also provide a basis for prioritizing verification and vali-

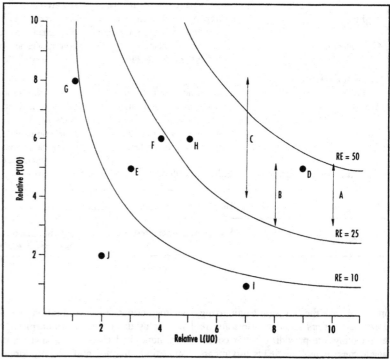

FIGURE 3. RISK-EXPOSURE FACTORS AND CONTOURS FOR THE SATELLITE-EXPERIMENT SOFTWARE. RE IS THE RISK EXPOSURE, P(UO) THE PROBABILITY OF AN UNSATISFACTORY OUTCOME, AND L(UO) THE LOSS ASSOCIATED WITH THAT UNSATISFACTORY OUTCOME. THE GRAPH POINTS MAP THE ITEMS FROM TABLE 3 WHOSE RISK EXPOSURE ARE BEING ASSESSED.

```
1. Objectives (the "why")
   ◆ Determine, reduce level of risk of the software fault-tolerance features causing unacceptable performance.
   ◆ Create a description of and a development plan for a set of low-risk fault-tolerance features.
2. Deliverables and milestones (the "what" and "when").
   ◆ By Week 3.
      1. Evaluation of fault-tolerance options
      2. Assessment of reusable components
      3. Draft workload characterization
      4. Evaluation plan for prototype exercise
      5. Description of prototype
   ◆ By Week 7.
      6. Operational prototype with key fault-tolerance features.
      7. Workload simulation
      8. Instrumentation and data reduction capabilities.
      9. Draft description, plan for fault-tolerance features.
   ◆ By Week 10
      10. Evaluation and iteration of prototype
      11. Revised description, plan for fault-tolerance features
3. Responsibilities (the "who" and "where")
   ◆ System engineer: G.Smith
     Tasks 1, 3, 4, 9, 11. Support of tasks 5, 10
   ◆ Lead programmer: C.Lee
     Tasks 5, 6, 7, 10. Support of tasks 1, 3
   ◆ Programmer: J.Wilson
     Tasks 2, 8. Support of tasks 5, 6, 7, 10
4. Approach (the "how")
   ◆ Design-to-schedule prototyping effort
   ◆ Driven by hypotheses about fault-tolerance-performance effects
   ◆ Use real-time operating system, add prototype fault-tolerance features
   ◆ Evaluate performance with respect to representative workload
   ◆ Refine prototype based on results observed
5. Resources (the "how much")
   $60K — full-time system engineer, lead programmer, programmer
          (10 weeks) * (3 staff) * $2k/staff-week)
   $0 — three dedicated workstations (from project pool)
   $0 — two target processors (from project pool)
   $0 — one test coprocessor (from project pool)
   $10K — contingencies
   $70K — total
```

FIGURE 4. RISK-MANAGEMENT PLAN FOR FAULT-TOLERANCE PROTOTYPING.

dation and related test activities by giving each error class a significance weight. Frequently, all errors are treated with equal weight, putting too much testing effort into finding relatively trivial errors.

◆ There is often a good deal of uncertainty in estimating the probability or loss associated with an unsatisfactory outcome. (The assessments are frequently subjective and are often the product of surveying several domain experts.) The amount of uncertainty is itself a major source of risk, which needs to be reduced as early as possible. The primary example in Table 3 and Figure 3 is the uncertainty in item C about whether the fault-tolerance features are going to cause an unacceptable degradation in real-time performance. If P(UO) is rated at 4, this item has only a moderate RE of 28, but if P(UO) is 8, the RE has a top-priority rating of 56.

One of the best ways to reduce this source of risk is to buy information about the actual situation. For the issue of fault

tolerance versus performance, a good way to buy information is to invest in a prototype, to better understand the performance effects of the various fault-tolerance features.

Risk-management planning. Once you determine a project's major risk items and their relative priorities, you need to establish a set of risk-control functions to bring the risk items under control. The first step in this process is to develop a set of risk-management plans that lay out the activities necessary to bring the risk items under control.

One aid in doing this is the top-10 checklist in Figure 3 that identifies the most successful risk-management techniques for the most common risk items. As an example, item 9 (real-time performance shortfalls) in Table 1 covers the uncertainty in performance effect of the fault-tolerance features. The corresponding risk-management techniques include

simulation, benchmarking, modeling, prototyping, instrumentation, and tuning. Assume, for example, that a prototype of representative safety features is the most cost-effective way to determine and reduce their effects on system performance.

The next step in risk-management planning is to develop risk-management plans for each risk item. Figure 4 shows the plan for prototyping the fault-tolerance features and determining their effects on performance. The plan is organized around a standard format for software plans, oriented around answering the standard questions of why, what, when, who, where, how, and how much. This plan organization lets the plans be concise (fitting on one page), action-oriented, easy to understand, and easy to monitor.

The final step in risk-management planning is to integrate the risk-management plans for each risk item with each other and with the overall project plan. Each of the other high-priority or uncertain risk items will have a risk-management plan; it may turn out, for example, that the fault-tolerance features prototyped for this risk item could also be useful as part of the strategy to reduce the uncertainty in items A and B (software errors killing the experiment and losing experiment-critical data). Also, for the overall project plan, the need for a 10-week prototype-development and -exercise period must be factored into the overall schedule, to keep the overall schedule realistic.

Risk resolution and monitoring. Once you have established a good set of risk-management plans, the risk-resolution process consists of implementing whatever prototypes, simulations, benchmarks, surveys, or other risk-reduction techniques are called for in the plans. Risk monitoring ensures that this is a closed-loop process by tracking risk-reduction progress and applying whatever corrective action is necessary to keep the risk-resolution process on track.

Risk management provides managers with a very effective technique for keeping on top of projects under their control: *Project top-10 risk-item tracking.* This technique concentrates management atten-

tion on the high-risk, high-leverage, critical success factors rather than swamping management reviews with lots of low-priority detail. As a manager, I have found that this type of risk-item-oriented review saves a lot of time, reduces management surprises, and gets you focused on the high-leverage issues where you can make a difference as a manager.

Top-10 risk-item tracking involves the following steps:

♦ Ranking the project's most significant risk items.

♦ Establishing a regular schedule for higher management reviews of the project's progress. The review should be chaired by the equivalent of the project manager's boss. For large projects (more than 20 people), the reviews should be held monthly. In the project itself, the project manager would review them more frequently.

♦ Beginning each project-review meeting with a summary of progress on the top 10 risk items. (The number could be seven or 12 without loss of intent.) The summary should include each risk item's current top-10 ranking, its rank at the previous review, how often it has been on the top-10 list, and a summary of progress in resolving the risk item since the previous review.

♦ Focusing the project-review meeting on dealing with any problems in resolving the risk items.

Table 4 shows how a top-10 list could have worked for the satellite-experiment project, as of month 3 of the project. The project's top risk item in month 3 is a critical staffing problem. Highlighting it in the monthly review meeting would stimulate a discussion by the project team and the boss of the staffing options: Make the unavailable key person available, reshuffle project personnel, or look for new people within or outside the organization. This should result in an assignment of action items to follow through on the options

chosen, including possible actions by the project manager's boss.

The number 2 risk item in Table 4, target hardware delivery delays, is also one for which the project manager's boss may be able to expedite a solution — by cutting through corporate-procurement red tape, for example, or by escalating vendor-delay issues with the vendor's higher management.

As Table 4 shows, some risk items are moving down in priority or going off the list, while others are escalating or coming onto the list. The ones moving down the list — like the design-verification and -validation staffing, fault-tolerance prototyping, and user-interface prototyping — still need to be monitored but frequently do not need special management action. The ones moving up or onto the list — like the data-bus design changes and the testbed-interface definitions — are generally the ones needing higher management attention to help get them

| Risk item | Monthly ranking | | | Risk-resolution progress |
	This	Last	No. of months	
Replacing sensor-control software developer	1	4	2	Top replacement candidate unavailable
Target hardware delivery delays	2	5	2	Procurement procedural delays
Sensor data formats undefined	3	3	3	Action items to software, sensor teams; due next month
Staffing of design V&V team	4	2	3	Key reviewers committed; need fault-tolerance reviewer
Software fault-tolerance may compromise performance	5	1	3	Fault-tolerance prototype successful
Accommodate changes in data bus design	6	—	1	Meeting scheduled with data-bus designers
Test-bed interface definitions	7	8	3	Some delays in action items; review meeting scheduled
User interface uncertainties	8	6	3	User interface prototype successful
TBDs in experiment operational concept	—	7	3	TBDs resolved
Uncertainties in reusable monitoring software	—	9	3	Required design changes small, successfully made

TABLE 4.
PROJECT TOP-10 RISK ITEM LIST FOR SATELLITE EXPERIMENT SOFTWARE.

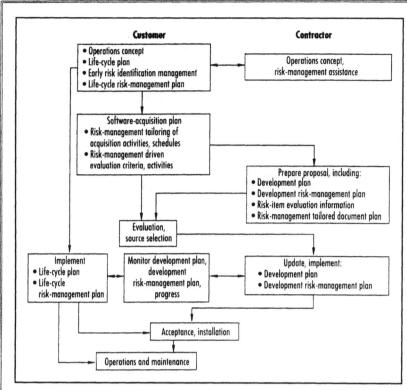

FIGURE 5. FRAMEWORK FOR LIFE-CYCLE RISK MANAGEMENT.

resolved quickly.

As this example shows, the top-10 risk-item list is a very effective way to focus higher management attention onto the project's critical success factors. It also uses management's time very efficiently, unlike typical monthly reviews, which spend most of their time on things the higher manager can't do anything about. Also, if the higher manager surfaces an additional concern, it is easy to add it to the top-10 risk item list to be highlighted in future reviews.

IMPLEMENTING RISK MANAGEMENT

Implementing risk management involves inserting the risk-management principles and practices into your existing life-cycle management practices. Full implementation of risk management involves the use of risk-driven software-process models like the spiral model, where risk considerations determine the overall sequence of life-cycle activities, the use of prototypes and other risk-resolution techniques, and the degree of detail of plans and specifications. However, the best implementation strategy is an incremental one, which lets an organization's culture adjust gradually to risk-oriented management practices and risk-driven process models.

A good way to begin is to establish a top-10 risk-item tracking process. It is easy and inexpensive to implement, provides early improvements, and begins establishing a familiarity with the other risk-management principles and practices. Another good way to gain familiarity is via books like my recent tutorial on risk management,[3] which contains the Air Force risk-abatement pamphlet[5] and other useful articles, and Robert Charette's recent good book on risk management.[4]

An effective next step is to identify an appropriate initial project in which to implement a top-level life-cycle risk-management plan. Once the organization has accumulated some risk-management experience on this initial project, successive steps can deepen the sophistication of the risk-management techniques and broaden their application to wider classes of projects.

Figure 5 provides a scheme for implementing a top-level life-cycle risk-management plan. It is presented in the context of a contractual software acquisition, but you can tailor it to the needs of an internal development organization as well.

You can organize the life-cycle risk-management plan as an elaboration of the "why, what, when, who, where, how, how much" framework of Figure 4. While this plan is primarily the customer's responsibility, it is very useful to involve the developer community in its preparation as well.

Such a plan addresses not only the development risks that have been the prime topic of this article but also operations and maintenance risks. These include such items as staffing and training of maintenance personnel, discontinuities in the switch from the old to the new system, undefined responsibilities for operations and maintenance facilities and functions, and insufficient budget for planned life-cycle improvements or for corrective, adaptive, and perfective maintenance.

Figure 5 also shows the importance of proposed developer risk-management plans in competitive source evaluation and selection. Emphasizing the realism and effectiveness of a bidder's risk-management plan increases the probability that the customer will select a bidder that clearly understands the project's critical success factors and that has established a development approach that satisfactorily addresses them. (If the developer is a noncompetitive internal organization, it is equally important for the internal customer to require and review a developer risk-management plan.)

The most important thing for a project to do is to get focused on its critical success factors.

For various reasons, including the influence of previous document-driven management guidelines, projects get focused on activities that are not critical for their success. These frequently include writing boilerplate documents, exploring intriguing but peripheral technical issues, playing politics, and trying to sell the "ultimate" system.

In the process, critical success factors get neglected, the project fails, and nobody wins.

The key contribution of software risk management is to create this focus on critical success factors — and to provide the techniques that let the project deal with them. The risk-assessment and risk-control techniques presented here provide the foundation layer of capabilities needed to implement the risk-oriented approach.

However, risk management is not a cookbook approach. To handle all the complex people-oriented and technology-driven success factors in projects, a great measure of human judgement is required.

Good people, with good skills and good judgment, are what make projects work. Risk management can provide you with some of the skills, an emphasis on getting good people, and a good conceptual framework for sharpening your judgement. I hope you can find these useful on your next project.　　　　　◆

REFERENCES

1. J. Rothfeder, "It's Late, Costly, and Incompetent — But Try Firing a Computer System," *Business Week*, Nov. 7, 1988, pp. 164-165.
2. B.W. Boehm, "A Spiral Model of Software Development and Enhancement," *Computer*, May 1988, pp. 61-72.
3. B.W. Boehm, *Software Risk Management*, CS Press, Los Alamitos, Calif., 1989.
4. R.N. Charette, *Software Engineering Risk Analysis and Management*, McGraw-Hill, New York, 1989.
5. "Software Risk Abatement," AFSC/AFLC pamphlet 800-45. US Air Force Systems Command, Andrews AFB, Md., 1988.

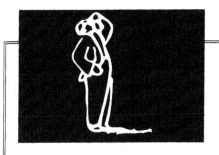

Achieving Higher SEI Levels

Michael K. Daskalantonakis, *Motorola*

◆ *Two years or more can pass between formal SEI assessments. An organization seeking to monitor its progress to a higher SEI level needs a method for internally conducting incremental assessments. The author provides one that has proven successful at Motorola.*

Many organizations have turned to the Software Engineering Institute's Capability Maturity Model to improve their software-engineering processes by setting goals to achieve higher SEI levels. This has created the need for an instrument and a process that can be used to evaluate an organization's current status relative to these goals.[1-3] At Motorola, we have developed a method for assessing progress to higher SEI levels that lets engineers and managers evaluate an organization's current status relative to the CMM and identify weak areas for immediate attention and improvement.[4] This method serves as an effective means to ensure continuous process improvement as well as grassroots participation and support in achieving higher maturity levels.

This progress-assessment process is not intended as a replacement for any formal assessment instruments developed by the SEI, but rather as an internal tool to help organizations prepare for a formal SEI assessment. Although I provide examples in terms of CMM version 1.1, both the self-evaluation instrument and the progress-assessment process are generic enough for use with any (similar) later version of the SEI CMM by updating the worksheets and charts used.

We began using the SEI Progress-Assessment method within Motorola's Cellular Infrastructure Group — an organization of more than 1,000 software engineers working on several projects and products for the cellular com-

Reprinted from *IEEE Software,* Vol. 11, No. 4, July 1994, pp. 17–24.

Score	Key activity evaluation dimensions		
	Approach	Deployment	Results
Poor (0)	• No management recognition of need • No organizational ability • No organizational commitment • Practice not evident	• No part of the organization uses the practice • No part of the organization shows interest	• Ineffective
Weak (2)	• Management has begun to recognize the need • Support items for the practice start to be created • A few parts of organization are able to implement the practice	• Fragmented use • Inconsistent use • Deployed in some parts of the organization • Limited monitoring/verification of use	• Spotty results • Inconsistent results • Some evidence of effectiveness for some parts of the organization
Fair (4)	• Wide but not complete commitment by management • Road map for practice implementation defined • Several supporting items for the practice in place	• Less fragmented use • Some consistency in use • Deployed in some major parts of the organization • Monitoring/verification of use for several parts of the organization	• Consistent and positive results for several parts of the organization • Inconsistent results for other parts of the organization
Marginally qualified (6)	• Some management commitment; some management becomes proactive • Practice implementation well under way across parts of the organization • Supporting items in place	• Deployed in some parts of the organization • Mostly consistent use across many parts of the organization • Monitoring/verification of use for many parts of the organization	• Positive measurable results in most parts of the organization • Consistently positive results over time across many parts of the organization
Qualified (8)	• Total management commitment • Majority of management is proactive • Practice established as an integral part of the process • Supporting items encourage and facilitate the use of the practice	• Deployed in almost all parts of the organization • Consistent use across almost all parts of the organization • Monitoring/verification of use for almost all parts of the organization	• Positive measurable results in almost all parts of the organization • Consistently positive results over time across almost all parts of the organization
Outstanding (10)	• Management provides zealous leadership and commitment • Organizational excellence in the practice recognized even outside the company	• Pervasive and consistent deployment across all parts of the organization • Consistent use over time across all parts of the organization • Monitoring/verification for all parts of the organization	• Requirements exceeded • Consistently world-class results • Counsel sought by others

Figure 1. Guidelines to rate CMM key activities in CMM version 1.1 or any later SEI CMM version. They were developed by modifying the Quality System Review scoring matrix guidelines to ensure that they address the spirit and themes considered in the CMM. All three evaluation dimensions included in this scoring matrix are equally weighted. You determine the score for a key activity by examining all three evaluation dimensions and their scoring guidelines simultaneously. An odd-numbered score is possible if some of, but not all, the criteria for the next higher level have been met.

munications business — in the second quarter of 1992. A year later, our organization was found to have achieved SEI level 2, the next higher SEI maturity level. This was primarily the result of strong senior-management support, backed by allocation of at least 10 percent of the progress-assessment participants' efforts within a given quarter, and engineer/manager actions taken to implement the process-improvement action plans. These action plans were generated and driven through the assessment method described here.

At Motorola, we found the progress-assessment method offers several benefits. It empowers engineers and managers working within a product group to conduct a self-evaluation relative to an SEI level and create their own list of findings and action plans. This ensures grass-roots involvement in the process and institutionalization of improvement. The process facilitates communication among those involved in this assessment and ensures that important information regarding processes and tools used within the product group is disseminated at the assessment meeting and at subsequent meetings. The process educates engineers and managers — the practitioners — regarding the key process areas and practices listed in the CMM. This increases their understanding of topics in which they may not have been involved in the past, such as software configuration management or software subcontractor management. This also increases the capability of the practitioners in terms of the software-engineering process, methods, tools, and technology. Finally, the progress-assessment process continuously prepares an organization for the next formal SEI assessment.

Some critics of the assessment instrument within Motorola's CIG have said that it focuses primarily on the key activities listed in the CMM without adequately covering other key practices (also called themes) such as the commitment and ability to perform. Responding to input from the CIG's Process Management Working Group, I decided to formally score and track only the key activities, while ensuring that the scoring guidelines used for determining the key activities' scores account for the additional practices listed in the CMM. For example, to achieve a rating of Marginally Qualified, the key-activity scoring guidelines in Figure 1 require that an organization show the existence of management commitment, have supporting items in place, and monitor and verify use. Also, the progress-assessment process specification requires that findings regarding these additional practices and their associated actions be identified and used as part of an SEI Progress Assessment. This ensures the necessary coverage of these practices.

ASSESSMENT INSTRUMENT

Each SEI level has several associated key process areas. The progress-assessment instrument lets you determine the scores associated with the SEI level your organization is trying to achieve. Each key process area contains several key activities. We created scoring guidelines for measuring how well an organization implements a specific key activity, basing them on several common CMM themes identified by Mark Paulk.[1]

 ♦ Commitment to perform
 ♦ Ability to perform
 ♦ Activities performed
 ♦ Monitoring implementation
 ♦ Verifying implementation

I then expanded and grouped these themes under three primary evaluation dimensions and developed criteria for evaluating them:

 ♦ *Approach.* Criteria here are the organization's commitment to and management's support for the practice, as well as the organization's ability to implement the practice.

 ♦ *Deployment.* The breadth and consistency of practice implementation across project areas are the key criteria here.

 ♦ *Results.* Criteria here are the breadth and consistency of positive results over time and across project areas.

Scoring. I used the evaluation dimensions and criteria to create guidelines for determining an integer score of 0-10 for each key activity, as Figure 1 shows. Although the guidelines are generic, the assessor can easily use them to determine the score of each specific key activity. This is simpler than having

SEI level 2—CMM v1.1 KPA: Software project tracking and oversight	Organization: ORG_NAME Date: 15/07/94 Average score: 4										
List of key activities	0	1	2	3	4	5	6	7	8	9	10
1. A documented software-development plan is used for tracking software activities and communicating status.							X				
2. The project's software development plan is revised according to a documented procedure.				X							
3. Senior management reviews and approves all commitments and commitment changes made to individuals and groups external to the organization.	X										
4. Approved changes to software commitments or commitments affecting software activities are explicitly communicated to the staff and managers of the software-engineering group and software-related groups.				X							
5. The project's software size is tracked and corrective actions are taken.							X				
6. The project's software costs are tracked and corrective actions are taken.	X										
7. The project's critical target computer resources are tracked and corrective actions are taken.						X					
8. The project's software schedule is tracked and corrective actions are taken.								X			
9. Software-engineering technical activities are tracked and corrective actions are taken.					X						
10. The software technical, cost, resource, and schedule risks are tracked throughout the life of the project.						X					
11. Actual measured data and replanning data for the project-tracking activities are recorded for use by software-engineering staff and managers.								X			
12. Software-engineering staff and managers conduct regular reviews to track technical progress, plans, performance, and issues against the development plan.				X							
13. Formal reviews, to address the accomplishments and results of project software engineering, are conducted at selected project milestones and at the beginning and completion of selected stages.			X								

Figure 2. A sample scoring worksheet. It can be used to summarize the score determined for the key activities of a given key process area, such as software project tracking and oversight, included in the SEI model. These scores are determined using the key-activity scoring guidelines shown in Figure 1.

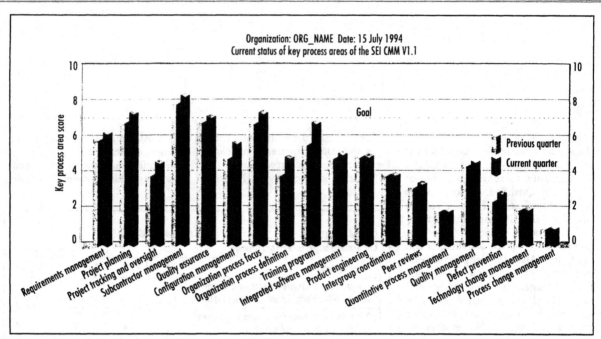

Figure 3. *Summarized progress report regarding SEI key process areas. Bars on the left correspond to the assessment results obtained the previous quarter. Bars on the right respond to the current quarter's results.*

a lengthy list of guidelines, such as one per key activity, which makes the scoring task more complex. The sample worksheet shown in Figure 2 is used to summarize the score obtained by using these guidelines. When applied at the project level, you translate the guideline "parts of the organization," as "subprojects" or "subsystems." When applied at the product-line, division, or group level, "parts of the organization" translates to "projects" or "project areas." Users of this scoring-guidelines matrix must ensure that they use the terms "commitment," "ability," "monitoring," and "verification" as described in the SEI model when determining a key activity's score.

To calculate the score for a specific key-process area, enter the score for each of its key activities in the worksheet shown in Figure 2. Average the individual key-activity scores to find the overall score for that key process area. Within Motorola, a score of 7 or higher for each key-process area at an SEI level i (1< i ≤ 5) indicates the organization will likely be assessed at SEI level i by a formal SEI assessment, assuming the organization has already been assessed as being at SEI level i–1. All the evaluation dimensions in Figure 1's scoring matrix carry equal weight when determining the score for a given key activi-

ty. Determine the key activity's score by examining all three evaluation dimensions and their scoring guidelines simultaneously.

Although each evaluation-dimension level represents a two-point increment, the score for a key activity can be an odd number if some of, but not all, the criteria for the next higher level are satisfied. For example, if some of the dimensions for a key process area are rated at the Fair level (4), while others are rated at the Marginally Qualified level (6), a score of 5 would be appropriate.

The average of the key process area scores for a given SEI level indicates how well the key process areas and activities corresponding to that level have been implemented within an organization. The key activities corresponding to each key process area in the CMM[3] are those listed in the sample worksheet. If multiple items are associated with an activity in the CMM, just consider them part of the package that describes the key activity when determining its score.

Low scores identify key activities and key process areas that need immediate attention to raise the organization's software-process capability. A low key-activity, key-process-area, or SEI-level score indicates a problem area that

needs immediate attention and improvement. The next section provides an example of how the problem areas are highlighted within those Motorola business units that already use this method.

DATA PRESENTATION

The organization's current status, as determined using the scoring guidelines shown in Figure 1, are summarized using bar charts and/or Kiviat plots. The bar chart in Figure 3 summarizes the overall status of the key-process-area implementation. Note that a progress assessment and the presentation of the results may be done for a specific SEI level only, instead of all SEI CMM levels at the same time. Typically this is the next higher SEI level the organization is trying to achieve.

You can use Kiviat charts to summarize the status of a key-process-area implementation for a specific SEI level. Figure 4 is an example of an organization's progress in implementing CMM level 2. Each axis starting at the center of the circle corresponds to a key-process area at that level. This chart indicates the progress achieved during the chosen interval — in this case the last quarter — in advancing from level 1 to level 2. The chart also indicates the key process areas at level 2 for which additional focus is necessary, as well as those for which the improvement efforts have already paid off.

The same applies to higher CMM levels. Suppose management is not satisfied with the progress made on Software Project Tracking and Oversight and wants to obtain additional information about the key activities that must be immediately addressed.

Information on implementation status is presented in a bar chart like the one shown in Figure 5. The lower bars on this chart clearly indicate the key activities of the Software Project Tracking and Oversight key process areas that need immediate improvement. These activities include revisions to the development plan, senior management review of external commitments, communication of approved commitment changes, software-cost tracking, tracking software-engineering

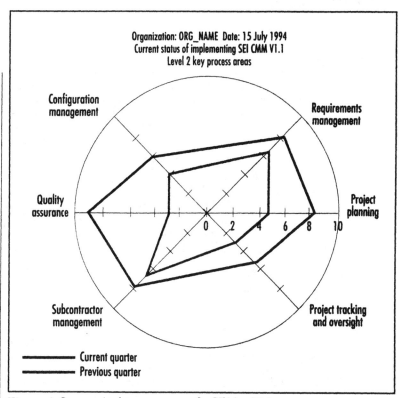

Figure 4. *Summarized progress report for SEI level 2 key process areas.*

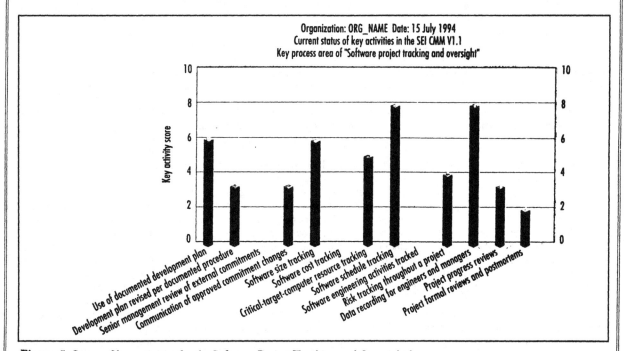

Figure 5. *Status of key activities for the Software Project Tracking and Oversight key process area.*

technical-activities, project-progress reviews, formal project reviews, and post-mortems. Addressing these items will lead to better performance against the target of reaching higher SEI process-capability levels.

PARTICIPANTS

To be effective, the assessment instrument must be championed and used by members of the organization conducting a progress assessment:

◆ *Organization management*. This role is generally taken by senior management. They are primarily responsible for understanding what is involved in an SEI progress assessment, indicating their support for the whole process, committing resources to implement the action plan created, and following up to ensure completion.

◆ *Progress-assessment champion*. This role is critical. A single individual is responsible for championing the whole process (for the specific time period that it is done), ensuring organization management's support, identifying who within the organization should participate, taking care of administrative items, and championing the action-plan implementation. The champion should be in a technically competent middle-management position that is well-respected within the organization. This role requires a lot of work, and the champion can be involved in progress assessment only for his or her particular organization.

◆ *Progress-assessment facilitator*. This person is responsible primarily for ensuring that the progress assessment runs smoothly, providing consulting support when necessary. The progress assessment includes not just assessment meetings but also action-plan creation and implementation as a result of these meetings. The necessary background for the facilitator includes experience in conducting assessments and audits of software organizations. The facilitator may be involved in several progress assessments for different organizations at the same time. The progress-assessment facilitator and progress-assessment champion must cooperate closely. The facilitator must be more familiar with the instruments involved and the SEI model used, and have overall experience in evaluating organizations, such as using Motorola's Quality System Review[5] or other audit mechanisms.

◆ *Progress-assessment participants*. The assessment participants are primarily technical and middle-management software people involved in day-to-day software development and maintenance activities. They are not necessarily limited to software developers, testers, and managers; they can also be people working in product management, marketing, or other positions that are part of the overall organization. They participate in the entire progress assessment, including meetings and action-plan implementation.

◆ *Organization-improvement champion*. This person initiates the progress-assessment process during the preparation stage. If no organization-improvement champion exists, one must be identified who will initiate this process. Typically, he or she is also the progress-assessment champion, at least initially, when the progress assessment is introduced to an organization. Once the progress assessment is established, the progress-assessment champion may be changed every quarter to ensure wider participation.

PROCESS

The progress-assessment process provides an ordered series of activities that guide the participants in the use of the progress-assessment instrument. The process consists of four stages: preparation, assessment meeting, action plan and commitment, and follow-up.

Preparation. Activities at this stage focus on obtaining management buy-in, if it is not already obtained, and preparing to conduct an effective SEI progress assessment.

1. The organization-improvement champion meets with organization management to present the benefits of introducing SEI progress assessments and recommends their use.

2. The organization-improvement champion identifies a progress-assessment champion.

3. The progress-assessment champion identifies a progress-assessment facilitator.

4. The progress-assessment champion and the progress-assessment facilitator determine the scope of the SEI progress assessment.

5. The progress-assessment champion and organization management select the progress-assessment participants from the projects and groups included in the scope of the SEI progress assessment.

Assessment meeting. During this stage, participants agree on a scoring for the key process areas and activities and a list of strengths and weaknesses in these areas.

1. The progress-assessment champion conducts an overview session for the assessment meeting participants.

2. The assessment-meeting participants prepare for the assessment meeting, record their scores and findings in the worksheets, and forward them to the progress-assessment facilitator.

3. The progress-assessment facilitator uses a spreadsheet (or other tool) to summarize assessment-meeting-participant scores before the meeting.

4. The progress-assessment facilitator identifies a recorder for the assessment meeting.

5. The progress-assessment facilitator moderates the assessment meeting.

> **THIS PROCESS SPEEDS IMPROVEMENT BY PROVIDING A WAY TO MEASURE AND TRACK IT.**

6. The recorder creates a draft list of scores and findings.

7. The progress-assessment champion moderates a review of this list.

8. The recorder updates and publishes the list.

9. The progress-assessment champion moderates a meeting with organization management and the progress-assessment participants where the scores and findings are presented.

Plan and commitment. At this stage the participants create the action plan, obtain commitments, and staff the plan according to the results of the assessment meeting.

1. The progress-assessment champion splits the progress-assessment participants into one team per key-process area. These teams generate draft action plans.

2. Each team meets with any existing organization key-process-area champions to ensure coordination and continuity of the action plans.

3. The draft action plans are reviewed and appropriately updated by the progress-assessment participants.

4. The progress-assessment champion ensures that the action plans are tracked using a project-management tool.

5. The progress-assessment champion moderates a meeting with organization management and progress-assessment participants, during which the action plans are presented and input is requested.

6. The action plans are updated on the basis of input by organization management.

7. Commitment templates for all action items are created and filled-in by the teams.

8. The progress-assessment champion ensures that individual meetings are scheduled with department managers to obtain their commitments.

9. Representatives of the teams participate in the meetings with department managers, finalize the commitment templates, and update their action plans appropriately.

Follow-up. During this final stage, participants ensure that the action plan is actually implemented and that sufficient progress is made, which is then reported to management.

1. Regular status meetings are conducted by each key-process-area team.

2. The progress-assessment champion conducts regular status meetings with the progress-assessment participants and provides status reports to organization management.

3. The organization-improvement champion identifies a new progress-assessment champion for next quarter's SEI progress assessment.

We have found that this process accelerates improvement by providing a way to measure it (the scoring guidelines) and track it (the presentation charts). This follows Motorola's approach to software measurement, which states: "Measurement is not the goal. The goal is improvement through measurement, analysis, and feedback."[6] The created action plans are shared with management, and requests for the necessary resources are made so that the actions can be implemented. This happens on a continuous basis, not just once every two years, which is the typical interval for formal SEI or other assessments. In fact, any actions necessary as a result of a formal SEI assessment or a Quality System Review may be folded into the already existing action plans developed through the use of SEI Progress Assessments.

This process also provides a driver for continuous process improvement, in line with the spirit of Motorola's Quality System Review and other process- and quality-improvement initiatives.

LESSONS LEARNED

Management buy-in is essential to a successful implementation of the progress-assessment instrument and process. We introduced both at CIG's monthly Software Process Improvement meeting, explaining what the assessment instrument is and proposing its use to assess current status relative to SEI level 2 and to drive organizational improvement. Motorola CIG's management adopted this proposal and asked that each product group conduct their own self-assessment using this instrument, then create action plans for improvement. Regular action-plan status meetings were also requested and conducted by management to track improvement achieved over time. In the months that followed, we learned several important lessons about implementing this progress-assessment method.

◆ Determine before conducting a progress assessment what its scope is. Also, determine what management level will be considered as "senior" for progress-assessment purposes (director and above, for example). You need this information so that participants can obtain a common understanding of how the SEI CMM description applies to their organization. It also ensures consistency in the use of the scoring guidelines in Figure 1.

◆ Ensure that sufficient coverage is achieved across software-development and -maintenance functions and groups involved. Do this by carefully selecting the participants in the progress assessment of a given quarter. A group of five to six people should be sufficient. However, a larger group of about 20 may be used if you need to increase buy-in within the organization and ensure that the action-plan implementation will be staffed properly. A mix of experienced people who have participated in past SEI Progress Assessments and inexperienced people is recom-

MANAGEMENT BUY-IN IS ESSENTIAL FOR SUCCESSFUL PROGRESS ASSESSMENTS.

mended. In the case of a larger group, special attention is required by the progress-assessment facilitator to ensure that the meetings are sufficiently under control.

♦ To ensure proper coverage of the SEI CMM, use the following guideline: *All* SEI CMM sections for a given key process area, not just the "Activities Performed," should be considered when using the scoring guidelines to determine a score, and when the list of findings and the action plan are created. For example, items under "Ability to Perform" that are not evident in the organization should be listed in the list of findings and subsequently addressed through the action plan created.

♦ The progress-assessment facilitator should use the following method to reach consensus on the score for a key activity and speed up the meeting: Determine what the average suggested score by the participants is, then move higher or lower based on comments by the participants. Do this by first obtaining the individual participant scores prior to the progress-assessment meet-ing, then use a spreadsheet to determine the mean, standard deviation, and so forth, in advance.

♦ Ensure that the entire progress assessment focuses more on identifying the organization's strengths and weaknesses (the findings) and the implementation of the action plan created and less on what a given key activity's score should be.

In addition to Motorola's Cellular Infrastructure Group, several Motorola business units have adopted the use of SEI Progress Assessments, including product groups within the Satellite Communications Group, Semiconductor Products Sector, the Land Mobile Products Sector, and the Automotive and Industrial Electronics Group. Thus far, these groups' experiences with SEI Progress Assessments support the lessons learned within the CIG.

After using the progress-assessment process for several quarters, we were able to formally document it, which implies that it reflects a practically implemented sequence of steps rather than a list of steps that would be nice to do but have not been implemented yet.

Having already achieved SEI level 2 in the second quarter of 1993, work is already in progress for achieving SEI level 3 within the CIG, with the SEI Progress Assessment process continuing to be the key driver. Benefits similar to those reported by Raymond Dion[7] are anticipated as a result of achieving higher SEI process-maturity levels.

The instrument and process used for implementing the SEI Progress Assessment method can also be used in conjunction with additional models of software capability, quality, customer satisfaction, software measurements,[8] and so on, such as the Quality System Review to assess progress relative to "higher levels" in that model. I encourage you to use the SEI Progress Assessment method within your own organization and to share your results with other software practitioners in professional conferences and publications. ♦

ACKNOWLEDGMENTS

I thank Allan Willey and Kim Dobson for pointing out the need for a progress-assessment method and asking that one be developed. I would also like to thank Motorola management, especially CIG's, for supporting the use of progress assessments; Motorola's practitioners for taking ownership of the instrument and process, successfully completing several quarterly progress assessments, and creating and implementing action plans to drive the improvement of their own product group/organization over time; and Bob Yacobellis, senior member of the technical staff and manager, Corporate Software Process Engineering Group, for his constructive review and comments regarding earlier versions of the SEI Progress Assessment method.

REFERENCES

1. M.C. Paulk et al., "Capability Maturity Model for Software," Tech. report CMU/SEI-91-TR-24, Software Eng. Inst., Pittsburgh, 1991.
2. M.C. Paulk et al., "Capability Maturity Model for Software, Version 1.1," Tech. report CMU/SEI-93-TR-24, Software Eng. Inst., Pittsburgh, 1993.
3. M.C. Paulk et al., "Capability Maturity Model, Version 1.1," *IEEE Software*, July 1993, pp. 18-27.
4. A. Topper and P. Forgensen, "More than One Way to Measure Process Maturity," *IEEE Software*, Nov. 1991, pp. 9-10.
5. Motorola Corporate Quality Council, "Motorola Corporate Quality System Review Guidelines," Revision 1, Literature # BR1202/D, Phoenix, Ariz., 1991.
6. M. K. Daskalantonakis, "A Practical View of Software Measurement and Implementation Experiences Within Motorola," *IEEE Trans. Software Eng.*, Nov. 1992, pp. 998-1010.
7. R. Dion, "Process Improvement and the Corporate Balance Sheet," *IEEE Software*, July 1993, pp. 28-35.
8. M.K. Daskalantonakis, V.R. Basili, and R.H. Yacobellis, "A Method for Assessing Software Measurement Technology," *Quality Engineering Journal*, Vol. 3, No. 1, 1990, pp. 27-40.

Address questions about this article to Daskalantonakis at Cellular Infrastructure Group, Motorola, Inc., 1501 West Shure Dr., Arlington Heights, IL 60004; dask@mot.com.

Successfully Applying Software Metrics

Robert B. Grady, Hewlett-Packard

What do you need to measure and analyze to make your project a success? These examples from many projects and HP divisions may help you chart your course.

The word *success* is very powerful. It creates strong, but widely varied, images that may range from the final seconds of an athletic contest to a graduation ceremony to the loss of 10 pounds. Success makes us feel good; it's cause for celebration.

All these examples of success are marked by a measurable end point, whether externally or self-created. Most of us who create software approach projects with some similar idea of success. Our feelings from project start to end are often strongly influenced by whether we spent any early time describing this success and how we might measure progress.

Software metrics measure specific attributes of a software product or a software-development process. In other words, they are measures of success. It's convenient to group the ways that we apply metrics to measure success into the four areas shown in Figure 1. This article contains four major sections highlighting examples of these areas.

Figure 1 also shows two arrows that represent conflicting pressures for data. For example, on one of the first software projects I managed, the finance department wanted me to use their system to track project costs, arguing that this would help me. I shortly learned that their system didn't give me the kind of information I needed to be successful. The reports weren't timely or accurate, and they didn't usefully measure progress. This was one of my first experiences with the opposing desires for information that can arise between a project manager and the division's management team. They wanted summary data across many diverse functions; I wanted data that would help me track day-to-day progress.

I soon realized that projects stand the best chance of success when the goals driving the use of different measures can be stated and mutually pursued. This article's examples are all from real projects, and they were chosen to show both viewpoints illustrated by the arrows in Figure 1. The examples also show how the possibly conflicting goals of a project team and of an organization can effectively complement each other. Finally, they are examples of things that *you* can measure to be more successful.

Project estimation and progress monitoring

Today there are dozens of software-estimation tools. Figure 1 suggests that such tools can be quite useful to project managers. These tools are now very sophisticated because they account for many possible project variables. Unfortunately, most of us are not much better at guessing the right values for these variables than we are at guessing total project schedules.

The basis for estimates. Most estimating tools are based on limited measurements. For example, the first three columns of Table 1 show measurements for my early 25,000-engineering-hour project, with and without nonengineering activities. (I finally tracked these measurements without using our normal accounting system.) Some of the data is useful for future estimates. For example, the percentages for supervision and administrative support would be reasonably accurate for other projects, particularly since they can be controlled. Even the time spent in different activities doesn't differ much from the averages for 132 more-recent Hewlett-Packard projects, although my team didn't collect the data in exactly the way that HP currently does.

Should you collect data like this for your projects? Since estimation models are based on such data, informally collecting it will help you track the validity of your inputs into any model. This data can give you useful insights into the accuracy of your estimates. The earlier you find differences, the more likely it is that management might accept schedule changes.

The bottom line. Higher level managers are usually not interested in as much detail as Table 1 presents. They want the bottom line: Is the project on schedule? Figure 2 shows how one HP lab tracked this across many projects.[1,2] Two ideas went into this graph. First, a schedule slip is the amount of time that a project schedule is moved to a later date. Second, average project progress for a

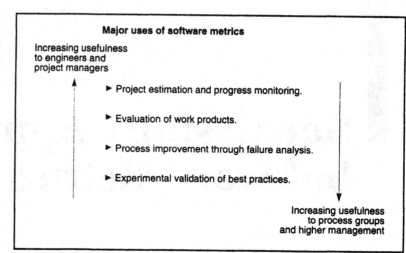

Figure 1. Major uses of software metrics and the conflicting pressures for data.

Table 1. Task breakdowns for a 25,000-engineering-hour software project over 2.5 calendar-years.

Tracked Times	Project %	Eng. Only %	Categories Currently Tracked	Approx. Project %	HP Average
Investigation	20	26	Reqs./Specs.	19	18
External/Internal Reference Specs	2	2	Design	16	19
Coding	19	23	Implement	32	34
Debugging	19	24			
Integration	11	14	Test	33	29
Quality Assurance	8	11			
Manuals	7				
Supervision	9			Not included	
Support	5				

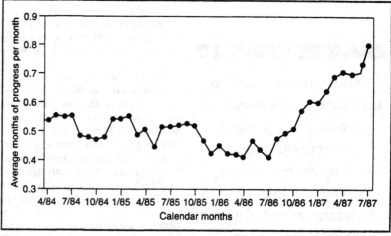

Figure 2. Development project progress for all software projects in one HP division.

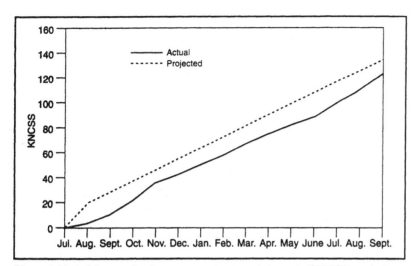

Figure 3. Plot of thousands of noncomment source statements (KNCSS) against time for project summarized in Table 1 (© 1987 Prentice-Hall, used with permission).

time period is defined as one minus the ratio of the sum of all project slips divided by the sum of project elapsed times.

For example, suppose you have a small lab with three projects. In a one-month period, the first project's manager believes that it is on schedule (its schedule doesn't change). Its slip is zero. The second project had a bad month. Its slip is one. The third project's manager expects the project will slip one week, for a slip of about one-quarter. The sum of the slips is 1.25. The sum of elapsed times is 3. Average project progress is therefore $1 - (1.25/3) = 0.58$.

The graph uses a moving average to smooth month-to-month swings. The lab first started plotting the graph around October 1985. They had enough historical data to show that they had only averaged about a half month of progress for every elapsed month. After monitoring the graph for a few months, the project teams gradually focused on more accurate schedules, and they improved their accuracy to an enviable point.[1,2]

Successful usage. The examples shown in Table 1 and Figure 2 were both successes. They show two things that you will see repeated in other examples:

- Lab management wanted limited, high-level summary data.
- Project-management data provided both confidence-building tracking information and a basis for better future estimates.

A major reason for success in both cases was that their end points — their goals — were measurable. Figure 2 graphically shows that the way the division estimated schedules hadn't changed for at least 1.5 years before they defined a way to measure progress. In the other example, Table 1, the data influenced dozens of my decisions. They included resource balancing, intermediate and final schedule commitments, test schedules, and technical writing schedules. Furthermore, I could confidently show and explain progress on a very large project in ways that few high-level HP managers had seen before.

Monitoring progress against estimates. There are two time-proven ways to track progress on a software project. The first is to track completed functionality (the features or aspects of the software product).

Tracking functionality. Despite often-expressed concerns about the usefulness of counting lines of code, I have found tracking code size against time to be very useful for managing projects. Figure 3 is a plot of thousands of noncomment source statements (KNCSS) against time for the project summarized in Table 1.[3]

KNCSS represents completed functionality here. It is reasonable to use during the coding and testing phases, particularly if you track coded NCSS separately from tested NCSS (not shown in Figure 3). I updated this graph every week to make sure the project was on track. I also tracked the status of modules designed for this project. This provided a link to our original estimates by exposing design areas significantly different from earlier plans.

More recently, HP has measured

FURPS criteria (functionality, usability, reliability, performance, and supportability) to complement simpler size-tracking metrics. (Grady[2] describes FURPS more completely.)

Finally, function points, another popular functionality measure, are computed from a combination of inputs, outputs, file communications, and other factors. They can be computed independently of source code, so some people find their added difficulty of use offset by this earlier availability. (Capers Jones' *Applied Software Measurement*, McGraw-Hill, New York, 1991, is a useful function-point reference.)

Found-and-fixed defects. Tracking functionality doesn't attract high-level management attention like the trends of found-and-fixed defects. This second method is very useful in monitoring progress in later development phases. These trends are also among the most important aids you have in deciding when to release a product successfully. Methods for analyzing such trends vary. Variations include simple trend plotting, sophisticated customer-environment modeling, and accurate recording of testing or test-creation times.

Using defect trends to make larger system-release decisions gives valuable confidence to higher level managers. They feel more comfortable when major release decisions are backed by data and graphs. Figure 4 shows the system test defects for a project involving over 30 engineers. It shows this project's status about one month before completion. The team derived the goal from past project experiences. One release criteria was for the defects/1,000-test-hours rate to drop and stay below the goal line for at least two weeks before release. The alternative projections were simple hand-drawn extrapolations using several of the past weeks' slopes. The team updated the graph every week. The weekly test hours were much fewer than 1,000, so the weekly ratios may give an impression that there were more defects than there really were.

HP has learned that the critical downward trend that Figure 4 displays is necessary to avoid costly postrelease crises. This project's downward slope continued, and the project released successfully. An opposite example was an HP software system released despite an absence of a clear downward defect trend. The result was a multimillion-dollar update shortly after release and a product with a bad quality reputation. This kind of mistake can cause

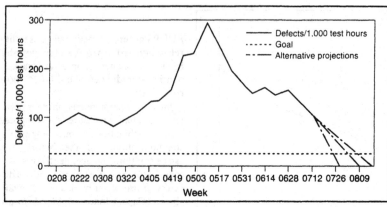

Figure 4. System-test defect trend for project involving over 30 engineers.

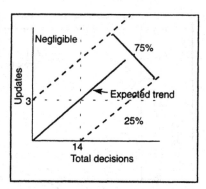

Figure 5. Trend analysis of number of source updates for system-level testing versus the number of decision statements per subroutine.

an entire product line's downfall. A recent article describes how one company learned this lesson the hard way.[4]

Plotting defect trends is one method where both project and high-level management have similar interests. While exact completion points may vary based on differing project goals, better decisions are possible when trends are visible. Those decisions will help to ensure project success.

Evaluation of work products

A work product is an intermediate or final output that describes the design, operation, manufacture, or test of some portion of a deliverable or salable product. It is not the final product. All software development finally results in a work product of code. While this section's brief examples center on code, the idea of extracting useful metrics from virtually any work product is the point to remember.

Because code can be analyzed automatically, it has been a convenient research vehicle for sophisticated statistical analysis. Unfortunately, this emphasis has created a strong bias in perceptions of metric applications. Many managers believe that useful metrics require time-consuming techniques outside of their normal decision-making processes. Even recently, one metrics expert told me that the minimum number of code metrics a project manager should monitor is around 20.

Cyclomatic complexity. Fortunately, HP has had good results when measuring just one code metric: cyclomatic complexity, which is based on a program's decision count. (The decision count includes

all programmatic conditional statements, so if a high-level-language statement contains multiple conditions, each condition is counted once.) One HP division especially saw this when they combined the metric with a visual image that graphically showed large complexity.[5] Graphs, and their source code cross references, help engineers understand problem locations and may provide insights for fixing them. The graphs excite managers because their availability encourages engineers to produce more maintainable software. This doesn't mean that the tool's numeric values are ignored: Complexity metrics give managers and engineers simple numerical figures of merit.

When considering engineering tool value, high-level managers want to know whether using such a tool yields better end products in less time. Project managers may have to look at other data like that shown in Figure 5 to build a strong case for tools.[6] This study concerned a project of 830,000 lines of executable Fortran code.

Those doing the study plotted the relationship between program-decision counts and the number of updates reflected by their source code control system. Seventy-five percent of the updates fell within the dashed lines. For their system, the number of updates was proportional to the number of decision statements. From their analysis, they drew a trend line. By knowing the cost and schedule effects of modules with more than three updates, they concluded that 14 was the maximum decision count to allow in a program. (Tom McCabe originally suggested 10, based on testing difficulty.[7])

You can do a similar analysis or you can accept these and similarly documented results and assume they apply equally well to your project. Then esti-

mate how using complexity tools can make your project more effective. Measure normal defect rates and both the engineering time and the calendar time to do fixes. Estimate how long it would take to run complexity tools. Finally, calculate your savings when you reduce complexity *before* your people start finding the defects in test. Grady[2] provides an economic justification for the purchase of complexity tools like these.

But the metrics expert who set a minimum of 20 code metrics was not totally wrong. Because cyclomatic complexity is a measure of control complexity, it is more valuable for control-oriented applications than for data-oriented ones. It works for both, but the characteristics of data-oriented applications suggest that you must consider other dimensions as well. Unfortunately, reported data-oriented results haven't been as thoroughly tested as those I've mentioned.

Design complexity. A promising metric for data-oriented complexity is fanout squared. The fanout of a module is the number of calls from that module. At least three studies have concluded that fanout squared is one component of a design metric that correlates well to probability of defects.[2,8,9] More importantly, fanout squared can be determined before code is created. Figure 6 on the next page shows the top-level structure chart of the most defect-prone module in a system. This module was the source of 50 percent of the system test defects, even though it had only 8 percent of the code. Its fanout squared was also the largest among the system's 13 top-level modules. In fact, postrelease defect densities were highly correlated to the fanout squared of the system's modules.

The figure shows a large number of

48

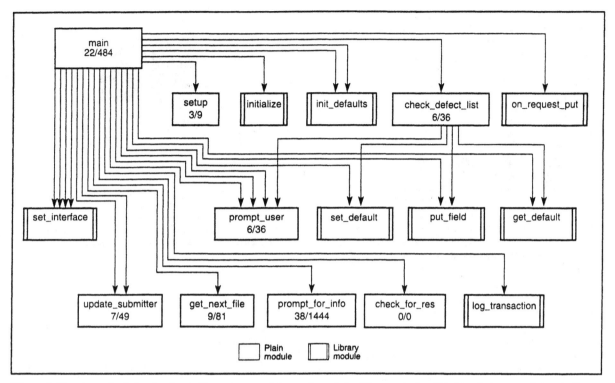

Figure 6. Structure chart showing fanout/fanout squared for each module. Diagram is simplified to show a complete set of connections for the main module only. Calls to system or standard utility routines are not shown or counted.

connections between *main* and the 15 other modules. The library modules don't call other modules, so no fanout is given for them. Note the fanout for *prompt_for_info*. With a fanout of 38 (and a fanout squared of 1,444), you can imagine its structure chart's complexity. Such large fanouts suggest that there is a missing design layer. Structure charts combine with fanout squared to give the same type of results as cyclomatic complexity and graphical views of control flow, only earlier.

Based on limited past experimental results, design complexity metrics may not be justified yet during design. However, if information like fanout squared were readily available as a byproduct of normal project tools, progress toward understanding design complexity would be faster. Meanwhile, measuring code complexity is desirable from both project and higher management viewpoints. Also, measuring design complexity in designs provides an important research opportunity.

More on successful usage. Cyclomatic complexity and fanout squared are just two types of work-product analysis. Automation recently introduced by the CASE (computer-aided software engineering) boom continues to expand engineers' comprehension of their work.

You can take advantage of complexity data to help your project in several ways. Like the Figure 5 example suggests, you can enforce a standard by computing complexity for all modules and not accepting any above some value. Another approach is to limit the number of modules above a given complexity level. Then make sure those modules are inspected and tested carefully. Another way is to require more documentation for such modules. Whichever way works best for you, it is certain that complexity information will help both you and your engineers to be more successful by providing information for better, more timely decisions.

Process improvement through failure analysis

I believe this third area from Figure 1 is the most promising for improving development processes. Failure analysis, and finding and removing major defect sources, offers the best short-term potential for guiding improvements.

Project defect patterns. There are several valuable approaches. One simple approach for project managers is to monitor the number of defects found during system test, code inspections, or design inspections. This data can be sorted by module, and special actions can be taken as soon as potential problem areas appear. For example, Figure 7 shows both prerelease system-test defects and defects for a product during the first six months after its release.[3]

Unfortunately, the project manager in this case didn't do anything different until after collection of postrelease data. The project manager then focused team effort on thorough inspections and better testing of the three most defect-prone modules. (While these modules were only 24 percent of the code, they accounted for 76 percent of the defects.) As a result, the team succeeded in greatly reducing the product's incoming defect rate by focusing on those three modules.

Software process defect patterns. Another type of failure analysis examines defect patterns related to development processes. This analysis affects enough people to generally require lab-level management sponsorship. Many HP divisions today start this analysis by cate-

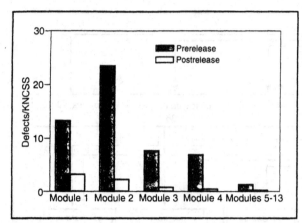

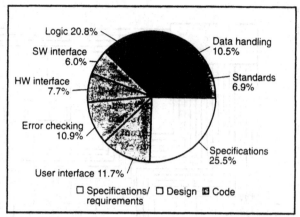

Figure 7. Analysis by code module for prerelease system-test defects and for those occurring during the first six months after the product's release (© 1987, Prentice-Hall, used with permission).

Figure 8. Top eight causes of defects for four Scientific Instruments Division projects at Hewlett-Packard.

gorizing their defects according to a three-level HP model used since 1987. The three levels are origin, type, and mode. Grady[2] describes several significant improvements achieved in divisions using this model. Figure 8 shows recent data for two levels of the model for yet another HP division (Scientific Instruments Division). The shading represents defect origin information, and the pie wedges are defect types. The data reflects the eight most frequently recorded causes of defects for four projects.

The division performed three post-project reviews to brainstorm potential solutions to their top four defect types. Several initiatives were launched. The first of these that yielded data for a full project life cycle recently concluded. The project team had decided to focus on user-interface defects. They had over 20 percent of that defect type on their previous project (even though the division-wide average was lower). They brainstormed the Figure 9 fishbone diagram and decided to create guidelines for user-interface de-

signs that addressed many of the fishbone-diagram branches.

Their results were impressive. They reduced the percentage of user-interface defects in test for their new year-long project to roughly 5 percent. Even though the project produced 34 percent *more* code, they spent 27 percent *less* time in test. Of course, other improvement efforts also contributed to their success. But the clear user-interface defect reduction showed them that their new guidelines and the attention they paid to

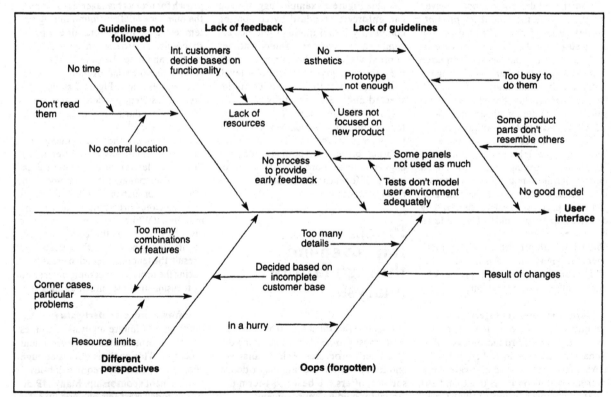

Figure 9. Fishbone diagram showing the causes of user-interface defects.

their interfaces were major contributors.

The examples you've seen in Figures 7, 8, and 9 show how a small investment in failure analysis can reap practical short-term gains. Ironically, the main limiter to failure-analysis success is that many managers still believe they can quickly reduce *total* effort or schedules by 50 percent or more. As a result, they won't invest in more modest process improvements. This prevents them from gaining 50 percent improvements through a series of smaller gains. Because it takes time to get any improvement adopted *organization-wide*, these managers will continue to be disappointed.

Experimental validation of best practices

This software metric use has been the most successful of the four listed in Figure 1. People have validated the success of important engineering practices (for example, prototyping,[10] reducing coupling, increasing cohesion,[9] limiting complexity,[6] inspections and testing techniques,[11] and reliability models[12]). This validation should lead to quicker, widespread acceptance of these "best" practices.

Of the four Figure 1 metric uses, project managers are least motivated to validate best practices because normal project demands have higher priority. On the other hand, these metrics have probably brought project managers the greatest benefits. The first example here is what high-level managers want to see. One HP division measured the data in Table 2 for different test and inspection techniques. The average efficiency of code reading/code inspections was 4.4 times better than other test techniques yield.[2,13] This data helps project managers to plan inspections for their projects and to convince their engineers of the merits of in-

Table 2. Comparison of testing efficiencies.*

Testing Type	Efficiency (Defects found/hour)
Regular use	0.210
Black box	0.282
White box	0.322
Reading/ Inspections	1.057

*Defect-tracking system lumped code reading and inspections into one category. About 80 percent of the defects so logged were from inspections.

spections by showing the benefits.

However, experience has shown that it takes many years to widely apply even proven best practices. It often takes local proof to convince engineers to change their practices. For example, Henry and Kafura first showed the fanout squared metric discussed earlier to be useful over 10 years ago (as a part of their information-flow metric).[8] Even then, they pointed out how such an early design metric would be useful during design inspections. Unfortunately, most software-developing organizations don't have standard design practices yet. Also, people haven't been convinced that it's worth the effort to do high-level design with the detail necessary to compute such measures.

Project managers might find Figure 10's graph useful for their projects. It shows all the fanout squared values for an HP product. If you had this information early in your project, you could focus inspections and evaluations on the high-value modules. Like cyclomatic complexity, fanout squared appears to have several very desirable properties:

- It is easy to compute.
- Graphical views (like Figure 6) do

reflect high complexity.
- The metric exposes a small percentage of a system's modules as potential problems.

Although this may be a significant future metric, it illustrates a dilemma. How much time can project managers or organizations spend proving such practices? As positive evidence grows and competitive pressures for higher quality grow, the motivation to apply promising new practices also increases. Not all validations of beneficial practices are as easy to measure as inspections. However, this is the road to progress. My advice to project managers is to invest some of your team's effort on improvements, but track and validate the benefits. My advice to high-level managers is to reserve some funds and encouragement to support such validations.

How do you apply software metrics to be successful? Review the four major uses of metrics, studying the project-level and management-level examples from successful projects. These examples lead to three recommendations for project managers:

- Define your measures of success early in your project and track your progress toward them.
- Use defect data trends to help you decide when to release a product.
- Measure complexity to help you optimize design decisions and create a more maintainable product.

Don't forget that other aspects contribute to successful metrics usage and project management beyond this article's examples. They include linking metrics to project goals, measuring product-related metrics, and ensuring reasonable collection and interpretation of data. Consider two more recommendations for strategic purposes:

- Categorize defects to identify product and process weaknesses. Use this data to focus process-improvement decisions on high-return fixes.
- Collect data that quantifies the success of best practices.

This is all useful advice, *but what do you need to measure to be successful?* It is difficult to reduce this answer to a small set of measures for high-level managers. Chapter 15 of Grady[2] discusses nine

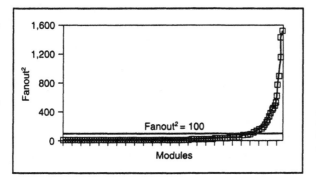

Figure 10. Fanout squared for a 250-module product, sorted by ascending fanout squared (which is more than 100 for only 10 percent of the modules).

useful management graphs. Finally, I suggest that project managers collect the following data:

- engineering effort by activity,
- size data (for example, noncomment source statements or function points),
- defects counted and classified in multiple ways,
- relevant product metrics (for example, selected measurable FURPS),
- complexity, and
- testing code coverage (an automated way of measuring which code has been tested).[2]

Understand how each of these relates to *your* success, and perform timely analyses to optimize your future. ∎

Acknowledgments

I especially thank Jan Grady and Debbie Caswell for their early reviews and suggestions when this article was just a way of organizing my ideas for a talk. I also thank other Hewlett-Packard and *Computer* reviewers for their helpful comments and suggestions. Finally, thanks to Brad Yackle, Mark Tischler, and the others at SID for sharing their failure-analysis results.

References

1. D. Levitt, "Process Measures to Improve R&D Scheduling Accuracy," *Hewlett-Packard J.*, Vol. 39, No. 2, Apr. 1988, pp. 61-65.

2. R. Grady, *Practical Software Metrics for Project Management and Process Improvement*, Prentice-Hall, Englewood Cliffs, N.J., 1992.

3. R. Grady and D. Caswell, *Software Metrics: Establishing a Company-Wide Program*, Prentice-Hall, Englewood Cliffs, N.J., 1987, pp. 31 and 110.

4. D. Clark, "Change of Heart at Oracle Corp.," *San Francisco Chronicle*, July 2, 1992, pp. B1 and B4.

5. W. Ward, "Software Defect Prevention Using McCabe's Complexity Metric," *Hewlett-Packard J.*, Vol. 40, No. 2, Apr. 1989, pp. 64-69.

6. R. Rambo, P. Buckley, and E. Branyan, "Establishment and Validation of Software Metric Factors," *Proc. Int'l Soc. Parametric Analysts Seventh Conf.*, 1985, pp. 406-417.

7. T. McCabe, "A Complexity Measure," *IEEE Trans. Software Eng.*, Vol. SE-2, No. 4, Dec. 1976, pp. 308-320.

8. S. Henry and D. Kafura, "Software Structure Metrics Based on Information Flow," *IEEE Trans. Software Eng.*, Vol. SE-7, No. 5, Sept. 1981, pp. 510-518.

9. D. Card with R. Glass, *Measuring Software Design Quality*, Prentice-Hall, Englewood Cliffs, N.J., 1990.

10. B.W. Boehm, T. Gray, and T. Seewaldt, "Prototyping vs. Specifying: A Multi-Project Experiment," *Proc. Seventh Int'l Conf. Software Eng.*, IEEE Press, Piscataway, N.J., Order No. M528 (microfiche), 1984, pp. 473-484.

11. L. Lauterbach and W. Randell, "Six Test Techniques Compared: The Test Process and Product," *Proc. Fourth Int'l Conf. Computer Assurances*, Nat'l Inst. Standards and Technology, Gaithersburg, Md., 1989.

12. M. Ohba, "Software Quality = Test Accuracy × Text Coverage," *Proc. Sixth Int'l Conf. Software Eng.*, IEEE Press, Piscataway, N.J., 1982, pp. 287-293.

13. T. Tillson and J. Walicki, "Testing HP SoftBench: A Distributed CASE Environment: Lessons Learned," *HP SEPC Proc.*, Aug. 1990, pp. 441-460 (internal use only).

Using Metrics to Manage Software Projects

Edward F. Weller

Bull HN Information Systems*

F ive years ago, Bull's Enterprise Servers Operation in Phoenix, Arizona, used a software process that, although understandable, was unpredictable in terms of product quality and delivery schedule. The process generated products with unsatisfactory quality levels and required significant extra effort to avoid major schedule slips.

All but the smallest software projects require metrics for effective project management. Hence, as part of a program designed to improve the quality, productivity, and predictability of software development projects, the Phoenix operation launched a series of improvements in 1989. One improvement based software project management on additional software measures. Another introduced an inspection program,[1] since inspection data was essential to project management improvements. Project sizes varied from several thousand lines of code (KLOC) to more than 300 KLOC.

The improvement projects enhanced quality and productivity. In essence, Bull now has a process that is repeatable and manageable, and that delivers higher quality products at lower cost. In this article, I describe the metrics we selected and implemented, illustrating with examples drawn from several development projects.

Project management levels

There are three levels of project management capability based on software-metrics visibility. (These three levels shouldn't be equated with the five levels in the Software Engineering Institute's Capability Maturity Model.) Describing them will put the Bull examples in perspective and show how we enhanced our process through gathering, analyzing, and using data to manage current projects and plan future ones.

First level. In the simplest terms, software development can be modeled as shown in Figure 1. Effort, in terms of people and computer resources, is put into a process that yields a product. All too often, unfortunately, the process can only be described

> **In 1989, Bull's Arizona facility launched a project management program that required additional software metrics and inspections. Today, the company enjoys improvements in quality, productivity, and cost.**

---

* Since writing this article, the author has joined Motorola.

Reprinted from *Computer*, Vol. 27, No. 9, Sept. 1994, pp. 27–33.

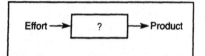

Figure 1. Software development level 1: no control of the development process. Some amount of effort goes into the process, and a product of indeterminant size and quality is developed early or (usually) late, compared to the plan.

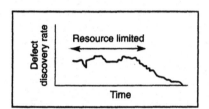

Figure 2. Defect discovery profile for lower development levels. The number of defects in the product exceeds the ability of limited resources to discover and fix defects. Once the defect number has been reduced sufficiently, the discovery rate declines toward zero. Predicting when the knee will occur is the challenge.

Figure 3. Software development at level 2: measurement of the code and test phases begins.

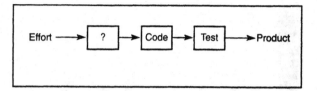

Figure 4. Software development level 3: control of the entire development process. You measure the requirements and design process to provide feedforward to the rest of the development as well as feedback to future planning activities.

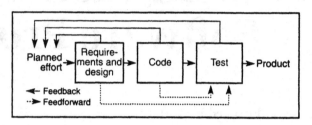

by the question mark in Figure 1. Project managers and development staff do not plan the activities or collect the metrics that would allow them to control their project.

Second level. The process depicted in Figure 1 rarely works for an organization developing operating-system software or large applications. There is usually some form of control in the process. We collected test defect data in integration and system test for many years for several large system releases, and we developed profiles for defect removal that allowed us to predict the number of weeks remaining before test-cycle completion. The profile was typically flat for many weeks (or months, for larger system releases in the 100- to 300-KLOC range) until we reached a "knee" in the profile where the defect discovery rate dropped toward zero (see Figure 2).

Several factors limit the defect discovery rate:

• Defects have a higher probability of being "blocking defects," which prevent other test execution early in the

integration- and system-test cycle.
• The defect discovery rate exceeds the development staff's capacity to analyze and fix problems, as test progresses and more test scenarios can be run in parallel.

Although this process gave us a fairly predictable delivery date once the knee was reached, we could not predict when the knee would occur. There were still too many variables (as represented by the first two boxes in Figure 3). There was no instrumentation on the requirements or design stages (the "?" in Figure 3).

Our attempts to count or measure the size of the coding effort were, in a sense, counterproductive. The focus of the development effort was on coding because code completed and into test was a countable, measurable element. This led to a syndrome we called WISCY for "Why isn't Sam coding yet?" We didn't know how to measure requirements analysis or design output, other than by document size.

We also didn't know how to estimate the number of defects entering into test. Hence, there was no way to tell how many weeks we would spend on the flat part of the defect-removal profile. Predicting delivery dates for large product releases with 200 to 300 KLOC of new and changed source code was difficult, at best.

A list of measures is available in the second-level model (Figure 3):

• effort in person-months,
• computer resources used,

• the product size when shipped, and
• the number of defects found in the integration and system tests.

Although these measures are "available," we found them difficult to use in project planning — there was little correlation among the data, and the data was not available at the right time (for instance, code size wasn't known until the work was completed). Project managers needed a way to predict and measure what they were planning.

Third level. The key element of the initiative was to be able to predict development effort and duration. We chose two measures to add to those we were already using: (1) size estimates and (2) defect removal for the entire development cycle.

Because the inspection program had been in place since early 1990, we knew we would have significant amounts of data on defect removal. Size estimating was more difficult because we had to move from an effort-based estimating system (sometimes biased by available resources) to one based on quantitative measures that were unfamiliar to most of the staff. The size measures were necessary to derive expected numbers of defects, which then could be used to predict test schedules with greater accuracy. This data also provided feedback to the planning organization for future projects.

To meet the needs of the model shown in Figure 4, we needed the following measures (italics designate changes from the prior list):

54

- effort in person-months,
- computer resources used,
- *estimated product size at each development stage*,
- product size *after coding*,
- *product size after each test stage*,
- number of defects *found in all development stages from inspections* (in this article, inspection defects refer to major defects), *unit test*, integration test, and system test, and
- *estimated completion date for each phase.*

The sidebar "Data collection sheet" shows a sample form used to compile data.

Project planning

Once the project team develops the first size estimate, the project manager begins to use the data — as well as historical data from our metrics database — for effort and schedule estimating. Several examples from actual projects illustrate these points.

Using defect data to plan test activities. We use the inspection and test defect databases as the primary defect-estimation source. The inspection data provides defect detection rates for design and code by product identifier (PID). Our test database can be searched by the same PID, so a defect depletion curve[2] for the project can be constructed by summarizing all the project's PIDs. (Several interesting examples in Humphrey[2] provided a template for constructing a simple spreadsheet application that we used to plan and track defect injection and removal rates.) Figure 5 shows such a curve for one project. The size and defect density estimates were based on experience from a prior project. The project manager estimated the unit and integration test effort from the defect estimates and the known cost to find and fix defects in test. The estimates and actual amounts are compared in the "Project tracking and analysis" section below.

Data collection sheet

This "Data collection sheet," developed by Kathy Griffith, Software Engineering Process Group project manager at Bull, compiles effort, size, defect, and completion data. Although the sheet is somewhat busy, only six data elements are estimated or collected at each development-cycle phase. The cells with XX in them indicate data collected at the end of high-level design; the cells with YY are derived from the XX data.

DATA COLLECTION SHEET

Project Name

Build
Product or Feature Group Identifier(s)
(PIDs, IDs, etc.)
Date of Initial Estimates

	REQ	HLD	LLD	CODE	LEV1	LEV2	LEV3	LEV4	GS	TOTAL
N&C Original KLOC Est										■
N&C Revised KLOC Est		XX								■
N&C KLOC Actuals	■									■
Effort - Estimate (PM)									■	
Effort - Revised (PM)		XX							■	
Effort - Actual (PM)		XX							■	
# Defects - Estimate		YY								
# Defects - Actual		YY								
Est Phase End Dates		XX								

GS = General Ship
HLD = High-Level Design
LLD = Low-Level Design

LEV1 = Unit, or Level 1, Test
LEV2 = Integration, or Level 2, Test
LEV3 = System, or Level 3, Test
LEV4 = Beta, or Level 4, Test

N&C = New and Changed
PID = Product IDentifier
PM = Person Months
REQ = Requirements Analysis

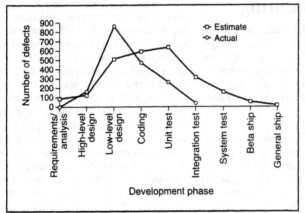

Figure 5. Estimated versus actual defect depletion curves.

different viewpoint, might have spotted the anomaly. Unit test data accuracy might have been questioned as follows:

- Are some of the errors caused by high-level design defects?
- Why weren't any design defects found in the integration test?

When the data was charted with the defect source added, the design-defect data discovery rate in the unit test was obvious. The inaccuracy of the integration test data also became apparent. A closer look at the project revealed the source of the defect data had not been collected.

We also questioned members of the design inspection teams; we found that key people were not available for the high-level design inspection. As a result, we changed the entry criteria for low-level design to delay the inspection for two to three weeks, if necessary, to let a key system architect participate in the inspection. Part of the change required a risk analysis of the potential for scrubbing the low-level design work started before the inspection.

Multiple data views. The data in Figure 6 helped the project manager analyze results from the integration test. The project team had little experience with the type of product to be developed, so a large number of defects were predicted. The team also decided to spend more effort on the unit test. After the unit test, the results seemed within plan, as shown in Figure 6a. During the integration test, some concern was raised that the number of defects found was too high. Once the data was normalized against the project size and compared to projections for the number of defects expected by the development team, the level of concern was lowered.

However, this project had a serious requirement error that was discovered in

the later stages of the system test; this demonstrated why it's important to look at more than the total number of defects or the defect density, even when the number of defects is below expectations. A closer look at the early development stages shows that very few requirements or high-level design defects were found in the inspections. The low-level design inspections also found fewer defects than expected. What the project members missed in the data analysis during the unit and integration tests was the large number of design errors being detected (see Figure 6b). This example demonstrates the value of independent data collection and analysis as soon as it is available.

An objective analysis, or at least an analysis that looked at the project from a

Using test cost. On one large project, the measured cost in the integration test was much higher than expected. Even though you know the cost of defects in test is high, an accurate cost tally can surprise you. If you haven't gathered the data for a project, the following example may convince you that the effort is worthwhile.

On this large project, it took

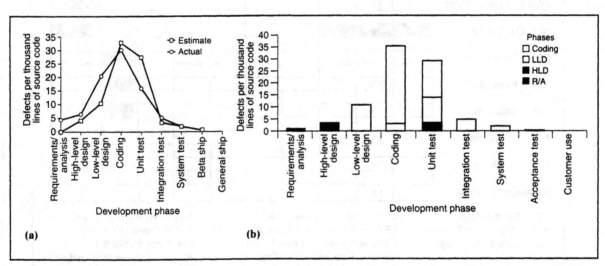

Figure 6. Projected versus actual number of defects found per thousand lines of code from inspections and test (a), and additional information when the defect source is included (b).

- 80 hours to find and fix the typical defect,
- 3.5 person-months to rebuild the product and rerun the test suite, and
- 8-10 calendar days to complete the retest cycle.

Three months' effort represents the fixed cost of test for this product area.

This analysis reemphasizes the need to spend more time and effort on inspecting design and code work products. How many additional hours should be spent inspecting the work products (design, code, and so forth) versus the months of effort expended in test?

Sanity check. Size estimates and software development attribute ratings are used as input to the Cocomo (Constructive Cost Model) estimating model.[3] (Joe Wiechec of Bull's Release Management group developed a Cocomo spreadsheet application based on Boehm[3] for schedule and effort sanity checks.) The accuracy of the effort estimate produced by Cocomo depends on accurate size estimate and software development attribute ratings (analyst capability, programmer capability, and so forth).

We compare the assumed defect rates and cost to remove these defects with the Cocomo output as a sanity check for the estimating process. Since project managers often assign attribute ratings optimistically, the defect data based on project and product history provides a crosscheck with the cost for unit and integration test derived from the Cocomo estimate. Reasonable agreement between Cocomo test-effort estimates and estimates derived from defect density and cost to find and fix per-defect figures confirm that attribute ratings have been reasonably revised. This sanity check works only for the attribute ratings, since both the Cocomo effort estimates and test cost estimates depend on the size estimate.

Project tracking

The keys to good project tracking are defining measurable and countable entities and having a repeatable process for gathering and counting. During the design phase, the metrics available to the project manager are

- effort spent in person-months,
- design-document pages, and
- defects found via work product re-

Table 1. Defect density inferences.

Defect Density Observation	Inferences
Lower than expected	Size estimate is high (good). Inspection defect detection is low (bad). Work product quality is high (good). Insufficient level of detail in work product (bad).
Higher than expected	Size estimate is low (bad). Work product quality is poor (bad). Inspection defect detection is high (good). Too much detail in work product (good or bad).

view, inspection, or use in subsequent development stages.

Interpreting effort variance. When effort expenditures are below plan, the project will typically be behind schedule because the work simply isn't getting done. An alternative explanation might be that the design has been completed, but without the detail level necessary to progress to the next development phase. This merely sets the stage for disaster later.

We use inspection defect data from design inspection to guard against such damaging situations. If the density falls below a lower limit of 0.1 to 0.2 defects per page versus an expected 0.5 to 1.0 defects per page, the possibility increases that the document is incomplete. When defect detection rates are below 0.5 defects per page, the preparation and inspection rates are examined to verify that sufficient time was spent in document inspection. We also calculate the inspection defect density using the number of major defects and the estimated KLOC for the project. If the defect density is lower than expected, either the KLOC estimate is high or the detail level in the work product is insufficient (see Table 1).

When trying to determine which of the eight possible outcomes reflect the project status, project managers must draw on their experience and their team and product knowledge. I believe the project manager's ability to evaluate the team's inspection effectiveness will be better than the team's ability to estimate the code size. In particular, a 2-to-1 increase in detection effectiveness is far less likely than a 2-to-1 error in size estimating.

When effort expenditures are above the plan and work product deliverables

are on or behind schedule, the size estimate was clearly lower than it should have been. This also implies later stages will require more effort than was planned.

In both cases, we found that the process instrumentation provided by inspections was very useful in validating successful design completion. The familiar "90 percent done" statements have disappeared. Inspections are a visible, measurable gate that must be passed.

Project tracking and analysis. Inspection defect data adds several dimensions to the project manager's ability to evaluate project progress. Glass[4] and Graham[5] claim that defects will always be a part of the initial development effort. (Glass says design defects are the result of the cognitive/creative design process, and Graham says errors are "inevitable, not sinful, and unintentional.") Humphrey presents data indicating that injection rates of 100 to 200 defects per KLOC of delivered code are not unusual.[6] Although we have seen a 7-to-1 difference in defect injection rates between projects, the variance is much less for similar projects.

For the same team doing similar work, the defect injection rate is nearly the same. The project analyzed in Figure 5 involved a second-generation product developed by many of the people who worked on the first-generation product. At the end of the low-level design phase, Steve Magee, the project manager, noticed a significant difference in the estimated and actual defect-depletion counts for low-level design defects. The estimate was derived from the earlier project, which featured many similar characteristics. There was a significant increase in the actual defect data. We

Measure	Value	Inference
Effort	Above plan	Project is larger than planned, if not ahead of schedule; or project is more complex than planned, if on schedule.
	Below plan	Project is smaller than estimated, if on schedule; or project is behind schedule; or design detail is insufficient, if on or ahead of schedule.
Defects Detected	Above plan	Size of project is larger than planned; or quality is suspect; or inspection detection effectiveness is better than expected.
	Below plan	Inspections are not working as well as expected; or design lacks sufficient content; or size of project is smaller than planned; or quality is better than expected.
Size	Above plan	Marketing changes or project complexity are growing — more resource or time will be needed to complete later stages.
	Below plan	Project is smaller than estimated; or something has been forgotten.

The percentage of design defects detected in code inspection on the first project was higher than we thought.

We were also concerned by the number of defects, which exceeded the total we had estimated even after accounting for the earlier detection. It seemed more likely that the size estimate was low rather than that there was a significant increase in defect detection effectiveness. In fact, the size estimate was about 50 percent low at the beginning of low-level design. The project manager adjusted his size estimates and consequently was better able to predict unit test defects when code inspections were in progress, and time for both unit and integration test.

Using defect data helped the project manager determine that design defects were being discovered earlier and project size was larger than expected. Hence, more coding effort and unit and integration test time would be needed.

Figure 7 shows the actual data as this project entered system test. Comparing the data in Figures 5 and 7 indicates a shift in defect detection to earlier stages in the development cycle; hence, the project team is working more effectively.

also had some numbers from the first project that suggested inspection effectiveness (defects found by inspection divided by the total number of defects in the work product) was in the 75 percent range for this team.

Again, we were able to use our inspection data to infer several theories that explained the differences. The defect shift from code to low-level design could be attributed to finding defects in the low-level design inspections on the second project, rather than during code inspections in the first project. A closer look at the first project defect descriptions from code inspections revealed that a third of the defects were missing functionality that could be traced to the low-level design, even though many defects had been incorrectly tagged as coding errors. Reevaluating the detailed defect descriptions brought out an important fact:

Defect data can be used as a key element to improve project planning. Once a size estimate is available, historical data can be used to estimate the number of defects expected in a project, the development phase where defects will be found, and the cost to remove the defects.

Once the defect-depletion curve for the project is developed, variances from the predictions provide indicators that project managers can examine for potential trouble spots. Table 2 summarizes these measures, their value (above or below plan), and the possible troubles indicated. These measures and those listed in Table 1 answer many of the questions in the design box in Figure 3.

One difficulty project managers must overcome is the unwillingness of the development staff to provide defect data. Grady[7] mentions the concept of public versus private data, particularly regarding inspection-data usage. Unless the project team is comfortable with making this data available to the project manager, it is difficult to gather and analyze the data in time for effective use.

I believe that continuing education on the pervasiveness of defects, and recog-

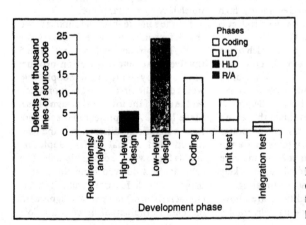

Figure 7. Actual defect density data for the project depicted in Figure 5.

nition that defects are a normal occurrence in software development, is a critical first step in using defect data more effectively to measure development progress and product quality. Only through collecting and using defect data can we better understand the nature and cause of defects and ultimately improve product quality. ∎

Acknowledgments

I thank John T. Harding and Ron Radice for their many hours of discussion on defect removal as a project management tool; Steve Magee, Fred Kuhlman, and Ann Holladay for their willingness to use the methods described in this article on their projects; Jean-Yves LeGoic for his excellent critique; Barbara Ahlstrand, Robin Fulford, and George Mann for inspecting the manuscript; and the anonymous referees for their helpful recommendations.

References

1. E. Weller, "Lessons from Three Years of Inspection Data," *IEEE Software*, Vol. 10, No. 5, Sept. 1993, pp. 38-45.

2. W. Humphrey, *Managing the Software Process*, 1990, Addison-Wesley, Reading, Mass., pp. 352-355.

3. B.W. Boehm, *Software Engineering Economics*, Prentice Hall, Englewood Cliffs, N.J., 1981.

4. R. Glass, "Persistent Software Errors: 10 Years Later," *Proc. First Int'l Software Test, Analysis, and Rev. Conf.*, Software Quality Engineering, Jacksonville, Fla., 1992.

5. D. Graham, "Test Is a Four Letter Word: The Psychology of Defects and Detection," *Proc. First Int'l Software Testing, Analysis, and Rev. Conf.*, 1992, Software Quality Engineering, Jacksonville, Fla.

6. W. Humphrey, "The Personal Software Process Paradigm," *Sixth Software Eng. Process Group Nat'l Meeting*, Software Eng. Inst., Carnegie Mellon Univ., Pittsburgh, 1994.

7. R. Grady, *Practical Software Metrics For Project Management and Process Improvement*, Prentice Hall, Englewood Cliffs, N.J., 1992, pp. 104-107.

Using Metrics in Management Decision Making

George Stark and Robert C. Durst, Mitre Corporation
C.W. Vowell, NASA Johnson Space Center

The metrics effort within NASA's Mission Operations Directorate has helped managers and engineers make decisions about project readiness by removing the inherent optimism of "engineering judgment."

O ver the years, NASA spacecraft and ground systems have become increasingly dependent on software to meet mission objectives. Figure 1 shows the growth in software size for several representative systems over time. The on-board software of unmanned spacecraft has grown from around 500 source lines of code (LOC) in Mariner 9 to an estimated 35,000 LOC for the Cassini spacecraft scheduled for launch in 1997. Software supporting on-board manned systems has grown from 16,500 LOC for the Apollo Saturn V to more than 500,000 LOC for the shuttle, and 900,000 LOC is projected for the space station data-management system. The ground systems used to train the astronauts and to monitor and control the spacecraft contain an average of more than one million LOC. Software supporting the mission control center has quadrupled in size over the last 10 years to more than 3 million executable LOC. For each of these systems, the amount of software has become the dominant factor contributing to increased system complexity. To better understand and manage any risks that might result from this increase in complexity, the Mission Operations Directorate (MOD) initiated a software metrics program in May of 1990.

The key requirement behind the development and implementation of the metrics initiative was to monitor a project's progress unobtrusively. To meet this requirement, the following four environmental criteria were established as essential to the definition of the metrics set. First, the metrics had to be relevant to the MOD development and maintenance environment. That is, they had to be relevant to large, real-time systems that involve multiple organizations and that are coded in multiple languages. Second, collection and analysis of the metrics had to be cost-effective. Third, multiple metrics were required during each reporting period to cross check the indications from any single metric and to provide a complete picture of project status. Fourth, the metrics needed to have a strong basis in industry or government practice for establishing "rule-of-thumb" thresholds for use by project managers.

Reprinted from *Computer*, Vol. 27, No. 9, Sept. 1994, pp. 42–48.

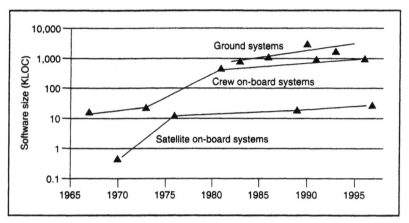

Figure 1. Software size for NASA projects has grown over time.

After defining the environmental criteria, we engaged in a three-step process to implement the software metrics initiative: definition, documentation, and education. For the definition step, we applied Basili's goal/question/metric paradigm[1] and the four environmental criteria to define metrics for software development and maintenance. The Basili technique involves establishing one or more organizational goals, posing questions that address the organization's progress toward meeting those goals, and defining measurements that can be collected to answer the questions. For example, we defined an organizational goal to minimize the effort and schedule used during software maintenance. We posed two questions to address this goal: Where are the resources going? How maintain-able is the system?

To answer these questions and still meet the four environmental criteria, we identified the following metrics: software staffing, service request (SR) scheduling, Ada instantiations, and fault type distribution. The software staffing and SR scheduling metrics provide insight into the total resources being applied to the project, while the Ada instantiations and fault type distribution metrics provide insight into the nature of the maintenance workload. (Ada instantiations provide insight into whether generics require repair or merely adaptation, and fault type distribution indicates what types of bugs are being identified and corrected.) To answer the maintainability question, we selected computer resource utilization, software size, fault density, software volatility, and design complexity. Working definitions of these and other metrics are included in the sidebar.

To document the metrics, we developed handbooks containing precise definitions and implementation details for project managers and engineers[2,3] and pulled together a set of stand-alone tools to aid in metrics analysis. Data was collected for six projects over two years to

---

Mission Operations Directorate software metrics descriptions

Ada instantiations — The size and number of generic subprograms developed and the number of times they are used within a project.

Break/fix ratio — Number of DRs resulting from a discrepancy report (DR) fix or a service request (SR) change divided by the total number of closed DRs + SRs over the same time period.

Computer resource utilization (CRU) — The percentage of CPU, memory, network, and disk utilization.

Design complexity — The number of modules with a complexity greater than an established threshold.

Development progress — The number of modules successfully completed from subsystem functional design through unit test.

Discrepancy report (DR) or **service request (SR) open duration** — The time lag from problem report or service request initiation to closure. A discrepancy report is a change made to software to correct a defect. A service request is a change made to software to add or enhance a capability.

DR/SR closure — Actual DR or SR receipts and closures by (sub)system by month.

Fault density — The open and total defect density (DRs normalized by software size) over time.

Fault type distribution — Percentage of defects closed with a software fix by type of fault (for example, logic, error handling, standards, interface).

Maintenance staff utilization — Engineering months per SR and per DR written by (sub)system.

Requirements stability — The trend of the total number of requirements to be implemented for the project over time.

Software reliability — The probability that the software "works" for a specified time under specified conditions.

Software size — The number of lines of code in the system that must be tested and maintained.

Software staffing — The number of software engineering and first-line management personnel directly involved with the software.

Software volatility — Percentage of modules changed per release.

SR scheduling — The length of time it takes to close an SR that requires a software change and the amount of engineering effort spent on SR closures.

Test case completion — The percentage of test cases successfully completed.

Test focus — The percentage of problem reports closed with a software fix.

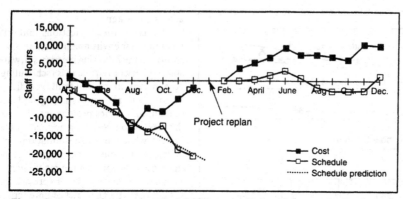

Figure 2. An earned-value chart for a MOD project helped keep cost and schedule on track.

test the process and to provide material for subsequent training. Finally, an education program was developed to ensure a common understanding of the metrics and their application. All MOD development and contractor personnel are trained using data from previous projects.

The following sections describe four specific decisions that were made using metrics data collected on MOD projects. We also provide a description of the metric toolkit and present some of our observations regarding metric data analysis and its real-world use.

Deciding to replan a project

The problem: How can I tell if my project is on schedule and within budget? MOD uses *earned value* to help answer this question. Earned value is a technique that combines the development progress metric, the staffing metric, and the expected cost of the project. A number of clearly identifiable development progress milestones are established, and a percentage of the cost and the expected number of staff-hours per calendar time to complete the task is allocated to each milestone. (Cost is tracked by staff-hours to protect contractor rate confidentiality.) The staff-hours value is "credited" only when the milestone is 100 percent complete. The total earned value equals the new milestones completed plus the prior completed milestones. Each month the earned value is reviewed. When enough data points are available, a linear extrapolation of the project schedule and cost is calculated. Management then

takes corrective action if there is a definite negative trend to the data.

Figure 2 shows an example earned-value graph by month for a project. This project began in April without earned-value measurement. Its scheduled completion date was October of the following year. In August, the project was baselined with earned value. The project was 13,200 hours behind schedule and 11,000 hours over budget (negative numbers indicate over budget or behind schedule). Because this was the first earned-value project in MOD, a decision to rebaseline was not made immediately. Instead, we gathered further metrics data and conducted supporting interviews with the project team.

By December, it was clear that action was required: The project was 20,000 hours behind schedule and over budget by almost 1,000 hours. (A reallocation of staffing resources in August accounted for the progress toward meeting budget, but the schedule continued to slip.) The dashed line in Figure 2 is a forecast based on the equation $y = mx + b$, where y is the hours earned and x is the month (that is, April = 1, May = 2, . . . , December = 9). The values for the slope (m) and the intercept (b) were calculated to be $m = -2,197$ and $b = 40$. Note that the slope is in units of staff-hours per month. Thus, assuming that there are 2,000 staff-hours in a staff-year, this slope indicates that the project schedule is slipping at a rate of more than one staff-year each month.

A review of the two most problematic subsystems showed some "requirements creep" and some staffing problems. The managers decided to review the requirements and replan the project. The review

and replan took one month; no original requirements were scrubbed. The new plan mitigated the requirements creep by incorporating the use of common software and commercial products available on the newly procured target platform. The new plan moved a small number of staff from maintenance to development and extended the original delivery date by two months. In October of the second year, a minor correction was made to the plan. As shown in the graph, this new plan delivered the system with the required functionality under budget (by 9,827 hours) and on schedule (1,500 hours ahead). Metrics collection made the problems visible, and the subsequent analysis drove these corrective decisions. A rough estimate of the cost avoidance from these decisions is calculated as (predicted schedule slip – actual schedule slip) × staff (or 9 months – 2 months) × 110 staff = 770 staff months.

Deciding to maintain or redesign software

The problem: How hard will it be for another organization to maintain this software? One approach to this question is to find relationships between the measurable characteristics of programs and the difficulty of maintenance tasks. Researchers have developed measures of software complexity that can be used to understand the structure of a software module. More than 100 complexity measurements have been proposed in the literature, but McCabe's cyclomatic complexity metric[4] is studied and used most often. McCabe defines the complexity of a program on the basis of its structure, using the number and arrangement of decision statements within the code. McCabe complexity is calculated as the number of decisions in the code plus one. Myers extended the metric to include predicates (for example, AND and OR) and decision-making statements in the calculation.[5] Because predicates do indeed create additional independent paths through a module, this metric is more comprehensive than its forerunner and is used within MOD.

Some researchers have expressed doubts about the validity of complexity measurement. These doubts have revolved around predictive models using the metrics and around the experimental designs used in some validation studies. Some practitioners, however, have found complexity measurement useful in planning for and assessing software development risks, in allocating resources during testing, and in managing maintenance efforts. Complexity measurement is implementable as part of a project's coding standard, since inexpensive tools are available to compute the values and report exceptions to the standard. The Software Engineering Laboratory at NASA's Goddard Space Flight Center has successfully used complexity measurement on a number of projects. The Safety Reliability and Quality Assurance organization at Johnson Space Center (JSC) has also applied the concepts successfully.

Within MOD, 16 systems currently in maintenance were analyzed. Seven of these systems were coded in C, four in Ada, and five in Fortran. For a given system, each software procedure was analyzed, and a cumulative distribution function was generated. There were typically several hundred to several thousand procedures in a system. Figure 3 shows the cumulative distribution functions of the extended McCabe complexity measure for 16 systems. (Note that the figure is a logarithmic scale on the x-axis.)

The figure indicates that 50 percent of system A functions had a complexity of less than or equal to 10, and 90 percent were less than or equal to 80. Based on published rules of thumb (for example, procedures should have McCabe complexity of less than 10) and the noticeable gap between the A and B systems and the other 14 systems, managers at JSC considered these two systems risk areas. They conducted a further investigation of these systems to determine the number of problem reports written since release, the number of users, and maintenance staff size. Management decided to retire system A and to find another approach to implement its function. An evaluation of commercial off-the-shelf products turned up a candidate that met more than 80 percent of system A functionality. This product has since been implemented and is now used by a majority of the users. Management decided to accept the risk on system B, since it was relatively error free and was developed, maintained, and used by a single organization. This result has allowed management to reallocate system A maintenance staff and thus concentrate additional effort in other areas.

For the systems in Figure 3, there was no statistical difference between lan-

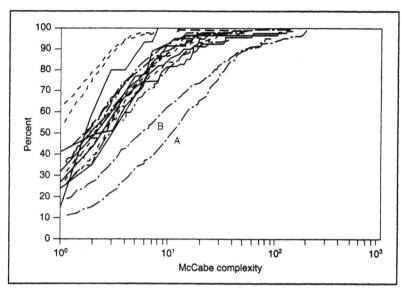

Figure 3. Cumulative distributions of the McCabe complexity measure revealed systems A and B as risk areas.

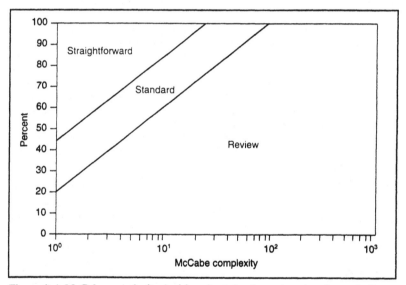

Figure 4. A McCabe complexity decision chart showing categories of complexity.

guages in terms of complexity. That is, the C systems studied were no more complex than the Ada or the Fortran systems. Thus, management used this graph to define categories of complexity. Figure 4 is a decision chart for use on new projects. Systems with distributions in the upper left-hand section of the chart are considered to have straightforward logic, systems that fall in the middle area are considered "standard complexity," and systems that fall to the right side of the chart are considered to be too logically

complex. When systems cross the boundary from standard to logically complex, the programming team is encouraged to review those modules. The logically complex systems are candidates for further review and possible reengineering. We are currently evaluating other techniques of complexity measurement (for example, Munson's relative complexity measure), but at this stage of the metrics program the extended McCabe metric is helping MOD managers make more informed decisions.

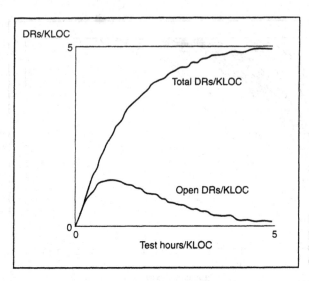

Figure 5. An ideal profile from subsystem defect-density testing.

Deciding when to integrate subsystems

The problem: How can I tell when my subsystems are ready to be integrated? We use the defect density metric to quantify the relative stability of a software subsystem and to identify any testing bottlenecks or possible overtesting by examining the fault density of the subsystem over time. There are three components to this metric: Total Density (T), Open Density (O), and Test Hours (H). The term *density* implies normalization by LOC. In practice,

T = Total number of software defects charged to a subsystem/KLOC,

O = Number of currently open subsystem software defects/KLOC, and

H = Active test hours per subsystem/KLOC.

The metric is then tracked as a plot of T and O versus H. A graph of T versus H indicates testing adequacy and code quality. Many problems are discovered early in the subsystem's testing phase, with increasingly fewer problems found as testing proceeds. Thus, the ideal graph begins with a near infinite slope and, as testing and debugging continues, approaches a zero slope. If the slope doesn't begin to approach zero, a low-quality subsystem or inefficient testing is indicated and should be investigated. The plot of O versus H indicates the problem-report closure rate. Again, more problems should be backlogged at the begin-

ning of test; then, as debuggers begin to correct the problems, the slope should become negative, indicating that the debuggers are working off their backlog. If the slope of the O-versus-H curve remains positive, it means the testers are finding faults faster than the debuggers can resolve them; the remedy is to halt testing until a new release can be delivered and the backlog of faults is reduced. An ideal defect density plot is shown in Figure 5.

Rules of thumb for this metric depend on the development environment and the organizational processes. The MOD rule of thumb is that total discrepancy reports (DRs) should be in the 5-per-KLOC range, with values between 3 and 10 considered normal. The test hours should be in the 2-per-KLOC range, with values between 1 and 10 considered normal. In general, the shape of the curves indicates the relative subsystem stability within a project. That is, by comparing the curves, one can determine if the subsystems are ready for integration. Total defects per KLOC should flatten out over time, and open defects per KLOC should decrease and approach zero. Too few defects or too few test hours may indicate poor test coverage or unusually high code quality, while too many of either may indicate poor code quality.

Data for the defect density metric is plotted as both total defects and open defects per KLOC versus test hours per KLOC by subsystem. On this project, we reviewed subsystems with increasing numbers of open defects, low test hours per KLOC, or no flattening of total de-

fects, because any of these conditions indicate a risk to successful deployment of the system.

Figures 6 and 7 plot defect density for two contrasting subsystems. Figure 6 matches the expected curves of Figure 5, indicating that subsystem E is mature and ready for integration. Comparison of subsystem H in Figure 7 with the expected profile shows differences that can be interpreted as risk signals indicating that the developers are having difficulty — that is, the total defect density is increasing, the open density is not decreasing, and very few test hours per KLOC have been expended. (The straight drop in defects/KLOC occurred when more code was added to the subsystem during test, as indicated by the software size metric.) Further, comparison with the other subsystems (for example, subsystem E from Figure 6) shows unequal testing and debugging of this subsystem. It is not ready for integration.

Based on this curve, MOD managers decided to allocate an additional 10 days of stand-alone testing for subsystem H. This decision lengthened the overall delivery schedule by three days, but without this additional testing, the integration process and the system-level testing would likely have been more difficult and time consuming. Note that analysis of this kind is not objective, nor is it completely quantitative. No universal thresholds or algorithms for subsystem acceptance are defined. However, we believe that the quantitative data provides support for higher quality subjective decision making.

Deciding whether a test schedule is reasonable

The problem: How can I tell if a test schedule makes sense? One way is to use historical data from previous projects as a reference. One can even account for "lessons learned" from previous projects in the analysis. The following example is from a project that immediately followed one that experienced significant code growth. In planning the follow-on project, the developers recalled that they had underestimated code size and therefore underestimated their test time requirements. The contractor responded by assuming similar code growth as before and increasing the planned number of test hours/KLOC. Unfortunately, this

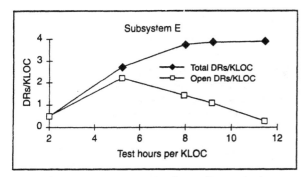

Figure 6. A subsystem defect-density profile that indicates there are no problems.

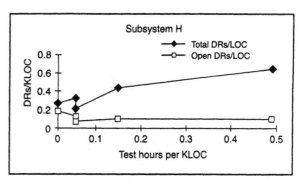

Figure 7. A subsystem defect-density profile indicating that corrective action is required.

was a major expense item and affected the product availability date. MOD wanted to take a different approach: control code growth and determine the test schedule.

The initial contractor schedules were available approximately one year before the start of testing. We performed a "sanity check" on the schedule and estimated a lower bound for the test schedule by factoring out the assumed code growth. (We divided the number of test hours requested by the code growth factor experienced on the previous project — LOC delivered/LOC planned.) We then estimated the months in test using the previous project's test-hour delivery rate (that is, test hours/calendar months). This yielded an estimate of 2.4 calendar months rather than the initial request of 6 months. Next, we estimated an upper bound for the test schedule by estimating the time required to deliver the full number of test hours based on the previous project's delivery rate. This resulted in an estimate of 7 months.

Management believed they could control requirements growth and other factors contributing to code growth so that the system would not experience the same growth as the previous delivery. To be conservative, they allowed for a growth factor of two, resulting in a 5-month test schedule. This reduced the contractor's schedule by one month, for an estimated savings of $200,000. Management reinforced the use of metrics by using metrics to closely monitor actuals versus plans on a monthly basis. By using the metrics as early indicators of changes in the project's status, management was able to hold code growth to a factor of 1.67. As a result, the project completed testing in slightly over 4 months, saving an estimated $300,000.

Metrics toolkit

Two characteristics that facilitated making the decisions described in the previous section were the ease of analysis and the consistency in the data collection. To ensure that these characteristics were present in the metrics program, we defined a standard suite of tools for use by analysts and project personnel. The toolkit supports analysis of the metrics to answer the questions and meet the goals that originally generated the metric set. Recall that answering a single question can require analysis of many metrics. Thus, it is important for the toolkit to collect and integrate data from multiple metrics. In our environment, the toolkit required a data repository element (for example, a database or spreadsheet), a cost/resource estimation tool, a size/complexity collection tool, and a reliability estimation tool.

The data repository element is based on a spreadsheet running on a desktop computer. The spreadsheet lets managers track planned and actual measurements. It also performs simple linear regression on individual metrics and provides graphical displays of the metrics data.

Additional cost and schedule information is provided by JSC's CostModeler[6] (an upgrade of JSC's CostModl). This tool helps a manager estimate the effort, cost, and schedule required to develop and maintain computer systems. CostModeler does not directly implement any specific cost estimation algorithm but instead lets users tailor appropriate models for their needs. It includes implementations of the JSC KISS (Keep it simple, stupid) model and four variations of Boehm's Cocomo (constructive cost model).

Another tool in the kit is Set Laboratories' UX-Metric, a commercial off-the-shelf code analysis tool that helps engi-

neers evaluate software complexity.[7] The tool supports several measures of complexity, including extended cyclomatic complexity, lines of code, span of variable reference, depth of nesting, number of interfaces, and Halstead software science measures.

Finally, we use the Statistical Modeling and Estimation of Reliability Functions for Software (SMERFS) tool for software reliability assessments. This tool is a public domain program available from the Naval Surface Warfare Center in Dahlgren, Virginia.[8] It implements 10 time-domain software reliability models, including those recommended by the American Institute of Aeronautics and Astronautics.[9] This tool allows analysts to forecast test durations, predict field failure rates based on test data, and track operational failure rates.

Although this toolkit is neither completely automated nor integrated in the sense that a user has a single entry point, all the components can share data. MOD project managers have found it useful for the metrics collection and analysis described above. The toolkit costs less than $1,000 and took less than a month to integrate and begin using.

Metrics, models, and decision making

Occasionally, we need to be reminded of the real meaning and use of metrics in our environment. The goal is to create a dialogue between managers and developers or between customers and suppliers. In general, the predictions made from the data have no element of statistical confidence. They are first and foremost design tools used to compare plans to actual results, to identify overly complicated parts, and to serve as input to the system's risk management.

The metrics and the models that use them need not be exact to be useful. Exact models are often so cumbersome and intractable that they are worthless to managers making decisions. Excellent and useful results are regularly obtained from simple models like those described above. Sometimes, however, such models give results that don't make sense in the environment. For example, in our original software reliability estimates we used a model that assumed that the number of lines of code in test was stable. The predictions from this model were not matching the observed failure rates in the project. Upon investigation we found that the size of the system under test was increasing incrementally. We changed to a model that accommodated software growth during test. The new model more closely matched the observed data, and the predictions from the model were useful for management decision making.

The point is that when the results from a model are not reasonable, these results are telling us something and need to be carefully examined: Either we've made a mistake in the mathematics, or the assumptions that define the model are bad. Sometimes an incorrect assumption is hard to notice. The model must be worked backward, manipulating the assumptions to give the best results, or a new approach must be taken.

Thus, metrics analysis begins with insight into the workings of the software development or maintenance processes. It continues with calculations from the conceptual models that reflect that insight. It results in answers to the original questions — answers that may affect decisions and change processes. Those portions of the metrics task that are computationally intensive, such as model execution, are best left to support tools such as those described in the toolkit. Some portions of the metrics task are best done by people. These are the portions that involve insight into the internal workings of the organization's processes. The insights gained by performing a Pareto analysis or debugging a model can result in improvements to the subject process as well as the model of that process. Thus, there is value to the organization in performing some of the metrics task "by hand." Remember, system integrity cannot be achieved without sound engineering applied to established software development and maintenance tasks.

The amount of code in NASA systems has continued to grow over the past 30 years. This growth brings with it the increased risk of system failure caused by software. Thus, managing the risks inherent in software development and maintenance is becoming a highly visible and important field. The metrics effort within MOD has helped the managers and engineers better understand their processes and products. The toolkit helps ensure consistent data collection across projects and increases the number and types of analysis options available to project personnel. The decisions made on the basis of metrics analysis have helped project engineers make decisions about project and mission readiness by removing the inherent optimism of "engineering judgment." ∎

References

1. V. Basili and H.D. Rombach, "Tailoring the Software Process to Project Goals and Environments," *Proc. Ninth Int'l Conf. Software Eng.*, IEEE CS Press, Los Alamitos, Calif., Order No. 767 (microfiche only), 1987, pp. 345-357.

2. NASA Johnson Space Center, *DA3 Software Development Metrics Handbook*, Version 2.1, JSC-25519, Houston, Texas, 1992.

3. NASA Johnson Space Center, *DA3 Software Sustaining Engineering Metrics Handbook*, Version 1.0, JSC-26010, Houston, Texas, 1992.

4. T.J. McCabe, "A Complexity Measure," *Trans. on Software Eng.*, Vol. SE-2, No. 4, 1976, pp. 308-320.

5. G. J. Myers, "An Extension to the Cyclomatic Measure of Program Complexity," *SIG-Plan Notices*, Vol. 12, No. 10, 1977, pp. 61-64.

6. B. Roush and R. Phillips, *CostModeler Version 1.0 User's Guide*, Software Development Branch, NASA Johnson Space Center, Houston, Texas, 1993.

7. SET Laboratories Inc., *UX-Metric*, Mulino, Ore., 1990.

8. W.H. Farr and O.D. Smith, "Statistical Modeling and Estimation of Reliability Functions for Software (SMERFS) User's Guide," NSWC TR 84-373 Rev 1, Naval Surface Warfare Center, Silver Spring, Md., 1988.

9. American Institute of Aeronautics and Astronautics, *Recommended Practice for Software Reliability*, ANSI/AIAA R-013-1992, Washington, D.C., 1993.

Chapter 2

What to Measure?

The papers

Using products to suggest measurement goals

William Hetzel, "The Measurement Process," in *Making Software Measurement Work: Building an Effective Software Measurement Program*, QED Publishing, Boston, Mass., 1993, pp. 25–56. Beginning from bottom-level detail, measuring work products can stimulate questions that help to set goals and change the development process.

Using project goals to suggest measures

Victor R. Basili and H. Dieter Rombach, "The TAME Project: Towards Improvement-Oriented Software Environments," *IEEE Trans. Software Eng.*, Vol. 14, No. 6, June 1988, pp. 758–773. The goal-question-metric paradigm offers a structure for using project goals and perspectives to suggest questions to be answered and characteristics to be measured.

Using process visibility to suggest measures

Shari Lawrence Pfleeger and Clement McGowan, "Software Metrics in the Process Maturity Framework," *J. Systems and Software*, Vol. 12, No. 3, July 1990, pp. 255–261. Process visibility is used to suggest what can or should be measured as part of a broader process improvement effort.

Measuring products

Edward N. Adams, "Optimizing Preventive Service of Software Products," *IBM J. Research and Development*, Vol. 28, No. 1, Jan. 1984, pp. 2–14. Analyzes a number of large software systems, showing that many software faults rarely lead to failures, while a small proportion of faults cause the most frequent failures.

Case study

Victor Basili and Scott Green, "Software Process Evolution at the SEL," *IEEE Software*, Vol. 11, No. 4, July 1994, pp. 58–66. The quality improvement paradigm is used to evaluate process effects on both products and people.

Editors' introduction

Once we understand why we need to measure, the next step is choosing the metrics themselves. This choice is neither obvious nor easy, as measurement can involve time and resources not always readily available. Although it is sometimes tempting to measure everything, in fact it is unrealistic and usually infeasible to do so. As we shall see later in Chapter 5, successful measurement programs usually begin with a small set of measures, and then expand as needs and goals change. Thus, it is important to have a rationale for choosing the metrics, not only to minimize resources but also to help us understand how the metrics information will be used. The papers in this chapter describe several techniques for determining which metrics are best for a given project.

A software project can be viewed from at least two perspectives: bottom-up and top-down. The bottom-up view begins with the products and tasks of software development, looking upwards at how each is related to the others and to the overall goals of the project. The top-down view starts instead with project goals, looking down at how each goal spawns a chain of activities and products that address it. Each perspective can be used as a framework for selecting appropriate metrics.

Bill Hetzel advocates the bottom-up approach in "The Measurement Process." He proposes that software development organizations begin the development process by collecting raw data on every work product developed and used. These data include feasibility studies, requirements documents, and design specifications, as well as more traditional code products. Then, the data are used to stimulate questions that help set goals and targets. Hetzel also introduces the basic steps involved in any software measurement effort.

By contrast, Victor Basili and Dieter Rombach propose a top-down approach in "The TAME Project: Towards Improvement-Oriented Software Environments." Their framework, known as the Goal-Question-Metric (GQM) paradigm, instructs organizations to phrase project goals as a set of questions; then, each question is analyzed to determine which measurements are needed to provide the answers. For example, to measure the effectiveness of a coding standard, we may have several questions to answer, addressing issues about who is using the standard and what we mean by productivity and quality. Each question suggests certain metrics, the values of which will help us to answer the questions and thus determine whether our goal is met. Figure 4 illustrates the type of tree that can be generated from a GQM analysis.

Table 2 shows part of a GQM analysis performed by Barnard and Price at AT&T to help them determine the effect of inspections. Notice that a single metric can refer to more than one question. For example, "average inspection rate" addresses both the quality of the inspected software and the effectiveness of the inspection process.

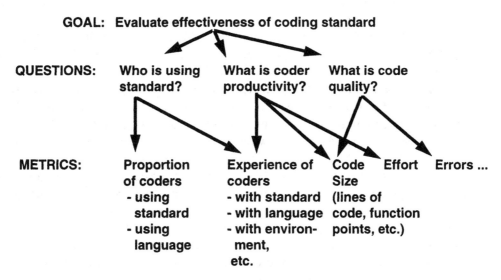

GOAL: Evaluate effectiveness of coding standard

QUESTIONS: Who is using standard?   What is coder productivity?   What is code quality?

METRICS: Proportion of coders
- using standard
- using language

Experience of coders
- with standard
- with language
- with environment, etc.

Code Size (lines of code, function points, etc.)

Effort

Errors ...

Figure 4. GQM tree (from Fenton and Pfleeger 1996).

Table 2. GQM analysis for effect of inspections (from Barnard and Price, *IEEE Software*, Mar. 1994).

Goal: PLAN
Question: How much does the inspection process cost?
Metric: Average effort per KLOC
Metric: Percentage of reinspections
Goal: MONITOR AND CONTROL
Question: What is the quality of the inspected software?
Metric: Average faults detected per KLOC
Metric: Average inspection rate
Metric: Average preparation rate
Goal: IMPROVE
Question: How effective is the inspection process?
Metric: Average effort per fault detected
Metric: Average inspection rate
Metric: Average preparation rate
Metric: Average lines of code inspected

Although opposite to one another, both the bottom-up and the top-down approach share several characteristics: For example, each is iterative and each allows feedback for continuous improvement.

Our third article in this chapter addresses the connection between process and measurement. The Software Engineering Institute's Capability Maturity Model (CMM) has focused attention on how process activities affect the resulting software. Although the CMM is a framework for evaluating the maturity of an organization's development process, it can also provide a starting point for deciding which metrics to use within that process. In "Software Metrics in the Process Maturity Framework," Shari Lawrence Pfleeger and Clement McGowan explain that measurement is possible only when the item to be measured is visible in the process. By drawing pictures of the process at each level of maturity, they describe how the picture suggests appropriate metrics.

The software life cycle does not end after analysis, design, and coding; maintenance can account for most of a product's resource expenditure, and maintenance activities must be devoted to improving software quality. In "Optimizing Preventive Service of Software Products," Ed Adams reports on the results of analyzing faults found in an IBM operating system. He relates faults to the time it takes for a fault to cause a failure that the user will experience, and shows that many software faults rarely lead to failures. On the other hand, a small proportion of faults cause the most frequent failures. Thus, a careful analysis of fault- and failure-based measurement data can help maintainers to understand which parts of the system are likely to cause the most failures. Preventive maintenance can then be directed at improving reliability by preventing failures, not just by correcting faults.

The last paper in this chapter is a case study which illustrates, once again, that prevention is better than cure. Victor Basili and Scott Green report on their success using the Quality Improvement Paradigm (QIP) at the NASA Goddard Space Flight Center Software Engineering Laboratory. QIP incorporates GQM. In the case described here, QIP was applied on a project implementing the Cleanroom methodology, which attempts to prevent rather than fix defects.

To probe further

S.D. Conte, H.E. Dunsmore, and V.Y. Shen, *Software Engineering Metrics and Models*, Benjamin Cummings, Menlo Park, Calif., 1986. A good review of available metrics for assessment and prediction, and a good discussion of the need for process models to support measurement.

W.B. Florac, *Software Quality Measurement: A Framework for Counting Problems, Failures and Faults*, Software Engineering Institute Technical Report CMU/SEI-92-TR-22, Pittsburgh, 1992. Contains a checklist of items to consider when defining software quality.

W.B. Goethert, E.K. Bailey, and M.B. Busby, *Software Effort Measurement: A Framework for Counting Staff-Hours*, Software Engineering Institute Technical Report CMU/SEI-92-TR-21, Pittsburgh, 1992. Contains a checklist of items to consider when defining an effort count.

NASA Goddard Space Flight Center Software Engineering Laboratory, *Software Measurement Guidebook*, National Aeronautics and Space Administration, SEL-94-002, July 1994. Describes the highly successful measurement program at NASA's Goddard Space Flight Center.

R.E. Park, *Software Size Measurement: A Framework for Counting Source Statements*, Software Engineering Institute Technical Report CMU/SEI-92-TR-20, Pittsburgh, 1992. Contains a checklist of items to consider when defining a lines-of-code count.

The Measurement Process

"Each measurement must have a linkage to a need."
Howard Rubin

"Measurement must be focused, based upon goals and models."
Vic Basili

"If we had management that knew what the right goals and
questions to ask were, we wouldn't need better measurement
nearly as badly as we do!"
Bill Hetzel

MEASUREMENT PARADIGMS

We emphasized in Chapter 1 that the number of potential software measures is very
large and greater than any organization's resources to systematically collect, present,
and use effectively. That requires us to prioritize and identify a rather small subset
to work on at any one time.

Accepting this basic fact has been a hard pill to swallow in most organizations.
Management thinks it can launch a measurement effort, define everything they'll
ever want or need to collect, and then just go forward and implement! That is almost
as wishful as expecting your systems group to somehow develop and implement all
the software systems you'll ever want or need.

Since we can't do everything at once, we need some practical guides for prioritizing and selecting the measures we will provide. In general, we have two basic approaches: *top-down* and *bottom-up*. The top-down approach starts with high-level
goals and needs and derives the measures needed to support them. The bottom-up
approach starts with measurable engineering observations and reality points and
builds up to management objectives and goals.

THE TOP-DOWN PARADIGMS

Much has been published about systematic top-down approaches to defining a measurement program. Two of the most visible and active contributors to the field of software measurement, Vic Basili and Howard Rubin, are prominent proponents. Their basic idea is that the measurement program should be built top-down and focused around clearly defined goals. The best known top-down model is Basili's GQM approach. Figure 2.1 illustrates the basic steps involved.

GQM starts with an identified set of desires or needs. A set of measurements to be collected is derived top-down from these needs by first identifying or listing a set of questions that if answered would establish whether the goals had been met or not. Measurements are then selected to provide answers or insight about each question.

Software goals often start out with a set of "quality factors": reliability, usability, maintainability, and so on. These factors were initially identified by Barry Boehm and the Rome Air Development Center in the 1970s as "components" of quality. To quantify the fuzzy notion of software quality, they tried to break down quality into a series of factors and subfactors (called criteria) and then identify specific metrics for each. The aim was to end up with a metrics set that collectively served to "measure" overall quality. I call this top-down approach the ILITY paradigm from the fact that most of the quality factors end in "ility."

1. *Development of goals* (The goals may be at a corporate, divisional, or project level and usually will address both productivity and quality concerns.)

2. *Generation of questions that define the goals* (A list of questions that need answers in order to know whether the goals have been met.)

3. *Identification of metrics (measures) that answer the questions* (A list of measures to be collected or tracked to answer the generated questions.)

Figure 2.1. Goal, Question, Metric steps.

Many folks got involved with the ILITY effort, and a lot was published about it. At one point a major technical report from Rome was published that had broken down over a dozen quality factors, more than two dozen subfactors, and over 200 specific measures. It included tables and forms to measure the 200+ items and a scheme to roll up all the results into one quality score or "figure of merit." The full ILITY model proved rather unwieldy and impractical to apply in the real world, but it has influenced and impacted many organizations and made its way into the draft *IEEE Standard for a Software Quality Metrics Methodology (P1061)* as the recommended approach for defining a set of quality metrics.

Many adaptations of GQM and the ILITY model have been made, and sufficient experience has been gained to demonstrate that a systematic approach is far superior to no approach or the informal, ad hoc, shotgun approaches that many organizations have tried. However, there are also some fundamental flaws and problems that must be recognized. The basic problem with any top-down method (whether for measurement, system development, or anything else) is who gets to define the top. The experience in many companies (especially the bigger ones), is that no one knows (or they are unable to agree) what the *right* set of goals should be. Companies often desperately need good measurement in order to *set* their goals! The GQM approach fails to recognize this, and it may not collect the measures needed to reshape the organization's goals or raise new and interesting questions. If management always knew the right goals to set and questions to ask, better measurements would not be so critical.

Top-down methods have also suffered from a lack of support and enthusiasm from the practitioners who must implement them. Some goals and questions are fairly easy to set but extremely difficult to measure effectively. Practitioners quickly recognize that the measures only address a small part of the goal and worry that managers will not interpret the metric information properly.

Yet another problem I've personally experienced with GQM is the tendency to "manipulate" the measured data. With the goals determined, there is a strong pressure for measurements that indicate or "show" progress. This may lead to "managing the news" or "finagling" the results to make management a little happier (after all, no one likes to set a goal and then see no progress). One wag went so far as to tag the approach "GAF" or "*G*oal, *A*nswer, *F*inagle," suggesting that more than a few organizations have abused their measurement program in the mistaken "service" of their management masters! Such practices are diametrically opposed to the true purpose of any really effective measurement activity. As Sophocles has told us "None love the bearer of bad news", and Fred Brooks adds "No one enjoys bearing bad news either, so it gets softened without real intent to deceive."

THE BOTTOM-UP MEASUREMENT ENGINEERING PARADIGM

In early 1991 Bill Silver and I collaborated on the design and introduction of an industry seminar on software measurement. As a part of that effort we conceived a new model built on the premise that the right place to start defining the set of needed measurements is at the engineering level integral with the software engineering process itself.

The approach is bottom-up and methodology based. It focuses on the basic *objects* that make up the core of all software engineering work: *work products* and the *people* who produce and use them. As software is specified and developed or enhanced, the people doing the job produce a series of work products. (The work products include such familiar items as feasibility studies, requirements documents, design specifications, code modules and components, test plans, tests and test reports, and user documents.) These work products are used in turn (sometimes by the same people who created them and sometimes by others) to produce new and changed work products. Eventually the work product created is a complete system for use by end users and customers.

The bottom-up measurement engineering paradigm specifies a base set of measurements to be collected on every work product developed and used (see Figure 2.2).

We need measures about the *inputs* (the resources, activities, and other work products that have been expended or used in completing the work product); the *outputs* (measures that describe and quantify the work item or items produced, such as their size and complexity); and the *results* (measures that quantify the experience and satisfaction with the work product and how good it is in terms of satisfying the people using it).

The point to stress is that these fundamental measures are required to answer just about *any* interesting question and are quite independent of what any organization's particular management goals and questions might be. This is true even if we are very familiar with our goals and can count on them not changing for a few months (or years) while we got our measurement program in place. This is not to say that it isn't important to know what your top-down goals are or that knowledge of such goals won't influence your selection of measures. It will and it should, but most of what we can really measure effectively is determined at the bottom, and we will argue that is the place where you should start.

The underlying principle behind the bottom-up measurement engineering model is that measurement's primary role is to support the engineering activity. In contrast to the top-down GQM approach, one might describe the model as a "MQG spiral." The important point to stress is that *measurements come first, not last*. The purpose of measurement is to stimulate questions and help provide knowledge and insight about the engineering activity. From such knowledge comes the ability to set goals and targets and to improve or change the process. Such changes, along with the natural forces for change brought on by new technology and various external influences, stimulate the need for new or modified measures that in turn raise new questions and so on around the MQG spiral (see Figure 2.3).

---

1. ***Input Measures***
   Information about the resources (people, computers, tools, other work products, etc.) applied and the process steps or activities carried out.

2. ***Output Measures***
   Information about the deliverables and work products that are created.

3. ***Results Measures***
   Information about the usage and effectiveness (perceived and actual) of the deliverables and work products in fulfilling their requirements.

Figure 2.2.   Fundamental software work product measurements.

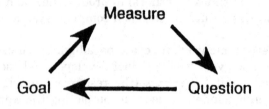

Figure 2.3. The MQG spiral.

Rather than start by asking managers what their goals are, we start by analyzing and modeling the software engineering activity to identify the fundamental measurements that all good projects should use. These measures are integrated into the engineering process and provided as a natural by-product of all software work.

When the bottom-up approach is used and measurements are defined (and engineered) as part of the engineering process, we obtain much more practitioner involvement and support. Practitioners correctly come to see the measurement effort as a basic part of all good technical work and are much less likely to fear and oppose it. We consider that strength a key element—thus the name "practitioner-based" measurement paradigm.

A key concept built into the paradigm from the start was to serve the practitioner first. Note the emphasis here on the word *service*. What the practitioner fears most (often with good reason) about measurement programs is the possibility that his or her performance will be displayed in a poor light or that management will somehow act inappropriately due to incomplete or misunderstood measures. To succeed, this fear of management control and misuse must be replaced with a recognition that the measurement activity is primarily aimed at serving the practitioner and that it is an activity that the practitioner controls and is responsible for—just as any other part of the software process!

Figure 2.4 displays the overall conceptual model. Software engineering is our discipline for the systematic production of a series of software-oriented work products. For each such work product we must define and provide measures that cover the three fundamental measurement needs: inputs (resources and activities that went into or will go into producing the work item), outputs (attributes that define and describe the work item, like its size and complexity), and results (measures that describe how the work item has been used and help assess its effectiveness and value).

Rather than asking management what they want or think they need, we engineer and instrument our processes to provide the basic data we know we can collect and use effectively, doing our best to prepare for the still unasked questions. The data is used by practitioners and first-line managers as meters and metrics to help make decisions nod avoid surprises. As it is gathered and analyzed it will trigger new questions and help to set new goals and objectives realistically. This in turn leads to changes in the process (new work products as well as new measures, meters, and metrics) and so on around our spiral.

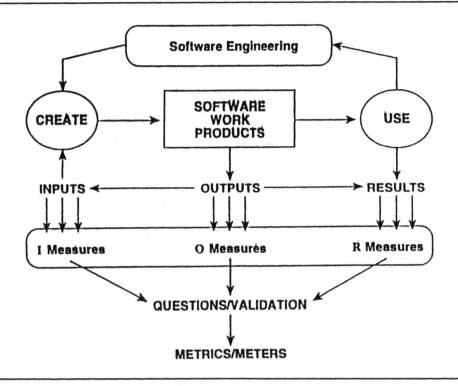

Figure 2.4. Measurement engineering bottom-up IOR model.

A basic goal is to stimulate new and interesting questions and to have the raw data at hand to answer most of the questions that do come up. We have discovered that most of management's needs can be satisfied easily if we've built in a strong, effective measurement program from the ground floor up. Conversely, trying to install measurements top-down does not work as well, especially when it loses or never even gains the strong support of the practitioners who have to implement it. (Of course we must always have the top-level commitment to make bottom-up, or for that matter any kind of measurement program work.)

We now realize that if we want well-run projects, if we want to avoid surprises and bad decisions with costly rework, if we want to learn from the past and engineer our software more and more effectively, then we really have no choice about providing the basic IOR measures. I should stress that such a bottom-up approach to measurement is not something the reader should view as new or surprising. Good measurement is a basic element of all good engineering. Software practices developed historically as an artistic craft (remember we started out *writing* programs) with little embedded measurement. As software grew in importance and consequence, management sought to impose measurement programs from the top to gain visibility and control. With the wisdom of hindsight we should now understand why this has not met with great success. If we really want to achieve an effective measurement program we must work from the bottom up and engineer measurement in every step of our emerging software engineering discipline.

- Focus on the software practitioner and the work products produced.
- Define and build in measures as part of the engineering activity bottom-up.
- Measure the inputs, outputs, and results (IOR) primitives for each work product.
- Use measures to create understanding, which drives questions and enables goal setting.
- Measure perceptions—what people who produce and use the work products think.
- Measure the use and results of the measurements.
- Understand that the measurement system will continuously evolve and change.
- Drive toward establishing validated process metrics and meters.
- Stimulate knowledge and prepare for the next question.
- Educate management to expect and require measurements as inputs to decisions and goal setting.

Some who have experimented with the measurement engineering approach have characterized it as Object-Oriented Measurement (OOM) to distinguish it from the Goal-Oriented Measurement implicit in the top-down approaches. The objects are the individual work products that analysts, developers, and maintainers produce. Each can be viewed as a self-contained item with its collection of input, outputs, and results measures that specify and describe it. People both create and use the objects, and their attributes and perceptions are a basic part of the input and results measurements.

Systematic measurement of each "object" allows for systematic measurement of the whole and turns out to be a most satisfactory philosophy and alternative for introducing and engineering an overall measurement effort. The paradigm provides the foundation philosophy behind this book. Subsequent chapters will flesh it out and illustrate it with various case studies and examples. Part II of the book takes each of the primary types of software work products (specifications, code, and test) and discusses appropriate bottom-up IOR measures in detail. Part III shows how the systematic collection of such measures can also serve the needs of managers (first line and executive) and customers for effective project, process, and product management.

THE BASIC MEASUREMENT PROCESS MODEL

Having introduced the bottom-up measurement engineering philosophy, let us now take a look at the basic process steps involved in any software measurement effort. For any set of measurements we might want to make, it is useful to identify four basic activities: *defining* what we want to measure, *collecting* the defined measures, *presenting* the collected information, and *using* the results to gain insight and take action.

Figure 2.5 displays these basic activities (define, collect, present, and use) as a simple process model that we will employ as a framework for systematic measurement engineering.

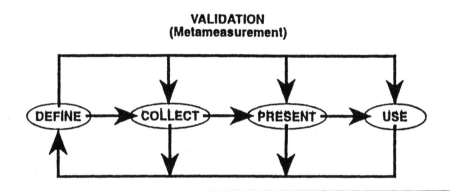

Figure 2.5.   A simplified process model.

It is of primary importance in all activities to ensure that we are accomplishing what we really wanted to. Is the definition precise? Are we collecting what was defined? Are we presenting it accurately? Is it having the effect we expected? This involves a fifth activity to measure the measurements and *validate* their effectiveness. As we will learn, it is surprisingly easy to collect, present, and even use incorrect measures. Validation is a key and never-ending activity that ensures our measured data is reasonable and our meters and metrics are appropriate.

Most readers will view the define, collect, present, and use activities as sequential steps (obviously we must define something before we collect it, and we have to collect and present it before we can use it). In reality each activity provides feedback and influences the other. For example, we'll often collect some information to observe trends before defining a new measure or discover that just presenting and using a measure for a while leads to new insights and questions that in turn brings about new or revised definitions. The model assumes such interactions are the norm with each of the activities overlapped and crossfeeding each other.

DEFINE

The logical first step in any systematic measurement process is one of *definition* or specification. Once we've identified a potential measure (whether top-down or bottom-up or some combination of both), we've got to define it carefully and make sure everyone understands just what is going to be collected and presented. Lack of careful specification is a common failing in many measurement programs. Most practitioners and managers new to measurement fail to realize how much information is really required to clearly define a new potential measure. Figure 2.6 lists some typical data elements that should be specified when a measurement is defined.

The specification should include a short description and a *handle* or shorthand name as well as details on how and when the measure is collected and its past and predicted values and value ranges. Additional information must be specified for any measure used or proposed as a candidate metric or meter. The existence of an organization metric or meter implies *use* within the organization for prediction, comparison, estimation, or control purposes. It is important that the usage relationship be fully specified and the validation information be available for anyone interested in using the metric or meter.

Handle:	A convenient shorthand name
Description:	Short description of what the measure is and the purpose for collecting
Observation:	How the measure is captured or collected
Frequency:	When the measure is collected
Scale:	Units of the measure
Range:	Minimum and maximum values observed or experienced
History:	What the measure has been like in the past
Expectation:	What the measure is expected to do in the future
Relationship:	How the measure is assumed to relate to the software process
Threshold:	Control or trigger values for metering action
Validation:	Backup data that validates the relationship strength and accuracy

Figure 2.6.   Elements of a measurement definition or specification.

Figure 2.7 provides an example of what a definition specification might look like for a lines of code measure in a hypothetical company. Such a definition does not have to be complete before collection (and in some cases even use) of the data can

Handle:	KLOC (Pronounced K—LOCK)
Description:	Thousands of lines of delivered new or modified code per project or system
Observation:	Measured by the automated tool KLOC-COUNTER whenever code is provided to integration test. See reference X for a more complete description of the tool.
Frequency:	Any time source code is modified or moved to the integration library
Scale:	Rounded to units of thousands of lines where a "line" is defined as a nonblank source code statement including comment lines, data definition lines, and any executable code.
Experience:	The measure has been used in pilot status for seven months. The range has run from a low of .8 (for a small enhancement project) to a high of 206 for the new billing system project.
Usage:	The measure is being used to support improved project estimation. Estimated KLOC is a required input to the project management estimation tool—ESTIMAN. Measuring actual KLOC delivered will help provide better estimates in the future.
Validation:	The project history database contains effort and KLOC data for a series of over 100 recent projects. A correlation study performed last year (See reference Y) showed a correlation of .82 between actual effort and measured KLOC. Only 12 percent of the projects varied by more than 20 percent over or under predicted effort. This means we should expect 9 out of 10 projects to be accurately estimated provided we can estimate or predict eventual KLOC delivered. It does not mean or imply that KLOC may be used to evaluate individual effort or productivity, only that total KLOC correlates reasonably well to total effort for a project.
Known Problems	Does not count or help estimate nondeliverable code like testware and drivers. Not supported with an automated tool on language A or platform B. Does not yet count deleted lines or changed lines on modifications.

Figure 2.7.   Sample definition for a Lines of Code measure.

start. Often it will be appropriate to collect loosely specified data on an informal or pilot basis. The data can then be studied and analyzed for patterns that enable us to define it more carefully or simplify the collection procedure. Quite often we will want to change the definition to meet pragmatic engineering constraints and allow for less costly and more automated collection.

We may also want to consider measures defined for short durations of time or to address very specific issues. Such impromptu measurements may be collected to help analyze or resolve particular questions. Once the issue has been satisfactorily answered, the measure can be set aside or put on the shelf until it is needed again.

COLLECT

The second major step in the systematic process is to *collect* measurement data. Implicit to the measurement engineering paradigm is the goal of seamlessly integrating the collection within or as a direct by-product of other, already existing software process steps. Our goal is to make collection as unobtrusive as possible; it must be efficient and perceived as *not* involving any extra or unnecessary steps.

Practitioners will quite properly resist collection activities that require significant manual effort or added steps. Automating the collection effort is often a critical success factor and should be done as a routine part of the development, testing, and maintenance activities. For example, many companies who measure lines of code call a line-counting tool whenever a module or component is checked in or turned over to integration for final testing and release. The source library and configuration management procedures invoke the tool as part of the check-in procedures and automatically log the result so that no extra effort is required from the practitioner.

As we stressed in the previous section, it is important to have clear definitions that are published and available to everyone on the project for any measures that are being collected. We recommend full disclosure to all involved even when the definition is very loose or fuzzy and the collection is only for a trial or evaluation period. The best way to ensure you are collecting good data is to feed back whatever you collect for review and validation as close to the source as possible. If the practitioners are not aware of what is being collected and don't review all the data you collect, you are almost assured of introducing bad data sooner or later.

The bottom-up paradigm assumes and relies on practitioners to be responsible and committed to a successful engineering-based measurement effort. They need to be part of the process and take responsibility to see that what is collected is reasonable and matches their engineering knowledge base. By feeding back any data whenever it is collected, we can avoid surprises and make sure this responsibility is met.

Measurement Data Collection Principles

- Unobtrusive
- Automated whenever possible
- Based on clear and unambiguous, published definitions
- Validated as collected (as close to the source as possible)
- Saved as a repository and for future validation or analysis purposes

---

If practitioner action is required to make a measurement or provide data, and you discover that some (or even many) of the practitioners are not cooperating, it is important to analyze the reasons. Ask the individuals involved what is happening. Are they aware of what is expected of them? Is it an education issue? Do they support providing the measure but just do not have the time? Or is it a matter of choosing to not cooperate and a lack of faith in the value or use of the measurement?

Exploring and analyzing why measurements are not collected accurately is a key part of collection. Measurement as a *service* means we must understand our customers and how they feel and work *with* them to achieve desired results.

It is also worthwhile to stress that a little analysis and creativity will often unearth alternative sources that may serve as substitutes for having to collect data at all or provide a much easier and more unobtrusive measure that approximates or highly correlates with the data that you really need.

Astronomers can't see black holes, but they assert their existence and analyze their properties on the basis of movements of visible objects around them. Similarly, we may not be able to directly "observe" certain software attributes because the relevant measures are not available or cost too much to obtain. But we may be able to show (through special analysis or industry research or data taken from other projects) that the attribute we want to look at is highly correlated with something much simpler that is readily available.

Some of the common alternative sources of measurement data include both objective and subjective information drawn from interviews and surveys, third-party databases, shared intra- or inter-company project data, and research or case study data in the published literature and conference proceedings.

PRESENT

Step 3 of the systematic process is to analyze, organize, and present the collected data so it can be used effectively. Over the years I have sat through many status meetings where people had good measurements (carefully defined and accurately collected), but failed to get their message across because of poor analysis. There is never a substitute for creative thinking! People need to focus on what the data means, how to interpret it, and what actions are being recommended. The presentation step is much more than just communicating data—it includes a high degree of judgment and creativity and the application of a broad array of analyses and modelling techniques. There are two key goals to be achieved: First, we must tabulate and array the information in a form that can be easily understood. Second, we want to encourage and support questions and conclusions about what the data means. That involves modeling and analysis to develop hypotheses and help understand the underlying relationships and implications.

For both there exists a fairly standard set of data manipulation, tabulation, and analysis techniques that are typically provided by standard spreadsheet software or commercial statistical packages. None of the capabilities are highly sophisticated, nor should they require the talents of a specialized analyst or statistician. What is required is a little training and experience to get comfortable with the package and a good foundation and awareness of basic data analysis techniques.

To illustrate the capabilities of such packages I've created a simple hypothetical example covering a few measurements that we might collect on the modules or program work products within an overall system design and development effort. Figure 2.8 displays a sample spreadsheet that might be produced in such a situation.

Resp	Module	Days	Start	Check In	Lines	Confidence	Changes	Test Defects
BH	DD11	21	3/15/92	3/29/92	405	Low	2	3
JB	CA1	8	2/9/92	2/26/92	145	High	0	0
JB	CA4	6	2/9/92	2/13/92	110	High	1	1
RC	U11	14	2/22/92	3/11/92	245	High	0	0
BH	U12	22	2/11/92	3/1/92	550	Medium	1	0
AM3	U13	6	3/5/92	4/22/92	401	High	0	0

Figure 2.8.   Example of a measurement spreadsheet.

Each module is represented as one row in the spreadsheet. As data on additional modules is collected, new rows are added. The columns denote the specific information and measures being collected on each module. Figure 2.8 includes the following information:

1. The initials of the assigned developer
2. The module name or identification
3. The number of days spent working on the module
4. The date work started
5. The date the module was first checked in to integration
6. The number of lines of code
7. A confidence measure reflecting the confidence in the module at check in (high, medium, or low)
8. The number of changes made after check in
9. The number of defects found after check in

Although this is a hypothetical example, the selected measures include at least a couple of each of the basic IOR elements: two **I**nput measures (resources and dates), two **O**utput measures that describe something about the module as a work product (lines of code and coder confidence), and two **R**esults or effectiveness measures (defects and changes that were made after check in). In any actual application other measures such as rework days spent, lines of code changed or reused, code complexity, user defects found, and so forth may need to be added. See Chapter 5 for a more complete discussion on applicable coding phase measurements and techniques.

Once the data is contained in a spreadsheet format it is very easy to view and present. All the packages make it very easy to display various tabulations and descriptive statistics. Figures 2.9, 2.10, and 2.11 show several typical outputs provided by the STATVIEW[1] package on my Macintosh. Each of these required only a few mouse clicks and a minute or two to produce.

---

[1]STATVIEW is a proprietary package marketed by Abacus Concepts of Berkeley, CA. Columns in the spreadsheet file typically denote selected I, O, or R measurements with rows used to enter one related set of observations. Alternatively the rows might be used to record data from different individuals within the same project or periodic observations over time.

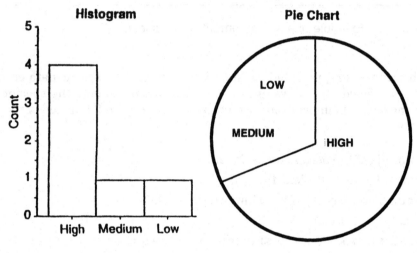

Frequency Table

Element:	Count:	Percent:	
High	4	66.667%	-Mode
Medium	1	16.667%	
Low	1	16.667%	

Figure 2.9. Displaying discrete measures.

The tables and plots in Figure 2.9 provide alternative presentations for column 7—the Coder Confidence measurement. This is a discrete category variable with choices of high, medium, and low. The different forms of presentation (frequency table, histogram, and pie chart) help us visualize the distribution of responses and better understand our data.

For continuous measures we can't use frequency tables (or histograms or pie charts) directly because the observed values are almost all different. What we can do is plot the observed values and try to describe or summarize the resulting distribution with various statistics (percentiles, median, mean, standard deviation). This is illustrated for the Lines of Code measure in our hypothetical example in Figures 2.10 and 2.11.

The first plot in Figure 2.10 is called a *scattergram*. Each of the six observed values for Lines of Code is shown as one point in the plot. The middle line through the plot is the computed average or *mean* value. Also shown are lines at plus and minus one *standard deviation* from the mean.

Below the scattergram is a *box plot*. The box plot is one of a variety of plotting techniques that helps focus attention on the distribution of a set of observed values. The bottom of the box is drawn as a line at the 25th percentile value (145) and the top at the 75th percentile value (405). The box thus contains the middle half of the distribution. The line inside the box is the median or 50th percentile value. The short lines above and below the box (called *whiskers* in statistical texts) help highlight any outer values (shown on the box plot as small circles). Box plots are most useful when comparing the distributions of several measures at once.

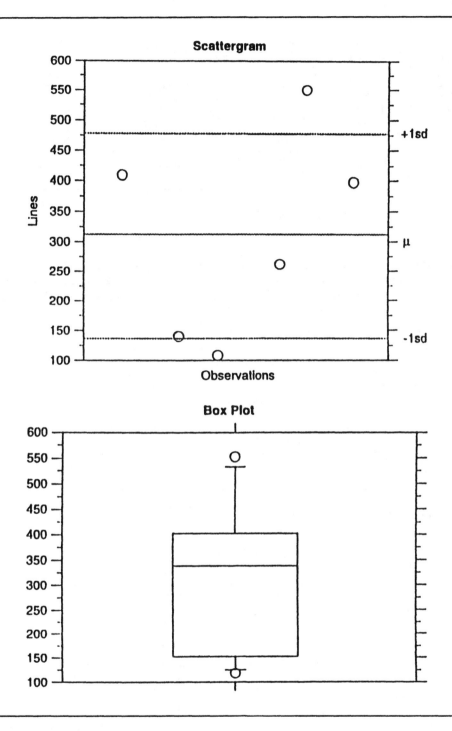

Figure 2.10.   Displaying continuous measures.

Figure 2.11 illustrates some of the common descriptive statistics that almost any presentation package will offer. This includes the mean (309) and standard deviation (171) as well as the minimum, maximum, range, and various percentile values. There is no entry for the mode (most common value) since all values were unique in this small sample set.

Mean:	Std. Dev.:	Std. Error:	Variance:	Coef. Var.:	Count:
309.333	171.087	69.846	29270.667	55.308	6
Minimum:	Maximum:	Range:	Sum:	Sum of Sqr.:	# Missing:
110	550	440	1856	720476	0
# < 10th %:	10th %:	25th %:	50th %:	75th %:	90th %:
1	113.5	145	323	405	535.5
# > 90th %:	Mode:	Geo. Mean:	Har. Mean:	Kurtosis:	Skewness:
1	•	265.347	223.462	-1.366	.13

Figure 2.11. Descriptive statistics.

Often it is desirable for presentation and analysis purposes to recode or classify a measurement into groups of values, thus converting it from a continuous measure into a discrete category measure. This is done to focus attention on the common groups of values and is another example of something that is very easy to do with most presentation tools. As an illustration, Figure 2.12 shows a frequency table and a histogram for the Lines of Code measurement recoded into one of five value ranges (0–100, 100–250, 250–500, 500–1000, and over 1000).

Frequency Table

Element:	Count:	Percent:
0–100	0	0%
100–250	3	50%
250–500	2	33.333%
500–1000	1	16.667%
Over 1000	0	0%

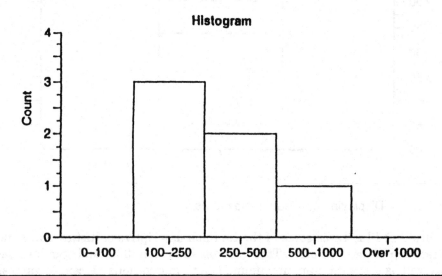

Figure 2.12. Recoded lines of code.

Another major benefit of having our measurement data in a spreadsheet or statistical package format is that many "what if," kinds of questions and relationships can be easily explored. The most common analyses performed are simple comparisons of one measure Against another. Figure 2.13 gives an example with a scattergram plot of the Lines of Code measure (column 7) versus the Days of Effort measure (column 3).

The points (or in this case, circles) show a general relationship (more lines requiring more effort), except for the 401 line user interface module (UI3), which took just six days. Such plots help us raise questions and "see" underlying relationships that might be present in the data. Once again, producing the scattergram requires only a couple of clicks and can easily be done for any pair of variables we might be interested in displaying.

The "strength" of the linear association between Lines of Code and Days can be measured by a statistic called the correlation coefficient. (The correlation coefficient for this data has a value of .71 reflecting the positive association that we can observe from the plot.) We can also perform a simple *regression analysis* and find the best straight line through the scattergram points (see Figure 2.14).

The line drawn through the data points is the computed "best" linear fit. The equation for the line is indicated above the plot and offers a "model" that we can use as a possible predictive metric. Based on our small sample of observations we would "predict" that the average 300-line module would require 12 to 13 days. (.03 x 300 + 3.44 = 12.44)

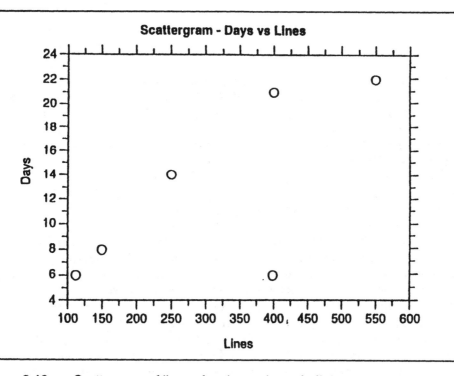

Figure 2.13.   Scattergram of lines of code vs. days of effort.

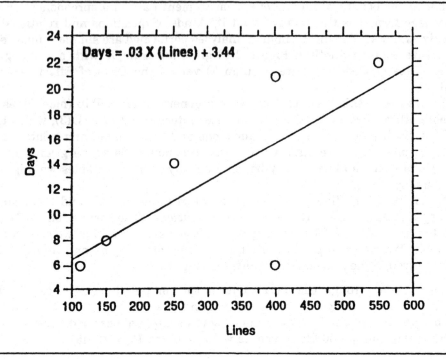

Figure 2.14.   Regression fit for Lines of Code vs. Days of Effort

Your statistical package regression analysis routine will also provide much more information—probably more than you need. In STATVIEW, tables are provided that give the standard error and confidence intervals for the slope and intercept, an analysis of variance and residual statistics if desired. You need not worry about understanding what all this means but it is nice to know it is there and occasionally you may want to take advantage of it.

Regression analysis can't be used on discrete or category measures like Coder Confidence. An alternative commonly employed is to present the data in the form of a contingency table. An example is shown in Figure 2.15.

If there were no relationship between Coder Confidence and the number of changes, the likelihood of falling within any column entry would be equally probable. For example, since three out of the six (half) of the observed number of changes is 0, we would also expect half of each of the Coder Confidence values (high, medium, and low) to have 0 changes. This expected number is what is shown in the expected values table. Differences between the observed and expected table entries can be used to measure or test for a possible relationship between Coder Confidence and changes.

This is done by computing the chi-square statistic or a contingency coefficient. As shown in the summary statistics table in Figure 2.15 the coefficient is .76. The chi-square test is significant at the .08 level, which means that statistically speaking the chances of this result occurring if the measures were not related are 8 out of 100.

Observed Frequency Table

	High	Medium	Low	Totals:
0	3	0	0	3
1	1	1	0	2
2	0	0	1	1
Totals:	4	1	1	6

Expected Values

	High	Medium	Low	Totals:
0	2	.5	.5	3
1	1.333	.333	.333	2
2	.667	.167	.167	1
Totals:	4	1	1	6

Summary Statistics

DF:	4	
Total Chi-Square:	8.25	p=.0828
G Statistic:	•	
Contingency Coefficient:	.761	
Cramer's V:	.829	

Figure 2.15. Contingency table analysis—Coder Confidence vs. changes.

Don't despair if you feel a little lost with all the statistical jargon. All the illustrations in this section are intended to *help* demonstrate how important having some automated data manipulation and presentation tools are to the successful measurement effort. *You need not (and should not) become bogged down in statistical analysis techniques and methods.* Certainly you can be successful without them. However, it is increasingly evident that most managers and practitioners are familiar with basic package data analysis and presentation techniques and expect them to be employed or at least available.

You should take advantage of this and plan on exploiting the power and ease of use of the presentation and analysis tools now available. It really doesn't make too much difference which one you choose—just pick one and take the time to learn and get comfortable with it.

I personally prefer the PC or workstation package approach that allows and supports a high level of individual hands-on work. As data is captured it should be entered in spreadsheet or standard data file format for easy use and manipulation. Design of the file organization and layout will eventually be required for the long run (especially as file sizes get large), but typically most groups start out experimentally and make many modifications as they go along. A big advantage of nearly all of the standard packages is that they support this flexibility and make later changes, re-grouping, or packaging of files easier. Thus, you shouldn't have to study or worry too much about setting things up "right" at the start.[2]

Besides the analytical modeling benefits, the tools will also give you lots of graphical options to help make your reports more colorful and interesting and allow you to get practitioners and managers *personally* involved in the presentation and analysis. This merging of the present and use activities is one of the clear trends in modern engineering measurement and something we'll have much more to say about in later chapters. It may well be the most important of all the many wonderful things the tools do for us!

One final point I'd like to stress again is the importance of viewing the measurement program dynamically and striving for continuous improvements in everything you present. You should make it a point to study and collect good (and bad) examples and save them for future use. I encourage keeping a scrapbook of interesting measurement presentations that you particularly like and dislike and that you encounter at various courses, conferences, or in reference materials such as this book. It is becoming more and more important to convert your data into graphical form to highlight trends and relationships. Any time you see a nice plot or graph, copy it and stick it in your scrapbook as a candidate for future application within your own organization. Better yet, swap scrapbooks with your friends and coworkers. Maybe we could even get some enterprising firm to start a new series of trading cards!

USE

The fourth in the process is getting customers to actually *use* the data and measurement information. Use should mean much more than just getting and reviewing a report or a presentation. What we seek is the triggering of new and more interesting questions and the direct use of information to help take action and make decisions. At the very minimum we want our measures to increase practitioner and manager knowledge and to help provide real insight and visibility for what is happening.

You can't *force* use, but you can make sure that information is presented and then measure what it is used for. In the systematic engineered measurement process I believe that everyone should start out measuring the usage of any measurements they collect. You should know who is getting which reports and what they do with them.

What we recommend is a regular periodic survey—perhaps every 6 to 12 months. This is an opportunity to ask what your customers want and need and to determine which reports or measures might be unnecessary or eliminated. Such a survey may be incredibly discouraging (when you find out most of what you collect and present is not being used for much of anything!), but measuring it is the key to helping you understand why and beginning to make changes that may be needed in your program.

---

[2]*Warning*: For most big projects you need some type of distributed network or server database. It is by no means a simple task to set this up and manage it properly. If your project is large and decentralized it will be important to think ahead carefully. If in doubt, seek out specialized help from others who have had to handle similar problems before.

To increase use you must be *responsive* and *timely*. This means getting data into the hands and heads of your customers before it is old hat or no longer useful to support decisions. The need for timely response is yet another argument for the kind of presentation tools discussed in the previous section. When employed properly they enable you to quickly create or change a report on demand—to answer the next question as soon as it arises! They also help you translate the raw data into forms that more closely relate to different customer needs and to respond whenever possible in the user's language and problem space. All of that encourages and supports growing usage and happy measurement customers.

Remember from Chapter 1 that use of measurement implies the existence of metrics and meters within the organization. The meters serve to control or trigger decisions, and the metrics support decision making by helping in estimation, prediction, or comparison. Measurements also help communicate and train people throughout the organization and support project and process improvement efforts with before, during, and after baselines. Track and publicize the uses that are working successfully, and strive to understand and improve those that aren't. As long as you can show a small but steady increase in real use of measurements over time, your program is headed in the right direction and will emerge as a success.

VALIDATION

The final step and one that spans and supports each of the others is the basic activity of validation and making sure that what we define, what we collect, what we present, and what we use results in effective products, projects, and processes for our company or organization. Measurement is not a political activity; its first and foremost goal is to portray reality accurately. The validation job is to make sure there is no accidental or deliberate distortion and that the use of measurement is effective in helping the organization to improve.

Validation involves many ongoing actions all aimed at making sure each step of the systematic measurement process is carried out properly. Two broad types of validation activities can be usefully distinguished. One is focused on the accuracy and completeness of data being defined and collected—does the data match reality? Are there any biases introduced? The second is concerned with showing that our measures can reliably be used in some externally beneficial way to make more effective decisions. Both types are important and difficult (time consuming) to conduct.

Shigeo Shingo stresses four principles as underlying the effective control of quality (see Figure 2.16). While these principles grew from Shingo's experience teaching production engineering to a generation of Toyota managers and were meant to be applied on a shop or factory floor, they apply equally well to validation activities and efforts. Good measurement engineering programs will pay heed to these principles and must invest substantial energy in ongoing validation.

---

1. Control upstream, as close to the source of the potential flaw as possible.
2. Establish controls in relation to the severity of the problem.
3. Think smart and small. Strive for the simplest, most efficient, and most economical.
4. Don't delay improvement by overanalyzing.

Figure 2.16. Shingo principles.

It does not take much to distort or kill the effectiveness of an entire program. We have learned through the school of hard knocks that a lot of effort must be invested in validity checking and validation. Even with excellent validation programs, it is seldom possible (or necessary) to get data much more accurate than within 10 percent to 20 percent of the "true" reality.

Part of the problem can usually be traced to sloppiness, poor procedures, and lack of communication. Fortunately, this is usually the major part and is generally quite correctable as long as someone is responsible and accountable for working on the problem. Another part lies in the basic human nature to fudge and rationalize personal views of reality. This is especially so when there are negative consequences to be faced and when the person feels it is unlikely that they will be exposed or called to task.

One side of every practitioner and manager knows that good and accurate information will really lead to a better job and better environment for everyone. The other side fears the consequences of any negative news and worries that it may be used in harmful or ill-considered ways. This creates a constant tug of war to get at reality and the truth—particularly when significant doses of bad news are involved.

There are lots of examples of the juggling problem throughout our industry. One classic example is the famous 90 percent complete syndrome where as much as 25 percent or more of the total project effort is required to complete what the project claims is the last 5 percent to 10 percent of the job. Another example is described by Putnam and Ware as "pouring from one pot to another." [Putnam 92 p. 98]

> It is far too easy to allocate some of the actual manmonths to one pot and some to another in order to match what somebody's planning assumptions were a year back. It may be hard to distort the total number of effort months for the whole organization, but within this total there can be a lot of pouring from one pot to another. A new project, in particular, is regarded as a lady bountiful. The general idea is to transfer folks there as quickly as possible to get billings up. Financial people seem to want a steady cash flow. The actual work, however, may not be ready for these people, so some of these manmonths are wasted. Later in the project when the effort is needed, these manmonths are no longer in the budget. The temptation is to play the same game with the next lady bountiful so as to complete the latest project.

Many more examples will be seen in case studies to come. It is the job of validation to anticipate this kind of fudging distortion and see that appropriate checks and balances are in place to avoid them. Many so-called "validation techniques" are available, but most boil down to careful checking and double-checking and a good dose of common sense.

The most important basic technique is the fundamental idea of feeding back any collected data right at the source or as close to the source as possible. The people supplying measurement data are in the best position to see if it has been captured incorrectly and rigorous source feedback can help breed individual responsibility for data accuracy.

Spot checks and audits that trace selected data to its source should be applied periodically as an overall check on the measurement effort. Outlier analysis focuses on understanding extreme and boundary values to surface special cases and avoid biasing of average results from the inclusion of a few points of bad data. Special calibration studies and sanity checks should be used to assure that results being obtained make sense and are repeatable. Encouraging everyone to look for and propose alternate data interpretations is a great way to avoid jumping to preliminary and wrong conclusions.

None of these techniques requires sophistication or special tools. What they share in common is a recognition that the organization must set aside ongoing effort into making sure that the measurement system is working and that everyone must be expected to be responsible and accountable for data validity and accuracy.

SUMMARY

This chapter has provided a foundation model for the measurement process. The reader should understand and be able to characterize the key features and elements of the bottom-up, practitioner-based measurement engineering paradigm as well as the five-step measurement process model.

We've stressed that the place to start engineering your measurement program is around the *work products* that are produced as a project proceeds, and that for each work product we need measurements of the *inputs,* the *outputs,* and the *results*.

We've also driven home the idea that measurement's primary role is the support of the working practitioner. Measurements should be integrated into all software work, and, fundamentally, measurements come *before* goals, not after.

We've provided a systematic model that can be used to engineer and structure a successful measurement effort. The steps of the model (define, collect, present, use, and validate) have been illustrated and shown to apply straightforwardly to most organizations.

Finally, we've stressed that a good measurement process will always be *changing*. New engineering techniques and new products will continually be forcing us to recalibrate and readjust our program. Even without such influences, we should constantly be raising new questions and striving for new or added insight. That leads to new metrics and meters and produces ongoing evolution and improvement of the process. The one constant we can count on is change, and our measurement program must be built from the start to support it.

Software is no longer a mysterious black art. We understand (even if we don't always do it) what is required to engineer it in an effective fashion. We also understand most of the measurements that need to be collected to support the effort and recognize that they must be built in from the bottom as the work process is defined and evolves. *Software measurements aren't something different or separate from software methodologies and techniques.* You don't first set up a process and *then* implement a measurement program. Good methods require and naturally support good measures, and hence most practical and useful measures should derive bottom-up, not top-down!

The TAME Project: Towards Improvement-Oriented Software Environments

VICTOR R. BASILI, SENIOR MEMBER, IEEE, AND H. DIETER ROMBACH

Abstract—Experience from a dozen years of analyzing software engineering processes and products is summarized as a set of software engineering and measurement principles that argue for software engineering process models that integrate sound planning and analysis into the construction process.

In the TAME (Tailoring A Measurement Environment) project at the University of Maryland we have developed such an improvement-oriented software engineering process model that uses the goal/question/metric paradigm to integrate the constructive and analytic aspects of software development. The model provides a mechanism for formalizing the characterization and planning tasks, controlling and improving projects based on quantitative analysis, learning in a deeper and more systematic way about the software process and product, and feeding the appropriate experience back into the current and future projects.

The TAME system is an instantiation of the TAME software engineering process model as an ISEE (Integrated Software Engineering Environment). The first in a series of TAME system prototypes has been developed. An assessment of experience with this first limited prototype is presented including a reassessment of its initial architecture. The long-term goal of this building effort is to develop a better understanding of appropriate ISEE architectures that optimally support the improvement-oriented TAME software engineering process model.

Index Terms—Characterization, execution, experience, feedback, formalizing, goal/question/metric paradigm, improvement paradigm, integrated software engineering environments, integration of construction and analysis, learning, measurement, planning, quantitative analysis, software engineering process models, tailoring, TAME project, TAME system.

I. INTRODUCTION

EXPERIENCE from a dozen years of analyzing software engineering processes and products is summarized as a set of ten *software engineering* and fourteen *measurement principles*. These principles imply the need for software engineering process models that integrate sound planning and analysis into the construction process.

Software processes based upon such *improvement-oriented software engineering process models* need to be *tailorable* and *tractable*. The tailorability of a process is the characteristic that allows it to be altered or adapted to suit

Manuscript received January 15, 1988. This work was supported in part by NASA under Grant NSG-5123, the Air Force Office of Scientific Research under Grant F49620-87-0130, and the Office of Naval Research under Grant N00014-85-K-0633 to the University of Maryland. Computer time was provided in part through the facilities of the Computer Science Center of the University of Maryland.

The authors are with the Department of Computer Science and the Institute for Advanced Computer Studies, University of Maryland, College Park, MD 20742.

IEEE Log Number 8820962.

a set of special needs or purposes [64]. The software engineering process requires tailorability because the overall project execution model (life cycle model), methods and tools need to be altered or adapted for the specific project environment and the overall organization. The tractability of a process is the characteristic that allows it to be easily planned, taught, managed, executed, or controlled [64]. Each software engineering process requires tractability because it needs to be planned, the various planned activities of the process need to be communicated to the entire project personnel, and the process needs to be managed, executed, and controlled according to these plans. Sound tailoring and tracking require *top-down measurement* (measurement based upon operationally defined goals). The goal of a *software engineering environment (SEE)* should be to support such tailorable and tractable software engineering process models by automating as much of them as possible.

In the *TAME (Tailoring A Measurement Environment) project* at the University of Maryland we have developed an improvement-oriented software engineering process model. The *TAME system* is an instantiation of this TAME software engineering process model as an ISEE (Integrated SEE).

It seems appropriate at this point to clarify some of the important terms that will be used in this paper. The term *engineering* comprises both development and maintenance. A software engineering *project* is embedded in some *project environment* (characterized by personnel, type of application, etc.) and within some *organization* (e.g., NASA, IBM). Software engineering within such a project environment or organization is conducted according to an overall software engineering *process model* (one of which will be introduced in Section II-B-3). Each individual software project in the context of such a software engineering process model is exeucted according to some *execution model* (e.g., waterfall model [28], [58], iterative enhancement model [24], spiral model [30]) supplemented by *techniques (methods, tools)*. Each specific instance of (a part of) an execution model together with its supplementing methods and tools is referred to as *execution process* (including the construction as well as the analysis process). In addition, the term *process* is frequently used as a generic term for various kinds of activities. We distinguish between *constructive* and *analytic* methods and tools. Whereas constructive methods and tools are concerned with building products, analytic

Reprinted from *IEEE Trans. Software Eng.*, Vol. 14, No. 6, June 1988, pp. 758–773.

method and tools are concerned with analyzing the constructive process and the resulting products. The body of experience accumulated within a project environment or organization is referred to as *experience base*. There exist at least three levels of formalism of such experience bases: *database* (data being individual products or processes), *information base* (information being data viewed through some superimposed structure), and knowledge base (knowledge implying the ability to derive new insights via deduction rules). The project personnel are categorized as either *engineers* (e.g., designers, coders, testers) or *managers*.

This paper is structured into a presentation and discussion of the improvement-oriented software engineering process model underlying the TAME project (Section II), its automated support by the TAME system (Section III), and the first TAME system prototype (Section IV). In the first part of this paper we list the empirically derived lessons learned (Section II-A) in the form of software engineering principles (Section II-A-1), measurement principles (Section II-A-2), and motivate the TAME project by stating several implications derived from those principles (Section II-A-3). The TAME project (Section II-B) is presented in terms of the improvement paradigm (Section II-B-1), the goal/question/metric paradigm as a mechanism for formalizing the improvement paradigm (Section II-B-2), and the TAME project model as an instantiation of both paradigms (Section II-B-3). In the second part of this paper we introduce the TAME system as an approach to automatically supporting the TAME software engineering process model (Section III). The TAME system is presented in terms of its requirements (Section III-A) and architecture (Section III-B). In the third part of this paper, we introduce the first TAME prototype (Section IV) with respect to its functionality and our first experiences with it.

II. Software Engineering Process

Our experience from measuring and evaluating software engineering processes and products in a variety of project environments has been summarized in the form of lessons learned (Section II-A). Based upon this experience the TAME project has produced an improvement-oriented process model (Section II-B).

A. Lessons Learned from Past Experience

We have formulated our experience as a set of software engineering principles (Section II-A-1) and measurement principles (Section II-A-2). Based upon these principles a number of implications for sound software engineering process models have been derived (Section II-A-3).

1) Software Engineering Principles: The first five software engineering principles address the need for developing quality *a priori* by introducing engineering discipline into the field of software engineering:

(P1) We need to clearly distinguish between the role of constructive and analytic activities. Only improved construction processes will result in higher quality software. Quality cannot be tested or inspected into software. An-alytic processes (e.g., quality assurance) cannot serve as a substitute for constructive processes but will provide control of the constructive processes [27], [37], [61].

(P2) We need to formalize the planning of the construction process in order to develop quality *a priori* [3], [16], [19], [25]. Without such plans the trial and error approach can hardly be avoided.

(P3) We need to formalize the analysis and improvement of construction processes and products in order to guarantee an organized approach to software engineering [3], [25].

(P4) Engineering methods require analysis to determine whether they are being performed appropriately, if at all. This is especially important because most of these methods are heuristic rather than formal [42], [49], [66].

(P5) Software engineers and managers need real-time feedback in order to improve the construction processes and products of the ongoing project. The organization needs post-mortem feedback in order to improve the construction processes and products for future projects [66].

The remaining five software engineering principles address the need for tailoring of planning and analysis processes due to changing needs form project to project and environment to environment:

(P6) All project environments and products are different in some way [2], [66]. These differences must be made explicit and taken into account in the software execution processes and in the product quality goals [3], [16], [19], [25].

(P7) There are many execution models for software engineering. Each execution model needs to be tailored to the organization and project needs and characteristics [2], [13], [16], [66].

(P8) We need to formalize the tailoring of processes toward the quality and productivity goals of the project and the characteristics of the project environment and the organization [16]. It is not easy to apply abstractly defined methods to specific environments.

(P9) This need for tailoring does not mean starting from scratch each time. We need to reuse experience, but only after tailoring it to the project [1], [2], [6], [7], [18], [32].

(P10) Because of the constant need for tailoring, management control is crucial and must be flexible. Management needs must be supported in this software engineering process.

A more detailed discussion of these software engineering principles is contained in [17].

2) Software Measurement Principles: The first four measurement principles address the purpose of the measurement process, i.e., why should we measure, what should we measure, for whom should we measure:

(M1) Measurement is an ideal mechanism for characterizing, evaluating, predicting, and providing motivation for the various aspects of software construction processes and products [3], [4], [9], [16], [21], [25], [48], [56], [57]. It is a common mechanism for relating these multiple aspects.

(M2) Measurements must be taken on both the software processes and the various software products [1], [5], [14], [29], [38], [40], [42]–[44], [47], [54]–[56], [65], [66]. Improving a product requires understanding both the product and its construction processes.

(M3) There are a variety of uses for measurement. The purpose of measurement should be clearly stated. We can use measurement to examine cost, effectiveness, reliability, correctness, maintainability, efficiency, user friendliness, etc. [8]–[10], [13], [14], [16], [20], [23], [25], [41], [53], [57], [61].

(M4) Measurement needs to be viewed from the appropriate perspective. The corporation, the manager, the developer, the customer's organization and the user each view the product and the process from different perspectives. Thus they may want to know different things about the project and to different levels of detail [3], [16], [19], [25], [66].

The remaining ten measurement principles address metrics and the overall measurement process. The first two principles address characteristics of metrics (i.e., what kinds of metrics, how many are needed), while the latter eight address characteristics of the measurement process (i.e., what should the measurement process look like, how do we support characterization, planning, construction, and learning and feedback):

(M5) Subjective as well as objective metrics are required. Many process, product and environment aspects can be characterized by objective metrics (e.g., product complexity, number of defects or effort related to processes). Other aspects cannot be characterized objectively yet (e.g., experience of personnel, type of application, understandability of processes and products); but they can at least be categorized on a quantitative (nominal) scale to a reasonable degree of accuracy [4], [5], [16], [48], [56].

(M6) Most aspects of software processes and products are too complicated to be captured by a single metric. For both definition and interpretation purposes, a set of metrics (a metric vector) that frame the purpose for measurement needs to be defined [9].

(M7) The development and maintenance environments must be prepared for measurement and analysis. Planning is required and needs to be carefully integrated into the overall software engineering process model. This planning process must take into account the experimental design appropriate for the situation [3], [14], [19], [22], [66].

(M8) We cannot just use models and metrics from other environments as defined. Because of the differences among execution models (principle P7), the models and metrics must be tailored for the environment in which they will be applied and checked for validity in that environment [2], [6]–[8], [12], [23], [31], [40], [47], [50], [51], [62].

(M9) The measurement process must be top-down rather than bottom-up in order to define a set of operational goals, specify the appropriate metrics, permit valid contextual interpretation and analysis, and provide feedback for tailorability and tractability [3], [16], [19], [25].

(M10) For each environment there exists a characteristic set of metrics that provides the needed information for definition and interpretation purposes [21].

(M11) Multiple mechanisms are needed for data collection and validation. The nature of the data to be collected (principle M5) determines the appropriate mechanisms [4], [25], [48], e.g., manually via forms or interviews, or automatically via analyzers.

(M12) In order to evaluate and compare projects and to develop models we need a historical experience base. This experience base should characterize the local environment [4], [13], [25], [34], [44], [48].

(M13) Metrics must be associated with interpretations, but these interpretations must be given in context [3], [16], [19], [25], [34], [56].

(M14) The experience base should evolve from a database into a knowledge base (supported by an expert system) to formalize the reuse of experience [11], [14].

A more detailed discussion of these measurement principles is contained in [17].

3) Implications: Clearly this set of principles is not complete. However, these principles provide empirically derived insight into the limitations of traditional process models. We will give some of the implications of these principles with respect to the components that need to be included in software process models, essential characteristics of these components, the interaction of these components, and the needed automated support. Although there is a relationship between almost all principles and the derived implications, we have referenced for each implication only those principles that are related most directly.

Based upon our set of principles it is clear that we need to *better understand* the software construction process and product (e.g., principles P1, P4, P6, M2, M5, M6, M8, M9, M10, M12). Such an understanding will allow us to *plan* what we need to do and improve over our current practices (e.g., principles P1, P2, P3, P7, P8, M3, M4, M7, M9, M14). To *make those plans operational*, we need to specify how we are going to affect the construction processes and their analysis (e.g., principles P1, P2, P3, P4, P7, P8, M7, M8, M9, M14). The *execution* of these prescribed plans involves the *construction* of products and the *analysis* of the constructive processes and resulting products (e.g., principles P1, P7).

All these implications need to be integrated in such a way that they allow for sound *learning and feedback* so that we can improve the software execution processes and products (e.g., principles P1, P3, P4, P5, P9, P10, M3, M4, M9, M12, M13, M14). This interaction requires the integration of the constructive and analytic aspects of the software engineering process model (e.g., principles P2, M7, M9).

The components and their interactions need to be formalized so they can be supported properly by an *ISEE* (e.g., principles P2, P3, P8, P9, M9). This formalization must include a *structuring of the body of experience* so that characterization, planning, learning, feedback, and improvement can take place (e.g., principles P2, P3, P8, P9, M9). An ideal mechanism for supporting all of these components and their interactions is *quantitative analysis* (e.g., principles P3, P4, M1, M2, M5, M6, M8, M9, M10, M11, M13).

B. A Process Model: The TAME Project

The TAME (Tailoring A Measurement Environment) project at the University of Maryland has produced a software engineering process model (Section II-B-3) based upon our empirically derived lessons learned. This software engineering process model is based upon the improvement (Section II-B-1) and goal/question/metric paradigms (Section II-B-2).

1) Improvement Paradigm: The improvement paradigm for software engineering processes reflects the implications stated in Section II-A-3. It consists of six major steps [3]:

(I1) Characterize the current project environment.

(I2) Set up goals and refine them into quantifiable questions and metrics for successful project performance and improvement over previous project performances.

(I3) Choose the appropriate software project execution model for this project and supporting methods and tools.

(I4) Execute the chosen processes and construct the products, collect the prescribed data, validate it, and provide feedback in real-time.

(I5) Analyze the data to evaluate the current practices, determine problems, record the findings, and make recommendations for improvement.

(I6) Proceed to Step I1 to start the next project, armed with the experience gained from this and previous projects.

This paradigm is aimed at providing a basis for corporate learning and improvement. Improvement is only possible if we a) understand what the current status of our environment is (step I1), b) state precise improvement goals for the particular project and quantify them for the purpose of control (step I2), c) choose the appropriate process execution models, methods, and tools in order to achieve these improvement goals (step I3), execute and monitor the project performance thoroughly (step I4), and assess it (step I5). Based upon the assessment results we can provide feedback into the ongoing project or into the planning step of future projects (steps I5 and I6).

2) Goal/Question/Metric Paradigm: The goal/question/metric (GQM) paradigm is intended as a mechanism for formalizing the characterization, planning, construction, analysis, learning and feedback tasks. It represents a systematic approach for setting project goals (tailored to the specific needs of an organization) and defining them in an operational and tractable way. Goals are refined into a set of quantifiable questions that specify metrics. This paradigm also supports the analysis and integration of

metrics in the context of the questions and the original goal. Feedback and learning are then performed in the context of the GQM paradigm.

The process of setting goals and refining them into quantifiable questions is complex and requires experience. In order to support this process, a set of *templates* for setting goals, and a set of *guidelines* for deriving questions and metrics has been developed. These templates and guidelines reflect our experience from having applied the GQM paradigm in a variety of environments (e.g., NASA [4], [17], [48], IBM [60], AT&T, Burroughs [56], and Motorola). We received additional feedback from Hewlett Packard where the GQM paradigm has been used without our direct assistance [39]. It needs to be stressed that we do not claim that these templates and guidelines are complete; they will most likely change over time as our experience grows. Goals are defined in terms of purpose, perspective and environment. Different sets of guidelines exist for defining product-related and process-related questions. Product-related questions are formulated for the purpose of defining the product (e.g., physical attributes, cost, changes, and defects, context), defining the quality perspective of interest (e.g., reliability, user friendliness), and providing feedback from the particular quality perspective. Process-related questions are formulated for the purpose of defining the process (quality of use, domain of use), defining the quality perspective of interest (e.g., reduction of defects, cost effectiveness of use), and providing feedback from the particular quality perspective.

• **Templates/Guidelines for Goal Definition:**

Purpose: To (characterize, evaluate, predict, motivate, etc.) the (process, product, model, metric, etc.) in order to (understand, assess, manage, engineer, learn, improve, etc.) it.

Example: To evaluate the system testing methodology in order to improve it.

Perspective: Examine the (cost, effectiveness, correctness, defects, changes, product metrics, reliability, etc.) from the point of view of the (developer, manager, customer, corporate perspective, etc.)

Example: Examine the effectiveness from the developer's point of view.

Environment: The environment consists of the following: process factors, people factors, problem factors, methods, tools, constraints, etc.

Example: The product is an operating system that must fit on a PC, etc.

• **Guidelines for Product-Related Questions:**

For each product under study there are three major subgoals that need to be addressed: 1) definition of the product, 2) definition of the quality perspectives of interest, and 3) feedback related to the quality perspectives of interest.

Definition of the product includes questions related to *physical attributes* (a quantitative characterization of the product in terms of physical attributes such as size, complexity, etc.), *cost* (a quantitative characterization of the resources expended related to this product in terms of effort, computer time, etc.), *changes and defects* (a quantitative characterization of the errors, faults, failures, adaptations, and enhancements related to this product), and *context* (a quantitative characterization of the customer community using this product and their operational profiles).

Quality perspectives of interest includes, for each quality perspective of interest (e.g., reliability, user friendliness), questions related to the *major model(s) used* (a quantitative specification of the quality perspective of interest), the *validity of the model for the particular environment* (an analysis of the appropriateness of the model for the particular project environment), the *validity of the data collected* (an analysis of the quality of data), the *model effectiveness* (a quantitative characterization of the quality of the results produced according to this model), and a *substantiation of the model* (a discussion of whether the results are reasonable from various perspectives).

Feedback includes questions related to *improving the product relative to the quality perspective of interest* (a quantitative characterization of the product quality, major problems regarding the quality perspective of interest, and suggestions for improvement during the ongoing project as well as during future projects).

• **Guidelines for Process-Related Questions**

For each process under study, there are three major subgoals that need to be addressed: 1) definition of the process, 2) definition of the quality perspectives of interest, and 3) feedback from using this process relative to the quality perspective of interest.

Definition of the process includes questions related to the *quality of use* (a quantitative characterization of the process and an assessment of how well it is performed), and the *domain of use* (a quantitative characterization of the object to which the process is applied and an analysis of the process performer's knowledge concering this object).

Quality perspectives of interest follows a pattern similar to the corresponding product-oriented subgoal including, for each quality perspective of interest (e.g., reduction of defects, cost effectiveness), questions related to the *major model(s) used*, and *validity of the model for the particular environment*, the *validity of the data collected*, the *model effectiveness* and the *substantiation of the model*).

Feedback follows a pattern similar to the corresponding product-oriented subgoal.

• **Guidelines for Metrics, Data Collection, and Interpretation:**

The choice of metrics is determined by the quantifiable questions. The guidelines for questions acknowledge the need for generally more than one metric (principle M6), for objective and subjective metrics (principle M5), and for associating interpretations with metrics (principle M13). The actual GQM models generated from these tem-

plates and guidelines will differ from project to project and organization to organization (principle M6). This reflects their being tailored for the different needs in different projects and organizations (principle M4). Depending on the type of each metric, we choose the appropriate mechanisms for data collection and validation (principle M11). As goals, questions and metrics provide for tractability of the (top-down) definitional quantification process, they also provide for the interpretation context (bottom-up). This integration of definition with interpretation allows for the interpretation process to be tailored to the specific needs of an environment (principle M8).

3) Improvement-Oriented Process Model: The TAME software engineering process model is an instantiation of the improvement paradigm. The GQM paradigm provides the necessary integration of the individual components of this model. The TAME software engineering process model explicitly includes components for (C1) the characterization of the current status of a project environment, (C2) the planning for improvement integrated into the execution of projects, (C3) the execution of the construction and analysis of projects according to the project plans, and (C4) the recording of experience into an experience base. The learning and feedback mechanism (C5) is distributed throughout the model within and across the components as information flows from one component to another. Each of these tasks must be dealt with from a constructive and analytic perspective. Fig. 1 contains a graphical representation of the improvement-oriented TAME process model. The relationships (arcs) among process model components in Fig. 1 represent information flow.

(C1) Characterization of the current environment is required to understand the various factors that influence the current project environment. This task is important in order to define a starting point for improvement. Without knowing where we are, we will not be able to judge whether we are improving in our present project. We distinguish between the constructive and analytic aspects of the characterization task to emphasize that we not only state the environmental factors but analyze them to the degree possible based upon data and other forms of information from prior projects. This characterization task needs to be formalized.

(C2) Planning is required to understand the project goals, execution needs, and project focus for learning and feedback. This task is essential for disciplined software project execution (i.e., executing projects according to precise specifications of processes and products). It provides the basis for improvement relative to the current status determined during characterization. In the planning task, we distinguish between the constructive and analytic as well as the "what" and "how" aspects of planning. Based upon the GQM paradigm all these aspects are highly interdependent and performed as a single task. The development of quantitatively analyzable goals is an iterative process. However, we formulate the four planning as-

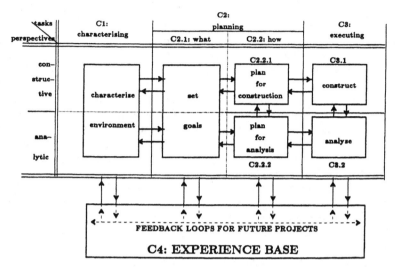

Fig. 1. The improvement-oriented TAME software process model.

pects as four separate components to emphasize the differences between creating plans for development and making those plans analyzable, as well as between stating what it is you want to accomplish and stating how you plan to tailor the processes and metrics to do it.

(C2.1) "What" Planning deals with choosing, assigning priorities, and operationally defining, to the degree possible, the project goals from the constructive and analytic perspectives. The actual goal setting is an instantiation of the front-end of the GQM paradigm (the templates/guidelines for goal definition). The constructive perspective addresses the definition of project goals such as on-time delivery, the appropriate functionality to satisfy the user, and the analysis of the execution processes we are applying. Some of these goals might be stated as improvement goals over the current state-of-the-practice as characterized in component C1. These goals should be prioritized and operationally defined to the extent possible without having chosen the particular construction models, methods and tools yet. The analytic perspective addresses analysis procedures for monitoring and controlling whether the goals are met. This analytic goal perspective should prescribe the necessary learning and feedback paths. It should be operationally defined to the extent allowed by the degree of precision of the constructive goal perspective.

(C2.2) "How" Planning is based upon the results from the "what" planning (providing for the purpose and perspective of a goal definition according to the GQM paradigm front-end) and the characterization of the environment (providing for the environment part of a goal definition according to the GQM paradigm front-end). The "how" planning involves the choice of an appropriately tailored execution model, methods and tools that permit the building of the system in such a way that we can analyze whether we are achieving our stated goals. The particular choice of construction processes, methods and tools

(component C2.2.1) goes hand in hand with fine-tuning the analysis procedures derived during the analytic perspective of the "what" planning (component C2.2.2).

(C2.2.1) Planning for construction includes choosing the appropriate execution model, methods and tools to fulfill the project goals. It should be clear that effective planning for construction depends on well-defined project goals from both the constructive and analytic perspective (component C2.1).

(C2.2.2) Planning for analysis addresses the fine-tuning of the operational definition of the analytic goal perspective (derived as part of component C2.1) towards the specific choices made during planning for construction (C2.2.1). The actual planning for analysis is an instantiation of the back-end of the GQM paradigm; details need to be filled in (e.g., quantifiable questions, metrics) based upon the specific methods and tools chosen.

(C3) Execution must integrate the construction (component C3.1) with the analysis (component C3.2). Analysis (including measurement) cannot be an add-on but must be part of the execution process and drive the construction. The execution plans derived during the planning task are supposed to provide for the required integration of construction and analysis.

(C4) The Experience Base includes the entire body of experience that is actively available to the project. We can characterize this experience according to the following dimensions: a) the degree of precision/detail, and b) the degree to which it is tailored to meet the specific needs of the project (context). The precision/detail dimension involves the level of detail of the experimental design and the level and quality of data collected. On one end of the spectrum we have detailed objective quantitative data that allows us to build mathematically tractable models. On the other end of the spectrum we have interviews and qualitative information that provide guidelines and "lessons learned documents", and permit the better formulation of goals and questions. The level of precision and detail affects our level of confidence in the results of the experiment as well as the cost of the data collection process. Clearly priorities play an important role here. The context dimension involves whether the focus is to learn about the specific project, projects within a specific application domain or general truths about the software process or product (requires the incorporation of formalized experience from prior projects into the experience base). Movement across the context dimension assumes an ability to generalize experience to a broader context than the one studied, or to tailor experience to a specific project. The better this experience is packaged, the better our understanding of the environment. Maintaining a body of experience acquired during a number of projects is one of the prerequisites for learning and feedback across environments.

(C5) Learning and Feedback are integrated into the TAME process model in various ways. They are based upon the experimental model for learning consisting of a set of steps, starting with focused objectives, which are turned into specific hypotheses, followed by running experiments to validate the hypotheses in the appropriate environment. The model is iterative; as we learn from experimentation, we are better able to state our focused objectives and we change and refine our hypotheses.

This model of learning is incorporated into the GQM paradigm where the focused objectives are expressed as goals, the hypotheses are expressed as questions written to the degree of formalism required, and the experimental environment is the project, a set of projects in the same domain, or a corporation representing a general environment. Clearly the GQM paradigm is also iterative.

The feedback process helps generate the goals to influence one or more of the components in the process model, e.g., the characterization of the environment, or the analysis of the construction processes or products. The level of confidence we have in feeding back the experience to a project or a corporate environment depends upon the precision/detail level of the experience base (component C4) and the generality of the experimental environment in which it was gathered.

The learning and feedback process appears in the model as the integration of all the components and their interactions as they are driven by the improvement and GQM paradigms. The feedback process can be channeled to the various components of the current project and to the corporate experience base for use in future projects.

Most traditional software engineering process models address only a subset of the individual components of this model; in many cases they cover just the constructive aspects of characterization (component C1), "how" planning (component C2.2.1), and execution (component C3.1). More recently developed software engineering process models address the constructive aspect of execution (component C3.1) in more sophisticated ways (e.g., new process models [24],[30], [49], combine various process dimensions such as technical, managerial, contrac-

tual [36], or provide more flexibility as far as the use of methods and tools is concerned, for example via the automated generation of tools [45], [63]), or they add methods and tools for choosing the analytical processes, methods, and tools (component C3.2.2) as well as actually performing analysis (component C3.2) [52], [59]. However, all these process models have in common the lack of completely integrating all their individual components in a systematic way that would permit sound learning and feedback for the purpose of project control and improvement of corporate experience.

III. Automated Support through ISEEs: The TAME System

The goal of an Integrated Software Engineering Environment (ISEE) is to effectively support the improvement-oriented software engineering process model described in Section II-B-3. An ISEE must support all the model components (characterization, planning, execution, and the experience base), all the local interactions between model components, the integration, and formalization of the GQM paradigm, and the necessary transitions between the context and precision/detail dimension boundaries in the experience base. Supporting the transitions along the experience base dimensions is needed in order to allow for sound learning and feedback as outlined in Section II-B-3 (component C5).

The TAME system will automate as many of the components, interactions between components and supporting mechanisms of the TAME process model as possible. The TAME system development activities will concentrate on all but the construction component (component C3.1) with the eventual goal of interfacing with constructive SEEs. In this section we present the requirements and the initial architecture for the TAME system.

A. Requirements

The requirements for the TAME system can be derived from Section II-B-3 in a natural way. These requirements can be divided into external requirements (defined by and of obvious interest to the TAME system user) and internal requirements (defined by the TAME design team and required to support the external requirements properly).

The first five (external) requirements include support for the characterization and planning components of the TAME model by automating an instantiation of the GQM paradigm, for the analysis component by automating data collection, data validation and analysis, and the learning and feedback component by automating interpretation and organizational learning. We will list for each external TAME system requirement the TAME process model components of Section II-B-3 from which it has been derived.

External TAME requirements:

(R1) A mechanism for defining the constructive and analytic aspects of project goals in an operational and quantifiable way (derived from components C1, C2.1, C2.2.2, C3.2).

We use the GQM paradigm and its templates for defining goals operationally and refining them into quantifiable questions and metrics. The selection of the appropriate GQM model and its tailoring needs to be supported. The user will either select an existing model or generate a new one. A new model can be generated from scratch or by reusing pieces of existing models. The degree to which the selection, generation, and reuse tasks can be supported automatically depends largely on the degree to which the GQM paradigm and its templates can be formalized. The user needs to be supported in defining his/her specific goals according to the goal definition template. Based on each goal definition, the TAME system will search for a model in the experience base. If no appropriate model exists, the user will be guided in developing one. Based on the tractability of goals into subgoals and questions the TAME system will identify reusable pieces of existing models and compose as much of an initial model as possible. This initial model will be completed with user interaction. For example, if a user wants to develop a model for assessing a system test method used in a particular environment, the system might compose an initial model by reusing pieces from a model assessing a different test method in the same environment, and from a model for assessing the same system test method in a different environment. A complete GQM model includes rules for interpretation of metrics and guidelines for collecting the prescribed data. The TAME system will automatically generate as much of this information as possible.

(R2) The automatic and manual collection of data and the validation of manually collected data (derived from component C3.2).

The collection of all product-related data (e.g., lines of code, complexity) and certain process-related data (e.g., number of compiler runs, number of test runs) will be completely automated. Automation requires an interface with construction-oriented SEEs. The collection of many process-related data (e.g., effort, changes) and subjective data (e.g., experience of personnel, characteristics of methods used) cannot be automated. The schedule according to which measurement tools are run needs to be defined as part of the planning activity. It is possible to collect data whenever they are needed, periodically (e.g., always at a particular time of the day), or whenever changes of products occur (e.g., whenever a new product version is entered into the experience base all the related metrics are recomputed). All manually collected data need to be validated. Validating whether data are within their defined range, whether all the prescribed data are collected, and whether certain integrity rules among data are maintained will be automated. Some of the measurement tools will be developed as part of the TAME system development project, others will be imported. The need for importing measurement tools will require an effective interconnection mechanism (probably an interconnection language) for integrating tools developed in different languages.

(R3) A mechanism for controlling measurement and analysis (derived from component C3.2).

A GQM model is used to specify and control the execution of a particular analysis and feedback session. According to each GQM model, the TAME system must trigger the execution of measurement tools for data collection, the computation of all metrics and distributions prescribed, and the application of statistical procedures. If certain metrics or distributions cannot be computed due to the lack of data or measurement tools, the TAME system must inform the user.

(R4) A mechanism for interpreting analysis results in a context and providing feedback for the improvement of the execution model, methods and tools (derived from components C3.2, C.5).

We use a GQM model to define the rules and context for interpretation of data and for feedback in order to refine and improve execution models, methods and tools. The degree to which interpretation can be supported depends on our understanding of the software process and product, and the degree to which we express this understanding as formal rules. Today, interpretation rules exist only for some of the aspects of interest and are only valid within a particular project environment or organization. However, interpretation guided by GQM models will enable an evolutionary learning process resulting in better rules for interpretation in the future. The interpretation process can be much more effective provided historical experience is available allowing for the generation of historical baselines. In this case we can at least identify whether observations made during the current project deviate from past experience or not.

(R5) A mechanism for learning in an organization (derived from components C4, C5).

The learning process is supported by iterating the sequence of defining focused goals, refining them into hypotheses, and running experiments. These experiments can range from completely controlled experiments to regular project executions. In each case we apply measurement and analysis procedures to project classes of interest. For each of those classes, a historical experience base needs to be established concerning the effectiveness of the candidate execution models, methods and tools. Feedback from ongoing projects of the same class, the corresponding execution models, methods and tools can be refined and improved with respect to context and precision/detail so that we increase our potential to improve future projects.

The remaining seven (internal) requirements deal with user interface management, report generation, experience base, security and access control, configuration management control, SEE interface and distribution issues. All these issues are important in order to support planning, construction, learning and feedback effectively.

Internal TAME requirements:

(R6) A homogeneous user interface.

We distinguish between the physical and logical user interface. The physical user interface provides a menu or command driven interface between the user and the TAME system. Graphics and window mechansims will be incorporated whenever useful and possible. The logical user interface reflects the user's view of measurement and analysis. Users will not be allowed to directly access data or run measurement tools. The only way of working with the TAME system is via a GQM model. TAME will enforce this top-down approach to measurement via its logical user interface. The acceptance of this kind of user interface will depend on the effectiveness and ease with which it can be used. Homogeneity is important for both the physical and logical user interface.

(R7) An effective mechanism for presenting data, information, and knowledge.

The presentation of analysis (measurement and interpretation) results via terminal or printer/plotter needs to be supported. Reports need to be generated for different purposes. Project managers will be interested in periodical reports reflecting the current status of their project. High level managers will be interested in reports indicating quality and productivity trends of the organization. The specific interest of each person needs to be defined by one or more GQM models upon which automatic report generation can be based. A laser printer and multicolor plotter would allow the appropriate documentation of tables, histograms, and other kinds of textual and graphical representations.

(R8) The effective storage and retrieval of all relevant data, information, and knowledge in an experience base.

All data, information, and knowledge required to support tailorability and tractability need to be stored in an experience base. Such an experience base needs to store GQM models, engineering products and measurement data. It needs to store data derived from the current project as well as historical data from prior projects. The effectiveness of such an experience base will be improved for the purpose of learning and feedback if, in addition to measurement data, interpretations from various analysis sessions are stored. In the future, the interpretation rules themselves will become integral part of such an experience base. The experience base should be implemented as an abstract data type, accessible through a set of functions and hiding the actual implementation. This latter requirement is especially important due to the fact that current database technology is not suited to properly support software engineering concepts [26]. The implementation of the experience base as an abstract data type allows us to use currently available database technology and substitute more appropriate technology later as it becomes available. The ideal database would be self-adapting to the changing needs of a project environment or an organization. This would require a specification language for software processes and products, and the ability to generate database schemata from specifications written in such a language [46].

(R9) Mechanisms allowing for the implementation of a variety of access control and security strategies.

TAME must control the access of users to the TAME system itself, to various system functions and to the experience base. These are typical functions of a security system. The enforced security strategies depend on the project organization. It is part of planning a project to decide who needs to have access to what functions and pieces of data, information, and knowledge. In addition to these security functions, more sophisticated data access control functions need to be performed. The data access system is expected to "recommend" to a user who is developing a GQM model the kinds of data that might be helpful in answering a particular question and support the process of choosing among similar data based on availability or other criteria.

(R10) Mechanisms allowing for the implementation of a variety of configuration management and control strategies.

In the context of the TAME system we need to manage and control three-dimensional configurations. There is first the traditional product dimension making sure that the various product and document versions are consistent. In addition, each product version needs to be consistent with its related measurement data and the GQM model that guided those measurements. TAME must ensure that a user always knows whether data in the experience base is consistent with the current product version and was collected and interpreted according to a particular model. The actual configuration management and control strategies will result from the project planning activity.

(R11) An interface to a construction-oriented SEE.

An interface between the TAME system (which automates all process model components except for the construction component C3.1 of the TAME process model) and some external SEE (which automates the construction component) is necessary for three reasons: a) to enable the TAME system to collect data (e.g., the number of activations of a compiler, the number of test runs) directly from the actual construction process, b) to enable the TAME system to feed analysis results back into the ongoing construction process, and c) to enable the construction-oriented SEE to store/retrieve products into/from the experience base of the TAME system. Models for appropriate interaction between constructive and analytic processes need to be specified. Interfacing with construction-oriented SEE's poses the problem of efficiently interconnecting systems implemented in different languages and running on different machines (probably with different operating systems).

(R12) A structure suitable for distribution.

TAME will ultimately run on a distributed system consisting of at least one mainframe computer and a number of workstations. The mainframes are required to host the experience base which can be assumed to be very large. The rest of TAME might be replicated on a number of workstations.

B. Architecture

Fig. 2 describes our current view of the TAME architecture in terms of individual architectural components and their control flow interrelationships. The first prototype described in Section IV concentrates on the shaded components of Fig. 2.

We group the TAME components into five logical lev-

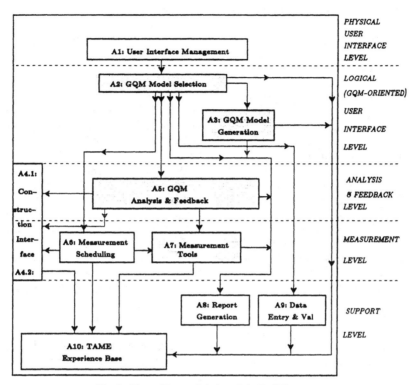

Fig. 2. The architectural design of the TAME system.

els, the physical user interface, logical user interface, analysis and feedback, measurement and support level. Each of these five levels consists of one or more architectural components:

• The Physical User Interface Level consists of one component:

(A1) The User Interface Management component implements the physical user interface requirement R6. It provides a choice of menu or command driven access and supports a window-oriented screen layout.

• The Logical (GQM-Oriented) User Interface Level consists of two components:

(A2) The GQM Model Selection component implements the homogeneity requirement of the logical user interface (R6). It guarantees that no access to the analysis and feedback, measurement, or support level is possible without stating the purpose for access in terms of a specific GQM model.

(A3) The GQM Model Generation component implements requirement R1 regarding the operational and quantifiable definition of GQM models either from scratch or by modifying existing models.

• The Analysis and Feedback Level consists of two components:

(A4.1) This first portion of the Construction Interface component implements the feedback interface between the TAME system and construction-oriented SEEs (part b) of requirement R11).

(A5) The GQM Analysis and Feedback component implements requirement R3 regarding execution and control of an analysis and feedback session, interpretation of the analysis results, and proper feedback. All these activities are done in the context of a GQM model created by A3. The GQM Analysis and Feedback component needs to have access to the specific authorizations of the user in order to know which analysis functions this user can perform. The GQM Analysis and Feedback component also provides analysis functions, for example, telling the user whether certain metrics can be computed based upon the data currently available in the experience base. This analysis feature of the subsystem is used for setting and operationally defining goals, questions, and metrics, as well as actually performing analyses according to those previously established goals, questions, and metrics.

• The Measurement Level consists of three components:

(A4.2) This second portion of the Construction Interface component implements the measurement interface between the TAME system and SEE's (part a) of requirement R11) and the SEE's access to the experience base of the TAME system (part c) of requirement R11).

(A6) The Measurement Scheduling component implements requirement R2 regarding the definition (and execution) of automated data collection strategies. Such strategies for when to collect data via the measurement tools may range from collecting data whenever they are needed for an analysis and feedback session (on-line) to collecting them periodically during low-load times and storing them in the experience base (off-line).

(A7) The Measurement Tools component implements requirement R2 regarding automated data collection. The component needs to be open-ended in order to allow the inclusion of new and different measurement tools as needed.

• The Support Level consists of three components:

(A8) The Report Generation component implements requirement R7 regarding the production of all kinds of reports.

(A9) The Data Entry and Validation component implements requirement R2 regarding the entering of manually collected data and their validation. Validated data are stored in the experience base component.

(A10) The Experience Base component implements requirement R8 regarding the effective storage and retrieval of all relevant data, information and knowledge. This includes all kinds of products, analytical data (e.g., measurement data, interpretations), and analysis plans (GQM models). This component provides the infrastructure for the operation of all other components of the TAME process model and the necessary interactions among them. The experience base will also provide mechanisms supporting the learning and feedback tasks. These mechanisms include the proper packaging of experience along the context and precision/detail dimensions.

In addition, there exist two orthogonal components which for simplicity reasons are not reflected in Fig. 2:

(A11) The Data Access Control and Security component(s) implement requirement R9. There may exist a number of subcomponents distributed across the logical architectural levels. They will validate user access to the TAME system itself and to various functions at the user interface level. They will also control access to the project experience through both the measurement tools and the experience base.

(A12) The Configuration Management and Control component implements requirement R10. This component can be viewed as part of the interface to the experience base level. Data can only be entered into or retrieved from the experience base under configuration management control.

IV. First TAME Prototype

The first in a series of prototypes is currently being developed for supporting measurement in Ada projects [15]. This first prototype will implement only a subset of the requirements stated in Section III-A because of a) yet unsolved problems that require research, b) solutions that require more formalization, and c) problems with integrating the individual architectural components into a consistent whole. Examples of unsolved problems requiring futher research are the appropriate packaging of the experience along the context and precision/detail dimension and expert system support for interpretation purposes. Examples of solutions requiring more formalization are the GQM templates and the designing of a software engineering experience base. Examples of integration problems are the embedding of feedback loops into the construction process, and the appropriate utilization of data access control and configuration management con-

trol mechanisms. At this time, the prototype exists in pieces that have not been fully integrated together as well as partially implemented pieces.

In this section, we discuss for each of the architectural components of this TAME prototype as many of the following issues as are applicable: a) the particular approach chosen for the first prototype, b) experience with this approach, c) the current and planned status of implementation (automation) of the initial approach in the first TAME system prototype, and d) experiences with using the component:

(A1) The User Interface Management component is supposed to provide the physical user interface for accessing all TAME system functions, with the flexibility of choosing between menu and command driven modes and different window layouts. These issues are reasonably well understood by the SEE community. The first TAME prototype implementation will be menu-oriented and based upon the 'X' window mechanism. A primitive version is currently running. This component is currently not very high on our priority list. We expect to import a more sophisticated user interface management component at some later time or leave it completely to parties interested in productizing our prototype system.

(A2) The GQM Model Selection component is supposed to force the TAME user to parameterize each TAME session by first stating the objective of the session in the form of an already existing GQM model or requesting the creation of a new GQM model. The need for this restriction has been derived from the experience that data is frequently misused if it is accessible without a clear goal. The first prototype implementation does not enforce this requirement strictly. The current character of the first prototype as a research vehicle demands more flexibility. There is no question that this component needs to be implemented before the prototype leaves the research environment.

(A3) The GQM Model Generation component is supposed to allow the creation of specific GQM models either from scratch or by modifying existing ones. We have provided a set of templates and guidelines (Section II-B-2). We have been quite successful in the use of the templates and guidelines for defining goals, questions and metrics. There are a large number of organizations and environments in which the model has been applied to specify what data must be collected to evaluate various aspects of the process and product, e.g., NASA/GSFC, Burroughs, AT&T, IBM, Motorola. The application of the GQM paradigm at Hewlett Packard has shown that the templates can be used successfully without our guidance. Several of these experiences have been written up in the literature [4], [16], [17], [39], [48], [56], [60], [61]. We have been less successful in automating the process so that it ties into the experience base. As long as we know the goals and questions *a priori*, the appropriate data can be isolated and collected based upon the GQM paradigm. The first TAME prototype implementation is limited to support the generation of new models and the modificaton of existing models using an editor enforcing the templates and guidelines. We need to further formalize the templates and guidelines and provide traceability between goals and questions. Formalization of the templates and providing traceability is our most important research issue. In the long run we might consider using artificial intelligence planning techniques.

(A4.1 and A4.2) The Construction Interface component is supposed to support all interactions between a SEE (which supports the construction component of the TAME process model) and the TAME system. The model in Fig. 1 implies that interactions in both directions are required. We have gained experience in manually measuring the construction process by monitoring the execution of a variety of techniques (e.g., code reading [57], testing [20], and CLEANROOM development [61]) in various environments including the SEL [4], [48]. We have also learned how analysis results can be fed back into the ongoing construction process as well as into corporate experience [4], [48]. Architectural component A4.1 is not part of this first TAME prototype. The first prototype implementation of A4.2 is limited to allowing for the integration of (or access to) external product libraries. This minimal interface is needed to have access to the objects for measurement. No interface for the on-line measurement of ongoing construction processes is provided yet.

(A5) The GQM Analysis and Feedback component is supposed to perform analysis according to a specific GQM model. We have gained a lot of experience in evaluating various kinds of experiments and case studies. We have been successful in collecting the appropriate data by tracing GQM models top-down. We have been less successful in providing formal interpretation rules allowing for the bottom-up interpretation of the collected data. One automated approach to providing interpretation and feedback is through expert systems. ARROWSMITH-P provides interpretations of software project data to managers [44]; it has been tested in the SEL/NASA environment. The first prototype TAME implementation triggers the collection of prescribed data (top-down) and presents it to the user for interpretation. The user-provided interpretations will be recorded (via a knowledge acquisition system) in order to accumulate the necessary knowledge that might lead us to identifying interpretation rules in the future.

(A6) The Measurement Scheduling component is supposed to allow the TAME user to define a strategy for actually collecting data by running the measurement tools. Choosing the most appropriate of many possible strategies (requirements Section III-A) might depend on the response times expected from the TAME system or the storage capacity of the experience base. Our experience with this issue is limited because most of our analyses were human scheduled as needed [4], [48]. This component will not be implemented as part of the first prototype. In this prototype, the TAME user will trigger the execution of measurement activities explicitly (which can, of course,

be viewed as a minimal implementation supporting a human scheduling strategy).

(A7) The Measurement Tools component is supposed to allow the collection of all kinds of relevant process and product data. We have been successful in generating tools to gather data automatically and have learned from the application of these tools in different environments. Within NASA, for example, we have used a coverage tool to analyze the impact of test plans on the consistency of acceptance test coverage with operational use coverage [53]. We have used a data bindings tool to analyze the structural consistency of implemented systems to their design [41], and studied the relationship between faults and hierarchical structure as measured by the data bindings tool [60]. We have been able to characterize classes of products based upon their syntactic structure [35]. We have not, however, had much experience in automatically collecting process data. The first prototype TAME implementation consists of measurement tools based on the above three. The first tool captures all kinds of basic Ada source code information such as lines of code and structural complexity metrics [35], the second tool computes Ada data binding metrics, and the third tools captures dynamic information such as test coverage metrics [65]. One lesson learned has been that the development of measurement tools for Ada is very often much more than just a reimplementation of similar tools for other languages. This is due to the very different Ada language concepts. Furthermore, we have recognized the importance of having an intermediate representation level allowing for a language independent representation of software product and process aspects. The advantage of such an approach will be that this intermediate representation needs to be generated only once per product or process. All the measurement tools can run on this intermediate representation. This will not only make the actual measurement process less time-consuming but provide a basis for reusing the actual measurement tools to some extent across different language environments. Only the tool generating the intermediate representation needs to be rebuilt for each new implementation language or TAME host enviroment.

(A8) The Report Generator component is supposed to allow the TAME user to produce a variety of reports. The statistics and business communities have commonly accepted approaches for presenting data and interpretations effectively (e.g., histograms). The first TAME prototype implementation does not provide a separate experience base reporting facility. Responsibility for reporting is attached to each individual prototype component; e.g., the GQM Model Generation component provides reports regarding the models, each measurement tool reports on its own measurement data.

(A9) The Data Entry and Validation component is supposed to allow the TAME user to enter all kinds of manually collected data and validate them. Because of the changing needs for measurement, this component must allow for the definition of new (or modification of existing) data collection forms as well as related validation (integrity) rules. If possible, the experience base should be capable of adapting to new needs based upon new form definitions. We have had lots of experience in designing forms and validations rules, using them, and learning about the complicated issues of deriving validation rules [4], [48]. The first prototype implementation will allow the TAME user to input off-line collected measurement data and validate them based upon a fixed and predefined set of data collection forms [currently in use in NASA's Software Engineering Laboratory (SEL)]. This component is designed but not yet completely implemented. The practical use of the TAME prototype requires that this component provide the flexibility for defining and accepting new form layouts. One research issue is identifying the easiest way to define data collection forms in terms of a grammar that could be used to generate the corresponding screen layout and experience base structure.

(A10) The Experience Base component allows for effective storage and retrieval of all relevant experience ranging from products and process plans (e.g., analysis plans in the form of GQM models) to measurement data and interpretations. The experience base needs to mirror the project environment. Here we are relying on the experience of several faculty members of the database group at the University of Maryland. It has been recognized that current database technology is not sufficient, for several reasons, to truly mirror the needs of software engineering projects [26]. The first prototype TAME implementation is built on top of a relational database management system. A first database schema [46] modeling products as well as measurement data has been implemented. We are currently adding GQM models to the schema. The experiences with this first prototype show that the amount of experience stored and its degree of formalism (mostly data) is not yet sufficient. We need to better package that data in order to create pieces of information or knowledge. The GQM paradigm provides a specification of what data needs to be packaged. However, without more formal interpretation rules, the details of packaging cannot be formalized. In the long run, we might include expert system technology. We have also recognized the need for a number of built-in GQM models that can either be reused without modification or guide the TAME user during the process of creating new GQM models.

(A11) The Data Access Control and Security component is supposed to guarantee that only authorized users can access the TAME system and that each user can only access a predefined window of the experience base. The first prototype implements this component only as far as user access to the entire system is concerned.

(A12) The Configuration Management and Control component is supposed to guarantee consistency between the objects of measurement (products and processes), the plans for measurement (GQM models), the data collected from the objects according to these plans, and the attached interpretations. This component will not be implemented in the first prototype.

The integration of all these architectural components is incomplete. At this point in time we have integrated the first versions of the experience base, three measurement tools, a limited version of the GQM analysis and feedback component, the GQM generation component, and the user interface management component. Many of the UNIX® tools (e.g., editors, print facilities) have been integrated into the first prototype TAME system to compensate for yet missing components. This subset of the first prototype is running on a network of SUN-3's under UNIX. It is implemented in Ada and C.

This first prototype enables the user to generate GQM models using a structured editor. Existing models can be selected by using a unique model name. Support for selecting models based on goal definitions or for reusing existing models for the purpose of generating new models is offered, but the refinement of goals into questions and metrics relies on human intervention. Analysis and feedback sessions can be run according to existing GQM models. Only minimal support for interpretation is provided (e.g., histograms of data). Measurement data are presented to the user according to the underlying model for his/her interpretation. Results can be documented on a line printer. The initial set of measurement tools allows only the computation of a limited number of Ada-source-code-oriented static and dynamic metrics. Similar tools might be used in the case of Fortran source code [33].

V. Summary and Conclusions

We have presented a set of software engineering and measurement principles which we have learned during a dozen years of analyzing software engineering processes and products. These principles have led us to recognize the need for software engineering process models that integrate sound planning and analysis into the construction process.

In order to achieve this integration the software engineering process needs to be tailorable and tractable. We need the ability to tailor the execution process, methods and tools to specific project needs in a way that permits maximum reuse of prior experience. We need to control the process and product because of the flexibility required in performing such a focused development. We also need as much automated support as possible. Thus an integrated software engineering environment needs to support all of these issues.

In the TAME project we have developed an improvement-oriented (integrated) process model. It stresses a) the characterization of the current status of a project environment, b) the planning for improvement integrated into software projects, and c) the execution of the project according to the prescribed project plans. Each of these

---

®UNIX is a registered trademark of AT&T Bell Laboratories.

tasks must be dealt with from a constructive and analytic perspective.

To integrate the constructive and analytic aspects of software development, we have used the GQM paradigm. It provides a mechanism for formalizing the characterization and planning tasks, controlling and improving projects based on quantitative analysis, learning in a deeper and more systematic way about the software process and product, and feeding back the appropriate experience to current and future projects.

The effectiveness of the TAME process model depends heavily on appropriate automated support by an ISEE. The TAME system is an instantiation of the TAME process model into an ISEE; it is aimed at supporting all aspects of characterization, planning, analysis, learning, and feedback according to the TAME process model. In addition, it formalizes the feedback and learning mechanisms by supporting the synthesis of project experience, the formalization of its representation, and its tailoring towards specific project needs. It does this by supporting goal development into measurement via templates and guidelines, providing analysis of the development and maintenance processes, and creating and using experience bases (ranging from databases of historical data to knowledge bases that incorporate experience from prior projects).

We discussed a limited prototype of the TAME system, which has been developed as the first of a series of prototypes that will be built using an iterative enhancement model. The limitations of this prototype fall into two categories, limitations of the technology and the need to better formalize the model so that it can be automated.

The short range (1–3 years) goal for the TAME system is to build the analysis environment. The mid-range goal (3–5 years) is to integrate the system into one or more existing or future development or maintenance environments. The long range goal (5–8 years) is to tailor those environments for specific organizations and projects.

The TAME project is ambitious. It is assumed it will evolve over time and that we will learn a great deal from formalizing the various aspects of the TAME project as well as integrating the various paradigms. Research is needed in many areas before the idealized TAME system can be built. Major areas of study include measurement, databases, artificial intelligence, and systems. Specific activities needed to support TAME include: more formalization of the GQM paradigm, the definition of better models for various quality and productivity aspects, mechanisms for better formalizing the reuse and tailoring of project experience, the interpretation of metrics with respect to goals, interconnection languages, language independent representation of software, access control in general and security in particular, software engineering database definition, configuration management and control, and distributed system architecture. We are interested in the role of further researching the ideas and principles of the TAME project. We will build a series of

evolving prototypes of the system in order to learn and test out ideas.

ACKNOWLEDGMENT

The authors thank all their students for many helpful suggestions. We especially acknowledge the many contributions to the TAME project and, thereby indirectly to this paper, by J. Bailey, C. Brophy, M. Daskalantonakis, A. Delis, D. Doubleday, F. Y. Farhat, R. Jeffery, E. E. Katz, A. Kouchakdjian, L. Mark, K. Reed, Y. Rong, T. Sunazuka, P. D. Stotts, B. Swain, A. J. Turner, B. Ulery, S. Wang, and L. Wu. We thank the guest editors and external reviewers for their constructive comments.

REFERENCES

[1] W. Agresti, "SEL Ada experiment: Status and design experience," in *Proc. Eleventh Annu. Software Engineering Workshop*, NASA Goddard Space Flight Center, Greenbelt, MD, Dec. 1986.
[2] J. Bailey and V. R. Basili, "A meta-model for software development resource expenditures," in *Proc. Fifth Int. Conf. Software Engineering*, San Diego, CA, Mar. 1981, pp. 107–116.
[3] V. R. Basili, "Quantitative evaluation of software engineering methodology," in *Proc. First Pan Pacific Computer Conf.*, Melbourne, Australia, Sept. 1985; also available as Tech. Rep. TR-1519, Dep. Comput. Sci., Univ. Maryland, College Park, July 1985.
[4] V. R. Basili, "Can we measure software technology: Lessons learned from 8 years of trying," in *Proc. Tenth Annu. Software Engineering Workshop*, NASA Goddard Space Flight Center, Greenbelt, MD, Dec. 1985.
[5] ——, "Evaluating software characteristics: Assessement of software measures in the Software Engineering Laboratory," in *Proc. Sixth Annu. Software Engineering Workshop*, NASA Goddard Space Flight Center, Greenbelt, MD, 1981.
[6] V. R. Basili and J. Beane, "Can the Parr curve help with the manpower distribution and resource estimation problems," *J. Syst. Software*, vol. 2, no. 1, pp. 59–69, 1981.
[7] V. R. Basili and K. Freburger, "Programming measurement and estimation in the Software Engineering Laboratory," *J. Syst. Software*, vol. 2, no. 1, pp. 47–57, 1981.
[8] V. R. Basili and D. H. Hutchens, "An empirical study of a syntactic measure family," *IEEE Trans. Software Eng.*, vol. SE-9, no. 11, pp. 664–672, Nov. 1983.
[9] V. R. Basili and E. E. Katz, "Measures of interest in an Ada development," in *Proc. IEEE Comput. Soc. Workshop Software Engineering Technology Transfer*, Miami, FL, Apr. 1983, pp. 22–29.
[10] V. R. Basili, E. E. Katz, N. M. Panlilio-Yap, C. Loggia Ramsey, and S. Chang, "Characterization of an Ada software development," *Computer*, pp. 53–65, Sept. 1985.
[11] V. R. Basili and C. Loggia Ramsey, "ARROWSMITH-P: A prototype expert system for software engineering management," in *Proc. IEEE Symp. Expert Systems in Government*, Oct. 23–25, 1985, pp. 252–264.
[12] V. R. Basili and N. M. Panlilio-Yap, "Finding relationships between effort and other variables in the SEL," in *Proc. IEEE COMPSAC*, Oct. 1985.
[13] V. R. Basili and B. Perricone, "Software errors and complexity: An empirical investigation," *ACM, Commun.*, vol. 27, no. 1, pp. 45–52, Jan. 1984.
[14] V. R. Basili and R. Reiter, Jr., "A controlled experiment quantitatively comparing software development approaches," *IEEE Trans. Software Eng.*, vol. SE-7, no. 5, pp. 299–320, May 1981.
[15] V. R. Basili and H. D. Rombach, "TAME: Tailoring an Ada measurement environment," in *Proc. Joint Ada Conf.*, Arlington, VA, Mar. 16–19, 1987, pp. 318–325.
[16] ——, "Tailoring the software process to project goals and environments," in *Proc. Ninth Int. Conf. Software Engineering*, Monterey, CA, Mar. 30–Apr. 2, 1987, pp. 345–357.
[17] ——, "TAME: Integrating measurement into software environments," Dep. Comput. Sci., Univ. Maryland, College Park, Tech. Rep. TR-1764 (TAME-TR-1-1987), June 1987.

[18] —, "Software reuse: A framework," in *Proc. Tenth Minnowbrook Workshop Software Reuse*, Blue Mountain Lake, NY, Aug. 1987.

[19] V. R. Basili and R. W. Selby, Jr., "Data collection and analysis in software research and management," in *Proc. Amer. Statist. Ass. and Biomeasure Soc. Joint Statistical Meetings*, Philadelphia, PA, Aug. 13-16, 1984.

[20] —, "Comparing the effectiveness of software testing strategies," *IEEE Trans. Software Eng.*, vol. SE-13, no. 12, pp. 1278-1296, Dec. 1987.

[21] —, "Calculation and use of an environment's characteristic software metric set," in *Proc. Eighth Int. Conf. Software Engineering*, London, England, Aug. 1985.

[22] V. R. Basili, R. W. Selby, and D. H. Hutchens, "Experimentation in software engineering," *IEEE Trans. Software Eng.*, vol. SE-12, no. 7, pp. 733-743, July 1986.

[23] V. R. Basili, R. W. Selby, and T.-Y. Phillips, "Metric analysis and data validation across Fortran projects," *IEEE Trans. Software Eng.*, vol. SE-9, no. 6, pp. 652-663, Nov. 1983.

[24] V. R. Basili and A. J. Turner, "Iterative enhancement: A practical technique for software development," *IEEE Trans. Software Eng.*, vol. SE-1, no. 4, pp. 390-396, Dec. 1975.

[25] V. R. Basili and D. M. Weiss, "A methodology for collecting valid software engineering data," *IEEE Trans. Software Eng.*, vol. SE-10, no. 3, pp. 728-738, Nov. 1984.

[26] P. A. Bernstein, "Database system support for software engineering," in *Proc. Ninth Int. Conf. Software Engineering*, Monterey, CA, Mar. 30-Apr. 2, 1987, pp. 166-178.

[27] D. Bjorner, "On the use of formal methods in software development," in *Proc. Ninth Int. Conf. Software Engineering*, Monterey, CA, Mar. 30-Apr. 2, 1987, pp. 17-29.

[28] B. W. Boehm, "Software engineering," *IEEE Trans. Comput.*, vol. C-25, no. 12, pp. 1226-1241, Dec. 1976.

[29] —, *Software Engineering Economics*. Englewood Cliffs, NJ: Prentice-Hall, 1981.

[30] —, "A spiral model of software development and enhancement," *ACM Software Eng. Notes*, vol. 11, no. 4, pp. 22-42, Aug. 1986.

[31] B. W. Boehm, J. R. Brown, and M. Lipow, "Quantitative evaluation of software quality," in *Proc. Second Int. Conf. Software Engineering*, 1976, pp. 592-605.

[32] C. Brophy, W. Agresti, and V. R. Basili, "Lessons learned in use of Ada oriented design methods," in *Proc. Joint Ada Conf.*, Arlington, VA, Mar. 16-19, 1987, pp. 231-236.

[33] W. J. Decker and W. A. Taylor, "Fortran static source code analyzer program (SAP)," NASA Goddard Space Flight Center, Greenbelt, MD, Tech. Rep. SEL-82-002, Aug. 1982.

[34] C. W. Doerflinger and V. R. Basili, "Monitoring software development through dynamic variables," *IEEE Trans. Software Eng.*, vol. SE-11, no. 9, pp. 978-985, Sept. 1985.

[35] D. L. Doubleday, "ASAP: An Ada static source code analyzer program," Dep. Comput. Sci., Univ. Maryland, College Park, Tech. Rep. TR-1895, Aug. 1987.

[36] M. Dowson, "ISTAR—An integrated project support environment," in *ACM Sigplan Notices (Proc. Second ACM Software Eng. Symp. Practical Development Support Environments)*, vol. 2, no. 1, Jan. 1987.

[37] M. Dyer, "Cleanroom software development method," IBM Federal Systems Division, Bethesda, MD, Oct. 14, 1982.

[38] J. Gannon, E. E. Katz, and V. R. Basili, "Measures for Ada packages: An initial study," *Commun. ACM*, vol. 29, no. 7, pp. 616-623, July 1986.

[39] R. B. Grady, "Measuring and managing software maintenance," *IEEE Software*, vol. 4, no. 5, pp. 35-45, Sept. 1987.

[40] M. H. Halstead, *Elements of Software Science*. New York: Elsevier North-Holland, 1977.

[41] D. H. Hutchens and V. R. Basili, "System structure analysis: Clustering with data bindings," *IEEE Trans. Software Eng.*, vol. SE-11, pp. 749-757, Aug. 1985.

[42] E. E. Katz and V. R. Basili, "Examining the modularity of Ada programs," in *Proc. Joint Ada Conf.*, Arlington, VA, Mar. 16-19, 1987, pp. 390-396.

[43] E. E. Katz, H. D. Rombach, and V. R. Basili, "Structure and maintainability of Ada programs: Can we measure the differences?" in *Proc. Ninth Minnowbrook Workshop Software Performance Evaluation*, Blue Mountain Lake, NY, Aug. 5-8, 1986.

[44] C. Loggia Ramsey and V. R. Basili, "An evaluation of expert systems for software engineering management," Dep. Comput. Sci., Univ. Maryland, College Park, Tech. Rep. TR-1708, Sept. 1986.

[45] M. Marcus, K. Sattley, S. C. Schaffner, and E. Albert, "DAPSE: A distributed Ada programming support environment," in *Proc. IEEE Second Int. Conf. Ada Applications and Environments*, 1986, pp. 115-125.

[46] L. Mark and H. D. Rombach, "A meta information base for software engineering," Dep. Comput. Sci., Univ. Maryland, College Park, Tech. Rep. TR-1765, July 1987.

[47] T. J. McCabe, "A complexity measure," *IEEE Trans. Software Eng.*, vol. SE-2, no. 4, pp. 308-320, Dec. 1976.

[48] F. E. McGarry, "Recent SEL studies," in *Proc. Tenth Annu. Software Engineering Workshop*, NASA Goddard Space Flight Center, Greenbelt, MD, Dec. 1985.

[49] L. Osterweil, "Software processes are software too," in *Proc. Ninth Int. Conf. Software Engineering*, Monterey, CA, Mar. 30-Apr. 2, 1987, pp. 2-13.

[50] F. N. Parr, "An alternative to the Rayleigh curve model for software development effort," *IEEE Trans. Software Eng.*, vol. SE-6, no. 5, pp. 291-296, May 1980.

[51] L. Putnam, "A general empirical solution to the macro software sizing and estimating problem," *IEEE Trans. Software Eng.*, vol. SE-4, no. 4, pp. 345-361, Apr. 1978.

[52] C. V. Ramamoorthy, Y. Usuda, W.-T. Tsai, and A. Prakash, "GENESIS: An integrated environment for supporting development and evolution of software," in *Proc. COMPSAC*, 1985.

[53] J. Ramsey and V. R. Basili, "Analyzing the test process using structural coverage," in *Proc. Eighth Int. Conf. Software Engineering*, London, England, Aug. 1985, pp. 306-311.

[54] H. D. Rombach, "Software design metrics for maintenance," in *Proc. Ninth Annu. Software Engineering Workshop*, NASA Goddard Space Flight Center, Greenbelt, MD, Nov. 1984.

[55] —, "A controlled experiment on the impact of software structure on maintainability," *IEEE Trans. Software Eng.*, vol. SE-13, no. 3, pp. 344-354, Mar. 1987.

[56] H. D. Rombach and V. R. Basili, "A quantitative assessment of software maintenance: An industrial case study," in *Proc. Conf. Software Maintenance*, Austin, TX, Sept. 1987, pp. 134-144.

[57] H. D. Rombach, V. R. Basili, and R. W. Selby, Jr., "The role of code reading in the software life cycle," in *Proc. Ninth Minnowbrook Workshop Software Performance Evaluation*, Blue Mountain Lake, NY, August 5-8, 1986.

[58] W. W. Royce, "Managing the development of large software systems: Concepts and techniques," in *Proc. WESCON*, Aug. 1970.

[59] R. W. Selby, Jr., "Incorporating metrics into a software environment," in *Proc. Joint Ada Conf.*, Arlington, VA, Mar. 16-19, 1987, pp. 326-333.

[60] R. W. Selby and V. R. Basili, "Analyzing error-prone system coupling and cohesion," Dep. Comput. Sci., Univ. Maryland, College Park, Tech. Rep., in preparation.

[61] R. W. Selby, Jr., V. R. Basili, and T. Baker, "CLEANROOM software development: An empirical evaluation," *IEEE Trans. Software Eng.*, vol. SE-13, no. 9, pp. 1027-1037, Sept. 1987.

[62] C. E. Walston and C. P. Felix, "A method of programming measurement and estimation," *IBM Syst. J.*, vol. 16, no. 1, pp. 54-73, 1977.

[63] A. I. Wasserman and P. A. Pircher, "Visible connections," *UNIX Rev.*, Oct. 1986.

[64] *Webster's New Collegiate Dictionary*. Springfield, MA: Merriam, 1981.

[65] L. Wu, V. R. Basili, and K. Reed, "A structure coverage tool for Ada software systems," in *Proc. Joint Ada Conf.*, Arlington, VA, Mar. 16-19, 1987, pp. 294-303.

[66] M. Zelkowitz, R. Yeh, R. Hamlet, J. Gannon, and V. R. Basili, "Software engineering practices in the U.S. and Japan," *Computer*, pp. 57-66, June 1984.

Software Metrics in the Process Maturity Framework

Shari Lawrence Pfleeger and Clement McGowan

The Contel Technology Center's Software Engineering Laboratory (SEL) has as one of its goals the improvement of software productivity and quality throughout Contel Corporation. The SEL's Process and Metrics Project addresses that goal in part by recommending metrics to be collected on each software development project throughout the corporation. This article suggests a set of metrics for which data are to be collected and analyzed, based on a process maturity framework developed at the Software Engineering Institute. Metrics are to be implemented step by step in five levels, corresponding to the maturity level of the development process. Level 1 metrics provide a baseline for comparison as improvements are sought. Level 2 metrics focus on project management. At the third level, metrics measure the products produced during development, while level 4 metrics capture characteristics of the development process itself to allow control of the process. Finally, the feedback loops of level 5's process metrics permit the metrics to be used to change and improve the development process.

1. INTRODUCTION

Dozens, if not hundreds, of software metrics are described in the software engineering literature [1]. The metrics chosen for a particular project play a major role in the degree to which the project can be controlled, but deciding which metrics to use is difficult. We can evaluate the purpose and utility of each metric only in light of the needs and desires of the development organization. Thus, we should collect data and analyze software metrics in the broad context of the software development process and with an eye toward understanding and improvement. It is for this reason that we at the Contel Technology Center's Software Engineering Laboratory have chosen a process maturity framework in which to place software metrics. Originating at the Software Engineering Institute, process maturity [2] describes a set of maturity levels at which an organization's development process takes place. Only when the

development process possesses sufficient structure and procedures does it make sense to collect certain kinds of metrics.

Thus, rather than recommend a large (and probably unwiedly) set of metrics to collect for each project throughout an organization, we recommend that metrics be divided into five levels, where each level is based on the amount of information made available by the development process. As the development process matures and improves, additional metrics can be collected and analyzed. In turn, the new information derived from the metrics allows the process to be controlled and enhanced. Thus, metrics collection begins at maturity level 1, moving on to the other levels only when dictated by a process that can support it.

This article explores the idea of process maturity and explains how process maturity levels are integrated naturally with metrics collection. We give examples of metrics at level, and we describe how the process and metrics program is working at Contel to improve the quality of our software.

2. PROCESS MATURITY LEVELS

The concept of process maturity is based on the notion that some development processes provide more structure or control than others. In effect, as certain characteristic process problems are solved by process methods and tools (e.g., configuration management), the process matures and can focus on other problems. Thus, maturity provides a framework in which to depict the several types of processes and to evaluate what kinds of metrics are best suited for collection in each type. The metrics, in concert with a variety of tools, techniques, and methods, are used to improve the process, increase the maturity level, and allow additional metrics collection to take place.

Figure 1 depicts the five levels of process and their characteristics. Assessing or determining the level of process maturity is the first step in deciding what metrics to collect.

Address correspondence to Shari Lawrence Pfleeger, Contel Technology Center, 15000 Conference Center Drive, P.O. Box 10814, Chantilly, VA 22021-3808.

Reprinted from *J. Systems and Software,* Vol. 12, S.L. Pfleeger and C. McGowan, "Software Metrics in the Process Maturity Framework," pp. 255–261, 1990, with kind permission from Elsevier Science–NL, Sara Burgerhartstraat 25; 1055 KV Amsterdam, The Netherlands.

Level	Characteristics	Metrics to Use
5. Optimizing	Improvement fed back to process	Process + feedback for changing process
4. Managed	Measured process (quantitative)	Process + feedback for control
3. Defined	Process defined, institutionalized	Product
2. Repeatable	Process dependent on individuals	Project
1. Initial	Ad hoc	Baseline

Figure 1. Process maturity levels related to metrics.

2.1 Level 1: Initial Process

The first level of process is termed *initial* and is characterized by an ad hoc approach to the software development process. That is, the inputs to the process are ill-defined, the outputs are expected, but the transition from inputs to outputs is undefined and uncontrolled. Similar projects may vary widely in their productivity and quality characteristics, because of lack of adequate structure and control. For this level of process maturity, the collection of metrics is difficult. Preliminary "baseline" project metrics should be gathered at this level to form a basis for comparison as improvements are made and maturity increases. The degree of improvement can be demonstrated in part by comparing new project measurements with the baseline ones. For example, initial measurements can be made of product size and staff effort, to determine a baseline rate of productivity; this rate can be compared with similar rates on subsequent projects. However, rather than concentrate on metrics and their meanings, the developers using a level 1 process should focus on imposing more structure and control on the process itself.

2.2 Level 2: Repeatable Process

The second process level, called *repeatable*, identifies inputs, outputs and, constraints. The requirements act as input, the code is output, and typical constraints are budget and schedule limits. The process is repeatable in the same way that a subroutine is repeatable: Proper inputs produce proper outputs, but we have no visibility into how the outputs are produced. Figure 2 depicts a repeatable process as an SADT diagram, where the incoming arrow on the left shows the input, the outgoing arrow on the right the output, and the arrow from the top the control or constraints. For example, the requirements may be the input to the process, with the software system as output. The control arrow represents constraints, such as schedule, budget, tools, standards, and other management control directives.

Only project-related metrics make sense at this level, since the activities within the actual transition from input to output are not available to be measured. Figure 3 illustrates the types of measures that make sense by associating measurable characteristics with each arrow. Notice that an additional arrow has been placed below the box to represent the personnel working on the project. Thus, for a repeatable process, we can measure the amount of effort needed to develop a system, the duration of the project, the size and volatility of the requirements, and the overall project cost, for example. The output can be measured in terms of its physical or functional size, and the resources used to produce that output can be viewed relative to size to compute productivity.

At Contel, we recommend that development organizations at the repeatable level include the following types of measures (the italicized metrics are examples of measures at this level; the metrics are defined and explained

Figure 2. SADT diagram of repeatable process.

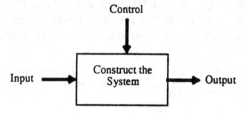

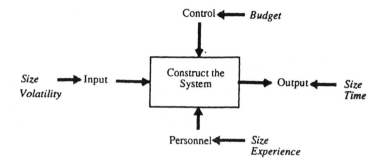

Figure 3. Measures for a repeatable process.

in detail in a technical report [3]):

- Software Size
  Noncommented source lines of code
  Function points
  Object and method count
- Personnel Effort
  Actual person-months of effort
  Reported person-months of effort
- Requirements Volatility
  Requirements changes

Several additional metrics may be desirable, depending on the characteristics of the project and the needs of project management. Many studies of project cost indicate that relevant technical experience and employee turnover can have a significant impact on overall project cost. Thus, the following items can be added to the level 2 metrics set at the discretion of management.

- Experience
  With domain/application
  With development architecture
  With tools/methods
  Overall years of experience
- Employee turnover

2.3 Level 3: Defined Process

The third process maturity level is called *defined*, because the activities of the process are clearly defined with entry and exit conditions, as depicted in Figure 4.

This additional structure means that we can examine the input to and output from each well-defined functional activity performed during development. That is, the intermediate products of development are well-defined and visible. This characteristic of the process allows us to measure characteristics of the intermediate products. Thus, the box of Figure 2 can be decomposed to view the activities necessary to construct the final system. Figure 4 describes three typical activities: design, build parts, and assemble. However, different processes may be partitioned into more distinct functions or activities. Figure 5 is an example of a simplified diagram suggesting the details of input, output, and control for each activity in a defined process.

Because the activities are delineated and distinguished from one another, the products from each activity can be measured and assessed, as shown in Figure 6. In particular, project managers can look at the complexity of each product. That is, we can examine the complexity of the requirements, design, code, and test plans, and assess the quality of the requirements, design, code, and testing.

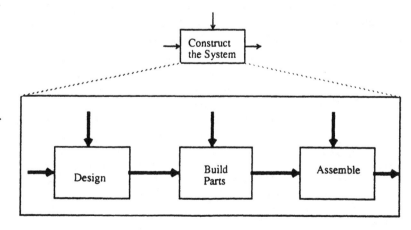

Figure 4. SADT diagram of defined process.

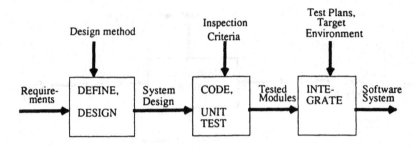

Figure 5. Example of a particular defined process.

In terms of complexity, we suggest that the following items be measured for a defined process:

- Requirements complexity
  Number of distinct objects and actions addressed in requirements
- Design complexity
  Number of design modules
  Cyclomatic complexity
  McCabe design complexity
- Code complexity
  Number of code modules
  Cyclomatic complexity
- Test complexity
  Number of paths to test
  If object-oriented development, number of object interfaces to test

One perspective from which to view the quality of the products is examination of the number of faults in each product and the density of defects overall. In addition, we can assess the thoroughness of testing. Thus, our recommended quality metrics include:

- Defects discovered
- Defects discovered per unit size (defect density)
- Requirements faults discovered
- Design faults discovered
- Code faults discovered
- Fault density for each product

We emphasize that this set does not represent the full spectrum of quality measures that can be employed. Issues of maintainability, utility, ease of use, and other aspects of quality software are not addressed by defect counts. However, defect analysis is relative easy to implement, and it provides a wide spectrum of useful information about the reliability of the software and the thoroughness of testing.

An additional product metric may be desirable. When customer requirements dictate that significant amounts of documentation be written (as often happens on government contracts), the number of pages of documentation may be a desirable measure to track and correlate with effort or duration. Thus, the set of product metrics may also include:

- Pages of documentation

2.4 Level 4: Managed Process

The *managed* process is the fourth level of maturity. Here, feedback from early project activities (e.g., problem areas discovered in design) can be used to set priorities for later project activities (e.g., more extensive review and testing of certain code). Because activities can be compared and contrasted, the effects of changes in one activity can be tracked in the others. In a managed process, the feedback determines how resources are deployed; the basic activities themselves do not change. As shown in Figure 7, this level allows measurements to be made across activities. For example, we can measure and evaluate the effects of major process factors such as reuse, defect-driven testing, and configuration management. The measures collected are used to control and stabilize the process, so that productivity and quality match expectations.

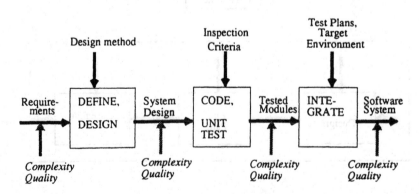

Figure 6. Measures for a particular defined process.

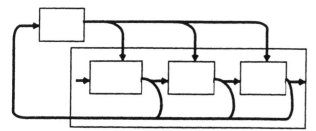

Figure 7. SADT diagram of managed process.

Figure 8 illustrates how a particular managed process might took. Metrics are used in feedback loops to report on the number of design defects and on the number and types of problems encountered with specific versions of the system. Then, project management uses the metrics information to make decisions about course corrections.

If the maturity of the process has reached the managed level, then process-wide metrics can be collected and analyzed. These metrics reflect characteristics of the overall process and of the interaction among major activities in the process, as shown in Figure 9. A distinguishing characteristic of a managed process is that the software development can be carefully controlled. Thus, a major characteristic of the recommended metrics is that they help management control the development process.

We recommend that the following types of data be collected for a managed process. In some cases, the actual metrics must be defined and analyzed to suit the development organization.

Process type. What process model is used in development? For example, the waterfall, prototype, and transformational development paradigms are very different. In concert with other product and process characteristics, the type of process may correlate highly with certain positive or negative consequences.

Amount of producer reuse. How much is designed for reuse? This measure includes reuse of requirements, design modules, and test plans as well as code. By de-

signing components for reuse, one project group may benefit from the effort of another group. Effort in understanding, creating, and testing code can be minimized, thus making the project easier to control. Furthermore, future projects can benefit from the reuse of components produced here.

Amount of consumer reuse. How much does the project reuse components from other projects? This measure includes reuse of requirements, design modules, and test plans as well as code. By using tested, proven components, effort can be minimized and quality can be improved.

Defect identification. How and when are defects discovered? Knowing whether defects are discovered during requirements reviews, design reviews, code walkthroughs, and reviews, integration testing or acceptance testing will tell us whether those process activities are effective.

Use of defect density model for testing. To what extent does the number of defects determine when testing is complete? Many organizations have no overall defect goals for testing the product. Thus, there is no way to judge the quality either of the testing or of the code. The use of defect density models has been shown to control and focus testing, as well as to increase the quality of the final product.

Use of configuration management. Is a configuration management scheme imposed on the development process? Configuration management and change control work to afford management a great deal of control over the development process. Traceability links can be used to assess the impact of alterations in some or all development activities or products.

Module completion over time. At what rates are modules being completed? Although ostensibly a prod-

Figure 8. Example of a managed process.

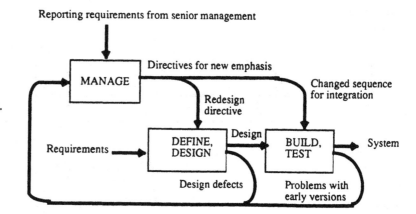

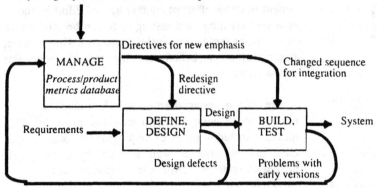

Reporting requirements from senior management

Directives for new emphasis

MANAGE
Process/product metrics database

Redesign directive

Changed sequence for integration

Requirements

DEFINE, DESIGN

Design

BUILD, TEST

System

Design defects

Problems with early versions

Distribution of defects, productivity of tasks, plans vs. actuals, resource allocation

Figure 9. Measures in a managed process.

uct metric, the rate at which modules are identified, designed, coded, tested, and integrated reflects the degree to which the process and development environment facilitate implementation and testing. If the rate is slow, the process may need improvement.

All of the process metrics described above are to be used in concert with the metrics discussed in earlier sections. Relationships can be determined between product characteristics and process variables to assess whether certain processes or aspects of the process are effective at meeting productivity or quality goals. The list of process measures is by no means complete. It is suggested only as an initial attempt to capture important information about the process itself.

2.5 Level 5: Optimizing Process

An *optimizing* process is the ultimate level of process maturity; it is depicted in Figure 10. Here, measures from activities are used to change and improve the process. This process change can affect the organization and the project as well. Results from one or more ongoing or completed projects may lead to a refined, different development process for future projects. In addition, a project may change its process before project completion, in response to feedback from early activities. The spiral model of development is such a process [5].

This dynamic tailoring of the process to the situation is indicated in the figure by the collection of process boxes labeled $T_0, T_1, \ldots, T_n$. At time T_0, the process is as represented by box T_0. However, at time T_i, management has the option of revising or changing the overall process. For example, the project manager may begin development with a standard waterfall approach. As requirements are defined and design is begun, metrics may indicate a high degree of uncertainty in the requirements. Based on this information, the process may change to one that prototypes the requirements and the design, so that we can resolve some of the uncertainty before substantial investment is made in implementation of the current design. In this way, an optimizing process gives maximum flexibility to the development. Metrics act as sensors and monitors, and the process is not only under control but is dynamic, too.

Studies by the Software Engineering Institute of 113 software development projects report that 85% of those surveyed were at level 1, 14% were at level 2, and 1% were at level 3. That is, none of the development projects had reached levels 4 or 5: the managed or optimizing levels. Based on these results, and the highly unlikely prospect of finding a level 5 project, our recommendations for initial metrics include only the first four levels.

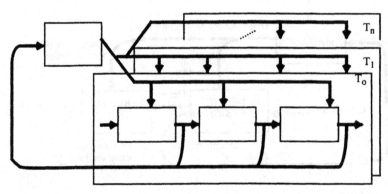

T_n

T_1

T_0

Figure 10. SADT diagram of optimizing process.

3. STEPS TO TAKE IN USING METRICS

Metrics are most useful only when implemented in a careful sequence of process-related activities. These activities lay the groundwork for effective project management by evaluating the needs and characteristics of development before identifying the appropriate metrics to collect. The typical development organization should take the following steps:

Assess the process. Working with a set of guidelines or with a process and metrics team, determine the level of process maturity desired (for a proposed project) or implemented (for an ongoing one).

Determine the appropriate metrics to collect. Once the process maturity level is known, decide which metrics to collect. For example, if level 2 is indicated by the process level, but the ongoing project currently collects no metrics data at all, then level 1 metrics may be suggested as a starting point, with level 2 metrics to be added at a later time.

Recommend metrics, tools, techniques. When the types of metrics are determined, identify tools and techniques to be used on the project. Choose these tools and techniques with the overall goals of the project in mind. Whenever possible, implement automated support for metrics collection and analysis as part of the project development environment. It is essential that metrics collection and analysis not impede the primary development activities; thus, metrics collection and analysis should be as unobtrusive as possible.

Estimate project cost and schedule. Having determined the process level and selected the development environment, estimate the cost and schedule of the project. By using measures implemented at levels 1 or 2, continue to monitor the actual cost and schedule during development.

Collect appropriate level of metrics. Oversee the collection of metrics.

Construct project data base. Design, develop and populate a project data base of metrics data. This data base can be used for analysis, where appropriate. Track the value of metrics over time, as recommended by Schultz [4] and others, to determine trends and to understand how project and product characteristics change.

Cost and schedule evaluation. When the project is complete, evaluate the initial estimates of cost and schedule for accuracy. Determine which of the factors may account for discrepancies between predicted and actual values.

Evaluate productivity and quality. Make an overall assessment of project productivity and product quality, based on the metrics available.

Form a basis for future estimates. Finally, incorporate the project metrics in a corporate or organizational metrics data base. This larger data base can provide historical information as a basis for estimation on future projects. In addition, the data base can be used to suggest the most appropriate tools and techniques for proposed projects.

We are following these steps today at Contel. As a result of our process and metrics program, a large Ada development project is collecting complexity information using automated tools. A tool development project using Objective C is counting objects and methods to track the size of the project; defects and their severity levels are also being monitored to assess the level of product quality. Likewise, satellite and telephone operations development groups are looking at a process maturity-based metrics approach to aid decisions about productivity and quality. Eventually, our corporate metrics data base will allow project managers to make decisions based on evidence from previous, similar projects.

4. EXPECTED BENEFITS

The increased understanding of the process and the control of the project offered by a process maturity approach outweigh the effort needed to capture, store, and analyze the information required. Objective evaluation of any new technique, tool, or method is impossible without quantitative data describing its effect. Thus, the use of metrics in a process maturity framework should result in

- enhanced understanding of the process.
- increased control of the process.
- a clear migration path to more mature process levels.
- more accurate estimates of project cost and schedule.
- more objective evaluations of changes in technique, tool, or method.
- more accurate estimates of the effects of changes on project cost and schedule.

REFERENCES

1. S. D. Conte, H. E. Dunsmore, and V. Y. Shen, *Software Engineering Metrics and Models*, Benjamin-Cummings, Menlo Park, California, 1986.
2. Watts Humphrey, *Managing the Software Process*, Addison-Wesley, Reading, Massachusetts, 1989.
3. Shari Lawrence Pfleeger, *Recommendations for an Initial Set of Metrics*, Contel Technology Center Technical Report CTC-TR-89-017, Chantilly, Virginia, 1989.
4. Herman P. Schultz, *Software Management Metrics*, Mitre Technical Report M88-1-ESD-TR-88-001, Bedford, Massachusetts, 1988.
5. B. W. Boehm, A Spiral Model of Software Development and Enhancement," *IEEE Computer*, May 1988.

Edward N. Adams

Optimizing Preventive Service of Software Products

The implementer of a large, complex software system cannot make it completely defect free, so he must normally provide fixes for defects found after the code is put into service. A system user may do preventive service by installing these fixes before the defects cause him problems. Preventive service can benefit both the software developer and the software user to the extent that it reduces the number of operational problems caused by software errors, but it requires the expenditure of the resources required to prepare, disseminate, and install fixes; and it can be the cause of additional software problems caused by design errors introduced into the code by fixes. The benefit from removing a given defect depends on how many problems it would otherwise cause. Benefits may be estimated by modeling problem occurrence as a random process in execution time governed by a distribution of characteristic rates. It is found that most of the benefit to be realized by preventive service comes from removing a relatively small number of high-rate defects that are found early in the service life of the code. For the typical user corrective service would seem preferable to preventive service as a way of dealing with most defects found after code has had some hundreds of months of usage.

Introduction

It is difficult to create a very large software product that is completely free of design errors (DEs). Accordingly, the software producer must provide means to correct user code for DEs not eliminated during product development. We term the process of correcting a user's code to eliminate a DE that is causing him a problem Corrective Service (CS) and the process of correcting his code to eliminate a DE that has not yet caused him a problem Preventive Service (PS).

Where a software system has many hundreds or thousands of users it is commonly the case that for every user problem caused by a previously unknown DE (a "discovery"), there will be several problems caused by already known DEs ("rediscoveries"). In such a situation, if all users would perform the PS to remove a DE soon after it is discovered, it would be possible to avert most of the user problems requiring CS to DEs in the product software. A program of thorough PS could be of considerable value to the software producer, since to the extent that it reduced his software product costs, it would permit him to realize higher effective product quality and to offer service at a lower price; and it could benefit the software user both in terms of lower cost and higher quality of software and in terms of a reduction in costs due to unscheduled interruptions of service caused by product software DEs.

However, PS like CS has its costs. It consumes the developer resources needed to prepare and distribute media for mass dissemination of the fixes, and it consumes user resources of operational time and staff to install fixes preventively. Moreover, PS is to some extent an original source of problems, since the code fixes themselves occasionally inject new DEs into the code.

The studies reported here were done over the period 1975–80 with the objective of developing means to estimate whether and under what circumstances PS is worthwhile to do. We report on

- The model we used to project the occurrence of user software problems;
- The results of fitting the model to historical error data;
- Our conclusions about how to carry out an optimum program of PS.

"Optimizing Preventive Service of Software Products," by E.N. Adams from *IBM J. Research and Development*, Vol. 28, No. 1, Jan. 1984, pp. 2–14, 1993,

The scenario for software service

Software service of the products we studied involved this series of events: The user of an IBM software product reported to an IBM Customer Engineer (CE) that he had a problem believed to be caused by a DE in the product. The CE diagnosed the source of the problem; if it was a DE in IBM code, he reported it to an IBM change team in a form called an APAR. The change team studied the APAR and, if the DE proved valid, prepared and sent to the user a code change that would avert the user's immediate problem.

Next the change team refined and tested the code change more comprehensively, and incorporated the finished version into a Program Temporary Fix (PTF), which is a vehicle for transmitting the changed module(s) of the product code. The change team transferred the PTF to another IBM group, which assembled PTFs on tapes for periodic distribution to users. Later an IBM development group might further process the PTFs and incorporate them into an updated version of the product. An IBM library facility distributed PTF tapes at frequent intervals, approximately monthly in the first months after First Customer Shipment (FCS) of the product. A PTF tape typically incorporated fixes for all significant errors found in the product up to a time one or two months before the tape was put in the library, and it took about a month to get the tapes from the distribution center to the average user. Accordingly, a user having the most recent PTF tape could assume that he had fixes for most errors discovered more than three months earlier.

Some users installed all PTFs preventively, some installed only selected PTFs, some just kept PTFs as an immediate source for fixes if need arose. Some users would install the PTFs only after waiting to see whether other users who had installed them had encountered new DEs caused by the fixes in the PTFs.

More often than not when a DE caused a user problem the problem proved to be a rediscovery. A rediscovery of a DE was somewhat easier to deal with than an original discovery, since much was already known about the DE and fixes for it were available. Even so a rediscovery was costly both to IBM and to the user.

For many products having large usership, problems caused by rediscoveries were more numerous than problems caused by original discoveries, even to the extent that they were the dominant factor in service cost. For such products the IBM service organization encouraged users to do prompt PS for all DEs. However, the users seemed more aware of the costs and risks of PS than they were persuaded of the benefits. (It is difficult to demonstrate the benefits realized from PS, since they must be quantified in terms of hypothetical events that PS is believed to have averted.) For whatever reason most users were unwilling to preventively install PTFs *en masse*.

Modeling the occurrence of errors

How to evaluate the benefits from PS is simple in principle. Some interval of time is required after a DE is discovered to prepare a change to the base code and install it in the users' versions of the code. Rediscoveries that occur in this time interval cannot be avoided; rediscoveries that would have occurred after this interval will be averted. One must determine the time interval between discovery and fix for the system arrangements in use and project what problems would have occurred after this interval. One then reckons what it is worth to avert these problems.

To carry through such an evaluation one needs means to project the numbers and times of the rediscoveries that would have followed each discovery. When we began our work little was known about the statistics of occurrence of rediscoveries, since no records were kept that summarized for a given DE the rediscoveries that followed it.

However, we had one piece of qualitative information that provided the key to understanding the time patterns of rediscovery. Persons familiar with the service scene reported that particular DEs were quite "virulent," causing problems to many users, but that many DEs were rather innocuous. We realized that if the "virulence" of a DE were a manifestation of the average rate at which the DE caused problems under operational circumstances, the times of rediscovery of a DE could be projected from its quantified virulence.

In accordance with this idea we adopted the following model for dealing with problem occurrence: In operational circumstances each DE in a product manifests a characteristic problem rate R. The occurrence of each problem caused by the DE, whether the original discovery or a rediscovery, is an event in a Poisson process, in which problem events occur at random times with an average rate R. The cumulative running time of all users plays the role of time in the Poisson process. The error rate of a product is the sum of the error rates associated with the individual DEs. The rates associated with different DEs may range over a wide spectrum of values, but the rate associated with a given DE remains unchanged until it is removed from the code by installation of a fix.

On this model the pattern in real time of the occurrence of software problems for a product is primarily a function of

- The rate of usership vs time,
- The number of DEs originally present in the product,
- The distribution of problem rates over the original DEs, and
- The schedule of installing fixes for DEs after they are discovered.

We sought historical error data for some older products in order to test whether we could estimate virulences and correlate them to patterns of rediscoveries. We soon learned of the work of Richard W. Phillips of IBM Poughkeepsie, who had collected and analyzed data on both product usage and times of original discovery for a number of products of interest to us. Phillips had determined the distribution of original discoveries against cumulative usage for these products and had found that the distribution was similar from one product to another. He had even determined an empirical formula for this distribution.

We found that Phillips' formula for the distribution of discoveries vs usage could be reproduced using our model if we assumed that the rate distribution, i.e., the relative numbers of DEs having each possible rate, was proportional to a particular inverse power of the rates. This finding confirmed the apparent usefulness of our model, so we used it in all our subsequent work.

Phillips was kind enough to make all of his data available to us so we began by studying them in detail. As we did so we saw that we would need a great deal of other data before we could establish whether discoveries and rediscoveries could be successfully projected.

Methods of data analysis and model calibration

We collected or created the following error statistics to use in applying our model to the analysis of error data for a number of software products:

- The average monthly product usage beginning with FCS,
- The number of original discoveries each month,
- The number of rediscoveries each month of each known DE.

The products we studied were all products such as operating systems comprised of hundreds of thousands of lines of code and used by many hundreds of users.

• Creating usage statistics
We needed to accurately determine the relation between usage and time for our products. The rate of usage by a user is his machine speed, and the total rate of usage at any time is the number of user machine speeds, so the cumulative usage U is the integral of

$$dU = N(T) \cdot F \cdot dT,$$

where $N(T)$ is the number of users at time T and F is the average machine speed.

Conceptually the machine speed value for determining usage would depend on the size of a user machine and the average number of shifts per day of usage. In practice we had no direct access to such detailed information about usage; the most we could hope to do was determine what user machines were running in a given month. The usage statistics available to us initially were indirectly arrived at estimates of the numbers of user machines at the end of each calendar quarter. These statistics proved to be insufficiently accurate for our purposes, so we developed our own usage estimates by analyzing records of service to software installed in IBM machines that were under contract for software service. The machines for which detailed records of software service were available to us were those in the United States inventory, so we limited our detailed study of error phenomena to users of these machines who bought software service from IBM. The U.S. inventory of machines accounted for about half of the total usage of our products. We reckoned usage in usage-months, a usage month being a chronological month multiplied by a machine speed.

To formulate usage month statistics we created for each machine a month by month record of which software products were serviced during a given month. We assumed that a product was in use for any month in which it required service, and during all months between two months in which it required service. When competing products such as different operating systems or different versions of the same operating system were in use during the same month—a common situation—we allocated the usage for that month among the pieces of competing software on the basis of the apparent level of service currently being required for each, and where successive versions of a product were in overlapping use, we phased out the older one in a timely fashion. In this manner we built for every machine in the U.S. inventory a putative month-by-month history of product use in which each machine contributed just one month of usage per month to the total usage statistics for all functionally similar products.

Some survey data were available from which we could determine for some products what the total usage had been at particular months. Our estimates checked well at times both early and late in product life.

• Taking account of machine size
We assumed originally that the machine size factor F in the usage reckoning should be the machine speed, and we adopted as a measure of machine speed a composite of cycle speed and memory size that had been developed in IBM. However, when we examined machine by machine error data for any single product, we found that problem rates for the same sized machines differed greatly and showed no tendency to distribute about a mean; typically a few machines had many problems, many machines had only a few problems. One obvious source of variation was that a machine on three-shift operation got credit for the same usage as a machine on one-shift operation, but the variations were much

greater than this mechanism could account for. When we learned that some of our users rented many machines, used the same software on each, and assigned to a single machine the task of reporting service problems for all, so that that one machine might be reporting the usage from dozens or hundreds of shifts a day, we realized that we were too far removed from actual operations to understand the error statistics for individual machines.

However, we needed a machine speed calibration. Phillips' discovery that product discovery curves were similar had led to a desire for a planning tool that could forecast the distribution in time of future problem occurrences for a product while it was still in development. For this purpose we determined a relation of the F factor in usage to machine speed that would make the rate distributions determined from different products as similar as possible. Assuming that F varied as a simple power of machine speed, we did a linear regression of data from a number of products to determine the best fit of that power. The resulting power was close to 0.5. We do not assign much meaning to the 0.5, but in our subsequent fittings of product data we used it so that our results were consistent with those of others.

● *Creating discovery statistics*
The problem rates associated with known DEs can only be known approximately and were estimated by statistical inference from the statistics of DE discovery and problem occurrence. For determining discovery times we had available APAR records, which contained the actual date of discovery of each DE. However, many of the APARs were submitted by users not in our user set, either users in other countries or users in internal IBM development groups. Since such APARs did not result from usage included in our usage statistics, it would be incorrect to count them as discoveries in our rate inference calculations. Accordingly we took as the date of DE discovery for our purposes the date of the first discovery by one of our users and created a statistical series "Discoveries by U.S. field users under service contract."

We also made minor adjustments to the discovery statistics of products for which there were successive releases in which a successor release contained essentially all of the code of the previous release. The adjustments in such cases were to count a few DEs found in successor releases as original in the earlier release, even though not found there before the release of the new code. We do not discuss the procedure for making these adjustments, which in any case affected only DEs having problem rates so low that they could remain undetected until release of successor software.

● *Creating problem statistics*
Our most accurate means of estimating the problem rates associated with a DE requires us to know the total number of problems, both original discovery and rediscoveries of the DE in a known period of usage. Such statistics had not been collected before our work, but fortunately there was a set of records from which the information to construct them could be extracted, viz., the weekly effort reports of the persons who service the products, the individual IBM Customer Engineers (CEs). Each CE prepared a weekly report about problems worked on that week. Each problem worked on was assigned a unique code number, which it kept for as long as the problem was open. The weekly report recorded the code number of each problem worked on during the week, what was done in regard to it, and, if the cause of a problem was finally diagnosed as an IBM DE, the APAR number of the DE causing the problem.

Gordon Jones and his associates in the IBM group involved in our task saw the possibility to determine rediscovery times by analyzing the CE effort reports. They developed a set of programs that searched the archival file of activity reports, pieced together all references to each problem number worked on, determined when each problem was closed for the last time, identified the APAR number of the DE that caused the problem, and determined whether the problem involved an original discovery or a rediscovery. Their programs built problem files from which we could determine for each DE in our products the date of the original discovery and the dates of each subsequent rediscovery.

● *Estimating problem rates associated with a DE*
We used two methods for estimating the rate associated with a DE. Each method gave a distribution of probabilities that the DE had each possible rate R.

Method 1: estimation from usage at time of discovery
On our model the probability that a given DE will cause a problem in usage interval dU is

$$R \, dU,$$

where R is the problem rate associated with the DE. The probability that a DE present in the code at FCS would remain there undetected after usage U is

$$e^{-RU},$$

and the probability that a DE having rate R would survive usage U without causing a user problem and be discovered for the first time in usage interval dU is

$$R \cdot e^{-RU} dU.$$

By Bayes' Theorem the probability that a given DE discovered for the first time at U has rate R is

$$\frac{P(R, 0) \, R \, e^{-RU} \, dU}{\sum_{R'} P(R', 0) \, R' \, e^{-R'U} \, dU},$$

in which $P(R, 0)$ is the probability for a DE to have rate R if we had no information about it.

The derivation of this formula may be seen as follows: The DE that caused the problem at U in dU must have some one of the possible rates. The numerator is the probability that the DE had the rate R and that it caused a problem at U in dU. The denominator is the sum of the independent probabilities that the DE had one of the possible rates and caused a problem at U in dU. The denominator, since it includes all possible ways for the event to occur, is the probability that the DE would be found at U in dU; so the fraction is the probability that the discovery came about in dU at U through the case in which DE has rate R.

If we set the factor $P(R, 0)$ equal to 1, as though all values of R are equally probable *a priori*, we get the probability density that the rate is in dR at R:

$$U^2 R e^{-RU}.$$

This function of R has a maximum at $R = 1/U$. The rate estimated from the maximum is just the reciprocal accumulated usage at the time the DE is discovered. The expected value of R is $2/U$, twice the value at maximum, which indicates that the distribution is skewed far toward higher values.

Method 2: estimation from usage at time of N problems
The probability that a DE having rate R will cause exactly N problems during cumulative usage U is

$$\frac{(UR)^N e^{-RU}}{N!}.$$

By the same kind of reasoning as for method 1, the probability that a DE found exactly N times during usage U has associated rate R is

$$\frac{(RU)^N e^{-RU} P(R, 0) \, dU}{\sum_{R'} (R'U)^N e^{-RU} P(R', 0) \, dU}.$$

If we take all R values as equally likely *a priori*, we find the probability density that the rate is in dR at R to be

$$\frac{U(RU)^N e^{-RU}}{N!}.$$

This function of R has its maximum at $R = N/U$ and expected value $(N + 1)/U$, which is $(N + 1)/N$ times the value at maximum. If N is large, the skew toward large values is much smaller percentagewise than in the distribution obtained by method 1.

• *Comparison of the two methods*
When many discoveries of a DE have occurred, the estimate of method 2 will have a much lower variance than that of

method 1 and is quite insensitive to the initial probability factors in the statistical formulas. For DEs having multiple discoveries it is presumably the more accurate estimate provided that the usage interval of analysis is one in which a negligible amount of PS was done.

If many users have removed a DE from their code, method 2 will give values of R that are too small in proportion as the usage by users who actually had the DE in their code is smaller than the total usage, since it counts the usage of those users who have actually stopped having the problems associated with these DEs. The uncertainty of estimate because of possible PS begins to be significant when the problem data are based on a period ending more than a few months after the time of discovery, and grows progressively greater the longer the time from discovery to the time of estimate. We show below data that provide evidence of the effect of PS on rates estimated by method 2.

The estimate by method 1 is not affected directly by the amount of PS done, but it is affected indirectly. If the estimate is made after much PS has been done, some of the discovered DEs will actually be DEs introduced by fixes. These secondary DEs will be assigned rates that are too low, and sometimes very much too low; and they will be used to impute low-rate DEs to the original distribution that were not actually there. To estimate the significance of this effect we need an estimate of how many secondary DEs are present. We report below a study we did with such a model, in which we found that the total number of originally present latent DEs estimated from late life data were about 15 percent higher when we did not take account of the creation of secondary DEs than when we did. We may take this as an estimate of the extent to which the original number of DEs of low rate is overestimated by method 1. Method 1 should not systematically overestimate or underestimate the number of DEs of high problem rate; however, its estimates of these numbers is quite sensitive to the initial probability factors $P(R, 0)$ in the formulas of statistical inference, so its results are subject to the uncertainties involved in assigning these factors.

• *Creating an empirical rate distribution*
We created an empirical rate distribution by adding together the rate distributions from the individual DEs found. For most purposes we estimated original rate distributions using method 2 and usage periods less than a year. We could estimate a rate distribution from the set of problems found in any continuous usage interval beginning with FCS. To do so we went through the following steps:

• We constructed a one-rowed table giving the numbers of DEs for which there were 1, 2, 3, · · · problems in that interval.

- We determined for each DE in the table the probability for its rate to take each value R of the distribution and assigned to each rate of the distribution a fractional number of DEs equal to that probability.
- We totaled up the contributions of fractional DEs for each value of R to get the estimated rate distribution for the DEs that had been found.
- We adjusted this distribution by dividing by

$$1 - e^{-RU},$$

which is the fraction of DEs of rate R originally present that would have been expected to be found in usage U. The adjusted distribution is our estimate of the rate distribution of DEs in the code as originally shipped.

A basic practical question was how to represent the distribution we were to fit. Given a known theoretical form for the distribution, we might have parameterized that form and chosen the parameters to attain a best fit. Having no established theory to provide such a form, we chose to derive a purely empirical distribution. A completely arbitrary distribution would have required an infinite number of parameters of fit, so we made the assumption that the distribution was smooth, so that if fitted at a number of points it could be inferred in between.

The empirical distribution we used was a set of discrete points, spaced at logarithmic intervals so that each rate above the lowest was larger than the one below it by a factor square root of 10. This distribution provided a point fairly close (within about a half of a Naperian interval) to any possible rate value in the range of values.

We experimented with a number of different choices of the discrete rate values and also studied fitting with different numbers of discrete values. We found that in general we required a range of several orders of magnitude in problem rates to represent the error patterns at all well; a minimum number of six rate values seemed needed and seven or eight seemed slightly better in some cases.

In practice we chose to parameterize the rate distribution in terms of *percentages* of DEs associated with each rate value plus the estimated total number of DEs present at FCS, hoping to be able to correlate the total number with the number of lines of new code.

- *Choosing the prior probability factors*
The rate distributions derived in the manner described are sensitive in part to the choice of the initial probability factors $P(R, 0)$. Unfortunately, there is no uniquely correct way to assign these factors. The results that are sensitive to these factors are rates assigned to a DE for which the problem

count is low; the rates assigned to a DE having only one problem are essentially determined by the prior probability factors.

When we began our work we chose these factors by assuming that all rates for a DE were equally likely *a priori*. To get a feeling about the underlying distribution we then performed this process:

- Determine a distribution from the data,
- Use the distribution arrived at as a new trial distribution to provide values for the $P(R, 0)$,
- Repeat until the distribution converges.

We would expect this procedure to converge to a distribution for which the actual data are more probable than any other data. While there is no reason to expect that the actual rate distribution would have that property, we expected it to be one for which the data are probable, so hoped the one converged on might be similar. Later, when we had distributions from a number of products and verified from Phillips' finding that they were similar, we felt it reasonable to use the average of several distributions to estimate the factors $P(R, 0)$.

In most of our work we used rates estimated by method 2 with problem data from the early field use of the code. These data include few discoveries of DEs having very low problem rates and no rediscoveries of them, so could give little empirical information about the true rates for these DEs. Since these DEs are by far the most numerous in the code, the *total number of original latent DEs* may be estimated very wrongly. Accordingly, we also made some determinations of the rate distribution using method 1 with discoveries over most of the usage life of the code. This analysis is known to overestimate the number of low-rate DEs, but because of our study of secondary DEs we felt that its value for the total number of latent DEs originally present might not be in error by a large factor.

Finally, by choosing our prior probability factors so that the two kinds of estimate of the rate distribution were fairly consistent, we sought to protect ourselves against getting these factors grossly wrong.

- *A study of secondary DEs*
All attempts to fit our simple model rate distribution to empirical problem data over the life of the code showed a systematic error of fit: The model with the best fitted parameters would give more early discoveries and fewer late discoveries than were actually observed. We thought that this failure of the modeling was probably caused at least in part by the fact that some of the later-found DEs had been injected into the code via the fixes for earlier-found DEs, as we could see from direct evidence.

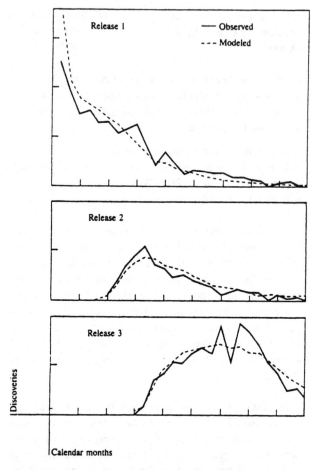

Figure 1 Monthly discoveries for products of Table 1. The actual and projected plots of discoveries vs time for three successive releases of a product. The discoveries are projected from the fitted numbers of original DEs for each release (not shown) and the mean of the three rate distributions.

We wanted to estimate approximately how much error the presence of secondary DEs would cause in estimating the parameters of the original rate distribution using an analysis that ignored these DEs. To this end we made a modified model that incorporated a representation of the introduction of secondary DEs as PS is done. This modified model was based on a number of overly simple assumptions, e.g., that a constant fraction of fixes introduced new DEs, that the new DEs had the same distribution of rates as newly shipped code, that the same constant fraction of users did PS at all times in the life of the code, that PS was done with a constant time lag after initial discovery, etc.

Since the treatment of PS was so artificial, we were not concerned to improve the fitting of empirical data in general, but only to determine whether we could find plausible values of fit parameters that would eliminate the systematic imbalance between early- and late-found DEs. We found that we could roughly account for the excess of long term discoveries

if we assumed that for each fix installed a new DE was generated with probability of the order of fifteen percent. Unfortunately the modified model involves so much that is arbitrary and overly simple that a detailed report on it would involve more explanation than the results justify. Apart from its value to give us an indication of how important secondary DEs were, it was of no greater value than the unmodified model.

Fitting the model parameters to some service histories

Having developed the sources of data and methods of analysis described above, we analyzed service data for a number of IBM products. Because of the commercial significance of the data and other sensitivities, we do not present original data nor identify individual products. We can characterize the products: Each was a release of an operating system, a large component of such a release, or a product of similar character in size and manner of use.

- *Fitted rate distributions*

Table 1 shows the fitted rate distribution for three successive releases of a single operating system. The reciprocal rate values, i.e., the mean times between user problems, are shown vs the percentage of DEs having this value. Here, as in all the data we present, we show only relative distributions.

- *Fitted total numbers of DEs present*

We do not present data on the estimated number of latent DEs present, since we did not find a way to get consistent and meaningful figures for this number. The difficulty we had is related to our inability to accurately determine the rates of DEs having very low problem rates. By varying the range of rates assumed possibly to be present and by varying the choice of the initial probability factors $P(R, 0)$, we could produce sets of fitting parameters that had widely different numbers of latent DEs but fit the problem data about equally well. These various fitted distributions varied almost entirely in the large numbers of DEs having very low problem rates; they all had about the same numbers of latent DEs present having high problem rates, these being the ones that accounted for the observed problem activity.

We had originally chosen to use the total number of latent DEs as a parameter, hoping to correlate it to the number of lines of new code in the product. Indeed, for a given set of rate parameters we did find that the number of latent DEs was crudely proportional to the number of lines of new code, but with deviations from proportionality of a factor of 2. However, it is clear that most of the fitted latent DEs did not correspond to real DEs of which our data could give knowledge. So the fitted total number of latent DEs is merely a fitting parameter whose values are to be understood only in connection with all other parameters used in a particular fit.

• Fitted discovery distributions

Figure 1 compares actual discoveries to fitted discoveries vs real time for each of the three releases of Table 1. Each fitted curve was projected from the model using as input data the monthly usage data for the release, the inferred total number of original latent DEs for the release, and the average of the three fitted rate distributions as given in the table. Since each of the three different distributions of discoveries vs real time is obtained from the same average rate distribution, it is clear that the main differences of shape derive from differences in the time pattern of usership. That the shapes are rendered fairly well in such a plot was Phillips' discovery.

Figure 1 shows that our model can capture the principal information needed to understand the smoothed trend of discoveries in real time. Although the time trends of fit are perhaps a little better than typical in this particular case, one can see that at some points there are errors of fit of the order of 30–50 percent, which is what one must expect when modeling in terms of such gross aggregates.

• Fitting rediscovery distributions

We did several studies of detailed rediscovery distributions. The format of such studies was to seek any plausible assumptions about what PS might have been done that would permit the model to reproduce the general trend of the rediscovery data. By using the model with secondary DEs we could almost always do such a fit within the accuracy that is to be expected for this kind of model. However, we do not present data showing these fits, since they are based on such arbitrary assumptions about PS that they are persuasive of little.

• Similarity of rate distributions of different products

Table 2 tabulates the distributions obtained from fitting problem data for the nine large products for which we had full life data at the time of the analysis. Among these were products used on both large and small machines. (It may be noted that the rate values used here are somewhat different from those used in Table 1. The differences are not important: Either set of values gives about as good a fit of the data.)

Examining the fitted rate data one can see that the numbers in the leftmost columns—the percentage of DEs in the lowest rate values—are very similar from product to product. These similarities are not meaningful, but merely reflect similarities of the initial probabilities used in the fitting as discussed above.

One can see that in the rightmost columns the variations along each column, from column to column, and from product to product also show similarities, although with much more variability of the data. These similarities are

Table 1 Problem rates for three releases of a product. The fitted distribution of problem rates is shown as a mean time between problem occurrences vs the percent of DEs in the corresponding rate class.

Rate class							
1	2	3	4	5	6	7	8
Mean time to problem occurrence in kmonths for rate class							
95	30	9	3	0.9	0.3	0.09	0.03
Fitted percentage defects in rate class by release							

Release								
1	24.1	26.4	28.8	13.5	3.0	2.9	1.1	0.2
2	21.3	23.2	25.5	13.8	5.0	7.4	3.3	0.5
3	21.9	24.1	27.5	16.2	3.9	4.0	2.1	0.2
Average	22.4	24.6	27.3	14.5	4.0	4.8	2.2	0.3

Table 2 Rate distributions for nine software products. These rate distributions were fitted using the same fit program and the same prior probability factors. The square root of machine speed rather than machine speed itself was used for reckoning usage of machines.

Rate class							
1	2	3	4	5	6	7	8
Mean time to problem occurrence in kmonths for rate class							
60	19	6	1.9	0.6	0.19	0.06	0.019
Fitted percentage defects in rate class by release							

Product								
1	34.2	28.8	17.8	10.3	5.0	2.1	1.2	0.7
2	34.3	28.0	18.2	9.7	4.5	3.2	1.5	0.7
3	33.7	28.5	18.0	8.7	6.5	2.8	1.4	0.4
4	34.2	28.5	18.7	11.9	4.4	2.0	0.3	0.1
5	34.2	28.5	18.4	9.4	4.4	2.9	1.4	0.7
6	32.0	28.2	20.1	11.5	5.0	2.1	0.8	0.3
7	34.0	28.5	18.5	9.9	4.5	2.7	1.4	0.6
8	31.9	27.1	18.4	11.1	6.5	2.7	1.4	1.1
9	31.2	27.6	20.4	12.8	5.6	1.9	0.5	0.0

meaningful, and the discrepancies between corresponding numbers in these columns are probably indicative of the actual variability of the rate distributions from product to product. Noisy these data are, but they suggest that rate distributions have considerable similarity of form from product to product.

Using the mean of these nine distributions, we calculated the total problem activity contributed by the DEs in each rate group. The result was that the few DEs in the set having the highest rate were responsible for more total problem rate

Table 3 Variation of fitted rates with usage interval. The rate distribution for this product was fitted using the total usage and cumulative discoveries as of the end of each month for 18 months. The apparent decreases in the right-hand columns show that the fraction of users having all of the most virulent DEs in their code diminishes after about month 7 or 8.

				Percentage of defects by rate class				
Class	1	2	3	4	5	6	7	8
Month								
1	23.1	24.7	26.5	14.6	4.4	4.5	2.0	0.3
2	23.1	24.8	26.5	14.6	4.3	4.4	1.9	0.3
3	23.2	24.9	26.6	14.6	4.3	4.3	1.8	0.3
4	23.2	24.9	26.6	14.5	4.3	4.3	1.9	0.4
5	23.2	24.9	26.6	14.6	4.3	4.3	1.6	0.5
6	23.3	25.0	26.8	14.8	4.4	4.0	1.4	0.3
7	23.3	25.0	26.8	14.8	4.4	4.0	1.3	0.3
8	23.3	25.0	27.0	15.1	4.5	3.8	1.1	0.3
9	22.9	24.7	26.8	15.4	5.0	3.9	1.1	0.2
10	23.4	25.1	27.0	15.1	4.7	3.7	0.9	0.1
11	23.3	25.0	26.9	15.3	5.2	3.4	0.7	0.0
12	23.7	25.4	27.1	14.8	5.1	3.2	0.6	0.1
13	23.9	25.6	27.0	14.7	5.4	2.9	0.5	0.1
14	24.4	25.9	26.9	14.4	5.4	2.6	0.4	0.1
15	24.6	26.1	27.0	14.2	5.3	2.5	0.3	0.1
16	24.9	26.3	27.0	14.0	5.2	2.2	0.3	0.1
17	25.2	26.5	26.8	14.0	5.1	2.0	0.3	0.1
18	25.4	26.7	26.9	13.8	5.0	1.9	0.3	0.1

than those in the set having the second highest rate, and that in general the DEs in any set were responsible for more problem activity than those in the set having the next highest rate. Thus the small numbers of DEs in the sets having the very highest rates account for nearly all of the problem potential of the code.

● *The effects of PS on fitted rates*
Table 3 illustrates how some effects of PS show up when we analyze data from progressively longer service intervals. The figure shows a table of the rate distribution obtained by fitting the cumulative problem data for a single product after each calendar month for 18 months. The inferred distributions are rather stable for the first seven or eight months, with no more than a suggestion of depletion of the percentages in the highest rate values, but after that time the numbers of DEs assigned to the three highest rate values diminish markedly.

That the numbers in the right-hand columns are fairly stable for the early months implies that as the user months accumulate, the numbers of problems assigned to the most virulent DEs increase in the same proportion, as though most of the users continue to have these DEs in their code.

After about seven months a change occurs, so that the numbers of DEs having high rates diminish markedly. This implies that the total number of problems reported against these DEs no longer increases in the same proportion as the usage, as though many of the users no longer have those virulent DEs in their code. Without looking at the raw data one cannot tell how completely the most virulent DEs had been eliminated, but it is as though their problem activity had been eliminated from most of the code.

We interpret these data to mean that during the first half year after FCS little if any PS was done, since the first DEs that PS would eliminate continued to be present essentially unchanged. We used a table such as this to estimate the amount of PS being done so that we could decide how many months of data could safely be used to determine an original rate distribution.

Discussion of the rate distribution
Several features of the distributions are of interest. First, the rate distributions are generically similar from product to product, as Phillips had discovered. To the extent that they are similar, we may conjecture that some process has shaped them so. If so, it should be a pervasive process, since these products had been produced at different places and times, by different people, and with significant differences of programming technology.

Second, the approximately linear slopes of the distributions at high rates are less steep than the simple model would suggest. If one considers that during the latter months of development the code is subjected to considerable usage, one might expect the numbers of the most virulent DEs to be reduced far below what is found, in fact that they would be approximately in the ratios of the exponential attenuation factors defined by their problem rates.

Reflecting on these matters and being aware that in fact considerable numbers of DEs are found during the development process, we realized that many must also be added during development. We developed an intuition that the characteristic shape of these distributions might just reflect the balancing during the development process between acts of creation and removal of high-rate DEs. Assume that as development proceeds new DEs are continually created, but at the same time existing ones are found and removed, and imagine that one can represent the evolution of the rate distribution by a pseudo-differential equation

$$\frac{d\,P(R)}{d\,t} = G - R_0\,P(R) - RP(R),$$

where $P(R)$ is the number of DEs per unit interval of rate R and "t" is a variable representing the passage of development "time." The term G represents the effective rate at which new DEs are created per unit of t; the term with R represents the probable fact that developers find DEs by activities similar in effect to running the code in the field; the term with R_0 reflects the assumption that developers also find DEs in ways that are unrelated to running it in the field. (We have evidence that they do, which need not be reviewed here.)

If development goes on long enough for the process described to come into balance for those DEs having very high problem rates, one may set the left-hand side to zero and solve for $P(R)$:

$$P(R) = \frac{G}{R + R_0}.$$

Since G itself could be expected to depend on R (it is plausible that the developer is more likely to create DEs of low virulence than DEs of high virulence), we cannot conclude the exact form by which the distribution should vary with R. However, these considerations suggest why $P(R)$ might well vary inversely with R somewhat as observed. So that we could relate this formula to the actual mean rate distribution of Table 2, we made a best fit of that distribution assuming $P(R)$ to be proportional to a power of $R + R_0$. To do this we associated with each discrete value except the lowest all the rates of the continuous distribution in the logarithmic interval from a 1/4 root of 10 below to 1/4 root of 10 above that discrete value. We associated with the lowest value all the states from rate 0 up to a factor 1/4 root of 10 above the lowest value. We obtained a best fit distribution

$$P(R) = \frac{G}{(R + 0.032)} 1.69$$

that fits the mean rate distribution closely. (There is a small glitch at the lowest rate point, undoubtedly related to the extra weight given by integrating the function all the way from 0.)

Optimizing preventive service

The rough level of modeling we have achieved is adequate as a guide to planning effective PS. We take it as axiomatic that PS is not to be done unless its benefits justify its cost. Generally speaking, the service costs that can be profitably avoided by PS are the result of problems caused by a small number of highly virulent DEs, most of which are found very soon after the code is put into service. The main question about any DE is whether to deal with it by PS or by CS.

The considerations in answering this question are much the same for the product producer and the product user. The user who has had no problem does not want to install a PTF if the risk from possible new DEs plus the costs of doing PS outweigh the expected gains from avoiding problems from the known DE. The producer must prepare a fix for the DE in any case, since he must provide CS to the user who discovered the DE, but he does not want to incur the additional

Discovery month

	1	2	3	4	5	6	7	8	9	10	11	12	13	14	15	16	17	18
1	7	0	0	0	0	0	0	0	0	0	0	0	0	0	0	0	0	0
2	29	9	0	0	0	0	0	0	0	0	0	0	0	0	0	0	0	0
3	44	26	7	0	0	0	0	0	0	0	0	0	0	0	0	0	0	0
4			19	6	0	0	0	0	0	0	0	0	0	0	0	0	0	0
5			24	15	5	0	0	0	0	0	0	0	0	0	0	0	0	0
6	88	52	28	17	12	4	0	0	0	0	0	0	0	0	0	0	0	0
7	103	61	33	20	14	10	4	0	0	0	0	0	0	0	0	0	0	0
8	117	69	38	23	16	11	8	3	0	0	0	0	0	0	0	0	0	0
9	132	78	42	26	18	13	9	7	3	0	0	0	0	0	0	0	0	0
10	147	87	47	29	20	14	10	8	6	2	0	0	0	0	0	0	0	0
11	162	95	52	32	22	15	11	9	7	5	2	0	0	0	0	0	0	0
12	176	104	57	35	24	17	12	9	7	6	5	2	0	0	0	0	0	0
13	191	113	61	38	25	18	13	10	8	6	5	4	2	0	0	0	0	0
14	206	121	66	41	27	19	14	11	8	7	5	4	3	1	0	0	0	0
15	220	130	71	44	29	21	15	12	9	7	6	5	4	3	1	0	0	0
16	235	139	76	47	31	22	16	12	10	8	6	5	4	3	3	1	0	0
17	250	147	80	50	33	24	17	13	10	8	6	5	4	4	3	3	1	0
18	264	156	85	52	35	25	18	14	11	9	7	6	4	4	3	3	2	1

Rediscovery month

Figure 2 Projected rediscoveries when DE is known. The number in the R row and D column is the projected number of rediscoveries made in month R caused by DEs discovered in month D. The numbers are projected for a hypothetical product that has steady month-by-month growth of usership on the assumption that all users use the initial version of the product.

expense of working up PTFs and distributing them to users unless the users will judge it worthwhile to put them in and will avert service calls by doing so.

There are at least two levels on which to approach the decision of whether to do PS. At the coarsest level, one relies on the statistical fact that early-found DEs are the virulent ones, so one does PS for all DEs found up to a certain value of usage, CS for all found later. The considerations as they might be weighed by the developer can be seen by studying a rediscovery matrix, an example of which is shown in Fig. 2. The rows and columns of the matrix are labeled by months reckoned from the time of FCS. The entry for row R and column D is the number of rediscoveries in the user base during month R caused by DEs discovered in month D. The total of the numbers in row R is the total number of rediscoveries expected in month R.

To construct such a matrix, assume a rate distribution, e.g., the one found from our work. Assign a number of initial latent DEs by the following procedure: Estimate the number of DEs to be found over the usage period of interest for the product of interest, perhaps on the basis of the number of lines of new code in the product; determine a number of initial latent DEs that will give the expected number of DEs for that amount of usage by direct projection from the model. The model is now calibrated to make the matrix.

125

Use the expected usage buildup for the code to calculate the number of DEs in each rate group that will be discovered in each month after the code is released. To get the column entries for a given month calculate the problem rate of all DEs found in that month as the sum of the number of DEs times the rate per DE. Now, using expected usages for later months, calculate entries for each row of the column as the problem rate of the column month times the number of months' usage for the row month. In the example of Fig. 2 all calculations assume that the initial version of the code is furnished to all users, no matter when they begin to use the code.

The significant trends in the rediscovery matrix are that the numbers grow steadily down a column and diminish strongly to the right across a row. The variation down the column reflects the continual entry of new users who can have problems; the decrease to the right reflects the diminishing virulence of DEs found in later months. It is easy to see that the large numbers all occur in the columns to the left, so that the preponderance of benefits of PS will come from avoiding problems in the leftmost columns.

The solid line in the figure is drawn with reference to a hypothetical PTF tape, made available by the end of month 3 and fixing all DEs found in months 1 and 2. The line encloses all problems whose occurrence can be affected by the fixes on the tape. The hatched area relates to rediscoveries during the period that users are installing fixes, which in this example is assumed to be two months. Some of the problems in the hatched area and all of those below it can be avoided by doing PS to remove the DEs on the tape; no other problems can be so avoided. The value of avoiding these problems must be the justification for doing PS with that tape.

We can construct the line that demarcates the problems affected by some other service vehicle by drawing a similar line with a column determined by the last month for which known DEs will be fixed and the row determined by the month in which the fixes become available to users. As one looks at various cases it becomes clear that, since one needs to eliminate the problems from only a few columns, a vehicle to do the most worthwhile PS can be built only a few months after FCS.

The service strategy for a developer is concerned with deciding what fixes to make available to users with which they can do PS. The optimum strategy for the developer depends on the details of his cost structure, but it is easy to see that he will find it beneficial to support PS to remove only the problems associated with a few columns on the left.

In making the matrix example, we assumed that all new users got the original version of the code unmodified to fix known DEs. The numbers in the rediscovery matrix would be different if, e.g., the developer arranged that each new user get a version of the code in which all available fixes have been installed. In that case one would modify the calculation so that the problem rate for the new users in a given month would be reduced appropriately, and would find that the numbers would not continue to increase down the columns, but would become constant past the month in which all new users have the fixes. For such a service strategy most of the numbers in the matrix will be smaller.

Calculations such as these charts illustrate may be useful in developing quantitative measures for the value of a particular service vehicle in the context of a given planning framework.

A user might approach the PS vs CS decision in a simpler way. He will benefit significantly from PS only if there is a significant chance that a DE he removes preventively would otherwise cause him a problem. Thus he might ask what is the mean time between problems for the DEs that a batch of fixes remove. To determine this one can follow the same calculation as above up to the point of estimating the total problem rate due to DEs found in a given month. If one now divides this quantity by the number of DEs that cause that rate, one gets the problem rate per DE found in a given month. In typical cases the user will find that after not many months the mean time to error for the DEs being fixed by new PTFs approaches the length of time he expects to run the code. The prospective benefit of removing such a DE is very small; and in view of the small chance that the fix will introduce a much more virulent DE, a prudent user will not put in the fix. For typical patterns of usership buildup the average problem rate per DE found in a given month is always about 0.75–0.8 times the reciprocal of the cumulative usage at the end of that month, so that, e.g., DEs found in the month that the cumulative usage reaches 3000 months have an average problem rate of the order 1 per 4000 months.

While the calculations for user and developer look quite different, they lead to much the same cutoff for doing PS, since both calculations are driven by the same underlying consideration: whether the probability of rediscovery justifies the cost of doing PS.

A more refined level of decision about PS can be made if the service organization keeps current records of which DEs caused each problem, since the decision can be made on a DE by DE basis rather than a month to month basis. Assume the developer records the times of occurrence of all problems associated with a given DE and a record of month by month usage of the product. He can then easily make a monthly estimate of the probable virulence of each known DE on the basis of accumulated usage and number of problems caused.

Given this estimate it is straightforward for either developer or user to determine for each DE whether the hazard it poses justifies PS.

One attractive fact about a DE by DE strategy is that application of fixes by all users can be restricted to just the small fraction of DEs for which it is profitable. Since most DEs, even if not fixed by PTF, are never rediscovered, one would like to avoid the cost of doing PS for them. A simple rule ensures this: Wait for at least one rediscovery before doing any PS. Everyone can afford this policy; a highly virulent DE will have its first rediscovery before the fixes could be disseminated anyhow, while a less virulent DE, for which a rediscovery comes only after several months, constitutes a small month by month risk to the users. Another attractive feature of dealing with individual DEs on the basis of estimated virulence is that one deals as efficiently with the (rare) highly virulent secondary DE as with an original DE.

In our judgment the fraction of DEs worth fixing is very small, probably less than ten per cent; and yet for a few DEs the payoff from PS is great. We are convinced that if one determines what PS to do on some such basis as sketched above, one can realize substantially better benefits from PS than are derived from either a fix all or a fix none strategy.

Concluding remarks
Our work suggests several useful things about the distribution of error rates in product code. First, most of the DEs present have mean times to discovery of hundreds to thousands of months when run on a single machine. Thus the typical DE requires very unusual circumstances to manifest itself, possibly in many cases the coincidence of very unusual circumstances. One may doubt that a testing group using a few machines and having only a few months to work could ever detect and remove all such DEs by purely empirical means. One may conclude that service will always be needed.

Second, if we are correct in our intuition about why the rate distributions in the products we studied were generically similar, we might expect the rate distributions in other large bodies of code to be similar also, at least so long as the methods of code development depend on empirical debugging. It may well be that as software engineering techniques improve, the population of DEs will balance at a lower level; but absent development methods that generate truly error-free code, the same sort of error rate distribution may well persist in future large products.

Third, to the extent that one can assume that the distribution of rates and the total number per thousand lines of code are similar for similar products, one can forecast the error behavior of a planned product. This can be of some use in planning for service. However, one must not expect high precision in such a forecast: There will be large percentage-wise variations in the small number of highly virulent DEs that dominate the early error behavior of the code. These variations will be even larger and less predictable for small products or products that are used sporadically.

Similarly, to the extent that one can represent the error phenomena in the user population by such a simple model, one can use the model for several types of quality control, but again one should do so without expectation of great precision in fitting and interpreting even after-the-fact error data, because the statistics of an actual product history will deviate from most probable values, because the statistical quantities used to interpret the history are subject to large errors of determination, and because the actual history depends on detailed circumstances not represented in the gross parameters. It may well be that our simple model, perhaps as modified to take account of secondary DEs, captures most of the significant regularities in the rate behavior of general pieces of code that can be represented without a lot of detailed information about the use of the product.

Relation of our work to that of others
The mathematical model and methods we used are simple and familiar. We based certain aspects of our work on the previous work of Richard W. Phillips of IBM Poughkeepsie, but did not make significant use of other work. We did look at some of the literature of reliability, where we found that the general notion of associating problem rates with DEs was a common one. Thus we present this work primarily for what we have learned about the empirical quantification of the error behavior of product quality code and for the implications that can be drawn from it about how to manage preventive service in such code.

Acknowledgments
In order to do this work we needed the assistance of many people in IBM, who helped us find and get access to the information we needed. We particularly acknowledge the generous assistance of Richard W. Phillips, who by sharing his ideas and the results of his pioneering work on discovery made our task much easier and enabled us to proceed directly along the most profitable path. We also acknowledge that although we present this paper as sole author, all of the work reported was done in collaboration with or depended directly on the results of Gordon Jones, Dan Price, Grant Wood, Alvin Blum, and the other members of their group, whose skill and perseverance in extracting problem data from a jungle of tapes, files, and reports made possible the creation of the problem statistics without which the work could not have been done.

Software Process Evolution at the SEL

VICTOR BASILI, *University of Maryland*
SCOTT GREEN, *NASA Goddard Space Flight Center*

◆ *The Software Engineering Laboratory has been adapting, analyzing, and evolving software processes for the last 18 years. Their approach is based on the Quality Improvement Paradigm, which is used to evaluate process effects on both product and people. The authors explain this approach as it was applied to reduce defects in code.*

S ince 1976, the Software Engineering Laboratory of the National Aeronautics and Space Administration's Goddard Space Flight Center has been engaged in a program of understanding, assessing, and packaging software experience. Topics of study include process, product, resource, and defect models, as well as specific technologies and tools. The approach of the SEL — a consortium of the Software Engineering Branch of NASA Goddard's Flight Dynamics Division, the Computer Science Department of the University of Maryland, and the Software Engineering Operation of Computer Sciences Corp. — has been to gain an in-depth understanding of project and environment characteristics using

process models and baselines. A process is evaluated for study, applied experimentally to a project, analyzed with respect to baselines and process model, and evaluated in terms of the experiment's goals. Then on the basis of the experiment's conclusions, results are packaged and the process is tailored for improvement, applied again, and reevaluated.

In this article, we describe our improvement approach, the Quality Improvement Paradigm, as the SEL applied it to reduce code defects by emphasizing reading techniques. The box on p. 63 describes the Quality Improvement Paradigm in detail. In examining and adapting reading techniques, we go through a systematic process of evaluating the candidate

Reprinted from *IEEE Software*, Vol. 11, No. 4, July 1994, pp. 58–66.

process and refining its implementation through lessons learned from previous experiments and studies.

As a result of this continuous, evolutionary process, we determined that we could successfully apply key elements of the Cleanroom development method in the SEL environment, especially for projects involving fewer than 50,000 lines of code (all references to lines of code refer to developed, not delivered, lines of code). We saw indications of lower error rates, higher productivity, a more complete and consistent set of code comments, and a redistribution of developer effort. Although we have not seen similar reliability and cost gains for larger efforts, we continue to investigate the Cleanroom method's effect on them.

EVALUATING CANDIDATE PROCESSES

To enhance the possibility of improvement in a particular environment, the SEL introduces and evaluates new technology within that environment. This involves experimentation with the new technology, recording findings in the context of lessons learned, and adjusting the associated processes on the basis of this experience. When the technology is notably risky — substantially different from what is familiar to the environment — or requires more detailed evaluation than would normally be expended, the SEL conducts experimentation off-line from the project environment.

Off-line experiments may take the form of either controlled experiments or case studies. Controlled experiments are warranted when the SEL needs a detailed analysis with statistical assurance in the results. One problem with controlled experiments is that the project must be small enough to replicate the experiment several times. The SEL then performs a case study to validate the results on a project of credible size that is representative of the environment. The case study adds

validity and credibility through the use of typical development systems and professional staff. In analyzing both controlled experiments and case studies, the Goal/Question/Metric paradigm, described in the box on p. 63, provides an important framework for focusing the analysis.

On the basis of experimental results, the SEL packages a set of lessons learned and makes them available in an experience base for future analysis and application of the technology.

Experiment 1: Reading versus testing. Although the SEL had historically been a test-driven organization, we decided to experiment with introducing reading techniques. We were particularly interested in how reading would compare with testing for fault detection. The goals of the first off-line, controlled experiment[1] were to analyze and compare code reading, functional testing, and structural testing, and to evaluate them with respect to fault-detection effectiveness, cost, and classes of faults detected.

We needed an analysis from the viewpoint of quality assurance as well as a comparison of performance with respect to software type and programmer experience. Using the GQM paradigm, we generated specific questions on the basis of these goals.

We had subjects use reading by stepwise abstraction,[2] equivalence-partitioning boundary-value testing, and statement-coverage structural testing.

We conducted the experiment twice at the University of Maryland on graduate students (42 subjects) and once at NASA Goddard (32 subjects). The experiment structure was a fractional factorial design, in which every subject applied each technique on a different program. The programs included a text formatter, a plotter, an abstract data type, and a database, and they ranged from 145 to 365 lines of code. We seeded each program with faults. The reading performed was at the unit level.

Although the results from both experiments support the emphasis on reading techniques, we report only the results of the controlled experiment on the NASA Goddard subjects because it involved professional developers in the target environment.

Figure 1 shows the fault-detection effectiveness and rate for each approach for the NASA Goddard experiment. Reading by stepwise abstraction proved superior to testing

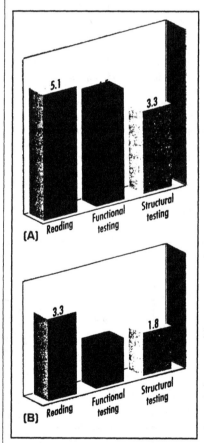

Figure 1. Results of the reading-versus-testing controlled experiment, in which reading was compared with functional and structural testing. **(A)** Mean number of faults detected for each technique and **(B)** number of faults detected per hour of use for each technique.

techniques in both the effectiveness and cost of fault detection, while obviously using fewer computer resources.

Even more interesting was that the subjects did a better job of estimating the code quality using reading than they did using testing. Readers thought they had found only about half the faults (which was nominally correct), while functional testers felt that had found essentially all the faults (which was never correct).

Furthermore, after completing the experiment, more than 90 percent of the participants thought functional testing had been the most effective technique, although the results clearly showed otherwise. This gave us some insight into the psychological effects of reading versus testing. Perhaps one reason testing appeared more satisfying was that the successful execution of multiple test cases generated a greater comfort level with the product quality, actually providing the tester with a false sense of confidence.

Reading was also more effective in uncovering most classes of faults, including interface faults. This told us

that perhaps reading might scale up well on larger projects.

Experiment 2: Validation with Cleanroom. On the basis of these results, we decided to emphasize reading techniques in the SEL environment. However, we saw little improvement in overall reliability of the development systems. Part of the reason may have been that SEL project personnel had developed such faith in testing that the quality of their reading was relaxed, with the assumption that testing would ultimately uncover the same faults. We conducted a small off-line experiment at the University of Maryland to test this hypothesis; the results supported our assumption. (We did this on a small scale just to verify our hypothesis before continuing with the Cleanroom experiment.)

Why the Cleanroom method? The Cleanroom method emphasizes human discipline in the development process, using a mathematically based design approach and a statistical testing approach based on anticipated opera-

tional use.[3] Development and testing teams are independent, and all development-team activities are performed without on-line testing.

Techniques associated with the method are the use of box structures and state machines, reading by stepwise abstraction, formal correctness demonstrations, and peer review. System development is performed through a pipeline of small increments to enhance concentration and permit testing and development to occur in parallel.

Because the Cleanroom method removes developer testing and relies on human discipline, we felt it would overcome the psychological barrier of reliance on testing.

Applying the QIP. The first step of the Quality Improvement Paradigm is to characterize the project and its environment. The removal of developer unit testing made the Cleanroom method a high-risk technology. Again, we used off-line experimentation at the University of Maryland as a mitigating approach.[4] The environment was a laboratory course at the university, and the project involved an electronic message system of about 1,500 LOC. The experiment structure was a simple replicated design, in which control and experiment teams are defined. We assigned 10 three-person experiment teams to use the Cleanroom method. We gave five three-person control teams the same development methodology, but allowed them to test their systems. Each team was allowed five independent test submissions of their programs. We collected data on programmer background and attitude, computer-resource activity, and actual testing results.

The second step in the Quality Improvement Paradigm is to set goals. The goal here was to analyze the effects of the Cleanroom approach and evaluate it with respect to process, product, and participants, as compared with the non-Cleanroom approach.

	Sample measures	Sample baseline	Sample expectation
Process	Effort distribution Change profile	Other 26% Code 21%	Increased design effort because of emphasis on peer-review process
Cost	Productivity Level of rework Impact of specification changes	Historically, 26 lines of code per day	No degradation from current level
Reliability	Error rate Error distribution Error source	Historically, seven errors per thousand lines of code	Decreased error rate

Figure 2. Sample measures, baselines, and expectations for the case studies investigating the Cleanroom method.

We generated questions corresponding to this goal, focusing on the method's effect on each aspect being studied.

The next step of the Quality Improvement Paradigm involves selecting an appropriate process model. The process model selected for this experiment was the Cleanroom approach as defined by Harlan Mills at IBM's Federal Systems Division, but modified for our environment. For example, the graduate-student assistant for the course served as each group's independent test team. Also, because we used a language unfamiliar to the subjects to prevent bias, there was a risk of errors due solely to ignorance about the language. We therefore allowed teams to cleanly compile their code before submitting it to the tester.

Because of the nature of controlled experimentation, we made few modifications during the experiment.

Cleanroom's effect on the software-development process resulted in the Cleanroom developers more effectively applying the off-line reading techniques; the non-Cleanroom teams focused their efforts more on functional testing than reading. The Cleanroom teams spent less time on-line and were more successful in making scheduled deliveries. Further analysis revealed that the Cleanroom products had less dense complexity, a higher percentage of assignment statements, more global data, and more code comments. These products also more completely met the system requirements and had a higher percentage of successful independent test cases.

The Cleanroom developers indicated that they modified their normal software-development activities by doing a more effective job of reading, though they missed the satisfaction of actual program execution. Almost all said they would be willing to use Cleanroom on another development assignment.

Through observation, it was also clear that the Cleanroom developers did not apply the formal methods associated with Cleanroom very rigorously. Furthermore, we did not have enough failure data or experience with Cleanroom testing to apply a reliability model. However, general analysis did indicate that the Cleanroom approach had potential payoff, and that additional investigation was warranted.

You can also view this experiment from the following perspective: We applied two development approaches. The only real difference between them was that the control teams had one extra piece of technology (developer testing), yet they did not perform as well as the experiment teams. One explanation might be that the control group did not use the available nontesting techniques as effectively because they knew they could rely on testing to detect faults. This supports our earlier findings associated with the reading-versus-testing experiment.

EVOLVING SELECTED PROCESS

The positive results gathered from these two experiments gave us the justification we needed to explore the Cleanroom method in case studies, using typical development systems as data points. We conducted two case studies to examine the method, again following the steps of the Quality Improvement Paradigm. A third case study was also recently begun.

First case study. The project we selected, Project 1, involved two subsystems from a typical attitude ground-support system. The system performs ground processing to determine a spacecraft's attitude, receiving and processing spacecraft telemetry data to meet the requirements of a particular mission.

ALMOST ALL THE CLEANROOM TEAM SAID THEY'D USE THE METHOD AGAIN.

The subsystems we chose are an integral part of attitude determination and are highly algorithmic. Both are interactive programs that together contain approximately 40,000 LOC, representing about 12 percent of the entire attitude ground-support system. The rest of the ground-support system was developed using the standard SEL development methodology.

The project was staffed principally by five people from the Flight Dynamics Division, which houses the SEL. All five were also working on other projects, so only part of their time was allocated to the two subsystems. Their other responsibilities often took time and attention away from the case study, but this partial allocation represents typical staffing in this environment. All other projects with which the Project 1 staff were involved were non-Cleanroom efforts, so staff members would often be required to use multiple develop-ment methodologies during the same workday.

The primary goal of the first case study was to increase software quality and reliability without increasing cost. We also wanted to compare the characteristics of the Cleanroom method with those typical of the FDD environment. A well-calibrated baseline was available for comparison that described a variety of process characteristics, including effort distribution, change rates, error rates, and productivity. The baseline represents the history of many earlier SEL studies. Figure 2 shows a sample of the expected variations from the SEL baselines for a set of process characteristics.

Choosing and tailoring processes. The process models available for examination were the standard SEL model,[5] which represents a reuse-oriented waterfall life-cycle model; the

IBM/FSD Cleanroom model, which appeared in the literature and was available through training; and the experimental University of Maryland Cleanroom model, which was used in the earlier controlled experiment.[4]

We examined the lessons learned from applying the IBM and University of Maryland models. The results from the IBM model were notably positive, showing that the basic process, methods, and techniques were effective for that particular environment. However, the process model had been applied by the actual developers of the methodology, in the environment for which it was developed. The University of Maryland model also had specific lessons, including the effects of not allowing developers to test their code, the effectiveness of the process on a small project, and the conclusion that formal methods appeared particularly difficult to apply and required specific skills.

On the basis of these lessons and the characteristics of our environment, we selected a Cleanroom process model with four key elements:

♦ separation of development and test teams,

♦ reliance on peer review instead of unit-level testing as the primary developer verification technique,

♦ use of informal state machines and functions to define the system design, and

♦ a statistical approach to testing based on operational scenarios.

We also provided training for the subjects, consistent with a University of Maryland course on the Cleanroom process model, methods, and techniques, with emphasis on reading through stepwise abstraction. We also stressed code reading by multiple reviewers because stepwise abstraction was new to many subjects. Michael Dyer and Terry Baker of IBM/FSD

provided additional training and motivation by describing IBM's use of Cleanroom.

To mitigate risk and address the developers' concerns, we examined backout options for the experiment. For example, because the subsystems were highly mathematical, we were afraid it would be difficult to find and correct mathematical errors without any developer testing. Because the project was part of an operational system with mission deadlines, we discussed options that ranged from allowing developer unit testing to discontinuing Cleanroom altogether. These discussions helped allay the primary apprehension of NASA Goddard management in using the new methodology. When we could not get information about process application, we followed standard SEL process-model activities.

We also noted other management and project-team concerns. Requirements and specifications change frequently during the development cycle in the FDD environment. This instability was of particular concern because the Cleanroom method is built on the precept of developing software right the first time. Another concern was that, given the difficulties encountered in the University of Maryland experiment about applying formal methods, how successfully could a classical Cleanroom approach be applied? Finally, there was concern about the psychological effects of separating development and testing, specifically the inability of the developers to execute their code. We targeted all these concerns for our postproject analysis.

Project 1 lasted from January 1988 through September 1990. We separated the five team members into a three-person development team and a two-person test team. The development

PROJECT RESULTS LED US TO EMPHASIZE PEER REVIEWS AND USE OF INDEPENDENT TESTING.

team broke the total effort into six incremental builds of approximately 6,500 LOC each. An experimenter team consisting of NASA Goddard managers, SEL representatives, a technology advocate familiar with the IBM model, and the project leader monitored the overall process.

We modified the process in real time, as needed. For example, when we merged Cleanroom products into the standard FDD formal review and documentation activities, we had to modify both. We altered the design process to combine the use of state machines and traditional structured design. We also collected data for the monitoring team at various points throughout the project, although we tried to do this with as little disturbance as possible to the project team.

Analyzing and packaging results. The final steps in the QIP involve analyzing and packaging the process results. We found significant differences in effort distribution during development between the Cleanroom project and the baseline. Approximately six percent of the total project effort shifted from coding to design activities in the Cleanroom effort. Also, the baseline development teams traditionally spent approximately 85 percent of their coding effort writing code, 15 percent reading it. The Cleanroom team spent about 50 percent in each activity.

The primary goal of the first case study had been to improve reliability without increasing cost. Analysis showed a reduction in change rate of nearly 50 percent and a reduction in error rate of greater than a third. Although the expectation was for productivity equivalent to the baseline, the Cleanroom effort also improved in that area by approximately 50 percent. We also saw a decrease in rework, as defined by the amount of time spent correcting errors. Additional analysis of code reading revealed that three fourths of all errors uncovered were found by only one reader. This prompted a renewed emphasis on mul-

QUALITY IMPROVEMENT PARADIGM: FOUNDATION FOR IMPROVEMENT

The Quality Improvement Paradigm is an effective framework for conducting experiments and studies like those described in the main text. It is an experimental but evolutionary concept for learning and improvement.[1]

The QIP has six steps:

1. Characterize the project and its environment.

2. Set quantifiable goals for successful project performance and improvement.

3. Choose the appropriate process models, supporting methods, and tools for the project.

4. Execute the processes, construct the products, collect and validate the prescribed data, and analyze the data to provide real-time feedback for corrective action.

5. Analyze the data to evaluate current practices, determine problems, record findings, and make recommendations for future process improvements.

6. Package the experience in the form of updated and refined models, and save the knowledge gained from this and earlier projects in an experience base for future projects.

The QIP uses two tools: the Goal/Question/Metric paradigm and the Experience Factory Organization.

GQM paradigm. The GQM paradigm is a mechanism used in the planning phase of the Quality Improvement Paradigm for defining and evaluating a set of operational goals using measurement.[2] It provides a systematic approach for tailoring and integrating goals with models of the software processes, products, and quality perspectives of interest, according to the specific needs of the project and organization.

You define goals in an operational, tractable way by refining them into a set of questions that extract appropriate information from the models. The questions, in turn, define the metrics needed to define and interpret the goals.

A goal-generation template helps in developing goals. The template specifies the essential elements: the object of interest (like product or process), the aspect of interest (like cost or ability

to detect defects), the purpose of the study (like assessment or prediction), the point of view from which the study is performed (like customer's or manager's), and the context in which the study is performed (like people-oriented or problem-oriented factors).

For example, two goals associated with the application of the Cleanroom method in the SEL were analysis of the Cleanroom process to characterize resource allocation from the project manager's point of view, and analysis of the Cleanroom product to characterize defects from the customer's point of view.

Experience Factory Organization. The Experience Factory Organization is an organizational structure that supports the activities specified in the QIP by continuously accumulating evaluated experiences, building a repository of integrated experience models that projects can access and modify to meet their needs.[3] The Experience Factory extends project-development activities by providing systematic

learning and packaging of reusable experiences. It packages experiences by building informal, schematized, formal, and automated models and measures of software processes, products, and other forms of knowledge, and distributes them through consultation, documentation, and automated support.

While project organization follows an evolutionary process model that reuses packaged experiences, the Experience Factory provides the set of processes needed for learning, packaging, and storing the project organization's experience for reuse. The Experience Factory Organization represents the integration of these two functions.

REFERENCES

1. V. Basili, "Quantitative Evaluation of Software Engineering Methodology," Tech. Report TR-1519, CS Dept., Univ. of Maryland, College Park, July 1985.
2. V. Basili and H. Rombach "The TAME Project: Towards Improvement-Oriented Software Environments," *IEEE Trans. Software Eng.*, June 1988, pp. 758-773.
3. V. Basili, "Software Development: A Paradigm for the Future," *Proc. Compsac*, IEEE CS Press, Los Alamitos, Calif., 1989.

---

tiple readers throughout the SEL environment.

We also examined the earlier concerns expressed by managers and the project team. The results showed increased effort in early requirements-analysis and design activities and a clearer set of in-line comments. This led to a better understanding of the whole system and enabled the project team to understand and accommodate changes with greater ease than was typical for that environment.

We reviewed the application of classical Cleanroom and noted successes and difficulties. The structure of independent teams and the emphasis on peer review during development was easy to apply. However, the devel-

opment team did have difficulty using the associated formal methods. Also, unlike the scheme in the classical Cleanroom method, the test team followed an approach that combined statistical testing with traditional functional testing.

Finally, the psychological effects of independent testing appeared to be negligible. All team members indicated high job satisfaction as well as a willingness to apply the method in future projects.

We packaged these early results in various reports and presentations, including some at the SEL's 1990 Software Engineering Workshop. As a reference for future SEL Cleanroom projects, we also began efforts to pro-

duce a document describing the SEL Cleanroom process model, including details on specific activities.[6] (The completed document is now available to current Cleanroom projects.)

Second case study. The first case study showed us that we needed better training in the use of formal methods and more guidance in applying the testing approach. We also realized that experiences from the initial project team had to be disseminated and used.

Again, we followed the Quality Improvement Paradigm. We selected two projects: one similar to the initial Cleanroom project, Project 2A, and one more representative of the typical FDD contractor-support environment,

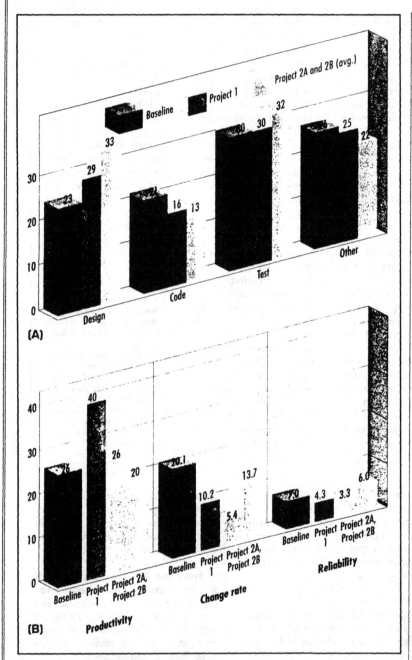

Figure 3. *Measurement comparisons for two case studies investigating Cleanroom. The first case study involved one project, Project 1. The second case study involved two projects, Projects 2A and 2B. (A) Percentage of total development effort for various development activities, and (B) productivity in lines of code per day, change rate in changes per thousand lines of code, and reliability in errors per thousand lines of code.*

Project 2B.

Project 2A involved a different subsystem of another attitude ground-support system. This subsystem focused on the processing of telemetry data, comprising 22,000 LOC. The project was staffed with four developers and two testers. Project 2B involved an entire mission attitude ground-support system, consisting of approximately 160,000 LOC. At its peak, it was staffed with 14 developers and four testers.

Setting goals and choosing processes. The second case study had two goals. One was to verify measures from the first study by applying the Cleanroom method to Project 2A, a project of similar size and scope. The second was to verify the applicability of Cleanroom on Project 2B, a substantially larger project but one more representative of the typical environment. We also wanted to further tailor the process model to the environment by using results from the first case study and applying more formal techniques.

Packages from the SEL Experience Factory (described in the box on p. 63) were available to support project development. These included an evolved training program, a more knowledgeable experimenter team to monitor the projects, and several in-process interactive sessions with the project teams. Although we had begun producing a handbook detailing the SEL Cleanroom process model, it was not ready in time to give to the teams at the start of these projects.

The project leader for the initial Cleanroom project participated as a member of the experimenter team, served as the process modeler for the handbook, and acted as a consultant to the current projects.

We modified the process according to the experiences of the Cleanroom team in the first study. Project 1's team had had difficulty using state machines in system design, so we changed the emphasis to Mills' box-structure algorithm.[7] We also added a more extensive

<table>
<tr><td colspan="6" align="center">**TABLE 1**
PROJECT COMPARISONS FOR SEL TECHNOLOGY EVALUATION</td></tr>
</table>

Evaluation aspect	Controlled experiments		Cleanroom case studies		
	Reading vs.testing	Cleanroom	Project 1	Project 2A	Project 2B
Team size	32 participants	Three-person development teams (10 experiment teams; five control teams); common independent tester	Three-person development team; two-person test team	Four-person development team; two-person test team	Fourteen-person development team; four-person test team
Project size and application	Small (145-365 LOC) sample Fortran programs	1,500 LOC, Fortran, electronic message system for graduate laboratory course	40,000 LOC, Fortran, flight-dynamics ground-support system	22,000 LOC, Fortran, flight-dynamics ground-support system	160,000 LOC, Fortran, flight-dynamics ground-support system
Results	Reading techniques appear more effective than testing techniques for fault detection	Cleanroom teams use fewer computer resources, satisfy requirements more successfully, and make higher percentage of scheduled deliveries	Project spends higher percentage of effort in design, uses fewer computer resources, and achieves better productivity and reliability than environment baseline	Project continues trend in better reliability while maintaining baseline productivity	Project reliability only slightly better than baseline while productivity falls below baseline

training program focusing on Cleanroom techniques, experiences from the initial Cleanroom team, and the relationship between the Cleanroom studies and the SEL's general goals. The instruction team included representatives from the SEL, members of the initial team, and Mills. Mills gave talks on various aspects of the methodology, as well as motivational remarks on the potential benefits of the Cleanroom method in the software community.

Project 2A ran from March 1990 through January 1992. Project 2B ran from February 1990 through December 1992. Again, we examined reliability, productivity, and process characteristics, comparing them to Project 1 results and the SEL baseline.

Analyzing and packaging results. As Figure 3 shows, there were significant differences between the two projects. Error and change rates for Project 2A continued to be favorable. Productivity rate, however, returned to the SEL baseline value. Error and change rates for Project 2B increased from Project 1 values, although they remained lower than SEL baseline numbers. Productivity, however, dropped below the baseline.

When we examined the effort distribution among the baseline and Projects 1, 2A, and 2B, we found a continuing upward trend in the percentage of design effort, and a corresponding decrease in coding effort. Additional analysis indicated that although the overall error rates were below the baseline, the percentage of system components found to contain errors during testing was still representative of baseline projects developed in this environment. This suggests that the breadth of error distribution did not change with the Cleanroom method.

In addition to evaluating objective data for these two projects, we gathered subjective input through written and verbal feedback from project participants. In general, input from Project 2A team members, the smaller of the two projects, was very favorable, while Project 2B members, the larger contractor team, had significant reservations about the method's application. Interestingly, though, specific shortcomings were remarkably similar for both teams. Four areas were generally cited in the comments. Participants were dissatisfied with the use of design abstractions and box structures, did not fully accept the rationale for having no developer compilation, had problems coordinating information between developers and testers, and cited the need for a reference to the SEL Clean-

room process model.

Again, we packaged these results into various reports and presentations, which formed the basis for additional process tailoring.

Third case study. We have recently begun a third case study to examine difficulties in scaling up the Cleanroom method in the typical contractor-support environment and to verify previous trends and analyze additional tailoring of the SEL process model. We expect the study to complete in September.

In keeping with this goal, we again selected a project representative of the FDD contractor-support environment, but one that was estimated at 110,000 LOC, somewhat smaller than Project 2B. The project involves development of another entire mission attitude ground-support system. Several team members have prior experience with the Cleanroom method through previous SEL studies.

Experience Factory packages available to this project include training in the Cleanroom method, an experienced experimenter team, and the *SEL Cleanroom Process Model* (the completed handbook). In addition to modifying the process model according to the results from the first two case studies, we are providing regularly scheduled sessions in which the team members and experimenters can interact. These sessions give team members the opportunity to communicate problems they are having in applying the method, ask for clarification, and get feedback on their activities. This activity is aimed at closing a communication gap that the contractor team felt existed in Project 2B.

The concepts associated with the QIP and its use of measurement have given us an evolutionary framework for understanding, assessing, and packaging the SEL's experiences.

Table 1 shows how the evolution of our Cleanroom study progressed as we used measurements from each experiment and case study to define the next experiment or study. The SEL Cleanroom process model has evolved on the basis of results packaged through earlier evaluations. Some aspects of the target methodology continue to evolve: Experimentation with formal methods has transitioned from functional decomposition and state machines to box-structure design and again to box-structure application as a way to abstract requirements. Testing has shifted from a combined statistical/functional approach, to a purely statistical approach based on operational scenarios. Our current case study is examining the effect of allowing developer compilation.

Along the way, we have eliminated some aspects of the candidate process; we have not examined reliability models, for example, since the environment does not currently have sufficient data to seed them. We have also emphasized some aspects. For example, we are conducting studies that focus on the effect of peer reviews and independent test teams for non-Cleanroom projects. We are also studying how to improve reading by developing reading techniques through off-line experimentation.

The SEL baseline used for comparison is undergoing continual evolution. Promising techniques are filtered into the development organization as general process improvements, and corresponding measures of the modified process (effort distribution, reliability, cost) indicate the effect on the baseline.

The SEL Cleanroom process model has evolved to a point where it appears applicable to smaller projects (fewer than 50,000 LOC), but additional understanding and tailoring is still required for larger scale efforts. The model will continue to evolve as we gain more data from development projects. Measurement will provide baselines for comparison, identify areas of concern and improvement, and provide insight into the effects of process modifications. In this way, we can set quantitative expectations and evaluate the degree to which goals have been achieved.

By adhering to the Quality Improvement Paradigm, we can refine the process model from study to study, assessing strengths and weaknesses, experiences, and goals. However, our investigation into the Cleanroom method illustrates that the evolutionary infusion of technology is not trivial and that process improvement depends on a structured approach of understanding, assessment, and packaging. ◆

ACKNOWLEDGMENTS

This work has been supported by NASA/GSFC contract NSG-5123. We thank all the members of the SEL team who have been part of the Cleanroom experimenter teams, the Cleanroom training teams, and the various Cleanroom project teams. We especially thank Frank McGarry, Rose Pajerski, Sally Godfrey, Ara Kouchadjian, Sharon Waligora, Harlan Mills, Michael Dyer, and Terry Baker for their efforts.

REFERENCES

1. V. Basili and R. Selby, "Comparing the Effectiveness of Software Testing Strategies," *IEEE Trans. Software Eng.*, Dec. 1987, pp. 1278-1296.
2. R. Linger, H. Mills, and B. Witt, *Structured Programming: Theory and Practice*, Addison-Wesley, Reading, Mass., 1979.
3. H. Mills, M. Dyer, and R. Linger, "Cleanroom Software Engineering," *IEEE Software*, Sept. 1987, pp. 19-24.
4. R. Selby, Jr., V. Basili, and T. Baker, "Cleanroom Software Development: An Empirical Evaluation," *IEEE Trans. Software Eng.*, Sept. 1987, pp. 1027-1037.
5. L. Landis et al., "Recommended Approach to Software Development: Revision 3," Tech. Report SEL-81-305, Software Engineering Laboratory, Greenbelt, Md., 1992.
6. S. Green, *Software Engineering Laboratory (SEL) Cleanroom Process Model*, Tech. Report SEL-91-004, Software Engineering Laboratory, Greenbelt, Md., 1991.
7. H. Mills, "Stepwise Refinement and Verification in Box-Structured Systems," *IEEE Software*, June 1988, pp. 23-36.

Address questions about this article to Basili at CS Dept., University of Maryland, College Park, MD 20742; basili@cs.umd.edu; or to Green at NASA/GFSC, Code 552.1, Greenbelt, MD 20771; segreen@gsfcmail.nasa.gov.

Chapter 3

How is Measuring Done?

The papers

Measurement tools and methods

Shari Lawrence Pfleeger and Joseph c. Fitzgerald, Jr., "Software Metrics Tool Kit: Support for Selection, Collection and Analysis," *Information and Software Technology*, Vol. 33, No. 7, Sept. 1991, pp. 477–482. Proposes a methodology for evaluating and classifying metrics tools that let a user build a tool kit tailored for project needs.

Using models

Sarah Brocklehurst and Bev Littlewood, "New Ways to Get Accurate Reliability Measures," *IEEE Software*, Vol. 9, No. 4, July 1992, pp. 34–42. Describes two comparison techniques for recalibrating reliability models to improve their accuracy.

Adopting and standardizing a method

Robert B. Grady and Tom Van Slack, "Key Lessons in Achieving Widespread Inspection Use," *IEEE Software*, Vol. 11, No. 4, July 1994, pp. 46–57. Identifies the four stages of Hewlett-Packard's technology adoption process, including measurement that demonstrates clear return on investment.

Case study

Michael K. Daskalantonakis, "A Practical View of Software Measurement and Implementation Experiences Within Motorola," *IEEE Trans. Software Eng.*, Vol. 18, No. 11, pp. 998–1,010. Describes Motorola's company-wide software metrics program to improve software with minimum resource expenditure.

Editors' introduction

Chapters 1 and 2 have helped us understand why we measure and what we choose to measure. In this chapter, we look at support for measurement: tools, models, and standards. It is important to remember that the primary responsibility of any developer is to produce a product, not to collect measurement data. Thus, it is essential that the job of metrics data collection and analysis be made as simple and as unobtrusive as possible by using tools, models, and standards. Models help us understand how the metrics relate to one another. Standards provide counting and collection rules to ensure consistency and completeness in our data. And by automating as much as possible, tools help speed up and standardize both collection and analysis. In particular, we can embed standards in our tools, allowing our counts to be as objective and consistent as possible.

In the first article, "Software Metrics Tool Kit: Support for Selection, Collection and Analysis," Shari Lawrence Pfleeger and Joe Fitzgerald provide a framework to help developers evaluate automated tools for metrics data collection, storage, and analysis. Using a faceted classification scheme commonly used for reuse repositories, they suggest a method of organizing keywords that describe a tool and its use. As tools are evaluated by a metrics team, their descriptions are placed in a tools database, and the keywords represent the evaluation findings. This framework lets users search for particular types of tools having specified characteristics; thus, the users can select and tailor a suite of metrics tools to meet their organizational and project needs.

Metrics are of little use without a context for understanding them. For this reason, we usually build models that tell us how the metrics relate to each other and to the artifacts they describe. Models are used most extensively in reliability measurement and prediction, where they tell us how failures and timing relate to our reliability assumptions and goals. But, as Figure 5 shows, different reliability models can predict very different behavior from the same data set. So we must look for ways to select an appropriate model, as well as ways to assure its accuracy.

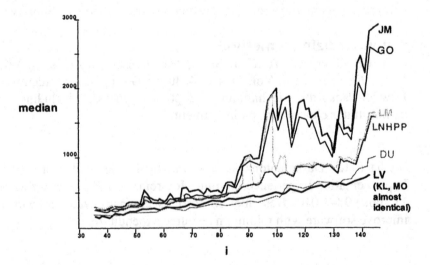

Figure 5. Data analyzed using several reliability growth models. The current median time to next failure is plotted on the y-axis against failure number on the x-axis (from Fenton and Pfleeger 1996).

In "New Ways to Get Accurate Reliability Measures," Sarah Brocklehurst and Bev Littlewood describe the problem of accuracy in measuring reliability. They believe that "it is now possible in most cases to obtain reasonably accurate reliability measures for software and to have reasonable confidence that this is the case in a particular situation, so long as the reliability levels required are relatively modest." Suggesting that no single reliability model is universally valid, they instead encourage engineers to select models most appropriate for a particular problem. The paper describes techniques for increasing model accuracy.

Standards and technology transfer are critical to good software measurement. Many measurement programs are started with good intentions—and data are collected and analyzed on pilot projects—but measurement does not become a widespread practice unless developers and engineers are convinced of its essential nature. Technology transfer in software engineering is a slow process.[1] Given the high cost and criticality of much of the software we build today, we cannot afford to wait that long; we must use measurement to understand effectiveness and then build a compelling argument for change.

In "Key Lessons in Achieving Widespread Inspection Use," Bob Grady and Tom Van Slack of Hewlett-Packard describe the process of software inspection adoption, using measurement to provide key insights about penetration and effectiveness. By standardizing the inspection process, H-P not only improves its software quality but ensures uniform measurement of defect data. According to Grady and Van Slack, H-P has experienced three of the four stages of the adoption process. The article details the history and implications of these stages, including the advantages of inspections and the success of manual (as opposed to automated) data collection.

Many of you may be familiar with the Malcolm Baldrige Award, presented annually by the United States government to American organizations with measurably high quality products. Motorola has received one of these prestigious awards, and the company has generously published the lessons it learned as it measured and improved its product quality. Our case study provides "A Practical View of Software Measurement and Implementation Experiences Within Motorola." Michael Daskalantonakis describes the multidimensional view of metrics that formed the basis for a Motorola-wide software initiative. The metrics were derived using the GQM paradigm that we encountered in Chapter 2. Daskalantonakis makes the important point that "...measurement is not the goal. The goal is improvement—through measurement, analysis, and feedback."

---

[1] S. Redwine and W. Riddle, "Software Technology Maturation," *Proc. 8th Int'l Conf. Software Eng.*, 1985, IEEE Computer Society Press, Los Alamitos, Calif., pp. 189-200.

To probe further

V.R. Basili and D. Weiss, "A Methodology For Collecting Valid Software Engineering Data," *IEEE Trans. Software Eng.*, Vol. 10, No. 3, 1984, pp. 728–738. The initial paper on the Goal-Question-Metric paradigm.

J.B. Dreger, *Function Point Analysis*, Prentice Hall, Englewood Cliffs, N.J., 1989. A handbook on how to collect and use function points.

T.C. Jones, *Applied Software Measurement: Assuring Productivity and Quality*, McGraw Hill, N.Y., 1992. Good overview of measurement, including much benchmark material for comparing your productivity and quality with industry averages.

P. Mellor, "Software Reliability Data Collection: Problems and Standards," in *Software Reliability*, Pergamon Infotech State-of-the-Art Series, Pergamon Press, London, pp. 165–181. Describes data collection requirements for quality and reliability evaluation.

P. Oman and J. Hagemeister, "Metrics for Assessing Software System Maintainability," *Proc. 1992 Conf. Software Maintenance*, IEEE Computer Society Press, Los Alamitos, Calif., 1992, pp. 337–344. Provides a taxonomy of maintainability characteristics and associated metrics that can be used to assess the source code quality.

S. Lawrence Pfleeger, "Measuring Software Reliability," *IEEE Spectrum*, Aug. 1992, pp. 56–60. Describes how viewpoints can affect definition and use of a measure.

Software metrics tool kit: support for selection, collection and analysis

S L Pfleeger and J C Fitzgerald, Jr

An approach is described to metrics tool evaluation that allows a project manager to select a customized set of metrics tools for inclusion in a metrics tool kit. The tool evaluation results are stored in a database organized according to a faceted classification. By providing descriptors of each facet, the manager can retrieve only that tool information relevant to the project at hand. Tools can then be compared and contrasted by assigning weights to a set of selection criteria. Finally, selected tools are combined in a tool kit that becomes part of the development environment.

software metrics, software quality, tool kits, software tools

Importance of software metrics

Software plays a major role in any business, from the systems used to provide new services to the necessary tracking and routing of information from one organization to another. Corporate success often depends on the quality of software-related products and on a business's ability to respond to its customers in a timely fashion and at a reasonable cost. Thus management and control of software development are paramount in assuring that software products are built on time, within budget, and in accordance with a stringent set of quality goals.

Software metrics are essential to understanding, managing, and controlling the development process. Quantitative characterization of various aspects of development involves a deep understanding of software development activities and their inter-relationships. In turn, the measures that result can be used to set goals for productivity and quality and to establish a baseline against which improvements are compared. Measurements examined during development can point to 'hot spots' that need further attention, analysis, or testing. Even during maintenance, metrics can reflect the effects of changes in size, complexity, and maintainability. Measurement also supports planning, as projections and predictions about future projects can be made based on data collected from past projects. Tools and strategies can be evaluated, and the development process and environment can be tailored to the situation at hand.

However, both management and software engineers often balk at the additional time and labour needed to support metrics data collection and analysis. For example, the Software Engineering Laboratory at the University of Maryland, USA, reports that data collection and analysis add 7 to 8% to the cost of a project[1], and DeMarco estimates that development costs increase between 5 and 10% when metrics collection is involved[2]. Thus tools and techniques must be available to software engineers to minimize the degree to which they are distracted by their metrics duties. Only then will metrics become a welcome part of software development.

The Contel Technology Center is addressing this need in several ways. As part of the Software Engineering Laboratory, the Software Metrics Project provides services and products to facilitate the use of metrics throughout the corporation. The authors recommend that the collection of metrics be tied to the maturity of the development process[3,4]. As discussed elsewhere[5,6], a project can measure only what is visible and appropriate. Thus an immature project (where requirements are not well known or understood) begins by measuring effort and time, so that a baseline can be established against which improvements can be compared. Next, when requirements are defined and structured, project management metrics establish general productivity measures. When the process is defined well enough to support it, a project adds product measurement; in this way, characteristics of intermediate products can be used to suggest the likely quality of the final product. If the project is mature enough to have a central point of control, then process measures with feedback to the controller or manager are appropriate. The feedback is used to make decisions about how to proceed at critical points in the process. Finally, the most mature projects can use process measures and feedback to change the process dynamically as development progresses.

Notice that the process maturity framework suggests metrics not only to monitor the activities in the development process, but also to help improve the process itself. By considering metrics as nested sets of measures related to process maturity, each level allows management more insight into and control over the process and its constituent products.

To support metrics collection and analysis, each development project is provided with a software metrics tool kit that can be tailored to individual project needs. The tool kit contains metrics tools to collect and analyse data

Mitre Corporation, 7525 Colshire Drive, McLean, VA 22102, USA

Reprinted from *Information and Software Technology*, Vol. 33, No. 7, Sept. 1991, S.L. Pfleeger and J.C. Fitzgerald, Jr., "Software Metrics Tool Kit: Support for Selection, Collection and Analysis," pp. 477–482, 1991, with kind permission from Elsevier Science–NL, Sara Burgerhartstraat 25; 1055 KV Amsterdam, The Netherlands.

appropriate for the project's process maturity, development environment, and management needs and preferences. Underlying the tool kit is a project metrics database. The database supports two activities. First, its contents can be used by the tools and by project managers to monitor and make decisions about the development process. Second, the database contents can be transferred to a corporate historical database. The corporate database is analysed to examine trends, make predictions, and set standards for future projects.

The remainder of this paper focuses on the development of the metrics tool kit. The way in which existing tools are evaluated is described, as are the methods used to make the evaluations available to project managers.

Evaluation philosophy

Many automated metrics tools are available today. They vary from simple analysers that count the number of decision points in a source listing to complex estimators of cost and schedule. Some tools are standalone, while others are embedded as part of a suite of computer-aided software engineering (CASE) tools. The authors have chosen to evaluate any tool that involves metrics data collection and analysis, whether commercially available or provided free to interested users. To do so, a two-stage approach to evaluation has been developed based on the work of Bohner[7]. The first stage, called a paper evaluation, reviews the product literature and documentation to determine

- the intent of the tool
- the type(s) of metrics supported by the tool
- the environment in which the tool is to be used
- the available interfaces between this tool and other tools
- the type of user interface provided by the tool

The results of the paper evaluation are used to suggest a small subset of metrics tools that deserve further investigation, based on particular needs. In particular, candidate tools are chosen for inclusion in a metrics tool kit; the tool kit is then built by the Software Metrics Project to assist software engineers in implementing the recommended metrics.

Once the candidate tools are selected for more detailed analysis, the actual tool (rather than its paper description) is installed and evaluated against a set of criteria. This second stage, called the extended evaluation, investigates each tool in depth. Tool characteristics examined include:

- speed
- data import and export capabilities
- quality of the user interface
- documentation
- tool accuracy
- vendor support
- cost

The paper and extended evaluations provide enough information to allow project managers to make informed decisions about the tools they wish to include in their project's development environment.

The paper evaluation is addressed in the next section. First, the general framework is discussed. Then, each characteristic is described in turn. Finally, the paper evaluation is illustrated with an example. The third main section discusses the extended evaluation. A rating form is displayed, showing the items included in the evaluation and the possible sources of information for each item. An example explains how the extended evaluation is performed.

An example of the use of the evaluations is described in the fourth section. In addition, it is explained how project managers have online access to the evaluations stored in an Oracle database. Updates and additions will be made as existing tools change and new ones are introduced. The fifth section describes the relevance of the metrics tool kits and tool evaluations to the ongoing work of the Software Metrics Project. Finally, conclusions are drawn about the types of metrics available for use today, their price, ease of use, and utility.

PAPER EVALUATION

Framework

The choice of metrics to be collected on a project is determined by the maturity of its software development process, the availability of data, and the needs of project management. To assist in the collection of metrics throughout the corporation, the Software Metrics Project develops a tool kit for each project, based on the metrics needs and the results of evaluations. A project manager specifies information about the project (e.g., its environment, methods, and metrics needs), and the evaluation database is used to suggest appropriate metrics tools.

The continuing tools survey gives an understanding of industry's ability to provide corporations with useful metrics tools. In discovering which tools need improvement, vendors can be directed towards making those improvements. Moreover, in collecting and storing tool information in a database, software managers can locate tools without having to perform individual evaluations themselves.

The first step in the evaluation process gathers information. Candidate tools are considered for inclusion in the tool kit. Information available on each tool is collected from the vendors, and existing third-party evaluations are sought. From the collection of information available for each tool, a paper evaluation is performed. The evaluation classifies the tool according to certain characteristics, described below, so that the entire body of tool evaluations forms a repository of tools information. Project managers can then query the repository to determine types of tools available, functionality, cost, and any other relevant information. The results of the paper evaluation are recorded at the top of a tool evaluation form, which captures the name of the tool, the vendor, and the date of the evaluation.

Tool classification

The next section of the evaluation classifies the tool according to several criteria. The classification scheme follows a methodology known as faceted classification. Facets are multiple independent indices used to identify groups of similar objects. That is, each facet characterizes an attribute of the object that cannot be described using any of the other facets. In this sense, facets are orthogonal. Such a scheme has been successful in classifying components for a reuse repository[8].

The classification scheme allows tool information to be stored and retrieved based on the interests and needs of the querying project manager. The indices or facets chosen are:

- Type: the type or purpose of the tool, such as cost estimation, code analysis, etc.
- Activity: the development step to which this tool can be applied, such as requirements, design, code, test, etc.
- Level: the minimum level of process maturity for which this tool may be appropriate.
- Method: the development method or technique supported by the type of tool being described (such as COCOMO, SADT, or Jackson System Development).
- Language: language dependencies of the tool (e.g., a code analyser might parse Ada and C, but not Cobol).
- Operating system: the operating system required for the tool to run.
- Platform: the hardware platform required for the tool to run, such as IBM PC or Vax.
- Target application: the system type that the tool is designed for, such as 'real time' or 'MIS' (management information system).

Each facet descriptor is entered in section 2 of the evaluation form. The entries for each descriptor are derived from vendor literature, discussions with vendor representatives, and/or evaluations reported in journals and trade publications. The facet characterization allows the description of every situation in which the tool can be used. Thus the form accommodates multiple descriptors for each facet. For example, if a tool runs on several platforms, under several operating systems, or with several design techniques, the facet descriptors can reflect these situations. For example, the evaluation for AdaMAT indicates that it runs both on a Vax and on a Rational platform. Similarly, it is noted on the form that AdaMAT can provide metrics for coding, testing, or maintenance.

A major benefit of faceted classification is the ease with which additional facets can be added to the scheme. Unlike hierarchical or other database structures, a faceted approach allows the existing information to be kept intact and the additional information needed to describe the new facet to be merely added. The only

1.0 The tool

Tool name:	Ada Metrics Analysis Tool (AdaMAT)
Vendor name:	Dynamics Research Corporation
Vendor address:	60 Frontage Rd Andover, MA 01810
Contact/phone #:	John Ragasta or John Rice/ 508–475–9090
Evaluation date:	05/21/90

2.0 Tool classification

Type	Activity	Level	Method	Language	Operating system	Platform	Target application
analysis	code maintenance test	2		Ada	R1000 VMS	Rational 100, 300C Vax	

3.0 Tool evaluation

Version:	1.0
Platform:	Rational 100
Operating system:	R1000
Cost:	Rational: $20,000 Vax: range from $5,000 to $25,000 depending on platform
Strengths:	Provides written feedback on potential problem areas in code, applies real software engineering principles (those that are both independent of and dependent on the Ada language itself)
Weaknesses:	Price; not available on PC platform as yet

TABLE 1.

Criteria	Raw score (1–10)	Weight (1–10)	Total
Performance/speed	can't objectively evaluate on heavily loaded Rational		
Data import/export	4		
User interface	7 (consistent with Rational)		
Documentation	5		
Tool accuracy	9		
Vendor support	8		
Cost	6		

Figure 1. Results of extended evaluation

restriction on new facets is that they be independent of existing facets. In other words, the aspect of the tool characterized by the new facet cannot be described by using a combination of descriptors with the old facets.

The tools evaluation information is stored in a database according to its faceted classification. Queries made in terms of facets allow project managers to read only those tool evaluations that suit their needs. For example, a manager of a project that is written in Ada on a Rational platform may need a tool that will generate complexity metrics for the project's code. Here the manager will set Type to 'complexity', Language to 'Ada', and Platform to 'Rational', and the result will be a list of tools that analyse complexity for Ada programs in the specified environment. The manager can be more specific, asking for instance for a Method of 'cyclomatic complexity' to get only those tools that implement McCabe's metric in the desired environment.

The top two sections of the evaluation report represent the information gathered in the paper evaluation step. The third section is used only for the extended evaluations.

EXTENDED EVALUATION

Evaluation criteria

The extended evaluation of a tool involves the use of a tool in a real-life setting. That is, a hands-on evaluation is done using Contel data with a functioning version of the tool (not a demonstration copy). The results of the evaluation are recorded in section 3 of the evaluation form, as shown in Figure 1. The first portion of this section contains information on the version, platform, and operating system of the tool as used in the hands-on evaluation. This information prevents inconsistencies in evaluation data across different platforms or as vendors release new versions of their tools.

Next are subjective evaluations of the tool's strengths and weaknesses; this part of the extended evaluation documents those issues not addressed in the more objective rating scheme that follows. The final portion of section 3 contains a summary table of the tool's objective evaluation. The criteria for evaluation fall into seven categories:

- Performance/speed: rates the execution of the tool in performing its calculations or analysis.
- Data import/export: refers to any means that the tool provides for importing/exporting data from/to other tools (the simpler data transfer mechanisms get higher scores).
- User interface: refers to ease of use and ease of learning the tool, so that it can be used effectively in an organization.
- Documentation: refers to the availability and overall quality of the documentation provided with the tool.
- Tool accuracy: rating given to judge a tool's accuracy in implementing a model for a certain metric (e.g., COCOMO for cost estimation) and the tool's flexibility in providing modifiable parameters to the model it implements.
- Vendor support: rating on the vendor's provision of support (e.g., an 800 number or help line), response time in answering questions, and the helpfulness of the information provided.
- Cost: criterion based on the cost for the corporation to use this tool on a company-wide scale, not just the single licence fee.

The criteria are arranged in tabular form, as shown. The left column contains the raw score the tool received in the evaluation, ranked from 1 (low) to 10 (high). The second column represents a weight given to each of the criteria. This weight is assigned by the project manager doing the evaluation. That is, each project will have different needs and goals, and therefore different desirable characteristics. Each possible rating (from 1 to 10) in each category is described in detail in a set of tables, so that there is no ambiguity between ratings. The rating definition tables are based on those reported by Bohner[7] and Reifer[9]. For example, vendor support is rated according to the table below:

(1) No response.
(2) Respond within five business days, calls processed on first come-first serve basis
(3) Respond within five business days, has call prioritization.
(4) Respond within four business days, calls processed on first come-first serve basis.
(5) Respond within four business days, has call prioritization.

(6) Respond within three business days, calls processed on first come-first serve basis.
(7) Respond within three business days, has call prioritization.
(8) Respond within two business days to all calls.
(9) Respond within one business day to all calls.
(10) Respond to problem at time of call.

By using the rating tables, a particular tool should be given the same rating by two different raters.

Evaluation tool and database

The evaluation database holds the results of all tool evaluations. A tool built on the database allows the project manager to tailor the evaluation to the needs of the project at hand, as shown in the example in the next section. The final score for each criterion is computed by multiplying the raw score by the assigned weights; if desired, the scores can be summed to yield a single number that represents the tool's overall rating. In this way, ratings can be compared and contrasted by the project manager and used to support final tool selection.

BUILDING TOOL KIT: EXAMPLE

The Software Metrics Program team uses the evaluation results to build a metrics tool kit tailored to a project's needs. To see how the tool kit is built, an example is presented.

Suppose manager A is beginning a software development project. According to the requirements, a system is to be developed using Objective C on a Sun workstation. Manager A consults with the Software Metrics Project team and decides that development will be at maturity level 3. According to the nested levels of metrics recommended, manager A plans to collect data for project management and project metrics. In particular, tools in the coding phase are required to analyse Objective C. The manager specifies queries by supplying descriptors for each facet of interest. For instance, the Language is Objective C, the Platform is a Sun, and the Activity is coding. The database responds with all tools described by these characteristics. Because manager A is concerned about software reliability, it may be important to know the complexity of intermediate products. The database can be queried for complexity tools in particular by specifying Type as complexity, along with the other facet descriptors.

Next, manager A reviews the evaluations of tools suggested as a result of the queries. It is up to the manager to select tools that are most appropriate for the needs of the project and that are consistent with any standards or guidelines set for the manager's organization. For example, the database may suggest a code analysis tool that reports a variety of Halstead metrics. However, the manager may decide that there is no need or requirement for such measurements on this project. Similarly, the manager must decide whether to use a tool that runs in the Sun environment with limited capability, rather than

1.0 Tool classification

TABLE 1. Metriscope

Criteria	Raw score (1–10)	Weight (1–10)	Total
Performance/speed	5	10	50
Data import/export	4	2	8
User interface	5	1	5
Documentation	5	1	5
Tool accuracy	9	2	18

Figure 2. Weighting of Metriscope tool by manager A

TABLE 1. CompleMetricks

Criteria	Raw score (1–10)	Weight (1–10)	Total
Performance/speed	2	10	20
Data import/export	3	2	6
User interface	5	1	5
Documentation	5	1	5
Tool accuracy	10	2	20

Figure 3. Weighting of CompleMetricks tool by manager A

TABLE 1. Metriscope

Criteria	Raw score (1–10)	Weight (1–10)	Total
Performance/speed	5	1	5
Data import/export	4	2	8
User interface	5	10	50
Documentation	5	8	40
Tool accuracy	9	1	9

Figure 4. Weighting of Metriscope tool by manager B

one that runs on another platform with increased capability.

Manager A is given the opportunity to weight each tool according to the project's priorities. For example, suppose that manager A is evaluating Metriscope, a tool to compute code complexity. Performance is important to the project manager, because the tool will be used repeatedly by many programmers on large code modules. The raw scores for Metriscope are listed in the first column, and manager A adds weights in the middle column, as shown in Figure 2. The totals for each criterion are calculated automatically.

By comparison, the same weights for the CompleMetricks tool yield the scores shown in Figure 3. It is important that manager A examines the scores for each criterion, not just the total score. It is clear that, on the basis of performance and speed, Metriscope is the tool of choice. However, several criteria may be important, and the manager must take each into account when making a final decision.

Similarly, manager B may examine the same tools, but with different priorities (see Figure 4). For example, manager A may have rated user interface low because the software engineers are familiar with metrics and the use of metrics tools. However, manager B's employees are using metrics for the first time, so user interface and documentation are more important.

In this way, tools can be compared and contrasted. The final decision on tool use is always left to the project manager.

Once the set of tools is chosen, their interaction with the development environment is considered. If the full complement of tools needed can run on a Sun workstation, then the software metrics team works with manager A to buy and use the tools on the workstation. Help is given in establishing a project historical database on the workstation, and the tools are supplemented with special-purpose code, if necessary, to populate the database with data collected. Finally, the metrics team helps manager A interpret the data and transfer the results to the corporate database for archival purposes.

However, some of the types of tools recommended may not be available for the Sun workstation. In this case, the metrics team identifies tools that run on an IBM PC and that meet manager A's requirements. The project historical database is built on the PC, and the PC is used to supplement the ongoing development on the Sun workstations. In this case, the data are transferred from the PC to the corporate database at project end. The PC is chosen as a platform for the tools because of its moderate cost and the abundance of metrics tools available to run on it.

Updates and additions will be made to the evaluation database as existing tools change and new ones are introduced. In addition, users of tools will be interviewed, and ratings changed to reflect experience with each tool. The strengths and weaknesses section of the tool evaluation report is likely to grow as user experiences are captured there.

CONCLUSIONS

The metrics tool evaluations performed have revealed only a limited number and kind of metrics tools available in the marketplace. Two general categories describe almost all of the tools on the market:

- project management and cost-estimation tools
- code analysis and testing tools

In this sense, the authors' work has identified several major areas in which other metrics tools are needed:

- requirements-related metrics tools (for complexity, completeness, uncertainty, etc.)
- process-related metrics tools
- maintainability metrics tools, including impact analysis tools

Moreover, the tools that exist vary widely in their functionality, sophistication of user interface, and price. The greatest lack of today's metrics tools is their inability to be integrated easily with one another or with the development environment in which they are placed. However, in spite of their limitations, the existing tools provide invaluable information about the way software is developed.

The goal of Contel's Software Metrics Project is to make metrics collection and analysis a natural and helpful part of the software development process. To that end, the software metrics evaluation database puts metrics tools information at the fingertips of those who need it. The resulting tool kits enable managers to integrate measurement into the development activities. In addition to its use for forecasting and scheduling, measurement is invaluable for providing the visibility into the process needed for informed decision-making about software development products and activities. Moreover, the measures provide a baseline against which improvement can be measured, so that goals for productivity and quality can be set and attained.

A major drawback to the tool kit approach is that the customization of tool kit to project is time-consuming, and coordination among tool kits can be difficult. Initially, the authors propose use of a standard set of tools (both commercial and home-grown) on an IBM PC, complete with uniform user interface and user's guide. However, if the project manager prefers another platform or another tool, inclusion of the same functionality can be a challenge. The authors have written a set of guidelines and counting rules to ensure consistency among the metrics that are collected, but they cannot always assure uniformity in interface or ease of use or understanding. Moreover, the price of using metrics tools varies greatly and is not always directly related to the amount of functionality provided by the tool. If the cost of metrics tools becomes prohibitive, the advantages of collecting and analysing data can be outweighed by the cost.

The Software Metrics Program will continue to evaluate and track the use of metrics tools throughout the corporation. Future plans include the development of analysis tools that, in concert with the corporate metrics database, will allow decisions to be made about metrics and metrics tools based on past successes. The authors plan to describe characteristics of the development process itself and incorporate those descriptors as facets in the database. In this way, tools will be selected based not only on development environment and tool strengths and weaknesses, but also on the type of development process or process activities.

REFERENCES

1 **Card, D and Glass, R** *Measuring software design quality* Addison-Wesley (1990)
2 **DeMarco, T** Comments at the 12th International Conference on Software Engineering, Nice, France (March 1990)
3 **Humphrey, W** *Managing the software process* Addison-Wesley (1989)
4 **Pressman, R** *Making software engineering happen* McGraw-Hill (1989)
5 **Pfleeger, S L** 'Recommendations for an initial set of software metrics' *Technical report CTC-TR-89-017* Contel Technology Center (1989)
6 **Pfleeger, S L and McGowan, C L** 'Software metrics in a process maturity framework' *J. Syst. Soft.* (July 1990)
7 **Bohner, S** 'Computer aided software engineering tools evaluation criteria' *Technical report CTC-TR-89-008* Contel Technology Center (1989)
8 **Prieto-Diaz, R and Freeman, P** 'Classifying software for reusability' *IEEE Software* (1987)
9 **Reifer Consultants, Inc.** 'Software tool/toolkit evaluation methodology' *Technical report RCI-TN-207* (April 1986)

New Ways to Get Accurate Reliability Measures

SARAH BROCKLEHURST and BEV LITTLEWOOD
City University, London

◆ *In spite of extravagant claims, no reliability model can be trusted to be accurate. Now, statistical techniques let you determine which model gives acceptable results.*

O ver the years, many software reliability models have been published, quite a few from our own Centre for Software Reliability. Unfortunately, no single model can be universally recommended. In fact, the accuracy of the reliability measures generated by the models varies dramatically: Some models sometimes give good results, some are almost universally awful, and none can be trusted to be accurate at all times. Worse, it does not seem possible to identify in advance those data sets for which a particular model is appropriate.[1]

This unsatisfactory situation has undoubtedly been the major factor in the poor adoption of reliability models. Users who have experienced poor results are once bitten, twice shy, unwilling to try new techniques.

It is with some trepidation that we claim our approach has largely eliminated these problems – our credo contains some caveats. We believe it *is* now possible *in most cases* to obtain *reasonably accurate* reliability measures for software *and to have reasonable confidence that this is the case* in a particular situation, so long as the reliability levels required are *relatively modest*. The italicized words here are important — there *are* some limits to what can be achieved — but these limits are not so restrictive that they should deter you from trying to measure and predict software reliability in an industrial context.

RELIABILITY AS A PREDICTION PROBLEM

In the form in which it has been most studied, the software-reliability problem involves dynamic assessment and prediction of reliability in the presence of that reliability growth which results from fault removal. This usually involves executing a program in an environment (test or real), observing failures, and fixing the faults

Reprinted from *IEEE Software*, Vol. 9, No. 4, July 1992, pp. 34–42.

that caused the failures. The expected failure behavior is therefore reliability growth, at least in the long term, although bad fixes that introduce new faults may cause short-term reversals.

Reliability-growth models use the data collected in this procedure, usually in the form of successive execution times between failures (or sometimes the number of failures in successive, measured time intervals), to estimate current reliability and predict future reliability growth.

What's important is that all questions of practical interest involve prediction. Even if you want to know current reliability, you are really asking about the future: In this case, about the random variable T, the time to the next failure. However you express reliability — as a rate of failure occurrence, the probability of surviving a specified mission without failure, the mean time to next failure, or any other convenient way — you are trying to predict the future.

So when you ask if a model is giving accurate reliability measures, you are really asking if it is predicting accurately. This is sometimes overlooked even in the technical literature, where authors have "validated" a model by showing that it can accurately explain past failure behavior and thereby claim that it is "accurate." The ability to capture the past accurately does not necessarily imply an ability to predict accurately. As Niels Bohr said, "Prediction is difficult, especially of the future."

NEW APPROACH

Consider the simplest prediction problem: estimating current reliability. Assume you have observed the successive interfailure times $t_1, t_2, \ldots, t_{i-1}$, and you want to predict the next time to failure, T_i. To do this, you use a model to obtain an estimate, $\hat{F}_i(t)$, of the true (but unknown) distribution function $F_i(t) \equiv P(T_i < t)$. If you knew the true distribution function, you could calculate any current reliability measure.

You start the program again and wait until it fails, which is a realization t_i of the random variable T_i. You repeat this operation for some range of i values. Informally,

you say that the model gives good results if what you *observe* tends to be in close agreement with what had been *predicted*.

Our approach is based on formal ways to compare prediction with observation.

Of course, this problem would be easier if you could observe the true $F_i(t)$ and compare it with the prediction, $\hat{F}_i(t)$. But you must somehow use only t_i, which is all you have. This is not a simple problem, and it is compounded because it is nonstationary — you want to predict accurately a sequence of different distributions, from each of which you will observe only one t_i.

However, you can make some simple comparisons. Suppose you need an accurate estimate of only the median of T_i, the value of T_i that is exceeded with probability 1/2. You could count what proportion of the actual t_i exceeded their predicted medians, and if this proportion is very different from 1/2, you can conclude that the median predictions were poor.

But this analysis does not tell you very much. Even if a series of predictions passed this test, it would give you confidence in the medians only. It does not tell you if other measures are accurate. What you really need is a way to detect any difference between prediction, $\hat{F}_i(t)$, and truth, $F_i(t)$.

U-plot. Our first technique aims to detect *systematic* differences between predicted and observed failure behavior. The u-plot, described in the box on p. 36, is a generalization of the median check.

The idea behind it is very similar to bias in statistics. In statistics, you use data to calculate an estimator of a population parameter. The estimator is unbiased if its average value is equal to the (unknown) parameter.

Of course, our case is more complex because we want to estimate a function, not just a number, at each stage, and because the problem's inherent nonstationarity means we can detect predic-

tion errors only over a sequence of different predictions.

In the event that the prediction errors are stationary — the nature of the error is the same at every stage — there will be a constant functional relationship between $\hat{F}_i(t)$ and $F_i(t)$. In such cases, you can use the u-plot to recalibrate the model — essentially training it to learn from its mistakes — and obtain more accurate predictions.

Recalibrating models to improve prediction accuracy exploits the fact that sometimes prediction errors are indeed approximately stationary. Clearly, there is always an unknown function, G_i, that will transform the predicted distribution into the true distribution. However, only sometimes is this function approximately the same in all cases: $G_i \approx G$ for all i.

When it is, you can estimate G using the comparison of earlier predictions against their corresponding observations and, by adjusting future predictions, improve their accuracy. In fact, the u-plot based on these earlier predictions is a suitable estimator of G.[2]

You adjust, or recalibrate, a model in four steps:

1. Obtain the u-plot, G_i^*, of predictions made before stage i. (It is better if G_i^* is a smoothed version of a joined-up, step-function u-plot, so our examples use a spline-smoothed version.)

2. Obtain $\hat{F}_i(t)$ from the raw (unrecalibrated) model for prediction at stage i.

3. Calculate the recalibrated prediction $\hat{\hat{F}}_i(t) \equiv G_i^*[\hat{F}_i(t)]$.

4. Repeat at each stage i.

This procedure is truly predictive, because it uses only the past to predict the future. You must believe neither that the recalibrated predictions will be better than the raw ones, nor that the prediction errors, G_i, are approximately stationary. You can use other techniques to compare and analyze prediction accuracy, including the prequential likelihood ratio, described next, which can show if recalibration has

> The ability to capture the past accurately does not necessarily imply an ability to predict accurately.

ASSESSING PREDICTIVE ACCURACY: *U*-PLOT

You use a *u*-plot to determine if predictions, $\hat{F}_i(t)$, are on average close to the true distribution, $F_i(t)$. For example, if you can show that the random variable T_i truly had the distribution $\hat{F}_i(t)$ — the prediction and the truth were identical — then the random variable $U_i = \hat{F}_i(T_i)$ will be uniformly distributed on (0,1). In statistics, this is called the probability integral transform.[1]

If you observe the realization t_i and calculate $u_i = \hat{F}_i(t_i)$, then u_i will be a realization of a uniform random variable. Doing this for a sequence of predictions gives a sequence $\{u_i\}$, which should look like a random sample from a uniform distribution. Any departure from the uniformity indicates some deviation between the predictions, $\{\hat{F}_i(t)\}$, and the truth, $\{F_i(t)\}$.

To find such departures, you plot a sample distribution function of $\{u_i\}$. This is a step function, constructed by placing points $u_1, u_2, \ldots, u_n$ (each of these is a number between 0 and 1) on the interval (0,1). Then, from left to right plot an increasing step function, with each step of height $1/(n+1)$ at each *u* on the abscissa. The resulting monotonically increasing function has a range (0,1). This is the *u*-plot.

If the $\{u_i\}$ sequence is truly uniform, the *u*-plot should be close to the line of unit slope. Any serious departure indicates inaccurate predictions. A common way to test if departures are significant is to compare them to tables for the Kolmogorov distance, the maximum vertical deviation of the plot from the line.[1] However, formal tests to prove significant departures are often unnecessary: As with the examples in this article, it is often clear from simply looking at the plots that the predictions are poor.

More important, informal inspections of *u*-plots can reveal a lot about prediction errors. For example, when predictions are consistently too optimistic, the model underestimates the chance of the next failure occurring before *t* (for all *t*). In such a *u*-plot, the *us* will bunch to the left of the (0,1) interval, giving a plot that is above the line of unit slope. Similarly, a *u*-plot that is entirely below the line indicates predictions that are too pessimistic. More complex *u*-plots can sometimes be interpreted in terms of the nature of the inaccurate predictions they represent.

REFERENCES
1. M.H. DeGroot, *Probability and Statistics*, Addison-Wesley, Reading, Mass., 1986.

produced better results than the raw model.

Even when a model gives predictions for a data set that have a good *u*-plot, there is no guarantee that the model is accurate in every way. In statistics, even if you have an unbiased estimator, you might still decide to use a biased one. For example, the unbiased estimator may have a large variance, so although its expected value is equal to the unknown parameter, its value in a particular case may be far from the expected value. This is the difference between what happens on average and what happens in a particular instance. Similar arguments apply to a good *u*-plot, which describes average behavior but can also mask large inaccuracies in particular predictions.

Prequential likelihood ratio. This deficiency led us to adopt a second technique, the prequential likelihood ratio, described in the box on p. 38.

The PLR lets you compare two models' abilities to predict a particular data source so that you can select the one that has been most accurate over a sequence of predictions. Unlike the *u*-plot, which is specific to a particular type of inaccuracy, the PLR is general — the model it selects as best is objectively best in a general way.[3] For example, it can detect when the predictions are too noisy and so are individually inaccurate, even when the *u*-plot looks good and the predictions seem unbiased.

We admit that both techniques are nontrivial, and you may find them very unfamiliar at first. This is not surprising, because traditional statistical methods have neglected prediction in favor of estimation. Techniques like PLR analysis have become available only recently. However, it is really very straightforward to use these techniques, which involve nothing more than simple graphical analysis.

THREE DATA SETS

Here we illustrate how to apply these techniques, using three sets of real failure data.

SS3 data set. Our first example uses the SS3 data set of 278 interfailure times, collected by John Musa.[4] This data set is unusual because all eight models we use for comparison seem to give extremely poor results as determined by the *u*-plot, but recalibration dramatically improves all eight. The box on p. 40 lists the models we used.

Figure 1a shows the raw data plotted as cumulative number of failures against total elapsed execution time. Figure 1b shows the successive predictions of the median next time to failure. The graph shows extraordinary disagreement among the models. The LV and KL models give results that are far more pessimistic than the other six. Although the graph applies to

the predicted medians only, if these are inaccurate, then other measures of reliability will also be inaccurate.

In fact, the *u*-plots in Figure 1c show that *all* predictions are extremely inaccurate; plots differ from the line of unit slope with very high statistical significance. The six models that approximately agree in Figure 1b are in fact much too optimistic — their *u*-plots are almost always above the line of unit slope. LV and KL, on the other hand, are too pessimistic — their *u*-plots are generally below the line of unit slope. These results suggest the true medians lie somewhere between the two clusters in Figure 1b.

Figure 1d shows log(PLR) plotted for each model against a reference model, DU. This analysis reveals that KL and LV are significantly superior to the other six models for this data set, even though we know them to be poor, too.

Because all the models give poor *u*-plots, we have no trustworthy predictions for this data set. Therefore, all models are candidates for recalibration. Figure 1e shows that recalibration brings much closer agreement in the predicted medians. And the *u*-plots of the recalibrated predictions in Figure 1f are an enormous improvement over the raw predictions. Now none of the deviations from the unit slope is statistically significant.

Figure 1g shows the log(PLR) plots of recalibrated versus raw predictions. The improvement in predictive accuracy is

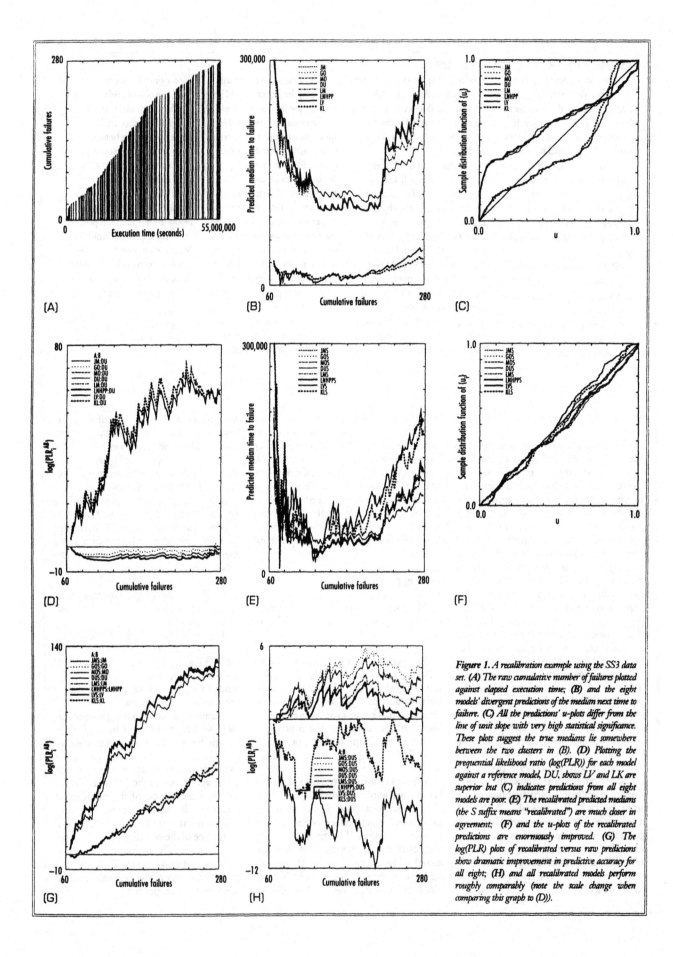

Figure 1. A recalibration example using the SS3 data set. (A) The raw cumulative number of failures plotted against elapsed execution time; (B) and the eight models' divergent predictions of the median next time to failure. (C) All the predictions' u-plots differ from the line of unit slope with very high statistical significance. These plots suggest the true medians lie somewhere between the two clusters in (B). (D) Plotting the prequential likelihood ratio (log(PLR)) for each model against a reference model, DU, shows LV and LK are superior but (C) indicates predictions from all eight models are poor. (E) The recalibrated predicted medians (the S suffix means "recalibrated") are much closer in agreement; (F) and the u-plots of the recalibrated predictions are enormously improved. (G) The log(PLR) plots of recalibrated versus raw predictions show dramatic improvement in predictive accuracy for all eight; (H) and all recalibrated models perform roughly comparably (note the scale change when comparing this graph to (D)).

ASSESSING PREDICTIVE ACCURACY: PLR

The prequential likelihood ratio is a way to decide which of a pair of prediction systems gives the most accurate results for a particular data source.

Figure A shows a true distribution (the probability density function) of the time to failure, T_j, and predictions of the PDF from two models, A and B. A is clearly better than B.

Eventually the failure occurs after time t_j. Obviously, you would expect t_j to lie in the main body of the true distribution (it is more likely to occur where $f_j(t)$ is larger). If you evaluate the two predictions at this value of t, you see there is a tendency for model A's prediction to be larger than model B's — model A's PDF tends to have more large values close to the large values of the true distribution than B's. This is what it means to say that A's predictions are closer to the truth than B's.

If model A's predictions are more accurate than B's, $\hat{f}_j^A(t_j)/\hat{f}_j^B(t_j)$ will tend to be larger than 1. The prequential likelihood ratio is simply a running product of such terms over many successive predictions:

$$PLR_i^{AB} = \prod_{j=k}^{j=i} \frac{\hat{f}_j^A(t_j)}{\hat{f}_j^B(t_j)}$$

and this should tend to increase with i if model A's predictions are better than B's. Conversely, B's superiority is indicated if this product shows a consistent decrease.

Of course, even if A is consistently more accurate than B, there is no guarantee that a single $\hat{f}_j^A(t_j)/\hat{f}_j^B(t_j)$ will always be greater than one. But you can expect the plot of PLR (or for convenience, its log) to exhibit overall increase with some fluctuation.

Usually, we are interested in comparing the accuracy of more than two prediction sequences. To do this, we select one arbitrarily as a reference and conduct pairwise comparisons of others against it, as above.

PLR is a completely general procedure for identifying the better of a pair of prediction sequences. Apart from the intuitive plausibility of PLR as a means of selecting between many competing prediction methods on a particular data source, support for this technique comes from a more formal asymptotic theory.[1]

REFERENCES

1. A.P. Dawid, "Statistical Theory: The Prequential Approach," *J. Royal Statistical Soc. A*, Vol. 147, 1984, pp. 278-292.

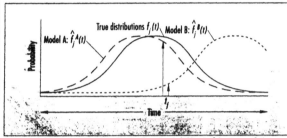

Figure A. The true probability density function (solid line) of the time to failure and the predicted PDFs from model A (long dashed line) and model B (short dashed line).

---

dramatic in all cases, but slightly less so for KL and LV. These two models were the best performing pair of the original eight — since they were not as bad as the other six, they had less room for improvement.

Figure 1h shows that all recalibrated models perform roughly comparably. In this graph, no single plot shows a consistent trend, compared with the corresponding plots in Figure 1d (note the scale change).

Clearly, recalibration had a dramatic effect on the accuracy of the predictions you can make about this data set. Faced with these results, a user would clearly make future predictions using one of the recalibrated versions of the models, possibly GOS (the S suffix designates a recalibrated model), although there is little difference between GOS and JMS or LMS.

As more data becomes available, of course, you must update the analysis and decide which, if any, predictions to trust. The most important advantage to this procedure is that it lets the data speak for itself and does not require the user to believe ahead of time that a model will give accurate predictions. Since such beliefs are highly questionable, this is an important new way to acquire confidence in reliability predictions.

CSR1 data set. The CSR1 data set, collected from a single-user workstation at the Centre for Software Reliability, represents some 397 user-perceived failures: genuine software failures, plus failures caused by usability problems, inadequate documentation, and so on.

Figure 2a shows the cumulative failure plot for the raw data; Figure 2b shows the median predictions from the eight models. Two things are striking: There is little evidence of reliability growth until about halfway through the data set, and again there is marked disagreement among the models when the growth does start.

In Figure 2c, the u-plots again show that all models perform poorly — all deviations from the unit slope are significant. More to the point, there are great differences in the nature of the prediction errors: JM, GO, LM, and LNHPP are too optimistic; KL and LV are pessimistic; and MO and DU have a pronounced S-shaped u-plot, intersecting the line of unit slope at about (0.5, 0.5). This indicates MO and DU predict the median time to failure accurately, but are too optimistic in estimating the probability of small times to failure and too pessimistic in estimating large times to failure.

The PLR analysis in Figure 2d shows that KL performs best overall, with LV second. The relatively poor performance of the other models is due partly to bias, as shown by the u-plots, and in some cases partly to noise, as evidenced by the great fluctuations in the medians in Figure 2b.

Once again, none of the raw predictions can be trusted according to the u-plot analysis, and these models are candidates for recalibration. Figure 2e shows the effect of recalibration on the median predictions. The change in medians from Figure 2b is in the right direction, according to the raw u-plots. The u-plots of the recalibrated predictions in Figure 2f confirm that there has indeed been an improvement. However, only KLS has a plot that does not significantly deviate from the line of unit slope (although MOS, DUS, LNHPPS, and LVS are only just significant).

While the u-plots for MOS and DUS improved a great deal, there is little change in the medians (Figures 2b and 2e). This is because the raw medians were very accurate, but other points on the raw predictive distributions were not, and these have been improved by recalibration.

Figure 2g shows a steady increase in all log(PLR) plots and confirms that, in all

---

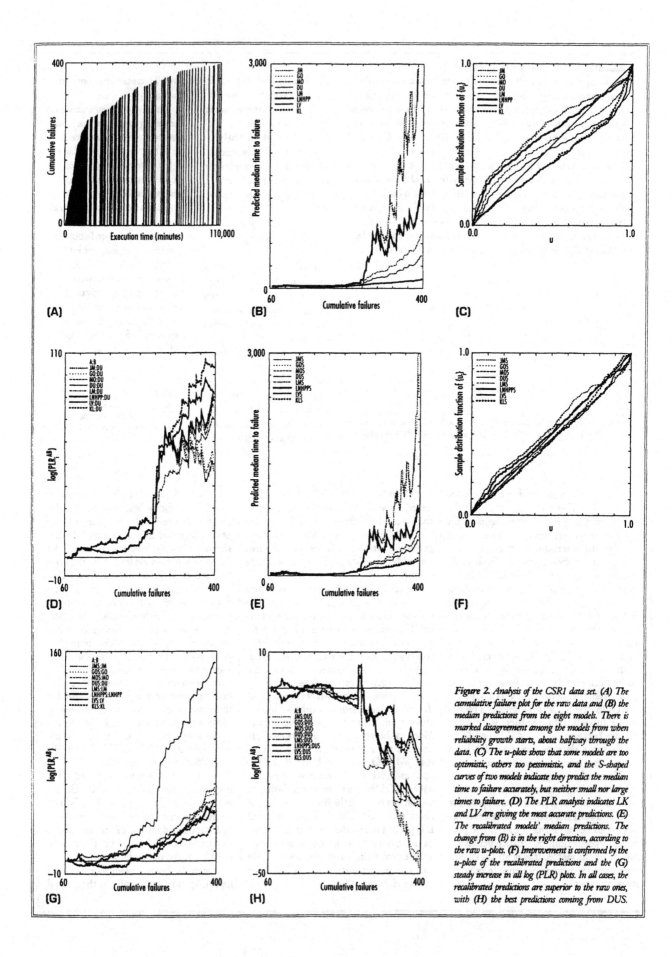

Figure 2. *Analysis of the CSR1 data set. (A) The cumulative failure plot for the raw data and (B) the median predictions from the eight models. There is marked disagreement among the models from when reliability growth starts, about halfway through the data. (C) The u-plots show that some models are too optimistic, others too pessimistic, and the S-shaped curves of two models indicate they predict the median time to failure accurately, but neither small nor large times to failure. (D) The PLR analysis indicates LK and LV are giving the most accurate predictions. (E) The recalibrated models' median predictions. The change from (B) is in the right direction, according to the raw u-plots. (F) Improvement is confirmed by the u-plots of the recalibrated predictions and the (G) steady increase in all log (PLR) plots. In all cases, the recalibrated predictions are superior to the raw ones, with (H) the best predictions coming from DUS.*

EIGHT MODELS

In applying our techniques, we used these eight reliability models:

• *Jelinski-Moranda* (JM): One of the earliest models, it assumes that failures occur purely at random and that all faults contribute equally to unreliability. It also assumes that fixes are perfect; thus, a program's failure rate improves by the same amount at each fix. (Z. Jelinski and P.B. Moranda, "Software Reliability Research," in *Statistical Computer Performance Evaluation*, W. Freiberger, ed., Academic Press, New York, 1972, pp. 465-484).

• *Goel-Okumoto* (GO): Similar to JM, except it assumes the failure rate improves continuously in time. (A.L. Goel and K. Okumoto, "Time-Dependent Error-Detection Rate Model for Software and Other Performance Measures," *IEEE Trans. Reliability*, Aug. 1979, pp. 206-211.)

• *Musa-Okumoto* (MO): Similar to GO, except it attempts to consider that later fixes have a smaller effect on a program's reliability than earlier ones. (J.D. Musa and K. Okumoto, "A Logarithmic Poisson Execution Time Model for Software Reliability Measurement," *Proc. Int'l Conf. Software Eng.*, IEEE CS Press, Los Alamitos, Calif., 1984, pp. 230-238.)

• *Duane* (DU): Developed for burn-in hardware testing, in which defective components are detected and replaced with good ones in the early days of use. Again, it assumes the failure rate changes continuously in time. (L.H. Crow, "Confidence Interval Procedures for Reliability Growth Analysis," Tech. Report 197, US Army Materiel Systems Analysis Activity, Aberdeen, Md., 1977.)

• *Littlewood* (LM): Similar to JM, except it assumes that different faults have different sizes (they contribute unequally to unreliability). It assumes larger faults tend to be removed early, so there is a law of diminishing returns in debugging. (B. Littlewood, "Stochastic Reliability Growth: A Model for Fault-Removal in Computer Programs and Hardware Designs," *IEEE Trans. Reliability*, Oct. 1981, pp. 313-320.)

• *Littlewood Nonhomogeneous Poisson Process* (LNHPP): Similar to LM, but assumes a continuous change in failure rate (instead of discrete jumps) when fixes take place. (D.R. Miller, "Exponential Order Statistic Models of Software Reliability Growth," *IEEE Trans. Software Eng.*, Jan. 1986, pp. 12-24.)

• *Littlewood-Verrall* (LV): Lets the size of the improvement in the failure rate at a fix vary randomly, representing the uncertainty about fault size and the efficacy of the fix. (B. Littlewood and J.L. Verrall, "A Bayesian Reliability Growth Model for Computer Software," *J. Royal Statistical Soc. C.*, Vol. 22, 1973, pp. 332-346.)

• *Keiller-Littlewood* (KL): Similar to LV, but uses a different mathematical form for reliability growth. (P.A. Keiller et al., "Comparison of Software Reliability Predictions," *Proc. IEEE Int'l Symp. Fault-Tolerant Computing*, IEEE CS Press, Los Alamitos, Calif., 1983, pp. 128-134.)

---

cases, the recalibrated predictions are superior to the raw ones. The greatest improvement is in DU, but this is largely because this model performs so poorly without recalibration. Figure 2h shows that after recalibration, the best predictions are coming from DUS, with KLS and LVS next best.

In this case, you would be advised to use DUS, bearing in mind that you must repeat this analysis at future stages in case there should be a reversal in fortunes among the models. Here, recalibration has turned the worst-performing model, DU, into the best, DUS.

> **Users should never believe claims that a particular model is universally reliable.**

In this analysis, we have deliberately taken no account of the fact that there seems to be little evidence of reliability growth until quite late — we have blindly applied the models and the recalibration procedure as a naive user would. Clearly, you could do some simple preprocessing to detect the early stationarity of the data, such as applying simple tests for trend. You could then exclude the early part of the data in applying the growth models. However, we do not introduce this complication here to save space.

CSR2 data set. Our third data set is a subset of the second — failures that are known to be due to software faults. The data displayed in Figure 3a is notable for several extremely large interfailure times, including one of 9,549 minutes. Although you might think that these large numbers are outliers that should be excluded from the data, such exclusion can only be justified in the face of real evidence.

Unfortunately, there is no obvious statistical test for outliers for nonstationary data. Because the problem of outliers may arise frequently in practice — and it has no obvious solution — we retained the possibly extreme values to show their effect on the models and the analysis.

The median predictions in Figure 3b show that the models respond to the large times differently. Four models (JM, LNHPP, GO, and LM) respond dramatically to a large time by making the next predicted median much larger, and this relative optimism continues for many predictions before dying away. Two models (LV and KL) seem completely unaffected by large times, exhibiting a much smoother and steadier median growth. Two others (MO and DU) are affected only slightly.

The *u*-plots in Figure 3c confirm that the models most affected by large times give very optimistic predictions. LV and KL are too pessimistic. The best *u*-plots come from MO and DU, but even these are poor. Once again, we have objective evidence that all these models are giving inaccurate results.

The PLR analysis in Figure 3d is greatly influenced by the ability of the models to cope with a very large time. LV and KL cope best because they give a predictive distribution that assigns fairly high probability to large times; DU is worst. If we were to omit the 9,549 observation and join the plots, KL and LV are still superior and there is little difference among the others.

The main point, though, is that on this evidence none of the predictions can be trusted and recalibration is appropriate. Figure 3e shows the recalibrated medians, which are in much closer agreement than the raw ones, although the large observa-

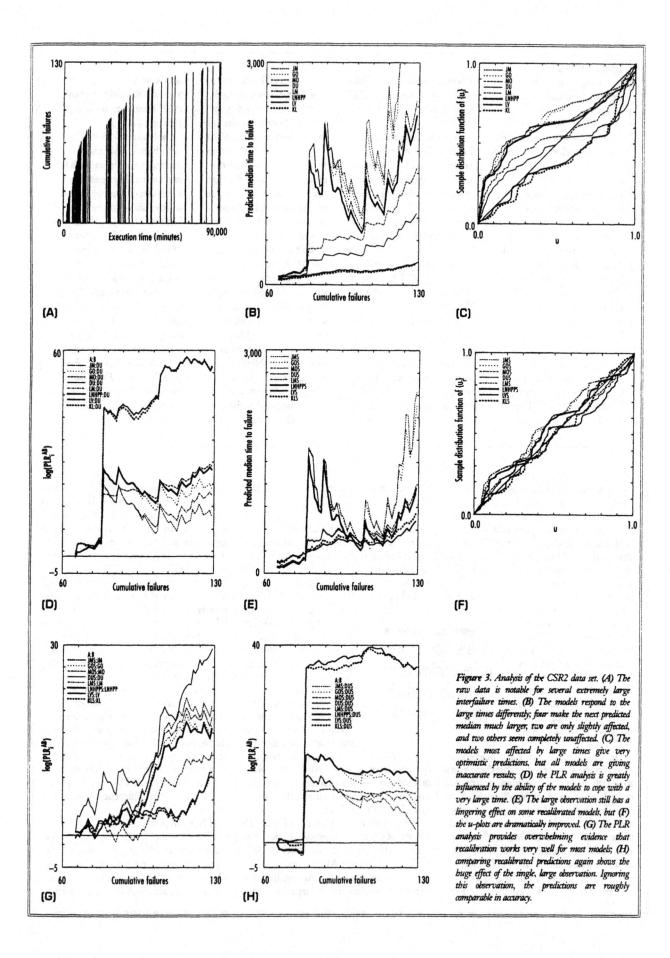

Figure 3. Analysis of the CSR2 data set. (A) The raw data is notable for several extremely large interfailure times. (B) The models respond to the large times differently; four make the next predicted median much larger, two are only slightly affected, and two others seem completely unaffected. (C) The models most affected by large times give very optimistic predictions, but all models are giving inaccurate results; (D) the PLR analysis is greatly influenced by the ability of the models to cope with a very large time. (E) The large observation still has a lingering effect on some recalibrated models, but (F) the u-plots are dramatically improved. (G) The PLR analysis provides overwhelming evidence that recalibration works very well for most models; (H) comparing recalibrated predictions again shows the huge effect of the single, large observation. Ignoring this observation, the predictions are roughly comparable in accuracy.

tion still has a lingering effect on some models. The u-plots in Figure 3f show a dramatic improvement — no deviations are statistically significant at the 10 percent level.

There is overwhelming evidence from the PLR analysis of recalibrated versus raw predictions in Figure 3g that recalibration is working very well for most models. It provides the least improvement for KL and LV, but these models needed the least improvement.

Finally, the comparison of recalibrated predictions in Figure 3h, shows again the huge effect of the single, large observation. If we take account of this single prediction, then once again the recalibrated LV and KL models are best, but all the evidence for their superiority comes merely from their ability to cope with this single observation. The different recalibrated predictions seem to be of roughly comparable accuracy if this observation is ignored, and that would seem to be a sensible procedure for anyone wishing to make further predictions on this data set.

The techniques we have described are important because they largely resolve a reliability modeling dilemma: Users are faced with a plethora of models, but none can be trusted to give accurate results always, and there is no way to select beforehand the model most appropriate for a particular application.

We cannot overemphasize that users should never believe claims for the universal validity of a particular reliability model. Indeed, we believe that the relatively poor adoption of reliability modeling has been caused in part by certain models being sold as panaceas.

We think our techniques provide a way to overcome these difficulties. We also think it is now possible to measure and predict reliability for the relatively modest levels needed in the vast majority of applications. Most important, the techniques give the user confidence that the results are sufficiently accurate for the program under examination. Users need not subscribe to dubious claims about a model's inherent plausibility to trust the reliability figures it generates.

In the examples we chose, the raw models perform badly. We deliberately chose these examples to show the power of the recalibration technique, but sometimes a model will perform reasonably well before recalibration. From a user's point of view, this is immaterial. Recalibration is easy to do and is genuinely predictive, so it should be applied as a matter of course. Then it is easy to use the analytical methods to find which version (raw or recalibrated) is performing best.

Although these techniques depend on rather novel and subtle statistical methods, we think their actual use and interpretation are comparatively straightforward. At the Centre for Software Reliability, we've developed software — available from us — to do these analyses.

Our approach is suitable for anyone contemplating measuring and predicting software reliability. Most of the time, the results are trustworthy. In rare cases in which none of the models work before or after recalibration, our techniques will serve as a warning.

Finally, a word of caution. Software is being used increasingly in safety-critical applications that demand a very high reliability. This poses enormous — possibly insurmountable — problems for system validation. We emphasize that all our techniques are designed for fairly modest reliability levels. Techniques that depend on reliability growth cannot assure very high reliability without infeasibly large observation periods. It has been argued that assuring ultrahigh reliability is even harder than we have suggested — that essentially it is impossible.[5] ◆

ACKNOWLEDGMENTS

This work was supported by the Commission of the European Communities' Strategic Programme for Research in Information Technology under project 3092 PDCS (Predictably Dependable Computing Systems).

REFERENCES

1. A.A. Abdel-Ghaly, P.Y. Chan, and B. Littlewood, "Evaluation of Competing Software Reliability Predictions," *IEEE Trans. Software Eng.* Sept. 1986, pp. 950-967.
2. S. Brocklehurst et al., "Recalibrating Software Reliability Models," *IEEE Trans. Software Eng.*, Apr. 1990, pp. 458-470.
3. A.P. Dawid, "Statistical Theory: The Prequential Approach," *J. Royal Statistical Soc. A*, Vol. 147, 1984, pp. 278-292.
4. J. Musa, "Software Reliability Data," tech. report, Data and Analysis Center for Software, Rome Air Development Center, Griffis Air Force Base, N.Y., 1979.
5. B. Littlewood, "Limits to Evaluation of Software Dependability," *Proc. 7th Annual Centre for Software Reliability Conf.*, B. Littlewood and N.E. Fenton. eds., Elsevier, London, 1991, pp. 81-110.

Address questions about this article to Brocklehurst at the Centre for Software Reliability, City University, London, EC1V OHB, UK; Internet s.brocklehurst@city.ac.uk.

Key Lessons In Achieving Widespread Inspection Use

Robert B. Grady and Tom Van Slack,
Hewlett-Packard

◆ *HP has distilled its experience in promoting inspections into a model of how technology adoption occurs and a metric of where it stands. Its managers know when and how to accelerate efforts to adopt inspections and other best practices. Experience has shown that the return on investment in technology-adoption efforts can be huge.*

Buying a house is one of the biggest decisions you ever make. When Bob and Jan bought their house, they worried about a lot of things, including the heating system, which used hot water instead of forced air. They had been told that some such heating systems used pipes that had to be replaced after 15 years. Although they were told the pipes in their house were OK, they decided to have the heating system inspected anyway. It turned out the house's pipes were leaking and had to be replaced. The $25 inspection fee was the best investment they ever made. The sellers had to buy a new heating system that cost more than 100 times the inspection cost.

Most software inspections won't yield a return on investment of 100 to 1. Depending on your business though, some can, and our data suggests that you can expect a yield of about 10 to 1.

This is the story of software-inspection adoption over time in Hewlett-Packard and the insights we have gained.

Inspection technology was adopted across our entire company in stages. Figure 1 shows three versions of an S-shaped curve of technology adoption that researchers have shown typically occurs.[1] The left-most curve shows rapid adoption and the fastest ROI. The other curves show much slower adoption rates. The figure illustrates that the adoption rate of a new practice can vary significantly. It also sug-

Reprinted from *IEEE Software*, Vol. 11, No. 4, July 1994, pp. 46–57.

gests four recognizable stages, which we defined for this article: experimental, initial guidelines, widespread belief and adoption, and standardization. HP's inspections program has progressed through three of these stages.

In this article, we address several key questions: What characterizes the four stages? What were the most important lessons learned? What situations led to failure or success? And most important, how can we apply what we learned to speed the adoption of other proven practices?

The lessons we relate here will give many of you who are directly or indirectly responsible for software process improvement more confidence that inspections apply to all software-development organizations.

INSPECTION INFLUENCES

It is easy to identify three major influences on HP software inspections. The first of these is historical. All engineers do reviews of some sort. In HP two of the more obvious hardware-related reviews were for hardware designs and printed circuit boards, both motivated by the need to reduce costly cycle times that also delayed time to market. The first HP software reviews — walkthroughs, really — were modeled on hardware reviews.

Then in 1976 Michael Fagan published his very influential "Design and Code Inspections to Reduce Errors in Program Development,"[2] in which he introduced the term *software inspections.* For the first time, Fagan presented data that helped managers better visualize inspection results. He also described the inspection process well enough that commercial classes soon followed. HP's first internal classes were created in the late '70s and widely taught by the early '80s.

The third influence was Tom Gilb. He extended Fagan's inspection process in several important ways that

represented a timely philosophical match with HP thinking. First, he was a strong proponent of inspecting early life-cycle artifacts more than code. Second, he extended Fagan's application of metrics to include measures of the inspection process itself. Finally, he described how to use these measures to motivate process improvement.[3] In 1990 HP combined these improvements and our accumulated experience with Fagan's methods to revise the inspection classes that are internally taught today.

The current HP inspection process is summarized in the box on p. 48. It is the result of more than 15 years of experience and improvements. The roles, steps, and results are well-understood and effective. The process works. By mapping the evolution of the program onto the four stages in Figure 1, we can better understand how adoption grew and how the program's success can be repeated by other process-improvement programs.

ADOPTION RATES VARY WIDELY, USUALLY PROGRESSING THROUGH FOUR STAGES.

EXPERIMENTAL (1976-1982)

In describing HP's early inspections experiences, we can appreciate how hard it is for archaeologists to reconstruct early history without any written records. In this case, we can at least summarize the memories of some of the people who were doing software then, but their recollections are bound to be fuzzy and biased.

Fagan's article provided a common point of departure for different HP groups. What were once isolated reviews initiated by former hardware engineers and project managers now became more organized efforts supported by managers in quality assurance and, occasionally, research and development. During this time, only a few HP divisions had quality-department staff with software backgrounds. Fagan's article gave even those who did not have software backgrounds something specific to work on with software people.

At this stage, our inspection process

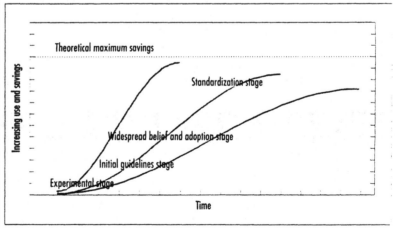

Figure 1. *Three versions of an S-shaped curve of technology adoption. The leftmost curve shows rapid adoption and the fastest ROI. The other curves show much slower adoption rates. We define four recognizable adoption stages: experimental, initial guidelines, widespread belief and adoption, and standardization.*

CURRENT HP INSPECTION PROCESS

The HP inspection process involves conducting a formal review of a document by a document owner and a team of peers. The review is led by a process chairperson, the moderator. The primary goal of the inspection process is to help the document owner and organization develop a high-quality product cost-effectively. Inspections ensure that documents are clear, self-explanatory, correct, and consistent with all related documents.

Five roles. There are five defined roles. Sometimes one person acts in more than one role.

♦ *Inspectors:* Find items (errors, omissions, inconsistencies, and areas of confusion) in a target document and issues (items beyond the scope of the inspection team).

♦ *Scribe:* Records items and issues found both before and during a logging meeting.

♦ *Owner:* Owns a document; identifies and fixes defects.

♦ *Moderator:* Manages the process; facilitates the inspection; reports statistics to the chief moderator; reports inspection's status and logged issues to management.

♦ *Chief Moderator:* Owns the inspection process; gathers and reports statistics across all inspections; drives inspection process improvements; serves as focal point for changes to inspections standards and checklists.

Some divisions also continue to use the *reader* role (a person who paraphrases a document during a logging meeting), particularly for complex code documents.

Seven steps. Table A shows the seven distinct steps in the HP inspection process, what happens, the people involved, and the time spent. This well-defined process represents a transformation of HP's earlier reviews and walkthroughs to an engineering process. Figure A shows how the process outputs are used to improve our products, inspections process, and development processes.

Occasionally the inspections process varies. For example, some divisions hold more formal meetings than others. In general, HP's culture leads to divisional autonomy and less

formality than in many other companies. One aspect that the current HP inspection process emphasizes, though, is that informality must not extend to the recording and tracking of meeting results.

The process step that varies the most is the cause/prevention step. Few divisions have successfully done this step before rework. The most successful adaptors of this step have the engineers who fix the defects enter causal information and short recommended actions when fixes are done. Then a separate failure-analysis activity takes data both from multiple inspections and from other test results to analyze and brainstorm solutions to frequently occurring or expensive problems.

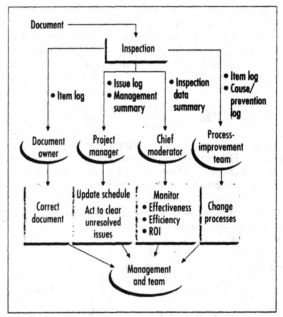

Figure A. *How HP uses the results from inspections.*

	Planning	Kickoff	Preparation	Logging meeting	Cause/prevention	Rework	Follow-up
What	Plan inspection and create packet	Brief team	Find items and issues	Find and log items and issues	Brainstorm cause(s) and recommend	Verify and fix defects	Release document
Who	Moderator and owner	Team	Team	Team	Team	Owner and moderator	Moderator and owner
Time	2 hrs.	1/2 hr.	2 hr.	1 1/2 hrs.	1/2 hr.	???	1/2 hr.

TABLE A — PROCESS STEPS AND CHARACTERISTICS OF HP SOFTWARE INSPECTION

used Fagan's checklist as a starting point and had code readers look at code from different perspectives. The emphasis was on code inspections.

Some inspections compared their metrics with Fagan's published metrics for engineering times, defect-finding rates, and defect types. Few matched Fagan's data closely enough for people to feel very positive about their results. Some of these start-ups failed. Many groups had little more than Fagan's article to go on, and for some projects this was not enough to reshape the team's dynamics, which sometimes involved strong egos and tendencies to criticize. Word of failures often spread faster than word of successes.

Some groups who believed in inspections persevered and tuned the process. Those who survived the start-up period became advocates for better company support. These groups found that better training, documentation, and a supportive atmosphere were necessary for successful inspections.

The experimental stage taught us that
♦ The initial use of new processes, methods, or tools depends heavily on visionary people who can look at someone else's results and see how they can be applied locally. This often means having the right person in the right place at the right time.
♦ If a division wants to lead in the adoption of best practices, it must foster visionary attempts and not penalize failures. A risk-averse environment does not grow leaders.
♦ Early success is fragile. Establishing a supporting infrastructure can make the difference between success and failure, and it can be difficult to convince people to try again.

INITIAL GUIDELINES (1983-1988)

This period marked a transition in HP not only for inspections but also for the use of many other software best practices. It is easier for us to reconstruct events in this period because by now HP had formed its Software Engineering Lab and Software Engineering Training. SEL started its Software Engineering Productivity Conferences in 1984, and SET started a newsletter, *SET News*. Their written records helped us reconstruct this period's key events and lessons.

In 1983, HP piloted an evolved version of an internal software-inspections class. SET was created to propagate such practices through training. It expanded class availability, and in 1984 more than 150 engineers took the class, and SET was offering train-the-trainer sessions. The SEPC proceedings helped us understand the outcomes from this training.

A paper presented at the first SEPC showed how one group had adapted Fagan's checklists to a specific HP division. By 1985 there was already a shift to reporting results in measurable terms, most commonly in defects found per hour that ranged from 0.24 up to 5.18. Most of the variation was probably caused by varying definitions and different software types and business applications. These variations did not matter much, because the repeated success stories at the conferences were strong reinforcing arguments that inspections did work, and they played a key role in building inspections momentum.

Besides centralized training and the SEPCs, three other key events occurred during this time. The first was a two-day course on the role of managers in software quality that every R&D manager was to take over the next one-and-a-half years. Taught mostly by their peers, this course was particularly important, because it exposed R&D managers with hardware backgrounds to the software-development process, which most were not familiar with. It gave them a much better understanding of what software developers do and led to stronger management support for process improvement.

The second key event was the creation of a productivity-manager position in most HP divisions. The primary responsibility of these new managers was to speed the adoption of best practices within a division. These managers formed a basic infrastructure to actively support division R&D improvements.

Finally, in 1986 our company president announced a Software 10X Improvement Program. This program challenged all HP R&D product labs to improve two key quality metrics by a factor of 10 — 12-month postrelease defect density and open critical and serious defects.

Combined with documented success stories, an infrastructure that provided a divisional conduit to support change, and freshly fanned management commitment, the 10X challenge was an additional incentive to adopt best practices quickly. A 1987 internal survey of quality managers showed that inspections were clearly their first choice to help them achieve the 10X goals.

This was an exciting time for HP software developers. During this stage we learned that
♦ Communicating successes effectively speeds both adoption and the improvement of the best practices themselves.
♦ Clearly defining who is responsible for process improvement speeds the adoption of best practices.
♦ Management training contributes to strong, sustained sponsorship.
♦ A high-level, compelling vision, like 10X goals that are directly tied to business challenges, helps ensure strong management sponsorship.
♦ Readily available training is nec-

> **GROUPS SURVIVING THE START-UP PERIOD BECAME ADVOCATES FOR BETTER SUPPORT.**

RETROSPECTIVE FROM INITIAL GUIDELINES STAGE

Let's look at the use of inspections by two different project teams within one division. Both team's firmware R&D engineers attended the 1984 version of the software-inspections course, which taught the Fagan method. It covered the reader role, discussed problems that can arise in inspection meetings, and how to achieve group consensus on defects. But it included little about how to use metrics to control and improve inspections, and there was not yet an infrastructure in place to support teams trying to use inspections.

Team 1 used the method to inspect code, and it helped them find defects. However, they felt that they weren't getting the ROI they should, but didn't know why (they didn't collect process metrics). Gradually they stopped using inspections. For one thing, the project manager thought they were too slow and people-intensive. For another thing, the team felt that inspecting noncode documents (requirements, specifications, designs, and test plans) took too long and didn't uncover enough major defects.

Team 2 used the method for code inspections and, like Team 1, tried to use the method for noncode documents. They experienced similar results, but instead of dropping inspections they set about improving the process. First they eliminated the reader, who used to paraphrase the document, and instead had the moderator step the team through the document. They adjusted the speed to the potential for defects. This helped the team focus the meeting on the document sections that had the most problems, and they achieved a better defect-finding rate.

Team 2 also experienced unproductive meeting discussions. To solve this, they eliminated discussion of whether or not a potential defect was really a defect. Instead, they had the inspector log any problem. After the meeting, the document author reviewed the log to decide if any follow-up discussion was needed. This also sped up the meeting and increased the number of potential major defects reported.

Finally, Team 2 had inspectors report their preparation time and the number of defects they found at the start of each inspection meeting. This helped ensure that every inspector spent enough time reviewing the document before the meeting. All these process changes resulted in more successful noncode inspections.

Despite the fact that both teams were in the same division, only one took the initiative to adjust the process. This happened in many parts of HP. Training by itself was not enough to ensure success, and an unsuccessful experience made it difficult to get groups like Team 1 to try inspections again.

---

essary to speed technology adoption, but it is not sufficient to sustain use (see the box above).

WIDESPREAD BELIEF AND ADOPTION (1989-1993)

By 1989 the 10X program was far enough along that divisions were reporting and corporate was summarizing data reasonably consistently.

While some progress was apparent, pressure had increased on the divisions to show how they planned to achieve the goals. An internal corporate-wide survey showed that every HP division was doing some form of inspection, although only 19 percent regularly did software-design reviews. The survey also showed strong confidence in inspections — more than 30 divisions picked inspections as a key practice in their effort to achieve their 10X goals.

While some divisions were working hard to implement widespread inspections, only five had plans for inspections training. It seemed clear that renewed corporate consulting efforts could help.

HP kicked off a new initiative specifically designed to

♦ improve the efficiency and effectiveness of inspections by implementing an inspection-moderator certification program, revising the training course, and instituting a company-wide technology-transfer plan

♦ improve R&D management awareness and commitment by developing a business case for inspections, marketing inspections, and monitoring division performance.

Four people from Corporate Quality worked part-time in close partnership with key practitioners to meet these goals. In early 1990, an internal inspections-practitioner workshop was held, and an outside consultant was hired to incorporate the best practices summarized there into an existing class. This formed the basis of a Moderator Training Class that soon followed. Meanwhile, an HP person created a "management pitch kit" on the business case for inspections.

These efforts culminated in a blitz campaign to promote inspections and the new training class across HP. Fagan and Gilb spoke at that summer's SEPC, and some of the key practitioner-workshop participants contributed four excellent papers. The blitz campaign created the awareness and management commitment to upgrade people's skills. This new commitment created demand for corporate, group, and divisional productivity and quality-assurance people.

HP responded by assigning both a full-time corporate inspections program manager and a full-time training specialist for one of the largest HP Groups (at HP, a Group is a collection of divisions in related businesses and may have more than 1,000 software engineers). This Group and corporate formed a partnership: Corporate provided guidance and funding. The Group championed improvements, adapted the moderator-training class for learning through practice, and modernized the inspections class. The Group felt that having these classes delivered externally was too expensive, so they planned to have their own people teach them. As Figure 2 shows, by early 1991, significant numbers of engineers were receiving the training.

These results did not come easily. The corporate approach to certifying moderators was based on the premise that there is one "best" way to do inspections and all the group had to do was push people toward it. But HP's divisions are independent and did not respond well to standardization. They didn't want to just be told what wasn't right, particularly when they saw their inspections working. They wanted flexibility, but they also wanted help in improving their processes. There was a constant struggle to hold management to their commitment to continuous improvement. What the divisions wanted was consulting support tailored to the Figure 1 adoption phase they were in.

Meanwhile, the training specialist was also having problems. One of the first classes "exploded" when a manager set up the class, then gave the engineers mixed signals about its importance versus other activities. Other classes included attendees who had tried inspections and not found them useful, and no one had told them how the methods in the new class might correct earlier problems. The training specialist came to the same conclusion as the corporate program manager: Consulting was needed to assess where a division was and to create an environment for success *before* training was done.

The consulting approach as it

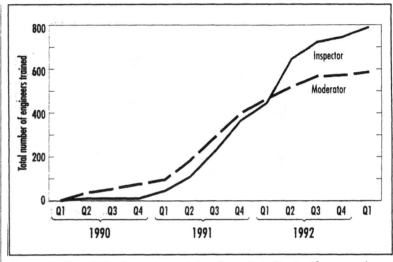

Figure 2. *Cumulative inspection training. By early 1991, significant numbers of engineers were receiving training.*

evolved in HP was adaptable to the needs of each division, which usually fell into three broad categories:

♦ Organizational commitment. Somebody — a key manager or key engineers — must be convinced that inspections could and should be done sooner instead of later.

♦ Advice and training on improving inspections. Often the local inspections champion was using a process that wasn't good enough for the division to feel that it was indispensable.

♦ Help in adapting the updated inspections approach to the division.

We then developed a consulting model structured to match and meet customer needs, provide appropriate training, and offer follow-up until the customer succeeds. It has five basic steps:

♦ Define the organizational business objective for doing inspections.

♦ Evaluate and influence the organization's readiness to do inspections.

♦ Create an infrastructure for success by identifying a local interested

person as chief moderator (who will also act as a champion).

♦ Benchmark the current process.

♦ Adjust the current process, train people, and consult to ensure success.

We knew from experience that the number of people trained is only a weak predictor of successful adoption. We wanted a stronger predictor, so we created a survey to determine the percentage of inspection penetration and effectiveness across HP. We defined a division's degree of penetration as the percentage of projects that held four or more inspections during a project's life, because one division had had great success when it asked teams to do four inspections before judging if inspections were worth the effort.

We had also consulted more with larger labs, and we wanted to see if they had higher penetration, so we arbitrarily broke the data into four different size groups. Figure 3 shows both the average penetration for different lab sizes and the percentage of the total HP population in each category. For example, labs with more than 75 software engineers represent more than 50 percent of HP's total software engineers, and they did four or more

DIVISIONS WANTED SUPPORT TAILORED TO THEIR ADOPTION STAGES.

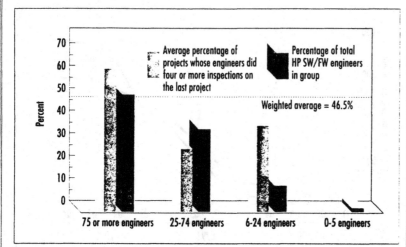

Figure 3. *1993 inspections penetration by number of division software and firmware developers. Labs with more than 75 software engineers represent more than 50 percent of HP's total software engineers, and they did four or more inspections on 63 percent of their projects in 1993.*

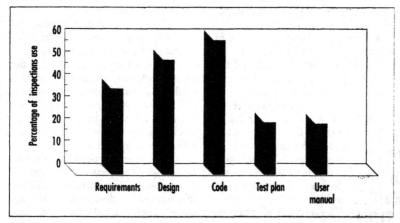

Figure 4. *1993 inspections use by document type in divisions with greater than 25 percent penetration. For this diagram, a project "used" inspections for a particular document if it inspected at least one document of that type.*

engineers, and they did four or more inspections on 63 percent of their projects in 1993.

The 1989 survey showed that every division was doing inspections, but it didn't ask how many projects did them, or how many were done per project. The 1993 data in Figure 3 more clearly shows that more than half the projects were either not using inspections or were just starting to use them. Fortunately, this graph is a lagging indicator. Many people trained in 1992 and 1993 were working on projects that simply hadn't completed four inspections yet. Although the average

penetration increased from 32 percent in 1992 to 46.5 percent in 1993, there is still much room for improvement.

The survey data does contain encouraging signs, however. Years of research show that the S-shaped diffusion curve takes off at about 10 to 25 percent adoption,[1] and more than 60 percent of the divisions responding had already achieved 25 percent penetration. Those who haven't are groups who can best benefit from continued consulting.

The survey also asked what documents are inspected. We strongly encourage the inspection of early documents, because these inspections help uncover defects that are very expensive if not found until later. We now analyze what percentage of different document types are inspected each year, but the 1993 survey asked only if projects inspected at least one noncode document of each type. For example, Figure 4 shows that 51 percent of the projects in divisions with greater than 25 percent penetration did at least one design inspection (and when all reporting divisions are included, the average is still 35 percent). This is much better than the 1989 average of 19 percent, and it suggests that recent training and consulting have helped increase early document inspections.

The survey clearly shows that inspection use is increasing, but the rate of increase varies. Because we are interested in how proven technologies such as inspections can be adopted faster, we looked more closely at one HP Group who has been very active during the last few years. This Group had a full-time person responsible for inspections and people who regularly both scheduled and did training. It also had high-level management support. One of the Group's key goals was to reduce rework, and using inspections was a major strategy to do this. Figure 5 shows the dramatic difference in the increased number of inspections done by this Group (74 percent) compared with the rest of HP (21 percent) from 1991 to 1992. We

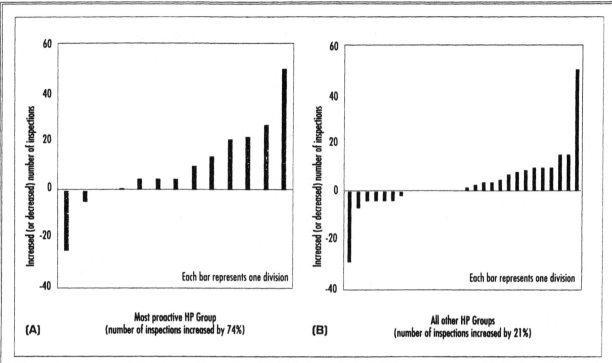

Figure 5. *Increasing divisional use of inspections. (A) This Group had a full-time person responsible for inspections, people who regularly both scheduled and did training, and high-level management support. (B) Compared with the rest of HP, the increase in inspections from 1991 to 1992 for the proactive Group was dramatic.*

also found that the most consistent difference between divisions that improved and divisions that remained unchanged or actually did fewer inspections was the presence or absence of a divisional chief moderator. Of the six divisions with the most growth in Figure 5a, every one had a chief moderator. It is clear that a good divisional infrastructure is as important as the Group and corporate ones.

Although we are still in the widespread belief and adoption stage, we have already learned that

♦ Training and process guidelines are not sufficient. Consulting with objectives tailored to divisions is also required. Find champions (for inspections, chief moderators) and sponsors. Work with divisions after training to ensure success.

♦ Few divisions can start with an optimal process. Learn the divisions' immediate wants and its long-term plans. Understand its processes and organizational constraints.

♦ Program-focused support makes a big difference in the adoption rate (Group-level people with full-time inspections responsibility, in this case).

♦ Good management process metrics are necessary to achieve and sus-

tain widespread use and effectiveness (see the box on p. 54).

STANDARDIZATION

It's not clear that there ever will be a single "standard" HP inspection process, but this is not the issue. What matters is that every project use some variation of a standard process in an efficient, cost-effective way.

The critical leadership roles during all other stages are those of champion and sponsor, and the standardization stage is no different. The first part of our standardization plan is to continue to *proactively identify and support champions and sponsors*, who will provide the technical and organizational leadership necessary for each group to assume long-term process ownership and responsibility.

We must arm these champions and sponsors with strong, persuasive messages. The second part of the standardization plan is to *reinforce management awareness with a strong inspections business case*. Many success stories have been presented at the SEPCs. Some of these stories have gone beyond measuring inspection defect-finding rates to comparing them with defect-finding rates in systems test. Although the

TABLE 1		
COST BENEFIT ANALYSIS OF DESIGN INSPECTIONS (ROI > 10 IN FIRST AND SUBSEQUENT YEARS)		
Items	Costs	Benefits
Training	48 engineering hours $1,650 (= approx. 25 eng. hrs.)	
Start-up costs	96 engineering hours 0.5 month	
Reduced defect-finding time		1,759 engineering hours
Reduced time to market		1.8 months

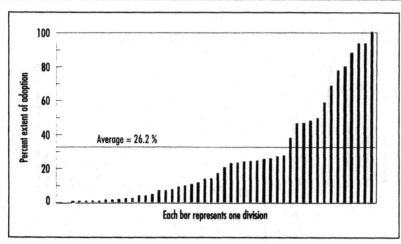

Figure 6. *Extent of inspections adoption, reflecting an increase from 20 percent adoption in 1992 to 26.2 percent adoption in 1993.*

The graph shows "Percent extent of adoption" on the y-axis (0 to 100) with a line marked "Average = 26.2 %". The x-axis notes "Each bar represents one division".

RETROSPECTIVE FROM WIDESPREAD BELIEF AND ADOPTION STAGE

The experiences in two divisions show how our thinking has gone beyond just implementing inspections to how inspections affect our products.

In the first division, code volume was growing rapidly. Fortunately, they had good historical labor and defect metrics, so the quality manager could make a strong case that future projects were in jeopardy unless they could substantially reduce testing effort and schedule by using inspections.

The division, which had a strong champion, also provided other incentives to adopt inspections. It conducted an exercise that had one team inspect a "clean" module written by one of its best engineers. The inspection uncovered three significant problems, so the engineers were convinced. And it was one of the first divisions to integrate real work products into its training class instead of canned examples and to train work groups together.

In three years, this division has done more than 180 inspections. The average time to find and fix major defects using inspections continues to be more than 10 times better than their old test methods, as reported by Dave Dickmann in a paper presented at an HP SEPC. They are getting more complex products to market far sooner than they would have using their old process.

The second division already enjoyed widespread use of inspections and it remained high even through several reorganizations. Inspections typically found 60 to 70 percent of the defects. However, a review of postrelease critical/serious defects showed no significant improvement in the division's products. To learn more, 13 project managers were asked about their backgrounds, their reasons for doing inspections, details about the inspections, what data was collected, and what follow-up occurred.[1]

What they learned was that a strong belief system had kept inspections alive, but the process was stagnant: It focused on code and other back-end work products; entry and exit criteria had relaxed; and there was seldom any attempt to use inspection data to change the process. This division learned that it must monitor the effectiveness of the inspection process by examining the quality of its products.

Questioning the process was a healthy exercise. The results created both motivation and direction for change. The key changes included a greater front-end emphasis and stronger metrics to drive process improvements and to monitor their inspections process.

REFERENCES

1. G. Shirey, "How Inspections Fail," *Software Practitioner*, May/Aug. 1993, pp 12-17.

rates vary from 4.4 times better up to 20 times better, they all make a strong business case.

Table 1 shows a cost-benefit analysis for design inspections, developed with well-documented HP and industry results. These numbers are for first-time application of design inspections on a six-person project to produce 50,000 lines of noncomment source statements. Because of space, we cannot detail the assumptions and calculations behind this analysis here, but we have published them elsewhere.[4] The ROI is a simple ratio of engineering time benefits divided by costs (1759/(48 + 25 + 96) = 10.4). Potential added revenue from faster time to market improves the ROI even more.

This is a much better return than many other R&D investments provide. In addition, there is little risk, and you needn't wait long for the initial investment to be paid off. Note that training and start-up costs occur only once per team, although there will be a small ongoing cost for a chief moderator. This type of analysis is important, because later adopters of new practices are more conservative and need stronger persuasion.

A software-organization's management must believe that inspections are important enough to develop them as a key part of their *core competence*, a set of skills that give a company a competitive edge. These skills represent collective learning that is "built through a process of continuous improvement and enhancement that may span a decade or longer."[5]

The third part of the standardization plan is to *continue building an infrastructure strong enough to achieve and hold software core competence*. At HP, the three layers of the infrastructure are corporate, group, and division. Their key roles are to train, consult, communicate, improve, and be responsible for the inspections process. We've seen that such an infrastructure maximizes the adoption rate and increases the odds that inspections are optimally done.

The fourth part of our standardiza-

DEFINING EXTENT-OF-ADOPTION METRIC

We created the extent-of-adoption measure to gauge company-wide progress against the three key program emphases: process maturity, depth of use, and breadth of use. The metric can range from 0 to 140, but we set all calculated values greater than 100 to a maximum value of 100. Briefly, the components of the equation

extent of adoption = inspection-process maturity
*(percentage of projects using inspections + weighted percentage of documents inspected) * constant

are as follows.

Inspection-process maturity. A constant from 1 to 14 based on a five-level model that details the practices early adopting divisions used to improve their peer-review processes. Model levels 1 and 2 are not really inspections, but informal peer desk reviews to formal walkthroughs. Level 3 is an industry-typical inspection process. Level 4 is a best-practice inspection process. And level 5 links formal inspections to a defect-prevention activity.

♦ *Level 1: Initial/ad hoc* (weight = 1): No established objective for doing reviews; individual peer review/desk-checking to informal walkthroughs done; no process documentation, training, or process infrastructure.

♦ *Level 2: Emerging* (weight = 3): Informal objective to find and remove defects; informal and formal walkthroughs done; process may be documented, some trained practitioners, and some awareness of need for infrastructure.

♦ *Level 3: Defined* (weight = 10): Stated objective to find and remove defects; formal inspections recommended on major projects; process documented, moderators trained, infrastructure in place, metrics collected; standards, templates, and checklists may not exist.

♦ *Level 4: Managed* (weight = 12): Stated objective to improve defect detection and removal earlier in the life cycle; formal inspections required on key documents for all major projects; process metrics used to improve process, defect cause information collected; standards, templates, and checklists exist for all key document types.

♦ *Level 5: Optimizing* (weight = 14): Stated objective to prevent defect introduction; organizational standard exists — and is adhered to — that defines which documents will be inspect-

ed under what conditions; defect-cause information is used in root-cause analysis to target changes to development process.

Percentage of projects using inspections. The percentage of projects that did four or more inspections on their last project. We picked four based on the experience of one division that had great success when it asked teams to do four inspections.

Weighted percentage of documents inspected. Several studies have measured the relative costs of fixing different types of defects, and our weights are based on their findings.[1] We then multiply these factors by the organization's percentage of projects using inspections for each document (we define a project as using inspection if it inspects at least one document of a particular type).

(5.7 * percentage of requirements + 2.5
* percentage of design + 2
* percentage of test + percentage of code)/11.2

We derived the percentage using the survey results in Figure 4 in the main text. For Figure 6 in the main text, because the survey only asked for the presence or absence of inspections for different document types on projects, the results overstate actual use. This measure has a factor of 11.2 so that its value also ranges from 0 to 100.

Constant = 0.05. Chosen to fit the extent-of-adoption metric into a range of 0 to 100 when the inspection process maturity factor is at a level 3 (weight of 10) and both the percentage of projects using and the weighted percentage of documents inspected are at their maximum values.

There is no scientific basis for assuming that a level 2 inspection process is three times better than a level 1 process or that a level 3 process is 10 times better, and so on. The maturity weights and their mathematical use in the extent-of-adoption metric are intended only to identify trends. As with all metrics created for one purpose, there is always the potential that some people might use this one for other purposes. To minimize the extent of potential distortions, we did a series of sanity checks that tested all combinations of the three factors at their high and low conditions. We then asked ourselves if the result seemed reasonable. To us, they did.

REFERENCES

1. R. Grady, *Practical Software Metrics for Project Management and Process Improvement*, Prentice-Hall, Englewood Cliffs, N.J. 1992.

---

tion plan is to *measure the extent of adoption*. We believe that consistently improving inspections use will visibly reduce defects and development times. We needed a measure that ties inspection results as closely as possible to such improvements. We created a measure consisting of three adoption components.

♦ *Depth* (percentage of projects using inspections). Some minimum number of inspections that signifies a project team seriously believes inspections are necessary (it is four now, but it may change).

♦ *Breadth* (weighted percentage of documents inspected). A weighting factor that accounts for the observation that inspecting early work products (requirements, designs) yields better returns than inspecting late ones (code).

♦ *Inspection-process maturity.* Not all inspections are equal. Today's inspections process is much more effective than Fagan's first method, so we add a simple weighting factor, as described in the box above.

So the formula we use to measure adoption, which we have found does separate the most effective divisions from the least effective is:

extent of adoption =
inspection-process maturity
* (percentage of projects using inspection
+ weighted percentage of documents inspected) * constant

This is how we produced the data in Figure 6. Imperfect as this metric is, it gives a baseline against which to track year-to-year progress. For example, the metric reflects an increase from 20 percent adoption in 1992 to 26.2 percent adoption in 1993. Most important, it includes the three major aspects that our experience shows contribute to reduced costs and development time.

ESTIMATING SAVINGS FROM INSPECTIONS

We derived the 1993 estimated savings of $21.5 million using the formula

estimated $ savings/year = % total costs saved * rework % * efficiency factor (.4) * total engineering costs

Percentage of total costs saved. Percentage for a work-product component only. It peaks at 100%.

Rework percentage. An internal HP software-development cost model estimates total rework at 33 percent. It is broken down into the work-product components shown in Table A.

Efficiency factor. Capers Jones says this varies from 30 percent to 75 percent.[1] Assume 40 percent for 1993 because our average maturity level is still relatively low.

Total engineering cost. Assuming 3,500 R&D software engineers at a cost of $150,000 per engineering year, total cost is $525 million.

Maximum possible savings from inspections. Total engineering cost ($525 million) times the rework percentage (33 percent) times the efficiency factor (60 percent) equals $105 million. (Some of this will be saved through other engineering techniques, so while this is a theoretical maximum, the practical maximum will be somewhat less. Also, while inspections substantially reduce costs, they don't totally

eliminate them. We use a 60 percent efficiency factor to simulate these combined effects).

Total savings. The sum of the savings from four major work products. Take the increase in the percentage of different types of inspections (for example, our 1993 survey showed design inspections had increased 33.8 percent), multiply it by how much of the total cost ($525 million) you assume the rework of a work product accounts for (11 percent in the case of design) and multiply that by an assumed 1993 efficiency factor of 40 percent. So 1993 design savings are

33.8% * (11% * $525M) * .4 = $7.81 million

These are very rough calculations, but they give us a way to translate our extent-of-adoption measure to company-wide savings. The estimated 1993 percentages came from the 1993 survey, which asked only about the presence or absence of different inspection types on projects, so the results overstate actual usage. The efficiency factor of only .4 at least somewhat makes up for this. Table A summarizes the savings estimate.

REFERENCES
1. C. Jones, *Programming Productivity*, McGraw-Hill, New York, 1986, p. 179.

TABLE A
ESTIMATED YEARLY SAVINGS ATTRIBUTABLE TO HP SOFTWARE INSPECTION

Work product	Estimated starting point	Estimated 1993	Percentage total cost saved	Rework percentage	Estimated $ savings per year
Specification	1%	29.5%	28.5%	17%	$10,175,000
Design	1%	34.8%	33.8%	11%	$7,808.000
Code	5%	42.3%	37.3%	4%	$3,133,000
Test plan	1%	17.1%	16.1%	1%	$338,000
Total		.		33%	$21,454,000

TABLE 2
KEY CONTRIBUTORS TO SUCCESSFUL INSPECTION ADOPTION

	Experimental	Initial guidelines	Widespread belief and adoption
Business factors		Compelling vision (10X)	Recognition of need for core competence
Organizational readiness	Local support infrastructure	Company-wide infrastructure (productivity managers) Company-wide communications (SEPC)	Inspections infrastructure (company, group, divisional levels) and metrics Needs assessment — organizational plans, readiness, constraints Consulting to set stage for success
People factors	Visionary people (champions) No penalties for failures (sponsorship)	Management training (sponsors) Local adaption	Proactive identification of champions and sponsors

Software inspections have taught us a lot about technology adoption. Table 2 summarizes the key lessons we learned in each stage. Where is HP on its S-shaped curve? To answer that, we must first compute the theoretical maximum savings. We estimate that roughly one third of all HP software costs are rework, and inspections can save 60 percent of these costs. For a company the size of HP, a conservative potential savings then is $105 million *per year*. (The box above explains how we arrived at these rough calculations.) Next, estimate how much the inspections program is already saving. Using data from our 1993 survey, we separately estimate savings for each document type and add them, for an estimated savings in 1993 of $21.4 million. Note that when these savings are translated to a lab of 100 engineers, they yield a bonus of more than four engineers to work on things other than rework (in every lab across the entire company). It's no wonder that a US government study concluded that it took an average of 15 to 20 years for new software technology to get to the point that it could be popularized and disseminated.[6] It has taken HP more than 15 years to reach this point, and we feel we still have almost 80 percent of the benefits yet to gain!

It is too late to speed up the earlier phases for inspections, but it is not too late to apply what we have learned. HP has created a set of software initiatives to accelerate company-wide adoption of a small number of software best practices, including inspections. These initiatives provide timely help to divisional pilot projects for these best practices and the corporate-level infrastructure we learned was so key to speeding technology adoption.

It is through experiences like those we describe here that we learn how to do things better. We now have a model for how technology adoption occurs, we know what to do to accelerate improvement, and we've been exposed to the typical problems we can expect. These experiences can be and are being applied to accelerate adoption of other best practices, and we've seen that the returns for such investments can be huge. ◆

ACKNOWLEDGMENTS

It is impossible to name everyone who played a major part in our program's success, but we would like to publicly thank the main contributors in recent years. These people helped customize and champion inspections at HP: Babs Brownyard, Neil Davies, Dave Dickmann, Clairmont Fraser, Bob Horenstein, Billy Knorp, Jean MacLeod, Debra Mallette, Rose Marchetti, Patsy Nicolazzo, Richard Peifer, Jerry Peltz, Steve Rodriguez, Jack Ward, David Wittall, and Dawn Yamine. In addition to some of them, others wrote some of the excellent papers that helped to sustain HP's interest and beliefs: Lee Altmayer, Frank Blakely, Mark Boles, Dave Decot, John DeGood, Joe Malin, Dan Miller, Alvina Nishimoto, Jim Nissen, Barbara Scott, Glen Shirey, Chris Smith, Yvonne Temple, Tim Tillson, Erik Torres, and Jack Walicki. We also thank the R&D labs that contributed their inspections-use data so we could develop the baseline inspections penetration, use, and extent-of-adoption metrics. Finally, we thank the 20 reviewers of this article for their comments, corrections, and enthusiasm, especially Jan Grady, Debbie Caswell, Cate Meyer, and Brian Sakai.

REFERENCES

1. E. Rogers, *Diffusion of Innovations, 3rd ed.*, Macmillan, New York, 1983.
2. M. Fagan, "Design and Code Inspections to Reduce Errors in Program Development," *IBM Systems J.*, No. 3, 1976, pp. 182-210.
3. T. Gilb, *Principles of Software Engineering Management*, Addison-Wesley, Reading, Mass., 1988.
4. R. Grady, *Practical Software Metrics for Project Management and Process Improvement*, Prentice-Hall, Englewood Cliffs, N.J., 1992.
5. C. Prahalad and G. Hamel, "The Core Competence of the Corporation," *Harvard Business Rev.*, May-June 1990, pp. 79-91.
6. S. Redwine and W. Riddle, "Software Technology Maturation," *IEEE Conf. Software Eng.*, Aug. 1985, pp. 189-200.

A Practical View of Software Measurement and Implementation Experiences Within Motorola

Michael K. Daskalantonakis, *Member, IEEE*

Abstract— The purpose of this paper is to describe a practical view of software measurement that formed the basis for a company-wide software metrics initiative within Motorola. A multi-dimensional view of measurement is provided by identifying different dimensions (e.g., metric usefulness/utility, metric types or categories, metric audiences, etc.) that were considered in this company-wide metrics implementation process. The definitions of the common set of Motorola software metrics, as well as the charts used for presenting these metrics, are included. The metrics were derived using the Goal/Question/Metric approach to measurement. The paper distinguishes between the use of metrics for process improvement over time across projects and the use of metrics for in-process project control. Important experiences in implementing the software metrics initiative within Motorola are also included.

Index Terms— Implementation experience, in-process project control, multidimensional view of measurement, practical view of measurement, process improvement, software metrics, software metrics infrastructure.

I. INTRODUCTION

THE PURPOSE of this paper is to describe a practical view of software measurement, that formed the basis for a company-wide software metrics initiative within Motorola. A *software metric* is defined as a method of quantitatively determining the extent to which a software process, product, or project posesses a certain attribute. This includes not only the formula used for determining a metric value, but also the chart used for presenting metric values, as well as the guidelines for using and interpreting this chart (and metric) in the context of specific projects.

To be practical, software metrics must be defined with their intended use in mind. Goal-oriented measurement (i.e., the identification of measurement goals and important characteristics to be measured before defining the metrics) [1]–[3] ensures such practicality because it provides not only metric definitions, but also the context for making interpretations of their values, so that engineers and managers are able to use them for making decisions.

Several companies are beginning to realize the important role that software metrics can play in planning and controlling software projects, as well as improving software processes, products, and projects over time. Such improvement results in increased productivity and quality, and reduced cycle time,

all of which make a company competitive in the software business. Although there are many examples of companies beginning to use metrics in industry (e.g., [4]–[6]), some are finding it a complex and difficult undertaking.

Results of an industry survey sponsored by Xerox and Software Quality Engineering [7] indicate that fewer than 10% classified it as positive and enthusiastic. In another survey conducted by Howard Rubin and Associates (mentioned in [8]), it is reported that two out of three measurement efforts started, failed, or discontinued after two years. These experiences indicate that the implementation of software metrics is a very complex issue that involves several dimensions. All these dimensions must be addressed through a practical view of measurement in order to increase the likelihood of successfully implementing software metrics within a company or project.

Section II of this paper provides a multidimensional view of software measurement and identifies different ways that software metrics can be used within software projects and a company. Section III discusses the use of metrics for process improvement over time, as well as the use of metrics for in-process project control. Section IV provides the author's experiences from implementing a software merics initiative within Motorola, in terms of the obstacles that were present and how they were addressed, the cost involved in implementing metrics, as well as the benefits obtained so far and expected over the next years. The conclusion is in Section V.

II. A MULTIDIMENSIONAL VIEW OF METRICS

The purpose of this section is to describe the prerequisites for successful metrics implementation and introduce the dimensions that must be considered when designing and implementing a successful metrics initiative. They should be considered by the function tasked to implement such an initiative.

It is important to understand that the likelihood of a successful metrics implementation increases significantly if several prerequisites are satisfied. These prerequisites specify [9] that the following (preferably automated) systems must be in place: a cost accounting system; a software configuration management system; and a problem reporting/corrective action system. These systems are considered prerequisites for metrics implementation because their existence greatly facilitates any metric data collection and analysis process. If these systems are not in place, the software organization has higher priority items that should be addressed before fully implementing metrics (although a scaled-down metrics initiative may be possible).

Manuscript received October 1, 1991; revised August 1, 1992. Recommended by R. Selby and K. Torii.

The author is with the Cellular Infrastructure Group, Motorola, Arlington Heights, IL 60004.

IEEE Log Number 9203769.

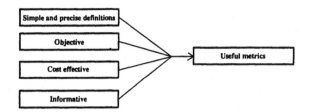

Fig. 1. Sample characteristics of useful metrics.

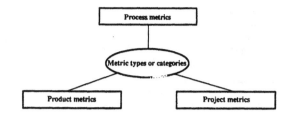

Fig. 2. An example of how software metrics can be classified (based on their intended use).

Also, since metrics are usually used in conjunction with a process that must be controlled and improved, documented processes that are in use should be in place before starting to define process control and improvement metrics. However, some metrics can be defined to be independent of the process used and in that case, there is no need to wait for a process to be defined. There are cases where the existence of metrics provides additional motivation to engineers and managers to go back and define the software processes used in order to improve them over time through the use of metrics.

The dimensions that must be considered when implementing a metrics initiative include the metric usefulness/utility, metric types or categories, metric audiences or users, metric user needs, and the levels of metric application. These dimensions are further described in the following subsections.

2.1. Metric Usefulness/Utility

There are several important characteristics that are associated with useful software metrics. Software metrics must be (Fig. 1):

simple to understand and precisely defined in order to facilitate consistency both in the calculation and the analysis of metric values;

objective (as much as possible) in order to decrease the influence of personal judgement to the calculation and analysis of metric values;

cost effective in order to have a positive return on investment (the value of the information obtained must exceed the cost of collecting the data, calculating the metric, and analyzing its values); and

informative in order to ensure that changes to metric values have meaningful interpretations (e.g., the fact that the estimation accuracy of project effort increased should imply that a better estimation technique was used).

2.2. Metric Types or Categories

Software metrics can be classified under different categories, although it is not unusual that the same metrics belong to more than one category. A classification of metrics based on their intended use follows (Fig. 2).

Process metrics are those that can be used for improving the software development and maintenance process. Examples of such metrics include the defect containment effectiveness associated with defect containment process (e.g., inspection and testing), the efficiency of such processes, and their cost.

Product metrics are those that can be used for improving the software product. Examples of such metrics include the

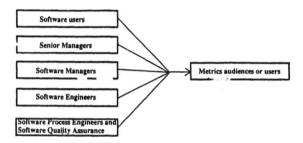

Fig. 3. Sample software metric audiences.

complexity of the design, the size of the source code, and the usability of the documentation produced.

Project metrics are those that can be used for tracking and improving a project. Examples of such metrics include the number of software developers, the effort allocation per phase of the project and the amount of design reuse achieved by the project.

2.3. Metric Audiences or Users

There are different potential audiences of software metrics and their primary interests in using metrics are also different (Fig. 3).

Software users are interested in the quality and value of the software products.

Senior Managers are interested in overall control and improvement across projects in the business unit.

Software Managers are interested in control and improvement of the specific software projects they manage.

Software Engineers are interested in control and improvement of the specific software project activities and work products in which they are involved.

Software Process Engineers and Software Quality Assurance are interested in a cross-section of what the four previous audiences are interested in (depending on whether they are working at the business unit level, or the project level).

2.4. Metric User Needs

A software metrics initiative must address the needs of all these potential metric audiences and users by (Fig. 4):

defining metrics and obtaining **consensus/acceptance** by the user community;

training metric users and providing **consulting** support for implementation; and

169

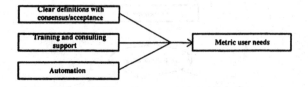

Fig. 4. Important metric user needs that must be addressed.

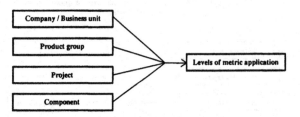

Fig. 5. Sample levels of metric application.

automating the data collection, analysis, and feedback process.

2.5. Levels of Metric Application

Such an initiative must also account for the different levels of measurement. Examples of such levels include (but are not limited to) (Fig. 5) the following.

The **company (or business unit) level,** at which data across several projects may be lumped together to provide a view of attributes such as productivity, quality, and cycle-time across projects.

The **product group level,** at which data across several projects in the same product area may be lumped together to provide a view of the same attributes, but within the product group.

The **project level,** at which data within the project is tracked and analyzed both in-process and post mortem in order to plan and control the project, as well as to improve similar projects across the business unit.

The **component level,** at which data within a component (e.g., subsystem) of a project is tracked and analyzed for managing the development of that component, as well as improving its quality over time.

This section implies that a software metrics initiative must be designed and implemented according to all of these levels and dimensions.

III. SOFTWARE METRICS INITIATIVE IN MOTOROLA

There are several reasons for starting Motorola's company-wide software metrics initiative. Studies published indicated to project participants and management, the usefulness of metrics in improving software engineering and management practices [21], [22]. Engineers and managers wanted to better understand the software development process and be able to determine necessary changes for productivity, quality, and cycle time improvement. They realized that this can be accomplished by measuring both the software development process and product, analyzing the metrics data collected, and

determining necessary changes that can lead to more sophisticated techniques for developing and maintaining software. Software managers and engineers have used software metrics as a method for determining progress towards quantified improvement goals, such as Motorola's six sigma quality goal of having no more than 3.4 defects per million of output units from a project.

It was apparent from the start of the metrics initiative (based also on observations from other companies) that software metrics implementation is a complex issue. There are several cultural and human issues that need to be addressed up front in order to assure the success of such an initiative. There is also a need to define and use software processes, focus on continuous process and product improvement, set quantitative goals, and measure the extent to which these goals are achieved. This implies software engineer and manager discipline, as well as acceptance of software measurement as an integral part of the software development process. It also implies the creation of an improvement mentality allowing presentation of data that may indicate significant problems for a project, and concentration on process improvement instead of evaluation of developers.

In addition to these issues, there were also several technical issues that needed to be addressed, such as the lack of common software metrics that are well defined, guidelines for data collection and interpretation, and tools for automating the use of metrics. A Metrics Working Group (MWG) with participation across Motorola's business units was established whose primary purpose was to define a minimal set of software metrics to be used company wide for measuring and eventually improving the quality of the developed software.

The Metrics Working Group has worked for three years intensively to define a common set of software metrics, and support the process of deploying the metrics within software development groups. This common set of metrics is defined in Section 3.1 and their use for tracking improvement over time across projects is explained. Additional processes and metrics were also defined by the Metrics Working Group (or adapted from already existing best practices in industry), so that software metrics are integrated within the process that they attempt to improve. Examples of such metrics associated with specific phases of the software development life cycle where they can be used are included in Section 3.2 and their use for in-process project control is explained. The Metrics Working Group has also created and deployed (through appropriate packaging with training and consulting activities) process and metric definitions for the formal software review and the software test processes using the Goal/Question/Metric approach [1]-[3].

In addition to process improvement over time and in-process project control, software metrics can also be used for measuring customer satisfaction and feeding this information to product designers, analyzing software performance and improving it during software design and development, benchmarking software development practices and results across companies, business units, and projects, etc. However, this paper focuses only on process improvement and in project control.

3.1. Use of Metrics for Process Improvement over Time

The overall philosophy of the company-wide software metrics initiative in Motorola has been: *Measurement is not the goal. The goal is improvement through measurement, analysis, and feedback.* This implies that quantitative improvement goals are identified and metrics data is not only collected, but it is also analyzed for providing improvement feedback to software engineers and managers. Senior management has supported this objective and has made software measurement a required practice by software development projects, as specified in the Quality Policy for Software Development (QPSD). This policy requires the use of metrics by software projects in the following measurement areas:

- delivered defects and delivered defects per size;
- total effectiveness throughout the process;
- adherence to schedule;
- estimation accuracy;
- number of open customer problems;
- time that problems remain open;
- cost of nonconformance;
- software reliability.

After continuous debate within the Metrics Working Group that lasted for about a year, the representatives of different business units agreed on a common set of metrics that addressed the measurement areas identified above. Software productivity was identified as an additional measurement area, and metrics were defined to address this area as well. The primary audience selected for these metrics was senior management, and the metrics were intended to be used primarily for tracking improvement over time, across projects. Although the metrics defined were not perfect, it was decided that it is better to start from a set of metrics addressing the measurement/improvement areas identified, and improve these metrics over time, instead of debating forever, trying to find perfect metrics.

The following definitions of terms are used for describing the metrics defined below.

Software problem: A discrepancy between a deliverable product of a phase of software development and its documentation, or the product of an earlier phase, or the user requirements. The *problem status* can be "open" (the problem has been reported), "closed available" (a tested fix is available to the customer), or "closed" (a tested fix has been installed at the customer site).

Error: A problem found during the review of the phase where it was introduced.

Defect: A problem found later than the review of the phase where it was introduced.

Fault: Both errors and defects are considered faults.

Failure: The inability of a functional software unit to perform its required function. A failure is caused by a defect encountered during software execution (i.e., testing and operation). Problem reports are created as a result of observing a software failure and when analyzed could result in identifying the defect(s) causing the failure.

Released software: Software that has entered the phase of beta test and operation.

Line of code: A physical source line of code, excluding lines that contain only comments or blanks. Lines of code are units of source size. There are two different counts of source size (total and delta). Total source size is the total size of the released software. Delta source size is the size of the source code added, deleted, and modified from the previous software release.

By mapping the measurement areas identified in the QPSD to improvement goals, and mapping these goals to corresponding characteristics (stated in the form of questions), and metrics, a simplified Goal/Question/Metric structure [1] was developed. The goals identified were:

Goal 1: Improve project planning.
Goal 2: Increase defect containment.
Goal 3: Increase software reliability.
Goal 4: Decrease software defect density.
Goal 5: Improve customer service.
Goal 6: Reduce the cost of nonconformance.
Goal 7: Increase software productivity.

The questions and metrics defined were based on practical considerations, such as the scope of the collected data (data primarily from the development organization), and the control over the reported problems (engineering perspective versus customer). Software projects were encouraged to broaden these definitions to take an end-to-end, customer view, and the metrics evolved in this direction over time. Following are the definitions of the common Motorola software metrics (in the context of the goals and questions), as well as a reference to the corresponding chart in Fig. 6 which is used for presenting the metric values. The charts in Fig. 6 are known within Motorola as "the 10–up software metrics charts." *Any data presented in charts within this paper are only for the purpose of providing examples, and should not be considered as representing actual project data.*

Goal 1: Improve Project Planning

Question 1.1: What was the accuracy of estimating the actual value of project schedule?

Metric 1.1: Schedule Estimation Accuracy (SEA) (chart 9)

$$\text{SEA} = \frac{\text{actual project duration}}{\text{estimated project duration}}.$$

Question 1.2: What was the accuracy of estimating the actual value of project effort?

Metric 1.2: Effort Estimation Accuracy (EEA) (chart 9)

$$\text{EEA} = \frac{\text{actual project effort}}{\text{estimated project effort}}.$$

Goal 2: Increase Defect Containment

Question 2.1: What is the currently known effectiveness of the defect detection process prior to release?

Metric 2.1: Total Defect Containment Effectiveness (TDCE) (chart 7)

$$\text{TDCE} = \frac{\text{number of pre-release defects}}{\text{number of pre-release defects} + \text{number of post-release defects}}.$$

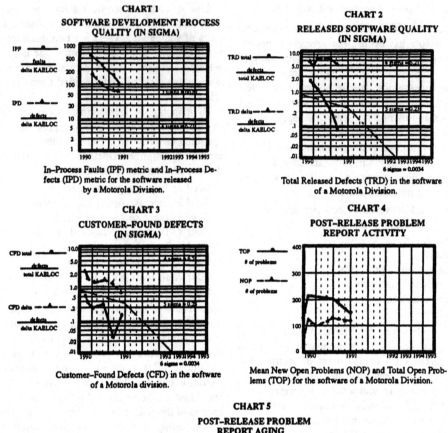

CHART 1
SOFTWARE DEVELOPMENT PROCESS QUALITY (IN SIGMA)

In–Process Faults (IPF) metric and In–Process Defects (IPD) metric for the software released by a Motorola Division.

CHART 2
RELEASED SOFTWARE QUALITY (IN SIGMA)

Total Released Defects (TRD) in the software of a Motorola Division.

CHART 3
CUSTOMER–FOUND DEFECTS (IN SIGMA)

Customer–Found Defects (CFD) in the software of a Motorola division.

CHART 4
POST–RELEASE PROBLEM REPORT ACTIVITY

Mean New Open Problems (NOP) and Total Open Problems (TOP) for the software of a Motorola Division.

CHART 5
POST–RELEASE PROBLEM REPORT AGING

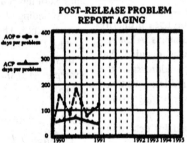

Mean Age of Open Problems (AOP) and mean Age of Closed Problems (ACP) for the software of a Motorola Division.

(a)

Fig. 6.   (a) Sample Motorola software metrics charts.

Question 2.2: What is the currently known containment effectiveness of faults introduced during each constructive phase of software development for a particular software product?

Metric 2.2: Phase Containment Effectiveness for phase i (PCEi) (chart 8)

$$PCEi = \frac{number\ of\ phase\ i\ errors}{number\ of\ phase\ i\ errors + number\ of\ phase\ i\ defects}.$$

Goal 3: Increase Software Reliability

Question 3.1: What is the rate of software failures, and how does it change over time?

Metric 3.1: Failure Rate (FR) (used at the project level only; not part of the 10–up charts)

$$FR = \frac{number\ of\ failures}{execution\ time}.$$

Goal 4: Decrease Software Defect Density

Question 4.1: What is the normalized number of in-process faults, and how does it compare with the number of in-process defects?

Metric 4.1a: In-Process Faults (IPF) (chart 1)

$$IPF = \frac{in\text{-}process\ faults\ caused\ by\ incremental\ software\ development}{assembly\text{-}equivalent\ delta\ source\ size}.$$

172

CHART 6
COST TO FIX POST–RELEASE PROBLEMS

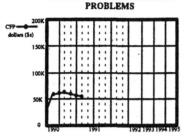

Cost to Fix post–release Problems (CFP)
within a Motorola Division.

CHART 7
TOTAL DEFECT CONTAINMENT EFFECTIVENESS

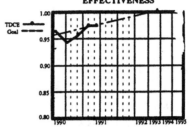

Total Defect Containment Effectiveness (TDCE)
for the projects of a Motorola division.

CHART 8
PHASE CONTAINMENT EFFECTIVENESS

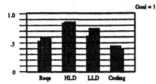

Phase Containment Effectiveness (PCE) for the
constructive phases of projects released in the
last twelve months within a Motorola Division.

Right: projects released in the last six months.
Left: projects released the prior six months.

CHART 9
ESTIMATION ACCURACY

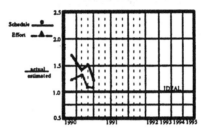

Schedule and Effort Estimation Accuracy (SEA and EEA) for
the initial estimates of a Motorola Division's software projects.

CHART 10
SOFTWARE PRODUCTIVITY

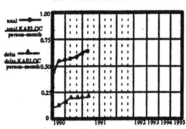

Software Productivity (SP) total and delta for
the projects of a Motorola Division.

(b)

Fig. 6. (b) Sample Motorola software metrics charts.

Metric 4.1b: In-Process Defects (IPD) (chart 1)

$$IPD = \frac{\text{in-process defects caused by incremental software development}}{\text{assembly-equivalent delta source size}}.$$

Question 4.2: What is the currently known defect content of software delivered to customers, normalized by assembly-equivalent source size?

Metric 4.2a: Total Released Defects total (TRD total) (chart 2)

$$TRDtotal = \frac{\text{number of released defects}}{\text{assembly-equivalent total source size}}.$$

Metric 4.2b: Total Released Defects delta (TRD delta) (chart 2)

$$TRDtotal = \frac{\text{number of released defects caused by incremental software development}}{\text{assembly-equivalent total source size}}.$$

Question 4.3: What is the currently known customer-found defect content of software delivered to customers, normalized by assembly-equivalent source size?

Metric 4.3a: Customer-Found Defects total (CFD total) (chart 3)

$$CFDtotal = \frac{\text{number of customer-found defects}}{\text{assembly-equivalent total source size}}.$$

173

Metric 4.3b: Customer-Found Defects delta(CFD delta) (chart 3)

$$CFDdelta = \frac{\text{number of customer-found defects caused by incremental software development}}{\text{assembly-equivalent total source size}}.$$

Goal 5: Improve Customer Service

Question 5.1: What is the number of new problems that were opened during the month?

Metric 5.1: New Open Problems (NOP) (chart 4)

$$NOP = \text{total new post-release problems opened during the month.}$$

Question 5.2: What is the total number of open problems at the end of the month?

Metric 5.2: Total Open Problems (TOP) (chart 4)

$$TOP = \text{total number of post-release problems that remain open at the end of the month.}$$

Question 5.3: What is the mean age of open problems at the end of the month?

Metric 5.3: (Mean) Age of Open Problems (AOP) (chart 5)

$$AOP = \text{(total time post-release problems remaining open at the end of the month have been open)}/ \text{(number of open post-release problems remaining open at the end of the month).}$$

Question 5.4: What is the mean age of the problems that were closed during the month?

Metric 5.4: (Mean) Age of Closed Problems (ACP) (chart 5)

$$ACP = \frac{\text{total time post-release problem closed within the month were open}}{\text{number of post-release problems closed within the month}}.$$

Goal 6: Reduce the Cost of Nonconformance

Question 6.1: What was the cost to fix post-release problems during the month?

Metric 6.1: Cost of Fixing Problems (CFP) (chart 6)

$$CFP = \text{dollar cost associated with fixing post-release problems within the month.}$$

Goal 7: Increase Software Productivity

Question 7.1: What was the productivity of software development projects (based on source size)?

Metric 7.1a: Software Productivity total (SP total) (chart 10)

$$SPtotal = \frac{\text{assembly-equivalent total source size}}{\text{software development effort}}.$$

Metric 7.1b: Software Productivity delta (SP delta) (chart 10)

$$SPdelta = \frac{\text{assembly-equivalent total source size}}{\text{software development effort}}.$$

These metrics are applicable primarily at the product group and business unit level and selected subsets are reported monthly (as part of quality reviews and reports) to corporate and senior management. The quality reports are created by the Software Quality Assurance groups within business units based on data collected from projects within these business units. The set of common Motorola software metrics has evolved over time, as feedback was obtained from metrics users. A metrics reference document defining these common metrics, including concrete guidelines for their interpretation and usage has been formally accepted by company-wide committees and is being deployed across the company, with many projects already using these metrics. This document is accompanied by an executive summary for a brief overview of the metrics.

After defining the common set of metrics, overall quantitative quality improvement goals for software processes and products were established. These goals have been stated using Motorola's six sigma quality concept as applied to software. Charts 1 and 2 of the 10–up charts are used for tracking these process and product quality goals. In addition to these goals, software projects and business units were encouraged to define their own improvement goals using the rest of the defined common metrics, based on where their current baseline (i.e., the range of achieved values) is, with respect to these metrics.

In addition to reporting the common software metrics, individual software projects conduct further analysis of metrics data for identifying areas for improvement. Defect data has been found quite useful in this process, because if classified by project phase introduced and by cause, it can lead to actions resulting in significant process and product improvements [13]. Estimation accuracy metrics have helped several projects to define and improve the techniques used for estimating software project schedule, effort, and quality. Software problem-related metrics have also helped projects to track the responsiveness to the needs of those reporting them, and make informed decisions about allocating resources for fixing them versus resources for new software development.

3.2. Use of Metrics for In-Process Project Control

The purpose of this section is to provide examples of how software metrics can be used in-process for project control. In-process project control is defined as the ability of software engineers and managers to make informed decisions regarding the current and projected status of a project and take corrective action if necessary. Much of the data collected for the purpose of reporting the 10-up software metric charts, described in the previous section for process improvement, can also be used while the project is still in progress (using different charts) in order to control that project. However, additional refined data is necessary in order to use metrics for in-process project control. Representative examples (but not an exhaustive list) of such use available from industry and piloted/used by projects

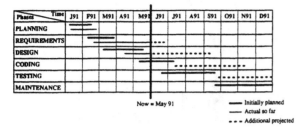

Fig. 7. A chart indicating the progress of planned activities for a project.

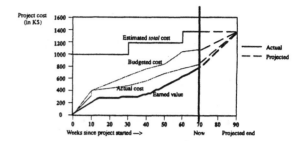

Fig. 8. A chart for tracking the earned value of the project (relative to the budgeted and actual cost).

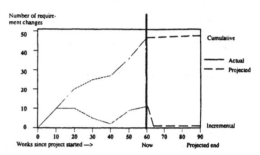

Fig. 9. Number of changes to the requirements document over time for a project.

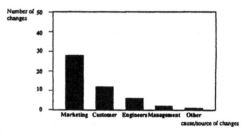

Fig. 10. Pareto chart for identifying major causes/sources of requirement changes in order to take corrective action (in-process).

within the company follow. *The data in the charts are only for providing examples, and should not be considered as actual data from projects.*

3.2.1. Life-Cycle Phase and Schedule Tracking Metric: The purpose of the chart in Fig. 7 is to track the progress of life-cycle phase/schedule progress. It indicates a sample use for tracking the current status of a software project. Management is informed that at the current date (May 1991), the project is supposed to be done with design, and coding should have already started. However, only a portion of the design has been completed so far. The project plan is revised based on the actual data so far, and the additional projected time to complete a phase (or milestone) is plotted. The collection of these charts generated throughout a project can provide also important historical metrics data for software managers. The activities included in the Gantt chart can be presented at a more refined level, depending upon the audience of the chart.

3.2.2. Cost/Earned Value Tracking Metric: The purpose of the chart in Fig. 8 [14] is to allow a manager to track in-process the following cost-related quantities (and update the project plan as necessary).

1) Estimated total cost of the project (estimated at 1000 K$ initially, revised to 1200 K$ at week 30, and revised again to 1350 K$ at week 60).
2) Budgeted cumulative cost of the project.
3) Actual cumulative cost of the project.
4) Earned value of the project (the sum of the budgeted cost for the activities already completed by the project). This value is a good indicator of the current project status.

This metric is important because it summarizes the actual progress of the project (what portion has been completed) and how that relates to the project budget/cost. Tracking these quantities allows the software manager to make informed decisions regarding the progress and viability of the project.

3.2.3. Requirements Tracking Metric: The purpose of the chart in Fig. 9 is to track in-process at the project level requirement changes and determine their impact on the project. Such requirement changes include addition of omitted requirements, and fixes of incorrectly captured requirements. Although enhancements to the software functionality that were not part of the initial scope of the project could also be considered as requirement changes, these changes should be tracked separately using another chart similar to Fig. 9.

If the manager using Fig. 9 determines that there is an unusually high number of requirement changes in the early stages of the requirement phase, the major cause of such changes can be determined in-process. This will allow corrective action to be taken, so that the changes to the requirements are minimized throughout the remaining part of the project. Fig. 10 is an example of a Pareto chart that can be used for this purpose. If marketing is identified as a major cause of requirement changes for adding omitted requirements or fixing incorrect requirements, the manager can enhance the interface with marketing and customers, and possibly use prototyping for ensuring that the required software functionality is understood and captured correctly.

3.2.4. Design Tracking Metric: Software managers are also interested in tracking the progress of designers in designing the software product. Fig. 11 can be used for this purpose. It tracks the cumulative number of requirements traceable into the design, over time. The assumption is that individual requirements are named so that they can be referenced. Another assumption is that a traceability matrix is used to indicate what requirements have already been addressed in the design created so far.

175

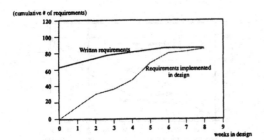

Fig. 11. Design creation progress metric for a software project.

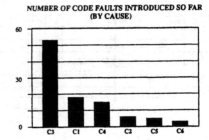

Fig. 12. Pareto chart for identifying what type of code faults is occurring most frequently, so that coders of additional modules can avoid their introduction in such modules.

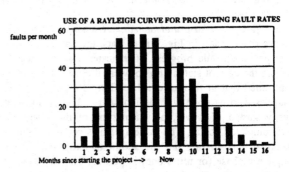

Fig. 13. Fault finding rate over the life-cycle of a software project.

The chart is used while the design is still under development for determining how complete the design is, and how fast it is created (design cycle-time). If the activity of design creation does not progress as fast as initially expected, the software manager determines the impact on schedule of subsequent phases, and the project plan is updated. Ideas on measuring software design complexity are included in [10] and [19].

3.2.5. Fault-Type Tracking Metric: The fault type tracking metric is used for analyzing code faults found with the objective to prevent the introduction of additional code faults. Once software coding has started and some of the modules have been implemented and are being reviewed and unit tested, code fault data starts to accumulate. This data can be analyzed in-process, while coding for additional modules progresses, in order to provide feedback to the coders of such modules regarding types of faults they should avoid introducing. Suppose that a software project uses Ada as the programming language, and the following cause categories for classifying code faults.

C1 — Incorrect or missing initialization of a variable.
C2 — Incorrect interface; call of an operation with the wrong parameters.
C3 — Logic problem, the control flow is wrong, the computation of a value is wrong.
C4 — Error handling problem, exception handled incorrectly, the operation has no recovery mechanism when an incorrect input is encountered.
C5 — The definition of a variable is incorrect, the fields of records are incorrectly defined
C6 — Other.

Fig. 12 is an example of a Pareto chart that can be created using these cause categories to classify code faults. The project participants identify C3 as the most frequently occurring type of code fault (so far), followed by C1. The recommendation is given to the coders working on the rest of the software modules to pay additional attention to the correctness of control flow, computation of values, and explicit initialization of all variables used within their modules. Tools can also be investigated that support the coders in their task by providing a graphical view of their modules, or prompting the coder for initializing any variable which is used without having been initialized yet.

Many additional metrics can be used in the coding phase for in-process project control (several of them automated through commercially available tools). For example, modules with high cyclomatic complexity [15] can be identified, and the manager can allocate additional resources for reviewing and unit testing these modules, or even rewrite them if they are unnecessarily complex.

3.2.6. Remaining Defects Metric: The chart in Fig. 13 [16] can be used in conjunction with a technique for estimating the number of faults remaining in a software project. This technique assumes that the fault finding rate for a software project has the shape of a Rayleigh curve that can be represented in the form of an equation. This equation provides the number of faults per month as a function of several known (or estimated) parameters from the project. A key parameter that must be estimated (based on historical fault data) is the total number of faults expected to be found over the life-cycle of the software product.

In the example of Fig. 13, if the software manager has data from the first months into the project, the Rayleight curve (and its corresponding equation) can be used for the purpose of projecting the fault finding rate over the remaining months of the software life-cycle. This fault finding rate can be used to project the number of faults to be found within a specified number of months. In this example, month 8 may correspond to the time that integration testing starts for the software project. Using the data so far (bars 1–7), and through fitting it in a Rayleigh curve, the projected remaining number of defects to be found in the software project can be estimated (based on the number for months 8–16).

3.2.7. Review Effectiveness Metric: The review effectiveness metric can be used to track review effectiveness and improve reviews and product quality over time. A control chart

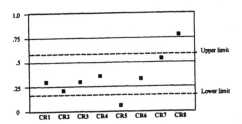

Fig. 14. Error density of source code reviewed within the project (or similar projects in the Division).

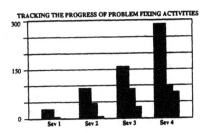

Fig. 15. Total open problems for the past three weeks of system testing for a software project.

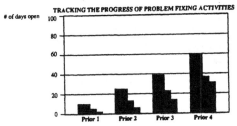

Fig. 16. Age of Open Problems for the past three months of system testing for a software project.

can be used in-process for identifying any potential problems with the review (inspection) process or the product reviewed. Fig. 14 is an example of such a chart, indicating the error density of source code reviewed so far within the project (or within similar projects in the Division) [17]. CRi indicates code review i. By using this chart in-process, the software manager determines that the review process used in CR5 must be examined further (by talking to the reviewers participating in the process). If the review process steps were followed, and the right people participated, the data for CR5 indicates that the quality of the code reviewed was relatively high. If the review process steps were not followed, and the right people did not participate as reviewers, it is an indicator that additional errors may exist in the code, and an additional review may be necessary.

By examining the same chart and attributes (in-process) for CR8, the software manager can make the following decisions. If the review process steps were not followed or the right people were not among the reviewers, an additional review and/or rewrite may be necessary for the code reviewed. However, if the process steps were followed and the right people were among the reviewers, most of the errors are likely to have been found. If the code reviewed was critical for the whole software product functionality, then a rewrite may be necessary (due to the high error density; fixes to errors found may have introduced additional faults in the code).

3.2.8. Problem Severity/Priority Tracking Metric: The problem severity/priority tracking metrics are used to track progress of fixing defects described in problem reports found in testing and make software release decisions. Total Open Problems are tracked overtime for problems of different severities (and/or priorities), so that the manager is able to determine whether or not major problems are being fixed, and whether or not the software project is getting closer to releasing the product, based on the release criteria used. An example of such release criteria for a large project may be that at release time all severity 1 (i.e., crash causing) and 2 (i.e., major functionality affected) problems found so far should be closed. Also, that no more than five problems of severity 3 (i.e., minor functionality affected) should exist, and no more than 15 problems of severity 4 (i.e., cosmetic) should exist in the software, all these problems will be communicated to the customers. Fig. 15 can then be used for making release decisions, in addition to tracking the progress of problem fixing activities (the three bars per severity correspond to the last three weeks before the data is reported).

Fig. 16 can also be used by the software manager in-process for tracking the Age of Open Problems metric by priority level, prioritizing resource allocation for problem fixing activities. If the age of priority 1 open problems is high, or is not dropping significantly over time, testing is disrupted (because the software crashes and tests cannot be executed). The manager can allocate the necessary resources for fixing such problems and is able to visualize what the impact is by examining Fig. 16.

An additional use of severity (and/or priority) data associated with problem reports and defects found in testing is to create a list of severity 1 and 2 defects found so far, and have a meeting with the designers and coders in order to identify where else in the software these same defects may exist. The output of this meeting can be used for fixing additional defects identified through this process, without waiting for testing (or the customers) to find them first.

In addition to the techniques discussed in this section, the Failure Rate metric can be used (in conjunction with a software reliability model [18]) for determining the current reliability level of the software and making release decisions. Also [20] provides additional examples of tracking quality-related attributes from a Software Quality Assurance perspective.

IV. EXPERIENCES FROM IMPLEMENTING MOTOROLA'S SOFTWARE METRICS INITIAVE

4.1. Software Metrics Infrastructure

Implementing a company-wide software metrics initiative can be a long term process. However, the benefits obtained for the company are certainly worth this effort. It was understood early in the process of implementing this initiative that there is a need for a *software metrics infrastructure*. A software metrics infrastructure is what needs to be put in place for he purpose of facilitating metrics implementation within business units. This consists of working groups with participation across the company (e.g., the Metrics Working Group), the deliverables, training workshops on metrics, tools automating metrics, consulting support for metric implementation within projects, etc. These items are further explained below.

In addition to the Metrics Working Group, a Metrics Users Group (MUG) has been established for sharing user experiences of implementing software metrics in projects. The Metrics Users Group has representation across business units, meets quarterly, shares experiences regarding the use of tools to automate metrics, and organizes demos of such tools. The group is also involved in organizing an Annual Software Metrics Symposium within the company.

Additional activities and outputs that are part of the software metrics infrastructure established by the Metrics Working Group follow.

- Clarifications of metric definition, interpretation, and use are provided by the Metrics Working Group during its regular meetings (the group meets twice a quarter since 1988), and they are "packaged" as part of the software metric documentation and training material for dissemination to metric users.
- In order to address the "training" and "consulting support" dimensions of metrics implementation, a two-day training workshop on software metrics has been developed and has been taught across the company in the past two years. Hands-on consulting activities by the instructor follow the training sessions if requested by the workshop participants. This has been found a very effective mechanism of software technology transfer.
- In order to address the "automation" dimension of metrics implementation, requirements for an automated metrics data collection, analysis, and feedback system were also created by the Metrics Working Group and were provided to tools groups involved in automating software metrics.
- Criteria for evaluating metrics tracking systems were also created for facilitating the process of selecting commercially available metric tools. A list of metric tools that exist within the company or are available form industry was created and disseminated to interested metric users.
- Support for further analysis of collected metric data has been provided to metric users through generic defect classification schemes and examples of using these schemes for creating process improvement recommendations.
- The Defect Prevention Process [13] has been recognized as an effective mechanism to ensure that process improvement is achieved through defect data analysis. This approach has been championed by the MWG and several projects have started using this approach.
- Guidelines to interested business units for creating a function responsible for implementing software metrics are also available and used. As any other activity, if no function is identified with the task of implementing metrics it is almost certain that it will not happen.
- A method for assessing software measurement technology [11] has been created and it is used for providing feedback

to projects about priority items that will further support metrics implementation.
- Customer satisfaction measurement through surveys (from a software perspective) is also encouraged through output of the Metrics Working Group.

4.2. Additional Implementation Experiences

An important lesson learned from the application of software measurement is that it is better to start from a set of metrics addressing important improvement areas, and evolve these metrics over time, instead of debating forever, trying to find perfect metrics. Another lesson is that as engineers and managers start using metrics, they realize the potential benefits of such use, and they start investigating additional ways to obtain even more benefits. The initial charts defined for presenting the common set of metrics were targeted toward senior management and the data presented was dependent on post-release data (primarily due to the need to minimize the cost associated with data collection). These charts are useful for providing an overview of the software quality status, and senior management has used them to track trends over time, as well as for benchmarking purposes.

Software engineers and managers who started using these charts expanded the use of metrics for in-process project control and feedback. As metrics data is collected within the software development process, the data should be analyzed in order to determine current project status and make projections of estimated status for the next phases of the project. This use within the project provides timely value to the engineers and software managers involved in the project. In addition to the initial 10–up software metric charts, in-process charts were defined and are used within software projects as explained in Section 3.2

In addition to the in-process charts, the Metrics Working Group has created process and metric definitions for the formal software review, and the software test processes. The metrics defined for controlling and improving the software review and test processes were developed through the application of the Goal/Question/Metric approach which was found very useful. The process and metric definitions are appropriately packaged in order to address the needs of different audiences, and training material has been developed and taught for the purpose of transferring this technology and ensuring its use by the product groups. A recent survey of software engineers and managers conducted indicates that a very high percentage (67% of those surveyed) use the software review package which was deployed by the Metrics Working Group over the last three years. Additional process/metrics packages will be investigated for processes such as the software design process and metrics for improving this process.

There have been several requests over time from metrics users across the company for a centralized location where metrics data can be stored and compared to data from other projects. However, the approach taken was that a metrics initiative is more manageable when it is *initiated* by encouraging localized (decentralized) data storage, analysis, and feedback, so that the data is close to its source. It makes more sense to use data when the context for the projects is known (e.g., products within a product group), as opposed to using data from projects in different product groups, projects of different size and complexity, etc. This is the reason why in addition to any metric data collected, data regarding the project from which this data was obtained should also be collected, stored, and used for analysis purposes. Decentralized databases storing data from local projects could be connected once the initiative is well established for providing benchmarking data to interested projects across the company.

A software metrics initiative should emphasize as its initial stages that the engineers and managers involved in the project are the best people to analyze the collected data, because they have expertise in the project domain and can interpret what the data indicates. An external consultant who has expertise in data analysis for process improvement and project control can help project participants to initiate such activities, and document some examples of how to do data analysis. It is best that this consultant be involved early in the project so that useful metrics are selected and the mechanisms are put in place to collect valid data and analyze them for improvement. Once this is done for a couple of projects, the project participants should take over, especially since the resources of software metric experts are limited (there is only a limited number of experts in this area that is available to date). The project participants should be able to champion data analysis and feedback once the metrics consultant has initiated these activities within the product group or business unit.

Another commonly found request to be expected when implementing software metrics is to pick only one metric to be used in a project, so that the cost is minimal. However, such use of a metric can be misleading, because it is really a set of metrics that should be tracked and analyzed in order to obtain a more accurate picture of several important attributes regarding a project or organization. If only one metric is used, projects can manage to optimize the values of that metric (indicating positive results). However, these projects may have significant problems that are not obvious by examining a single metric.

There is a cost involved when implementing a software metrics initiative. There are approximately eight participants present in the Metrics Working Group meetings (twice a quarter). There are also about 15 people present in the Metric Users Group meetings (quarterly). These people are involved at least on a part time basis within their organizations in implementing software metrics. Cost is also involved in terms of implementing software metric tools, but it can be minimized by avoiding duplication of effort.

There is an example within a Motorola Division where the resources used were 3 persons per year for approximately 350 software engineers (less than 1% of resources). In an example from another Division, the resources used were 0.75 person-years per year for approximately 70 engineers (about 1% of the resources). Cost associated with post-release metric data collection has been insignificant compared to the benefits. The cost associated with in-process metric data collection can be higher, but such cost can be minimized through automation. In general, the overall cost is acceptable and justified. The benefits obtained so far through quality, productivity, and cycle-time improvement (which are expected to continue in the future), are well worth the investment made.

There are several additional benefits that have been obtained so far from implementing software metrics. People have started thinking more seriously about software process and quality. The data has helped projects understand the extent of the problems they were facing and motivate them to improve. The metrics have helped establish local baselines (i.e., ranges of achieved data values), and focus on actions with quantitative results. There are cases of significant quality and productivity improvements due to implementing several software engineering practices, including metrics.

For example, the focus within a Motorola Division on improving software quality (and tracking results through metrics) has achieved 50X reduction in released software defect density within 3.5 years. However, it is important to understand that presenting the 10–up software metric charts did not improve quality by itself. It is the quality initiative taken as a result of analyzing the data in the charts that made the difference.

There are also many indirect benefits from implementing software metrics, including cases where the use of metrics has helped to improve ship-accpetance criteria, and schedule estimation accuracy. Software development groups are expected to learn from their mistakes from previous projects (through post-mortem analyses) and take action to avoid them. It is also expected that as a result of improving software quality, there will be significant improvement in Total Customer Satisfaction. Another long range benefit expected (which has been actually achieved so far within Motorola) is significant cost reduction due to improved quality. This results from reduced rework and the use of resources for new software development instead of fixing problems. In addition to cost reduction, reduced cycle time is also expected.

Software metrics is only one of the initiatives taken in the area of software quality. Additional initiatives include the use of a Quality System Review for software, Senior Management Forums for software, Software Engineering Institute assessments, software engineering education, technology transfer, and benchmarking/use of best practices. Motorola has been awarded the First Malcolm Baldrige National Quality Award in 1988 for its successful efforts and results on improving quality in all aspects of its business.

V. CONCLUSION

By addressing the areas discussed in this paper, Motorola has been successful in the implementation of a company-wide software metrics initiative with minimum resources. The level of expertise in using metrics varies across software development projects, but increases over time. However, additional work is necessary for ensuring that the software metrics initiative is institutionalized across all software development projects. Results from the use of metrics (documented in the proceedings of the Annual Software Metrics Symposium) indicate several examples where benefits have been achieved.

It is important to remember that metrics can only show problems and give ideas as to what can be done. It is the actions taken as a result of analyzing the data that bring the results. This is the reason why it is critical for metrics users to understand that measurement is not the goal. The goal is improvement, through measurement, analysis, and feedback.

ACKNOWLEDGMENT

Motorola's Software Process Engineering Group (SPEG) within Software Research and Development (SRD) has championed the use of metrics across the company over the last four years. The work presented in this paper was done while the author was working in that group. The author would like to acknowledge the contribution to this work by many Motorolans who participated in the Software Quality Subcommittee (SQSC) of the Software Engineering Technology Steering Committee, and its Metrics Working Group over time. All these people have been significant contributors ensuring that software metrics are used for driving software process and product improvement over time. The author would like to recognize explicitly the contributions of Dr. R. H. Yacobellis (Manager of the Software Process Engineering Group) in supporting the metrics initiative from a management perspective. Also, Dr. V. R. Basili (Professor of Computer Science, University of Maryland at College Park) who provided consulting support to the Metrics Working Group and ensured a continuous focus on creating output that is of value to its customers (i.e., metric users across Motorola).

REFERENCES

[1] V.R. Basili and D.M. Weiss, "A methodology for collecting valid software engineering data," *IEEE Trans. Software Eng.*, vol. SE-10, pp. 728–738, 1984.

[2] V.R. Basili and H. D. Rombach, "Tailoring the software process to project goals and environments," in *Proc. Ninth Int. Conf. Software Engineering*, 1987.

[3] ———, "The TAME project: Towards improvement-oriented software environments," *IEEE Trans. Software Eng.*, vol. SE-14, pp. 758-773, June 1988.

[4] S.L. Pfleeger, J.C. Fitzgerald, and A. Porter, "The CONTEL software metrics program," in *Proc. First Int. Conf. Applications of Software Measurement*, Nov. 1990.

[5] F.E. McGarry, "Results of 15 years of measurement in the SEL," in *Proc. Fifteenth Annual Software Engineering Workshop*, NASA/Goddard Space Flight Center, Nov. 1990.

[6] R. B. Grady and D.L. Caswell, *Software Metrics: Establishing a Company-Wide Program.* Englewood Cliffs, NJ: Prentice Hall, 1987.

[7] B. Hetzel, "The software measurement challenge," in *Proc. First Int. Conf. Applications of Software Measurement*, Nov. 1990.

[8] G. Miluk, "Cultural barriers to software measurement," in *Proc. First Int. Conf. Applications of Software Measurement*, Nov. 1990.

[9] F.J. Buckley, "Rapid prototyping a metric program," in *Proc. First Int. Conf. Applications of Software Measurement*, Nov. 1990.

[10] ———, "Rapid prototyping a metrics program," in *Proc. First Int. Conf. Applications of Software Measurement*, Nov. 1990

[11] V.R. Basili and D.H. Hutchens, "An empirical study of a syntactic complexity family," *IEEE Trans. Software Eng.*, vol. SE-9, pp. 664–672, 1983.

[12] M.K. Daskalantonakis, V.R. Basili, and R.H. Yacobellis, "A method for assessing software measurement technology," *Quality Engineering J. American Society for Quality Control*, vol. 3, 1990–91.

[13] C. Jones, *Applied Software Measurement–Assuring Productivity and Quality.* New York: McGraw-Hill, 1991.

[14] R.G. Mays *et al.*, "Experiences with defect prevention," *IBM Syst. J.* vol. 29, 1990.

[15] D. Youll, *Making Software Development Visible.* New York: Wiley Series in Software Engineering Practice, 1990.

[16] S.D. Conte, H.E. Dunsmore, and V.Y. Shen, *Software Engineering Metrics and Models.* Benjamin/Cummings, 1986.

[17] L. Putnam, *Quantitative Software Management (QSM) Approach.* McLean, VA: Quantitative Software Management, 1990.

[18] J. Kelly and J. Sherif, "An analysis of defect densities found during software inspections," Fifteenth Annual Software Engineering Workshop, Goddard Space Flight Center, Greenbelt, Maryland, Nov. 1990.

[19] J.D. Musa, A. Iannino, and K. Okumoto, *Software Reliability–Measurement, Prediction, Application.* New York: McGraw-Hill, 1987.

[20] D. Card and R. Glass, *Measuring Software Design Complexity.* Englewood Cliffs, NJ: Prentice Hall, 1990.

[21] B. Glick, "An SQA quality tracking methodology," in *Proc. Int. Conf. Software Maintenance,* Nov. 1990.

[22] V.R. Basili and R.W. Selby, "Comparing the effectiveness of software testing strategies," Univ. Maryland, College Park, *Tech. Rep. TR-1301,* May 1985.

[23] B. W. Boehm, "Understanding and controlling software costs," *IEEE Trans. Software Eng.*, vol. 14, Oct. 1988.

[24] J. Brian Dreger, *Function Point Analysis.* Englewood Cliffs, NJ: Prentice-Hall, 1989.

Chapter 4

How are Metrics Used?

The papers

Classification tree analysis: Identifying high-risk components

Adam A. Porter and Richard W. Selby, "Empirically Guided Software Development Using Metric-based Classification Trees," *IEEE Software*, Vol. 7, No. 2, Mar. 1990, pp. 46–54. By classifying components into target classes based on historical data, high-risk components can be identified early in the life cycle.

Multiple metrics graphs: Assessing overall improvement

Shari Lawrence Pfleeger, Joseph C. Fitzgerald, Jr., and Dale A. Rippy, "Using Multiple Metrics for Analysis of Improvement," *Software Quality J.*, Vol. 1, No. 1, Mar. 1992, pp. 27–36. Appropriately chosen metrics can be graphically combined to display a composite view of the process against which to measure improvement.

Tuning the process

Watts S. Humphrey, Terry R. Snyder, and Ronald R. Willis, "Software Process Improvement at Hughes Aircraft," *IEEE Software*, Vol. 8, No. 4, July 1991, pp. 11–23. Beginning at CMM level 2, Hughes implemented the assessment team's initial recommendations to show substantial improvement in the development process.

Tuning the product

Paul W. Oman, "A Case Study in SQA Audits," *Software Quality J.*, Vol. 2, No. 1, Mar. 1993, pp. 13–27. By evaluating software products, processes, and SQA functions, SQA audits ensure that defined quality standards are followed and are effective.

Predicting performance

John C. Munson and Taghi M. Khoshgoftaar, "Measuring Dynamic Program Complexity," *IEEE Software*, Vol. 9, No. 6, Nov. 1992, pp. 48–55. A relative complexity measure is used to combine the features of many different complexity metrics and then predict performance and reliability.

Contrasting products

Don Coleman et al., "Using Metrics to Evaluate Software System Maintainability," *Computer*, Vol. 27, No. 8, Aug. 1994, pp. 44–49. Describes the use of maintainability metrics to assess the effects of maintenance changes, rank subsystem complexity, and compare the quality of subsystems.

Case study

Joel Henry et al., "Improving Software Maintenance at Martin Marietta," *IEEE Software*, Vol. 11, No. 4, July 1994, pp. 67–75. Using data collected throughout a major project, common statistical methods are used to assess and evaluate improvements in maintenance.

Editors' introduction

The first three chapters have helped us understand why we measure, what data we collect, and how the measuring is done. Now that we have a repository of measurement data, this chapter tells us how we analyze and present the data to the various audiences who need to know about our projects, products, and processes.

We begin with a problem that is common to all who gather data: distilling large numbers of measures down to the key few that tell us what we need to know. In "Empirically Guided Software Development Using Metric-Based Classification Trees," Adam Porter and Rick Selby use classification tree analysis to organize large vectors of data into decision trees based on targets or goals. Based on their assumption that most defects are found in a relatively small percentage of a system's modules, Porter and Selby present an example where their technique automatically generates classification trees that identify high-risk modules. One advantage of this technique is its ability to deal with different measurement scales and with missing data.

Often, measurement information must be displayed to people who are not software engineers and who want single indicators that represent the values of several metrics in combination. Shari Lawrence Pfleeger, Joe Fitzgerald, and Dale Rippy deal with this problem by describing the use of multiple metrics graphs. Their technique for "displaying metrics in a way that preserves the integrity and meaning of each but allows a composite view and a balancing of goals" was used to compare software products and to view the change in software quality over time. Figure 6 shows an example of how the Contel Corporation used multiple metrics graphs to depict the essential elements of software switch quality, while generating an overall quality measure represented by the polygon connecting the dots. It requires no software expertise to know that the smaller the polygon, the higher the switch quality.

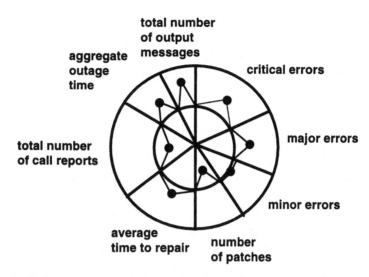

Figure 6. Multiple metrics graph for evaluating switch software (from Pfleeger, Fitzgerald, and Rippy 1992).

As we have seen, measurement is an essential part of process improvement. Many organizations invest heavily in a process improvement scheme. The SEI Capability Maturity Model, TickIT, ISO-9000, Bootstrap, and SPICE are some commonly used process improvement frameworks. It is easy to tell whether certain prescribed activities are being done, but much harder to know if the processes are effective and the products are really improving. Measurement can help make this improvement more visible. The paper by Watts Humphrey, Terry Snyder, and Ronald Willis shows quantitative evidence of the gains made as Hughes Aircraft's Software Engineering Division progressed from CMM level 2 to level 3. "Software Process Improvement at Hughes Aircraft" follows the process of assessing the maturity level with a description of the results and benefits of the assessment. The authors list 11 lessons learned as Hughes improved its process.

The ultimate evidence of good process is good product. In "A Case Study in SQA Audits," Paul Oman discusses the use of software quality assurance audits to show that a software product adheres to accepted standards. Oman's approach involves evaluating a development organization's products, process maturity, and the mechanisms to control development. Emphasizing the gathering and reporting of data, he then shows how his approach was applied at three companies.

Software development requires a large investment in time and people, so early understanding of likely outcomes is desirable, if not essential. But it is not always easy to know from early development products what the ultimate product quality is likely to be. For example, although we measure reliability in terms of Mean Time To Failure (MTTF) for an operational system, we cannot afford to wait until the system is complete to know if it has acceptable reliability. Similarly, we cannot wait until delivery to know how a product will perform. John Munson and Taghi Khoshgoftaar address this problem in "Measuring Dynamic Program Complexity." Using factor analysis of 16 different measures, they generate relative and functional complexity measures that can be used in reliability and performance prediction.

Next, Don Coleman and his colleagues describe "Using Metrics to Evaluate Software System Maintainability." Their maintainability metrics, derived from several underlying models and applied to data at Hewlett-Packard, are used to assess the effects of maintenance changes, rank subsystem complexity, and compare the quality of subsystems.

Whenever we select and apply a metric, it is important to evaluate the effectiveness of the metric as well as of the information it conveys. That is, there are ways to improve the metric and its use, in addition to focusing on process and product improvement. This chapter's case study looks at how measurement was applied to software maintenance problems at Martin Marietta. In "Improving Software Maintenance at Martin Marietta," Joel Henry and his colleagues use data collected throughout a major project. Common statistical methods are used to assess and evaluate improvements in maintenance. In each case, they discuss the utility of the measure, and they explain how the measure is used or changed to address the overall goal of improving software maintenance.

To probe further

D. Ash et al., "Using Software Maintainability Models to Track Code Health," *Proc. 1994 Int'l Conf. Software Maintenance*, IEEE Computer Society Press, Los Alamitos, Calif., 1994, pp. 154–160. Describes the use of metrics to track maintainability in industrial software systems undergoing code change.

D. Card and R.L. Glass, *Measuring Software Design Complexity*, Prentice Hall, N.J., 1991. Describes the need for measuring software design complexity and how such a measure was developed and used at NASA's Software Engineering Laboratory.

T. DeMarco, *Controlling Software Projects*, Dorset House, N.Y., 1983. Seminal book on why measurement is needed for project management. Many project management metrics are described, as well as their analysis and use.

Empirically Guided Software Development Using Metric-Based Classification Trees

Adam A. Porter and *Richard W. Selby*, University of California at Irvine

Identifying high-risk components early in the life cycle is an efficient way to improve quality. This method automatically generates a measurement-based map to those components.

Accerding to the 80/20 rule, about 20 percent of a software system is responsible for 80 percent of its errors, costs, and rework. As Barry Boehm and Philip Papaccio[1] have advised:

"The major implication of this distribution is that software verification and validation activities should focus on identifying and eliminating the specific *high-risk* problems to be encountered by a software project, rather than spreading [the] available early-problem-elimination effort uniformly across trivial and severe problems."

However, it is difficult to identify problematic components early in the life cycle. In this article, we examine a solution that casts this as a classification problem. The proposed approach derives models of problematic components, based on their measurable attributes and those of their development processes. These measurement-based models provide a basis for forecasting which components are likely to share the same high-risk properties,

such as being error-prone or having a high development cost. Developers can use these classification techniques to localize the troublesome 20 percent of the system.

We have developed a method of generating measurement-based models of high-risk components automatically and a methodology for its application to large software projects. The method, *automatic generation of metric-based classification trees*, uses metrics from previous releases or projects to identify components that are likely to have some high-risk property, based on historical data.

Software metrics are measures of components and their development processes.[2,3] Localizing likely problem areas lets developers focus their resources and tools on those components that are likely to possess high-risk properties.

We chose automatic classification-tree generation over other classification methods because the resulting models are

Reprinted from *IEEE Software*, Vol. 7, No. 2, Mar. 1990, pp. 46–54.

straightforward to build and interpret. Moreover, you can customize classification trees by using different metrics to classify different component classes in different development environments.

We are implementing our method in a tree-generation system, a prototype of which we have developed. We intend to integrate the system with Amadeus,[4] a measurement and empirical analysis system being developed to support techniques for measuring, modeling, and empirically analyzing large systems and processes.

Classification trees

Classification trees are one way to identify high-risk[5] components. The trees use metrics to classify components, such as modules, according to how likely they are to have certain high-risk properties. Classification trees let developers orchestrate the use of several metrics, so the trees serve as *metric-integration frameworks*. Example metrics that may be used in a classification tree are source lines, data bindings, cyclomatic complexity, data bindings per 100 source lines, and number of data objects referenced. Figure 1 shows an example tree.

You can model those high-risk properties that interest you. For example, you may want to identify modules whose error rates are likely to be above 30 errors per 1,000 source lines; whose total error counts are likely to be above 10; whose maintenance costs are likely to require between zero to 10 man-hours of effort; or whose error counts of error type X are likely to be above zero, where X might mean interface, initialization, or control errors.

Each of these properties defines a *target class* — the set of modules likely to have that property. Our system generates automatically a classification tree to classify the modules in each target class, based on

data from previous releases and projects. Our system generates classification trees through a recursive algorithm that selects metrics that best differentiate between modules within a target class and those outside it.[6] If you want to focus resources on high-payoff areas, you might use several classification trees to support your analysis.

Metric-based classification trees have several benefits:

• You can specify the target classes of modules to be identified.

• They are generated *automatically* using past data.

• The generation process is extensible

— you can add new metrics.

• They serve as metric-integration frameworks because they use multiple metrics simultaneously to identify a particular target class and may incorporate any metric from all four measurement abstractions: nominal, ordinal, interval, and ratio.

• They prioritize data-collection efforts and quantify diminishing marginal returns.

• You can calibrate the tree-generation algorithm to new projects and environments using historical data.

• You can apply the tree-generation algorithm to large systems.

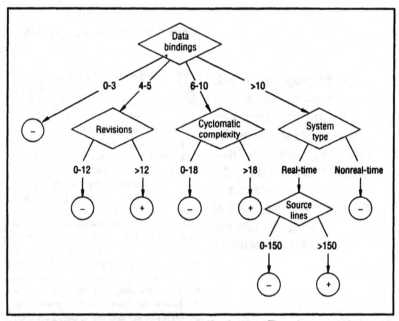

Figure 1. Example hypothetical metric-classification tree. There is one metric at each diamond-shaped decision node. Each decision outcome corresponds to a range of possible metric values. Leaf nodes indicate if a module is likely to have some property, such as being error-prone or containing errors in a certain class (in the figure, "+" means likely to have errors of type X and "–" means unlikely to have errors of type X).

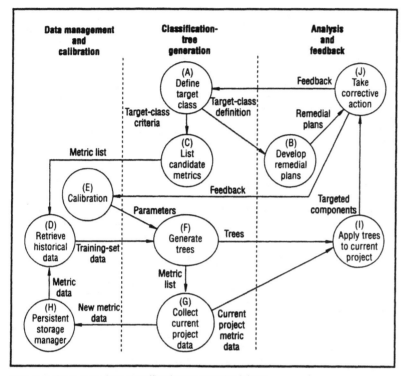

Figure 2. Overview of the classification-tree methodology.

We are developing a multiphase methodology for integrating the automatic generation of metric-based classification trees into large-system development and evolution. We are basing our methodology on lessons we are learning in two validation studies, using data from the National Aeronautics and Space Administration[6] and Hughes Aircraft.[7]

Empirical classification methodology

Figure 2 shows an overview of our classification method and its three main activities: data management and calibration, classification-tree generation, and analysis and feedback of newly acquired information. Our classification method is an iterative process, the steps of which are labeled with capital letters in Figure 2. Because this approach is automated, you can easily build and evaluate trees at many points in the project's life cycle, obtaining frequent feedback about the product's state.

Classification-tree generation. This central activity constructs classification trees and prepares them for analysis and feedback. It is during this phase that you define the target classes by establishing criteria to differentiate between members and nonmembers of the target classes (step A). For example, you could define a target class of error-prone modules as those modules whose total errors are in the top 10-percent range of historical data.

You then specify the remedial plans, such as further testing and analysis, to be applied to those components likely to be in the target class (step B).

The system then guides the creation of a list of candidate metrics for inclusion in the classification trees and passes it to the historical database for retrieval (step C). A default candidate metric list contains all the metrics for which data is available from previous releases and projects.

The system then feeds historical metric data and calibration parameters into the tree-generation algorithm (steps D and E).[6] The tree-construction process develops characterizations of those modules within and outside the target class based on measurable attributes of past modules (step F).

Classification trees may incorporate metrics that capture a module's features and interrelationships, as well as the process and environment in which the module was constructed. They may include objective and subjective metrics. Any of the many automated data-collection tools can feed candidate metrics into the tree-generation system, thus minimizing the effect of data collection on development.

When the trees have been generated, the system begins collecting the metrics used in the classification-tree decision nodes on the current project modules (step G). This data is stored for future use (step H) and passed, with the classification trees, to the analysis and feedback activity (steps I and J).

You may define target classes and generate classification trees at any stage of development and maintenance. However, before you can apply a tree to classify modules on your project, you must collect the metric data required by the tree for your modules. For example, suppose you want to apply our method at the end of module coding and testing to identify modules likely to have integration-test errors. To do so, you must include in the candidate metric list only those metrics that are available at or before the end of module coding and testing, or the resulting tree may call for metrics that cannot be collected on the current modules until some future phase.

Data management and calibration. These activities retain and manipulate historical data and tailor classification-tree parameters to the development environment. You may calibrate the tree-generation parameters, such as the sensitivity of the tree-termination criteria, to your environment (step E). We have described the tree-generation parameters and how to calibrate them elsewhere.[6-7] The calibration parameters examined in our earlier study[6] that resulted in the most accurate trees were the log-based, information theory evaluation function heuristic; either

25-percent or 40-percent tolerance in the tree-termination criteria; octile ordinal groupings of metrics; including all available metrics in the candidate set; and including historical metric data on all available modules in the training set.

The tree-generation algorithm builds classification trees based on metric values for a group of previously developed modules. We call this set of metric values a training set (step D). The metric values for the training set and the current project are stored in a persistent storage manager (step H).

Analysis and feedback. This part of the method leverages the information resulting from the tree generation by applying it in the development process.

It is important that you determine what remedial actions should be applied to modules classified as likely members of the target class (step B). For example, if you want to identify modules that are likely to contain a certain error type, you should prescribe the testing or analysis techniques that are designed to detect errors of that type, or you should describe how to redesign and reimplement the modules. Developing plans early in the process allows time to train people and build support tools, and discourages the application of ad-hoc remedies.

The system feeds the metric data collected for modules in the current project into the classification trees to identify modules likely to be in the target class (step I).

Once identified, you can apply the remedial plans developed earlier to the targeted modules (step J). As you apply the remedial plans, you may have insight into new target classes you should identify or into how to fine-tune the generation parameters. You can feed these insights back into the target-class definition and data-calibration activities.

Validation studies

We have developed environment-independent tool prototypes to automatically generate metric-based classification trees. These tools embody the tree-generation algorithm and the supporting data-manipulation capabilities. These tools are only preliminary versions.

Table 1.
Interface-error data.

Metric	A	B	C	D	E	F	G	H	I	J	K	L
Interface errors	3	2	10	1	2	9	1	3	6	2	3	0
Class	−	−	+	−	−	+	−	−	+	−	−	−

We have conducted one validation study and are undertaking a second that uses the classification-tree methodology and the supporting tool prototypes. The studies are intended to determine the feasibility of the approach and to analyze the trees' accuracy, complexity, and composition.

The first study used project data from 16

Automated generation of classification trees is well suited to the volumes of data you encounter in large-system development and evolution.

NASA systems.[6] The 16 systems ranged in size from 3,000 to 112,000 lines of Fortran. In this study, the classification trees were to identify two target classes: modules with high development effort or those with high faults. In both cases, "high" was defined to mean the top 25-percent relative to past data. We collected 74 candidate metrics on the more than 4,700 modules in the systems, capturing perspectives such as development effort, faults, changes, design style, and implementation style. Our prototype system automatically generated and evaluated 9,600 classification trees, based on several parameters. On average, the trees correctly classified 79.3 percent of the modules according to whether or not they were in the target class, which was an encouraging initial accuracy rate.

We are conducting a second study to identify error-prone and change-prone components in a Hughes maintenance system that contains more than 900 components and 100,000 lines.[7]

Example application

This example uses a training set of 12 modules and three candidate metrics collected on each module. To explain the example and underlying calculations completely, we have kept the number of modules in the training and test sets and the number of metrics collected on each module very small.

In practice, however, automated generation of classification trees is well suited to the volumes of data you encounter in large-system development and evolution. For example, in the NASA study, some of the training sets included more than 4,000 modules and 70 metrics.

Interface errors. Our example scenario finds the managers of project X concerned about a spate of newly uncovered interface errors in the most recently released version of the system. Because project X is being developed iteratively, they decide to use classification trees to localize the modules in the next release that are likely to suffer from many similar errors.

The modules from earlier system releases comprise the training set. As Table 1 shows, an examination of interface error data for the training-set modules reveals that three modules — C, F and I — have a relatively high number of interface errors. The managers define the target class to include modules with at least six interface errors (step A). As Table 1 shows, such modules are positive in-

Table 2.
Raw training-set data.

Metric	A	B	C	D	E	F	G	H	I	J	K	L
						Module						
Module function	I	I	F	I	F	I	P	P	P	I	F	F
Data bindings	2	9	6	13	10	15	6	15	20	4	17	16
Design revisions	11	9	11	0	5	4	2	10	5	7	1	0
Class	−	−	+	−	−	+	−	−	+	−	−	−

Table 3.
Recoded training-set data.

Metric	A	B	C	D	E	F	G	H	I	J	K	L
						Module						
Module function	β	β	α	β	α	β	γ	γ	γ	β	α	α
Data bindings	α	β	α	β	β	γ	α	γ	γ	α	γ	γ
Design revisions	γ	γ	γ	α	β	β	α	γ	β	β	α	α
Class	−	−	+	−	−	+	−	−	+	−	−	−

Module function	α = File management (F);	β = User interface (I);	γ = Process control (P)
Data bindings	α = 0 ≤ x ≤ 7;	β = 8 ≤ x ≤ 14;	γ = x ≥ 15
Design revisions	α = 0 ≤ x ≤ 3;	β = 4 ≤ x ≤ 8;	γ = x ≥ 9

stances of the target class, while modules with fewer interface errors are negative instances.

The managers decide to do additional testing and analysis on those modules in the current release that are likely target-class members. They decide to apply code reading by stepwise abstraction to those future modules likely to have interface errors. Empirical studies have indicated that stepwise abstraction is effective in detecting interface errors (step B).[8] By outlining remedial plans before they generate and apply the tree, the developers can receive training in the chosen techniques and build the support tools they will need.

Candidate metrics and calibration. Next, the developers choose three candidate classification metrics: module function, data bindings (a measure of module interrelationships[9]), and design revisions (step C).

Data for these three metrics are retrieved for each training-set module from a historical database (steps D and H). Table 2 shows these data. As part of the data calibration, the system recodes this raw metric data, assigning each metric one of three possible values (step E). Table 3 shows these recoded data. The recoding groups the metric values into mutually exclusive and exhaustive ranges.

In this example, the metric values for data bindings and design revisions were clustered statistically to produce three ranges. The metric value for module function must, by definition, be one of three values.

Tree generation. The system can now begin to generate a classification tree (step F). The inputs to the tree-generation algorithm include the training set and a list of candidate metrics and their recoded values for the training-set modules.

The tree-generation algorithm begins by selecting one metric from the candidate set, which it will use to partition the training set. If the candidate metric has n possible values then, for $1 \leq k \leq n$, the kth subset of the partition contains those modules with value k. In this example, each metric was calibrated to have three outcomes, so n equals 3 for each metric.

Metric-selection function. After examining all the candidate metrics, the system places one at the tree's root. Each subset created by that partition becomes a child of the root. To determine which metric to place at the root, the system uses a metric-selection function to evaluate each candidate. This function evaluates the homogeneity of the subsets that result from using the metric as a partition: It assesses the degree to which the metric partitions modules into subsets that contain modules of the same class. The selection function favors those metrics that yield homogeneous partitions because the purpose of classification trees is to distinguish target-class members from nonmembers.

The metric-selection function uses an evaluation function F to measure the homogeneity of a single subset. In our example

$$F(p_i, n_i) = -\frac{p_i}{p_i + n_i}\log_2\frac{p_i}{p_i + n_i} - \frac{n_i}{p_i + n_i}\log_2\frac{n_i}{p_i + n_i}$$

where p_i and n_i correspond to the number of positive and negative instances in the subset.[6,10] $F(p_i, n_i)$ returns values in the range [0,1], with smaller values indicating greater homogeneity.

Next, the metric-selection function calculates a weighted average over each subset. The metric returning the lowest value

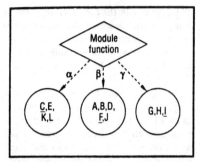

Figure 3. A partial tree using module function as the candidate metric. The metric-selection function E({A,B,...,L}, Module Function) returns 0.801. Positive target class instances are underlined.

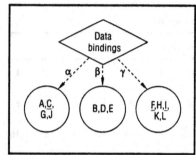

Figure 4. A partial tree using data bindings as the candidate metric. The metric-selection function E({A,B,...,L}, Data Bindings) returns 0.675. Positive target class instances are underlined.

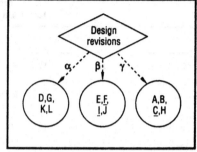

Figure 5. A partial tree using design revisions as the candidate metric. The metric-selection function E({A,B,...,L}, Design Revisions) returns 0.603. Positive target class instances are underlined. This metric is selected and its leftmost child becomes a leaf node labled "– ."

is selected for the tree. In our example, the metric-selection function, given module set C and candidate metric A yielding v subsets, is

$$E(C,A)=\sum_{i=1}^{v} weight_i * F(p_i, n_i)$$

where p_i and n_i are the number of positive and negative instances of the target class in the ith subset and the weighting factor, $weight_i$, is the fraction of modules in C that are elements of subset i, as determined by

$$weight_i = \frac{p_i + n_i}{|C|}$$

where $|C|$ is the number of modules in the set C.

Partially built trees. Figure 3 shows a partially built tree with module function as the candidate metric. Modules having the ith metric value are shown as the ith child of the root. Modules that are positive instances of the target class are shown underlined. Module function has three possible values, which correspond to the three children of the root node.

Figures 4 and 5 display partially built trees with data bindings and design revisions as the candidate metrics. In our example, design revisions has the lowest metric-selection function value and so will be placed at the root of the tree. Table 4 shows the calculation of the metric-selec-

tion function, E({A,B,...,L}, design revisions), for design revisions.

In Figure 5, the design-revisions metric has partitioned the training set into three

---

> *The purpose of classification trees is to distinguish members of the target class from nonmembers.*

---

subsets. Now, each child node is tested against a termination criteria. Our example uses a simple criteria, called zero-percent tolerance, which requires that tree construction end on a path when all (100

percent) the modules in the node are members of the same class. If the criteria is met, the node becomes a leaf and is labeled with the class of its members. Otherwise, the metric used at its parent node is deleted from the list of candidate metrics and the construction process is applied recursively to the node. In Figure 5, the left child node meets the termination criteria, becomes a leaf, and is labeled with a negative symbol (–), which indicates that modules following this path are not likely to be members of the target class.

In Figures 6 and 7, tree generation continues, building on the second child of the root node. In Figure 6, the module-function metric classifies the modules in this subset, but the data-bindings metric in Figure 7 returns a more homogeneous value, so it is selected at this node. Figure 7 shows that each child node meets the termination criteria, so tree generation con-

Table 4.
Calculation of metric selection function using the design-revisions metric to partition the modules.

	p	n	total	*weight*	$F(p,n)$	*weight* $* F(p,n)$
Child 1	0	4	12	.333	0.0	0.0
Child 2	2	2	12	.333	1.0	.333
Child 3	1	3	12	.333	.811	.270
Sum						.603

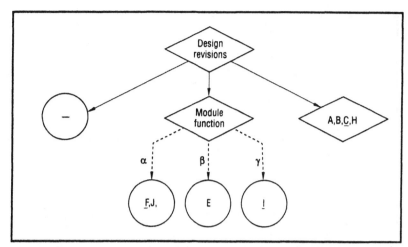

Figure 6. A partial tree using module function as the candidate metric. The metric-selection function E({E,F,I,J}, Module Function) returns 0.500. Positive target class instances are underlined.

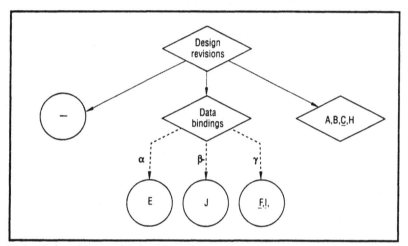

Figure 7. A partial tree using data bindings as the candidate metric. The metric-selection function E({E,F,I,J}, Data Bindings) returns 0. Positive target class instances are underlined. This metric is selected, yielding three leaf nodes labeled, from left to right, "–," "–," and "+."

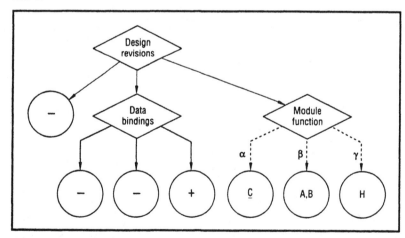

Figure 8. A partial tree using module function as the candidate metric. The metric-selection function E({A,B,C,H}, Module Function) returns 0. Positive target class instances are underlined.

tinues on the third child of the root.

Figure 8 shows that this time the module-function metric returns a more homogeneous value than the data-binding metric shown in Figure 9, so it is chosen. Because its children meet the termination criteria, tree construction halts. Figure 10 shows the completed tree. In general, a metric (except for the root metric) may appear in the tree more than once, and some of the candidate metrics may not be used in the tree at all.

Applying the tree. The developers are now ready to apply the classification tree to the version of the system currently under development (step I). The data for the three metrics in the tree are collected for the current version of the system (step G), recoded, and run through the classification tree to target those modules likely to suffer from many interface errors.

> *By creating valid descriptions of error-prone module classes, we have a basis for identifying such modules in the future.*

Table 5 lists the raw data and Table 6 lists the recoded data for three current modules: *M, N,* and *O.*

To determine those modules in the current version likely to be high-risk, you start at the root of the tree and, based on the metric's value at that node, follow one of the branches. You repeat this step until you encounter a leaf. A module is classified as likely to be a member of the class labeled at the leaf node.

Figure 11 shows the path taken when classifying module *N.* Module *N* is targeted as likely to have many interface errors, based on past project training data. Modules *M* and *O* are classified as unlikely to have many interface errors, so you can initiate the corrective action planned earlier, which in this example is the application of code reading by stepwise abstraction, on module *N* (step J).

Table 5.
Raw test-set data.

	Module		
Metric	M	N	O
Module function	P	I	I
Data bindings	3	16	9
Design revisions	0	7	12

Table 6.
Recoded test-set data.

	Module		
Metric	M	N	O
Module function	γ	β	β
Data bindings	α	γ	β
Design revisions	α	β	γ

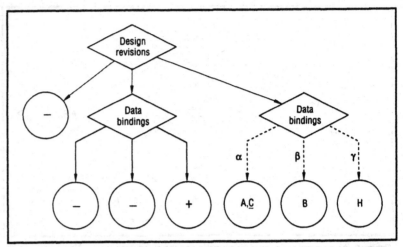

Figure 9. A partial tree using data bindings as the candidate metric. The metric-selection function E({A,B,C,H}, Data Bindings) returns 0.500. Positive target class instances are underlined. For this example, the metric module function is selected (see Figure 8), and it produces three children labeled "+," "−," and "−."

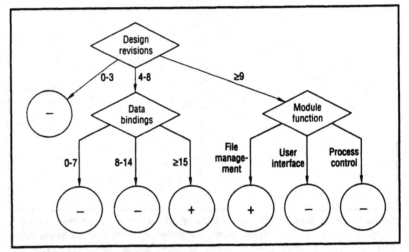

Figure 10. The completed classification tree.

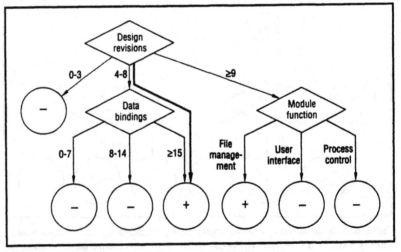

Figure 11. Applying the classification tree on module *N*.

Empirically based approaches can provide added visibility and insight into large systems and their development processes. One way these techniques can by used is to characterize classes of modules. By creating valid descriptions of module classes (such as error-prone, having a high development cost, requiring rework, or containing some specified class of error), we have a basis for identifying similar modules in a future project. Information about potentially high-risk modules can then be fed back into development and maintenance processes to focus limited resources on high-payoff areas, efficiently improving the overall quality and cost of the software produced.

We are refining our proposed approach, addressing issues such as

• the effectiveness of classification trees on a wider range of module classes,

• how to fine-tune the tree-generation algorithms and calibration process, and

• the integration of the classification-tree tools into the Amadeus measurement and empirical analysis system.

Research in these areas will help us improve measurement-based development and evolution processes, so researchers and practitioners can understand and control software development more effectively. ❖

192

Acknowledgments

This work was supported in part by the National Science Foundation grant CCR-8704311 with cooperation from the US Defense Dept.'s Advanced Research Projects Agency under ARPA order 6108, program code 7T10, National Aeronautics and Space Administration grant NSG-5123, NSF grant DCR-8521398, the University of California's Micro program, Hughes Aircraft, and TRW. We thank Kent Madsen, Doug Schmidt, and the anonymous referees for their comments on earlier versions of this article.

References

1. B.W. Boehm and P.N. Papaccio, "Understanding and Controlling Software Costs," *IEEE Trans. Software Eng.*, Oct. 1988, pp. 1,462-1,477.

2. V.R. Basili, *Tutorial on Models and Metrics for Software Management and Engineering*, CS Press, Los Alamitos, Calif., 1980.

3. V.R. Basili, R.W. Selby, and T.Y. Phillips, "Metric Analysis and Data Validation Across Fortran Projects," *IEEE Trans. Software Eng.*, Nov. 1983, pp. 652-663.

4. R.W. Selby et al., "Classification Tree Analysis Using the Amadeus Measurement and Empirical Analysis System,"*Proc 14th Software Eng. Workshop*, NASA Goddard Space Flight Center, Greenbelt, Md., 1989.

5. *Tutorial: Software Risk Management*, Barry Boehm, ed., CS Press, Los Alamitos, Calif., 1989.

6. R.W. Selby and A.A. Porter, "Learning from Examples: Generation and Evaluation of Decision Trees for Software Resource Analysis," *IEEE Trans. Software Eng.*, Dec. 1988, pp. 1,743-1,757.

7. R.W. Selby and A.A. Porter, "Software Metric Classification Trees Help Guide the Maintenance of Large-Scale Systems," *Proc. Conf. Software Maintenance*, CS Press, Los Alamitos, Calif., 1989.

8. V.R. Basili and R.W. Selby, "Comparing the Effectiveness of Software Testing Strategies," *IEEE Trans. Software Eng.*, Dec. 1987, pp. 1278-1296.

9. R.W. Selby, "Generating Hierarchical System Descriptions for Software Error Localization," *Proc. Second Workshop Software Testing, Verification, and Analysis*, CS Press, Los Alamitos, Calif., 1988.

10. J.R. Quinlan, "Induction of Decision Trees," *J. Machine Learning*, Vol. 1, No. 1, 1986, pp. 81-106.

Using multiple metrics for analysis of improvement*

SHARI LAWRENCE PFLEEGER[1], JOSEPH C. FITZGERALD Jr.[2]
and DALE A. RIPPY[3]

[1]*MITRE Corporation, 7525 Colshire Drive, McLean, Virginia, VA 22102 USA;* [2]*GTE Laboratories,*
40 Sylvan Road, Waltham, Massachusetts, USA; [3]*GTE Telephone Operations, Irving, Texas, USA*

To make global decisions about a project or group of projects, it is necessary to analyse several metrics in concert, as well as changes in individual metrics. This paper discusses several approaches to collective metrics analysis. First, classification tree analysis is described as a technique for evaluating both process and metrics characteristics. Next, the notion of a multiple metrics graph is introduced. Developed initially as a way to evaluate software switch quality, a multiple metrics graph allows collections of metrics to be viewed in terms of overall product or process improvement.

Keywords: software metrics, product improvement, process improvement

1. Introduction

Software plays a major role in many organizations, from the systems used to provide new services to the tracking of resources and opportunities. Organizational success depends on the quality of products and on an ability to respond to customers (internal or external) in a timely fashion and at a reasonable cost. Thus, management and control of software development are paramount in assuring that software products are built on time, within budget and in accordance with a stringent set of quality goals.

Software metrics are essential to understanding, managing and controlling the development and maintenance processes. Quantitative characterization of various aspects of these processes involves a deep understanding of software development and maintenance activities and their interrelationships. In turn, the measures that result can be used to set goals for productivity and quality and to establish a baseline against which improvements are compared. Measurements examined during development can point to 'hot spots' that need further attention, analysis or testing. During maintenance, metrics can reflect the effects of changes in size, complexity and maintainability. Measurement also supports planning, as projections and predictions about future projects can be made based on data collected from past projects. Tools and strategies can be evaluated, and the development process and environment can be tailored to the situation at hand. In particular, characterization and analysis of the various development and maintenance activities, viewed in

---

* This work was done while the authors were affiliated with Contel Technology Center, Chantilly, Virginia, USA.

concert with metrics, can tell us which measures and activities are appropriate in which contexts and for solving which problems.

Decisions based on process and metrics characteristics are made at many levels, from the designers and programmers who build a system to the high-level managers who must determine if a given project is better (in terms of productivity and quality) than previous projects. Presenting metrics and process information to the highest levels of management is a problem; there is little need for these managers to be mired down in extreme detail about code and interfaces. At the same time, the lowest level project members need the detail in order to make quick decisions about how to proceed on their daily tasks. A metrics program that can address the full range of needs is more attractive – and will be more accepted in the corporate culture – than one that is highly specialized or focused only on a small set of project members or managers.

At the Contel Technology Center, these metrics and process analysis needs were addressed in several ways. The Software Metrics Project provided services and products to facilitate the use of metrics throughout the corporation. We recommended that the collection of metrics be tied to the maturity of the development process. As discussed in (Pfleeger, 1989) and (Pfleeger and McGowan, 1990), a project can measure only what is visible and appropriate. Thus, an immature project (where requirements are not well-known or understood) begins by measuring effort and time, so that a baseline can be established against which improvements can be compared. Next, when requirements are defined and structured, project management metrics establish general productivity measures. When the process is defined well enough to support it, a project adds product measurement; in this way, characteristics of intermediate products can be used to suggest the likely quality of the final product. If the project is mature enough to have a central point of control, then process measures with feedback to the controller or manager are appropriate. The feedback is used to make decisions about how to proceed at critical points in the process. Finally, the most mature projects can use process measures and feedback to change the process dynamically as development progresses.

Notice that the process maturity framework suggests metrics not only to monitor the activities in the development process but also to help improve the process itself. By considering metrics as nested sets of measures related to process maturity, each level allows management more insight into and control over the process and its constituent products. Use of and need for metrics help define a migration path from one maturity level to the next.

To support metrics collection and analysis, we provided development projects with a software metrics toolkit tailored to individual project needs (Pfleeger and Fitzgerald, 1991). The toolkit contained metrics tools to collect and analyse data appropriate for the project's process maturity, development environment, and management needs and preferences. Underlying the toolkit was a project metrics database. The database supported two activities. First, its contents could be used by the tools and by project managers to monitor and make decisions about the development process. Second, the database contents could be transferred to a Contel corporate historical database. The corporate database, containing both metrics information and process descriptions, allowed us to analyse and examine trends, make predictions, and set standards for future projects.

This paper focuses on the way in which we presented some of the metrics information to those who need to use it to assess project and product quality: project managers, developers and customers. We begin by explaining how several metrics are more useful when viewed in concert with other metrics, rather than by themselves. We discuss two techniques that allowed us to depict a group of metrics at once, while also permitting us to track general improvement of a process or product over time. Next, we show an example of how one of the techniques was used by Contel to evaluate the quality of switch software provided by several different vendors. Finally, we explain how these techniques can be used to depict a variety of related metrics.

2. Viewing several metrics at once

Software metrics programs often prescribe a set of metrics to reflect project, process and product characteristics that are important in controlling or evaluating all or part of the software development process. Viewed in isolation, each metric describes a particular characteristic that can be compared with a goal or norm. Examined individually over time, these measurements can be helpful in noting trends and predicting future characteristics or outcomes. However, viewed in combination, measurements can provide a picture of the balance between quality and cost that is often difficult to determine in other ways.

It has been known for a long time that when a set of characteristics is important, optimizing on a single one usually leads to unacceptable results in the others (Weinberg and Schulman, 1974). Thus, it is important to be able to view several metrics in context and to be able to balance the goals of one against the others. Several attempts have been made to combine several metrics into one comprehensive number. For example, Card and Glass describe a complexity metric that is a composite of different aspects of complexity (Card and Glass, 1990), while Munson and Khoshgoftaar apply a similar technique to aid in project management decisions (Munson and Khoshgoftaar, 1990). However, there are many problems with such an equational approach, where the individual metrics are lost and the meaning of the composite is often unclear. For this reason, we have chosen to use two techniques that display metrics in a way that preserved the integrity and meaning of each but allows a composite view and a balancing of goals.

3. Classification trees

The first approach, called 'classification tree analysis', has been used by Porter and Selby (1990) to determine which collection of metrics acts as the best predictor of a certain situation. For example, suppose that for each of n projects a set of k measurements is made. We may want to examine these measurements to see which ones are the best indicators of high cost or poor quality, as measured by high project cost or high number of errors, for instance. We can consider each project to be a vector with $k + 1$ elements: the k measurements for the project plus the target descriptor of cost or quality. By performing a classification tree analysis on the n vectors, we can generate a decision tree that shows us which of the measurements, viewed collectively, are good predictors of the target value(s).

To see how the analysis might work, consider an example where a large set of measurements has been made for each project in a given collection of projects. These measurements can include not only typical metrics such as complexity or lines of code, but also descriptions of process characteristics, such as amount of reuse, use of a defect density model for testing, or use of prototyping for requirements. The target characteristic of interest is quality, measured here by the number of errors per thousand lines of code. We say that a project is of poor quality if it has more than five errors

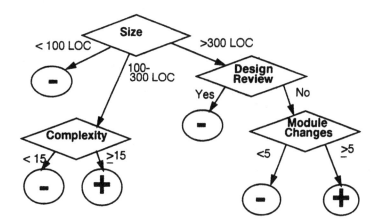

Fig. 1. Example of classification tree.

per thousand lines of code. Then, we perform a classification tree analysis to determine which measurements are the best predictors of poor quality. The result is a decision tree, such as that shown in Fig. 1.

In the example, a circled minus sign indicates high quality (i.e. five or fewer errors per thousand lines of code), while a circled plus means that the quality is low. The decision tree tells us that size of a module (in lines of code), its cyclomatic complexity, subjection to a design review and the number of changes acts as the best indicators of whether the quality will be low. In particular, low quality is likely in the following cases:

1. If the module has between 100 and 300 lines of code and a complexity of 15 or more;
2. If its design has not been reviewed and the module has changed at least five times.

Using the classification tree technique, the individual metrics retain their identities, but additional information is imparted by viewing them in the composite.

Such a view of metrics and process is valuable to many classes of project participants. Designers and programmers can use the results as guidelines in evaluating individual modules: module size and complexity must not exceed certain limits without good reason. Project managers who are pressed for time or resources can limit design reviews only to those modules likely to be subject to change. Higher-level managers can institute process and metrics standards based on the analysis: design reviews in certain situations, use of complexity analysis tools and increased use of configuration management, for example. In a sense, then, everyone wins: metrics and process characteristics are tracked because everyone sees their obvious benefit in increasing control and minimizing project risk.

4. Muliple metrics graphs

A second technique for depicting combinations of metrics is called a 'multiple metrics graph' (Pfgleeger *et al.* 1991); it is a variation of a Kiviat diagram or graph (Morris and Roth, 1982). The Kiviat diagram, originally used to depict characteristics reported in simulations, displays characteristics on slices of a large, circular pie, as shown in Fig. 2. The pie is divided into equal slices, one

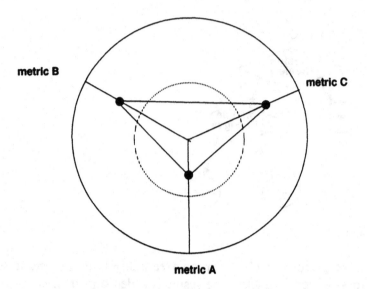

Fig. 2. Kiviat diagram with three metrics.

for each measurement or characteristics to be presented. The inner circle represents a goal or minimum, and the outer circle represents a maximum. A point is placed on the line representing the metric, indicating its position with respect to the goal. Finally, the points are connected, so that the resulting polygon is in some sense an indication of overall performance.

In a multiple metrics graph, the pie is divided into unequal slices (unlike the Kiviat graph), so that the size of the slice (that is, the number of degrees in the arc) represents the importance of the metric. Thus, the larger the slice, the more important the metric. A small, concentric circle represents the goals for each metric. Within each slice, a point is placed in the centre (equidistant from the adjacent radii) to represent the degree to which the goal is met. The centre of the pie represents the best case; the outer edge of the pie is the worst case. The goal and radius are normalized among slices so that the goal arcs form a circle. Finally, a line is drawn from the representative point to the intersection of the goal line and radii forming each side of the pie slice.

To understand how the final diagram looks, let us examine an example. Suppose we are working on a project where three metrics, A, B and C, are of great importance. For example, A could represent programmer productivity, B the quality of the product (in terms of errors per thousand lines of code), and C the complexity of the code. The metrics must be chosen so that the smaller the number, the better. For instance, the productivity measure may be the reciprocal of lines of code per person-month. Once the metrics are determined, goals can be set for each of the three metrics. The project manager or customer may determine that quality is most important, productivity second, and complexity third. When asked to weight the three metrics, the manager assigns 50 points (of 100) to quality, 30 to productivity and 20 to complexity.

Correspondingly, we draw a multiple metrics graph with slices of 180 degrees (0.50 × 360 degrees), 108 degrees (0.30 × 360), and 72 degrees (0.20 × 360), respectively, as shown in Fig. 3. The dashed circle inside the pie represents the goals for each of the three metrics. In each pie slice, we place a point to represent the performance of the project with respect to the goal. For instance, productivity is better than the target set for it, so the point is inside the dashed circle, close to the

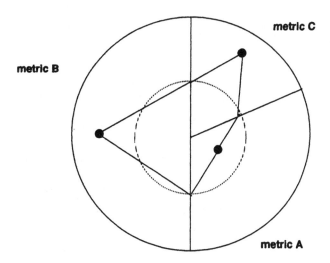

Fig. 3. Example multiple metrics graph.

centre of the pie. A line from the centre of the pie to the outer circle (through the middle of the arc forming the slice) represents the set of possible productivity results; the closer to the centre, the better the performance for that metric. The point representing actual performance is placed on the line in direct correspondence to the best and worst values for the metric, represented by the centre and outer circle endpoints of the line, respectively.

On the other hand, metrics B and C are not within the goals set for them, so the point is placed between the inner (dashed) circle and the pie's outer circle. Next, lines are drawn from each of the representative points to the places where the goal arc meets the edges of the slice. In this way, the area of the resulting quadrilateral for each metric represents the degree to which goals are met: the smaller the area, the better. The polygon formed by uniting the three quadrilaterals represents the overall performance of the project or products.

This aspect of the multiple metrics graph is significantly different from Kiviat diagrams. Kiviat pie slices are always the same size, and the points representing each metric are connected to each other. The area of the resulting polygon for a Kiviat diagram has no meaning with respect to performance, and it is dependent on the relative position of the metrics around the circle. In a multiple metrics graph, the meaning of the areas is clear, and the order of the metrics around the circle is not significant. Over time, the area of the polygon and the areas of the individual quadrilaterals in a multiple metrics graph can be tracked to see whether performance overall and with respect to the individual characteristics is improving and in what ways.

5. A longitudinal example of multiple metrics graphs

To see how multiple metrics graphs can be useful in evaluating metrics over time, we present a small example of how three interrelated metric values can change. Suppose a major software system is composed of three subsystems: A, B and C. We want to track the number of errors in each subsystem that cause failures during a given time interval, t_i. That is, as a failure occurs, the source of the failure

Table 1. Example data collected over time

Time interval	t_1	t_2	t_3	t_4
Errors in A	8	8	7	5
Errors in B	7	3	3	3
Errors in C	8	8	5	5

is identified and noted as being in either A, B or C. Table 1 contains data for four time intervals (t_1 through t_4).

For each column of Table 1, we can draw a multiple metrics graph to represent the relative importance and performance of the three measurements. To do this, we must ask the manager to answer three important questions:

1. What is the goal for each metric?
2. What is the expected maximum for each metric?
3. What is the relative importance of each metric with respect to the others?

In the first case, the manager may say that it is desirable to have at most five errors per subsystem in the time interval. This choice is reflected in the goal circle, which is set to have a unit radius. The manager may say that no more than 10 errors are expected per subsystem (perhaps based on past history), so the radius of the outer circle is set to two.

Suppose the manager answers the third question by saying that the functionality and criticality of the software in subsystem A is three times as important as in subsystem B, and that subsystem C is twice as important as B. We can use this information to determine the size of the pie slices; the slice for A is half the circle, for B one sixth, and for C one third.

Finally, we graph the data from Table 1, and the results are shown in Fig. 4.

In this case, it is relatively easy to see that improvements are being made over time in each of the three error counts. However, the overall impact is not easily seen until we compare the graphs and corresponding areas of the polygons. From t_1 to t_2, a major reduction is made in the count of errors in B, so that the count betters the goal value established for it. However, since the pie slice representing subsystem B occupies only one sixth of the overall area of the graph, the reduction in the area of the polygon is fairly small: only 0.4 (i.e., $3.69 - 2.69$). A much bigger improvement is seen from t_2 to t_3: no further reduction is noted in subsystem B, but errors are reduced in A and C. Because A occupies half of the graph and C one third, this reduction results in a large reduction in the overall quality index: from 3.29 to 2.57, for a difference of 0.72. That is, from t_2 to t_3, a drop in three errors improved the quality almost twice as much as the same drop in errors from t_1 to t_2! Thus, the graph reflects more than the sum of the metrics it contains; it can also show the influence of priorities.

This characteristic of multiple metrics graphs is one of the aspects that distinguishes it from Kiviat graphs and traditional approaches to metrics evaluation. In addition, the graph allows the evaluator to see which dimensions are responsible for the increase in quality and which still require improvement. For example, despite the clear overall improvement from t_1 to t_3, it is clear that subsystem A has not yet met its goal. It is not until t_4 that the polygon fits inside the goal circle, so that quality is deemed satisfactory.

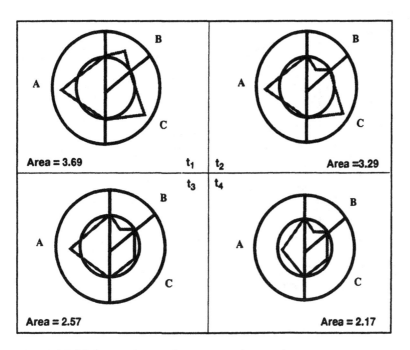

Fig. 4. Multiple metric graphs compared over time.

6. Example: security certification and switch vendor software quality

The multiple metrics graph approach was used at Contel in several contexts. For instance, we have depicted the results of software security certifications using a multiple metrics graph for a government customer. Measures of confidentiality, integrity and availability were included, so that overall security could be viewed in each of the three dimensions, as well as in the aggregate. For Contel's telephone operations division, we helped to evaluate the quality of the digital switch software supplied to us by several vendors by viewing metrics of importance on a multiple metrics graph. In the latter case, seven of the eight metrics used are supplied by the vendors themselves, and the eighth (the total number of output messages) is derived from error messages catalogued automatically in the various telephone regions. Figure 5 shows which metrics are used to assess the quality of the switches.

Previous attempts by Bellcore and others to access switch quality were rejected, since the software quality index generated by weighting important measures and summing them yielded a single figure that was difficult for the vendors to interpret and to understand over time. By using the multiple metrics graphs, the vendors can see how they have improved and where more work is needed. A single quality index number can be generated, and it is directly related to the area of the overall polygon. By overlaying one month's multiple metrics graph over that of the previous month, the vendors can see changes in each dimensions, i.e. in each pie slice. By overlaying one vendor's graph over another's, equivalent switches can be compared and buying decisions supported.

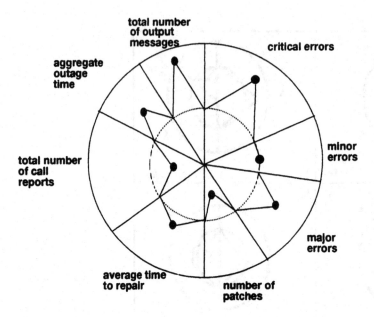

Fig. 5. Example of switch software evaluation.

7. Conclusions

The goal of any metrics project is to make metrics collection and analysis a natural and helpful part of the software development process. To that end, both classification tree analysis and multiple metrics graphs enable managers to integrate measurement into development activities and into the decision-making process. The classification trees support decision-making, not only in terms of what metrics are the best predictors of a particular characteristic (such as cost or quality) but also of the process activities that are most effective in certain situations. Similarly, the multiple metrics graphs provide a baseline against which improvement can be measured, so that goals for productivity and quality can be set and attained.

The Contel Software Metrics Project applied both classification trees and multiple metrics graphs to the variety of situations in which metrics were used at Contel. To support the automation of the analysis, we used commercial software (CART™, from California Statistical Software, Inc.) to generate classification trees. We developed our own software to draw multiple metrics graphs from data stored in Lotus 1–2–3 spreadsheets. Since our project metrics databases were collections of such spreadsheets, our software enabled us to select appropriate measures, assign weights, and draw the graphs automatically. In this way, metrics collection, reporting and analysis were easy, and managers and customers used the information to make informed decisions about software and the system and processes affected by it.

The use of these tools and techniques were instrumental in changing the culture of the development and maintenance processes at Contel. They provided project managers with more understanding of the process and thus with more control. The ultimate benefits of using the tools and techniques included decreased risk, improved processes and better quality products.

References

Card, D. and Glass, R. (1990) *Measuring Software Design Quality*, Prentice Hall, Englewood Cliffs, New Jersey.

Morris, M.F. and Roth, P.F. (1982) *Computer Performance Evaluation*, Van Nostrand.

Munson, J.C. and Khoshgoftaar, T. (1990) Applications of a relative complexity metric for software project management, *Proceedings of AOWSM-2*, Portland, Oregon.

Pfleeger, S.L. (1989) *Recommendations for an initial set of software metrics*, CTC-TR-89-017, Contel Technology Center.

Pfleeger, S.L. and McGowan, C.L. (1990) Software metrics in a process maturity framework, *Journal of Systems and Software*, **12**(7), 255–61.

Pfleeger, S.L., Fitzgerald Jr, J.C. and Rippy, D.A. (1991) Software metrics reporting: presentation of multiple metrics for analysis of improvement, *Proceedings of the Third Annual Oregon Workshop on Software Metrics*. Silver Falls, Oregon.

Pfleeger, S.L. and Fitzgerald, J.C. (1991) A software metrics toolkit: support for selection, collection and analysis, *Information and Software Technology*, **33**(7), 477–82.

Porter, A.A. and Selby, R.W. (1990) Empirically guided software development using metric-based classification trees, *IEEE Software* **7**(2), 151–60.

Weinberg, G.M. and Schulman, E.L. (1974) Goals and performance in computer programming, *Human Factors*, **16**(1), 53–65.

Software Process Improvement at Hughes Aircraft

WATTS S. HUMPHREY, *Software Engineering Institute*
TERRY R. SNYDER *and* RONALD R. WILLIS, *Hughes Aircraft*

◆ *In just two years, Hughes' Software Engineering Division progressed from level 2 to level 3. Here's how they did it, how much it cost, and what they gained.*

In 1987 and 1990, the Software Engineering Institute conducted process assessements of the Software Engineering Division of Hughes Aircraft in Fullerton, Calif. The first assessment found Hughes' SED to be a level 2 organization, based on the SEI's process-maturity scale of 1 to 5, where 1 is worst and 5 is best.[1]

This first assessment identified the strengths and weaknesses of the SED, and the SEI made recommendations for process improvement. Hughes then established and implemented an action plan in accordance with these recommendations. The second assessment found the SED to be a strong level 3 organization.

The assessment itself cost Hughes about $45,000, and the subsequent two-year program of improvements cost about $400,000. Hughes found that the investment improved working condi- tions, employee morale, and the perfor- mance of the SED as measured in project schedule and cost. Hughes estimates the resulting annual savings to be about $2 million.

In this article, we outline the assessment method used, the findings and recommen- dations from the initial assessment, the ac- tions taken by Hughes, the lessons learned, and the resulting business and product consequences.

We write this article in the broad interest of software-process improvement, particu- larly its costs and benefits. Because its assess- ments are confidential, the SEI cannot pub- licize costs and benefits until it has amassed a large body of data. So, during the second as- sessment in 1990, Watts Humphrey and Terry Snyder agreed to write an article – Humphrey to provide material on the as- sessment process and Hughes to provide material on results and benefits.

Reprinted from *IEEE Software*, Vol. 8, No. 4, July 1991, pp. 11–23.

Background. The SED is one division in Hughes' Ground Systems Group. Although it is the largest dedicated software organization in the Ground Systems Group and provides contract support for many other divisions, there are other (project-related) software organizations in the group.

The SED, formed in 1978, primarily works on US Defense Dept. contracts. It employs about 500 professionals. Of these, 41 percent have 10 to 20 years experience in software and 12 percent have 20 or more years experience. The assessments described here examined only the work of the SED in Fullerton; the findings and recommendations are pertinent only to that organization. However, Hughes has capitalized on this experience to launch a broader process-improvement effort.

At the time of the 1990 assessment, the SEI had conducted 14 assessments and observed 18 self-assessments. As a result, it had gained a great deal of experience on effective methods for identifying the actual state of practice in software organizations. It is thus our opinion that the overall effect of misunderstandings and errors on these assessments was modest.

ASSESSMENT PROCESS

A process assessment helps an organization characterize the current state of its software process and provides findings and recommendations to facilitate improvement. The box on pp. 14-15 explains the SEI's process-improvement paradigm, its supporting process-maturity structure, and the principles of process assessment.

Hughes assessments. The two Hughes assessments were conducted by teams of SEI and Hughes software professionals. In both assessments, all the team members

> A process assessment helps an organization characterize the current state of its software process and provides findings and recommendations to facilitate improvement.

were experienced software developers. The 1987 assessment was conducted by a team of seven: one from Hughes and six from the SEI. The 1990 assessment team included nine professionals: four from Hughes and five from the SEI. Two of the authors, Watts Humphrey and Ronald Willis, were members of both teams.

The SED team members prepared a list of candidate projects for review by the entire assessment team during training. The entire team then selected projects that it felt reasonably represented the development phases, typical project sizes and applications, and the major organization units. Six projects were reviewed in the 1987 assessment and five in 1990. Only one project was included in both assessments.

Before the assessment, the Hughes SED manager, Terry Snyder, and the SEI's process-program director, Watts Humphrey, signed confidential agreements covering the ground rules for the assessments. The key points in these agreements were:

♦ The SEI and the assessment team members were to keep the assessment results confidential. Hughes could use the assessment results in any way it chose.

♦ The SED manager agreed to participate in the opening and closing assessment meetings.

♦ In addition to the regular team members, the SED manager agreed that Hughes would provide needed support to handle the assessment arrangements and to lead the work on the follow-up action plan.

♦ The SED manager also committed Hughes to developing and implementing appropriate action plans in response to the assessment recommendations. If Hughes deemed that action was not appropriate, it was to explain its reasons to the assessment team.

After the SEI agreed to consider conducting an assessment:

♦ A commitment meeting was held with the SEI and the SED manager and his staff to agree on conducting the assessment and to establish a schedule.

♦ For both assessments, Hughes and the SEI selected the assessment team members, and the SEI trained them in its assessment method. These two-day training programs were held at the SEI, where the entire assessment team was familiarized with the assessment process and prepared for the on-site period.

♦ The on-site assessment was conducted.

♦ A detailed, written report of the assessment findings and recommendations was prepared and a briefing on the recommendations was delivered to the SED management team and all the assessment participants. In both assessments, the SED manager invited senior corporate executives to attend the briefing. Because he did not know the findings in advance, this involved some risk. However, the added understanding provided by these briefings contributed materially to the launching of a Hughes corporate-wide process-improvement initiative modeled on the SED's work.

♦ The SED developed and implemented an action plan based on these recommendations.

Maturity levels. In 1987, the assessments focused on the responses to the level 2 and level 3 questions: Because the assessment period is intentionally limited to four days, we decided to devote our attention to those areas most pertinent to the organization's perceived maturity level. This was possible because the SEI assessment process uses the questionnaire to help focus on the most informative interview topics.

In the 1990 assessment, the team briefly reviewed the level 2 responses and then interviewed the project representatives on the questions at levels 3, 4, and 5. In areas where the project responses differed or where the response pattern was atypical, the team requested more information. Because these discussions were on Tuesday afternoon and the additional materials were needed by Thursday morning, the representatives were told to bring only available working materials and not to prepare anything special.

As a consequence, we believe the team determined an organizational maturity level with a fair degree of accuracy in both the 1987 and 1990 assessments. There is, of course, the possibility that some questions were not discussed in sufficient detail to identify all misunderstandings or errors.

1987 ASSESSMENT

The first SEI assessment of six Hughes projects was conducted November 9-12, 1987. The final report, including recommendations, was presented in January 1988.

Recommendations. The assessment team made seven recommendations.

Quantitative process management. The assessment team found that the professionals working on the assessed projects gathered a significant amount of data on many aspects of the process. While this was important in moving the organization toward a managed software process (level 4), much of the long-term potential value of this data was lost because it was kept in multiple, disparate databases. Furthermore, the lack of a central location for this data made it difficult for project managers and professionals to know what data was available, what data should be gathered, and how it could most effectively be used for product and process improvement.

The team recommended that the SED establish the goal of achieving quantitative process management. To establish the foundation for statistical process management, this goal should include:

♦ Establishing a centralized database to include current and future data on cost estimates, cost experience, error data, and schedule performance. Additional process data should be included as it is gathered.

♦ Establishing uniform data definitions across projects.

♦ Augmenting the process definitions to include those key measures and analyses required at each major project milestone,

together with appropriate responsibilities.

♦ Providing the resources needed and the responsibility assignments required for gathering, validating, entering, accessing, and supporting the projects in analyzing this data.

Process group. The team recommended that the SED establish a technical group to be the focal point for process improvement. This group's initial tasks would be to lead the development of action plans for accomplishing the assessment team's recommendations, to lead, coordinate, and track the implementation of the action plans, and to establish the centralized process database.

Requirements. The team found that the SED generally was not involved in early system definition. Whenever software considerations were not integrated into systems engineering early in the system-definition phase, the software specifications often were ambiguous, inconsistent, untestable, and subject to frequent last-minute changes. Because in general the quality of a software product cannot exceed the quality of its requirements, the team perceived this as a critical problem.

The team recommended that the SED be involved in the specification development for all new Hughes software-intensive projects. It also suggested that systems-engineering groups attend applicable software-engineering courses.

Quality assurance. Although the existing software quality-assurance organization at Hughes performed several necessary functions, it suffered from widely different views of its usefulness and could not fully contribute to the software-development process because it was understaffed and its personnel were not adequately trained.

To strengthen the role of SQA, the

> In general the quality of a software product cannot exceed the quality of its requirements, so the team recommended the SED be involved in specification development.

team recommended a training program that would include software-engineering principles, Hughes standard procedures, phases of the life cycle, and the functions of SQA personnel. It was also recommended that the value added by SQA be clarified for program management so it could better understand the need to allocate resources to it.

Training. The team found that Hughes had a comprehensive, company-sponsored software-engineering training program. However, the team also found that certain training categories were either not available or not being used adequately. Key examples were training for assistant project managers, review leaders, and requirements specification.

The team recommended that Hughes review its software-training requirements. The review was to conclude with plans for restructuring the current training programs, providing new subjects, creating a training priority structure, and using new training methods as appropriate. It was also recommended that Hughes consider a required training program.

Review process. Although Hughes had made provision for technical reviews during the development process, they were not performed uniformly across all projects. So the team recommended that Hughes reassess its current review practices and determine how to assure a consistent and uniform review practice at appropriate points in the software-development process. The objective was to improve product quality, reduce reliance on testing, and improve overall project predictability and productivity.

Working relationship. During the assessment, the working relationship with the Defense Dept.'s Defense Contract Administrative Services department was often

SEI PROCESS ASSESSMENT PROCEDURES

To make orderly improvement, development and maintenance organizations should view their process as one that can be controlled, measured, and improved. This requires that they follow a traditional quality-improvement program such as that described by W. Edwards Deming.[1]

For software, this involves the following six steps:

1. Understand the current status of their process.

2. Develop a vision of the desired process.

3. Establish a list of required process-improvement actions in priority order.

4. Produce a plan to accomplish these actions.

5. Commit the resources and execute the plan.

6. Start over at step 1.

The SEI has developed a framework to characterize the software process across five maturity levels. By establishing their organization's position in this framework, software professionals and their managers can readily identify areas where improvement actions will be most fruitful.

Many software organizations have found that this framework provides an orderly set of process improvement goals and a helpful yardstick for tracking progress. Some acquisition groups in the US Defense Dept. are also using this maturity framework and an associated SEI evaluation method called the Software Capability Evaluation to help select software contractors.

Maturity framework. Figure A shows the SEI's software process-maturity framework. The SEI derived this empirical model from the collective experiences of many software managers and practitioners. The five maturity levels

♦ reasonably represent the historical phases of evolutionary improvement of actual software organizations,

♦ represent a measure of improvement that is reasonable to achieve from the prior level,

♦ suggest interim improvement goals and progress measures, and

♦ make obvious a set of immediate improvement priorities once an organization's status in the framework is known.

While there are many aspects to these transitions from one maturity level to another, the overall objective is to achieve a controlled and measured process as the foundation for continuous improvement.

Assessment. The process-maturity framework is intended to be used with an assessment method. A process assessment is a review of an organization's software process done by a trained team of software professionals. Its purpose is to determine the state of the organization, to identify the highest priority process issues, and to facilitate improvement actions.

The assessment process facilitates improvement by involving the managers and professionals in identifying the most critical software problems and helping them agree on the actions required to address these problems.[2] The basic objectives of an assessment are to

♦ learn how the organization works,

♦ identify its major problems, and

♦ enroll its opinion leaders in the change process.[3]

In SEI assessments, five or six projects are typically selected as representative samples of the organization's software process. The guiding principle for selecting projects is that they represent the mainstream software business for the organization.

On-site period. The on-site assessment period is an intense

Level	Characteristics	Key challenges	Result
5 Optimizing	• Improvement fed back into process • Data gathering is automated and used to identify weakest process elements • Numerical evidence used to justify application of technology to critical tasks • Rigorous defect—cause analysis and detect prevention	• Still human-intensive process • Maintain organization at optimizing level	Productivity & quality
4 Managed	(Quantitative) • Measured process • Minimum set of quality and productivity measurements established • Process database established with resources to analyze its data and maintain it	• Changing technology • Problem analysis • Problem prevention	
3 Defined	(Qualitative) • Process defined and institutionalized • Software Engineering Process Group established to lead process improvement	• Process measurement • Process analysis • Quantitative quality plans	
2 Repeatable	(Intuitive) • Process dependent on individuals • Established basic project controls • Strength in doing similar work, but faces major risk when presented with new challenges • Lacks orderly framework for improvement	• Training • Technical practices (reviews, testing) • Process focus (standards, process groups)	
1 Initial	(Ad hoc/chaotic process) • No formal procedures, cost estimates, project plans • No management mechanism to ensure procedures are followed, tools not well integrated, and change control is lax • Senior management does not understand key issues	• Project management • Project planning • Configuration management • Software quality assurance	Risk

Figure A. The SEI process-maturity framework.

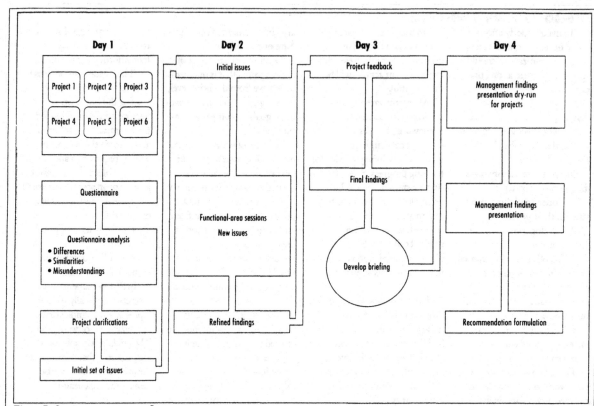

Day 1

Project 1   Project 2   Project 3

Project 4   Project 5   Project 6

Questionnaire

Questionnaire analysis
- Differences
- Similarities
- Misunderstandings

Project clarifications

Initial set of issues

Day 2

Initial issues

Functional-area sessions

New issues

Refined findings

Day 3

Project feedback

Final findings

Develop briefing

Day 4

Management findings presentation dry-run for projects

Management findings presentation

Recommendation formulation

Figure B. On-site assessment process flow.

four "half-days" : The team members are involved for more than half of each 24 hours, generally starting at 7:30 a.m. and not concluding until 10:00 or 11:00 p.m. No one has time to perform normal duties during this phase.

While this is a potentially stressful activity, the extensive training prepares the team members to make a highly productive effort and to build the cohesion and team spirit required to achieve consensus on the complex issues encountered. The dedication and enthusiasm of the assessment team also significantly contributes to their credibility to the organization and to acceptance of the findings.

Figure B shows the flow of the on-site activities during SEI process assessments. Each on-site assessment starts with a presentation to the manager, staff, and all the assessment participants. This

meeting covers the assessment ground rules, assessment principles, and the schedule.

The assessment team then meets in closed session to review the questionnaire responses in preparation for the first round of discussions with project leaders. Project managers and functional experts are interviewed to clearly determine the key issues behind their responses to an SEI questionnaire.[4]

Next, a private discussion is held with each project leader to clarify any issues identified by the assessment team during its review of project responses and to request explanatory materials, if appropriate.

Next, a full day is devoted to discussions with software practitioners from selected technical areas such as requirements and high-level design, and code and unit test. Typically, about six professionals are selected from across

the organization for each functional area. These functional area representatives are selected with the following criteria:

♦ Be considered an expert in the technical area by his or her peers.

♦ Be assigned to, and working on, one or more mainstream projects at the site (not necessarily a project included in the assessment).

♦ Be considered an opinion leader in the organization.

A second round of individual project leader meetings is then held to review the supporting materials, resolve remaining issues, and review the preliminary assessment findings. On the last day, a findings briefing is presented to senior management and all the assessment participants.

The final assessment activity is the preparation and presentation of a written report

and recommendations to the site manager and staff. The recommendations highlight the assessment team's view of the highest priority items for immediate action. Following the assessment, the organization prepares and implements an action plan. In accordance with the agreement, the SEI reviews and comments on these plans.

REFERENCES

1. W.E. Deming, *Out of the Crisis*, MIT Center Advanced Eng. Study, Cambridge, Mass., 1982.
2. R.A. Radice et al., "A Programming Process Study," *IBM Systems J.*, No. 2, 1985, pp. 91-101.
3. D.H. Kitson and W.S. Humphrey, "The Role of Assessment in Software Process Improvement," Tech. Report CMU/SEI-89-TR-3, Software Eng. Inst., Carnegie Mellon Univ., Pittsburgh, 1989.
4. W.S Humphrey and W. Sweet, "A Method for Assessing the Software Engineering Capability of Contractors," Tech. Report CMU/SEI-87-TR-23, Software Eng. Inst., Carnegie Mellon Univ., Pittsburgh, 1987.

identified as ineffective or counterproductive. It was thus recommended that the SED work to im~~rove~~ this relationship.

Actions taken. Within two months of the January 1988 recommendations briefing, Hughes developed an action plan to implement the recommended improvements. As predetermined, the assessment site coordinator was the primary author for the action plan, although many people contributed to the decision and approval process.

Because implementation of the proposed actions was estimated to require a 2-percent increase in division overhead rate, it took three more months (until June 1988) to get the action plan and required funding approved by Ground Systems Group management. In so doing, top management became committed to the improvement program.

For the most part, the 1988 action plan was implemented on schedule and under budget. It took 18 months and was completed just one month before the 1990 reassessment.

Action plan. The 1988 action plan began with a one-page summary of the assessment life cycle and the projects assessed. It then listed the goals and put the action plan in the context of a Ground Systems

---

3.1 FORM SOFTWARE ENGINEERING PROCESS GROUP

3.1.1 Summary of the SEI Findings. Decentralization of the software organization into geographically isolated projects and even into separate product line divisions has impaired progress in software-technology development. Such decentralization has already affected quality-indicator data collection leading to multiple, disparate databases.

3.1.2 Requirements. The following are necessary attributes of the desired solution.

a. An organizational entity, the software-engineering process group (SEPG), exists and has the following attributes:
- serves as the focal point for software process improvement
- leader has technical credibility and influence
- staff is experienced
- initial staff size is three people
- eventual staff size is 2 percent to 3 percent of software developers
- staff is rotated every 2 to 3 years

b. The SEPG performs the following functions:
- lead development and implementation of the SEI action plan
- define/improve technical and management software practices
- lead definition of standards for software processes/products
- establish and maintain the software-process database
- initiate the definition, collection, analysis of process data
- facilitate periodic assessment of software-engineering process
- identify and promote the organization's technology needs
- establish requirements and plans for training
- research, develop, and transfer new technology
- define requirements for process automation (i.e. tools)
- facilitate periodic management reviews on state of practice

3.1.3 Responsibilities.
Manager, Software Engineering Division, forms SEPG and assigns SEPG leader, approves SEPG charter, provides funding for SEPG activities, and periodically reviews SEPG progress. Leader, Software Engineering Process Group, develops SEPG charter, develops and implements plans to accomplish 3.1.2, and recruits and selects full-time technical staff for the SEPG.

3.2 IMPLEMENT QUANTITATIVE PROCESS MANAGEMENT

3.2.1 Summary of the SEI Findings. Although data on projects is collected, it is kept in multiple, unrelated databases. The lack of a central focal point for data makes it difficult to know what data is available, what data should be gathered, and how it can be most effectively used for product and process improvement.

3.2.2. Requirements. The following are necessary attributes of the desired solution:

a. A centralized database exists that has the following attributes:
- standardized data definitions across all projects
- fed by all projects
- sufficient data element types to statistically manage the software-development process

b. Software process and product standards exist that specify when and what data to collect to be able to statistically manage the software-development process.

c. Software process and product standards exist that specify analyses to be performed at each project milestone, together with appropriate responsibilities, to be able to statistically manage the software-development process.

d. An organization exists (SEPG) that provides the following services:
- gathers, validates, and enters data into the database
- controls access to the database
- supports projects in analyzing the data

e. Formal means exist to enforce these requirements.

3.2.3. Responsibilities.
Leader, Software Engineering Process Group, assigns responsibility for 3.2.2a through 3.2.2.d, ensures implementation of 3.2.2.e.

3.3 FILLS GAPS IN TRAINING PROGRAM
3.3.1 Summary of the SEI Findings. Although there is clear evidence of commitment to training, there are unfilled gaps in certain areas, opportunities for more effective training, and not enough required training (as opposed to optional training).

3.3.2 Requirements. The following are necessary attributes of the desired solution:

a. A report based on review of current training needs and training effectiveness exists and is used to modernize the existing training program. The report contains the following:

Figure 1. *Section 3 of Hughes SED 1988 action plan. The action plan lists tasks as process-requirements specifications in the context of the Ground Systems Group.*

Group organizational improvement strategy.

The plan then detailed five improvement tasks, written as process-requirement specifications:

♦ Form a software-engineering process group.

♦ Implement quantitative process management.

♦ Fill in the gaps in training.

♦ Standardize an effective review process.

♦ Move toward a software-engineering discipline.

Figure 1 shows a part of the plan's wording. As the figure shows, the plan specified testable conditions for each task that, if met, would satisfy the recommended process improvements. The plan also avoided specifying solutions, to allow implementation flexibility.

Two of the SEI's recommendations were not included in the action plan because they involved organizations not under SED control. The first, to strengthen SQA, dealt with a function that was in another division of Hughes. Although the SED was striving to regain a centralized SQA function that would be under its control, it had not yet achieved that reorganization and therefore could not guarantee the outcome. (Later, the SED did achieve a centralized SQA organization.)

. recommended restructuring of current training program
. unfilled gaps in training curriculum
. training priorities
. recommended changes to existing training methods
b. A training curriculum exists that contains all training that is currently defined plus the following additional training subjects:
. associate program manager (APM)
. review leader (for internal reviews)
. use of engineering techniques in software development
. understanding and using software practices and procedures
. how to write good software-requirements
. how to test at the software-requirements level
. how to test at the unit level
. software quality assurance
. practical guide to the use of performance analysis
c. A directive exists that specifies training requirements in terms of specific subjects versus job position and that these training requirements be considered in annual performance evaluations.

3.3.3 Responsibilities.
Leader, Software Engineering Process Group, leads the effort to accomplish 3.3.2.a, 3.3.2.b, and 3.3.2.c.
Manager, Software Engineering Division, approves and enforces the training practice developed as a result of 3.3.2.c.

3.4 STANDARDIZE AN EFFECTIVE REVIEW PROCESS

3.4.1 Summary of the SEI Findings. While Hughes does include provision for reviews during the development process, reviews do not appear to be uniformly performed across projects.

3.4.2 Requirements. The following are necessary attributes of the desired solution:
a. Review standards exist as part of the directive system. They include the following:
 ᠄ overall review practice (i.e., what reviews, when, who is responsible)
. specific criteria to be used in each review
. procedures for conducting reviews

. required data collection and reporting from reviews
b. Required training curriculum includes review-leader training.

3.4.3 Responsibilities.
Leader, Software Engineering Process Group, leads the effort to accomplish 3.4.2.a and 3.4.2.b.
Manager, Software Engineering Division, approves and enforces the standards developed as a result of 3.4.2.b.

3.5 MOVE TOWARD SOFTWARE -ENGINEERING DISCIPLINE

3.5.1 Summary of the SEI Findings. Software engineering is not uniformly treated as an engineering discipline. There are several aspects to this problem, including lack of early software involvement in systems definition, lack of the use of experimentation (i.e., prototyping) as an engineering tool, and skipping software-development steps when schedule pressures increase. On several of the projects studied, software engineering is appropriately addressing these systems-engineering concerns, and software engineering is treated as an engineering discipline; however, on other projects, this was found not to be the case.

3.5.2 Requirements. The following are necessary attributes of the desired solution:
a. Software-development plans for all new projects include an approved budget and task for software-engineering participation in system design and software-requirements specification.
b. System engineers are invited and attend appropriate software-engineering training classes.
c. All required software-development steps are carried out, regardless of schedule pressure.

3.5.3 Responsibilities.
Software Associate Program Managers (APMs) implement 3.5.2.a and 3.5.2.c.
Manager, Software Engineering Division, ensures 3.5.2.a and 3.5.2.c.
Leader, Software Engineering Process Group, leads the effort to accomplish 3.5.2.b.

The second recommendation not included, to improve relations with Defense Contract Administrative Services, again dealt with an organization over which the SED had no control. To negotiate an effective interface with the DCAS was not something Hughes could guarantee, so it was excluded from the action plan. (However, an effective interface was later negotiated.)

The action plan then estimated the labor for implementation to be 100 man-months over 18 months, divided into six major functions:

♦ process-group leader: 8 percent,
♦ process definition: 6 percent,
♦ technology development: 28 percent,
♦ quantitative-process management: 41 percent,
♦ training: 16 percent, and
♦ review-process standardization: 1 percent.

Budget cuts later reduced the 100 man-months of labor to 78. Not included in these estimates were other direct charges for such things as computers, office space, and training facilities, and the existence of certain services such as training and central computer facilities.

Process group. In June 1988, the idea of an SEPG was relatively new at the SEI. Although the concept was well-understood, the implementation was assumed to require that certain roles be organized into a separate function focused on process-technology improvement.

At first, Hughes didn't understand the process-group concept very well, so it tried to implement this SEI approach literally. Also, Hughes' experience with centralizing technology improvement was that, over time, walls of miscommunication developed, leading to just the opposite of technology transfer.

However, on further examination, it was found that the SED, a high level 2 organization with significant progress toward level 3, already had formal roles in place for many process-group functions. All but three functions (action-plan implementation, technology transfer, and development of a required training policy) were either in place or being formed independently of the action plan. Hughes just didn't call it a process group.

To implement the action plan, Hughes issued a bulletin that created the process group, named the existing major functions, and named the person responsible for each function. The bulletin was enlightening to those who understood both what already existed and the SEI's concept of a process group because it made the concept tangible.

The process group, however, was not yet complete. Three key additions brought it all together as an effective focus for process improvement:

♦ Technology steering committee. Although the technology steering committee already existed, Hughes did not fully understand its role as a process-group driving function. Given the newly established functions and responsibilities, the process group did not have one person as a leader but instead was directed by the technology steering committee. Thus, it became the committee's job to develop technology road maps, assess current technology, evaluate the overall direction, and make general technology-policy decisions.

♦ Technology management. Hughes' practices and procedures addressed people management, project management, resource management, and management of other *things*, but not management of *technology*. One of the first improvements was to formalize the management of technology, as with any other corporate resource. This was done through brainstorming and consensus decision making. The plans were recorded as a new practice, technology management.

♦ Technology transfer. A new job function, head of technology transfer, was created and staffed with a full-time person. It was soon clear that the establishment of this function was the most profound action in the entire improvement process. It is not clear if the very positive effect of this action was due to the person's abilities, the existence of the function, or just the timing — but without a doubt this function had more effect than any other single improvement.

Among other things, the head of technology transfer coordinated self-assessments, developed a questionnaire glossary, became the local expert in the SEI maturity questionnaire, became a member of the Software Productivity Consortium's technology-transfer advisory group, developed an SPC technology-transfer plan, briefed senior management on the state of process maturity, maintained a database of technology used on each project and an awareness of what technology each project needed, facilitated technology transfer among projects, ran a special-interest group on process improvement, supported the corporate-wide technology-transfer program, and served on the practices and procedures change-review board, the training policy committee, and the technology steering committee.

Two other additions to the process group that were very helpful were a training committee to periodically review training requirements and their effectiveness and a special-interest group on process improvement. These groups met as needed to find and fix process problems.

Quantitative process management. Before the 1988 action plan, the SED collected "quality indicators" in response to a company-wide push for total quality management. These indicators were error or defect counts, categorized into types, shown in bar graphs with descending importance, and used in postanalyses to isolate where improvement was needed. Each project collected its own data in its own format.

> The action plan estimated the labor for implementation to be 100 man-months over 18 months. Budget cuts later reduced the 100 man-months of labor to 78.

The new approach called for senior management to be briefed every month on the health of each project. To do this, information was collected from each project and compiled into a report that included the project's accomplishments, problems, program trouble reports, quality indicators, scope changes, resource needs, and lessons learned. Also presented were plots of actual versus planned values over time to show the project's schedule, milestones, rate chart, earned value, financial/labor status, and target-system resource use.

The SED implemented a new, division-wide quantitative process-management function and selected one person to be its champion. It standardized the data collected and the reports produced with it, centralized its error-and-defect database, and established a technology center for process-data analysis.

This effort firmly ingrained error-and-defect data collection and analysis into the Hughes culture. It provided the capability required for level 3 maturity and serves as a foundation for future improvement. But time and budget constraints caused it to fall short of achieving all the goals. Some capabilities not achieved are

♦ collecting historical data to support predictions,

♦ projecting analyses within the context of division-wide data,

♦ automating data collection and reporting, and

♦ optimizing data collection based on business needs.

Training gaps. The SED also implemented an organizational policy for required training. Although a policy for required training was not achievable the first time it was tried in 1985, by 1988 the time was right to make it work. (Hughes made training a job requirement, not a promotion requirement, thus solving the equal-employment-opportunity problem that stalled the 1985 effort.)

The company's thrust in continuous measurable improvement and total quality management, combined with the SED manager's personal belief in training resulted in a new policy that required training for all software engineers in the divi-

sion. To support the new requirement, the SED implemented a training-records database that recorded the training status of each employee yearly, at about the time of performance appraisals, and it established a training committee to periodically review training requirements and effectiveness.

Before the 1988 action plan, the SED's internal formal training classes included 17 on modern programming practices, 51 on programming languages and CASE tools, and three on job-specific topics. Enrollment was first-come, first-served. Although training was encouraged and well attended, it was not required.

Although the action plan suggested specific additions to the training program, the SED surveyed its employees to establish what new training was needed. Based on that survey, it added classes on project management, internal reviews, requirements writing, requirements- and unit-level testing, and quality assurance. All these courses had been developed and conducted several times by the 1990 reassessment.

The training programs were open to all engineering functions. Attendance was advertised to and encouraged for all engineers. As of November 1989, 20 percent (174) of the attendees at the training classes were from organizations outside the SED.

Standardized reviews. Before the 1988 action plan, Hughes had established an overall technical-review practice, review criteria, review reporting, data-collection procedures, and the requirement to have a quality-evaluation plan for each project.

Despite these practices, the assessment revealed that the review process was inconsistent. The 1988 action plan included a standard procedure for conducting reviews as well as the training of review leaders in how to conduct reviews. Both were

> The SED implemented a new, division-wide quantitative process-management function and selected one person to be its champion.

completed in 1989.

Software-engineering discipline. The 1988 action plan required that software engineers be involved in the system-engineering process, that system engineers become more involved with software, and that software engineers use traditional engineering techniques such as prototypes and experimentation.

The SED could not require that the system-engineering organization implement these changes because system engineering was not under its control.

Instead, the plan required that the SED participate in the system-engineering process, with the realization that some system-engineering organizations might be reluctant to accept its help. In those cases where software engineers were involved with system design, considerably fewer problems occurred and better products resulted.

1990 REASSESSMENT

Early in 1989, Hughes asked the SEI to conduct a second assessment of the SED. The SEI's resources are limited and it can conduct only a few assessments per year, but the opportunity to evaluate a major software organization at two points in its process-improvement program interested the SEI greatly.

The findings and recommendations from the second assessment indicated that substantial improvements had been implemented. From level 2 in 1987, Hughes had progressed to being a strong level 3, with many activities in place to take it to level 4 and 5.

Improvements included the formation of a process group, key training actions, and a comprehensive technical review process. The assessment concluded that Hughes had achieved a strong position of

	TABLE 1		
COMPARISON OF RESPONSES TO LEVEL 2 AND LEVEL 3 QUESTIONS			
(PERCENTAGE OF POSITIVE RESPONSES)			

Question	1987 assessment	1990 assessment	Average response (from *State of the Practice*)
Level 2			
2.1.4 Is a formal procedure used to make estimates of software size?	50	100	33
2.2.2 Are profiles of software size maintained for each software configuration item over time?	83	100	36
Level 3			
1.1.7 Is there a software-engineering process group or function?	50	100	69
1.2.3 Is there a required software-engineering training program for software developers?	50	100	44
1.2.5 Is a formal training program required for design- and code-review leaders?	0	100	12
2.4.13 Is a mechanism used for controlling changes to the software design?	50	100	100
2.4.19 Is a mechanism used for verifying that the samples examined by software quality assurance are truly representative of the work performed?	33	100	69
2.4.21 Is there a mechanism for assuring the adequacy of regression testing?	33	80	23

software-process leadership and had established the foundation for continuing process improvement.

The assessment team also found that the professional staff was committed to high-quality software work and that it demonstrated disciplined adherence to the established process.

Findings. The SEI made five basic findings in the second assessment:

♦ The SED's role in the Ground Systems Group. The software-engineering process was constrained by lead program managers' misunderstandings of software issues.

♦ Requirements specifications. The SED had become involved in specifying software requirements for some, but not all, projects.

♦ Process data. The SED had made substantial progress in gathering data, but the progress still required solidification. For example, it needed more assistance for data application and analysis. (Although data analysis at the project level was maturing, division-wide data analysis was limited.)

♦ Process automation. The SED had improved its CASE technologies, but the team found that improvement in six areas would reduce the drudgery and labor of recurring tasks: unit-test procedure generation, execution and analysis of regression tests, path-coverage analysis, CASE-tool evaluation, tool expertise, and tool- and method-effectiveness evaluation.

♦ Training. Training was identified as an organizational strength. However, the team found that additional training was needed to help the projects effectively use the process data being gathered.

Recommendations. The team made six recommendations.

Process awareness. Enhance the awareness and understanding of the software process within lead divisions and Ground Systems Group management.

Process automation. Establish a project-oriented mechanism to assess tool needs and effectiveness, develop or acquire automation support where needs assessment justi-

fies its use, provide ongoing information on CASE availability and capabilities, and make tools expertise available to the projects.

Process-data analysis. Expand the process-data analysis technology to include error projection, train employees to analyze project-specific process data, develop a division-wide context for interpreting project-specific data, and ensure that process data is not used to evaluate individuals.

Data-collection/-analysis use. Optimize process data collection and analysis to best benefit product and business results.

Requirements process. Continue efforts to increase participation in the software-requirements process, update SED bidding practice to require SED input and participation in requirements generation, and increase the skill level of software engineers in writing requirements.

Quality assurance. Ensure adequate SQA support for SED software efforts. In particular, it should ensure that Ground Systems Group SQA practices are consistently applied on all efforts in which the SED is responsible for the software and that the level of SQA effort is sufficient to support each project's needs.

ASSESSMENT COMPARISON

The SEI has compiled data on all the assessments it has conducted in its *State of the Software Engineering Practice.*[2] Tables 1 and 2 detail the two Hughes assessment results compared with the state-of-the-practice data for level 2 and level 3 questions. (Because there was insufficient data on level 4 and 5 questions at the time of the state-of-the-practice report, we cannot include this comparison.)

To provide a valid comparison between the two SED assessments, we used the same SEI questionnaire in both assessments. In 1987, the SED met the level 2 criteria in all important aspects. As Table 1 shows, of the six projects assessed, there were only four negative answers to two of the 12 key level 2 questions. In other words, of 72 answers, 68 were yes. In 1987, the SED could not answer yes to many key level 3 questions, as Table 1 also shows. Table 2 shows the more interesting

changes in the key level 4 questions between the two assessments.

We drew several conclusions from these results. First, in 1987 there was not agreement among projects on some organization-wide questions. For example, in Table 1 questions 1.1.7, 1.2.3, and 1.2.5 concern the total organization, not individual projects. In all cases, these responses should have been 0 percent. Similarly, in Table 2, questions 1.3.4, 2.3.1, 2.3.8, and 2.4.2 relate to the entire organization. Here, the numbers should have been 0 percent for the first three and 100 percent for 2.4.2.

Second, the analysis and error-projection activities asked about in the level 4 questions typically are difficult and require extensive training and support. Because the intent is to focus attention on the key error causes, to build understanding of these critical factors, and gradually to establish the means to control them, considerable data analysis and experience is required before proficiency can be expected.

LESSONS LEARNED

Hughes learned 11 important lessons from the SED process-improvement ef-

fort, listed here in order of importance.

Management commitment. The path to improvement requires investment, risk, time, and the pain of cultural change. Delegation is not strong enough to overcome these roadblocks. Commitment is. Process improvement should be tied to the salary or promotion criteria of senior management.

Pride is the most important result. Improvements are one-time achievements, but pride feeds on itself and leads to continuous measurable improvement. When the whole organization buys into the improvement and sees the results unfold, it gains a team esprit de corps and from that, pride. Hughes' people pulled together to improve the entire organization's software process and they all share in the success.

Increases in maturity decrease risk. Another important benefit (and goal) of process maturation is decreased risk of missing cost and schedule estimates. The two concepts of risk and process maturity are closely coupled. As an organization matures, its performance in meeting planned costs and schedules improves.

Question		1987 assessment	1990 assessment
TABLE 2 **COMPARISON OF RESPONSES TO LEVEL 4 QUESTIONS** **(PERCENTAGE OF POSITIVE RESPONSES)**			
1.3.4	Is a mechanism used for managing and supporting the introduction of new technologies?	16	100
2.2.5	Are design errors projected and compared to actuals?	16	20
2.2.6	Are code and test errors projected and compared to actuals?	16	20
2.2.14	Is test coverage measured and recorded for each phase of functional testing?	83	100
2.3.1	Has a managed and controlled process database been established for process metrics data across all projects?	50	100
2.3.2	Are the review data gathered during design reviews analyzed?	16	100
2.3.3	Is the error data from code reviews and tests analyzed to determine the likely distribution and characteristics of the errors remaining in the product?	16	20
2.3.4	Are analyses of errors conducted to determine their process-related causes?	83	100
2.3.8	Is review efficiency analyzed for each project?	50	100
2.4.2	Is a mechanism used for periodically assessing the software-engineering process and implementing indicated improvements?	83	100

The indicator the SED uses for cost risk, and the indicator for which there is historical data available, is a cost-performance index, which is calculated as CPI = BCWP/ACWP, where BCWP is the budgeted cost of work performed and ACWP is the actual cost of work performed.

The CPI has shown a steady improvement, from 0.94 in July 1987 to 0.97 in March 1990. In other words, in July 1987 the SED averaged about 6 percent actual costs over budgeted costs; in March 1990 it had reduced this average to 3 percent. This 50-percent reduction nets Hughes about $2 million annually. These values are averages for all SED projects at the time.

When considering all the direct labor, support, overhead, travel, and equipment costs for the assessment and improvement costs, these first-year benefits are five times the total improvement expenditures.

Assuming that the Hughes maturity is at least maintained, these financial benefits should continue to accrue. Furthermore, the improved contract performance makes Hughes' estimates of software cost more credible during contract negotiations.

The benefits are worth the effort and expense. When the improvement effort was begun in 1988, Hughes was not sure what the benefits would be, other than achieving the next higher level on the process-maturity model. However, Hughes received a handsome return on its investment: The quality of work life has improved, and the company's image has benefited from the improved performance.

The SED has experienced very few crises at the Ground Systems Group facility since applying a mature process to each project. Although volatile requirements continue to be a persistent engineering problem, the effect of shifting requirements on cost and schedule is under con-

trol and reliably predictable.

A less quantifiable result of process maturity is the quality of work life. Hughes SED has seen fewer overtime hours, fewer gut-wrenching problems to deal with each day, and a more stable work environment. Even in the volatile aerospace industry in California, software-professional turnover has been held below 10 percent.

Software technology center is key. A software technology center works most effectively when most of the development, project management, administration, technology development, training, and marketing are housed in one organization.

The size and focus of such a central organization makes it possible to afford, for example, an SEPG that focuses on technology improvement, a full-time person in charge of technology transfer, an organization-wide data-collection and -analysis service, independent software research and development, and a CASE center. All these are important contributors to improving process maturity.

A coherent culture exists at level 3. A coherent organizational culture results from the cumulative effect of a long-lived organization with a common purpose, environment, education, and experience base. You can quickly sense the nature of an organization's culture when you hear people speaking in the same technical language, sharing common practices and procedures, and referring to organizational goals as their own.

At level 3, Hughes found that the common culture helped foster an esprit de corps that reinforced team performance. In fact, Hughes concluded it needed to achieve a common process across the organization, to establish an organization-wide training program, and to enable buy-in of organizational goals. Although it is difficult to precisely phrase a question to determine if an organization does or does

not have such a positive culture, an assessment team can agree whether or not team members experienced it during an assessment.

A focal point is essential. Disintegrated, asynchronous improvement is not only inefficient but also ineffective for solving organization-wide problems. Although there is still the need for cell-level improvement teams, there must also be an organizational focal point to plan, coordinate (integrate), and implement organization-wide process improvements. The SEI calls this focal point an SEPG. Hughes calls it the technology steering committee, others might call it an engineering council. Whatever the name, there must be a focal point.

Technology transfer is essential. The establishment of a technology-transfer function was judged the most profound of the actions taken.

Software-process expertise is essential. In 1987, the SEI questionnaire and a few SEI professionals were all the expert help there was. Now there is a growing literature on software process, a draft capability maturity model, and an improved draft questionnaire. Many SEI people are experts in software process, and even more people in industry have become experts in software process.[1]

To understand and use the available knowledge, process-improvement teams must become process experts and they must be able to interpret the assessment questionnaire in the context of the organization. For example, the SED wrestled over the ambiguity of the phrase "first-line managers" in the questionnaire. In the Hughes organization, "manager" is used only for the third promotion level and above in the line-management hierarchy, but this isn't what the SEI meant. After discussions with the SEI over the meaning of the phrase, Hughes concluded that it meant the first supervisory position for software engineers, a position Hughes called group head.

Because group heads did not sign off on schedules and cost estimates, Hughes

> Hughes SED has seen fewer overtime hours, fewer gut-wrenching problems to deal with each day, and a more stable work environment.

considered changing their practices to require the heads to do so. However, Hughes found that some software projects have eight people, while others might include an entire lab of 250 people with several sections and many groups. It thus did not always seem appropriate to have group heads approve schedules and cost estimates.

Hughes finally concluded that "first-line manager" in the Hughes culture meant associate project manager, the person who is in charge of software development on a project (no matter what level), and the one who negotiates and approves schedules and cost estimates with the program manager, documenting those agreements in a work authorization and delegation document. Hughes SED thus translated the question "Do software first-line managers sign off on their schedules and cost estimates?" as "Do associate project managers approve work authorization and delegation documents?"

An action plan is necessary. An action plan based on process-maturity assessment recommendations will not necessarily move an organization to the next stage of maturity. Assessment recommendations come from a brainstorming and consensus-building team process that, because of the nature of the process and the time limitations, can address only the top priority recommendations (about 10 out of 36 in the last assessment). Furthermore, action plans tend to not include many people-oriented changes (such as getting people to buy in on changes) that are needed for progress.

The only ones questioning the value of level 2 are those who have not achieved it. To an organization that has achieved it, level 2 capabilities seem obvious and indispensable. It is simply a natural, responsible way of conducting business.

When compared with those of the general population of SEI-assessed organizations, it is clear that the 1987 Hughes improvement efforts started from a very strong base. Based on the SEI data, the Hughes process in 1987 was in approximately the 90th percentile of all organizations studied.[2]

It is also clear that given sufficient management emphasis and competent, skilled, and dedicated professionals, significant improvement in software process is possible. Improvements like those made at Hughes' SED can significantly help a software organization's overall business performance. The SEI assessment of Hughes' SED formed the bases for a sustained improvement effort.

Finally, improvement is reinforcing. As each improvement level is reached, the benefits are demonstrated and the opportunities for further improvement become clear. ◆

ACKNOWLEDGMENTS
· We thank Ken Dymond, Larry Druffel, George Pandelious, Jeff Perdue, and Jim Rozum for their helpful review comments. We very much appreciate Dorothy Josephson's support in preparing the manuscript and the able editorial assistance of Linda Pesante and Marie Elm. The comments and suggestions of Carl Chang and the anonymous referees were also a great help in converting our manuscript into a finished article.
   This work was sponsored by the US Defense Dept.

REFERENCES
1. W.S. Humphrey, *Managing the Software Process*, Addison-Wesley, Reading, Mass., 1989.
2. W.S. Humphrey, D.H. Kitson, and T.C. Kasse, "The State of Software-Engineering Practice: A Preliminary Report," Tech. Report CMU/SEI-89-TR-1, Software Eng. Inst., Carnegie Mellon Univ., Pittsburgh, 1989.

A case study in SQA audits

PAUL W. OMAN*

Software Engineering Test Laboratory, Department of Computer Science, University of Idaho, Moscow, Idaho 83843, USA

Received December 1991

Software quality assurance (SQA) audits are becoming a standard practice in corporations seeking to enter contractual relations with other organizations, or just evaluating their own state of readiness. This paper describes one approach to conducting SQA audits. Excerpts from reports of actual audits conducted on several organizations engaged in software development are used to show how an audit is conducted and what can be achieved through the auditing process. The paper is not meant to be a definitive answer or guide to doing SQA audits. Rather, it serves as an annotated case study of how SQA audits can be conducted with an emphasis on data gathering and reporting.

Keywords: quality assurance, software audits

1. Introduction

Software quality assurance (SQA) is the planned and systematic arrangement of actions necessary to establish confidence that a software product conforms to accepted technical requirements (IEEE, 1990a). The IEEE Computer Society and the International Organization for Standardization have several published standards relative to software quality assurance (IEEE, 1986a, 1989; ISO, 1987) and software reviews (IEEE, 1990b). In addition, there are related standards and guidelines for configuration management (IEEE, 1987a, 1990), verification and validation (IEEE, 1986b), and software project management (IEEE, 1987b). All of these plans and guidelines provide the basic form for evaluating the quality of software and software processes, but they don't give the details necessary actually to perform an audit of the software quality assurance preparedness of an organization.

The purpose of this paper is to show an approach to SQA audits: the external evaluation of an organization's software products, software process maturity, and software quality assurance function. The principles and techniques described here are consistent and compatible with the methods and requirements set forth in the IEEE Standard for Software Reviews and Audits (IEEE, 1990b). While the standard provides the overall guidelines and format, this paper gives an insight into how

* Dr Paul W. Oman is an associate professor of computer science at the University of Idaho, and an independent software consultant who specializes in software analysis. He is the director of the Software Engineering Test Lab within the UI College of Engineering, where he conducts research in software development methods, CASE tools, and software maintainability issues. Oman has published over 50 articles and reports on software tools, software development, and computer science education. He has a PhD in computer science and is a member of the IEEE, IEEE Computer Society, and ACM.

they can be applied. Further, the principles and techniques described in this paper have been used to conduct actual SQA audits of some corporations engaged in software development. Excerpts from the reports of those audits are presented here as a case study of data gathering and reporting techniques used while conducting an SQA audit. However, the individual data values and results from those reports have been changed to protect the proprietary information and integrity of those corporations.

2. Software quality assurance audits

We derive the definition for SQA audits from the IEEE Standard for Software Review and Audits (IEEE, 1990b):

> '*Audit*: An independent evaluation of software products or processes to ascertain compliance to standards, guidelines, specifications, and procedures based on objective criteria . . .'
> '*Review*: An evaluation of software element(s) or project status to ascertain discrepancies from planned results and to recommend improvement . . .'
> '*Software element*: A deliverable or in-process document produced or acquired during software development or maintenance . . .'

From these definitions it is apparent that an SQA audit is an independent evaluation of an organization's (1) software products, (2) software processes, and (3) software quality assurance functions. The following subsections deal with each of these three areas. Note, however, that prior to conducting an SQA audit it is essential that the appropriate standards and guidelines that govern the organization(s) being audited are identified. Where explicit requirements are lacking, the existing ANSI/IEEE and ISO standards can be used as a baseline.

2.1. *Auditing and reviewing software products*

When auditing an organization's SQA effectiveness, an analysis of its software products for (at least) the following attributes should be included:

1. overall code structure and organization;
2. maintainability aspects and code change traceability;
3. extent of the verification and validation (V&V) process and documentation;
4. compliance with standards; and
5. comparison with modern programming practices.

For purposes of software analysis, select a mixture of key high- and low-level programs to provide broad coverage of the areas (or projects) which are being audited. If this is not possible, use random selection through the pool of available programs (or suites of programs). Do *not* analyse just the software initially provided by the corporate engineers. Always ask for something they have not provided.

Analyse each of the programs by

1. tracing the execution from the main routine down to the third level of subprogram calls.

Record flowcharts, subprogram call charts, and I/O interfaces during this trace to provide an overall picture of the code structure, flow of control, and data flow;

2. checking for consistency and traceability by comparing the data gathered from the above trace to the code's supporting documentation;
3. noting style and maintenance characteristics, and classifying the degree of subprogram coupling and cohesion. Coupling is the intermodule control and data connections; cohesion is the intramodule strength (Pressman, 1992). For high maintainability and reusability it is necessary to have low coupling and high cohesion.
4. using a metrics extractor (such as PC-Metric, SET Laboratories, 1988, used in the following examples) to calculate code quality and complexity metrics;
5. comparing the source code to documented V&V results to determine the extent of the V&V effort.

Figure 1 contains excerpts from a software audit done on the XYZ Corporation within the last 5 years. The audit report contains sections discussing code structure and style, complexity and maintainability, documentation, traceability, and compliance with standards. It ends with actual conclusions and recommendations from the audit report. Although extensive, this example is not meant to be an exhaustive account of what should be included in an audit of software products. Rather, it is simply an example of what can be accomplished in a period of a few days. The text of the report shown in the following section is from an actual audit, but characteristic details have been changed to protect the confidentiality of the organizations involved in the audit.

2.1.1 *Exerpts from a software product audit*

General observations. In general, all of the programs exhibit characteristics typical of code written in the 1960s and 1970s even though much development work has occurred in the last 10 years. Large portions of the code can be traced to origins in the 1960s and 1970s. For example, the FLOSPEC main program has a comment dated 1963 and the TRANSIT main program has an output statement with a 1977 date. For the most part, new coding efforts (i.e. revised, rebuilt, and new subprograms) are similar in style and organization to the old code.

FLUIDS, written by the ABC Company in the mid 1980s, contains roughly half old code and half new code. The old code is characteristic of early unstructured programs, but the new code is generally well written with block structured language constructs. On the other hand, SPACES, written by PDQ Corporation in the late 1980s, has the style and structure typical of the 1970s. It does not use block structured language features and its appearance is indistinguishable from the older programs.

With the exception of FLUIDS, the supporting documentation and V&V traceability for the code is out of date or incomplete. The documentation and V&V effort has not kept pace with the code modifications and new code development.

Code structure and style. With the exception of FLUIDS, which does contain structured language constructs, the overall structure and style of the code reflects the programming practices used prior to the advent of structured programming techniques, even though much of the code was written in the late 1980s:

1. short (less than six characters) variable names

Table 1. Code complexity/maintainability statistics.

	Number of subprograms	Subprogram averages for			Exceptions	
		LOC	B/L	Span	per cent	average
FLUIDS	189	79	10	9	47	3.3
FLOSPEC	34	108	10	9	59	3.2
FDYNA	85	74	11	10	67	3.1
TRANSIT	101	113	16	14	62	3.8
MINTRON	44	163	29	24	69	5.0
SERVICE	48	133	34	17	65	4.9
SPACES	2	1170	161	147	100	3.5

Subprograms   main program, subroutines, and functions
LOC   average lines of code per subprogram
B/L   average number of branches and loops per subprogram
Span   average 'life' of a variable (in statements)
Exceptions   unusual, non-standard, or poor programming practices
Exc. per cent   percentage of subprograms containing exceptions
Exc. average   average number of exceptions per subprogram

2. no indentation to show blocking and nesting
3. lack of block structure emulation (D and D' structures)
4. high subprogram coupling (extensive common couplings)
5. low subprogram cohesion (coincidental and logical cohesion)
6. long subprograms (in excess of 1000 lines)
7. multiple entry and exit points (content couplings)
8. excessive use of unconditional branching in and out of loops
9. high level of loop nesting
10. high variable span (in excess of 200 lines)
11. high loop span (in excess of 1200 lines)

FLUIDS, the notable exception to the above profile, contains extended variable name, indentation and spacing to highlight block structures, smaller subprograms, lower loop and variable spans, and less unstructured branching.

Code complexity and maintainability.   A summary of each program's code complexity and quality attributes calculated by PC-Metric is shown in Table 1. These data were extracted from the PC-Metric complexity reports generated using the tool's default values for exceptions reporting. The programs are listed in increasing order of measured complexity. As can be seen from the table, FLUIDS has the least complexity, while SPACES exhibits the most complexity.

FLUIDS is the only program in which less than half of the subprograms contain exceptions. SPACES has the highest complexity. It is a monolithic program written with numerous unstructured branches and long loops (one loop spans 1208 lines of code). It can be concluded from these data that these programs do not conform to modern day programming practices and standards. Further, maintenance endeavours would be hampered by the code structure and style characteristics. (See Table 1.)

Supporting documentation and traceability. The supporting documentation for the XYZ programs is either missing or out of date. Much new code has been written without accompanying documentation. For the old code, the description of the I/O, calling sequence, and flow control described in the user's manuals and programming manuals are incorrect because they do not correspond to the source code listings. The original documentation, typically dated in the mid-1970s, was adequate, but several iterations of code change, without accompanying documentation change, have rendered the existing documentation incorrect and potentially risky.

Following are examples demonstrating the inconsistencies and incompleteness of the supporting documents for the XYZ programs that were analysed. (This is not a complete list of recorded anomalies.)

FDYNA The description in the programmer's manual does not correspond to the actual code listing which contains statements dated 2/13/86 and 6/16/87. Further, the last document describing the historical development of FDYNA is dated 7/15/85, although several changes have been made since then.

SPACES The new programmer's manual describes calls to two subroutines which are *not* included in the code and fails to document others which *are* called by the program.

MINTRON The description in the programmer's manual does not correspond to the actual code listing which contains numerous modifications. Further, comments within MINTRON, describing how the program works, are at odds with the actual execution of MINTRON. Evidence can be seen in SKEW subroutine where header comments refer to non-existent subprograms.

TRANSIT The code contains extensive modifications dated 12/86, 6/87, and 1/89, while the programmer's manual is dated 10/86 and the last applicable memoranda is dated 3/20/87. The subprogram calling sequence described in the supporting documentation does not correspond to the actual code execution. Further, the main program code writes two conflicting version dates, one prints 'January 1980' and the other prints '1 AUG 1988'.

Verification and validation traceability. Following is a comparison of the documented V&V efforts with respect to source code changes in FDYNA, SPACES, MINTRON, FLUIDS, and TRANSIT, FLOSPEC and SERVICE were not analysed in this manner.

FDYNA The most recent V&V documentation is a one page memoranda which describes an independent review of the V&V effort described in another memoranda. The independent review concludes that the calculations are correct but the documentation is out of date. Also, the source code listing contains modifications which are not addressed in any V&V documentation.

SPACES There are no V&V reports for SPACES. The one page summary sheet for SPACES refers to comparisons with independent data, but these efforts are not documented.

MINTRON The two most recent V&V documents are internal memoranda showing that changes have been made to MINTRON without subsequent V&V tests. Both memoranda describe parameter and dimension changes made to the source code and then conclude 'these changes have no effect on the validation status of MINTRON'.

FLUIDS The only applicable V&V documents are two internal ABC corporate memoranda. The first document validates the use of FLUIDS for fluid flow analysis, while the second compares the results obtained from FLUIDS to those from FLUIFLO, a similar program. It should be noted that these efforts were conducted by the ABC Corporation on data unrelated to the XYZ corporate applications.

TRANSIT   The latest applicable documents are two internal memoranda. Both memoranda discuss changes but provide no evidence of V&V efforts. Further, the code contains modifications dated after the memoranda were written.

Compliance with standards.   On the whole, this set of programs does not meet applicable government and industrial standards, for the following reasons:

1. Plans for software quality assurance are missing.
2. Software V&V plans and reports are missing, inadequate, or out of date.
3. Code structure and style does not conform to present day programming practices.
4. User documentation does not follow a consistent form, nor is it up to date.
5. Programmer documentation does not follow a consistent form, nor is it up to date.
6. Requirements and design specifications for newly developed codes are missing.

Further, these codes do not comply with XYZ corporate standards for one or more of the following reasons.

(a) V&V plans for all procured software are required but non-existent.
(b) Requirement specifications and user manuals are required for all existing and procured software, but several are missing.
(c) Requirements and design specifications are required for all newly developed software, but are non-existent.
(d) Only software with a status of 'Verified' and 'Stable' can be used within the design stages of 'Critical' projects, and yet there are documented instances where this is not being adhered to.

Conclusions.   Most of the programs were written in the 1970s (or derived from such code) and are typical of the coding techniques used prior to the advent of structured programming methodology. This is to be expected of codes with origins in the 1960s and 1970s, but surprising when encountered in the new code written in the 1980s. Proper training in present-day software engineering techniques and structured programming principles has been lacking. As a result these codes are not considered acceptable or maintainable by today's standards.

The lack of source code control is evidenced by undocumented and unverified source code changes. That is, the code contains modifications not described in supporting documentation. Rarely is there documented traceability for what the modification was, who implemented the modification, and who retested the modified code. This, in turn, is evidence that a formal sign-off mechanism is not used (or not enforced) for version control.

The lack of unified coding standards can be seen in the style variations implemented throughout the old code and evidenced by the new SPACES code. It is clear that mechanisms for the use of indentation, variable naming, commenting, structure, and the other coding characteristics listed in the standards documents have not been used.

Recommendations

1. Update the set of software tools used to develop and maintain code. Tools for version control,

style and maintainability assessment, complexity measurement, re-engineering, and automated documentation should be investigated.

2. Institute a formal training program on structured program techniques and software engineering principles.
3. Implement a consistent software V&V plan.
4. Use a source code control system to enforce modification traceability of recent changes.
5. Implement a formal regression testing function that is tied to the source code control system.
6. Adopt uniform coding standards that are compatible with present day coding practices and software tools.
7. Adopt minimum documentation requirements compatible with existing ANSI/IEEE standards.

2.2. *Evaluating the software process maturity*

The Software Engineering Institute (SEI) at Carnegie Mellon University devised a software process maturity framework (Humphrey, 1988, 1990) and a survey with which to measure an organization's software process maturity. This process maturity framework can be used to assess (or audit) an organization's software processes. According to the SEI framework, an organization's software development and management proceeds through five stages of maturity:

1. *Initial*: the base level that all organizations exhibit.
2. *Repeatable*: process control functions are implemented to ensure that a repeatable level of software quality be attained from project to project.
3. *Defined*: the process control functions employed at level 2 are now formally defined and supporting technology is used.
4. *Managed*: comprehensive process measurement techniques are now used, beyond those of simple cost and schedule performance monitoring.
5. *Optimizing*: collected data supports continued improvement and optimization of the process.

The five levels of process maturity have been defined and documented in work performed by Watts Humphrey (1988) and the SEI (1991). In these studies, a software process maturity assessment instrument was devised and validated with DoD contractors carrying software management and/or development responsibilities. Some characteristics of this study are worth pointing out: (i) Seventy-six per cent of the contractors assessed in the original survey fell into the initial level; (ii) Only four corporations were observed at level 3; and (iii) No organizations were observed at levels 4 or 5.

Since the survey of DoD organizations, some of those companies have advanced to level 3 and a few are approaching level 4. But establishing the true status of an organization's software process maturity requires a complete assessment along the lines of the SEI procedures. That is beyond the scope of a simple (and quick) SQA audit, so for our purposes it is adequate to use a subset of the SEI survey in order to *estimate* the process maturity level.

The complete survey and instructions for application (SEI, 1991) are available from the SEI at Carnegie Mellon University. For initial auditing purposes a subset of the level 2 and level 3 questions can be used to determine the organization's approximate maturity level. The survey is completed by answering yes or no to each of the questions with respect to: (a) A single representative project; and/or (b) All projects within the organization. A preponderance of positive responses to questions

Table 2. Positive responses to key questions on software process maturity.

	Any 1 project (%)	All internal projects (%)	All external projects (%)
2nd level questions (Repeatable)	58	8	16
3rd level questions (Defined)	42	0	0

of a given level is sufficient evidence to claim that the process maturity rests at that level. So for auditing purposes, a preponderance of affirmative responses to the level 2 or 3 questions indicates that the process maturity lies at (or approaches) that level. Note, however, that this approximation can – and should – be verified by the organization's self-assessment of its process maturity.

The following section contains excerpts from an abridged software process maturity audit applied to the XYZ Corporation within the last 5 years. Again, characteristic details have been changed to protect the organization being evaluated.

2.2.1 Excerpts from a process maturity audit

Assessment method. This section describes the application of an abridged software maturity assessment survey based on the original work by the SEI. Key questions used in determining if corporations have achieved the Repeatable and Defined levels of software process maturity were taken from the SEI survey and applied to:

1. a single representative XYZ software project;
2. all XYZ software projects as a whole; and
3. all externally contracted software projects.

The survey was given to an XYZ quality assurance engineer working on software related quality assurance, and verified through independent evaluation by two members of the auditing team. There was 96 per cent agreement between the XYZ engineer's assessment and that of the auditing team.

Survey results. Results of the survey are summarized in Table 2. Each column shows the percentage of positive responses to key questions related to Repeatable and Defined process maturity. A preponderance of affirmative responses at any one level is sufficient evidence of process maturity at that level.

Results of the survey indicate that the XYZ software process maturity approaches Repeatable status for a single well-controlled project. For all projects taken as a whole, and all external development projects, the software process maturity is clearly at the initial level. For all projects, between 84 and 92 per cent of the responses to questions on Repeatable behaviour (second level) were negative; 100 per cent of the responses to questions on Defined behaviour (third level) were negative. Therefore, existing XYZ process maturity does not exceed the first (Initial) level (see Table 2.)

The initial level of the SEI framework represents the base level in which all corporations begin their software management and development. To attain Repeatable status certain functions must be implemented to ensure that controlled software quality is replicated from project to project. Initial software process maturity is characterized in the SEI assessment literature as having an 'ad *hoc*, or possibly chaotic, process'. Organizations at this level proceed with developing software without formalized procedures, cost estimation, and software project plans. Tools for software quality are not well integrated into the software development/management function, nor are they uniformly applied. The SEI literature suggests that Initial-level organizations need to address: (1) project management; (2) senior management oversight; (3) quality assurance; and (4) change control. Therefore, all of these points should be addressed in the XYZ management hierarchy and SQAP.

Conclusions from the survey. From the results of the process maturity assessment, and from interviews with XYZ employees, the following conclusions can be drawn:

1. Source code control systems have not been used.
2. Coding standards for style and maintainability do not exist.
3. Software interface constraints and requirements for controlling software across a variety of computing platforms and contractors do not exist.
4. The formalism of moving software from 'experimental' status to 'operational' status is not well defined.
5. Measurements of code quality and complexity have not been employed.
6. Measurements of software maintenance effort, software development effort, and programmer productivity have not been employed.
7. Models and mechanisms for measuring defect density and software reliability have not been employed.

Recommendations

1. Implement a source code control system to monitor source code modifications.
2. Create uniform standards for programming style, structure, documentation, and interface requirements.
3. Formalize the relationship between the program library and code status (experimental, operational, production). Ensure that all code within the library has a designated status.
4. Apply a program of software process metrics to measure (a) effort and expense relative to software development and maintenance, and (b) software quality relative to defect intensity, code complexity, and code reliability.
5. Use process metrics to establish procedures for estimating software maintenance and development costs. Undertake cost/benefit analyses of all major software suites to determine if software maintenance is cost effective.
6. Institute a formal training program on coding standards and practices for all engineers involved with software maintenance and development.

2.3. *Assessing the SQA function*

An organization's software quality assurance function consists of:

1. Software management administrative lines of control;
2. Documents comprising the software management plan;
3. Mechanism for software configuration control (including documentation).

These elements comprise the organizational mechanisms to manage and control software. An assessment of these components, together with an assessment of the process maturity (discussed in the previous section), provides a means for auditing an organization's SQA function. This section discusses how to assess these remaining components.

2.3.1 *Assessing SQA management*

The assessment of the management and administration of SQA starts by obtaining (or creating) an organizational hierarchy chart relative to software development and management. Look for positions of Quality Assurance Director and the Vice-President (or Director) for Software Development. Examine the relationship between these two administrators and make sure they are both accountable for software quality. To affect software quality assurance, the quality assurance (QA) engineers should report up through the SQA Director who communicates with the VP in charge of software development to implement quality assurance controls downward to the development projects. QA engineers should not be placed under the supervisors of engineering projects. Time and budget constraints frequently lead project supervisors to overrule or ignore suggestions from subordinate QA engineers. Having the QA engineers report to the QA Director (or directly to the VP for software development) assures that high-level management will at least be cognizant of possible QA problems.

Auditing the software management lines of control is generally a simple matter of checking that the appropriate QA reporting lines of authority have been established and that personnel involved with the use and development of software are properly trained. For example, QA engineers should be well versed in the Software Quality Assurance Plan, Software Management Plan, Configuration Management Plan, and any other documents pertaining to the control and use of software. Also, check to make sure that software managers are well trained in the SQAP, SMP and CMP, as well as all documents pertaining to the development and maintenance of software. Spot checks and pointed questions will reveal much in the way of training and preparedness.

Section 2.3.2 contains excerpts from an example audit looking at the software-related management lines of the XYZ Corporation within the last 5 years. Again, characteristic details have been changed to protect the organization being audited.

2.3.2 *Excerpts from a management audit*

Observations on administrative lines of authority. The director of Engineering QA is on the same administrative level as the Engineering VP; the SQA engineers report to the engineering project managers; the office of Configuration Management appears to be under the Engineering VP, with subordinate functions of Software Configuration Control and Software Management. The position and responsibility of Configuration Management is at the same level as engineering project managers. This restricts Configuration Management (and its subordinate functions of Configuration Control and Software Management) to horizontal observation and evaluation of engineering processes. Hence, neither the Configuration Manager nor the Software Manager have influence over software development and management conducted in engineering projects. It is not clear who has responsibility for software quality assurance within engineering projects. The relationship between the Configuration Manager and the QA office is not specified and the relationship between the QA Director and the individual project's QA departments is not clear.

Observations on software related training facilities. The XYZ facilities for training personnel on software related issues consist of a training office and an automated training-tracking system. The training office is responsible for co-ordinating – not conducting – training sessions and required readings across all XYZ projects involving software. The actual training falls under the auspices of the individual project managers, but the training office is responsible for: (1) coordinating training sessions; (2) tracking the progress of those training mechanisms; and (3) recording the status of training for each member of the technical staff.

The tracking system is automated and appears to be fully functional. It was tested by the auditing team with a series of *ad hoc* queries, with results verified by examination of physical records and interviews with the technical staff. In every tested instance, the automated tracking system was accurate and up-to-date with respect to training materials and records. It is questionable, however, if this degree of accuracy can be maintained with existing staffing (2.5 personnel) as the corporation pursues its projected personnel increase of doubling within the next 2 years. The new personnel, combined with new procedures to address added functions and manpower, will cause an accelerating need for training.

Recommendations

1. Move the SQA engineers and the Configuration Management Office under the direction of the QA Director to create a unified QA programme.
2. Provide the QA Director with authority to establish and enforce corporate standards for software development, coding, and documentation.
3. Ensure that both the QA Director and the Engineering VP have a thorough knowledge of software quality assurance procedures.
4. Plan for increasing the training office staff in accordance to the expected manpower ramp-up within the next 6 months to 12 months.

2.3.3 *Assessing software management plans and documentation*

The organization's software management plan should be well documented and should require the set of minimum (or recommended) documentation outlined in the applicable standards (e.g. ANSI/IEEE). The plan should also incorporate configuration management aspects and/or refer to a stand-alone Configuration Management Plan. Assessing the quality of an organization's software management plan is essentially just ensuring that it meets the minimum intent behind the applicable standards.

Section 2.3.4 contains excerpts from an analysis of the XYZ Corporation's SQAP documentation. The audit was conducted within the last 5 years. Again, characteristic details have been changed to protect the organization.

2.3.4 *Excerpts from a SQAP audit*

Observations. All XYZ software management is controlled by the directives contained in the Contract Policy Manual, the Software Management Plan, and the Guidelines for the Control of Software document. Each of these documents is addressed below.

The XYZ Corporation has no separate Software Quality Assurance Planning document, so the set of documents described above must be considered to comprise that function. As a body, this document set does *not* meet all applicable documentation requirements as specified by the ANSI and IEEE standards.

Contract Policy Manual (CPM). This document is a general overview of the contractor management structure; it references other documents, but contains no list of referenced or applicable documents. It contains one paragraph introductions to the Engineering Management Plan, the Configuration Management Plan, and the Software Management Plan. It also has a broad overview of the Product Quality Assurance Plan, but details are not provided. Recommendations with regard to the Contract Policy Manual.

1. The CPM should contain a list of referenced and applicable documents.
2. The CPM should contain details on who is responsible for monitoring and administering the plans it references.

Software Management Plan (SMP). The Software Management Plan is required by ANSI and IEEE standards. It generally adheres to those requirements, but contains instances of vague and/or inaccurate wording that need correction. Recommendations with regard to the Software Management Plan:

1. Provide a reference list of all cited and applicable documents.
2. For each function outlined in the plan, specify who is responsible for implementing that function and how it will be monitored.
3. Develop a uniform plan for management and quality assurance of externally contracted software that will be adhered to by all participating organizations.
4. Adopt the definitions embodied within the ANSI and IEEE standards to ensure compliance with all pertinent regulations.
5. Omit the exclusionary provisos and require independent review of all existing software.
6. Specify that independent validation review shall be done by someone not involved with the code's design and implementation.
7. Specify that changes to existing software, undergo the same level of baselining and V&V efforts applied to newly developed software.
8. Provide guidelines for minimally adequate regression testing.

Guidelines for the Control of Software (GCS). The Guidelines for the Control of Software outlines procedures for software use, control, documentation, and development. It is vague and imprecise. Recommendations with regard to the Guidelines for the Control of Software:

1. Clarify the parties responsible for implementing and monitoring this document.
2. Clarify the parties responsible for software approval.
3. Adopt the ANSI/IEEE definitions and outlines for Requirement Specifications and User's Manuals.
4. Include a V&V report and a programmer's manual as required documentation.
5. *All* changes to software should be monitored and controlled via a source code control system and a formal regression testing procedure. Implement software baselining within a source code control system and a formal mechanism for regression testing.

2.3.5 *Assessing configuration management*

An organization's configuration management function consists of: (1) Configuration Manager's position and duties; (2) Configuration Management Plan (CMP); (3) Facilities for software libraries and version control; and (4) Mechanisms for software control and distribution over a variety of computing environments. Two of these aspects will not be dealt with in detail here. The Configuration Manager's function has already been addressed in the previous discussion of management lines of authority; and the form and function of configuration management plans are well documented elsewhere (IEEE, 1990b,c).

The following paragraphs discuss the software library function and the problem of distributed computing over a variety of computing environments. It's difficult to suggest strict guidelines for auditing these functions – what is reasonable and prudent must be decided relative to the critical nature of the software being managed.

Software libraries.   The software library should be more than just a repository for source and/or object code. A source code control system, configuration management system, and object code library should be implemented (with appropriate control procedures) to ensure that multiple copies of source and executable code do not contaminate production systems. Ideally, the software library should be viewed as an integrated collection of control systems that protect the organization's software investment. When auditing an organization's configuration management function the following should be looked for:

1. A *source code control system* that archives one version of the source code and maintains update records of all modifications to that source code. Source code control data (such as embedded version identification, date and time stamps, and update log) should be provided as automated features of the system.
2. A *configuration management system* that works as an 'intelligent' function that knows different configurations of host and/or target platforms, and configures the software under development for each of the known configurations. This permits fast and controlled system portability from platform to platform.
3. An *object code library* that allows only the most recently verified and validated version of the code to be used in the development of a production system. Code that has not undergone V&V should not be allowed in the object code library.

Distributed computing.   Most corporate software development and support spans several different computer platforms such as mainframe clusters, multi-windowed workstations, desktop PCs, and remote supercomputers. But formal plans for controlling software quality in a distributed, multi-platform computing environment are rarely generated, even though they are desperately needed.

Assessing an organization's SQA function should include a test of their awareness of this problem. The Configuration Management Plan and the Software Quality Assurance Plan should address this issue, or at least refer to another document that does. There are three problems which should be addressed by such a plan:

1. How will software be distributed and controlled over multiple platforms and participating organizations?
2. How will shared software be integrated and maintained across several platforms and organiza-

tions?

3. How will shared software be screened against software viruses and worms?

Following are some recommendations about what to do and look for when auditing an organization involved in distributed software management:

1. Suggest that the organization create a plan for software version control over a distributed computing environment with multiple contributors.
2. Look for uniform coding standards for interface constraints and requirements, coding and commenting style, code structure, and other coding characteristics.
3. Check to see if there exists a formal program of regression testing for all code modifications. Make sure it includes V&V assessment for each of the supported platforms.
4. Suggest that line-by-line code reviews for safety-critical code are appropriate.

3. Summary and conclusions

Software quality assurance audits are becoming a common practice in corporations seeking to enter contractual relations with another organization, or just evaluating their own state of readiness. This paper was not meant to be a definitive answer or guide to doing SQA audits. Rather, it was intended to show an example of how it can be done, with an emphasis on metrics and measurement.

Following are some points to keep in mind when considering, preparing for, or conducting an SQA audit:

1. SQA audits should always be done by someone external to the organization being audited.
2. SQA audits should not be undertaken by anyone unfamiliar with the applicable standards. (An audit without standards makes no sense.)
3. The level of detail (depth) of an audit is solely dependent upon the allotted time. Given sufficient time, even line-by-line code reviews are possible and sometimes desirable.
4. SQA audits should include evaluations of an organization's software products, software processes, and software quality assurance functions.
5. The evaluation of software products should include analyses of the overall code structure and organization, maintainability aspects and code change traceability, traceability of the V&V process and documentation, compliance with applicable standards, and comparison to modern programming practices.
6. The evaluation of software process maturity should be based on an established framework and assessment technique, such as the SEI process maturity framework.
7. Assessing an organization's software quality assurance function requires looking at their software management administrative lines of control, documents comprising the software management plan, and mechanism for software configuration control, as well as the maturity of their in-place software development and maintenance processes.

References

IEEE (1986a) *IEEE Guide for Software Quality Assurance Planning*, IEEE Std. 983-1986, IEEE Computer Society, IEEE, Inc., 345 East 47th Street, New York, NY 10017.

IEEE (1986b) *IEEE Standard for Software Verification and Validation Plans*, IEEE Std. 1012-1986, IEEE Computer Society, IEEE, Inc., 345 East 47th Street, New York, NY 10017.

IEEE (1987a) *IEEE Guide to Software Configuration Management*, IEEE Std. 1042-1987, IEEE Computer Society, IEEE, Inc., 345 East 47th Street, New York, NY 10017.

IEEE (1987b) *IEEE Standard for Software Project Management Plans*, IEEE Std. 1063-1987, IEEE Computer Society, IEEE, Inc., 345 East 47th Street, New York, NY 10017.

IEEE (1989) *IEEE Standard for Software Quality Assurance Plans*, IEEE Std. 730-1989, IEEE Computer Society, IEEE, Inc., 345 East 47th Street, New York, NY 10017.

IEEE (1990a) *IEEE Standard Glossary of Software Engineering Terminology*, IEEE STd. 610. 12-1990, IEEE Computer Society, IEEE, Inc., 345 East 47th Street, New York, NY 10017.

IEEE (1990b) *IEEE Standard for Software Reviews and Audits*, IEEE Std. 1028-1088, IEEE Computer Society, IEEE, Inc., 345 East 47th Street, New York, NY 10017.

IEEE (1990c) *IEEE Standard for Software Configuration Management Plans*, IEEE Std. 828-1990, IEEE Computer Society, IEEE, Inc., 345 East 47th Street, New York, NY 10017.

ISO (1987) *Quality Management and Quality Assurance Standards*, ISO 9000 to 9004 (inclusive), ISO Technical Committee, International Organization for Standardization, ISO/TC 176, Case Postal 56, CH-1211, Geneva, Switzerland, 1987.

Humphrey, W. (1988) Characterizing the software process: A maturity framework. *IEEE Software*, 5(2), 73–79.

Humphrey, W. (1990) *Managing the Software Process* (Addison-Wesley, Reading, MA).

Pressman, R. (1992) *Software Engineering: A Practitioner's Approach*, 3rd edition (McGraw-Hill, New York).

SEI (1991) SEI Technical Reports #SEI-91-TR-24 and #SEI-91-TR-25, Carnegie Mellon University, Pittsburgh, PA 15213, USA.

SET Laboratories (1988) *PC-Metric*, SET Laboratories Inc., PO Box 868, Mulino, OR 97042.

MEASURING DYNAMIC PROGRAM COMPLEXITY

Relative complexity
combines the features of
many complexity metrics
to predict performance
and reliability.

JOHN C. MUNSON
University of West Florida
TAGHI M. KHOSHGOFTAAR
Florida Atlantic University

Too many performance and reliability models treat programs like black boxes whose internal attributes don't differ from one application to another. But a program's performance varies, depending on the complexity of the input. Software metrics are a good way to tell if a model accurately predicts performance. Since a program's performance depends on complexity, a metric must accurately measure complexity and the internal nature of a program.

Some people take metrics as a simple solution for understanding very complex problems, which is like pouring crude oil into a gas tank. Metrics require considerable refinement and distillation before you can use them in cost, performance, and reliability models. To use complexity metrics as predictors of program reliability and performance attributes, you must understand the program's underlying complexity domains.

But often the pressures to deliver a product dominate quality concerns. Selecting the right metrics and correctly interpreting the results take time and effort. There are more than a hundred or so metrics to choose from, and each, according to its author, clearly outperforms and eclipses the others. In truth, they measure many of the same things. Our research leads us to believe that existing metrics probably measure no more than four or five distinct

Reprinted from *IEEE Software*, Vol. 9, No. 6, Nov. 1992, pp. 48–55.

types of complexity. Assuming this is true, the best metric would represent as much variance in these underlying complexity domains as possible.

From a mathematical or statistical perspective, the problem with most metrics is that they are simple linear compounds of other metrics. For example, Maurice Halstead's program-vocabulary metric η is the sum of $\eta 1$ (unique operator count) and $\eta 2$ (unique operand count). If you know the two measures of $\eta 1$ and $\eta 2$ on a program module, their sum offers no additional information.

Another problem with metrics is that what they measure overlaps considerably. Consider lines of code and statement count. Clearly, the more lines of code a program has the more program statements it may contain. In some languages, this correspondence is one to one.

Some have tried to develop a metrics taxonomy to clarify the nature of the underlying complexity domains.[1] One classification, for example, divides metrics into those that measure static attributes (like lines of code) and those that measure dynamic attributes (like the number of control-structure executions at runtime). These taxonomies fail to reflect the actual variation of the metrics if applied to the development of mathematical models. Our technique shows the variability of a metric to reveal the complexity domains, ultimately representing complexity as a numerical value called relative complexity.

Relative complexity aggregates many similar metrics into a linear compound metric that describes a program. Since relative complexity is a static measure, we expand it by measuring relative complexity over time to find a program's functional complexity. And since relative complexity gives feedback on the same complexity domains that many other metrics do, developers can save time by choosing one metric to do the work of many.

Complexity metrics, such as relative complexity, are valuable only if they can describe ways a program can vary. In the past, complexity metrics have not been applied successfully to predictive models for software development, because different program modules have substantially different metric values. Relative complexity reflects each module's contribution to a system's total complexity,[2] so you can compare modules with different sets of values. For example, module A might have many lines of code and low cyclomatic complexity; whereas, module B might have fewer lines and higher cyclomatic complexity. These modules clearly differ in their complexity profiles, but are not directly comparable. If we can compare the programs by a single metric, we can identify complex programs, which require more development effort — and usually contain more errors — at an earlier stage of development.

A direct relationship between relative complexity and measures of program quality and performance[3,4] does not imply that complexity causes errors. Further, simplifying the structure of a program will not automatically decrease errors or changes. Simple or complex, bad code is bad code.

We believe, however, that all things being equal regarding programmer ability, relative complexity is a good predictor of poor-quality modules. We generally found that highly complex modules contain labyrinthine control structures and bushy logic. On the basis of this, we believe complexity metrics should enhance existing software reliability and performance models.

METRICS COLLECTED BY THE ADA METRIC ANALYZER

Statements	The number of executable statements in the unit, counted from the parse tree by counting each statement node.
η_1	The number of unique operators referenced in a unit, including all semantic and arithmetic operators and all procedures and functions.
N_1	The count of references to the operators in the unit.
η_2	The count of the number of unique operands referenced in the unit, including any object used by the operator.
N_2	The total count of all references to the operands in the unit.
$V(g)$	Thomas McCabe's cyclomatic complexity.
Size	The count of all the nodes in the parse tree generated by the parser.
MaxDepth	The length of the longest branch in the tree generated by the parser.
MaxOrder	The count of the largest number of edges from a single node in the parse tree.
MeanOrder	Calculated from the maximum order and the minimum order as $$\text{mean} = (\text{maximum} + \text{minimum})/2.$$
MaxLevel	The maximum level of nesting in the unit. Nesting is defined as a procedure/function defined within another procedure/function or a begin-end block defined within another begin-end block.
Inputs	The number of input parameters to the procedure or function. Any parameter declared as an input is counted as an input regardless of whether or not the value is referenced.
Outputs	The number of output parameters defined for a procedure or function, including the return value for a function.
InCalls	The number of times in the code that the procedure or function is called, including internal (recursive) and external calls.
OutCalls	The total number of calls (not just unique calls) made to other routines from this one.
BW	Les Balady's bandwidth metric. A value based on McCabe's cyclomatic complexity, adjusted for the added complexity of nested Ifs instead of just the number of Ifs in the code.

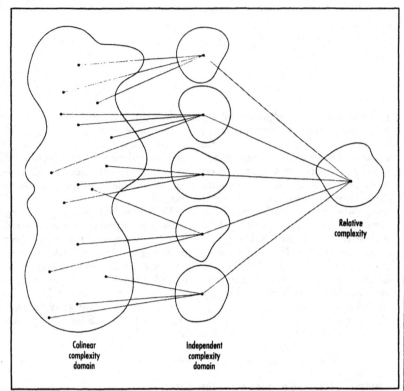

Figure 1. *Factor-analysis reduces 16 metrics to five complexity domains and ultimately to one metric, relative complexity.*

FACTOR ANALYSIS

Factor analysis aims to describe the relationships among variables in terms of a few underlying, but understandable, random factors. The factor model argues that, if you were to group variables so that all within the group are highly correlated but have relatively small correlations with variables in other groups, then in each group there is probably an underlying factor that is responsible for the correlation. You could characterize a program's complexity with a simple function of a small number of variables, each representing an uncorrelated measure of the program's attribute.

We used factor analysis to reduce 16 complexity metrics (described in the box on page 49) to a set of five independent complexity domains. (See Figure 1.) These domains are the basis for a conceptual model of complexity, consisting of the independent complexity domains of control, size, modularity, effort or information content, and data structure.[5] Any program could have characteristic measures on each of these domains. Consider, for example, a single program. We might measure 16 complexity metrics: c_1, c_2, c_3, ..., c_{16}. The factor model would map these

16 metrics onto five uncorrelated measures; f_1, ..., f_5.

The primary question in factor analysis is, is the data consistent with a prescribed structure? In this case, the prescribed structure is our five complexity domains. Once you have a factor pattern, you must interpret the common factors — which is the burden of the observer, not the factor analysis. Usually, you can easily observe the relationships of variables grouped by their association with a common factor and name this set. For example, in this study, Thomas McCabe's cyclomatic complexity and Thomas Gilb's logical complexity are distinctly associated with the control domain. Thus, factor analysis is a clustering technique.

Table 1 shows the results of applying factor analysis to the data from the 16 metrics produced by our Ada metric analyzer. The metric-analyzer system has 106 modules, and for each we obtained 16 raw metric values. Table 1's factor pattern shows the relationship between each of the raw metrics and the five domains produced by factor analysis. The larger the number, the stronger the relationship between a metric and a domain. For example, the cyclomatic complexity metric $V(g)$ has a

value of 0.951 on control and relatively small values elsewhere. Thus, it is most closely associated with control. The metrics and their associated domains are in boldface in the table.

We called the first domain in the table "control" because the metrics clustered together by factor analysis relate to program-control issues. These domain names are arbitrary, but we have seen similar patterns in other studies and believe that certain raw complexity metrics are associated with certain domains in an emerging complexity model.

Each of the five factors shown in Table 1 has an eigenvalue representing that domain's variance. The sum of all 16 resulting eigenvalues equals the number of metrics (16). Thus, the first factor, control, with its eigenvalue of 3.964, accounts for just under 25 percent of the total variance observed in the raw metrics.

MAPPING TO RELATIVE COMPLEXITY

Even after reducing 16 metrics to five domains, it is still difficult to compare modules. The next step is to map the five domains to a single domain, relative complexity, which characterizes the complexity of each module as a single value.

Factor analysis has another benefit besides clustering metrics: it yields a factor-score coefficient matrix. This matrix maps a set of raw, standardized, complexity metrics to the underlying factor domains. It is from these new measures of program complexity that we derived the relative complexity measure, ρ. For each program, we input a raw data vector of complexity metrics to the factor analysis, which converts it to a new standardized metrics vector. Then, for each standardized data vector, you can calculate a new vector of factor scores.

The relative complexity of the factored modules is

$$\rho_i = \lambda_1 f_{1i} + \lambda_2 f_{2i} \ldots + \lambda_m f_{mi}$$

where λ_j is the eigenvalue associated with the jth factor domain and f_{ji} is the factor score of the ith module on the jth factor. Each eigenvalue represents the relative contribution of its associated factor to the total variance explained by all factors. In essence, the relative-complexity metric is a weighted sum of the individual factor scores. In this context, the relative-complexity metric represents each raw complexity metric in proportion to the amount of unique variation it contributes.

Statistically, the underlying distribution of ρ's is both interesting and tractable. These represent observations from a normally distributed population with a zero mean and a variance of

$$V(\rho) = \sum_{i=1}^{m} \lambda_i^2$$

where m represents the number of factors in the factor pattern.

The actual values of the relative-complexity metric are not quite digestible by the typical metrics consumer because they range from negative to positive numbers. So we scaled the metric

$$\rho_i' = 10\frac{\rho_i}{\sqrt{V(\rho)}} + 50$$

so that it has a mean of 50 and a standard deviation of 10.

The relative-complexity metric classifies modules by complexity and provides a mechanism for ordering them. Our research has established that it is a stable measure. We examined its sensitivity for modules of sample programs from a larger population. We found the metric was not overly sensitive to subtle variations in complexity values of associated programs. If relative complexity is to be used for classification, it should be robust — and we believe it is.[6]

COMPLEXITY OVER TIME

The relationship between the relative-complexity metric and reliability and performance is significant for several reasons.

♦ You can collect these metrics early in the life cycle.

♦ To the extent that you can establish a definitive relationship between metrics and reliability and performance, you can use these metrics as adjuncts to reliability and performance modeling.

Reliability and quality models for a system under development must reflect the changing nature of the program, as designers subject it to various levels of testing. Programs tend to become more complex as systematic changes are made during test and validation. A mathematical reliability model must reflect this increasing complexity. A major problem in modeling failure, in terms of the extended reliability models we propose, is describing the nature of the failed system. A complete system might consist of a hundred or more program modules, each a candidate for modification during testing.

To describe a system's complexity at any point in time, we must know which version of each module was in the failed program. Consider a system composed of n modules, $m_1, m_2, m_3, \ldots, m_n$. Let m_j^i m_j^i represent the ith version of the jth module. So the first build of the system includes the set of modules

$$< m_1^1, m_2^1, m_3^1 \ldots m_n^1 >$$

You can represent this configuration more succinctly by simply recording the superscripts as vectors. Thus, versions of a sys-

Metric	Control	Size	Information content	Modularity	Data structure
$V(g)$	**0.951**	0.114	0.181	-0.041	-0.039
Statements	**0.949**	0.164	0.219	-0.058	-0.036
N_1	**0944**	0.141	0.200	-0.092	-0.072
OutCalls	**0.933**	0.141	0.021	0.036	-0.004
MaxDepth	-0.027	**0.971**	-0.020	-0.040	-0.042
η_2	0.059	**0.969**	0.076	-0.071	-0.004
N_2	0.244	**0.946**	0.065	-0.058	-0.020
Size	0.371	**0.908**	0.034	-0.034	-0.034
MaxOrder	0.062	0.084	**0.919**	0.132	-0.040
MeanOrder	0.058	0.085	**0.918**	0.133	-0.036
BW	0.248	-0.048	**0.857**	-0.101	0.084
η_1	0.258	0.021	**0.676**	-0.277	0.024
MaxLevel	0.089	-0.029	-0.161	**0.764**	-0.112
Outputs	-0.195	-0.118	0.168	**0.741**	0.162
InCalls	0.001	0.024	-0.182	-0.163	**0.791**
Inputs	-0.112	-0.106	0.247	0.244	**0.743**
Eigenvalues	3.964	3.733	3.162	1.370	1.240

TABLE 1
FACTOR PATTERN FOR METRIC ANALYZER

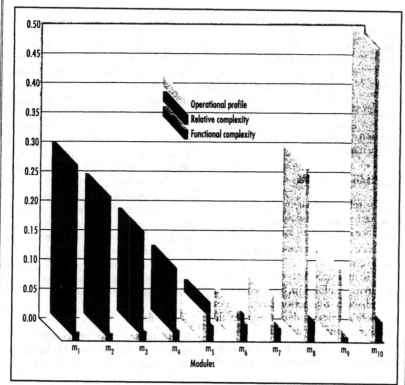

Figure 2. *Operational profile and relative complexity for low functional complexity.*

where v^n_i represents an element from the configuration vector v^n described earlier.

DYNAMIC COMPLEXITY

Unlike mechanical or electronic systems, like a jet engine, in which all components operate together, we can't test a software system simply by activating it. Software systems have many independent components, and different inputs take distinct paths through them. Hence, as stated earlier, the dynamic complexity of the system depends on input. The operational or functional complexity of the system also changes in response to varying input. Given the association between module complexity and errors, it follows that as applications change over time, so too will the likelihood of faults.

In software development, an operational profile describes the set of interactions among modules and the probabilities that they will occur. When a software system runs an application, an operational profile is represented by the probabilities, $p^i_1, p^i_2, ..., p^i_n$. For our purposes, p_i represents the probability that the ith module is executing at any moment.

The functional complexity φ of the system running that application is then

$$\varphi = \sum_{i=1}^{n} p_i \rho_i$$

This is simply the expected value of relative complexity under a particular operational profile. We expect the operational profile for a program to change over time. In other words, for each time interval i, an operational profile exists represented by the probabilities $p^i_1, p^i_2, ... p^i_n$ .. This is distinctly the case during testing, when designers subject the program to numerous test suites to exercise different functions. Unfortunately, this is generally the same time that reliability modeling data is collected.

Given the relationship between complexity and embedded errors, the failure intensity should rise as the functional complexity increases. For the ith time interval, the functional complexity of the system may be represented by

tem under development might look like

$$v^1 = 1,1,1,...,1$$
$$v^2 = 2,2,1,...,1$$
$$v^3 = 2,3,1,...,1$$
$$v^4 = 3,3,2,...,2$$
$$\vdots$$

So the ith entry in the vector v^n would represent the version number of the ith module in the nth build of the system.

Equally important to our efforts to predict complexity is capturing complexity metrics during development. Our continuing research in complexity metrics leads us to believe that metric analyzers must be refined to improve our ability to capture data during development. The relative-complexity metric can be enhanced with augmented coverage of the complexity domains.

We have devised a way to compute the relative complexity of various releases of a system. We first compute relative complexity for the modules in the first build of a software system v^1. The factor-score coefficient matrix of the modules in this first system does not change subsequently, but serves as a baseline for measuring changes in program complexity.

Associated with the ith program module m^1_i at the first build of a program is a corresponding relative complexity value of ρ^1_i. By definition, the relative complexity ρ of the program system will be

$$\rho^1 = \sum_i \rho_i v^1_i = 0$$

at this first build. As time progresses, system complexity tends to rise.[7] Thus, the relative complexity of the nth version of a system may be represented by a nondecreasing function of a module's relative complexity as follows:

$$\rho^1 = \sum_i \rho_i v^1_i \geq 0$$

$$\varphi_i = \sum_{j=1}^{n} p_j^1 \rho_j^{v_j^1}$$

under the assumption that a new system build at the end of the ith time interval fixes a program error. If you choose an application so that the probability of running a complex module is high, the functional complexity will be large. Figures 2 and 3 show this.

Figure 2 shows an operational profile of a program in which most of the time is spent in modules of relatively low complexity. Figure 3 shows an operational profile of a program in which a good deal of time is spent in modules of relatively high complexity. While the relative complexities of the systems in Figures 2 and 3 are identical, their operational profiles are very different.

PERFORMANCE AND FUNCTIONAL COMPLEXITY

We plan to add more complexity domains to the underlying complexity domain model to represent even more aspects of variability. Some of the newly emerging domains, such as control-flow and data-structure complexity, clearly relate to system performance. For example, if you use lines of code to measure complexity, you might mistakenly appraise two programs, one of 20 lines with two nested loops and one of 100 lines with no loops. The 20-line program would probably run longer, but the lines-of-code metric wouldn't catch that. If you add a second metric, the cycles in the control-flow graph, you can tell more about the programs.

There is also a strong relationship between measures of system performance and functional complexity.[8] That is, as a program's functional complexity increases because of the nature of the input, its processing capability decreases. For example, we ran the pretty-print program from the Ada software repository against three inputs: our metric analyzer, the program itself, and the style-checker from the Software Engineering Institute.

At the outset, we computed the relative complexity of each module in the pretty-print system. We then ran pretty-print against the three test Ada programs to ob-

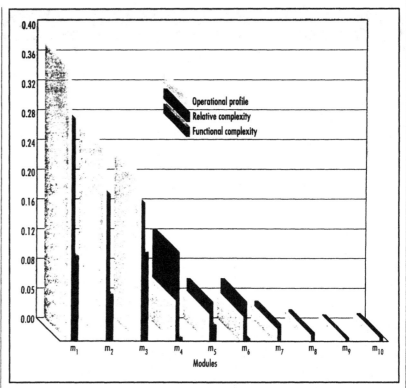

Figure 3. Operational profile and relative complexity for high functional complexity.

tain its operational profile. With the operational profile and the relative complexity of each module, we calculated the functional complexity of each module on each of the three inputs. Table 2 shows these values ordered by the relative complexity of the modules.

The values presented in Table 2 represent only a subset of the programs, whose functional complexity is generally greater than 0.25. Even with this subset, we can make some interesting observations.

For example, module 35 has a relative complexity of 67.73. This is almost two standard deviations above the mean of 50. For each of the three input scenarios, the program spent about one third of its time executing that module as evidenced by its profile values. This module clearly has the greatest functional complexity of any of the modules. The functional complexity of each of the executions was above a value of 59. This means that the dominant modules in the operational profile

were almost one standard deviation above the mean of 50. This program is clearly running its more complex modules for this input.

As we ran this program against the three test Ada programs, its functional complexity changed to fit the program it was processing. As functional complexity increased, processing (in CPU time per line) also increased. We found very high correlations between functional complexity and these processing times as an arbitrary measure of system performance.

The important point here is that the variation in a system's performance is not static. A system's performance does not decrease strictly because of the workload. Rather, performance degradation is strongly related to the functional complexity of the task. This being the case, we should be able to model aspects of performance early in the life cycle to anticipate performance variability before a system begins service.

TABLE 2
RELATIVE COMPLEXITY AND FUNCTIONAL COMPLEXITY FOR THREE ENVIRONMENTS

Module	ρ	System 1		System 2		System 3	
		φ	Profile	φ	Profile	φ	Profile
1	43.58	0.23	0.005	0.31	0.007	0.42	0.009
2	45.55	0.66	0.015	0.36	0.007	0.83	0.018
3	46.11	1.38	0.030	1.55	0.033	1.78	0.038
4	46.36	0.26	0.006	0.13	0.002	0.25	0.005
5	46.56	0.40	0.009	0.16	0.003	0.31	0.006
6	46.70	0.48	0.010	0.43	0.009	0.50	0.010
7	46.85	0.14	0.003	0.11	0.002	0.13	0.002
8	47.35	4.84	0.102	4.18	0.088	4.34	0.091
9	47.39	0.35	0.008	0.25	0.005	0.25	0.005
10	47.64	1.04	0.022	0.83	0.017	1.01	0.021
11	47.74	2.79	0.059	2.36	0.049	2.38	0.049
12	48.33	0.28	0.006	0.15	0.003	0.21	0.004
13	48.56	0.56	0.012	0.33	0.006	0.48	0.009
14	48.69	0.21	0.004	0.11	0.002	0.13	0.002
15	48.77	2.03	0.042	2.03	0.041	2.29	0.047
16	49.18	0.36	0.007	0.34	0.006	0.55	0.011
17	49.44	0.24	0.005	0.27	0.005	0.29	0.006
18	50.64	0.42	0.008	0.43	0.008	0.98	0.013
19	50.72	0.45	0.009	0.29	0.005	0.49	0.009
20	51.97	2.02	0.039	1.94	0.037	2.25	0.043
21	53.14	0.98	0.019	1.02	0.019	1.04	0.019
22	53.60	0.41	0.008	0.40	0.007	0.41	0.007
23	54.50	0.20	0.004	0.16	0.002	0.26	0.004
24	54.88	0.29	0.005	0.27	0.004	0.29	0.005
25	55.85	0.23	0.004	0.27	0.004	0.42	0.007
26	56.45	0.26	0.005	0.27	0.004	0.31	0.005
27	56.96	0.69	0.012	0.75	0.013	0.86	0.015
28	57.61	0.98	0.017	0.79	0.013	1.07	0.018
29	58.91	0.39	0.007	0.35	0.006	0.39	0.006
30	59.30	0.38	0.007	0.34	0.005	0.36	0.006
31	62.02	0.30	0.005	0.36	0.005	0.40	0.006
32	62.75	1.51	0.024	1.63	0.025	1.76	0.028
33	65.32	1.58	0.024	1.06	0.016	1.28	0.019
34	66.18	0.96	0.015	0.76	0.011	0.79	0.011
35	67.73	21.71	0.321	24.71	0.364	25.11	0.370
36	68.73	3.56	0.052	2.49	0.036	2.75	0.040
37	75.23	0.77	0.010	0.84	0.011	1.44	0.019
38	96.31	2.93	0.031	1.51	0.015	1.89	0.019

Complexity metrics provide substantial information about the differences in the systems being modeled, and metric models will probably be integrated into extensions of existing reliability and performance models. The key to the eventual success of such models lies not in the way they are formulated, but in how accurately they predict system behavior. We are preparing to use our methods to measure the reliability of the space shuttle's on-board flight software.

Metric models generally fail to account for at least two things. Systems become more complex over time, both during test and validation and in maintenance, and the dynamic complexity of a system at any moment is a function of its operational profile. Thus, a program may exercise its most complex or its least complex functions, depending on the input.

Performance modeling aims to predict system behavior accurately in response to varying input. A major problem is that software undergoes several stages of testing during development. At each stage, corrections and modifications are made with the hope of increasing its reliability. But a modification, or series of modifications, could lead to a deterioration in performance. The important statistical issue is how to model and describe changes in performance as a result of the modification.

On the basis of our recent research, we believe that relative complexity is a stable and reasonable tool for comparing and classifying programs. Unlike other metrics, relative complexity simultaneously combines all attribute dimensions of all complexity metrics. We have established that complexity metrics, including the relative-complexity metric, are closely associated with quality measures. By combining the set of complexity metrics for each life-cycle phase into a single, comprehensive metric, we can determine quality measures for a final program product using complexity measures from the design or possibly even the specification phases.[9]

Perhaps the most important feature of the relative-complexity metric is that you can generalize it. As more complexity metrics are developed, the relative-complexity metric can incorporate them. We have concluded that there are relatively few domains in the complexity problem space. If raw complexity metrics are suitably chosen to reflect all aspects of the underlying complexity domains, then the concept of relative complexity should provide a reasonable means of ordering programs by complexity. We realize, however, that the relative-complexity metric represents a static measure of a dynamic system. Functional complexity, on the other hand, measures a system in operation, which is crucial to getting an accurate prediction of a dynamic system's complexity. ◆

ACKNOWLEDGMENTS

This work was supported in part by a research grant from the State of Florida High Technology and Industry Council Applied Grants Program.

REFERENCES

1. V. Cote et al., "Software Metrics: An Overview of Recent Results," *J. Systems and Software*, Mar. 1988, pp. 121-131.
2. J.C. Munson and T.M. Khoshgoftaar, "Applications of a Relative Complexity Metric for Software Project Management," *J. Systems and Software*, Vol. 12, No. 3, 1990, pp. 283-291.
3. T.M. Khoshgoftaar and J.C. Munson, "Predicting Software Development Errors Using Complexity Metrics," *IEEE J. Selected Areas in Communications*, Feb. 1990, pp. 253-261.
4. J.C. Munson and T. M. Khoshgoftaar, "Regression Modeling of Software Quality: An Empirical Investigation," *J. Information and Software Technology*, Mar. 1990, pp. 105-114.
5. J.C. Munson and T.M. Khoshgoftaar, "The Dimensionality of Program Complexity," *Proc. Int'l Conf. Software Engineering*, IEEE CS Press, Los Alamitos, Calif., 1989, pp. 245-253.
6. J.C. Munson and T.M. Khoshgoftaar, "The Relative Software Complexity Metric: A Validation Study," *Proc. Conf. Software Engineering*, Cambridge University Press, Cambridge, UK, 1990, pp. 89-102.
7. R.I. Leach, "Software Metrics and Software Maintenance," *J. Software Maintenance*, June 1990, pp. 133-142.
8. W.H. Shaw et al., "A Software Science Model of Compile Time," *IEEE Trans. Software Eng.*, 1989, pp. 543-549.
9. D.N. Card and W.W. Agresti, "Measuring Software Design Complexity," *J. Systems and Software*, June 1988, pp. 185-197.

Address questions about this article to Munson at the CS Division, University of West Florida, Pensacola, FL 32514; Internet jmunson@dcs119.dcsnod.uwf.edu; or to Khoshgoftaar at the CS and Eng. Dept., Florida Atlantic University, Boca Raton, FL 33431; Internet taghi@cse.fau.edu.

Using Metrics to Evaluate Software System Maintainability

Don Coleman and Dan Ash, Hewlett-Packard

Bruce Lowther, Micron Semiconductor

Paul Oman, University of Idaho

With the maturation of software development practices, software maintainability has become one of the most important concerns of the software industry. In his classic book on software engineering, Fred Brooks[1] claimed, "The total cost of maintaining a widely used program is typically 40 percent or more of the cost of developing it." Parikh[2] had a more pessimistic view, claiming that 45 to 60 percent is spent on maintenance. More recently, two recognized experts, Corbi[3] and Yourdon,[4] claimed that software maintainability is one of the major challenges for the 1990s.

These statements were validated recently by Dean Morton, executive vice president and chief operating officer of Hewlett-Packard, who gave the keynote address at the 1992 Hewlett-Packard Software Engineering Productivity Conference. Morton stated that Hewlett-Packard (HP) currently has between 40 and 50 million lines of code under maintenance and that 60 to 80 percent of research and development personnel are involved in maintenance activities. He went on to say that 40 to 60 percent of the cost of production is now maintenance expense.

The intent of this article is to demonstrate how automated software maintainability analysis can be used to guide software-related decision making. We have applied metrics-based software maintainability models to 11 industrial software systems and used the results for fact-finding and process-selection decisions. The results indicate that automated maintainability assessment can be used to support buy-versus-build decisions, pre- and post-reengineering analysis, subcomponent quality analysis, test resource allocation, and the prediction and targeting of defect-prone subcomponents. Further, the analyses can be conducted at various levels of granularity. At the component level, we can use these models to monitor changes to the system as they occur and to predict fault-prone components. At the file level, we can use them to identify subsystems that are not well organized and should be targeted for perfective maintenance. The results can also be used to determine when a system should be reengineered. Finally, we can use these models to compare whole systems. Comparing a known-quality system to a third-party system can provide a basis for deciding whether to purchase the third-party system or develop a similar system internally.

Reprinted from *Computer*, Vol. 27, No. 8, Aug. 1994, pp. 44–49.

Recent studies in metrics for software maintainability and quality assessment have demonstrated that the software's characteristics, history, and associated environment(s) are all useful in measuring the quality and maintainability of that software.[5-7] Hence, measurement of these characteristics can be incorporated into software maintainability assessment models, which can then be applied to evaluate industrial software systems. Successful models should identify and measure what most practitioners view as important components of software maintainability.

A comparison of five models

We recently analyzed five methods for quantifying software maintainability from software metrics. The definition, derivation, and validation of these five methods has been documented elsewhere.[7] Only a synopsis of the five methods is presented here:

- *Hierarchical multidimensional assessment models* view software maintainability as a hierarchical structure of the source code's attributes.[6]
- *Polynomial regression models* use regression analysis as a tool to explore the relationship between software maintainability and software metrics.[8]
- *An aggregate complexity measure* gauges software maintainability as a function of entropy.[5]
- *Principal components analysis* is a statistical technique to reduce collinearity between commonly used complexity metrics in order to identify and reduce the number of components used to construct regression models.[7]
- *Factor analysis* is another statistical technique wherein metrics are orthogonalized into unobservable underlying factors, which are then used to model system maintainability.[5]

Tests of the models indicate that all five compute reasonably accurate maintainability scores from calculations based on simple (existing) metrics. All five models and the validation data were presented to HP Corporate Engineering managers in the spring and summer of 1993. At that time it was decided that the hierarchical multidimensional assessment and the polynomial regression models would be pursued as simple mechanisms for maintainability assessment that could be used by maintenance engineers in a variety of locations. HP wanted quick, easy-to-calculate indices that "line" engineers could use at their desks. The following subsections explain how these methods were applied to industrial systems.

HPMAS: A hierarchical multidimensional assessment model. HPMAS is HP's software maintainability assessment system based on a hierarchical organization of a set of software metrics. For this particular type of maintainability problem, Oman and Hagemeister[6] have suggested a hierarchical model dividing maintainability into three underlying dimensions or attributes:

(1) The *control structure*, which includes characteristics pertaining to the way the program or system is decomposed into algorithms.

(2) The *information structure*, which includes characteristics pertaining to the choice and use of data structure and dataflow techniques.

(3) *Typography, naming, and commenting*, which includes characteristics pertaining to the typographic layout, and naming and commenting of code.

We can easily define or identify separate metrics that can measure each dimension's characteristics. Once the metrics have been defined and/or identified, an "index of maintainability" for each dimension can be defined as a function of those metrics. Finally, the three dimension scores can be combined for a total maintainability index for the system. For our work, we used existing metrics to calculate a deviation from acceptable ranges and then used the inverse of that deviation as an index of quality.

Most metrics have an optimum range of values within which the software is more easily maintained. A method called *weight and trigger-point-range analysis* is

---

Software maintenance definitions

Definitions for software "maintenance" and "maintainability" are many, but they are fairly consistent in scope and intent. Here are the IEEE standard definitions:[1]

Maintenance: The process of modifying a software system or component after delivery to correct faults, improve performance or other attributes, or adapt to a changed environment.

Maintainability: The ease with which a software system or component can be modified to correct faults, improve performance or other attributes, or adapt to a changed environment.

Consistent with these definitions, the maintenance process can be divided into three areas of focus:[1]

Corrective maintenance: Maintenance performed to correct faults in hardware or software.

Adaptive maintenance: Software maintenance performed to make a computer program usable in a changed environment.

Perfective maintenance: Software maintenance performed to improve the performance, maintainability, or other attributes of a computer program.

Reference

1. IEEE Std. 610.12-1990, "Glossary of Software Engineering Terminology," in *Software Engineering Standards Collection*, IEEE CS Press, Los Alamitos, Calif., Order No. 1048-06T, 1993.

used to quantify maintainability by calculating a "degree of fit" from a table of acceptable metric ranges. When the metric value falls outside the optimum range, it indicates that maintainability is lower; hence, there is a deviation (or penalty) on the component's contribution to maintainability. The optimum range value, called the *trigger point range*, reflects the "goodness" of the program style. For example, if the acceptable range for *average lines of code* (aveLOC) is between 5 and 75, values falling below 5 and above 75 serve as the trigger points for what would be classified as poor style. If the measured average lines of code value lies within the acceptable range, there is no penalty. If the metric value falls outside the trigger point range but is close to the bounds (trigger points), we then apply a proportional deviation, which can run up to 100 percent (the maximum penalty). The weighted deviation is computed by multiplying the calculated deviation by a weighted value between zero and one, inclusive. The metric attributes are combined based on the assumption that the dimensional maintainability is 100 percent (highly maintainable); they are then reduced by the deviation percentage of each metric. Dimension maintainability is calculated as

$$DM_{dimension} = 1 - \frac{\sum w_i D_i}{\sum w_i}$$

The overall maintainability index is the product of the three dimensions. Multiplying the three dimensions' maintainability gives a lower overall maintainability than averaging does, which underscores the fact that deviation in one aspect of maintainability will hinder other aspects of the maintenance effort, thus reducing maintainability of the entire system.

HPMAS was calibrated against HP engineers' subjective evaluation of 16 software systems, as measured by an abridged version of the AFOTEC (Air Force Operational Test and Evaluation Center) software quality assessment instrument.[9] HPMAS maintainability indices range from 0 to 100, with 100 representing excellent maintainability.

Polynomial assessment tools. Regression analysis is a statistical method for predicting values of one or more response (dependent) variables from a collection of predictor (independent) variables. For purposes of software maintainability assessment, we need to create a polynomial equation by which a system's maintainability is expressed as a function of the associated metric attributes. We have used this technique to develop a set of polynomial maintainability assessment models.[8] These models were developed as simple software maintainability assessment methods that could be calculated from existing metrics. Since these models were intended for use by maintenance practitioners "in the trenches," the models were again calibrated to HP engineers' subjective evaluation of the software as measured by the abridged version of the AFOTEC software quality assessment instrument.[9] That is, the independent variables used in our models were a host of 40 complexity metrics, and the dependent variable was the (numeric) result of the abridged AFOTEC survey.

Approximately 50 regression models were constructed in an attempt to identify simple models that could be calculated from existing tools and still be generic enough to apply to a wide range of software systems. In spite of the current research trend away from the use of Halstead metrics, all tests clearly indicated that Halstead's volume and effort metrics were the best predictors of maintainability for the HP test data. The regression model that seemed most applicable was a four-metric polynomial based on Halstead's effort metric and on metrics measuring extended cyclomatic complexity, lines of code, and number of comments:

Maintainability = 171
$- 3.42 \times \ln(aveE)$
$- 0.23 \times aveV(g')$
$- 16.2 \times \ln(aveLOC) + aveCM$

where *aveE*, *aveV(g')*, *aveLOC*, and *aveCM* are the average effort, extended V(G), average lines of code, and number of comments per submodule (function or procedure) in the software system.

Preliminary results indicated that this model was too sensitive to large numbers of comments. That is, large comment blocks, especially in small modules, unduly inflated the resulting maintainability indices. To rectify this, we replaced the *aveCM* component with percent comments (*perCM*), and a ceiling function was placed on the factor to limit its contribution to a maximum value of 50.[10] Also, because there has been much discussion of the nonmonotonicity of Halstead's effort metric (it is not a nondecreasing function under the concatenation operation), we reconstructed the model using Halstead's volume metric instead. Thus, the final four-metric polynomial now used in our work is

Maintainability = 171
$-5.2 \times \ln(aveVol)$
$-0.23 \times ave\ V(g')$
$-16.2 \times \ln(aveLOC)$
$+(50 \times \sin(\sqrt{2.46 \times perCM}))$

This polynomial has been compared to the original model using the same validation data. The average residual between the effort-based model and the volume-based model is less than 1.4.

Applying the models to industrial software

A software maintainability model is only useful if it can provide developers and maintainers in an industrial setting with more information about the system. Hence, the data used to test and validate our models consisted entirely of genuine industrial systems provided by Hewlett-Packard and Defense Department contractors. The examples are presented here to show how these models can aid software maintainers in their decision making. The data presented in the following subsections is real and unaltered, except that proprietary information has been removed.

Using HPMAS in a pre/postanalysis of maintenance changes. Over several years of software maintenance, systems tend to degrade as the number of "patches" to them increases. To combat this increase in entropy, a pre/postanalysis can be used to ensure that the maintainability of a system does not decline after each maintenance modification. To exemplify this, an existing HP subsystem, written in C for the Unix platform, was analyzed using HPMAS prior to perfective maintenance modification. Once the modification was complete, the modified subsystem was analyzed by HPMAS and the results were compared to determine if there was any detectable change in the maintainability of the subsystem. Table 1 contains an overall analysis of the changes made to the subsystem.

The HPMAS maintainability index in Table 1 shows that the maintainability of the subsystem was essentially unchanged (a 0.4 percent increase) even though the perfective maintenance changes had actually increased the complexity of the system. Specifically, 149 lines of code, two modules, and 29 branches were added to the system. Although the maintenance engineer denied that functionality increased, a visual inspection of the source code revealed that increased error checking had, in fact, been added to the code. For example, the original version of module Function_F, shown in section 2 of Table 2, contained 12 error-screening checks, while the modified version contained 16 error checks. (Throughout this discussion, function names have been changed to protect Hewlett-Packard proprietary information.)

Table 2 contains a module-by-module comparison of the pre- and post-test maintainability indices for the subsystem. The table is divided into four sections to demonstrate the distribution of maintenance changes. The first section of the table contains the modules that were not modified during the maintenance task. The second section contains modules that were slightly modified but which retained their original module names. The third section contains modules that have been modified and renamed. (The modules in this section were matched by visually inspecting the post-test system to identify any reused comments, variables, or control flow used in the pretest system.) The last sec-

tion contains modules in the pretest system that could not be matched to any module in the post-test system. (Visual inspection of the code revealed that the post-test components contained reused code from the pretest system, but they could not be matched to any one post-test component.) Thus, the last section represents an area of the program where the subsystem was repartitioned, resulting in a new subsystem organization.

This type of postmaintenance analysis can provide the maintenance staff with a wealth of information about the target

system. For example, section 1 of Table 2 consists of unchanged components with relatively high HPMAS maintainability scores. If these components remain unchanged over several maintenance modifications, they might be considered for a reusability library. Components in the second section address the system goal but have not yet reached the refinement of those in the first section. Their HPMAS metrics are generally lower than those in the first section, and they have changed less than ± 5 percent from the pre- to postanalysis.

Table 1. Comparing pre- and post-test results shows how much maintenance modification changes a subsystem.

	Pretest	Post-test	Percent Change
Lines of code	1,086.00	1,235.00	13.4
Number of modules	13.00	15.00	15.4
Total V(g′)	226.00	255.00	12.8
HPMAS maintainability index	88.17	88.61	0.4

Table 2. Module-by-module comparison of pre- and postanalysis results.

Section	Pretest Analysis		Post-test Analysis		Percent Change
	Name	Metric	Name	Metric	
1	Function_A	93.83	Function_A	93.83	0.0
	Function_B	93.82	Function_B	93.82	0.0
	Function_C	92.96	Function_C	92.96	0.0
	Function_D	84.41	Function_D	84.41	0.0
2	Function_E	86.24	Function_E	89.00	3.2
	Function_F	65.58	Function_F	67.27	2.6
	Function_G	88.06	Function_G	85.83	−2.5
3	Function_H	78.41	Function_H′	83.05	5.9
	Function_I	72.85	Function_I′	63.15	−13.3
	Function_J	67.75	Function_J′	66.43	−1.9
	Function_K	68.83	Function_K′	66.67	−3.1
4	Function_L	80.68			
	Function_M	78.78			
			Function_N	85.08	
			Function_O	80.75	
			Function_P	79.68	
			Function_Q	69.68	

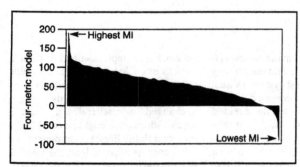

Figure 1. Maintainability index plot for 714 files that make up a software system with 236,000 lines of code.

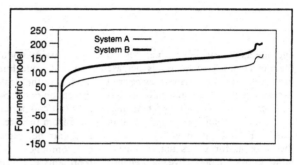

Figure 2. Using the four-metric model to compare maintainability of two software systems.

The last two sections contain the most extensive changes to the subsystem. Components in these two sections represent a large burden to the maintainer, essentially representing a repartition of the problem. This is evidenced by the renaming of components, lower HPMAS metric values, and unmatchable pre- and post-test components. The maintenance engineer renamed all of the components in section 3 (presumably because he thought the original names did not adequately describe them) and substantively changed their functionality. Section 4 contains old components that could not be matched to components in the new system. They represent the largest burden to the maintenance effort because (1) the new components are untested, (2) the structure of the system has changed, requiring all documentation and diagrams for this system to be updated, and (3) all maintainers who were familiar with the pretest system are unfamiliar with the post-test system.

Using polynomials to rank-order module maintainability. To detect differences in subsystem maintainability, the four-metric polynomial was applied to a large third-party software application sold to HP. The system consists of 236,000 lines of C source code written for a Unix platform. The software complexity metrics were calculated on a file-by-file basis, and a maintainability index was calculated for each file.

The file-by-file analysis of the 714 files constituting the software system is shown in Figure 1. This histogram shows the maintainability (polynomial) index for each file, ordered from highest to lowest. The index for each file is represented by the top of each vertical bar; for negative indices, the value is represented by the bottom of the bar. The maintainability analysis for this system showed that the file maintainability scores (or indices) range from a high of 183 to a low of –91.

All components above the 85 maintainability index are highly maintainable, components between 85 and 65 are moderately maintainable, and components below 65 are "difficult to maintain." The dotted line indicates the *quality cutoff* established by Hewlett-Packard at index level 65.[10] Although these three quality categories are used by HP, they represent only a good "rule of thumb."

The figure shows that 364 files, or roughly 50 percent of the system, fall below the quality-cutoff index, strongly suggesting that this system is difficult to modify and maintain. Prior to our analysis, the HP maintenance engineers had stated that the system was *very* difficult to maintain and modify. Further analysis proved

that change-prone and defect-prone subsystem components (files) could be targeted using the ranked order of the maintainability indices.

In a subsequent study, a similar analysis was conducted on another third-party subsystem and compared against a maintainability index profile for a proprietary HP system (an example is shown in the next subsection). Based on that comparison, HP decided to purchase the third-party software.

Using polynomials to compare software systems. The polynomial models can also be used to compare whole software systems. We analyzed two software systems that were similar in size, number of modules, platform, and language (see Table 3).

The first system, A, is a third-party acquisition that had been difficult to maintain. (Again, the names of the two systems have been changed to protect proprietary information.) The second system, B, had been cited in internal Hewlett-Packard documentation as an excellent example of state-of-the-art software development. The four-metric polynomial model was used to compare the two systems to see the differences in their maintainability profiles. HP maintenance engineers, already experienced with the systems, were asked to comment on the maintainability of each system.

The results of the polynomial model shown in Table 3 corroborate the engineers' informal evaluation of the two software systems. The A system yielded a maintainability index of 89; while clearly above our acceptability criteria, it is considerably lower than the 123 maintainability index calculated for system B. This corresponds to the mediocre evaluation A received from the Hewlett-Packard engineers and the high praise B received from the engineers working on that system. We performed a more

Table 3. A polynomial comparison of two systems corroborated an informal evaluation by engineers.

	A	B
HP evaluation	Low	High
Platform	Unix	Unix
Language	C	C
Total LOC	236,275	243,273
Number of modules	3,176	3,097
Overall maintainability index	89	123

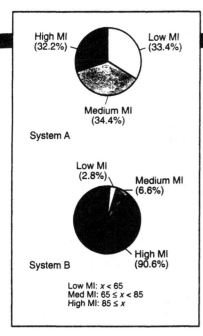

High MI
(32.2%)

Low MI
(33.4%)

Medium MI
(34.4%)

System A

Low MI
(2.8%)

Medium MI
(6.6%)

High MI
(90.6%)

System B

Low MI: $x < 65$
Med MI: $65 \le x < 85$
High MI: $85 \le x$

Figure 3. Comparison of two systems, with high-, medium-, and low-maintenance lines of code expressed in percentages.

granular analysis by calculating the polynomial on a module-by-module basis. Figure 2 shows a plot of the ordered results. The B system (the thick line) consistently scored higher than the A system for all but one module. The significant gap between the two plots accentuates the fact that the A system is less maintainable.

Figure 3 contains two pie charts showing the distribution of lines of code in the three maintainability classifications (high, medium, and low). The upper pie chart, representing the A system, illustrates the nearly equal distribution of code into the three classifications. The lower pie chart, representing the B system, shows that a significant portion of this system falls in the high maintainability classification. The B system contains only 15 components, representing 2.8 percent of the lines of code, that fall below the quality cutoff. The A system, on the other hand, contains 228 components, representing 33.4 percent of the lines of code, that fall below the quality cutoff. Hence, using lines of code to compare the two systems reveals that although their overall maintainability index is adequate, the B system is likely to be much easier to maintain than the A system. This result corresponds to the Hewlett-Packard evaluations.

To date we have conducted an automated software maintainability analysis on 11 software systems. In each case, the results from our analysis corresponded to the maintenance engineers' "intuition" about the maintainability of the (sub)system components. But in every case, the automated analysis provided additional data that was useful in supporting or providing credence for the experts' opinions.

Our analyses have assisted in buy-versus-build decisions, targeting subcomponents for perfective maintenance, controlling software quality and entropy over several versions of the same software, identifying change-prone subcomponents, and assessing the effects of reengineering efforts.

Software maintainability is going to be a considerable challenge for many years to come. The systems being maintained are becoming increasingly complex, and a growing proportion of software development staff is participating in the maintenance of industrial software systems. Our results indicate that automated maintainability analysis can be conducted at the component level, the subsystem level, and the whole system level to evaluate and compare software. By examining industrial systems at different levels, a wealth of information about a system's maintainability can be obtained. Although these models are not perfect, they demonstrate the utility of such models. The point is that a good model can help maintainers guide their efforts and provide them with much needed feedback. Before developers can claim that they are building maintainable systems, there must be some way to measure maintainability. ∎

References

1. F.P. Brooks, *The Mythical Man–Month: Essays on Software Engineering*, Addison–Wesley, Reading, Mass., 1982.

2. G. Parikh and N. Zvegintzov, *Tutorial on Software Maintenance*, IEEE CS Press, Los Alamitos, Calif., Order No. 453, 1983.

3. T. Corbi, "Program Understanding: Challenge for the 1990s," *IBM Systems J.*, Vol. 28, No. 2, 1989, pp. 294-306.

4. E. Yourdon, *The Rise and Fall of the American Programmer*, Yourdon Press Computing Series, Trenton, N.J., 1992.

5. J. Munson and T. Khoshgoftaar, "The Detection of Fault-Prone Programs," *IEEE Trans. Software Eng.*, Vol. 18, No. 5, May 1992, pp. 423-433.

6. P. Oman and J. Hagemeister, "Metrics for Assessing Software System Maintainability," *Proc. Conf. Software Maintenance*, IEEE CS Press, Los Alamitos, Calif., Order No. 2980-02T, 1992, pp. 337-344.

7. F. Zhuo et al., "Constructing and Testing Software Maintainability Assessment Models," *Proc. First Int'l Software Metrics Symp.*, IEEE CS Press, Los Alamitos, Calif., Order No. 3740-02T, 1993, pp. 61–70.

8. P. Oman and J. Hagemeister, "Construction and Testing of Polynomials Predicting Software Maintainability," *J. of Systems and Software*, Vol. 24, No. 3, Mar. 1994, pp. 251-266.

9. *Software Maintainability — Evaluation Guide*, AFOTEC Pamphlet 800-2 (updated), HQ Air Force Operational Test and Evaluation Center, Kirkland Air Force Base, N.M., Vol. 3, 1989.

10. D. Coleman, "Assessing Maintainability," *Proc. 1992 Software Eng. Productivity Conf.*, Hewlett-Packard, Palo Alto, Calif., 1992, pp. 525–532.

Don Coleman is a project manager with Hewlett-Packard Corporate Engineering. He works in the area of software maintainability assessment and defect analysis.

Dan Ash is a firmware engineer for Hewlett-Packard Boise Printer Division. He specializes in font technology and embedded systems.

Bruce Lowther is a software engineer at Micron Semiconductor. He works in object-oriented development, focusing on software reusability and software quality. He is a member of the IEEE Computer Society.

Paul Oman is an associate professor of computer science at the University of Idaho where he directs the Software Engineering Test Lab. He is a member of the IEEE Computer Society.

Readers can contact the authors through Paul Oman, Software Engineering Test Lab, University of Idaho, Moscow, Idaho 83843, e-mail oman@cs.uidaho.edu.

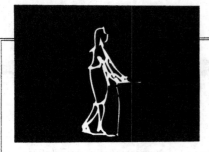

Improving Software Maintenance at Martin Marietta

JOEL HENRY, *East Tennessee State University*
SALLIE HENRY, DENNIS KAFURA, *and*
LANCE MATHESON, *Virginia Tech*

◆ *Using data collected throughout a major project, the authors apply common statistical methods to quantitatively assess and evaluate improvements in a large contractor's software-maintenance process. Results show where improvements are needed; examining the change in statistical results lets you quantitatively evaluate the effectiveness of the improvements.*

T he process used to develop and maintain software significantly affects the cost, quality, and timeliness of software products. The impact is so significant that software-process improvement is seen by some as the most important approach to software-product improvement.[1]

In 1990, General Electric Corp. began a four-year study of the software-maintenance process in the Government Electronic Systems Division, which is now owned by Martin Marietta and which includes the Computer Program Projects Group. The study's goal was the improvement of perfective-maintenance activities within the CPPG. Perfective maintenance involves adding functionality to a software product after it has been delivered to the customer. We determined that a project-level savings of only five percent would be worth hundreds of thousands of dollars per maintenance project. We believe that such benefits are not unique to Martin Marietta. Other organizations can also apply our analysis techniques to realize similar savings.

One area of study sought answers to three questions:

♦ How can we quantitatively assess the maintenance process?

♦ How can we use that assessment to improve the maintenance process?

♦ How do we quantitatively evaluate the effectiveness of any process improvements?

We selected a process-assessment methodology developed by Joel Henry[2] that follows Total Quality Manage-

Reprinted from *IEEE Software*, Vol. 9, No. 4, July 1994, pp. 67–75.

ment principles and is based on Watts Humphrey's Process Maturity Framework. It lets you use a process-modeling technique based on control-flow diagrams to define an organization's maintenance process. After collecting process and product data throughout the maintenance process, you analyze it using parametric and nonparametric statistical techniques. The statistical-analysis results and the process model help you assess and guide improvements in the organization's maintenance process.

The method uses common statistical tests to quantify relationships among maintenance activities and process and product characteristics. The relationships, in turn, tell you more about the maintenance process and how requirements changes affect the product.

We recognize that the statistical strength of the relationships will vary from organization to organization, and that the specific regression equations, correlations, and contingency tables are not universally applicable either.

However, the statistical relationships, when used with a well-defined and well-documented software-process model, will nearly always show where process improvement is needed, regardless of the organization. Of course, the exact improvement activity implemented depends heavily on the organization's goals, resources, and existing software process.

MAINTENANCE PROCESS

The CPPG manages the maintenance of a large portion of the software that supports a major ship-defense system. The system consists of both hardware and software and enjoys a long legacy of successful operation. It is controlled by more than 10 programs (called element programs) executing on separate platforms that accept input from external sensors and operators. Extensive communication among programs via a high-speed network takes place during operation. The system has undergone more than 20 years of maintenance. These efforts are aimed largely at incorporating functional upgrades and correcting defects.

Upgrades and defect corrections are implemented in specific product releases. A product release is implemented under a contract that specifies a set of functional enhancements called upgrade items. Implementing a product enhancement follows an eight-step process:

♦ System engineers analyze the impact and interpret the meaning of each upgrade item.

♦ This analysis is examined at the preliminary design review, after which detailed design of the upgrade items takes place.

♦ The detailed designs are examined at the critical design review.

♦ Customer representatives and management initiate implementation, if they judge that the critical design review has been successfully completed.

♦ Specification changes originating after the critical design review are submitted to a review board of project-management, system-engineering, configuration-management, and customer representatives. The board reviews estimates supplied by project managers of how the proposed changes will affect the project's cost, schedule, and programs.

♦ Each approved specification change receives a computer-program change number, which appears as a comment on each line of code added or changed to implement that specification change. Programmers also record how many lines of code are added, deleted, or changed.

♦ The responsible groups record detailed information about implementation effort, test results, and final status for each specification change.

♦ The project-management organization, software subcontractor, metrics group, testing groups, and CPPG's upper-level management all collect data during the product-enhancement effort.

As part of this study, we captured and analyzed data about upgrade items for, and upgrade-specification changes to, the largest program in the system, the control program, during this product enhancement. We validated our results by cross-referencing data, performing automated analysis of the delivered source code, and interviewing people.

The data provides measures at three levels: the system level (a high-level view of all element programs), the element level (a view of each program), and the specific product and activity level. Both product and process measures are available at each level.

Product measures at the system level include the number of upgrades to be implemented, the number of defects detected, and the number of corrected and uncorrected errors

TABLE 1 ESTIMATED EFFORT TO IMPLEMENT UPGRADE ITEMS AS PERCENTAGE OF ACTUAL	
Upgrade item	Estimate of person-months as a percentage of actual
1	43.36%
2	27.05%
3	48.04%
4	53.13%
5	53.21%
6	252.56%
7	101.37%
8	46.51%
9	43.31%
10	106.75%
11	15.59%
12	22.37%
13	14.61%

along with their operational priority for each program. Product measures at the element level include the number of individual requirements, number of specification changes per upgrade item, number of written requests for clarification of functionality, and magnitude of impact on the element program. The finest level of measurement records both the estimate and the actual impact on each module in the system and the number of source lines of code added, changed, and deleted per upgrade-item specification change and module. Additional measures, such as the change in module size, the percentage of the module altered, and the mean number of modules changed per specification change, are computed from these basic measures.

Process measures are collected from the same three levels of detail. System-process measures include effort expended, progress toward product-enhancement milestones, and task-completion rates per element. Element-level process measures include effort expended, progress, and task-completion status, but focus on upgrade items, specification changes, and error corrections within the element. The most specific level of process measurement includes effort expended per activity, work product, and progress. Effort expended measures the data captured per activity, such as unit-test time, and per work product, such as number of days spent correcting each module for each error corrected.

ASSESSMENT RESULTS

We used three common statistical techniques — multiple regression, rank correlation, and Chi-square tests of independence in two-way contingency tables — to assess the effectiveness of process improvements made. For each of the following areas, we describe the specific process-improvement goal (which we had established before the assessment), the quantita-

TABLE 2 RESULTS OF REGRESSION ANALYSIS				
Prediction time	Dependent variable	Independent variables	R^2	P-value
PDR	Actual person-months	Contract estimate of person-months Number of PDR Spec changes	0.82	0.0011
CDR	Actual person-months	Contract estimate of person-months Number of PDR Spec changes CDR estimate of changed LOCs	0.91	0.0001

tive assessment of the existing process, the process improvement, and our evaluation of that improvement. We based our evaluation of a process improvement on the observed change in statistical relationships. In our study, P-value measures the probability of assuming a relationship exists when in fact no relationship exists. R^2 measures the amount of variability in one data set that is explained by another data set. The criteria established to evaluate relationships is a maximum P-value of 0.05 and a minimum R^2 value of 0.80.

Upgrade items. The contract for the product enhancement under investigation defined multiple upgrade items. The contract also contained an estimate of the effort, in person-months, needed to implement each upgrade item. System Engineering produced the estimates using a proprietary procedure based on historical data. Table 1 shows the contract estimates of the person-months needed to implement each upgrade item as a percentage of the actual person-months expended. For example, the estimate of the number of person-months needed to implement upgrade item 3 was 48.04 percent of the actual person-months expended, less than half the actual person-months needed to implement the upgrade.

At two critical points in the maintenance process we analyzed the upgrade items to improve the accuracy

of our effort estimates: immediately following preliminary- and critical design review. We suspected that design-review data, used in conjunction with historical information, could predict the actual effort needed.

Applying multiple-linear regression, we derived two predictive equations, the first using data available at preliminary design review and the second data at critical design review. Table 2 presents the results. The data items included in the regression equations were chosen using stepwise-regression techniques, which select the most statistically significant independent variables from the set of available independent variables.

Analysis of the prediction errors (residuals) determined that we could construct prediction intervals. This ability increases organizational confidence in the regression equations. CPPG currently uses prediction intervals to show management the variability of actual upgrade-item effort.

Improvement efforts focused on increasing the accuracy of the proprietary estimation technique. We made changes to significant factors in the estimation technique based on our improvement results. We expected this type of improvement to affect the R^2 value of the regression equation, increasing it toward 1.0. At the same time, the P-value should decrease, reflecting the increased accuracy of the regression equation. We also expected a change in the number of indepen-

TABLE 3 SPECIFICATION-CHANGE CHARACTERISTICS BY ORIGINATION PERIOD					
Origination period	Number of specification changes	Average changed LOCs per specification change	Average modules changed per specification change	Average changed LOCs per module per specification change	Average LOCs per person-day as a percentage of CDR-specification-change average LOCs per person-day
PDR	13	1,371.5	7.2	342.6	99.5%
CDR	17	1,012.2	9.7	137.1	100.0%
Post-CDR	61	84.4	1.8	44.9	72.4%

dent variables that make a statistically significant contribution (as measured by the P-value associated with each independent variable) to the accuracy of the regression equation. Logically, improved initial estimates would begin to account for the variability explained by some of the independent variables.

Follow-up research confirmed these expectations. The accuracy of the regression equation as measured by R^2 improved. However, three different effects on the independent variables occurred. The P-value of the initial estimate decreased significantly, meaning this independent variable contributed even more to the accuracy of the predictive equation. This result demonstrates that the estimation method did improve. The importance of the number of changes to the functional specification of the upgrade items remained statistically significant, demonstrated by only a slight increase in its associated P-value.

The P-value of the estimated changed LOCs increased dramatically, indicating this variable contributed less to the predictive equation. In effect, this independent variable no longer affected the regression equation's accuracy as the improvements were implemented. These results demonstrate three general points:

♦ Improving the accuracy of initial

effort estimates diminishes the importance of some independent variables used to predict that effort, as shown by the increase in the P-value of the estimated number of changed LOCs. Logically, the initial estimate should take into account problems and changes occurring throughout the process, thus reducing the need to reestimate during the process.

♦ Some independent variables continue to make statistically significant contributions to the prediction accuracy as demonstrated by the small P-values associated with the number of changes to the functional specification of the upgrade items. These independent variables are difficult to account for in the initial estimate but contribute significantly to the amount of effort required to complete a software project.

♦ As you would expect, the significance of the initial estimate increases dramatically when the initial estimation's accuracy improves.

Upgrade-specification changes. Specification changes made after the critical design review significantly affect both the process and the product. Twice as many specification changes occurred after the critical design review for the analyzed product enhancement than at the critical- and preliminary design reviews. These later specification

changes must be distributed to, and their implementation coordinated among, many different groups, including system engineering, project management, subcontractors, quality assurance, testing groups, and configuration management.

While these specification changes cause a great deal of frustration and confusion for all groups involved in the maintenance process, no quantitative analysis of this type of specification change had previously been performed. Each group collected specification-change data important to its specific task, but did little or no postproject analysis of the data. In addition, the groups did not share data and often kept separate and sometimes conflicting copies of the data. Consequently, no one knew the quantitative effect on the maintenance process and the software product of specification changes made after critical design review.

We knew that late specification changes were more costly and much more difficult to implement, test, and control. Our goal was to reduce their effects on the maintenance process by quantifying the effects of upgrade-specification changes and obtaining quantitative evidence for the causes of this impact.

Ninety-one upgrade-specification changes were written during the product enhancement. We separated by origination time period into preliminary-design-review, critical-design-review or postcritical-design-review

FOLLOW-UP RESEARCH CONFIRMED THAT THE ESTIMATION METHOD DID IMPROVE.

TABLE 4		
CHANGED LOCs PER PERSON-DAY VS. TOTAL CHANGED LOCs		
	≤ Median changed LOCs	> Median changed LOCs
≤ Median LOCs changed per person-day	33	13
> Median LOCs changed per person-day	4	41

TABLE 5		
CHANGED LOCs PER PERSON-DAY VS. CHANGED LOCs PER MODULE		
	≤ Median changed LOCs	> Median changed LOCs
≤ Median LOCs changed per person-day	42	3
> Median LOCs changed per person-day	4	42

groups. The characteristics of each group are shown in Table 3, which gives

♦ The productivity (measured by average source lines of code per person-day) of upgrade-specification changes made after the critical design review was only 72.4 percent of that for specification-changes made at the critical design review.

♦ Postcritical-specification changes have less effect on the programs (measured by the average LOCs changed, average modules changed, and average changed LOCs per module) than specification changes made at the preliminary- or critical design review.

The Mann-Whitney rank-sum test showed that a statistically significant difference existed between postcritical-design-review specification changes made after the critical design review and those done at the preliminary design review and critical design review. This difference would be reflected in the average LOCs changed per person-day, total LOCs changed, and LOCs changed per module. The existence of such a difference is not surprising. However, quantifying its amount and showing that it is statistically significant will require further assessment and improvement.

We constructed contingency tables to analyze the relationship between changed LOCs and productivity for all upgrade-specification changes. We created the tables using the median values of changed LOCs per person-day, total changed LOCs, and changed LOCs per module. The contingency tables appear as Tables 4 and 5. The P-values for both tables are less than 0.005, allowing us to reject the hypothesis that changed LOCs per person-day are independent of either total changed LOCs or changed LOCs per module.

According to the information in Tables 4 and 5 and an analysis of our organization's process, it appeared that the overhead required to document and process specification changes,

which had a small effect on the control program, significantly decreased the productivity achieved when implementing specification changes. Using all upgrade-specification changes, we fitted a regression equation that predicted person-days required from changed LOCs incurred. The R^2 of this equation is 0.94 and the P-value is less than 0.0001. The y-intercept, representing the number of person-days expended for each specification change regardless of size, was quite high. This intercept indicates that each specification change requires significant overhead, which decreases the productivity of specification changes that require few changed LOCs.

We focused our process-improvement efforts on reducing the number of *small* specification changes, which we identified by the LOCs rewritten and modules changed on the programs. While we agreed that a process improvement that reduces specification changes occurring late in the process would be most beneficial, we knew that eliminating all late specification changes would be nearly impossible. We held a second critical design review and agreed to group related specification changes into larger work packages. In this case, we expected the productivity of specification changes occurring after the critical design

review to approach that of specification changes originating at the preliminary- and critical design reviews.

The improvement was evaluated from a statistical standpoint using contingency tables that test if productivity — measured in LOCs added, changed, and deleted per person-day — is independent of the change's size, measured in LOCs. The contingency tables showed less dependence between the size of change and productivity, but the variables were not independent. We suspected contingency tables do not detect improvement until the change in row and column values is large. We evaluated process improvement by the relative rise in the mean (as a percentage of the previous productivity) and the median number of changed LOCs per person-day and the decrease in variance of the specification changes' size. Adding a second critical design review enhanced productivity, but the inherent difficulties of late specification changes remain. Further improvement in this area may prove very difficult.

Module impact. All LOCs added or changed are commented with a program change number. These program change numbers let you trace the effect of specification changes and error corrections to source code on

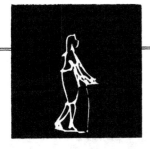

either a procedural or modular basis.

We captured the number of errors corrected per module following integration testing, as well as the number of upgrade items and upgrade-specification changes that affected each module. We also captured the percentage of changed LOCs in the module and the number of person-days expended per module to implement upgrade-specification changes.

Test results showed some modules contained many errors and others contained very few. Further, the modules containing many errors were not consistently error-prone across product-enhancement efforts. During the investigation step, personnel involved in the process advanced many different explanations for the test results, but we found no quantitative evidence to support any of them.

The process-improvement goal was to detect more errors earlier in the life cycle. Reliability in this context meant the error-proneness of modules as measured by errors corrected per module. If relationships existed, the

relationships were to be quantified.

We applied rank correlation to determine the association between errors corrected per module and the impact of upgrade items per module. We measured the impact on modules by the number of upgrades and upgrade-specification changes affecting a module and the percentage of the module changed. We measured the impact on the maintenance process by the number of person-days expended implementing upgrade-specification changes per module. Strong rank correlation existed between errors corrected per module and upgrade-item impact, as shown by the rank-correlation coefficients in Table 6.

We also wanted a simple module classification, according to upgrade impact, to predict which modules will have more or fewer errors than a specified number. We created contingency tables using the median values of errors corrected and the number of upgrades and upgrade-specification changes affecting a module. The contingency tables appear in Tables 7 and

8 and both have P-values of less than 0.005.

The rank-correlation coefficients show significant correlation exists between errors corrected and upgrade-item impact. This strong correlation suggests modules can be ranked using upgrade impact, which can then predict the ranking of modules based on errors corrected. To detect errors prior to the lengthy and expensive test phases, modules predicted to be error-prone can be selected for inspection during the coding phase. Module ranking can also be used to select modules for additional unit- and module-integration testing before system testing.

Table 7 shows that selecting modules based on an upgrade-item impact greater than the median would correctly identify 26 of the 28 modules (93 percent) with error rates above the error median. Of the 31 modules selected with an upgrade impact greater than the median, 26 (84 percent) actually had more than the median number of errors per module.

We focused our improvement efforts on those modules that received more than the median number of upgrades or specification changes, targeting them for walkthroughs and additional testing. The number of errors corrected early in the life cycle should alter subsequent statistical analysis.

Applying statistical techniques after our improvement efforts showed that the number of errors detected and removed did not necessarily change the results of our contingency-table analysis unless very effective walkthroughs and testing were performed on the selected modules.

Modules receiving more than the median number of upgrades typically still required more than the median number of error corrections. The errors corrected after unit testing must be reduced significantly, resulting in a very small range of errors corrected per module, before contingency-table analysis indicates the independence of

TABLE 6
CORRELATION BETWEEN ERRORS
CORRECTED AND UPGRADE IMPACT

	Number of upgrades	Number of upgrade spec changes	Percentage of module changed	Number of person-days
Number of errors corrected	0.803	0.855	0.767	0.808

TABLE 7
NUMBER OF DEFECTS VS. UPGRADE-ITEM IMPACT

	≤ Median number of upgrade items impacting	> Median number of upgrade items impacting
≤ Median number of errors corrected	22	5
> Median number of errors corrected	2	26

row and column classification. In this case, the effectiveness of process improvement must be evaluated by changes in the median and mean number of errors corrected per module following integration testing.

Reexamination of these values following code walkthroughs and additional unit testing showed a significant decline in the median and mean number of errors corrected per module, a simple but important statistical result. The diminished median and mean values reflect an effective process improvement.

Though we had hoped the contingency tables would suggest independence between upgrade-item impact and error-proneness, they did not. This supports the assertion that the majority of errors introduced during the implementation of functional upgrades are removed during code walkthroughs and unit testing. We concluded that the decrease in the mean and median number of errors corrected per module demonstrates an important process improvement. The contingency tables indicate that inspection and testing processes can be further improved.

Engineering-test phase. The programs written by a software subcontractor undergo two different test phases following delivery to the contractor. During the first, the engineering-test phase, programs that received upgrade items are tested to detect errors and ensure the specified functionality is achieved. During the second, the test phase, the entire system is qualified for demonstration to the customer.

The engineering-test phase is important to the maintenance process because it is the last phase in which adequate time remains to correct errors. The tests executed in this phase specifically target the upgrade items and upgrade-specification changes. This phase tests the ability of the programs to provide the functionality described in the specification documents and establishes the reliability of

TABLE 8
NUMBER OF DEFECTS VS.
UPGRADE SPECIFICATION-CHANGE IMPACT

	≤ Median number of upgrade spec changes impacting	> Median number of upgrade spec changes impacting
≤ Median number of errors corrected	25	3
> Median number of errors corrected	6	22

TABLE 9
ENGINEERING-TEST-PHASE RESULT CORRELATION

Upgrade-item characteristics	Rank correlation			Linear correlation
	Tests failed	Defects detected	Total tests	Total tests
Modules changed	−0.031	0.439	0.594	0.633
Person-days	0.087	0.152	0.703	0.737
Spec changes	−0.366	0.084	0.257	0.027
LOCs changed	0.207	0.495	0.740	0.860

the upgrade items implemented in the current product enhancement as well as the reliability of the entire software product.

Our process-improvement goal was to increase the effectiveness of defect detection during this phase. The improvements arose from an investigation of upgrade-item characteristics that influence the engineering-test results, primarily the number of defects detected.

We applied rank-correlation and linear-correlation analysis to determine the relationship between upgrade-item characteristics and engineering-test results. The correlation of tests failed, tests run, and defects detected appears in Table 9. The correlation of upgrade-item characteristics with either tests failed or defects detected is very low. Both the rank- and linear-correlation of total tests is statistically significant, suggesting a relationship between total tests and the upgrade characteristics of modules changed, person-days, and LOCs changed.

Further investigation of this phase

showed very low first-test failure rates for all upgrade items affecting the control program for the product enhancement under analysis. Eleven of the upgrade items had first-test failure rates of 4.2 percent or less. Both historical data and management input supported the view that first-test failure rates had typically been much higher for the control program.

Analysis of the organization's maintenance process was key to explaining the quantitative results of Table 9 and the low first-test failure rate. To detect defects earlier in the maintenance process, the engineering-test group supplied the subcontractor with the tests to be executed during the engineering-test phase. The subcontractor then used these tests to verify the program before the phase began.

The rank correlation between the number of upgrades and errors detected in the subcontractor test phase is 0.72, which suggests the subcontractor detected the defects and repaired the errors uncovered using the tests supplied by the engineering-test group. This supports the assertion that errors

| TABLE 10 |||||
| RANK CORRELATION BETWEEN POSTDELIVERY DEFECTS DETECTED AND VARIOUS MEASURES OF UPGRADE IMPACT |||||
	Functional upgrades	Upgrade spec. changes	LOCs added	Predelivery defects detected
Number of postdelivery defects detected	0.916	0.902	0.939	0.911

were detected earlier in the product-enhancement effort.

The number of defects detected during the engineering-test phase does not correlate with any upgrade-item characteristic. This is because the tests run during the engineering-test phase were run in the immediately preceding phase by the subcontractor. This duplication is expensive and unneeded.

The process-improvement strategy chosen by the CPPG helped modify the role of the engineering-test group and the activities performed during the engineering-test phase. First, the engineering-test phase now focuses on enhancement-to-enhancement regression testing, which is not currently performed anywhere else in the maintenance process. Second, the engineering-test group monitors the tests run by the subcontractor and requires detailed reports describing the activities and outcome of these tests.

While we have yet to completely evaluate this improvement, statistical relationships remain between the upgrade-item measures and the number of tests run and defects detected in the subcontractor-test phase. We believe these relationships will persist until very effective error-removal activities are implemented in earlier phases of the maintenance process. When they are implemented, the relationships should become statistically insignificant when measured in the regression-testing phase, demonstrating that defects are detected and errors removed during the subcontractor-test phase.

The shift to this form of regression testing by the CPPG testing group provides an extra level of testing not previously available. Regression testing improves the overall quality of the delivered product, a result we expect postdelivery measures will confirm.

Postdelivery product impact. After the CPPG delivers a product-enhance-ment product, the customer performs all subsequent maintenance until a new product enhancement is delivered. The customer collects and stores in a large database any defects found following product-enhancement delivery.

Within each of the programs that comprise the software, defect and error-correction data are collected and sorted by functional group. Error-correction data includes an ID number, description, program, functional group, date reported, and priority from one (highest) to five (lowest).

Both the customer and Martin Marietta show significant interest in the reliability of upgrade items. The customer benefits from having reliability information for each functional group based on upgrade data, while the CPPG can assess the reliability of delivered software following improvements made to its software process.

We suspected that the number of defects found before delivery had a significant affect on reliability — which we defined in this context as the error-proneness of functional groups, measured by defects detected per functional group. Our process-improvement goal therefore was to reduce the postdelivery defects detected by the customer per functional group. Specifically, we wanted to quantify the impact of functional upgrades on the reliability of functional groups.

We captured and collected the number of defects detected per functional group from the customer database over a nine-month period following a product-enhancement. At delivery, we collected the number of upgrades and upgrade-specification changes affecting each functional group. We also collected the total number of LOCs added, changed, and deleted; the total number of person-days spent implementing upgrade items; and the number of predelivery defects.

We applied rank correlation to investigate the association between upgrade impact and number of defects detected per functional group following delivery. Strong rank correlation exists between postdelivery defects detected, functional upgrades, upgrade specification changes, LOCs added, and predelivery defects detected, as shown by the rank-correlation coefficients in Table 10. This strong correlation suggests that ranking functional groups based on upgrade-impact measures accurately predicts their ranking based on postdelivery defects detected.

Our process-improvement efforts consisted of additional walkthroughs at the module level and other measures that focused test activities on the functional groups significantly impacted by upgrade items. A reduction in postdelivery defects did occur, but this reduction had only a minor impact on the rank correlations. We found this occurred because a constant reduction in postdelivery defects across all functional groups above the median did not change the rank of the functional groups according to postdelivery defects detected. Process improvement quickly moved functional groups with postdelivery defects near the original median down below the original median, but few groups began close enough to the median to make such a move. Groups with postdelivery defects far above the original median will remain above it until extremely effective process improvement is accomplished. Judging the effectiveness of process improvements in this way hid the substantial improvement actually accomplished.

Although the median number of defects per functional group remained steady across programs, the mean number showed a significant reduction across all programs. Clearly, functional groups with postdelivery defects above the median contain a large number of defects and inflate the mean. Equally important, the standard deviation of postdelivery defects also decreased significantly, showing less variability across functional groups.

While strong rank correlation shows that further improvements can be made, these correlations do not indicate that improvements already made have been ineffective.

These results show that process improvement can have a significantly positive impact on product reliability, as measured by customer-detected defects. This impact could remain hidden if simply evaluated by the rank correlations between upgrade impact and postdelivery impact. A thorough view of upgrade-impact data quickly points out the effectiveness of the process improvement. Although software organizations desire rapid, dramatic improvement (reflected in correlations approaching zero), our results suggest that the effectiveness of some process-improvement types is slow but steady over time.

The assessment results presented here clearly show where process improvements can be applied within the organization. The effectiveness of these improvements can be evaluated by carefully examining changes in the strength of statistical relationships following the improvement.

We have learned three important points concerning process-improvement evaluation. First, statistical techniques must be applied with care. A single technique may not evaluate the true effect of the process improvement. For example, considering only the median and rank correlation of upgrade impact on postdelivery product reliability fails to highlight the improvement clearly shown by the reduction of the mean and standard deviation.

Second, in some cases process improvement must be very effective to significantly alter statistical results. The contingency tables used to classify modules as error-prone change little until effective process improvement removes nearly all the defects. In this case, a steady reduction in the median number of errors corrected per module indicates steady process improvement.

Third, process improvement affects linear-regression results in different ways. In our study, the regression equations' accuracy increased, but effects on the importance of individual independent variables differed.

Although we concentrate on perfective maintenance, the techniques presented here quantify the relationships in the software-development process as well. Perfective maintenance, like software development, begins by specifying the functionality to be produced in the software product. Specification changes occur throughout the development of new software in the same way they occur during perfective maintenance. The nature and strength of these relationships may differ between perfective maintenance and software development, but the techniques we presented describe how to instrument, analyze, and interpret them.

The results of our analysis have been reviewed and interpreted by developers and project management, yielding suggestions for improvements in the maintenance process. Many of these improvements have been made. In addition, a central database has been developed to store maintenance measures, and analysis tools have been installed to support continued process assessment and improvement. ◆

REFERENCES

1. W.S. Humphrey, *Managing the Software Process*, Addison-Wesley, Reading, Mass., 1989.
2. J.E Henry, *An Integrated Approach to Software Process Assessment*, doctoral dissertation, Virginia Polytechnic Institute and State University, Blacksburg, Va., 1993.

Address questions about this article to Joel Henry at Department of Computer Science, East Tennessee State University, Johnson City, Tennessee; henryj@etsu.east-tenn-st.edu

Chapter 5

How is the Metrics Program Improved?

The papers

Learning from existing programs

Stan Rifkin and Charles Cox, *Measurement in Practice*, SEI Technical Report CMU/SEI-91-TR-16, Software Engineering Institute, Pittsburgh, 1991, pp. 1–7. Summarizes the common characteristics of eleven of the best measurement programs in the United States in the early 1990s.

Evaluating metrics programs

Ross Jeffery and Mike Berry, "A Framework for Evaluation and Prediction of Metrics Program Success," *Proc. 1st Int'l Software Metrics Symp.*, IEEE Computer Society Press, Los Alamitos, Calif., 1993, pp. 28–39. Uses four criteria (context, inputs, process, and outputs), to evaluate and compare three metrics programs' effectiveness.

Improving standards

Shari Lawrence Pfleeger, Norman Fenton, and Stella Page, "Evaluating Software Engineering Standards," *Computer*, Vol. 27, No. 9, Sept. 1994, pp. 71–79. Analyzes typical software engineering standards, comparing them with other engineering standards and proposing a framework that is used in an actual development environment.

Validating measures

Norman F. Schneidewind, "Methodology for Validating Software Metrics," *IEEE Trans. Software Eng.*, Vol. 18, No. 5, May 1992, pp. 410–422. Uses six criteria for ensuring that a software metric properly assesses, controls, and predicts software quality.

Considering the impact of measurement

Tom DeMarco, "Mad About Measurement," *Why Does Software Cost So Much?*, Dorset House, N.Y., 1995, pp. 11–25. Describes the use of measurement in three ways: behavior modification, steering, and discovery.

Case study

Daniel J. Paulish and Anita D. Carleton, "Case Studies of Software Process Improvement Measurement," *Computer*, Vol. 27, No. 9, Sept. 1994, pp. 50–57. Uses a basic set of measures to understand and improve software development at Siemens.

Editors' introduction

The metrics process can and should be viewed as part of a larger software development process. It can, therefore, be considered as a possible candidate for process improvement. We should continue to question the value of activities and products in an effort to make the process more effective. In this chapter, we examine existing software measurement programs to determine what we can learn from them and how we can improve them.

In the early 1990s, Stan Rifkin and Charlie Cox conducted a survey of measurement programs in the United States. Their results, published as a Software Engineering Institute technical report, describe the eleven best measurement programs in the US. The first few pages of their report, summarized here, distill the common practices of those eleven successful efforts into guidelines for an effective measurement program.

The Rifkin and Cox guidelines were derived a posteriori, after having examined commonalities among several programs. A more objective, a priori approach is suggested by Ross Jeffery and Mike Berry in "A Framework for Evaluation and Prediction of Metrics Program Success." They propose evaluation criteria based on four dimensions: context (environment), inputs (resources), process (development and maintenance of the metrics program), and products (outputs of the program). Using these perspectives, Jeffery and Berry rate the past success and possible future success of metrics programs in three companies.

We noted earlier that standards can provide unity, consistency, and objectivity to software development, and in particular to measurement data. Many standards are produced by committees with good intentions—but not necessarily with demonstrated improvement. The United Kingdom's SMARTIE project aimed to provide a measurement-based framework for evaluating the effectiveness of software engineering standards and methods. In "Evaluating Software Engineering Standards," Shari Lawrence Pfleeger, Norman Fenton, and Stella Page describe the framework and how it can help to improve the objectivity and effectiveness of standards. Accompanying the framework is a case study, explaining how a change in data collection standards could improve a large corporation's ability to assess its software quality.

When we define metrics, we must be sure that they in fact capture the characteristics we are interested in understanding. Metrics validation is the process of verifying that a metric indeed reflects its intended associated attribute. In other words, validation makes sure that we are measuring what we say we are measuring. Validation techniques are controversial, and there are many conflicting points of view about what is appropriate validation. In his "Methodology for Validating Software Metrics," Norman Schneidewind proposes a validation technique based on six criteria, each of which is keyed to a particular quality function. When placed in the methodology framework, the end result is a process that "integrates quality factors, metrics, and quality functions." The author shows how statistical methods can validate metrics, and he gives an example of how this is done.

There are many ways to use measurements, and each has an effect on many people. Likewise, process activities and changes affect people and the way in which they do their jobs. In the past, measurement-based studies have focused on processes and products, rather than on people and their effectiveness. Much of the reluctance to evaluate people is due to fear that developers will adjust their behaviors to "make the numbers look good." Indeed, Weinberg and Schulman describe a classic experiment that showed that programming teams could always optimize their performance with respect to a single success criterion, but always at the expense of the other goals.[1]

We want our measurement studies to reflect actual, customary behavior, not behavior contrived to alter the measured results. Several pioneers have done studies to try to capture reality, and Bill Curtis reminds us that we need to perform our studies in realistic settings.[2] Dewayne Perry, Nancy Staudenmayer, and Larry Votta have begun a series of measurement-based experiments to record typical behavior and enhance process understanding.[3] For example, by observing and measuring behavior, they show that many project delays occur as one developer waits for another to complete a task. Measurement plays a key role in making this problem visible. The solution is fairly simple and low-tech: Developers are assigned to two projects at a time, so that an individual can work on one project while waiting for a task to finish on the other project.

Many of our models, particularly for cost and schedule estimation, include parameters to reflect the differences in developer experience and expertise. The models incorporate the assumption that more experienced developers produce better code more quickly than less-experienced staff. But we have few rigorous studies to confirm that the assumption is indeed true, or to help us understand exactly what contributes to differences in performance and quality. Tom DeMarco and Tim Lister encourage work with a focus on the role of people, by presenting examples[4] of how morale, surroundings, and team attitude contribute to good products and projects. We point out here the need for more research, but we acknowledge the sociological problems that are involved in setting up valid experiments and case studies.

In particular, we must be sensitive to the way in which our measurement and its goals can affect individuals. In "Mad About Measurement," Tom DeMarco cautions us to consider the impact of measurement on people. He points out that there are three main approaches to measurement:

---

[1] G.M. Weinberg and E.L. Schulman, "Goals and Performance in Computer Programming," *Human Factors*, Vol. 16, No. 1, 1974, pp. 70-77.
[2] B. Curtis, "By the way, did anyone study any real programmers?" in *Empirical Studies of Programmers* (R. Soloway and S. Iyengar, eds.), Ablex Publishing, Norwood, N.J., 1986, pp. 256–262.
[3] D.E. Perry, N.A. Staudenmayer, and L.G. Votta, "People, organizations and process improvement," *IEEE Software*, Vol. 11, No. 4, July 1994, pp. 36–45.
[4] T. DeMarco and T. Lister, *Peopleware*, Dorset House, N.Y., 1987.

- We collect data for discovery, so that we understand how the development process works and how it relates to products and resources, or
- We can use measurement for steering, so the collected data guides us in our decision-making, and
- We can use measurement to modify human behavior.

But DeMarco warns us that when we use measurement for behavior modification, we must take great care. The double entendre in the title of his essay reflects the double-edged sword that metrics provides. We can be enthusiastic about measurement, or we can be angry about it. As researchers and practitioners, we should be sure that the former does not instill the latter in those people who are helping us measure and improve software.

Our final case study examines the ongoing collaboration between the Software Engineering Institute and Siemens Corporation. In "Case Studies of Software Process Improvement Measurement," Dan Paulish and Anita Carleton describe research into process improvement using Siemens software development organizations as study sites. Based on their preliminary findings, the authors make several recommendations about process improvement. Of particular interest is the set of metrics used to characterize and distinguish the participating organizations.

To probe further

B. Kitchenham, L. Pickard, and S.L. Pfleeger, "Using Case Studies for Process Improvement," *IEEE Software*, July 1995. Explains how measurement, when used to support case studies, can help improve the overall development and maintenance processes.

K. Moeller and D.J. Paulish, *Software Metrics: A Practitioner's Guide to Improved Product Development*, IEEE Computer Society Press, Los Alamitos, Calif., 1993. Describes the metrics program at Siemens Corporation, including results about productivity and quality.

T. Pearse and P. Oman, "Maintainability Measurements on Industrial Source Code Maintenance Activities," *Proc. 1995 Int'l Conf. Software Maintenance*, IEEE Computer Society Press, Los Alamitos, Calif., 1995, pp. 295–303. Describes pre- and post-metrics–based analyses of four maintenance activities showing code improvements, flaws in the metric models, and implications for programmer behavior.

S. Lawrence Pfleeger, "Lessons Learned in Building a Corporate Metrics Program," *IEEE Software*, Vol. 10, No. 3, pp. 67–74. Explains how a large telecommunications company created a successful measurement program.

S. Rifkin and C. Cox, *Measurement in Practice*, SEI Technical Report CMU/SEI-91-TR-16, Software Engineering Institute, Pittsburgh, 1991. A description of eleven of the best measurement programs in the US in the early 1990s.

Measurement in Practice

by Stan Rifkin and Charles Cox[*]

Abstract: A few organizations have reputations for implementing excellent software measurement practices. A sample of these organizations was surveyed in site visits. Clear patterns of practices emerged and they are reported at a consolidated, "lessons learned" level and in more detailed case studies.

1. Introduction

The Software Engineering Institute (SEI) Software Process Program encourages the use of measurement[1] to aid the management of software development and maintenance.[2] As part of our encouragement, we seek to expose software practitioners and managers to the greatest benefits and best operation of measurement programs. Measurement is critical to the software process maturity framework[3] promulgated by the SEI, and this relationship provided additional impetus to collect excellent measurement practices.

This report presents the results of site surveys of 11 divisions of 8 organizations that have gained reputations for having excellent[4] measurement practices. While these organizations are considered leaders in software measurement, this is by no means an exhaustive list. By publishing these results, we hope to encourage other organizations to increase the effectiveness of their measurement programs.

We visited one or more divisions of the following organizations (in alphabetical order): Contel, Hewlett Packard, Hughes Aircraft, IBM, McDonnell Douglas, NASA, NCR, and TRW.

---

[*]Current affiliations: Stan Rifkin, Master Systems Inc., PO Box 8208, McLean, Virginia 22106; Charles Cox, Naval Weapons Center, Code 3108, China Lake, California 93555.

[1] The terms "measurement," "measures," and "metrics" are used interchangeably. "Measurement" includes the categories of process, product, and project.

[2] "Development" is used in the remainder of this report to mean both development and maintenance.

[3] Watts S. Humphrey, "Characterizing the software process: A maturity framework," *IEEE Software*, 73-79, March 1988; and *Managing the Software Process*, Watts S. Humphrey, Addison-Wesley, 1989.

[4] "Excellent" is used in the same sense as "excellent companies" in *In Search of Excellence*, Thomas J. Peters and Robert H. Waterman, Jr., Warner, 1982, namely, "continuously innovative", p. 13.

"Measurement in Practice" by S. Rifkin and C. Cox from SEI Technical Report CMU/SEI-91-TR-16, 1991, pp. 1–7. Reprinted with permission.

2. Results

Persistent patterns emerged from our discussions with measurement leaders, and we found numerous interrelationships among the patterns. There were two patterns that ran through all the organizations: errors have been decriminalized, and measurement is part of something larger.

2.1. Decriminalization of Errors

The organizations we interviewed discuss, analyze, examine, study, and evaluate errors, failures, defects, shortfalls, and problems. These organizations expressed the belief that one of the most effective ways to improve quality and productivity is to eliminate currently known errors. They seek to eliminate those errors in ways that insure they will not occur again—by improving the underlying software development process that produced the error in the first place.

We saw this decriminalization of errors in many ways. Project estimates included expected defect rates, and actual rates were closely tracked. Senior management project reviews dealt in detail with causes of deviating from cost, schedule, and quality targets. Project managers became experienced in planning corrective actions that kept actual defects under control. Defect prevention teams regularly looked for root causes of errors and suggested process improvements. Customer support personnel took the customer's point of view and, therefore, had a broad definition of failure ("any problem the customer is having").

In a word, defects were made public. No one was surprised by them. Everyone was working to eliminate them. Errors were talked about in the hallways and around the water coolers. These organizations believe that if you cannot see errors, you cannot eliminate them.

2.2. Measurement Is Part of Something Larger

These organizations developed their programs in the first place within the context of overall software improvement (though not necessarily *process* improvement). Measurement was an integral part of a culture of quality in the organizations; it was not added on, appended, or made to stand alone.

One of the most impressive integrations was with an organization that had a corporate standard requiring that each new product at release have a defect density lower than the mature product it replaced. The only way to know whether the new product had a lower defect density was to measure the mature product and to measure the new product. And if the measurement of the new product was made only just before the release decision, there would not have been enough time to take corrective action. Accordingly, this organization learned to track the defect density profiles over the whole development cycle in time to plan and execute corrective actions, if required. This organization now knows a great deal about how to set quality goals, the shape and behavior of defect density profiles over the development and field life cycle, and which corrective actions work and which do not.

In other words, measurement was used to aid understanding of the software development life cycle. It was part of a bigger picture, part of a culture of quality improvement.

2.3. Patterns

We observed a small set of patterns that were consistent across numerous organizations surveyed, though not every element of these patterns was found in every surveyed organization. One aspect bears repeating: the patterns are overlapping and interrelated. For example, taking an evolutionary approach and understanding that adoption takes time are related: one is urged to take an evolutionary approach in light of the observation that adoption takes time.

The patterns fell along four dimensions: the content of the measures, matters regarding people, the measurement program, and how the program was implemented. Each dimension is elaborated below in the following sections.

2.4. Measures

2.4.1. Start Small
Several organizations collect just one datum, one measure: defects. They present and analyze this one measure in many ways, and they manage software development based on the measure. Other organizations collect in the range of 10 to 20 measures, concentrating on information that has to be collected for other purposes (such as for cost accounting).

All organizations emphasized measures that were conspicuously practical, that incurred low collection cost and effort, and that could be presented simply (i.e., were fundamental or were a binary function of fundamental measures). Typical starter sets included measures of effort (labor hours), size (lines of code), and quality (defects).

2.4.2. Use a Rigorously Defined Set
All organizations agonized over the precise definitions of the measures they wanted to collect. Typically, they first defined the uses of the measures and then prepared draft definitions that were circulated to the stakeholders or their representatives for review. Many organizations concentrated on defining sets that could be collected by machine.

Some organizations prototyped their definitions by using the draft definitions on a pilot project for a short time to see if any unanticipated concerns arose.

2.4.3. Automate Collection and Reporting
Those interviewed advised us to minimize as much as possible the impact of measurement on software developers by defining measures that could be collected automatically. We noted that most organizations planned for, developed, and provided automated tool support for measurement as early as possible. Many organizations had automated line counters, and some organizations had front-ends to traditional time card accounting systems; these front-ends would strip off a code indicating where in a project's work breakdown structure the reported labor hours were being spent.

Many organizations used existing automated tools such as spreadsheet software, software configuration management systems, and text presentation systems linked to numerical information in other files to assist in report generation.

2.5. People

2.5.1. Motivate Managers

Our interviewees said that managers must be motivated to learn the value of measurement as a management tool and to accept the added responsibility (and cost) of performing measurement. Appropriate rewards and recognition need to be established at all levels of the organization in order to encourage and sponsor measurement efforts.

Many organizations saw that if line management liked what the measurement program was producing, then by "natural selection" the effort would survive, grow, and prosper. Accordingly, line management has been the primary user of many of the measurement programs surveyed.

One motivation for using measurement is the support measurement provides for decisions. In meetings with upper management or with customers, measurement reports can substantiate the schedule needed for changes, the time and resources required for incorporating proposed changes, and other typically controversial issues.

2.5.2. Set Expectations

Measurement can be used for many purposes. In order to set expectations, the goals of measurement must be focused and articulated. The most common foci were on cost, schedule, and quality. One common goal was to ascertain where additional resources could be applied in order to improve the software product or process.

Again, we found that the emphasis was on collecting information that had to be collected for another purpose anyway. These organizations were careful not to over-promise the benefits of measurement. Measurement thereby gained acceptance as part of the "standard practice" of software development and management, as opposed to an art practiced by staffers who might not be involved in the day-to-day experience of software design and production.

2.5.3. Involve All Stakeholders

Measurement is used in different ways at different levels and, therefore, is perceived differently by its users and by those measured. Organizations with successful programs found it important during formative stages to include all stakeholders in the discussions of the goals, uses, and definitions.

Some organizations had proclaimed measurement standards or definitions unilaterally and found that such proclamations were resisted, particularly at the practitioner level. Later, these organizations had to re-engineer their measurement programs in order to involve all stakeholders.

Involving all stakeholders is one step toward earning trust (see 2.5.5). By acknowledging that measurement is a "loaded" subject in the eyes of those who may have had negative experiences with measurement (SAT scores, school grades, job performance evaluations, etc.), the successful measurement programs have worked to include software practitioners in the early stages of measurement definition.

2.5.4. Educate and Train

It is important to educate and train all persons who are affected by measurement. Training materials need to be tailored to the level and responsibilities of the target groups. It is typical for organizations to target measurement training courses for different audiences: an overview course for those who need to know why they are—or should be—involved in a measurement program, an analysis course for managers and development staff, and an implementation course for those responsible for preparing, entering, and validating the input data. Several organizations stated that the payoff in measurement is its use for evaluating the software process; training is required to take advantage of that use.

2.5.5. Earn Trust
A fear of software developers and managers is that the results of measurement will be used to rate individuals, projects, and/or divisions. A common practice to allay such concerns was to make results anonymous so that at each succeeding level of aggregation it was not possible to identify the specific reporting units. For example, presentations that contain multiple projects refer to those projects as Project A, Project B, etc. Usually, the staff associated with each project knows which data are its own, but cannot match the other coded project designations with real projects.

On a par with the rating issue is the concern that no harm come to the bearer of bad tidings—that the truth not be penalized. The earlier problems surface, the easier and less costly it is to deal with them. This need for candor extends all the way from the sources of the data to those who report on the results of the analyses.

2.6. Program

2.6.1. Take an Evolutionary Approach
Because measurement is part of a culture change, it must be viewed as part of a continuous journey. Measurement can be viewed as an application of both standard management practices and the scientific method. The most successful programs we observed supported experimentation and innovation (both with measurement and with software development), self-actualization, and improvement of technology and process. To support evolution, there is a need to plan for regular reviews of all aspects of the measurement program (goals, implementation, use, delivery, cost-effectiveness, etc.).

One of the ways this was manifested was in the changing focus of the organization's measurement program. As development problems made visible by the measurement program were being resolved, new issues were being raised that called for a modification of the measurement effort. These changes were needed to obtain the information required to analyze the new concerns and then to determine whether the changes implemented were successful in remedying the problems.

2.6.2. Plan to "Throw One Away"
The evolutionary approach can, by itself, imply the need to throw away some or all of the first measurement program (a paraphrase of one of "Brooks' Laws"[5]). Several organizations pilot tested their measurement system, knowing that some parts of it would survive scrutiny and that other parts would have to be revised. Along these lines, pilot programs do more than just prove a new technology, they also help identify those items that lack merit and should be dropped from the program. Futher, pilot programs help organizations learn how to change, how to implement new technologies independent of the content.

Virtually every organization surveyed is using a different measurement set than it used a few years ago. For some, this represented throwing away the program and starting over.

---

[5] *The Mythical Man Month*, F. Brooks, Addison-Wesley, 1975.

2.6.3. Get the Right Information to the Right People
The value of even the best measurement programs will be diminished if the people who have managerial authority do not receive the information that will help guide their decision making. Measurement reports must be relevant, timely, and limited to that information needed at the particular level of the recipient.

2.6.4. Strive for an Initial Success
Carefully choose the initial projects to be measured. The whole program will be judged by an assessment of the early return on investment. Many organizations achieved continuing support for measurement by targeting projects based on their potential for a successful measurement program.

Naturally, this factor has to be balanced with an accurate set of expectations about what measurement can and cannot deliver (see Section 2.5.2).

2.7. Implementation

2.7.1. Add Value
Adding value implies that something must result from the measurement effort. The increase in knowledge and understanding as a result of measurement must be translated into action by managing and developing software in better and smarter ways.

Some organizations cautioned not to promise more than could be delivered, especially early in the life of a measurement program when there is an insufficient base of data upon which to support inferences. It was easier for some organizations to add value because they bound the program's costs by concentrating on data that had to be collected in any case.

2.7.2. Empower Developers to Use Measurement Information
Measurement can help developers in their interchange with both external and internal customers. The ability to quantify concerns helps developers and customers reach a common understanding as to where viewpoints and definitions differ. Further, armed with historical measurement information, developers can respond to customer request for change with reasoned analyses of the impact of those changes upon the program.

In a few organizations, we heard about the following kind of statement made by a development manager to a customer: "I am going to work very hard to make the changes by the time you need them, but historically, based on the figures I have just given you, it will take longer than your imposed deadline. I recommend that you modify your plans in light of our history."

2.7.3. Take a "Whole Process" View
The application of measurement to development is just one piece, though an important one, of the development mosaic. An understanding of the whole system development process, as well as of measurement, is required for beneficial use of the technology. Also, measurement information must be tempered by good judgment. For example, one organization found that it had planned to improve a particular area of software development only to discover–while developing its business case for the improvement–that software development accounted for a very small portion of the system development cost.

Also, persons experienced in software process improvement advise others considering a program of continuous improvement to be careful to stabilize the development process before trying to change it, whether the change is suggested by measurement or not.

2.7.4. Understand that Adoption Takes Time

Measurement and process improvement take time. They take more than just defining and establishing a program. They require a change in attitude, a shift in culture, and these do not happen quickly. The change can take years and must be continually reinforced to survive and grow.

2.8. Benefits

We saw evidence that measurement has been beneficial to:

- Support management planning by providing insight into product development and by quantifying trade-off decisions
- Support understanding of both the development process and the development environment
- Highlight areas of potential process improvement as well as objectively characterize improvement efforts

The table in Appendix A indicates a few of the specific benefits experienced by the organizations surveyed, and the actual case studies in that appendix provide more detail about the benefits.

A Framework for Evaluation and Prediction of Metrics Program Success

Ross Jeffery and Mike Berry

University of New South Wales

Abstract

The need for metrics programs as a part of the improvement process for software development and enhancement has been recognized in the literature. Suggestions have been made for the successful implementation of such programs but little empirical research has been conducted to verify these suggestions. This paper looks at the results of three metrics programs in three different software organizations with which the authors have worked, compares the metrics program development process in those organizations with an evaluation framework developed from the literature, and suggests extensions which may be needed to this framework.

1. Introduction

It has been recognized for some time that software process and product improvement can be achieved through a successful metrics program. For example, Grady and Caswell [7] propose "software metrics will help you to develop better software in your organization". On a slightly different tack, Fenton [4] argues that software engineering is "more an ideology than a discipline (because) measurement has been almost totally ignored", and adds that perhaps software is "out of control" because we do not measure.

Arguments concerning the need for measurement in software engineering draw on conventional wisdom and comparisons with other forms of engineering and science in which measurement is central. It is difficult to imagine that these arguments can be refuted, but it is perhaps also difficult to propose and validate the necessary organizational requirements for the establishment of a successful metrics program. In reviewing the literature, the recommendations fall into one of four perspectives; *context, inputs, process, and products*

By *context* we mean the environment in which the metrics program is developed and operated; *inputs* are factors or resources that are applied to the metrics program; *process* is the method used to develop, implement, and maintain the program; and *products* are the measures taken, reports produced and other output of the program.

Most authors appear to concentrate their recommendations in one area. For example, Grady and Caswell [7] have a *process* perspective when they list ten steps to success for a measurement program. Fenton [4] classifies these ten steps into four categories and also provides an additional general set of rules that we have classified into our four perspectives as follows:

Context
• have clearly stated objectives and goals
• have realistic assessments of pay-back period

Inputs
• resource the program properly
• allocate resources to training to motivate and sustain interest.

Process
• let the objectives determine the measures
• have an independent metrics team
• create a metrics database
• use automatic tools wherever possible
• do not use the program to assess individuals
• use measures only for pre-defined objectives

Products
• facilitate actions to be taken on basis of observed measurements

At the 1987 and the 1989 International Function Point Users Group meetings other authors provided additional insights. For example, Rubin [10] suggests a *context* perspective when he states that the goals of the measurement program must be congruent with the goals of the business. He adds a *product* perspective when he suggests that the measures must offer clarity of interpretation and use, and that the end result must provide clear benefits to the management process at the chosen management audience levels

Brown [2] provides a *context* perspective when she states that it is important to have senior management commitment. She also adds to Grady & Caswell's [7] *process* perspective with suggestions to make sure everyone knows what is being measured and why, and to develop and publish a firm implementation plan. Garrett [5] concentrates on the *context* perspective when he suggests that an environment be created in which the measured staff can participate in the development of the measures, that there is a quality environment established by management, and that the development processes are stable. Musa et. al. [9] argue that in addition it is also important to determine the required granularity (*context*), provide feedback on results (*products*), and to clean and use the data promptly (*process*).

Selby et al. [11] provide three principles (of a *process* nature) for the guidance of those undertaking measurement programs with the objective of process improvement:

• Make measurement active by integrating measurement and process,
• Provide capabilities for users to explain events and phenomena associated with the project,
• Provide an extensible integration framework for the addition of new techniques.

De Marco [3] emphasises the *input* perspective with recommendations for resourcing the measurement team. He suggests a minimum of three people half time be assigned to the team, and a pilot project be established in which learning can occur. Basili [1] underlined the *context* perspective. When looking at failures in metrics programs Verdugo (reported in Fenton [4]) lists the following reasons for lack of success:

• Lack of clear definition of the purpose of the program
• Personnel resistance due to perception of it being a negative commentary on their performance
• Data collection burden was added to already burdened staff
• Program reports failed to generate management action
• Management support withdrawn because program seemed problematic and generating "no-win" situations.

The objective of this research was to provide validation of these suggestions, and possible extensions, based on a study of three separate organizations. The authors were closely involved in the establishment of metrics programs in these three organizations over the years 1986 to 1992. Thus, this research takes recommendations derived (in some cases) from single organisations (Hewlett Packard, Royal Bank of Canada,

AT&T, General Electric) and tests their validity in other contexts.

2. Assessment Criteria for the Case Studies

It is proposed to review the case studies using a framework synthesised from the literature referenced above and based on the four perspectives. The literature proposes a largely unstructured list of program imperatives. In this section we gather these imperatives under the four perspectives .

From the literature the following questions are suggested:

Context
C1. Were the goals of the measurement program congruent with the goals of the business?
C2. Could the measured staff participate in the development of the measures?
C3. Had a quality environment been established?
C4. Were the processes are stable?
C5. Could the required granularity be determined and was the data available?
C6. Was the measurement program tailored to the needs of the organisation?
C7. Was senior management commitment available?
C8. Were the objectives and goals clearly stated?
C9. Were there realistic assessments of pay-back period?

Inputs
I1. Was the program resourced properly?
I2. Were resources allocated to training?
I3. Were at least 3 people assigned to the measurement program?
I4. Was research done?

Process
A. Process Motivation and objectives
PM1. Was the program promoted through the publication of success stories and encouraging exchange of ideas?
PM2. Was a firm implementation plan published?
PM3. Was the program used to assess individuals? (Demotivating)
B. Process Responsibility and metrics team
PR1. Was the metrics team independent of the software developers?
PR2. Were clear responsibilities assigned?
PR3. Was the initial collection of metrics sold to the data collectors?
C. Process data Collection
PC1. Were the important initial metrics defined?
PC2. Were tools for automatic data collection and analysis developed?
PC3. Was a metrics database created?
PC4. Was there a mechanism for changing the measurement system in an orderly way?

PC5. Was measurement integrated into the process?

PC6. Were capabilities provided for users to explain events and phenomena associated with the project?

PC7. Was the data cleaned and used promptly?

PC8. Did the objectives determine the measures?

D. Process Training and awareness

PT1. Was adequate training in software metrics carried out?

PT2. Did everyone know what was being measured and why?

Products

P1. Were the measures clear and of obvious applicability? ("facilitate actions to be taken on basis of observed measurements")

P2. Did the end result provide clear benefits to the management process at the chosen management audience levels

P3. Was feedback on results provided to those being measured?

P4. Was the Measurement system flexible enough to allow for the addition of new techniques?

P5. Were measures used only for pre-defined objectives?

3. The Organizational Settings

Measurement without context can be quite misleading, and for that reason the following data is provided on the organizations involved. In order to maintain the confidentiality of these organizations they are referred to simply as Organizations A, B, and C.

Organization A is a large information systems group of over 1000 staff within a large company in the banking and finance industry. Within that group, the systems development group have responsibility for requirements determination, design, construction and maintenance of all software systems for the company. The metrics program in the group was the responsibility of the measurement and control group and was established to achieve a very limited but well defined goal over a defined time period. The initiative described in this paper was to establish a metrics program to:

1. capture project size, characteristics, elapsed time and effort data,

2. use that data to construct a simple prototype estimation tool,

3. define and document an estimation process for inclusion in the general software process already defined for the organization,

4. develop a staff training program covering the estimation methodology, tool and metrics program

5. refine the estimation methodology and tool over time as more data was collected

With the possible exception of number five, the goals were achieved on schedule and within budget. Goal five has been elusive for this organization.

Organization B was also in the banking and finance industry. The number of information technology staff was somewhat more than company A. The goals of the metrics program were similar to Organization A, except that steps 2, 4 and 5 were not included. It also differed in terms of (1) a higher interest in the measurement of software development productivity, and (2) the organizational commitment to the measurement initiative, and understanding of it, was lower. It was viewed more as a research program with less control and loosely specified goals. The program was largely unsuccessful in this organization and was disbanded within three years of commencement.

Organization C was in the transportation industry. At the time the measurement system was introduced, the organization was in a major growth phase positioning itself to meet an anticipated leap in demand. To handle the anticipated demand from its clients, the I.T. organisation tripled in size in three years from 300 to 900 staff. A Project Office was established to provide support to Project Managers and to prepare management reports; the Measurement program was established within the Project Office.

The Measurement program grew out of an earlier Function Point Counting program which had been running for two years. Attempts had been made to provide productivity rates for estimation using function points and effort recorded in a project database. While these early results were not published due to concerns about data quality, there was support from some senior managers for a new measurement program. Because of a realisation that a measurement program that provided isolated-views had the potential to be misleading, it was decided that an integrated measurement program would be undertaken. This involved capturing as many measures of the systems delivery process and products as possible and storing them in an integrated database from which queries could be answered and reports produced.

At its peak, the measurement team consisted of an architect, a functional analyst, a data analyst and a statistician. When the size of the project became apparent, management requested that work be suspended in order to produce what was called the Interim Measurement system. The Interim system was put together in three months and provided a variety of views of the development process and products from existing data sources. Reports were produced on a regular basis and provided to management. There were major concerns about the reliability of the data. The Interim

Measurement system was closed down after 15 months in operation.

4. Criteria Scoring Scheme

In order to structure the analysis and discussion concerning the case studies it was necessary to establish a framework and scoring mechanism that could be applied. We have done this using subjective criteria scoring by the authors based on their participation in the organizations. The score is a zero through three rating which concerns the extent to which the criteria suggested in the literature were met in the particular case study environment. Because the literature provides no indication of relative importance of any criteria, equal weighting has been applied to each of them in the analysis. Thus the scheme used was:

CRITERIA SCORING SCHEME:
0 = did not meet any of the requirement
1 = met some of the requirement
2 = met most of the requirement
3 = fully met the requirement

The criteria scoring scheme is at least ordinal in its measurement of the success phenomena. It is even possible, but unlikely, that the resultant organizational scores could be interval or ratio as the scale classification is dependant on the relationship between the measure itself and the phenomena of interest (success). This is untested at this point in time.

The authors did apply an importance weighting scale of their own [8], but the results did not add to the meaning to the data and have therefore been omitted from this paper.

5. Organization Scores

5.1 Context

In this section each criteria is evaluated and scored for each of the three organizations. This provides the case study information concerning the metrics program as well as the scoring to be used in later analysis.

C1. Were the goals of the measurement program congruent with the goals of the business?
Org. A (score = 2)

Improvement of the estimation process was a well established goal at all levels of management in the organizational segment. Better quantitative management of this process was seen as important by a majority of managers.
Org. B (score = 1)

There was only a weak link between the measurement program goal and organizational goals. The measurement activities were seen as a more professional manner of business rather than linked to organizational goals.
Org. C (score = 2)

The mission of the business was to become an efficient implementor of computer-based solutions for its clients. For the software developers, this translated to a performance improvement program with goals of improving productivity, product quality and client service. Measurement was an integral part of this performance improvement strategy.

C2. Could the measured staff participate in the development of the measures?
Org A (score = 1)

The measurement activities discussed here concerned project size, characteristics, elapsed time and effort data. Little participation occurred.
Org. B (score = 1)

Again the initial data collection was limited. A few project leaders were consulted but participation was limited.
Org. C (score = 1)

At the start of the measurement program a Joint Application Design session was held with participants ranging from Senior Analyst level to Executive Management. Few of the participants at that time could articulate their need for information apart from statistics for project estimation. Thereafter, the products of the interim measurement system were decided by the System Architect. It was intended that the products of the integrated measurement system would be developed by the users themselves using the populated metrics database.

C3. Had a quality environment been established?
Org. A (score = 2)

The measurement and control group had responsibility for quality although sophisticated quality measurement was not carried out. An improvement paradigm was in operation in the organization resulting in favourable attitudes toward methods aimed at improvement.
Org. B (score = 0)

There was no quality measurement in place in the organizational sector nor little recognition of improvement as necessary.
Org. C (score = 1)

The organisation was in the process of implementing a number of quality-related elements. However, there was no formal Quality Assurance program at that time.

C4. Were the processes stable?

Org. A (score = 3)

The software process was well defined and stable. Measurement was being used to add defined estimation methods to that process but had no destabilizing effect.

Org. B (score = 0)

Software processes were under development during the same time period. The measurement activities were viewed as experimental along with the new process definition work.

Org. C (score = 0)

Both software development and management processes were highly unstable (changing monthly) while the organisation came to terms with new methodology, tools, reporting requirements, organisation structure and people.

C5. Could the required granularity be determined and was the data available?

Org. A (score = 2)

Granularity was recognized as an important factor and some definition work was carried out. In the time available it was not possible to collect sufficient data at the desired granularity but this limitation was recognized and worked around as best as possible.

Org. B (score = 0)

Consideration was given to the issue but no solution was possible in the time frame with the objectives and resources.

Org. C (score = 0)

Granularity was a major issue both for data collection and reporting. Much of the data had been aggregated and the levels of aggregation were inconsistent. Low levels of granularity meant that there insufficient data points for meaningful analysis: high levels meant mixing development environments and losing relevance.

C6. Was the measurement program tailored to the needs of the organisation?

Org. A (score = 3)

The need was well defined and measurement tailored to that need.

Org. B (score = 1)

Measurement was only loosely connected to need. Tailoring was attempted but proved difficult with limited resources.

Org. C (score = 1)

In terms of assisting with the performance improvement program, there was insufficient linking of measures with actions. To some extent the program was tailored to meet a political need for justifying the high investment in the organisation.

C7. Was senior management commitment available?

Org. A (score = 3)

The project was carried out with full senior management commitment. The manager responsible for software in the organization provided program budget and maintained close contact with the initiative.

Org. B (score = 0)

Management commitment was present only at one level above the project leader. The program was relatively short lived.

Org. C (score = 1)

There was little public demonstration of a commitment to measurement by senior management, although informal statements of support were given to the metrics team. The program was sponsored by the Systems Delivery Manager who was convinced of its value, however, support from his subordinate managers was patchy. When the Systems Delivery Manager left that position, the program lost its sponsorship.

C8. Were the objectives and goals clearly stated?

Org. A (score = 3)

The objectives were contained in a consultant contract specifying deliverables, duration and cost. In this way goals were demonstrably clear.

Org. B (score = 0)

The project was seen by management as containing a high level of uncertainty which resulted in imprecise and informal specification of goals.

Org. C (score = 0)

Explicit statements of goals and objectives were not agreed at the outset. Instead the program was undertaken with the twin hopes that information could be extracted provided sufficient data could be analysed and that the information could then be translated into action.

C9. Were there realistic assessments of pay-back period (e.g. 2 years)?

Org. A (score = 1)

The limited scope of the project meant that cost and duration were fixed and small. Payback was obvious in these circumstances but benefits were not formally compared with costs.

Org. B (score = 0)

This factor was not considered at the time of the work.

Org. C (score = 1)

The metrics team knew how long it would take to build the integrated measurement system and populate it with sufficient data to be useful. Management, however, were under political pressure to provide early assessments of returns on investment. This led to the Interim Measurement system. When the financial crisis came, it was the lack of benefits in the short-term and the knowledge that more time and expense were required that led to cancellation of the project.

5.2 Inputs

I1. Was the program resourced properly?
Org. A (score = 3)

Two contract consultants and two organizational staff carried out most of the work excluding programming of the estimation tool which used other organizational staff.

Org. B (score = 1)

One part-time contractor and one staff member were allocated to the project. Part way through the project the organization's staff member was changed. The new member did not have the understanding of the project, nor the organizational support to carry the work.

Org. C (score = 2)

One fulltime experienced System Architect, a fulltime statistician/data analyst, functional and data analyst on as required basis. The architect also had to do training, promotion of measurement, field queries about reports.

I2. Were resources allocated to training?
Org. A (score = 3)

The contractors were funded to research, develop and deliver the necessary training material, with additional resources from the training department.

Org. B (score = 0)

Training was not considered up until the time the project was cancelled.

Org. C (score = 1)

Training was part-time as emphasis was on the development of the integrated measurement system.

I3. Were at least three people assigned to the Measurement program?
Org. A (score = 3)

Yes

Org. B (score = 2)

No, only two.

Org. C (score = 3)

Yes.

I4. Was research done?
Org. A (score = 3)

The narrow focus of the project allowed extensive industry and academic research to be carried out before the project was commenced.

Org. B (score = 1)

Because the project was not well focussed and the goals were imprecise, research was limited by the extent to which relevant areas could be defined.

Org. C (score = 1)

Research fell into two areas: the formal analysis and modelling was regarded as research into the software development environment and processes. Most of the guidelines and information came from conferences and publications of the International Function Point Users

Group. No academic research was used - the project personnel were unaware of the academic work.

5.3 Process

A. Motivation and objectives
PM1. Was the program promoted through the publication of success stories and encouraging exchange of ideas?
Org. A (score = 1)

This occurred only through the training programs. This meant that many personnel were unaware of the initiative and thus not able to participate.

Org. B (score = 0)

Not only were success stories not published but staff disagreed on the measures being taken. Thus productivity figures were in dispute and accusations of errors in the metrics database led to tension between organizational segments.

Org. C (score = 1)

Promotional presentations were made to all levels of staff within the commercial division at the start of the program. Presentations of products were made to management. There were no success stories and little exchange of ideas. Basically people were told what they were getting and what they had to do as data capturers.

PM2. Was a firm implementation plan published?
Org. A (score = 3)

The measurement project was controlled as a fixed price, fixed duration, well defined deliverables project. All the parties to the project were well aware of their requirements.

Org. B (score = 0)

The implementation was never defined clearly. Many alternative methods were under consideration, resulting in imprecise deliverables.

Org. C (score = 1)

There was a project plan that showed when specific deliverables for the current phase would be ready. However, there was no firm plan for implementation of the integrated system. The interim system just grew with new ideas

PM3. Was the program used to assess individuals?
Org. A (Score = 3)

The aim of the program was to assist individuals through better estimation support. No assessment was involved.

Org. B (Score = 1)

There was a worry about assessment which resulted in the disagreement concerning project productivity. The imprecise goals meant that assessment was not ruled out by staff.

Org. C (Score = 2)

There was no attempt to assess individual team members, although this was requested by some managers. However, there was a proposal to use the output from the measurement system for the Management by Objectives program. This was seen to be a positive element as it would ensure management interest in the program. Unfortunately, the interest was mostly manifested as lack of trust in the application of the measures and concern about data quality.

B. Responsibility and metrics team

PR1. Was the metrics team independent of the software developers?

Org. A (Score = 3)

Yes. Responsibility and work was carried out by the measurement and control department.

Org. B (Score = 2)

Mostly. The measurement staff were largely separated from development by their location in a research type group. There was some development work in this group involving new tools. These projects were measured.

Org. C (Score = 2)

Mostly. The metrics team were responsible to the projects office manager who reported to the Systems Delivery manager.

PR2. Were clear responsibilities assigned?

Org. A (Score = 3)

Yes. Responsibility for research, methodology development, data collection, training, etc was clearly defined and allocated.

Org. B (Score = 1)

As there was only one organizational member full time on the project it was clearly his responsibility. However, tasks were insufficiently defined to allow responsibility to be clear.

Org. C (Score = 1)

No. It was clear that the measurement system architect was responsible for designing and implementing the system from the technical point of view. However, the responsibility of his managers and the user managers was unclear. Every non-technical issue had to be negotiated, with the usual resolution being maintenance of the status quo.

PR3. Was the initial collection of metrics sold to the data collectors?

Org. A (Score = 1)

There was some attempt via the estimation courses and the limited presentations to convince people of the need for quality data. However, these usually occurred some time after data collection was well established and the metrics database reasonably populated.

Org. B (Score = 0)

This was not carried out in this organization.

Org. C (Score = 1)

There was some attempt via the function point analysis courses and the limited presentations to convince people of the need for quality data. Two problems undermined the selling process: the constant growth of staff numbers and the tendency of project managers not to allocate sufficient time for the collection activities.

C. Collecting data

PC1. Were the important initial metrics defined?

Org. A (Score = 2)

The initial metrics set was very limited. Size and elapsed time were well defined but effort was less clearly defined.

Org. B (Score = 1)

Clear and precise definitions of size and effort were not established.

Org. C (Score = 1)

The Function Point score of a new system was regarded as the base measure, while lines of code were regarded as more important for existing systems. There was no agreement as to what were the most important quality-related metrics.

PC2. Were tools for automatic data collection and analysis developed?

Org. A (Score = 1)

Some automation of effort data was in place.

Org. B (Score = 1)

Some automation of effort data was in place.

Org. C (Score = 2)

An automated tool was available for Function Point Analysis and Effort recording. There was some automation of the recording of production incidents and in the later stages the recording of service requests by clients was automated.

PC3. Was a metrics database created?

Org. A (Score = 3)

The database was established under control of the measurement and control group, and contained the initially defined metrics.

Org. B (Score = 1)

A database was established, but not well controlled or populated.

Org. C (Score = 1)

The goal of the integrated measurement system was the creation and maintenance of metrics database. The interim measurement system pulled together data from a variety of databases to produce reports.

PC4. Was there a mechanism for changing the measurement system in an orderly way?

Org. A (Score = 1)

In that the measurement system came under the control of a central group, the capacity for orderly change was present. However, it was not defined how this should occur and was difficult to achieve.

Org. B (Score = 0)

No mechanism was present.

Org. C (Score = 0)

No. The interim system was changed whenever new data was available or management requested a new report. The integrated system was oriented to loading a database from which the users could prepare their own reports.

PC5. Was measurement integrated into the process?

Org. A (Score = 1)

Most of that data was hand calculated outside the process.

Org. B (Score = 1)

Most of that data was hand calculated outside the process.

Org. C (Score = 1)

This was the direction, however, much of the data used was specifically entered for measurement purposes.

PC6. Were capabilities provided for users to explain events and phenomena associated with the project?

Org. A (Score = 2)

The mechanism employed was one of consultation between measurement and control and the project staff. This appeared to work well but was labour intensive and thus delayed achievement of other measurement goals.

Org. B (Score = 0)

Not present.

Org. C (Score = 1)

An online tool was available that surveyed the environment in which a system was developed. This allowed developers to provide some additional information. However, there was nothing that enabled developers to provide textual information.

PC7. Was the data cleaned and used promptly?

Org. A (Score = 1)

There was some concern about data quality. Measurement and control took responsibility for the data and used consultation with project staff to try to clean it where possible. Reporting was not extensive.

Org. B (Score = 0)

Data quality was suspect, but insufficient resources were available to clean the data. Almost no reporting occurred.

Org. C (Score = 1)

The quality of the data was always suspect, however, there were insufficient resources for cleaning it. Reports were prepared and distributed within two weeks of the end of the accounting period. This was regarded as acceptable for a batch system.

PC8. Did the objectives determine the measures?

Org. A (Score = 2)

Almost entirely except that availability of measures had some influence on the extent of metrics collected.

Org. B (Score = 1)

In part only because the objectives were not clearly defined.

Org. C (Score = 1)

The initial goals of the organisation were to improve production and this was reflected in the reports produced. The metrics team were consulted as to what could constitute measurable objectives: in this case, it was the availability of measures that helped determine what could be chosen as goals.

D. Training and awareness

PT1. Was adequate training in software metrics carried out?

Org. A (Score = 2)

One of the consultants was used extensively for this purpose in measurement and control. The other consultant was used extensively for training project leaders.

Org. B (Score = 0)

No training was carried out.

Org. C (Score = 1)

Some training in function point analysis was carried out.. Managers were not trained in the use of the metrics.

PT2. Did everyone know what was being measured and why?

Org. A (Score = 1)

Only limited knowledge of the program existed in the organization.

Org. B (Score = 0)

Knowledge of the program was limited to a handful of people.

Org. C (Score = 1)

Only the commercial division was targeted for measurement. Within that division, the lack of continuous education and promotion meant that many newcomers were unaware. It is considered significant that the program was cancelled by a newly promoted manager from another division who had no contact with the measurement program until that point.

5.4 Products

P1. Were the measures clear and of obvious applicability?

Org. A (Score = 2)

Although not universally accepted throughout the organization, there was very little dissension from the nature and application of the measures.

Org. B (Score = 0)

They could have been except for the lack of clear goals and hence application.

Org. C (Score = 1)

In the opinion of the author, little attempt was made by managers to understand and apply the measures even though the relevance of some metrics e.g. hours per function point seems clear.

P2. Did the end result provide clear benefits to the management process at the chosen management audience levels

Org. A (Score = 1)

There were observed deficiencies in the end result, however most goals were achieved. The evolution of the measurement program was not planned, however, and this may be the major reason for its recent lack of obvious success.

Org. B (Score = 0)

There were no obvious benefits of the work .

Org. C (Score = 0)

It is difficult to point to a single management decision that was actually supported by the measurement system. This is not to say that they could not have been however.

P3. Was feedback on results provided to those being measured?

Org. A (Score = 0)

The goal of the program did not anticipate feedback to project managers, but rather input to project management decisions. This was the nature of the program rather than a necessary deficiency of the program.

Org. B (Score = 0)

Not at all.

Org. C (Score = 1)

In the beginning reports were only produced for the divisional level. This was deliberate in order to make them less personal. When reports were later produced at department and project level they were not allowed to distributed outside the department/project because of "sensitivity". Where trends were apparent or something needed highlighting, this was done via a commentary attached to the report.

P4. Was the Measurement system flexible enough to allow for the addition of new techniques?

Org. A (Score = 0)

As mentioned above, the flexibility and extent to which this program could evolve was perhaps its major weakness.

Org. B (Score = 0)

The program was never successful enough to warrant evolution.

Org. C (Score = 1)

The interim measurement system was inflexible and code had to be changed to cater for even simple changes such as project type. The integrated system was planned to be flexible and table driven.

P5. Were measures used only for pre-defined objectives?

Org. A (Score = 3)

Although this was the case, it may be that the only reason for this was that there was very little publicity given to the measures taken.

Org. B (Score = 1)

Because of concern and disagreement over the accuracy of the data, the measures became a focus for disagreement on relative productivity for different technologies. Although productivity measurement was originally anticipated, the objective in this area did not include this type of conflict.

Org. C (Score = 0)

No, there was no control on the interpretation or use that could be made of figures once published. In one instance, while one manager was quoting productivity figures as evidence for efficacy of a CASE tool, another was using the same figures as evidence of the quality of the staff.

6. Quantitative Results

Using the organizational scores to each question as documented in section 5, the following scores are obtained:

Context

	Organisation Score		
	A	**B**	**C**
C1. Goals	2	1	2
C2. Participation	1	1	1
C3. Quality Environment	2	0	1
C4. Stable Processes	3	0	0
C5. Data availability	2	0	0
C6. Needs driven	3	1	1
C7. Mgt. Commitment	3	0	1
C8. Stated objectives	3	0	0
C9. Pay-back period	1	0	1
	---	---	---
TOTAL	20	3	7

Inputs

	Organisation Score		
	A	**B**	**C**
I1. Resourcing	3	1	2
I2. Training	3	0	1
I3. Team size	3	2	3
I4. Research	3	1	1
	---	---	---
TOTAL	12	4	7

Process

	Organisation Score		
	A	**B**	**C**
A. Motivation			
PM1. Promotion	1	0	1
PM2. Plan	3	0	1
PM3. Individuals	3	1	2
B. Responsibility			
PR1. Independence	3	2	2
PR2. Responsibilities	3	1	1
PR3. Data collectors	1	0	1
C. Collecting data			
PC1. Initial metrics	2	1	1
PC2. Automatic tools	1	1	2
PC3. Metrics database	3	1	1
PC4. System change	1	0	0
PC5. Process integration	1	1	1
PC6. Explanations	2	0	1
PC7. Data use	1	0	1
PC8. Objectives-driven	2	1	1
D. Training & awareness			
PT1. Training	2	0	1
PT2. Awareness	1	0	1
	---	---	---
TOTAL	30	9	17

Products

	Organisation Score		
	A	**B**	**C**
P1. Applicability	2	0	1
P2. Clear benefits	1	0	0
P3. Feedback	0	0	1
P4. Flexibility	0	0	1
P5. Application	3	1	0
	---	---	---
TOTAL	6	1	3

Table 1. Raw criteria scores

7. Discussion

In comparing these three measurement programs, it was clear before quantitative comparison that Organization A was the most successful of the three and Organization B was the least successful. Organization A's program continues relatively successfully today whereas the programs in B and C were disbanded. These observations are supported by the scores for each category of criteria. A normalized comparison is given in Table 2 in which each organization is compared in terms of percent of possible total perfect score.

However this analysis may be inappropriate for the data collected as discussed in section 4 above [12]. Further refinement of the measurement technique and testing of the resultant scores will be necessary to resolve this. The same picture is available in Table 3 in which an assumption of ordinal-only scales has been made. In this table the data is presented as a count of the number of occurrences of each score category. In this table we see Organization A scoring higher overall with better performance in the Context and Input categories.

	Organization		
	A	**B**	**C**
Context	74	11	26
Inputs	100	33	58
Process	62	19	35
Products	40	7	20

Table 2. Organization score

Score	Organization		
	A	**B**	**C**
Context			
3	4	-	-
2	3	-	1
1	2	3	5
0	-	6	3
Inputs			
3	4	-	1
2	-	1	1
1	-	2	2
0	-	1	-
Process			
3	5	-	-
2	4	1	3
1	7	7	12
0	-	8	1
Product			
3	1	-	-
2	1	-	-
1	1	1	3
0	2	4	2
Total			
3	14	-	1
2	8	2	5
1	10	13	22
0	2	19	6

Table 3. Organization Score by category

From these tables we see that Organization A has been more successful in all categories and relatively more successful in the areas of *context* and *inputs*. Organizations B and C have been relatively more successful internally in the areas of *input* and *process*.

Organization A's major weakness was in program evolution. The framework signals this in the low response to questions C2 Participation, PM1 Promotion, PR3 Data Collectors, PC2 Automatic Tools, PC4 System Change, PC5 Process Integration, and P4 Flexibility. Low scores in these characteristics reveal that post development evolution will be difficult since the necessary pre-conditions are almost entirely absent. The high overall scores on context and input shows that the framework reflects the successful strategies used to set up the program. The lower scores in process and particularly product indicate significant problems in the future success of the program.

Organization B scored very low in all categories. The program was not successful in set up or operation and had no opportunity to evolve.

Organization C reveals a very low context score along with relatively low inputs. This aligns well with the establishment problems that were encountered. The higher input score allowed the organization to establish an interim system but this failed because of the context, process and product factors. It was far more successful than Organization B and this is reflected in the higher values in all categories. The low scores in process and product align well with the program's demise.

Overall the framework appears promising for measurement program evaluation and success prediction. Set up success aligns with scores in context and input categories. Evolution and benefits success is broadly linked to process and product scores.

8. Possible Extensions

Although the results obtained are in agreement with the subjective evaluation of the relative success of the three programs and the categorical totals confirm and explain the authors opinions, it is proposed that the following criteria might be added to the evaluation framework based on the experience obtained in these three programs.

Context

1. Identify who has responsibility for obtaining benefits from the measurement program. The measurement program will usually be designed to benefit a production unit of the organization. Costs will be incurred by the measurement group and can be controlled within that group. Unless responsibility attaches for the achievement of planned benefits it

creates an environment in which it is possible that they will not be realized.

2. Ensure that management experience & training are sufficient to use the measurement products. The concepts introduced in a measurement program may be quite new to sections of management and outside their prior training. This factor is also important to ensure benefits are realized.

3. Build a participatory management style. Because measurement can be seen as a threat, successful involvement is more likely under a participatory style culture.

4. Ensure a supportive industrial climate applies. By this we mean an environment which might be characterized as friendly, common values, shared goals, trust, high level of respect of technical staff for managers, and so on.

5. Ensure the level of technical difficulty (software complexity, communications, interfacing) is within the capacity of the developers. This requirement is for adequate training of the measurement staff.

Inputs

6. Use external consultants where needed to get additional experience and authority. The program in Organization C could have had a different course if additional authority and experience were available to influence to set up and input values.

Process

7. State the criteria at the outset of the program for evaluating program achievements. This criteria is suggested as being important in the framework because it adds clarity of purpose to the program definition.

Products

8. Ensure chosen metrics are relevant and acceptable to target community. In all cases studied there was insufficient attention to the relevance of the metrics to the target community. This factor is suggested in order to focus attention on this detail.

9. Conclusions

This paper has suggested a metrics program evaluation and prediction framework. The framework contains four categories of questions which were validated using the case study method in three organizations. This validation showed that the framework appears to provide an effective mechanism to evaluate reasons for success and failure in metrics programs. As such it is also likely that the framework could be used to predict likely success or failure and as a vehicle to assist management in the establishment of successful programs.

The data available was insufficient to (1) provide an independent and validated measure of the variables. The authors were linked with the metrics programs in these organizations and measurement bias is therefore possible, (2) determine if the framework and weightings would have sufficient granularity and robustness when evaluating programs which were more similar in their strengths and weaknesses, (3) provide other than a certain ordinal measurement scheme, thus severely limiting the analysis that can be carried out, (4) test the model in a predictive setting. For these reasons it is appropriate to further test the framework against a larger data set, preferably containing different software industry organization types.

10 References

[1] V. Basili, "Recent Advances in Software Measurement", *Proc. 12th International Conference on Software Engineering*, IEEE Computer Society, 1990

[2] D. Brown. "Function Point Implementation", *Proc. 1987 Spring Conference of IFPUG*, International Function Point Users Group, Scottsdale Arizona, 1987.

[3] T. DeMarco, *Controlling Software Projects: Management, Measurement and Estimation*, Yourdon Press, New York, 1982.

[4] N. Fenton, *Software Metrics: A Rigorous Approach*, Chapman & Hall, London, 1991.

[5] W.A. Garrett, "Proving Application Development Productivity and Quality", *Proc. 1989 Spring Conf. of IFPUG*, International Function Point Users Group, San Diego, 1989.

[6] R. Grady, *Practical Software Metrics for Project Management and Process Improvement*, Prentice-Hall, New Jersey, 1992.

[7] R. Grady and Caswell, *Software Metrics: Establishing a Company-Wide Program*, Prentice-Hall, New Jersey, 1987.

[8] R. Jeffery and M. Berry, A Case Study Evaluation of A Proposed Framework for Evaluation and Prediction of Metrics Program Success, *ITRC Report #9301*, Information Technology Research Centre, UNSW, February, 1993.

[9] J.D. Musa, A. Iannino, & K. Okumoto, *Software Reliability: Measurement, Prediction, Application*, McGraw-Hill, New York, 1987

[10] H.A. Rubin "Critical Success Factors for Measurement Programs", *Proc. 1987 Spring Conference of IFPUG*, International Function Point Users Group, Scottsdale, Arizona, 1987.

[11] R. Selby, A. Porter, Schmidt, & Berney, "Metric Driven Analysis and Feedback Systems for Enabling Empirically Guided Software Development", *Proc. 13th Intn'l Conf. on S'ware Eng.*, IEEE Computer Society, 1991.

[12] H. Zuse, *Software Complexity*, Walter de Gruyter, Berlin, 1991.

Evaluating Software Engineering Standards

Shari Lawrence Pfleeger, Norman Fenton, and Stella Page
Centre for Software Reliability

Given the more than 250 software engineering standards, why do we sometimes still produce less than desirable products? Are the standards not working, or being ignored?

Software engineering standards abound; since 1976, the Software Engineering Standards Committee of the IEEE Computer Society has developed 19 standards in areas such as terminology, documentation, testing, verification and validation, reviews, and audits.[1] In 1992 alone, standards were completed for productivity and quality metrics, software maintenance, and CASE (computer-aided software engineering) tool selection. If we include work of the major national standards bodies throughout the world, there are in fact more than 250 software engineering standards. The existence of these standards raises some important questions. How do we know which practices to standardize? Since many of our projects produce less-than-desirable products, are the standards not working, or being ignored? Perhaps the answer is that standards have codified approaches whose effectiveness has not been rigorously and scientifically demonstrated. Rather, we have too often relied on anecdote, "gut feeling," the opinions of experts, or even flawed research, rather than on careful, rigorous software engineering experimentation.

This article reports on the results of the Smartie project (Standards and Methods Assessment Using Rigorous Techniques in Industrial Environments), a collaborative effort to propose a widely applicable procedure for the objective assessment of standards used in software development. We hope that, for a given environment and application area, Smartie will enable the identification of standards whose use is most likely to lead to improvements in some aspect of software development processes and products. In this article, we describe how we verified the practicality of the Smartie framework by testing it with corporate partners.

Suppose your organization is considering the implementation of a standard. Smartie should help you to answer the following questions:

- What are the potential benefits of using the standard?
- Can we measure objectively the extent of any benefits that may result from its use?
- What are the related costs necessary to implement the standard?
- Do the costs exceed the benefits?

Reprinted from *Computer*, Vol. 27, No. 9, Sept. 1994, pp. 71–79.

To that end, we present Smartie in three parts. First, we analyze what typical standards look like, both in software engineering and in other engineering disciplines. Next, we discuss how to evaluate a standard for its applicability and objectivity. Finally, we describe the results of a major industrial case study involving the reliability and maintainability of almost two million lines of code.

Software engineering standards

Standards organizations have developed standards for standards, including a definition of what a standard is. For example, the British Standards Institute defines a standard as

A technical specification or other document available to the public, drawn up with the cooperation and consensus or general approval of all interests affected by it, based on the consolidated results of science, technology and experience, aimed at the promotion of optimum community benefits.[2]

Do software engineering standards satisfy this definition? Not quite. Our standards are technical specifications available to the public, but they are not always drawn up with the consensus or general approval of all interests affected by them. For example, airline passengers were not consulted when standards were set for building the A320's fly-by-wire software, nor were electricity consumers polled when software standards for nuclear power stations were considered. Of course, the same could be said for other standards; for example, parents may not have been involved in the writing of safety standards for pushchairs (strollers). Nevertheless, the intention of a standard is to reflect the needs of the users or consumers as well as the practices of the builders. More importantly, our standards are not based on the consolidated results of science, technology, and experience.[3] Programming languages are declared to be corporate or even national standards without case studies and experiments to demonstrate the costs and benefits of using them. Techniques such as cleanroom, formal specification, or object-oriented design are mandated before we determine under what circumstances they are most beneficial. Even when scientific analysis and evaluation

exist, our standards rarely reference them. So even though our standards are laudably aimed at promoting community benefits, we do not insist on having those benefits demonstrated clearly and scientifically before the standard is published. Moreover, there is rarely a set of objective criteria that we can use to evaluate the proposed technique or process.

Thus, as Smartie researchers, we sought solutions to some of the problems with software engineering standards. We began our investigation by posing three simple questions that we wanted Smartie to help us answer:

- On a given project, what standards are used?
- To what extent is a particular standard followed?
- If a standard is being used, is it effective? That is, is it making a difference in quality or productivity?

What is a standard — and what does it mean for software engineering?

Often, a standard's size and complexity make it difficult to determine whether a particular organization is compliant. If partial compliance is allowed, measurement of the degree of compliance is difficult, if not impossible — consider, for example, the ISO 9000 series and the 14 major activities it promotes.[4] The Smartie project suggests that large standards be considered as a set of smaller "ministandards." A ministandard is a standard with a cohesive, content-related set of requirements. In the remaining discussion, the term *standard* refers to a ministandard.

What is a good standard?

We reviewed dozens of software engineering standards, including international, national, corporate, and organizational standards, to see what we could learn. For each standard, we wanted to know

- How good is the standard?
- What is affected by the standard?
- How can we determine compliance with the standard?
- What is the basis for the standard?

"Goodness" of the standard was difficult to determine, as it involved at least three distinct aspects. First, we wanted to know whether and how we can tell if the standard is being complied with. That is, a standard is not a good standard if there is no way of telling whether a particular organization, process, or piece of code complies with the standard. There are many examples of such "bad" standards. For instance, some testing standards require that all statements be tested "thoroughly"; without a clear definition of "thoroughly," we cannot determine compliance. Second, a standard is good only in terms of the success criteria set for it. In other words, we wanted to know what attributes of the final product (such as reliability or maintainability) are supposed to be improved by using the standard. And finally, we wanted to know the cost of applying the standard. After all, if compliance with the standard is so costly as to make its use impractical, or practical only in certain situations, then cost contributes to "goodness."

We developed a scheme to evaluate the degree of objectivity inherent in assessing compliance. We can classify each requirement being evaluated into one of four categories: reference only, subjective, partially objective, and completely objective. A reference-only requirement declares that something will happen, but there is no way to determine compliance; for example, "Unit testing shall be carried out." A subjective requirement is one in which only a subjective measure of conformance is possible; for example, "Unit testing shall be carried out effectively." A subjective requirement is an improvement over a reference-only requirement, but it is subject to the differing opinions of experts. A partially objective requirement involves a measure of conformance that is somewhat objective but still requires a degree of subjectivity; for example, "Unit testing shall be carried out so that all statements and the most probable paths are tested." An objective requirement is the most desirable kind, as conformance to it can be determined completely objectively; for example, "Unit testing shall be carried out so that all statements are tested."

Clearly, our goal as a profession should be to produce standards with require-

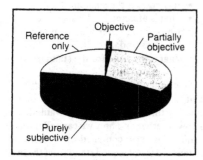

Figure 1. Degree of objectivity in software engineering standards' requirements.

Figure 2. A comparison of (a) BS4792 standard for safe pushchairs, with 29 requirements, and (b) DEF STD 00-55 for safe software, with 115 requirements, shows that software standards place more emphasis on process than on the final product.

ments that are as objective as possible. However, as Figure 1 illustrates, the Smartie review of the requirements in software engineering standards indicates that we are a long way from reaching that goal.

To what do our standards apply?

To continue our investigation, Smartie researchers reviewed software engineering standards to determine what aspect of software development is affected by each standard. We considered four distinct categories of requirements in the standards: process, internal product, external product, and resources. Internal product requirements refer to such items as the code itself, while external product requirements refer to what the user experiences, such as reliability. For examples of these categories, we turn to the British Defence Standard DEF STD 00-55 (interim),[5] issued by the Ministry of Defence (second revision in 1992) for the procurement of safety-critical software in defense equipment. Some are internal product requirements:

- Each module should have a single entry and exit.
- The code should be indented to show its structure.

Others are process requirements:

- The Design Team shall validate the Software Specification against Software Requirements by animation of the formal specification.

while some are resource requirements:

- All tools and support software . . . shall have sufficient safety integrity.
- The Design Authority shall demonstrate . . . that the seniority, authority, qualifications and experience of the staff to be employed on the project are satisfactory for the tasks assigned to them.

Typical of many software standards, DEF STD 00-55 has a mixture of all four types of requirements.

Are software standards like other standards?

Standardization has made life easier in many disciplines. Because of standard voltage and plugs, an electrical appliance from Germany will work properly in Italy. A liter of petrol in one country is the same as a liter in another, thanks to standard measurement. These standards, products of other engineering disciplines, offer lessons that we can learn as software engineers. So the next step in the Smartie process was to examine other engineering standards to see how they differ from those in software engineering. In particular, we asked

- Is the mix of product, process, and resource roughly the same?
- Is the mix of objective and nonobjective compliance evaluation roughly the same?

The answer to both questions is a resounding no. To show just how different software engineering standards are, Figure 2 compares the British standard for pushchair safety with DEF STD 00-55, a

software safety standard.

The figure shows what is true generally: Software engineering standards are heavy on process and light on product, while other engineering standards are the reverse. That is, software engineering standards reflect the implicit assumption that using certain techniques and processes, in concert with "good" tools and people, will necessarily result in a good product. Other engineering disciplines have far less faith in the process; they insist on evaluating the final product in their standards.

Another major difference between our standards and those of other engineering disciplines is in the method of compliance assessment. Most other disciplines include in their standards a description of the method to be used to assess compliance; we do not. In other words, other engineers insist that the proof of the pudding is in the eating: Their standards describe how the eating is to be done, and what the pudding should taste like, look like, and feel like. By contrast, software engineers prescribe the recipe, the utensils, and the cooking techniques, and then assume that the pudding will taste good. If our current standards are not effective, it may be because we need more objective standards and a more balanced mix of process, product, and resource requirements

The proof of the pudding: Case studies

The Smartie framework includes far more than we can describe here — for example, guidelines for evaluating the experiments and case studies on which the standards are based. We address all of these issues in Smartie technical reports, available from the Centre for Software Reliability. For the remainder of this article, we focus on an aspect of Smartie that distinguishes it from other research on standards: its practicality. Because Smartie includes industrial partners, we have evaluated the effectiveness of Smartie itself by applying it to real-life situations. We present here two examples of the Smartie "reality check": (1) applying the framework to written standards for a major company and (2) evaluating the use of standards to meet specified goals.

Both examples involve Company X, a large, nationwide company whose services depend on software. The company is interested in using standards to enhance its software's reliability and maintainability. In the first example, we examine some of the company's programming standards to see if they can be improved. In the second example, we recommend changes to the way data is collected and analyzed, so that management can make better decisions about reliability and maintainability.

Reality check 1: How good are the written standards? We applied the Smartie techniques to a ministandard for using Cobol. The Cobol standard is part of a larger set of mandated standards, called programming guidelines, in the company's system development manual.

Using the guidelines reputedly "facilitate[s] the production of clear, efficient and maintainable Cobol programs." The guidelines were based on expert opinion, not on experiments and case studies demonstrating their effectiveness in comparison with not following the guidelines. This document is clearly designed as a standard rather than a set of guidelines, since "enforceability of the standards is MANDATORY," with "any divergence" being "permanently recorded."

We focused on the layout and naming conventions, items clearly intended to make the code easier to maintain. Layout requirements such as the following can be measured in a completely objective fashion:

- Each statement should be terminated by a full stop.
- Only one verb should appear on any one line.
- Each sentence should commence in

column 12 and on a new line, second and subsequent lines being neatly indented and aligned vertically.... Exceptions are ELSE which will start in the same column as its associated IF and which will appear on a line of its own.

Each line either conforms or does not, and the proportion of lines conforming to all layout requirements represents overall compliance with the standard.

On the other hand, measuring conformance to some naming conventions can be difficult, because such measurements are subjective, as is the case with

- Names must be meaningful.

The Smartie approach recommends that the standard be rewritten to make it

---

The Smartie framework has guidelines for evaluating the case studies on which the standards are based.

---

more objective. For example, improvements might include

- Names must be English or scientific words which themselves appear as identifiable concepts in the specification document(s).
- Abbreviations of names must be consistent.
- Hyphens must be used to separate component parts of names.

Conformance measures can then use the proportion of names that conform to the standard. Analysis of the commenting requirements also led to recommendations that would improve the degree of objectivity in measuring conformance.

Reality check 2: Do the standards address the goals? Company X collects reliability and maintainability data for many of its systems. The company made available to Smartie all of its data relating to a large system essential to its business.

Initiated in November 1987, the system had had 27 releases by the end of 1992. The 1.7 million lines of code for this system involve two programming languages: Cobol (both batch Cobol and CICS Cobol) and Natural (a 4GL). Less than a third of the code is Natural; recent growth (15.2 percent from 1991 to 1992) has been entirely in Cobol. Three corporate and organizational goals are addressed by measuring this system: (1) monitoring and improving product reliability, (2) monitoring and improving product maintainability, and (3) improving the overall development process. The first goal requires information about actual operational failures, while the second requires data on discovering and fixing faults. The third goal, process improvement, is at a higher level than the other two, so Smartie researchers focused primarily on reliability and maintainability as characteristics of process improvement.

The system runs continuously. Users report problems to a help desk whose staff determines whether the problem is a user error or a failure of the system to do something properly. Thus, all the data supplied to Smartie related to software failures rather than to documentation failures. The Smartie team received a complete set of failure information for 1991-92, so the discussion in this section refers to all 481 software failures recorded and fixed during that period. We reviewed the data to see how data collection and analysis standards addressed the overall goal of improving system reliability and maintainability. In many cases, we recommended a simple change that should yield additional, critical information in the future. The remainder of this section describes our findings.

A number is assigned to each "fault" report. We distinguish a fault (what the developer sees) from a failure (what the user sees).[6] Here we use "fault" in quotation marks, since failures are labeled as faults. A typical data point is identified by a "fault" number, the week it was reported, the system area and fault type, the week the underlying cause was fixed and tested, and the actual number of hours to repair the problem (that is, the time from when the maintenance group decides to clear the "fault" until the time when the fix is tested and integrated with the rest of the system). Smartie researchers analyzed this data and made several recommendations about how to improve data collection and analysis to

Existing closure report

Fault ID: F752
Reported: 18/6/92
Definition: Logically deleted work done records appear on enquiries
Description: Causes misleading information to users. Amend Additional Work Performed RDVIPG2A to ignore work done records with flag-amend = 1 or 2

Revised closure report

Fault ID: F752
Reported: 18/6/92
Definition: Logically deleted work done records appear on enquiries
Effect: Misleading information to users
Cause: Omission of appropriate flag variables for work done records
Change: Amend Additional Work Performed RDVIPG2A to ignore work done records with flag-amend = 1 or 2

get a better picture of system maintainability. Nevertheless, the depth of data collection practiced at Company X is to be applauded. In particular, the distinction between hours-to-repair and time between problem-open ("week in") and problem-close ("week out") is a critical one that is not usually made in maintenance organizations.

The maintenance group designated 28 system areas to which underlying faults could be traced. Each system area name referred to a particular function of the system rather than to the system architecture. There was no documented mapping of programs or modules to system areas. A typical system area involved 80 programs, with each program consisting of 1,000 lines of code. The fault type indicated one of 11, many of which were overlapping. In other words, the classes of faults were not orthogonal, so it was possible to find more than one fault class appropriate for a given fault. In addition, there was no direct, recorded link between "fault" and program in most cases. Nor was there information about program size or complexity.

Given this situation, we made two types of recommendations. First, we examined the existing data and suggested simple changes to clarify and separate issues. Second, we extracted additional information by hand from many of the programs. We used the new data to demonstrate that enhanced data collection could provide valuable management information not obtainable with the current forms and data.

Issue 1: Faults versus failures. Because the cause of a problem (that is, a fault) is not always distinguished from the evidence to the user of that problem (that

is, a failure), it is difficult to assess a system's reliability or the degree of user satisfaction. Furthermore, with no mapping from faults to failures, we cannot tell which particular parts or aspects of the system are responsible for most of the problems users are encountering.

• *Recommendation*: Define fault and failure, and make sure the maintenance staff understands the difference between the two. Then, consider failure reports separate from fault reports. For example, a design problem discovered during a design review would be described in a fault report; a problem in function discovered by a user would be described in a failure report.

Issue 2: Mapping from program to system area. Use of system areas to describe faults is helpful, but a mapping is needed from program name to system area. The current information does not reveal whether code in one system area leads to problems in another system area. The batch reporting and integration into the system of problem repairs compounds this difficulty because there is then no recorded link from program to fault. This information must have existed at some point in the maintenance process in order for the problem to be fixed; capturing it at the time of discovery is much more efficient than trying to elicit it well after the fact (and possibly incorrectly).

• *Recommendation*: Separate the system into well-defined system areas and provide a listing that maps each code module to a system area. Then, as problems are reported, indicate the system area affected. Finally, when the cause of the problem is identified, document the

names of the program modules that caused the problem.

Issue 3: Ambiguity and informality inherent in the incident closure reports. The description of each problem reflects the creativity of the recorder rather than standard aspects of the problem. This lack of uniformity makes it impossible to amalgamate the reports and examine overall trends.

• *Recommendation:* The problem description should include the manifestation, effect, and cause of the problem, as shown in Figure 3. Such data would permit traceability and trend analysis.

Issue 4: Fault classification scheme. Because the scheme contains nonorthogonal categories, it is difficult for the maintainer to decide in which category a particular fault belongs. For this reason, some of the classifications may be arbitrary, resulting in a misleading picture when the faults are aggregated and tracked.

• *Recommendation:* Redefine fault categories so that there is no ambiguity or overlap between categories.

Issue 5: Unrecoverable data. By unrecoverable, we mean that the information we need does not exist in some documented form in the organization. For example, most of the problem report forms related a large collection of faults to a large collection of programs that were changed as a result. What appears to be unrecoverable is the exact mapping of program changes to a particular fault. On the other hand, some information was recoverable, but with great difficulty. For example, we re-created size information

Table 1. Recoverable (documented) data versus nonrecoverable (undocumented) data.

Recoverable	Nonrecoverable
Size information for each module Static/complexity information for each module Mapping of faults to programs Severity categories	Operational usage per system (needed for reliability assessment) Success/failure of fixes (needed to assess effectiveness of maintenance process) Number of repeated failures (needed for reliability assessment)

manually from different parts of the data set supplied to us, and we could have related problem severity to problem cause if we had had enough time.

• *Recommendation:* The data in Table 1 would be useful if it were explicit and available to the analysts.

Figures 4 through 8 show what we can learn from the existing data; Figures 9 through 11 (page 78) show how much more we can learn using the additional data.

Since we have neither mean-time-between-failure data nor operational usage information, we cannot depict reliability directly. As an approximation, we examined the trend in the number of "faults" received per week. Figure 4 shows that there is great variability in the number of "faults" per week, suggesting that there is no general improvement in system reliability.

The chart in Figure 5 contrasts the "faults" received with the "faults" addressed and resolved ("actioned") in a given week. Notice that there is wide variation in the proportion of "faults" that are actioned each week. In spite of the lack-of-improvement trend, this chart provides managers with useful information; they can use it to begin an investigation into which "faults" are handled first and why.

Examining the number of "faults" per system area is also useful, and we display the breakdown in Figure 6. However, there is not enough information to know why particular system areas generate more "faults" than others. Without information such as size, complexity, and operational usage, we can draw no definitive conclusions. Similarly, an analysis of "faults" by fault type revealed that data and program faults dominated user, query, and other faults. However, the fault types are not orthogonal, so again there is little that we can conclude.

Figures 7 and 8 show, respectively,

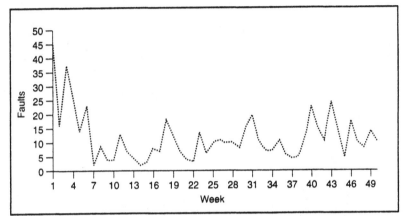

Figure 4. Reliability trend charting the number of faults received per week.

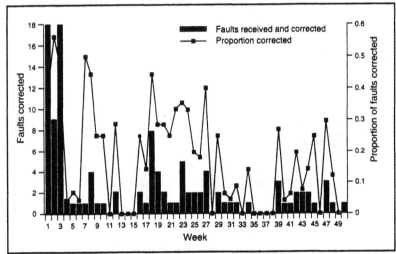

Figure 5. Charting the faults received and acted upon in the same week helps show how Company X deals with software failures.

mean time to repair fault by system area and by fault type. This information highlights interesting variations, but our conclusions are still limited because of missing information about size.

The previous charts contain only the information supplied to us explicitly by Company X. The following charts reflect additional information that was recovered manually. As you can see, this re-

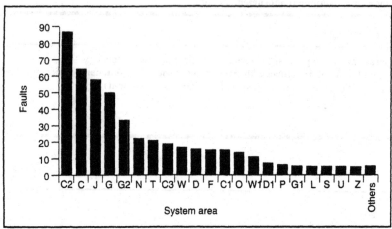

Figure 6. Plotting the number of faults per system area helps isolate fault-prone system areas.

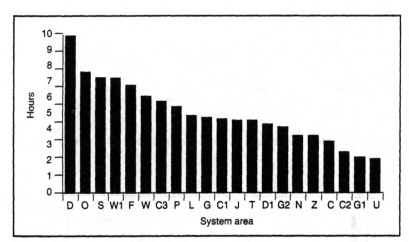

Figure 7. Mean time to repair fault (by system area).

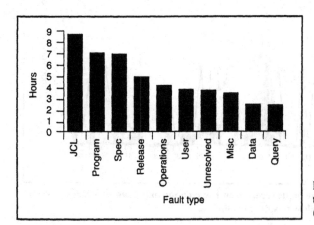

Figure 8. Mean time to repair fault (by fault type).

examined. Recall that Figures 4, 5, and 6 revealed limited information about the distribution of "faults" in the overall system. However, by adding size data, the resulting graph in Figure 10 shows the startling result that C2 — one of the smallest system areas (with only 4,000 lines of code) — has the largest number of "faults." If the fault rates are graphed by system area, as in Figure 11, it is easy to see that C2 dominates the chart. In fact, Figure 11 shows that, compared with published industry figures, each system area except C2 is of very high quality; C2, however, is much worse than the industry average. Without size measurement, this important information would not be visible. Consequently, we recommended that the capture of size information be made standard practice at Company X.

These charts represent examples of our analysis. In each case, improvements to standards for measurement and collection are suggested in light of the organizational goals. Our recommendations reflect the need to make more explicit a small degree of additional information that can result in a very large degree of additional management insight. The current amount of information allows a manager to determine the status of the system; the additional data would yield explanatory information that would allow managers to be proactive rather than reactive during maintenance.

Lessons learned in case studies

The Company X case study was one of several intended to validate the Smartie methodology, not only in terms of finding missing pieces in the methodology, but also by testing the practicality of Smartie for use in an industrial environment (the other case studies are not complete as of this writing). The first and most serious lesson learned in performing the case studies involved the lack of control. Because each investigation was retrospective, we could not

- require measurement of key productivity and quality variables,
- require uniformity or repetition of measurement,
- choose the project, team, or staff characteristics that might have eliminated confounding effects,

covered information enriches the management decisions that can be made on the basis of the charts.

By manually investigating the (poorly documented) link between individual programs and system areas, we examined the relationships among size, language, and system area. Figure 9 shows the variation between CICS Cobol and Natural in each of the main system areas

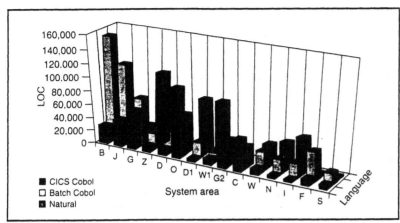

Figure 9. System structure showing system areas with more than 25,000 lines of code and types of programming languages.

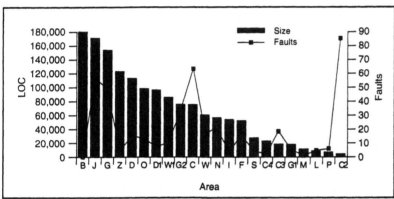

Figure 10. System area size versus number of faults.

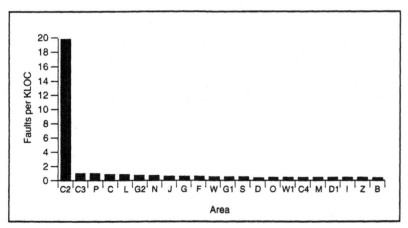

Figure 11. Normalized fault rates.

- choose or rewrite standards so that they were easy to apply and assess,
- choose the type of standard, or
- establish a baseline condition or environment against which to measure change.

The last point is the most crucial. Without a baseline, we cannot describe with confidence the effects of using (or not using) the standards. As a consequence, a great deal of expert (but nevertheless highly subjective) judgment was necessary in assessing the results of the case studies. It is also clear that a consistent level of control must be maintained throughout the period of the case study. There were many events, organizational and managerial as well as technical, that affected the outcome of the case study, and about which we had no input or control. In particular, lack of control led to incomplete or inconsistent data. For example, a single problem report usually included several problems related only by the time period in which the problems occurred. Or the description of a single type of problem varied from report to report, depending on the documentation style of the maintainer and the time available to write the description. With such inconsistency, it is impossible to aggregate the problem reports or fault information in a meaningful way; it is also impossible to evaluate the root causes of problems and relate them to the use of standards. Indeed, the very lack of standards in data collection and reporting inhibits us from doing a thorough analysis.

A final difficulty with our assessment derives from the lack of information about cost. Although we have Company X data on the time required to fix a problem, the company did not keep careful records on the cost of implementation or maintenance at a level that allows us to understand the cost implications of standards use. That is, even if we can show that using standards is beneficial for product quality, we cannot assess the trade-offs between the increase in quality and the cost of achieving that quality. Without such information, managers in a production environment would be loath to adopt standards, even if the standards were certifiably effective according to the Smartie (or any other) methodology.

We learned a great deal from reviewing standards and administering case studies. The first and most startling result of our work is that many standards are not really standards at all. Many "standards" are reference or subjective requirements, suggesting that they are really guidelines (since degree of compliance cannot be evaluated). Organizations with such standards should revisit their goals and revise the standards to address the goals in a more objective way.

We also found wide variety in conformance from one employee to another as well as from one module to another. In one of our case studies, management assured us that all modules were 100 percent compliant with the company's own structured programming standards, since it was mandatory company practice. Our review revealed that only 58 percent of the modules complied with the standards, even though the standards were clearly stated and could be objectively evaluated.

A related issue is that of identifying the portion of the project affected by the standard and then examining conformance only within that portion. That is, some standards apply only to certain types of modules, so notions of conformance must be adjusted to consider only that part of the system that is subject to the standard in the first place. For example, if a standard applies only to interface modules, then 50 percent compliance should mean that only 50 percent of the interface modules comply, not that 50 percent of the system is comprised of interface modules and that all of them comply.

More generally, we found that we have a lot to learn from standards in other engineering disciplines. Our standards lack objective assessment criteria, involve more process than product, and are not always based on rigorous experimental results.

Thus, we recommend that software engineering standards be reviewed and revised. The resulting standards should be cohesive collections of requirements to which conformance can be established objectively. Moreover, there should be a clearly stated benefit to each standard and a reference to the set of experiments or case studies demonstrating that benefit. Finally, software engineering standards should be better balanced, with more product requirements in relation to process and resource requirements. With standards expressed in this way, managers can use project objectives to guide standards' intention and implementation.

The Smartie recommendations and framework are practical and effective in identifying problems with standards and in making clear the kinds of changes that are needed. Our case studies have demonstrated that small, simple changes to standards writing, and especially to data collection standards, can improve significantly the quality of information about what is going on in a system and with a project. In particular, these simple changes can move the project from assessment to understanding. ∎

Acknowledgments

We gratefully acknowledge the assistance of other participants in the SERC/DTI-funded Smartie project: Colum Devine, Jennifer Thornton, Katie Perrin, Derek Jaques, Danny McComish, Eric Trodd, Bev Littlewood, and Peter Mellor.

References

1. *IEEE Software Engineering Technical Committee Newsletter*, Vol. 11, No. 3, Jan. 1993, p. 4.

2. British Standards Institute, *British Standards Guide: A Standard for Standards*, London, 1981.

3. N. Fenton, S.L. Pfleeger, and R.L. Glass, "Science and Substance: A Challenge to Software Engineers," *IEEE Software*, Vol. 11, No. 4, July 1994, pp. 86-95.

4. International Standards Organization, *ISO 9000: Quality Management and Quality Assurance Standards — Guidelines for Selection and Use*, 1987 (with ISO 9001 - 9004).

5. Ministry of Defence Directorate of Standardization, *Interim Defence Standard 00-55: The Procurement of Safety-Critical Software in Defence Equipment, Parts 1-2*, Glasgow, Scotland, 1992.

6. P. Mellor, "Failures, Faults, and Changes in Dependability Measurement," *J. Information and Software Technology*, Vol. 34, No. 10, Oct. 1992, pp. 640-654.

Methodology For Validating Software Metrics

Norman F. Schneidewind, *Senior Member, IEEE*

Abstract— We propose a comprehensive metrics validation methodology that has six validity criteria, which support the quality functions assessment, control, and prediction, where quality functions are activities conducted by software organizations for the purpose of achieving project quality goals. Six criteria are defined and illustrated: association, consistency, discriminative power, tracking, predictability, and repeatability. We show that nonparametric statistical methods such as contingency tables play an important role in evaluating metrics against the validity criteria. Examples emphasizing the discriminative power validity criterion are presented. A metrics validation process is defined that integrates quality factors, metrics, and quality functions.

Index Terms—Metrics validation methodology, metrics validation process, nonparametric statistical methods, quality functions, validity criteria.

I. INTRODUCTION

WE believe that software metrics should be treated as part of an engineering discipline—metrics should be evaluated (validated) to determine whether they measure what they purport to measure prior to using them. Furthermore, if metrics are to be of greatest utility, the validation should be performed in terms of the quality functions (quality assessment, control, and prediction) that the metrics are to support.

We propose and illustrate a validation methodology whose adoption, we believe, would provide a rational basis for using metrics. This is a comprehensive metrics methodology that builds on the work of others: these have been validation analyses performed on specific metrics or metric systems for the purpose of satisfying specific research goals. Among these validations are the following: 1) function points as a predictor of work hours across different development sites and sets of data [1]; 2) reliability of metrics data reported by programmers [3]; 3) Halstead operator count for Pascal programs [10]; 4) metric-based classification trees [16]; and 5) evaluation of metrics against syntactic complexity properties [17].

Our approach to validation has the following characteristics: (i) The methodology is general and not specific to particular metrics or research objectives. (ii) It is developed from the point of view of the metric user (rather than the researcher), who has requirements for assessing, controlling, and predicting quality. To illustrate the difference in viewpoint, we can make an analogy with the automobile industry: the manufacturer has an interest in brake lining thickness as it relates to stopping distance, but from the driver's perspective, the only meaningful metric is stopping distance! (iii) It consists of six

Manuscript received December 19, 1990; revised January 15, 1992. Recommended by M. V. Zelkowitz. This work was supported by the Naval Surface Warfare Center, and by the Army Operational Test and Evaluation Center.
The author is with the Naval Postgraduate School, Monterey, CA 93943.
IEEE Log Number 9107760.

mathematically defined criteria, each of which is keyed to a quality function, so the user of metrics can understand how a characteristic of a metric, as revealed by validation tests, can be applied to measure software quality. (iv) The six criteria are: association, consistency, discriminative power, tracking, predictability, and repeatability. (v) It recognizes that a given metric can have multiple uses (e.g., assess, control, and predict quality) and that a given metric can be valid for one use and invalid for another use. (vi) It defines a metrics validation process that integrates quality factors, metrics, and functions.

This paper is organized as follows. First, in Section II a framework is established which pulls together the concepts and definitions of quality factor, quality metric, validated metric, quality function, validity criteria, and a metrics validation process. These concepts and definitions are integrated by the use of a metrics validation process chart. In this section we show how validity criteria support quality functions. Next, in Section III we indicate why nonparametric statistical methods are applicable to and compatible with the validity criteria. This is followed in Section IV by an example of metrics validation, using the discriminative power validity criterion. Lastly, in Section V some comments are made about future research directions.

II. FRAMEWORK

The framework of our metrics methodology consists of the following elements, which are keyed to Fig. 1: the quality factor, quality metric, validated metric, quality functions, validity criteria, and metrics validation process. In Fig. 1 we use the notation (*Project, Time, Measurement*) to designate the project, time (e.g., life-cycle phase), and type of measurement (quality factor, quality metric). We use V to designate the project in which a metric is validated, and A to designate the project in which the metric is applied.

This diagram is interpreted as follows:

- The events and time progression of the validation project are depicted by the top horizontal line and arrow. This time line consists of Project 1 with metric M collection in Phase $T1$ (step 1); factor F collection in Phase $T2$ (step 2); and validation of M with respect to F in Phase $T2$ (step 3).
- The events and time progression of the application project are depicted by the bottom horizontal line and arrow. This project is later in chronological time than the validation project, but has the same phases $T1$ and $T2$. This time line consists of Project 2 with metric collection M' in Phase $T1$ (step 4); application of M' to assess, control, and predict quality in Phase $T1$ (step 5); collection of

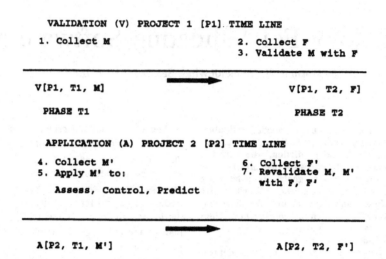

VALIDATION (V) PROJECT 1 [P1] TIME LINE

1. Collect M   2. Collect F
                                                3. Validate M with F

V[P1, T1, M]   ⟶   V[P1, T2, F]

PHASE T1   PHASE T2

APPLICATION (A) PROJECT 2 [P2] TIME LINE

4. Collect M'   6. Collect F'
5. Apply M' to: 7. Revalidate M, M'
                                                   with F, F'
   Assess, Control, Predict

A[P2, T1, M']   ⟶   A[P2, T2, F']

Fig. 1. Metrics validation process.

factor F' in Phase $T2$ (step 6); and revalidation of M and M' with respect to F and F' in Phase $T2$ (step 7).
• Metric M' is the same metric as M, but in general it has different values, since it is collected in a different project. The same statement applies to F' and F.

Each element is defined and described in greater detail in the following subsections.

A. Quality Factor

A quality factor F (hereafter referred to as "factor" or "F") is an attribute of software that contributes to its quality [13], where software quality is defined as the degree to which software possesses a desired combination of attributes [14]. For example, reliability (an attribute that contributes to quality) is a factor. A factor can have values such as the error counts $F_1, \ldots, F_n$ in a set of software components (i.e., an element of a software system, such as module, unit, data, or document [13]). We define F to be a type of metric that provides a direct measure of software quality [6]. This means that F is an intrinsic indicator of quality as perceived by the user, such as errors in the software that result in failures during operation. We denote F as the factor in V, and F' as the factor in A. F and F' are shown as collected at points 2 and 6, respectively, in Fig. 1.

B. Quality Metric

A quality metric M (hereafter called "metric" or "M") is a function (e.g., cyclomatic complexity $M = e - n + 2p$) whose inputs are software data (elementary software measurements, such as the number of edges e and number of nodes n in a directed graph), and whose output is a single numerical value M that can be interpreted as the degree to which software possesses a given attribute (cyclomatic complexity) that may affect its quality (e.g., reliability) [15]. For example, if there are two components 1 and 2 with $M_1 = 3$ and $M_2 = 10$, this may indicate that the reliability of 1 may be greater than the reliability of 2. Whether this is the case depends upon whether M is a valid metric (see below). We define M to be an indirect

measure of software quality [2], [6]. This means that M may be used as a substitute for F when F is not available, as is the case during the design phase. M is shown as collected at point 1 in Fig. 1.

It is important to recognize that in general there can be a many-to-many relationship between F and M. For expository purposes, we limit our examples to one-to-one or one (F) to many (M) relationships.

C. Validated Metric

A validated metric is one whose values have been shown to be statistically associated with corresponding factor values (e.g., $M_1, \ldots, M_n$ have been statistically associated with $F_1, \ldots, F_n$ for a set of software components $1, \ldots, n$) [13]. A validation test of M with respect to F is shown at point 3 in Fig. 1. We denote M' as a validated metric. Since M is validated with respect to F, it is necessarily the case that F is valid. Therefore we say that F is valid by definition as a result of wide acceptance or historical usage (e.g., error count).

Since F is a direct measure of quality, it is preferred over M whenever it is possible to measure F sufficiently early in the life cycle to permit quality to be assessed, controlled, and predicted (see below). However, since this is usually not the case, the need for validation arises. We also note that since the cost of finding and correcting errors grows rapidly with the life cycle, it is advantageous to have approximate early (leading) indicators of software quality. (Analogously, one could posit that the Dow Jones stock price average (M) is an approximate leading indicator of the gross national product (F) in the American economy and conduct a validation test between the two.) Thus we can formulate the following policy with respect to software measurement: when it is feasible to measure and apply F, use it; otherwise, attempt to validate M with respect to F and, if successful, use M'.

D. Quality Functions

Quality functions are activities conducted by software organizations for the purpose of achieving project quality goals.

Both product and process goals are included. The quality functions that are pertinent to this metrics methodology are: assessment, control, and prediction.

1) Quality Assessment: Quality assessment is the evaluation of the relative quality of software components. "Relative quality" is the quality of a given component compared with the quality of other components in the set (e.g., if M' is cyclomatic complexity, the quality of component 1, with $M' = 3$, may be better than the quality of component 2, with $M' = 10$). Validated metrics are used to make a relative comparison of the quality of software components. The purpose of assessment is to provide software managers with a rational basis for assigning priorities for quality improvement and for allocating personnel and computer resources to quality assurance functions. For example, priorities and resources would be assigned on the basis of relative values (or ranks) of M' (i.e., the most resources would be assigned to the components with the highest (lowest) values (or ranks) of M'). M' is shown collected at point 4 in Fig. 1, and used for assessment at point 5.

2) Quality Control: Quality control is the evaluation of software components against predetermined critical values of metrics (i.e., the value of M' that is used to identify software which has unacceptable quality [13]) and the identification of components that fall outside quality limits. We denote M'_c as the critical value of M'. Validated metrics are used to identify components with unacceptable quality. The purpose of control is to allow software managers to identify software that has unacceptable quality sufficiently early in the development process to take corrective action. For example, $M'_c = 3$ would be used as a critical value of cyclomatic complexity to discriminate between components that contain errors and those that do not.

Control also involves the tracking of the quality of a component over its life cycle. For example, if M' is cyclomatic complexity, an increase from 3 to 10, as the result of a design change, would be used to indicate possible degradation in quality. M' is shown as collected at point 4 in Fig. 1, and used for control at point 5.

3) Quality Prediction: Quality prediction is a forecast of the value of F at time $T2$ based on the values of $M'_1, M'_2, \ldots, M'_n$ for components $1, 2, \ldots, n$ at time $T1$, where "time" could be computer execution time, labor time, or calendar time. Validated metrics (e.g., size and complexity) are used during the design phase to make predictions of test or operational phase factors (e.g., error count). The purpose of prediction is to provide software managers with a forecast of the quality of the operational software, and to flag components for detailed inspection whose predicted factor values are greater than (or less than) the target values (determined from requirements analysis). M' is shown as collected at point 4 in Fig. 1, and used for prediction at point 5.

E. Validity Criteria

Validity criteria provide the rationale for validating metrics—they are the specific quantitative relationships that are hypothesized to exist between factors and metrics. Validity criteria, in turn, are based on the principle of validity, which defines the general quantitative relationship between factors and metrics that must exist for the validity criteria to be applied. First, we provide definitions relating to the principle of validity. Then we define the principle of validity. Lastly, we define each validity criterion and provide an example of its application.

1) Definitions:

$$R[M] : \text{Relation } R \text{ on vector } \boldsymbol{M} \text{ for } V[P1, T1, M] \tag{1}$$

$$R[F] : \text{Relation } R \text{ on vector } \boldsymbol{F} \text{ for } V[P1, T2, F] \tag{2}$$

$$R[M'] : \text{Relation } R \text{ on vector } \boldsymbol{M}' \text{ for } A[P2, T1, M'] \tag{3}$$

$$R[F'] : \text{Relation } R \text{ on vector } \boldsymbol{F}' \text{ for } A[P2, T2, F'] \tag{4}$$

where R could be, for example, an order relation such as: Magnitude $[M_1 < M_2 \ldots < M_n]$ and Magnitude $[F_1 < F_2 \ldots < F_n]$ involving n values (data points) for M and F.

2) Principle of Validity:

$$\text{IF } R[M] \Leftrightarrow R[F]$$

is validated statistically with confidence level α and, for certain validity criteria, with threshold value β_i,

$$\text{THEN } \{R[M] \Leftrightarrow R[F]\} \Rightarrow \{R[M'] \Rightarrow R[F']\}? \tag{5}$$

In other words, does the mapping $M \Leftrightarrow F$, validated on Project 1, imply a mapping $M' \Rightarrow F'$ on Project 2? We assume (5) to be true at point 5 in Fig. 1. Once F' is collected at point 6, we revalidate (or invalidate) (5) by repeating the validation test using aggregated M and M', validated with respect to aggregated F and F' at point 7.

We note that a metric may be valid with respect to certain validity criteria, and invalid with respect to other criteria. Each validity criterion supports one or more of the quality functions assessment, control, and prediction, which were described above. The validity criteria—association, consistency, discriminative power, tracking, predictability, and repeatability—are applied at point 3 of Fig. 1. The particular criteria that are used depend on the quality functions (one or more) that are to be supported.

The validation procedure requires that threshold values β_i be selected for certain validity criteria. The criterion used for selecting these values is reasonableness (i.e., judgment must be exercised in selecting values to strike a balance between the one extreme of causing an M, which has a high degree of association with F, to fail validation, and the other extreme of allowing an M of questionable validity to pass validation).

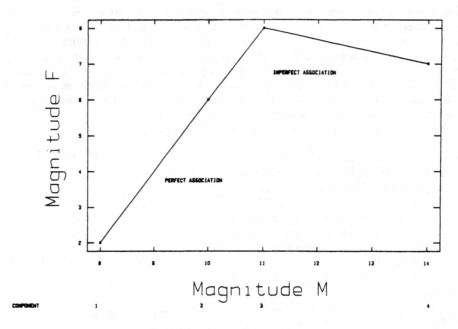

Fig. 2. Association validity criterion.

A short simple numerical example follows the definition of each validity criterion for the purpose of illustrating the basic concepts of the validity criteria. For illustrative purposes, F is error count and M is cyclomatic complexity, or complexity for short, in the examples. Also, to keep the examples simple we use small sample sizes; these sample sizes would not be acceptable in practice. As noted previously, given $\{F\}$ and $\{M\}$, it is possible to have an M_j in $\{M\}$ predict multiple F's in $\{F\}$, or to have an F_i in $\{F\}$ predicted by multiple M's in $\{M\}$. However, in order to simplify the examples, only the one-to-one case will be illustrated.

3) Association: The variation in F explained by the variation in M, which is given by R^2 (coefficient of determination), where R is the linear correlation coefficient, must exceed a specified threshold, or

$$R^2 > \beta_a, \text{ with specified } \alpha. \qquad (6)$$

This criterion assesses whether there is a sufficient linear association between F and M to warrant using M as an indirect measure of F. This criterion supports the quality assessment function as follows.

If the elements of vector M, corresponding to components $1, 2, \ldots, n$, are ordered by magnitude, as illustrated in Table I, can we infer a linear ordering of F with respect to M for the purpose of assessing differences in component quality? In other words, does the following hold?

$$\text{Magnitude}[M_1 < M_2 \ldots < M_i \ldots < M_n] \Leftrightarrow$$
$$\text{Magnitude}[F_1 < F_2 \ldots < F_i \ldots < F_n] \qquad (7)$$

and $(M_{i+1} - M_i) \propto (F_{i+1} - F_i)$ for $i = 1, 2, \ldots, n-1$.

The data of Table I are plotted in Fig. 2 to contrast perfect with imperfect association.

Since there is seldom perfect linear magnitude ordering between F and M (i.e., $R = 1.0$), we use (6) to measure

TABLE I
VALIDATION PROJECT

Component	M (magnitude)	M (rank)	F (magnitude)	F (rank)
1	8	1	2	1
2	10	2	6	2
3	11	3	8	4
4	14	4	7	3

the degree to which (7) holds. For example, if $R = 0.9$ and $\alpha = 0.05$, then 81% of the variation in F (error count) is explained by the variation in M (complexity), with an acceptable confidence level. If this relationship is demonstrated over a representative sample of components, and if β_a has been established as 0.7, we could conclude that M is associated with F and can be used to compare magnitudes of complexity obtained from different components to assess the degree to which they differ in quality (e.g., the difference in complexity magnitude between component 2 and component 1 (10–8) is proportional to their differences in quality in Table I).

The resultant M' would be used to assess differences in the quality of components on the application project.

4) Consistency: The rank correlation coefficient r between F and M must exceed a specified threshold, or

$$r > \beta_c, \text{ with specified } \alpha. \qquad (8)$$

This criterion assesses whether there is sufficient consistency between the ranks of F and the ranks of M to warrant using M as an indirect measure of F [9]. This criterion supports the quality assessment function as follows.

If the elements of vector M, corresponding to components $1, 2, \ldots, n$, are ordered by rank as illustrated in Table I, can we infer an ordering of F with respect to M for the purpose

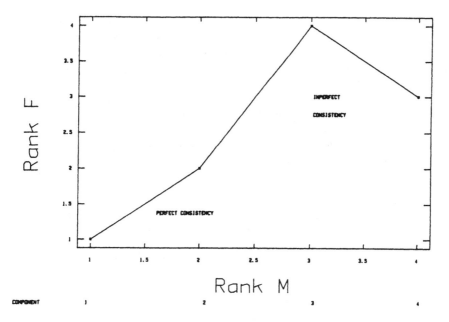

Fig. 3. Consistency validity criterion.

of assessing the rank order of component quality? In other words, does the following hold?

$$\text{Rank}[M_1 < M_2 \ldots < M_i \ldots < M_n] \Leftrightarrow$$
$$\text{Rank}[F_1 < F_2 \ldots < F_i \ldots < F_n]. \quad (9)$$

The data of Table I are plotted in Fig. 3 to contrast perfect with imperfect consistency for the same set of components.

Since there is seldom perfect rank ordering between F and M (i.e., $r = 1.0$), we use (8) to measure the degree to which (9) holds. For example, if $r = 0.8$ and $\alpha = 0.05$, there is an 80% ranking between F and M, with an acceptable confidence level. If this relationship is demonstrated over a representative sample of components, and if β_c has been established as 0.7, we could conclude that M is consistent with F and can be used to compare ranks of complexity obtained from different components to assess the degree to which they differ in relative quality (e.g., component 2 quality is lower (higher complexity) than component 1 quality in Table I).

The resultant M' would be used to assess relative quality of components on the application project.

5) Discriminative Power: The critical value of a metric M_c must be able to discriminate, for a specified F_c, between elements (components $1, 2, \ldots, i, \ldots n$) of vector F [17] in the following way:

$$M_i > M_c \Leftrightarrow F_i > F_c \text{ and}$$
$$M_i \leq M_c \Leftrightarrow F_i \leq F_c \quad (10)$$

for $i = 1, 2, \ldots, n$ with specified α.

This criterion assesses whether M_c has sufficient discriminative power to warrant using it as an indirect measure of F_c. This criterion supports the quality control function as follows.

Would M_c, as illustrated in Table II, partition F for a specified F_c as defined in (10)? For example, the data from

TABLE II
VALIDATION PROJECT

$M_c = 10$ $F_c = 2$	$M \leq M_c$	$M > M_c$
$F \leq F_c$	$O_{11} = 1$	$O_{12} = 0$
$F > F_c$	$O_{21} = 1$	$O_{22} = 2$

$O_{ij} = $ count of observations in cell i, j.

O_{11}, O_{22}: correct classifications.

O_{12}, O_{21}: incorrect classifications.

Table I is used in Table II, with $M_c = 10$ and $F_c = 2$. We see that discriminative power is not perfect in Table II (i.e., $O_{21} \neq 0$). If it is desired to flag components with more than two errors ($F > F_c$) for detailed inspection and if $M_c' = 10$ (complexity) is validated, it would be used on the application project to control quality (i.e., discriminate between acceptable and unacceptable components), as shown in Fig. 4. One purpose of Fig. 4 is to identify trends in quality (e.g., a persistent case of components being in the unacceptable zone).

Since there is seldom a perfect discriminator M_c for F_c (i.e., $O_{12} = O_{21} = 0$ in Table II), we use an appropriate statistical method (e.g., chi-square contingency table [7], [8], [12]) and representative sample of components to measure the degree to which (10) holds.

6) Tracking: M must change in unison with F for a given component i at times $T_1, T_2, \ldots T_j, \ldots, T_m$ as follows:

$$M_i(T_{j+1}) > M_i(T_j) \Leftrightarrow F_i(T_{j+1}) > F_i(T_j)$$
$$M_i(T_{j+1}) = M_i(T_j) \Leftrightarrow F_i(T_{j+1}) = F_i(T_j)$$
$$M_i(T_{j+1}) < M_i(T_j) \Leftrightarrow F_i(T_{j+1}) < F_i(T_j) \quad (11)$$

with specified α.

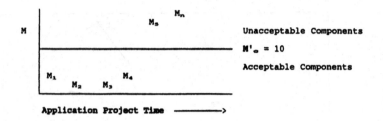

Fig. 4.   Application of metrics to quality control (discriminative power) for components 1, 2, ... n.

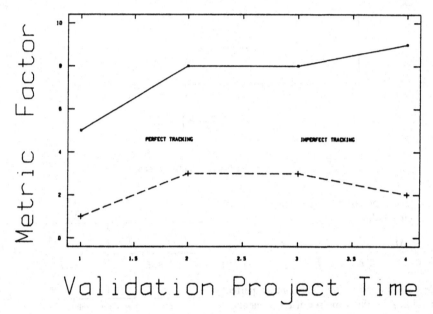

Fig. 5.   Tracking validity criterion (component i).

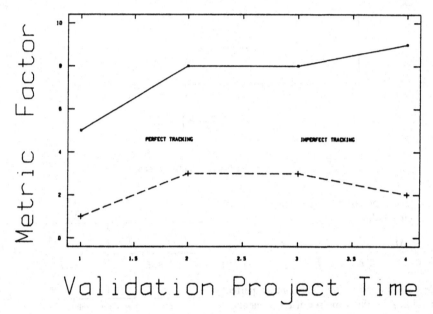

Fig. 6.   Application of metrics to quality control (tracking) for component i at times 1, 2, ..., m.

This criterion is illustrated graphically in Fig. 5 to contrast perfect with imperfect tracking, where factor and metric values are plotted against project time.

This criterion assesses whether M is capable of tracking changes in F (e.g., as a result of design changes) to a sufficient degree to warrant using M as an indirect measure of F. This criterion supports the quality control function as follows.

Would changes in M track changes in F as defined in (11)? If M is validated, then a vector $M_i'(T_j)$ consisting of the values $M_i'(T_1), M_i'(T_2), \ldots, M_i'(T_j), \ldots, M_i'(T_m)$ of component i, measured at times $T_1, T_2, \ldots, T_j, \ldots, T_m$ would be used to track quality on the application project. For example, if complexity M_i' is valid for tracking error count F, M_i' would be used as shown in Fig. 6, where quality increases from T_1

to T_2, stays the same from T_2 to T_3, and decreases thereafter.

Since there is seldom perfect tracking of F by M, we use an appropriate statistical method (e.g., binary sequences test [8]) and representative sample for component i to measure the degree to which (11) holds.

7) Predictability: A function of M, $f(M)$, where M is measured at time $T1$, must predict F, measured at time $T2$, with an accuracy β_p or

$$\left| \frac{Fa_{T2} - Fp_{T2}}{Fa_{T2}} \right| < \beta_p \qquad (12)$$

where Fa_{T2} is the actual value, and Fp_{T2} is the predicted value.

This criterion is illustrated graphically in Fig. 7 to contrast perfect with imperfect prediction, where $f(M)$, formulated at $T1$, will either turn out to be equal to Fa at $T2$ (perfect Predictability), or be equal to Fp^+ or Fp^- (imperfect Predictability).

This criterion assesses whether $f(M)$ can predict F with required accuracy. This criterion supports the quality prediction function as follows.

If (12) holds, would the following hold?

$$Fp_{T2} = f(M_{T1}) \Rightarrow Fp_{T2}' = f(M_{T1}') \qquad (13)$$

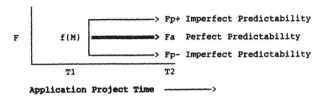

Fig. 7.   Application of metrics to quality prediction (predictability) for a component.

where vector $Fp_{T2} = [F_1, F_2, \ldots, F_n]_{T2}$ and vector $M_{T1} = [M_1, M_2, \ldots, M_n]_{T1}$ for components $1, 2, \ldots, n$, and Fp'_{T2}, and M'_{T1} are similarly defined. In other words, do we have:

$$\left| \frac{Fa'_{T2} - Fp'_{T2}}{Fa'_{T2}} \right| < \beta_p. \tag{14}$$

For example, if a function f relating error count with complexity can be identified (e.g., regression analysis) that is a good predictor of F (i.e., satisfies (12)), then we would use the same f as the predictor of F' to predict error count from complexity on the application project.

Since there is seldom a perfect f (i.e., $Fp_{T2} = Fa_{T2}$), we use (12) to measure the degree to which f predicts F.

8) Repeatability: The success rate of validating M for a given validity criterion i must satisfy:

$$N_{is}/N_i > \beta_{is} \tag{15}$$

where N_{is} is the number of validations of M for criterion i, and N_i is the total number of trials for criterion i.

This criterion assesses whether M can be validated on a sufficient percentage of trials to have confidence that it would be a dependable indicator of quality in the long run. We use "trials," because validation could be performed with respect to projects, applications, components, or some other appropriate entity.

F. Metrics Validation Process

Given that there must be a validation project V and an application project A, as shown in Fig. 1, this requirement gives rise to what we call the "fundamental problem in metrics validation." This problem arises because there could be significant time lags, product and process differences, and differences in goals and environments [5] between the following phases of the validation process (see Fig. 1):

1) $V[P1, T1, M]$ and $V[P1, T2, F]$
2) $V[P1, T2, F]$ and $A[P2, T1, M']$
3) $A[P2, T1, M']$ and $A[P2, T2, F']$.

An important characteristic of the methodology is expressed by the following:

$$\text{IF } V[P1, T1, M] \Leftrightarrow V[P1, T2, F]$$
$$\text{THEN } A[P2, T1, M'] \Rightarrow A[P2, T2, F']. \tag{16}$$

From (16), it follows that at point 3 in Fig. 1, M is validated in V. Whether M' will actually be valid in A will not be known until point 7. Thus it is worthwhile to discuss some of the practical difficulties of adhering to (16) and possible remedies.

With respect to phase 1), the product or process may have changed so much between $T1$ and $T2$ that M, collected at $T1$, may no longer be representative of F. If this is the case, M should be collected again at $T2$ to validate against F. The advantage of collecting M at $T1$ is that it may be easier and less expensive than at $T2$, because M can be collected as a by-product of compilation and design and code inspections.

The same considerations apply with respect to phase 3), except that now the concern is with whether M' collected at $T1$ should be used for revalidation at $T2$. However, note that it is mandatory that M' be collected at $T1$ to have an early indication of possible quality problems (that is a key concept of our methodology!).

With respect to phase 2), we can achieve a degree of stability in the validation process if the following procedure is employed:

a) Select V and A to be as similar as possible with respect to application and development environments.

With respect to phases 1)–3) considered jointly, we can achieve a degree of stability in the validation process if procedure a) is employed, plus the following two additional procedures:

b) Select the same life cycle phase for $T1$ in V and A.
c) Select the same life cycle phase for $T2$ in V and A.

We recognize that it may be infeasible to implement these procedures. If this is the case, it means that there is a higher risk that M validated at point 3 in Fig. 1 will not remain valid at point 5.

III. NONPARAMETRIC STATISTICAL METHODS FOR METRICS VALIDATION

Nonparametric statistical methods are used to support metrics validation, because these methods have important advantages over parametric methods. Indeed, it would be infeasible to validate metrics in many situations without their use. This is the case, because the assumptions that must be satisfied to employ nonparametric methods are less demanding than those that apply to parametric methods. This might lead to the conclusion that nonparametric methods are less rigorous than parametric methods. Despite this possible perception, nonparametric methods allow us to develop very useful order relations concerning the relative quality of components. The validity criteria which use nonparametric methods are shown in Table III. The advantages of nonparametric methods over parametric methods, which are important for metrics validation, are the following:

TABLE III
VALIDITY CRITERIA PROPERTIES

Criterion	Scale	Method	Measurement Property
Association	Interval	Parametric	Difference
Consistency	Ordinal	Nonparametric	Higher/Lower
Discriminative Power	Nominal	Nonparametric	High/Low
Tracking	Nominal	Nonparametric	Increment
Predictability	Interval, Ratio	Parametric	% Accuracy
Repeatability	Ratio	Parametric	% Success

TABLE IV
EXAMPLE DATA

Project Application	Procedures (with errors)	Statements	Errors
1. String Processing	11 (5)	136	10
2. Directed Graph Analysis	31 (12)	430	27
3. Directed Graph Analysis	1 (1)	13	1
4. Data Base Management	69 (13)	1021	26
	112 (31)	1600	64

Number of procedures: 112 total, 31 with errors, 81 with no errors.

Number of source statements: 2007 total, 1600 included in metrics analysis.

Language : Pascal on all projects.

Programmer: Single programmer. Same programmer on all projects.

- Given the noisiness of metrics data, the fact that the assumptions are less restrictive is a big advantage.
- No assumption is necessary about distribution (e.g., data does not have to be normally distributed).
- We can use the nominal scale (i.e., component A is high quality, component B is low quality) and location statistics like the median [11]. The *Discriminative Power* validity criterion is based on this measurement property. Similarly, we can use the nominal scale to indicate whether an incremental change in a metric tracks (yes/no) an incremental change in a factor. The *Tracking* validity criterion is based on this measurement property.
- We can use the ordinal scale (i.e., component A is higher quality than component B) and order statistics such as ranks. The *Consistency* validity criterion is based on this measurement property. For example, ranks of random variables [3] can be used rather than the values themselves, thus relaxing the assumptions about data relationships (e.g., linearity), while providing a measure of quality (e.g., ranking of components) that is useful to the software manager. In other words, the fact that the data is not as "well-behaved" as we might believe it should be does not necessarily mean that it is less useful.

TABLE V
CONTINGENCY TABLE

	Complexity ≤ 3	Complexity > 3	
No Errors	75	6	81
Errors	10	21	31
	85	27	112

TABLE VI
PROJECTS 1, 2, 3, AND 4

C_c	χ^2	α
1	22.32	2.30E-6
2	32.14	1.44E-8
3	**41.60**	**1.26E-10**
4	26.80	2.26E-7

112 Procedures (81 with no errors, 31 with errors)

In fact, when we consider that many useful applications of metrics can be derived from the ability to classify components as being "higher quality" or "lower quality," we realize that the information provided by nonparametric analysis is supportive of this approach.

Despite the advantages of nonparametric methods, certain validity criteria lend themselves to the use of parametric methods. These are shown in Table III. "Association," which measures the difference in component quality, uses the interval scale. "Predictability" uses the interval scale to predict a factor value and the ratio scale for measuring prediction accuracy. Lastly, "Repeatability" uses the ratio scale for measuring metric validation success.

Appendix A summarizes the quality function, validity criterion, purpose of valid metric, and statistical method.

IV. EXAMPLE OF VALIDATING METRICS

The following example is provided to illustrate the validation of M with F and the identification of an M_c which would be used in the quality control function. Also, we show how to conduct a cost-sensitivity analysis on M_c in order to identify its optimal value (i.e., the minimum cost M_c across a range of assumptions about the cost of using M_c).

The data used in the example validation tests were collected from actual software projects. The "Discriminative Power" validity test is illustrated.

A. Purpose of Metrics Validation

The purpose of this validation is to determine whether cyclomatic number (complexity (C)) and size (number of source statements (S)) metrics, either singly or in combination, could be used to control the factor reliability as represented by the factor error count (E). A summary of the data is shown

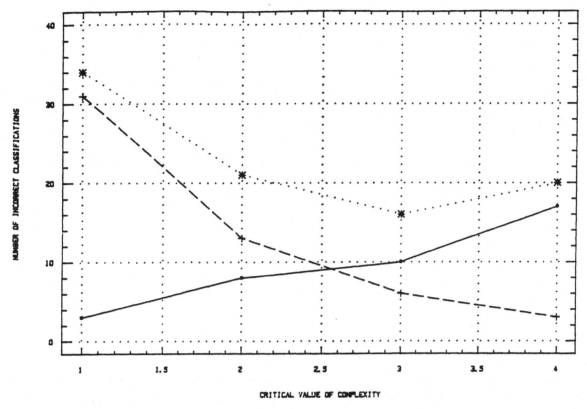

Fig. 8. Incorrect classification (complexity).

in Table IV, and the detailed data listing can be found in Appendix B.

Using the conventions of Fig. 1, the following is the notation applicable to this example:

Metric: C, S collected at point 1, Fig. 1.
Factor: E, collected at point 2, Fig. 1.
Critical Value of Metric: C_c, S_c validated at point 3, Fig. 1.
V[Projects 1, 2, 3, 4: Design; C, S]
V[Projects 1, 2, 3, 4: Test; E]

B. Discriminative Power Validity Test

We divide the data into four categories, as shown in Table V, according to a critical value of C, C_c, so that a chi-square test can be performed to determine whether C_c can discriminate between procedures with errors and those with no errors [4].

From the high value of chi-square (41.60) (see Table VI) and the very small significance level (1.26E-10) in the samples, we infer that $C_c = 3$ could discriminate between procedures with errors (low-quality software) and those without errors (high-quality software).

Table V shows how good a job $C_c = 3$ does to discriminate between procedures with errors and procedures with no errors: 75 of 81 with no errors, and 21 of 31 with errors are correctly classified.

C. Sensitivity Analysis of Critical Value of Complexity

In order to see how good a discriminator C_c is for this example, we observe the number of misclassifications that result for various values of C_c : (i) Type 1 ("error procedures," classified as "no error procedures"), and (ii) Type 2 ("no error procedures," classified as "error procedures"). This is shown in Fig. 8. As C_c increases Type 1 misclassifications increase, because an increasing number of high complexity procedures, many of which have errors, are classified as having "no errors." Conversely, as C_c decreases Type 2 misclassifications increase, because an increasing number of low complexity procedures, many of which have no errors, are classified as having "errors." The total of the two curves represents the "misclassification function." It has a minimum at $C_c = 3$, which is the value given by the chi-square test (see Table VI). The chi-square test will not always produce the optimal C_c,

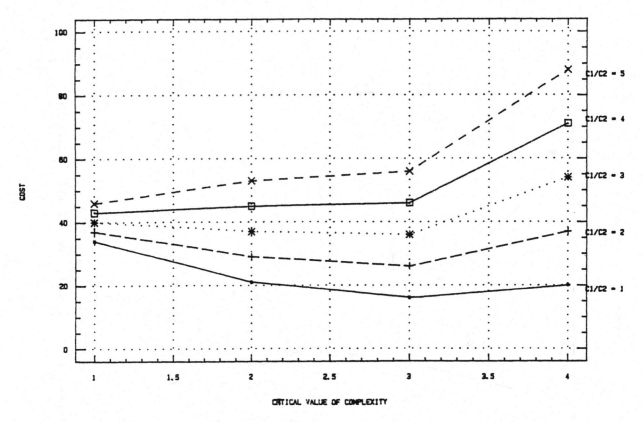

Fig. 9. Cost of incorrect classification (complexity).

but the value should be close to optimal.

The foregoing analysis assumes that the costs of Type 1 and Type 2 misclassifications are equal. This is usually not the case, since the consequences of not finding an error (i.e., concluding that there is no error when, in fact, there is an error) would be higher than the other case (i.e., concluding that there is an error when, in fact, there is no error). In order to account for this situation, the number of Type 1 misclassifications for given values of C_c is multiplied by $C1/C2$ ($C1/C2 = 1, 2, 3, 4, 5$), which is the ratio of the cost of Type 1 misclassification to the cost of Type 2 misclassification. These values are added to the number of Type 2 misclassification to produce the family of five "cost" curves shown in Fig. 9. Naturally, with the higher cost of Type 1 misclassifications taking effect, the optimal C_c (i.e., minimum cost) decreases. However, even at $C1/C2 = 5, Cc = 3$ is a reasonable choice.

A "Contingency Table" was also developed for S, leading to $S_c = 13$. The same type of sensitivity analysis was performed on S_c. It was found that the optimal is $S_c = 15$, as opposed to $S_c = 13$, as given by the chi-square analysis.

We conclude that C and S are valid with respect to the "Discriminative Power" criterion, and either could be used to distinguish between acceptable ($C \leq 3, S \leq 13$) and unacceptable quality ($C > 3, S > 13$) for this and similar applications when this data can be collected. However, only one is needed (i.e., C is highly correlated with S). It should be noted that it is less expensive to collect S than C.

V. SUMMARY AND FUTURE RESEARCH

We described and illustrated a comprehensive metrics validation methodology that has six validity criteria, which support the quality functions of assessment, control, and prediction. Six criteria were defined and illustrated: association, consistency, discriminative power, tracking, predictability, and repeatability. These criteria are important because they provide a rationale for validating metrics; in practice, this rationale is frequently lacking in the selection and application of metrics. With validated metrics we have a basis for making decisions and taking actions to improve the quality of software. We showed that quality factors, metrics, and functions can be integrated with our metrics validation process. We developed a framework which pulls together the concepts and definitions of quality factor, quality metric, validated metric, quality function, validity criteria, and the metrics validation process. We showed that nonparametric statistical methods play an important role in evaluating whether metrics satisfy the validity criteria. An example of the application of the methodology was presented for the discriminative power validation criterion. The discriminative power criterion allows the metrics user to control the production of highly reliable software by providing thresholds of acceptable quality.

Future research is needed to extend and improve the methodology by finding an answer to the following question: to what extent are metrics that have been validated on one project, using our criteria, valid measures of quality on future projects—both similar and different projects?

Appendix A is given in Table VII.

TABLE VII
APPENDIX A

Quality Function	Validity Criterion	Purpose of Valid Metric	Statistical Method
Quality Assessment	Association	Assess differences in quality	1. Coeff. of Determination $R^2 > \beta_a$. 2. H0: Population Correlation Coeff. = 0. 3. H0: Population Correlation Coefficient $> \sqrt{\beta_a}$. 4. Linear Partial Correlation Coeff. (Metric Normalization. Accounting for Size). 5. Population Correlation Coefficient Confidence Interval. 6. Factor Analysis (Tests of Independence).
Quality Assessment	Consistency	Assess relative quality	1. Rank Correlation Coefficient $r > \beta_c$.
Quality Control	Discriminative Power	Control Quality (discriminate between high and low)	1. Mann-Whitney Comparison of Average Ranks of Two Groups of components. 2. Chi-square Contingency Table for Finding Critical Value of Metric. 3. Short-Cut Technique for Finding Critical Value of Metric: Maximize $O_{11}O_{22}$. 4. Sensitivity Analysis of Critical Value of Metric. 5. Krusal-Wallis Test of Average Metric Rank Per Given Value of Quality Factor. 6. Discriminant Analysis (Use of a Single Metric's Mean as Discriminator).
Quality Control	Tracking	Control quality (track changes)	1. Binary Sequences Test and Wald-Wolfowitz Runs Test.
Quality Prediction	Predictability	Predict quality	1. Scatter Plot to Investigate Linearity. 2. Linear Regression. a. Test Assumptions b. Examine Residuals 3. Find Confidence and Prediction Intervals. 4. Test for Predictability $<$ Threshold (β_p) and Repeatability $>$ Threshold (β_{is}). 5. Non-linear Regression. 6. Multiple Linear Regression. a. Test Assumptions b. Examine Residuals c. Test for Predictability $<$ Threshold (β_p) and Repeatability $>$ Threshold (β_{is}).
All Quality Functions	Repeatability	Ensure metric validated with specified success rate	Ratio of Validations to Total Trials $>$ Threshold (β_{is})

APPENDIX B

Appendix B is given in Table VIII.

TABLE VIII
APPENDIX B—PROCEDURES WITH NO ERRORS

C	S	E	Project	C	S	E	Project
2	6	0	1	1	3	0	4
1	8	0	1	1	3	0	4
1	11	0	1	1	3	0	4
1	4	0	1	1	5	0	4
3	18	0	1	1	5	0	4
3	15	0	1	1	6	0	4
1	3	0	2	1	9	0	4
1	3	0	2	1	6	0	4
1	3	0	2	1	8	0	4
1	3	0	2	1	9	0	4
1	3	0	2	1	9	0	4
1	3	0	2	2	4	0	4
1	3	0	2	2	7	0	4
1	3	0	2	2	9	0	4
1	5	0	2	4	56	0	4
1	5	0	2	1	24	0	4
1	5	0	2	2	13	0	4
1	13	0	2	2	13	0	4
1	3	0	2	2	10	0	4
1	3	0	2	2	9	0	4
1	3	0	2	2	12	0	4
1	3	0	2	5	21	0	4
1	3	0	2	5	49	0	4
1	3	0	2	3	19	0	4
1	3	0	2	4	20	0	4
1	2	0	4	2	6	0	4
1	2	0	4	2	12	0	4
1	7	0	4	2	9	0	4
1	5	0	4	2	10	0	4
1	7	0	4	1	21	0	4
1	5	0	4	4	21	0	4
1	5	0	4	3	11	0	4
1	5	0	4	2	13	0	4
1	5	0	4	3	14	0	4
1	4	0	4	7	19	0	4
1	3	0	4	2	15	0	4
1	3	0	4	2	10	0	4
1	3	0	4	2	17	0	4
1	3	0	4	3	19	0	4
1	3	0	4	3	15	0	4
				2	15	0	4

(Continued)
C	S	E	Project	C	S	E	Project
2	34	2	2	13	49	5	4
4	19	1	2	4	19	1	4
5	30	2	2	4	27	1	4
				4	17	2	4

C : Complexity
S : Number of source statements (excluding comments)
E : Error count

Procedures with Errors

C	S	E	Project	C	S	E	Project
2	14	1	1	4	26	1	2
6	26	5	1	16	94	8	2
5	7	2	1	2	13	1	3
5	21	1	1	6	83	1	4
2	6	1	1	5	28	1	4
1	3	1	2	8	37	5	4
1	11	1	2	3	13	2	4
1	8	1	2	3	16	1	4
2	15	3	2	7	34	1	4
8	45	3	2	5	24	1	4
4	18	1	2	4	18	3	4
6	54	3	2	5	35	2	4

ACKNOWLEDGMENT

The author thanks the referees for their many useful comments and suggestions that have greatly improved this paper. He also thanks the members of the IEEE Standard for a Software Quality Metrics Methodology Working Group for many useful discussions and debates that helped inspire this work.

REFERENCES

[1] A. J. Albrecht and J. E. Gaffney, Jr., "Software function, source lines of code, and development error prediction: a software science validation," *IEEE Trans. Software Eng.*, vol. SE-9, pp. 639–648, Nov. 1983.
[2] A. L. Baker *et al.*, "A philosophy for software measurement," *J. Syst. Software*, vol. 12, no. 3, pp. 277–281, July 1990.
[3] V. R. Basili, R. W. Selby, Jr., and T.-Y. Phillips, "Metric analysis and data validation across Fortran projects," *IEEE Trans. Software Eng.*, vol. SE-9, pp. 652–663, Nov. 1983.
[4] V. R. Basili, and D. H. Hutchens, "An empirical study of a syntactic complexity family," *IEEE Trans. Software Eng.*, vol. SE-9, pp. 664–672, Nov. 1983.
[5] V. R. Basili and H. D. Rombach, "The TAME project: toward improvement-oriented software environments," *IEEE Trans. Software Eng.*, vol. 14, pp. 759–773, June 1988.
[6] M. E. Bush and N. E. Fenton, "Software measurement: a conceptual framework," *J. Syst. Software*, vol. 12, no. 3, pp. 223–231, July 1990.
[7] D. N. Card, G. T. Page, and F. E. McGarry, "Criteria for software modularization," in *Proc. 8th Int. Conf. on Software Eng.*, Aug. 1985, pp. 372–377.
[8] W. J. Conover, *Practical Nonparametric Statistics.* New York: Wiley, 1971.
[9] S. D. Conte, H. E. Dunsmore, and V. Y. Shen, *Software Engineering Metrics and Models.* Menlo Park, CA: Benjamin/Cummings, 1986.
[10] L. Felician and G. Zalateu, "Validating Halstead's theory for Pascal programs," *IEEE Trans. Software Eng.*, vol. 15, pp. 1630–1632, Dec. 1989.
[11] N. E. Fenton and A. Melton, "Deriving structurally based software metrics," *J. Syst. Software*, vol. 12, no. 3, pp. 177–187, July 1990.
[12] J. D. Gibbons, *Nonparametric Statistical Inference.* New York: McGraw-Hill, 1971.
[13] *IEEE Standard for a Software Quality Metrics Methodology* (draft), no. P-1061/D21, Apr. 1, 1990.
[14] *IEEE Standard Glossary of Software Engineering Terminology*, ANSI/IEEE Std. 729–1983.
[15] *IEEE Glossary of Software Engineering Terminology* (draft), no. P729/610.12/D8, Mar. 30, 1990.
[16] A. A. Porter and R. W. Selby, "Empirically guided software development using metric-based classification trees," *IEEE Software*, vol. 7, no. 2, pp. 46–54, Mar. 1990.
[17] E. J. Weyuker, "Evaluating software complexity measures," *IEEE Trans. Software Eng.*, vol. 14, pp. 1357–1365, Sept. 1988.

2

MAD ABOUT MEASUREMENT

Not previously published.

This essay is adapted from a keynote address I gave to the 5th International Conference on Applications of Software Measurement in La Jolla, Calif., November 9, 1994. The audience that day was large and warm, and much of the presentation was born on the stage, child of the magic that sometimes happens with a great audience.

Having worked during much of the last decade and a half in the area of software metrics, I find myself more and more troubled by the role of this now prominent component of our industry. The title I have chosen for this essay is meant to betray some of my ambivalence on the subject. The title can be read in two opposite ways, leaving one to wonder, Is the author madly positive about the success of software measurement? or Is he positively mad that our measurement hasn't really paid off? The answer is yes, I am. Both.

Any book you pick up on the subject of software metrics (my own *Controlling Software Projects* [1] included) is likely to be in the madly positive category. There is a mantra that runs through these books, something along the lines of "Look, here is *yet another* wonderful metric that could show you useful things about how your organization or project is doing." Many of the metrics are indeed compelling. The aggregate message, however, is what has begun to bother me. That message is

> Metrics Are Good.
> More Would Be Better.
> Most Is Best.

Though never stated in so many words, this message is everywhere. It is at the heart of metrics books, conferences, seminars, and articles. You can hardly focus on the literally hundreds of metrics proposed by Basili, Boehm, DeMarco and Lister, Gilb, Grady and Caswell, Jones, Matsubara, McCabe, Putnam, Rubin, and others without wondering uneasily if you really oughtn't to be collecting *all* of them. God, no.

This may seem obvious, but somebody really ought to say it: Metrics cost a ton of money. It costs a lot to collect them badly and a lot more to collect them well.

HOW MUCH IS ENOUGH?

In early 1984, my colleague Tim Lister and I visited what was then one of America's premier computer makers. We lectured and consulted there for a week. One of the things we noticed immediately was a culture of interruption in the software group. That meant developers could rarely work for more than a few minutes at a time on any one task. To call their attention to this, we suggested they begin to measure the length of work periods, uninterrupted chunks of time in which the developer could work obsessively on one thing and one thing only. This would involve some bookkeeping about each interruption, but it would have the positive effect of focusing attention on the value of extended chunks, and the frustration caused by the interruptions. The company agreed.

Years later, I called a contact in the company on another matter and was astounded to learn that they were still tracking interrupts. The rate had stabilized within a few months and all the value of building interrupt awareness had long since been realized. But they were still writing down the time and the cause of each interrupt.

I am sorry to say that that once great company is now not nearly so great. I do hope that Tim Lister and I were not the direct cause

Since I have been as guilty as anyone in overselling the idea of software metrics, it is perhaps incumbent on me to set the record straight on just how metrics data collection makes sense. Here is my best shot at it:

DeMarco's Mea Culpa Premise

I can only think of one metric that is worth collecting now and forever: defect count. Any organization that fails to track and type defects is running at less than its optimal level.

There are many other metrics that are worth collecting *for a while*. Each time you introduce and begin collecting a new metric, you need to put in place a mechanism to cease collecting that metric at some time in the future.

Many of the most useful metrics should be collected only on a sampling basis.

MEASUREMENT: AT ITS BEST AND AT ITS WORST

Sure, measurement costs money, but it does have the potential to help us work more effectively. At its best, the use of software metrics can inform and guide developers, and help organizations to improve. At its worst, it can do actual harm. And there is an entire range between the two extremes, varying all the way from function to dysfunction. It may be useful to bound this range with an example from each extreme.

First, the positive: Metrics could be defined as the discipline of counting things and observing and profiting from patterns found among the things we count. That is also a pretty fair definition of *science*. My sense of what science is has been affected over this last year by a new friendship with the biologist Uldis Roze, author of *The North American Porcupine* [2]. Much of what we know about porcupines today, about their habits and habitat, comes from painstaking (and often painful) research performed by Uldis Roze. You can't listen for long to the man describe his work without becoming aware of the central role of counting in porcupine research. He counts quills under trees to guess how much time the animals spend in each type of tree. He counts populations, numbers in their litters, death rates due to various kinds of injury and illness, droppings, bone fractures, quill density in various parts of the body ... anything that will hold still, he counts it.

Over dinner one night with our families, Uldis told a story to make that very point: He told of a little girl, ten years old, who had shown a budding interest in science. Her father, also a biologist, wondered what he could do to encourage her interest. Since her birthday was coming up, he thought about what kind of gift would be right: a microscope, perhaps? Or a chemistry set? But those seemed far too glitzy for his notion of what real science was. Finally, he hit upon the idea of giving her a click-counter. He set her to work in the nearby woods, counting anything she wanted to discover what she could about the natural world.

That image has stayed with me ever since, a symbol of the practice of science (and of metrics) at its best. I offer it as a guidepost to mark one end of the function/dysfunction spectrum: a little girl in the forest, bent on discovery, with a click-counter in her hand.

As an example of metrics at their worst, consider the case of the Soviet nail factory that was measured on the basis of the number of nails produced. The factory managers hit upon the idea of converting their entire factory to production of only the smallest nails, tiny brads. Some commissar, realizing this as a case of dysfunction, came up with a remedy. He instituted measurement of *tonnage* of nails produced, rather than numbers. The factory immediately switched over to producing only railroad spikes. The image I propose to mark the dysfunction end of the spectrum is a Soviet carpenter, looking perplexed, with a useless brad in one hand and an equally useless railroad spike in the other.

Now where does your organization stand along this spectrum? Are you closer to the little girl with the click-counter, or closer to the carpenter staring inn puzzlement at the two useless nails? Are you closer to function or dysfunction? Don't be too quick to answer. Dysfunction is far more common than you may think.

To help you place yourself and your organization, you need to understand why you collect metrics in the first place. I observe there are at least three different reasons we collect metrics as follows:

1. to discover Acts about our world
2. to steer our actions
3. to modify human behavior

We might arrange these, too, in a spectrum:

Behavior Modification ———— Steering ———— Discovery

Though I haven't yet given a formal definition of what I mean by *dysfunction,* I think you can sense that it is toward the left side of this spectrum where dysfunction is most likely to occur, and toward the right side where dysfunction is least likely; we may err in our attempts to discover, but we are not prone to systemic dysfunction. The middle ground, Steering, lies between the extremes in its propensity toward dysfunction.

Where does the discipline of software metrics lie on this spectrum? Well, we certainly started off, in the 1970s, to measure in order to discover. Indeed, we begin most presentations on measurement with some appropriate paean to Discovery. For instance, the following quote crops up in the first chapter or two of most measurement books:

> *When you can measure what you are speaking about, and express it in numbers, you know something about it; but when you cannot measure it, when you cannot express it in numbers, your knowledge is of a meager and unsatisfactory kind: it may be the beginning of knowledge, but you have scarcely, in your thoughts, advanced to the stage of science.* [Lord Kelvin, 1891]

In other words, Lord Kelvin suggests that we measure to know. My own quote "You can't control what you can't measure" implies that we measure to steer. But I'm beginning to wonder.

When we measure productivity, for example, we don't really do it to discover what our productivity is or to steer ourselves consistent with our actual productive capacity. When we measure productivity, we are stating loud and clear that we want productivity to increase. It's a goal. Similarly, when we measure defects, we are stating that we want the number of defects to be reduced. Neither of these statements is a bad goal in itself. But the measurements that lead toward them are neither Discovery nor Steering metrics. They are squarely in the camp of Behavior Modification, which leads me to the first of what will eventually become five Disquieting Thoughts About Software Metrics:

DT#I: Have we practitioners of software metrics little by little gotten out of the Discovery and Steering business and into the Behavior Modification business?

If so we are increasingly exposed to the possibility of dysfunction, of unwittingly causing outcomes that are squarely at odds with our goals.

Measurement programs, from the simplest to the most elaborate, all have the same goal: to make the organization more effective. But can we really say, after all these years of focusing on measurement, that organizations that do measure their software processes are on the whole more efficient than those that don't? There are a few impressive counterexamples, Microsoft and Apple to name just two companies that make no systematic use of software measurement. During the last decade, a period of triumphant ascendancy of software metrics as a discipline, these two companies have done just fine without. They aren't the only ones either. The entire small-cap sector is not known for its measurement practices, yet the solid vitality of the American economy since 1980 leas come almost entirely from these small companies.

Compare two organizations known respectively for measurement and nonmeasurement: IBM and Microsoft. What we know is that a propensity toward lots of software measurement at IBM is part of a larger pattern of activities that are prominent there and that have almost no counterpart at Microsoft: IBM is keen on the Software Engineering Institute's Capability Maturity Model (CMM), and Microsoft isn't. IBM has "fat book" methodologies, and Microsoft doesn't. IBM generates an enormous quantity of documentation as part of its software lifecycle, and Microsoft generates almost none. IBM is dedicated to ISO-9000 compliance and certification and Microsoft has simply thumbed its nose at ISO-9000.

What do the SEI's model, elaborate methodologies, copious documentation, and ISO-9000 compliance all have in common? Together, they can be interpreted as signs of *institutionalization*. Organizations characterized by all of these factors are the ones we tend to call "institutions," and the organizations that practice none of the above are something else. IBM is an institution, and Microsoft is a very large economic organism trying its best not to be an institution.

Considering software metrics in light of this pattern leads to my second Disquieting Thought About Software Metrics:

DT#2:   Is all of our measurement effort just part of a trend toward institutionalization?

I suspect there is at least some truth to that grim conjecture. Certainly, the companies best represented at metrics conferences and tutorials tend to be the most institutional ones. If that's true, it's bad news. I never wanted to be part of the institutionalization of anything, and I suspect you didn't either.

MEASUREMENT DYSFUNCTION

In this section, I present three brief examples of measurement dysfunction and, finally, a definition. My intention here is first to show you some of the patterns of dysfunction, and second to impress upon you that dysfunction is more prevalent than we like to acknowledge; dysfunction is not the exception to the rule, but the rule itself [3]. Two of the examples come from software measurement and one from outside our field.

Hitachi

The first example is taken from Hitachi Software. The dysfunction detected there is particularly depressing as it happened in the context of an altogether admirable bit of good science and good discovery measurement conducted by Hitachi's then Chief Scientist Tomoo Matsubara. In the late 1970s, Matsubara had begun to suspect that early detected defects could be a positive indication of as-yet-undetected defects. This relationship works particularly well if applied at a well-defined project checkpoint, say, end of unit test. The more defects you'd already found in your module through unit testing, according to Matsubara's rule, the more there were still to be found. Although counterintuitive, we now know this to be true in general and a powerful tool for assessing quality of a partly debugged product. It provides a reliable prediction of what Matsubara calls "latent defects." [4]

Hitachi moved quickly to exploit this relationship by tracking defects detected during the early testing, predicting latent defects still in the product, and then tracking the late integration testing process by comparing defects detected against latent defects suspected to be still in the code. This technique enabled them to produce a "quality-progress diagram," which they used to predict progress toward acceptable quality and to control project endgame activities (see Fig. 1).

No dysfunction yet. The scheme proved workable on a number of projects and eventually became integral to Hitachi's measurement program.

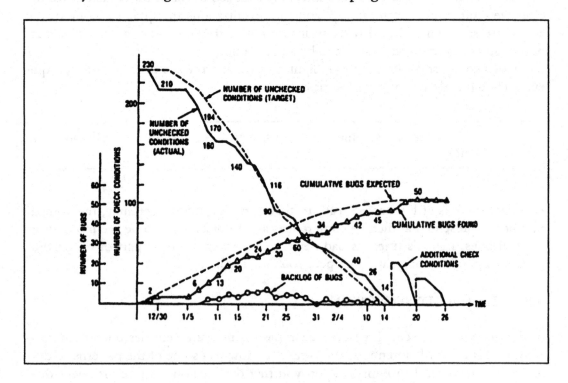

Figure 1. Hitachi's quality-progress diagram.

In March 1989, I received an astonishing letter from a young friend who was working under Matsubara at Hitachi. He reported that they had begun to detect a most curious misuse of the latent defect mechanism. Programmers had come to understand that more defects shown during unit test caused management to predict still more yet to be found. That translated to pressure on those workers to find an expected number of latent defects as the project neared its ship date. Consciously or unconsciously, developers began holding back defects found during unit test. Holding back a defect benefits the individual developers in three ways: They look good at the end of unit test, since their modules appear relatively defect free; they have fewer latent defects ascribed to their code, hence less pressure later; and they have one or two defects ready to produce during integration testing when management clamors for more: "Here's a defect I just found, Boss" they say, artfully neglecting to mention that they just found it in a pocket. Holding back defects benefits the developer, but doesn't benefit the organization at all. It is a clear example of dysfunction.

Sears

My second example of dysfunction is from outside the software field. You probably have already heard about it: the 1992 confession by marketing giant Sears, Roebuck, & Co. that the company "may have acted against its customers' best interests" in selling them unneeded product maintenance programs. In brief, the sales commission structure had given salespeople an incentive to sell more maintenance agreements, and the salespeople had done just that, selling far more than customers could really use. In June 1992, Sears addressed an open letter to its customers apologizing for the way the incentives had worked to their detriment and offering reimbursement. Guided by their commission scheme, the salespeople had acted in a way that, as Sears later acknowledged, was directly opposed to the company's real goals—another example of measurement dysfunction at work.

About the time of the Sears fiasco, I happened to be returning a pair of ski gauntlets to L.L. Bean in Freeport, Maine. The gauntlets had begun to come apart at a seam. I have an old engineers bias that seams should be stronger than the material they join, and so I was unsatisfied. But I was also a bit sheepish. After all, these gloves had served me well for two whole seasons. I explained the problem to the customer service agent, including my feeling about the required integrity of seams. And then I asked her if I was being unreasonable. "What do you think?" I asked. She looked down at my sales slip to catch my name. "Mr. DeMarco, it doesn't matter what I think. It only matters what *you* think, and you think the seams ought to be stronger than the fabric. So we're going to take these gauntlets back and give you a new pair or your money back, and we're going to tell the makers to strengthen their seams."

What was L.L. Bean doing that Sears had neglected? Somehow, L.L. Bean had caused this young employee to put herself in founder Leon L. Bean's shoes, to ask herself, "How would Mr. Bean handle this customer? How would he want me to act?" Sears instead had its salesfolk asking themselves, "How does the commission plan want me to act?"

United States Army

My final example contains only a suspicion of dysfunction. It is prompted by a speech presented by General Peter A. Kind of the United States Army to the Software Technology Conference of April 12, 1994, in Salt Lake City, Utah [5]. In this address, General Kind extolls the Army's record in instituting a program of software reuse. The program was difficult to implement but, on the whole, General Kind argues, a great success:

> *Does reuse reduce cost? In the Advanced Field Artillery Tactical Data System it avoided $40 million. The Tactical Communications Interface avoided $5 million, and the Army Command and Control System avoided $480 million. That's a total of $525 million in those three programs.*

Wow. Sounds impressive, and perhaps it is. But I wonder where those numbers came from. They didn't come directly from General Kind who, for all his qualities as a good general, probably makes no pretense of being a whiz with software metrics. They were given to him, I suspect, by workers several levels below. You have to ask the question, Were those workers made more secure in their jobs or in their budgets or in their control of power by the findings they reported? Almost certainly they were. Now imagine yourself in exactly that position. You have been asked to produce a metric showing the savings of reuse, and, by the way, no harm done if the results show *really huge* savings. How would you go about it? Here's a possibility: You measure the cost of producing any particular piece of code, count the number of total times it is used, and compute:

$$\text{Net Saving} = \text{Cost to Produce} \times (\text{Number of Uses} - 1)$$

So, if there is a module that cost $1 million to produce and it is used fifty times, the net saving is $49 million.

What could possibly be wrong with this? Well, two things. First, it has the dangerous characteristic that the saving is directly proportional to the original production cost. So, if you spend $2 million to produce the very same module instead of $1 million, your saving would jump from $49 million to $98 million. Spend a little more, and you save a lot more.

The second problem is that the calculation doesn't include any indication of benefit. So, a monstrously overpriced module that has little or no benefit might be added to a system that itself has no benefit just to produce a "saving" of enormous proportion.

This is saving in the grand tradition of Blondie who tells Dagwood, "Dagwood, I saved us $300 today by buying three hats at half price." It leaves the American taxpayer musing, along with Dagwood, "Why do I feel so poor in spite of all this saving?"

Of course, I can't prove that the Army used precisely this calculus to arrive at its reported saving, but I suspect they did. If so, it is another example of measurement dysfunction:

meas.ure.ment dys.func.tion *n* : compliance with the letter of a motivational scheme in such a way as to achieve exactly the opposite of that scheme's underlying goals and intentions

"BUT THEY DIDN'T ACT PROFESSIONALLY!"

In each of these cases of measurement dysfunction or suspected dysfunction (even including the Soviet nail factory), you could argue that the workers didn't act professionally, that they really shouldn't have allowed the measurement scheme to influence them to the detriment of the organization's real goals and intentions. But they did. And they always will.

You can't have it both ways on professionalism. You can't expect workers to be totally professional and also expect them to allow themselves to be explicitly motivated by simplistic metric indicators of good performance. Even that prototypical example of professionalism, the medical doctor, will not act professionally if he or she is also trying to work to the numbers: maximizing patients seen per hour, drugs prescribed, specialists referred, sutures and bandages saved, and a host of other numerical indications of success.

The numerical indications of success are what W. Edwards Deming calls "extrinsic motivators." Things like professionalism, pride of workmanship, identification with true organizational success, and pleasure in work well done are "intrinsic motivators." As Deming points out, extrinsic motivators tend to drive out intrinsic motivators. When you direct people to work to the numbers, they do just that. Lost in the shuffle are their own intrinsic values and your organization's real goals and imperatives. The result is sure to be dysfunction.

Case Studies of Software-Process-Improvement Measurement

Daniel J. Paulish, Siemens Corporate Research

Anita D. Carleton, Software Engineering Institute

Siemens software-development organizations are case-study sites in a research project with the Software Engineering Institute. The effort has yielded suggestions for promoting software-process improvement.

S oftware measurement is becoming integral to improving software development. The approach begins with a documented software-development process. A business enterprise — on the basis of its strategic objectives — establishes goals to improve the process over a specified period of time. Then it defines measures to periodically gauge progress in achieving the improvement goals. When the data collected indicates development-process problems, the enterprise can formulate corrective actions and compare them to determine the best return on investment for software-process improvement.

Figure 1 shows how measures play a key role in a closed-loop feedback mechanism for incremental improvements to the software-development process over time.[1] These process improvements result in higher quality products, thus increasing the business enterprise's competitiveness.

In this article, we describe an ongoing research project conducted jointly by Siemens and the Software Engineering Institute. Siemens software-development organizations in Germany and the United States are case-study sites at which we measure the effect of methods to improve the software-development process. To observe and quantify the impact of software-process improvement, we must measure the performance of a software-development organization over time. Comparison of performance across organizations is very difficult, since organizations define measures and collect performance data in different ways. However, we can separately track performance improvement in each organization if it defines measures consistently and develops similar products.

We have defined basic measures for performance of a software-development organization. We limited ourselves to a small number of simple measures to reduce the complexity of collecting, analyzing, and maintaining the performance data.

Improving the software-development process improves the quality of software products and the overall performance of the software-development organization.[2] However, as Figure 2 shows,[3] process is only one of several controllable factors in improving software quality and organization performance. Others include the skills and experience of the people developing the software, the technology used (for example, CASE tools), product complexity, and environmental characteristics such as schedule pressure and communications.

Reprinted from *Computer*, Vol. 27, No. 9, Sept. 1994, pp. 50–57.

Organization performance depends on the complexity of the products being produced, the activities of the development organization, the development environment used, and the business situation. For example, different performance in productivity should be expected for different types of development such as new-product development, enhancement, migration, conversion, or maintenance. Business environmental factors such as whether the business is profitable and external regulatory requirements also affect an organization's performance. We do not try to establish what is good performance or compare organizations' performance. Instead, we track changes in performance over time within a specific organization.

Motivation

Many software-engineering organizations today want to improve their software-development processes to improve product quality and development-team productivity and reduce product development time, thereby increasing competitiveness and profitability. However, few know the best way to improve their development process. The wide assortment of available methods, such as configuration management, defect prevention process, function-point analysis, quality function deployment, software-quality assurance, software-reliability engineering, and total quality management, often leaves managers confused about which methods to introduce at which times in their process evolution.

The motivation to improve a software process usually results from a business need such as strong competition, external regulation, or a call for increased profitability. After assessing its current practices and process maturity, an organization often initiates approaches to improve a software-development process, as shown in Figure 3. The selection and successful implementation of improvements depend on many variables, such as the current process maturity, skills base, organization, and business issues such as cost, risk, and implementation speed. Predicting the success of a specific improvement is difficult because of environmental variables external to the method: staff skills, acceptance, training effectiveness, and implementation effi-

ciency. Once the improvement is in place, the organization must determine whether the method was implemented successfully, whether the process is mature enough to consider implementing additional methods, and whether the selected method is appropriate in the current process maturity level and environment.

Process-improvement method

A *software-process-improvement method* is an integrated collection of procedures, tools, and training for increasing product quality, improving development-team productivity, or reducing development time. A software-process-improvement method can support a *key process area* of the Capability Maturity Model (CMM) or improve the effectiveness of key practices within a key process area.[4]

Some outcomes of an improved software-development process could include

- fewer product defects found by customers,
- earlier identification and correction of defects,
- fewer defects introduced during development,
- faster time to market, and
- better predictability of project schedules and resources.

Software-process-improvement methods often require a significant investment in training and effort. Often, considerable barriers in an organization must be overcome before a measurable impact results from the improved process. In this article, we also summarize some lessons learned from organizations that experienced implementation barriers.

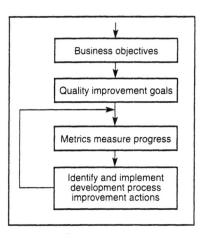

Figure 1. Software measurement approach.

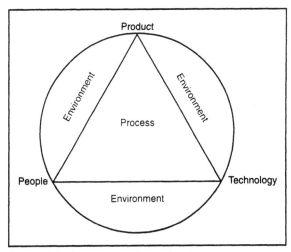

Figure 2. Software quality determinants.

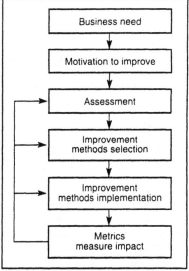

Figure 3. Process-improvement approach.

Table 1. Primary data.

Measure	Units of Measurement
Defects	Number of defects found per phase
Product size	Lines of code (LOC)
Effort	Staff-hours
Actual schedule duration time	Months per phase
Estimated schedule duration time	Months per phase

Table 2. Environmental data.

Measure	Units of Measurement
Staff size	Number of people
Staff turnover	Percentage of people who left in last 12 months
Maturity level	Estimate or from assessment: 1 to 5
Morale	Subjective response class: poor, average, good, excellent

Case-study approach

At the Siemens software-development organizations selected as case-study sites, we made a limited number of basic measurements to capture current performance in development-team productivity, process maturity, and product quality. We will continue to observe the sites for the next few years, collecting measurement data and conducting interviews at least annually.

Site selection. In selecting sites, we wanted

- a large variety of application domains, organization sizes, and product complexity;
- organizations in both the US and Germany;
- organizations where we had personal contacts; and
- organizations relatively dedicated to software-process improvement.

The case-study sites selected process-improvement methods based on their current maturity level, skills base, organization structure, and business issues. Initially, we visited each development organization twice. We will revisit them about once a year to recalculate the basic measurements. This will provide quantitative data about the effect of the selected process-improvement methods. We have docu-

mented lessons learned so far from the implementation of the process-improvement methods. In particular, we observed "soft" factors such as quality culture, motivation, and the effect on staff morale.

Interview and data collection approach. We collected the data for the case study from site interviews and documentation supplied by each case-study site. Each initial site visit consisted of an overview of the project (approximately one hour) and a one- to two-hour interview. The interview questions addressed the software-development practices, process, and environment; the software-process-improvement methods used and planned; and currently used performance measures.

A few months after the initial interview, we asked each site to establish a measurement baseline to determine its current performance. (We describe the data requested in the next section.) The baseline data was confidential and in some cases too sensitive for discussion outside the organization. The degree of difficulty that each organization experienced in generating the performance data varied considerably, depending on its maturity level and previous application of quantitative measurement approaches.

On the basis of our follow-up interviews and measurement data collected so far, we anticipate that over a period of four to five years the organizations will see an improvement in performance data. This time span is a consequence of the

relatively long product-development cycle times. Since performance is normally calculated for a project or product release, the data can be observed only by successive releases over time.

The data collected from a case-study site will often be for recent projects for which field defect data has been collected for one year. Thus, the term *site* does not imply a strict physical location. In some locations, multiple projects may be reported, while some projects may be managed over multiple physical sites, often within several countries.

Performance measures

With the request to the case-study sites to provide data, we included the performance measures we present here. We suggested that the organizations provide data according to these measures, although we would welcome data using differently defined measures. What the study requires is consistent data reporting over time. This assumes that the products developed by the organizations will be of similar complexity over the observation time period (three to five years), which is reasonable since the sites are all involved with maintaining mature products as well as developing newer versions of these products. Most sites that supplied data used the definitions provided, or they had already been tracking similar data because of previously shared software measurement training across Siemens business units. We suspect that the data is more accurate from the organizations that have established measurement programs, as compared with organizations that collected the data for the first time for this study.

Primary data. Table 1 summarizes the primary data we collected for each software-development organization. This data is similar to SEI-recommended core measures.[5] The initial baseline data should be collected for the last major product software release used by customers in the field for at least one year.

The number of *defects* found per phase and the total should be collected. Each organization will have unique defect-counting rules, describing what is a defect and during which activities defects are counted. For guidance, we recommend Florac's work,[6] in which a software defect is defined as any flaw or imperfection in a software work product or process. When found in executable code, a defect is frequently called a *fault* or *bug*.

Product size is measured using function points[7] or lines of code. Park[8] provides a lines of code (LOC) measurement definition. The measurement should be made at the time of product release to customers. The reported measure is the count of lines of code, excluding comment and blank lines.

Effort is assessed using the organization's existing accounting and time-reporting procedures. Effort should include the work performed by all staff involved with software development, including test, quality assurance, and documentation generation. Effort should be counted for the duration of the phases in product development from the beginning of high-level design to one year after first customer delivery. Goethert, Bailey, and Busby[9] give guidance on effort counting.

Schedule duration time for the implementation and qualification testing phases is reported. We define the schedule cycle time as the calendar time from the start of high-level design to first customer delivery, or the sum of the schedule duration times for the implementation and qualification testing phases. In addition to the actual time required for the last release, the organization should report the times estimated for these phases prior to implementation — that is, the estimated schedule.[9]

Environmental data. Measurement of characteristics of the development environment helps in identifying key influences on development-organization performance and in understanding the context in which the products were developed. The data collected will be somewhat "soft": Environmental measures are somewhat poorly defined and less commonly applied. These measures may change as an organization gains more experience. Table 2 summarizes the basic environmental measures.

Organization *staff size* should be measured at the time of the baseline measurements or at a recent convenient point (for example, last month or last quarter). The count should include staff members who perform the work included in the effort measure. For example, software engineers, testers, quality specialists, and documentation specialists should be counted. The count should include full-time, permanent employees, not temporary contractors or part-time employees.

Staff turnover should be measured as an indicator of organization stability. We define staff turnover as the percentage of staff members who have left the organization within the 12 months before the time of the baseline staff size measurement, divided by the staff size.

A high staff turnover could be the result of downsizing or extreme business conditions that result in organizational stress. This measure gives insight into how long staff members remain within the organization. If many new hires replace the staff members who left, an organization may have training and staff-assimilation challenges. Some organizations may also wish to calculate staff turnover separately for management and technical staff.

The software-process *maturity level* of the organization should be determined in accordance with the Capability Maturity Model. We suggested that the case-study organizations conduct self-assessments around the time of the baseline measurements, and then biannually thereafter. If an assessment had been done within the last two years, we asked the organization to report the assessment level. If not, we asked for a current estimate of process maturity level. This data helps in correlating the process-improvement methods an organization selects with its process maturity.

A measure of an organization's *staff morale* helps in determining whether this significantly influences its performance. Morale is not easy to measure. However, some organizations conduct periodic morale and opinion surveys, making such

data readily available. If it is not, the organization should estimate current morale. Since this is a subjective metric, we suggest a four-level response scheme: poor, average, good, and excellent.

Performance measures. We calculated basic software-development organization performance measures from the primary data summarized in Table 3. We will recalculate the measures for each successive project, release, or product, and compare them with the measures of the prior project, release, or product to observe the performance improvement within an organization.

We calculate the first two organization performance measures from the defects primary data. *Defect detection distribution* is the percentage of faults found in each development phase. *Defect rate* is the number of defects for each development phase divided by the product size in thousands of lines of code (KLOC). The defect rates should decrease for later phases of the product-development process. If the number of users is large, almost all product defects will be found during its lifetime, and many will be found during the first year of use. The defect rate for the field-use phase is thus a reliable measure of product quality.[10] Exceptions to this are cases when the number of users is small or when a product's quality is so poor that users quickly stop using it (and hence stop reporting errors). The *defect insertion rate* is the sum of the defect rates over all phases.

Project productivity is a basic organization performance measure. A common method of calculating it is to divide the product size by the effort. Organizations that develop multiple releases for the same product may wish to count *delta lines of code* for their release productivity calculation. Delta lines are changed and added lines of code for a release, as compared with the prior release. An organization must also define rules for handling reused code. Integrating previously tested code in new products greatly en-

Table 3. Organization performance measures.

Measure	Units of Measurement	Primary Data Used
Defect detection distribution	Percentage of defects found per phase	Defects
Defect rate	Defects/KLOC per phase	Defects, product size
Project productivity	LOC/staff-hour	Product size, effort
Schedule cycle time	Months	Actual schedule duration time
Schedule adherence	Percent (estimated minus actual)/estimated	Actual and estimated schedule duration times

Table 4. Primary data summary.

Measure	Definition	Units	Nominal Value	Range
Defects	Count of defects found during implementation, qualification testing, and field-use phases	Number of defects found per phase	Implementation: 1400, qualification testing: 650, field use: 180	Implementation: 120-6300, qualification testing: 130-2500, field use: 1-450
Product size	Lines of code (LOC) count, excluding comment and blank lines	LOC	1.6M	150K-5M
Effort	Staff-hours required for product development through first year of field use	Staff-hours	300K	15K-750K
Actual schedule duration time	Schedule time used per phase	Months per phase	Implementation: 14, qualification testing: 7	Implementation: 4-20, qualification testing: 2-16
Estimated schedule duration time	Schedule time estimated per phase	Months per phase	Implementation: 13, qualification testing: 5	Implementation: 4-22, qualification testing: 2-13

hances productivity, and development staff should be encouraged to reuse code. Productivity could also be calculated using function points rather than lines of code. In some cases, project productivity calculated using the total product size is called product productivity. If delta lines of code are counted, the project productivity is often called process productivity.

Schedule cycle time is calculated by adding the actual schedule duration times for the implementation and qualification testing phases of the project. *Schedule adherence* is a measure of the organization's ability to develop products on time and meet commitments. Schedule adherence is the difference between the estimated schedule duration time and the actual schedule duration time, divided by the schedule duration time, calculated as a percentage. A negative number indicates a schedule slip; a positive number indicates that the development was done more quickly than estimated.

Other common measures of organization performance that we did not use in our project include development cost, which can be calculated as the effort multiplied by the average hourly labor rate for the project. Profitability and customer satisfaction also are sometimes used to measure organization performance. (Methods to calculate these measures are available elsewhere.[1])

Baseline performance data

For the metrics baseline from each case-study site, we asked each contact person to fill out a data-input form with the primary data, environmental data, and organization performance measures. Since the goal of the project is to observe organization performance over time, the definitions of the measures can be unique to each case-study site, as long as they are consistent over time. We suggested that each organization calculate the measurement baseline with a recent product release used by customers in the field for one year.

We made the following observations concerning the collection of the baseline performance data:

• All organizations considered the performance data to be proprietary and con-fidential. Some thought the data was so sensitive that they refused to supply it for the study, although they participated in the interviews. These organizations claimed they needed to protect the data to control customer communications and interactions. We suspect some feared use of the data for comparison across organizations. We also suspect this fear may be greater in organizations that have multiple development sites in several countries. The corporate effort to help organizations perform self-assessments also encountered this barrier of fear of comparison with others, particularly across national borders.

• Many organizations had difficulty collecting the performance data. Organizations with established metrics programs had the least difficulty. Some organizations were collecting such data for the first time, and used the case-study project as a motivator for measurement application. Another difficulty occurred in organizations that work on many product releases simultaneously, often with the same staff. For example, a staff member may be asked to maintain a previously released software version and help with the design of future releases and im-

312

Table 5. Environmental data summary.

Measure	Definition	Units	Nominal Value	Range
Staff size	Current number of software engineers, testers, quality specialists, and documentation specialists	Number of people	450	25 to 1,600
Staff turnover	Percent (number of staff members who have left in last 12 months)/staff size	Percentage of people who left	14	4 to 21
Maturity level	CMM levels 1 to 5 from last assessment or estimate	1 to 5	2	1 to 4
Morale	Subjective estimate of staff morale	Poor, average, good, or excellent	Average	Average to good

plementation of the current release. In such cases, it was often difficult to collect performance data that accurately separated effort, time, and defects among the various releases. Organizations often use this multiple-release strategy to meet customer needs — that is, to reduce the time increments between releases when schedule cycle times are long. In general, this is a complexity issue that concerns the organization's management.

• Most organizations adhered to the measurement definitions we provided. This may be a result of corporate training and standards developed over the past few years for measurement application.

• The environmental data was controversial and difficult to determine, as we anticipated. For organizations that had not yet conducted an assessment, the maturity-level estimates tended to differ significantly, depending on who the point-of-contact asked within the organization. In general, newer staff tended to estimate the maturity level lower than staff who had worked longer in the organization.

Tables 4 through 6 present the primary data, environmental data, and organization performance measures as a summary and composite of all the organizations that reported data. In the tables, the fourth column gives composite nominal values averaged over all the reported projects; the fifth column gives the ranges of values collected. There are undoubtedly differences among the organizations concerning definition of measures and the accuracy of the data collected. The composite data merely identifies rough performance indicators and demonstrates the diversity among the case-study

sites. The interpretation is complicated by the fact that not all organizations reported data for all measures.

Our overall observation of the case-study sites during the first year of the project demonstrated to us the need for a stable, supportive environment to best realize a significant improvement in organization performance. Business and organizational changes generally hindered the software-process-improvement progress made by some of the case-study sites. These changes included top management replacement, downsizing, and reorganizations. Despite these distractions, half the case-study sites obtained ISO 9001 certification during the first year of the study, and all the organizations made progress in achieving this goal.

In addition to beginning the Siemens study, the Software Engineering Institute has completed an initial study of 13 organizations' experience over the past nine years with software-process improvement.[11] The 13 organizations comprise Department of Defense contractors, commercial organizations (including one of the Siemens case-study sites), and military organizations. Table 7 summarizes some of the data collected in this study to show that organizations engaged in software-process improvement over extended periods can achieve dramatic results.

Common implementation problems

On the basis of our case-study work so far, we have identified common bar-

riers to the implementation of software-process-improvement methods. Here we summarize them and suggest ways to overcome them.

Getting started. Some organizations had difficulty getting started with software-process improvement and the methods they selected. We encouraged these organizations to undergo assessment because it is a proven technique for identifying priorities and getting buy-in across the organization. We also encouraged them to establish a software engineering process group. We provided guidance and contact information for SEI-associated Software Process-Improvement Network organizations and more experienced Siemens development organizations.

Staff turnover. Some of the organizations underwent downsizing (layoff) that created software-engineering staff turnover. This leads to a difficult environment for software-process improvement, since improvement requires initial and sustained investment, and the effects may not be measurable for a few years. We have also observed that in any organization there are champions and advocates of software-process improvement. If these individuals are laid off or their priorities change as a result of downsizing, the introduction of new software-process-improvement methods is more difficult. We encouraged organizations that were downsizing to consider profitability goals as part of the initiation and planning for software-process improvement. Only one of the case-study organizations had previously

Table 6. Organization performance measures summary.

Measure	Definition	Units	Nominal Value	Range
Defect detection distribution	Percentage of defects found during implementation, qualification testing, and field-use phases	Percent of defects found per phase	Implementation: 63, qualification testing: 29, field use: 8	Implementation: 23 to 68, qualification testing: 27 to 78, field use: 4 to 35
Defect rate	Defects divided by product size per phase	Defects/KLOC per phase	Implementation: 0.8, qualification testing: 0.6, field use: 0.2	Implementation: 0.2 to 1.7, qualification testing: 0.3 to 1.2, field use: 0.008 to 0.36
Project productivity	Product size divided by effort	LOC/staff-hour	5	2.6 to 6.7
Schedule cycle time	Sum of schedule duration times for implementation and qualification testing phases	Months	21	6 to 36
Schedule adherence	Percent (estimated schedule duration time minus actual schedule duration time)/estimated schedule duration time	Percent	−17	−42 to −13

used profitability measures with software development, although all organizations were affected by overall business profitability goals. We also observed that large staff turnover currently appears to be a greater problem in the US than in Germany.

Dedicated resources. Some of the organizations used part-time resources, usually line managers or improvement teams, to implement software-process-improvement methods. Although greatly dependent on the organization's size and the individuals' specific skills and influence, part-time effort is usually not as effective as full-time dedicated resources. We encouraged organizations to appreciate the return on investment of process improvement. We suggested they introduce some of the methods as a pilot project until they were generally recognized as successful. The most effective software engineering process groups often had a full-time team leader supported by team members who were first-line managers dedicating approximately 20 percent of their time to process improvement. These managers had control of resources that could be applied to process improvement as required.

Management support. We have generally observed that management support is necessary for software-process improvement. To help overcome lack of management interest, we offered point-of-contacts support in communicating to their management the benefits of process improvement. The need for management support and buy-in at all levels of the organization seemed to be a more important issue in the US than in Germany. Organizations that provided generalized quality training (for example, TQM) were generally more supportive of software-process improvement.

Time restrictions. Some organizations had difficulty finding the time to work on software-process improvement because they had extreme commitments to deliver customer products. We pointed out

Table 7. Software-process-improvement results (1987-1993).[11]

Measure	Median	Range
Productivity gain per year	35 percent	9 to 67 percent
Early detection gain per year (defects discovered pre-test)	22 percent	6 to 25 percent
Yearly reduction in time to market	19 percent	15 to 23 percent
Yearly reduction in post-release defect reports	39 percent	10 to 94 percent
Business value of software-process-improvement investment (value returned on each dollar invested)	5.0	4.0 to 8.8

that delivery dates had high priority, but when the release was completed, effort must be put into software-process improvement to avoid future emergencies.

Here we can present only limited results because of our short time observing the case-study sites. Nevertheless, we can make some preliminary recommendations to organizations wishing to improve their software-development process.

• Use the Capability Maturity Model as a guide for software-process improvement. The CMM was relatively easy for organizations to understand and apply to their situations. It provides a framework showing which methods to use, based on current maturity.

• Conduct an assessment to start a software-process-improvement program. Assessment is a very powerful method for identifying priorities for improvement and building consensus within the organization.

• Pick a few process-improvement methods and implement them effectively. Many organizations make the mistake of initiating too many process-improvement activities, so none gets implemented well.

• Pay attention to the implementation of the method as much as or more than the method itself. For sustained improvement over time, the selected methods must be implemented well. Good implementation includes good training and management.

• Keep in mind that some process-improvement methods are easier to introduce and implement than others. For example, defect prevention requires prior implementation of defect detection. Also, inspections may be easier to introduce than a metrics program. (Further recommendations and discussion of this subject are available elsewhere.[12])

We found that cultural factors are substantial. Although the case-study sites are quite diverse organizations with differing products and development processes, the greatest difference appears to be between organizations in Germany and the US. In many cases, German and US sites selected and implemented the same software-process-improvement methods, often using the same training courses and trainers.

However, the way that the methods were introduced and the level of acceptance were very different. This implies that an organization's cultural characteristics have a significant impact on its success with adopting software-process-improvement methods. Software-engineering managers and other staff members involved with organizational change (for example, software engineering process group members) should pay particular attention to cultural characteristics when implementing process-improvement methods. ■

References

1. K.-H. Möller and D.J. Paulish, *Software Metrics: A Practitioner's Guide to Improved Product Development*, 1993, IEEE CS Press, Los Alamitos. Calif., Order No. 3035.

2. W.S. Humphrey, *Managing the Software Process*, Addison-Wesley, Reading, Mass., 1989.

3. M.I. Kellner and J.W. Over, "A Software Quality Improvement Framework." *Proc. Software Eng. Forum*, Olivetti Information Services, Milan, Italy. 1992.

4. M.C. Paulk et al., "Capability Maturity Model for Software, Version 1.1," Tech. Report CMU/SEI-93-TR-24. ESD-93-TR-177, Software Eng. Inst., Carnegie Mellon Univ., Pittsburgh, 1993.

5. A.D. Carleton et al., "Software Measurement for DoD Systems: Recommendations for Initial Core Measures," Tech. Report CMU/SEI-92-019, ESC-TR-92-019, Software Eng. Inst., Carnegie Mellon Univ., Pittsburgh, 1992.

6. W.A. Florac. "Software Quality Measurement: A Framework for Counting Problems. Failures and Faults." CMU/SEI-92-TR-22, ESC-TR-92-22, Software Eng. Inst., Carnegie Mellon Univ., Pittsburgh, 1992.

7. A.J. Albrecht and J.E. Gaffney, "Software Function, Source Lines of Code and Development Effort Prediction: A Software Science Validation." *IEEE Trans. Software Eng.*, Vol. SE-9, No. 6, Nov. 1983, pp. 639-648.

8. R.E. Park, "Software Size Measurement: A Framework for Counting Source Statements," Tech. Report CMU/SEI-92-TR-20, ESC-TR-92-20, Software Eng. Inst., Carnegie Mellon Univ., Pittsburgh, 1992.

9. W.B. Goethert, E.K. Bailey, and M.B. Busby, "Software Effort Measurement: A Framework for Counting Staff-Hours," Tech. Report CMU/SEI-92-TR-21. ESC-TR-92-21, Software Eng. Inst., Carnegie Mellon Univ., Pittsburgh, 1992.

10. P. Jilek, K.-H. Möller, and D.J. Paulish, "The Use of Metrics for Software Development," *Proc. Ninth World Conf. Computer Security, Audit, and Control*, Elsevier Advanced Technology, London, 1992.

11. J. Herbsleb et al., "Benefits of CMM-Based Software-Process Improvement: Initial Results," CMU/SEI-94-TR-13, ESC-TR-94-013, Aug. 1994, Software Eng. Inst., Carnegie Mellon Univ., Pittsburgh, 1994, p.15.

12. R.D. Austin and D.J. Paulish, "A Survey of Commonly Applied Methods for Software Process Improvement," Tech. Report CMU/SEI-93-TR-27, ESC-TR-93-201, Software Eng. Inst., Carnegie Mellon Univ., Pittsburgh, 1993.

Epilog

The papers in this collection present a snapshot of current software measurement practice. Additional information is being made available all the time, particularly through Internet and World Wide Web (WWW) activities. Organizations such as the Center for High-Integrity Software System Assurance at the US National Institute of Standards and Technology and the US Software Engineering Institute maintain Web home pages that list a great deal of resource material on measurement. The UK Centre for Software Reliability maintains a home page that includes a bibliography of relevant material, and the US Department of Defense and US Army provide access to a host of useful documents and references.

We browsed the Net in early 1996 and discovered a host of universities and commercial home pages that describe the use and availability of metrics and metric tools. We suggest that you use a search service, such as Digital Equipment Corporation's AltaVista (http://www.altavista.digital.com) or Yahoo! Corporation's new search engine (http://www.yahoo.com), and run a query on "software metrics" to see what is available.

The reasons for measurement are manifold and important. The candidate metrics are numerous, too, and it is not yet clear that we have defined the most appropriate ones for the problems at hand. Still, the papers in this book demonstrate the fact that measurement is an essential and useful part of software development and maintenance. The next steps are to remain skeptical of the status quo, and to assess and refine our measurement activities so that we get the most "bang for the buck." We will know we are a mature software engineering activity when developers and maintainers no longer ask why they must measure or even what they must measure but instead assume that measurement is good science and good practice. The result will be a demonstrable increase in software quality, utility, and functionality. Our legacy will be not mountains of unanalyzed, unintelligible data but instead a safer, more comfortable world in which quality software is taken for granted.

Glossary[1]

Attribute—a characteristic of an entity.

Baseline—a set of measures that have been formally reviewed and agreed upon, and thereafter serve as the basis for further maintenance and development.

Cohesion—the degree to which the tasks of a software module are functionally related.

Coupling—a measure of the intermodule connectedness, or interdependence, of software modules.

Complexity—the degree to which a software module has design or implementation characteristics that are difficult to understand and verify.

Cyclomatic complexity—a graph theoretic measure of the branch complexity of a software module estimating the number of independent paths through a strongly connected graph representing the module. Also referred to as McCabe's V(g), after its inventor, Tom McCabe.

Data flow complexity—a measure of design or source code complexity based on the intra- and intermodule data paths defined in the design or code.

Data structure complexity—a measure of design or source code complexity based on the data structures defined in the design or code.

Defect—an anomaly in a software product.

Defect density—a measure of the tendency for a software module to contain defects, usually normalized by some size measure, for example, defects/LOC.

Direct metric—a metric applied during development or during operations that represents a software quality factor (for example, mean time to software failure for the factor reliability).

Entity—an item that is part of a software development process, product or resource.

---

[1] Adapted from IEEE Standard 610.12-1990, *Standard Glossary of Software Engineering Terminology*, Standard 982.1-1988, *Standard Dictionary of Measures to Produce Reliable Software*, and Standard 1061-1992, *Standard for a Software Quality Metrics Methodology*.

Error—a human action that results in software containing a fault.

Factor—a particular aspect of an attribute (an attribute may comprise several factors).

Failure—a software failure occurs when a functional software unit can no longer perform its required function or cannot perform that function within specified limits.

Fan-in—the number of calls or references to a given code module.

Fan-out—the number of calls or references from a given code module.

Fault—an accidental condition in a software module (for example, incorrect step, process, or data definition) that causes the software system to fail.

Flowgraph—a graphical representation of the flow of control through a software systems design or source code implementation.

Function points—a measure of the "functions the software is to perform" based on requirements information on external inputs, external outputs, logical internal files, external interface files, and external inquiries. Developed by A.J. Albrecht of IBM.

Halstead metrics—a set of code metrics introduced by Maurice Halstead based on the unique and total numbers of operators and operands observed in source code.

Hybrid metric—a combination of two or more different measures to collapse existing measurement domains or estimate a new measurement domain.

KLOC—lines of code, in thousands.

KSLOC—source lines of code, in thousands.

LOC—lines of code.

Measure—a mapping from the empirical (real) world to a formal (mathematical) world.

Measurement—the act or process of applying a measure (that is, applying the mapping); a figure, extent, or amount obtained by measuring.

Measurement scale—a class of measure that suggests appropriate uses of the measure; typical scales are nominal, ordinal, interval, and ratio.

Metrics framework—a technique used for organizing, selecting, communicating, and evaluating the required quality attributes for a software system; a hierarchical breakdown of factors, subfactors, and metrics for a software system.

Metric—a particular mapping; for example, both lines-of-code and object count are mappings that can be used as size measures.

MTBF—Mean Time Between Failures, a reliability measure.

MTTF—Mean Time To Failure, a reliability measure.

Predicate—a logical datum used for branch control, a decision node.

Predictive metric—a metric applied during development and used to predict the values of a factor.

Primitive metric—a simple mapping, usually on something that is directly countable.

Process step—any task performed in development, implementation, or maintenance.

Process metric—a metric to measure characteristics of a method, technique, or tool used to develop, implement, or maintain a system.

Product metric—a metric to measure the characteristics of a product of development, such as requirements, designs, code, documentation, or test cases.

SLOC—source lines of code.

Test coverage—the degree to which a given test or set of tests exercises the components of a software system (for example, branch coverage, statement coverage).

V(g)—see cyclomatic complexity.

IEEE Computer Society Press Publications

The world-renowned Computer Society Press publishes, promotes, and distributes a wide variety of authoritative computer science and engineering texts. These books are available in two formats: 100 percent original material by authors preeminent in their field who focus on relevant topics and cutting-edge research, and reprint collections consisting of carefully selected groups of previously published papers with accompanying original introductory and explanatory text.

Submission of proposals: For guidelines and information on CS Press books, send e-mail to cs.books@computer.org or write to the Acquisitions Editor, IEEE Computer Society Press, P.O. Box 3014, 10662 Los Vaqueros Circle, Los Alamitos, CA 90720-1314. Telephone +1 714-821-8380. FAX +1 714-761-1784.

IEEE Computer Society Press Proceedings

The Computer Society Press also produces and actively promotes the proceedings of more than 130 acclaimed international conferences each year in multimedia formats that include hard and softcover books, CD-ROMs, videos, and on-line publications.

For information on CS Press proceedings, send e-mail to cs.books@computer.org or write to Proceedings, IEEE Computer Society Press, P.O. Box 3014, 10662 Los Vaqueros Circle, Los Alamitos, CA 90720-1314. Telephone +1 714-821-8380. FAX +1 714-761-1784.

Additional information regarding the Computer Society, conferences and proceedings, CD-ROMs, videos, and books can also be accessed from our web site at www.computer.org.